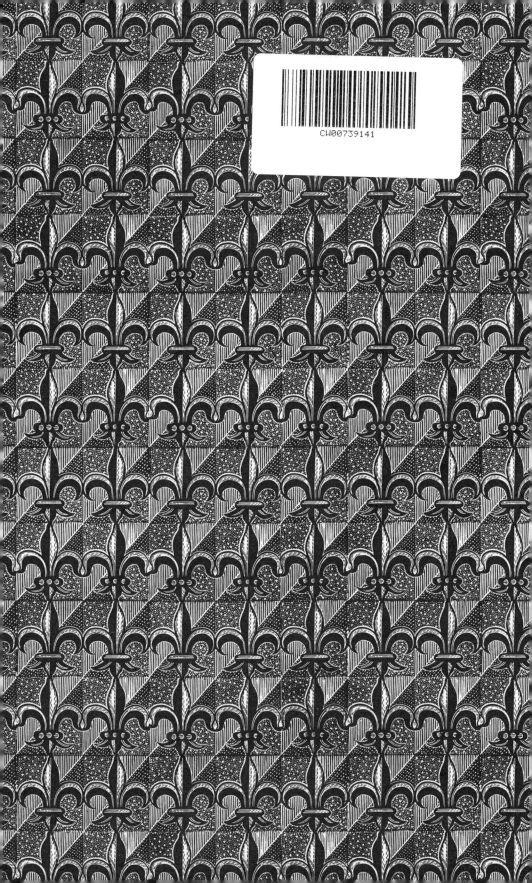

THE LITERARY
COMPANION
TO DOGS

For Barbara,
Xmas '93
X

Also edited by Christopher Hawtree

Night and Day
Graham Greene, *Yours Etc: Letters to the Press*
1936 (with Charles Moore)
John Meade Falkner, *The Nebuly Coat* (World's Classics)
John Hampson, *Saturday Night at the Greyhound* (Hogarth Press)

as James Finch
A Bullet from Hell

THE LITERARY COMPANION TO DOGS

From Homer to Hockney

Sniffed out by
Christopher Hawtree

*'Sometimes I think they understand
every word we say!'*

('Pont')

SINCLAIR-STEVENSON

First published in Great Britain in 1993
by Sinclair-Stevenson
an imprint of Reed Consumer Books Ltd
Michelin House, 81 Fulham Road, London SW3 6RB
and Auckland, Melbourne, Singapore and Toronto

Copyright in the compilation and editorial matter © 1993 by Christopher Hawtree

Permission to reproduce copyright material in
this anthology is acknowledged between
pages 871–874 of this edition.

The right of Christopher Hawtree to be identifed as editor of this work
has been asserted by him in accordance
with the Copyright, Design and Patent Act 1988

A CIP catalogue record for this book
is available at the British Library
ISBN 1 85619 324 1

Typeset by CentraCet, Cambridge
Printed and bound in Great Britain
by Mackays of Chatham plc,
Chatham, Kent

Beware of dogs

Paul's Epistle to the Philippians

Preface and Acknowledgements

The chief fact today I think is the development & discovery of Tinker's character – all in the right direction. He has taken a long walk by the river the avenue & the Park; his spirit is great, but almost under control. He fell into the river twice; jumped out again; circled madly with a black poodle, & investigated several garden gates, which seem to have a fascination for him. He is a human dog, aloof from other dogs.

Virginia Woolf, *Diary*: 15 October 1917

CURIOUS, THE WAY in which ideas come to mind. Perhaps they are there all along, but this chrestomathy began with a wet Sunday afternoon in Hamburg and another reading of Virginia Woolf's diary, from which leapt this paragraph whose ring of truth is characteristic of that remarkable work. With it came a reflection upon the diverse ways in which dogs animated her life and writing; and, from that, their appearances in the works of authors whom she relished.

Many of these authors will be found in the following pages, together with some of whom she might have disapproved. The more one reads, the more one becomes aware of the democracy of the dog: it would be a dull spirit that did not savour diversity, and one hopes that this collection will send readers in at least some of the directions which its compilation required. One can only agree with Hemingway that Ouida's *Pierrot: A Dog of Flanders*, once a staple of every schoolroom, is completely unreadable but her pamphlet *Dogs* remains vigorous stuff; one could fill a volume apiece with Horace Walpole and Sir Walter Scott. In the meanwhile, thinking of Walpole's word 'dogmanity', one can only agree with Virginia Woolf's remark, in her notes to *Flush*, that 'the whole question of dog's relation to the spirit of the age, whether it is possible to call a dog Elizabethan, another Augustan, another Victorian, together with the influence upon dogs of the poetry and philosophy of their masters, deserves a fuller discussion than can here be given it.'

With this in mind, the volume is arranged chronologically by subject rather than by sections given over to – say – food, death, cats as friend and foe, movies, the stage, tales of great endeavour and acts of hopeless folly: readers will make such connections for themselves as Argus chimes down the ages. In some cases – among them, George Eliot, John Brown and A. C. Swinburne – the authors have been brought alongside, such was their commenting upon one another. Annotation has been kept to a minimum, the contents of a chrestomathy speaking for themselves rather than labelled as dry exhibits in a museum.

Shortly before his death, Graham Greene (whose feelings about dogs were ambiguous) suggested that I should indeed compile such a volume, and Katherine Duncan-Jones provided congenial surroundings while I both began and finished work.

That is, if such work can ever be said to be finished. One begins to see dogs everywhere, and I am grateful to my publisher, Christopher Sinclair-Stevenson, for calling me to heel, for, in chasing leads, there is a risk of going barking mad. Emily Kerr and Sophie Ovenden brought the typescript into shape with admirable care and despatch.

It is only natural that anybody who compiles a chrestomathy should wish to give an impression of omniscience, but such work can prove an education, one which is partly a matter of canvassing opinion – even of calling in old favours, and sometimes of barter. Such is the trading among chrestomathists as they collide in the lobby of the excellent London Library that it often resembles the floor of the old Stock Exchange, and I must thank those assailed there and diverted from their own labours by my wild cry of '. . . dogs': D. J. Enright (supernatural etc.), Jeremy Lewis (office life), Christopher Silvester (interviews/Parliament), Charles Sprawson (swimming), Peter Vansittart (London etc.) and A. N. Wilson (clergy), while Dr Francis Wheen's parallel – and unparalleled – work on cats and catmen prompted much exchanging of faxes.

The usual gratitude is offered to the staff of the aforementioned London Library, and to the Bodleian Library, the British Museum Reading Room, Hove Public Library, the New York Public Library and Westminster Reference Library.

Others prevented me from saying, with Shakespeare, that 'I've watched so long that I'm dog-weary': Jonathan Aldous, Fareed Ali, Ophelia Ali, Mark Amory, Lady Clare Asquith, Dr Toby Barnard, Julian Barnes, the late Robert Baxter, Michael Bloch, Susan Boyd, William Boyd, Noël Brookes, Anne Chisholm, Ron Cortie, Michael

Davie, Madeleine Enright, C. J. Fox, the late Roy Fuller, Sandy Gall, Professor Donat Gallagher, Mary Gallagher, Alex Greville-Sims, Jan Hawtree, Kenneth Hillier, John Hughes, Richard Ingrams, Ian Irvine, John Wyse Jackson, Lewis Jones, Stanley Leff, Petra Lewis, Dr Philip Mansel, Bryan Marlow, David Marr, Michael Mason, Douglas Matthews, Joseph Mitchell, Hugh Montgomery-Massingberd, Brian Oatley, Charles Orwin, the late Miss Pepper, Corine Richards, George Robertson, Candice Rodd, Judith Rossner, Vikram Seth, Sebastian Shakespeare, Professor Michael Shelden, Bobby Short, Joan Smith, Graham Swift, D. J. Taylor, Ian Thomson, David Twiston Davies, John Updike, Dr Keith Walker, John Wells, Dr Stephanie West, Anthony Wheale, Ashley White, Beatrice Wilson, Edward Wilson, Emily Wilson, Dr Hanneker Wirtjes, Isabel Wolff – and the unknown American in the British Museum who put me onto *Beautiful Joe* and confessed that she still weeps at the movie of *Old Yeller*.

I am grateful to Professor Frederick Karl for revealing that, as a graduate student, he helped anonymously to compile an authoritative veterinary manual in order to fund his studies. Buchan and Heather Hillier provided secretarial help, and it would be churlish not to acknowledge the part played by Toshiba BD–3110, which never once groaned at the amount of books placed face-down on its glass screen and more than justifies each year's written-down value.

I would be glad to hear, via the publisher, from anybody who knows of any 'good bits'.

Textual Note: both original-spelling and modernized texts have been used (except that the long 's' has been emended): dogges are suggested but do not dominate. American and English spellings are retained.

Song lyrics have been excluded (one has to know the tune), but attention should be drawn to 'The Day Off' in Stephen Sondheim's *Sunday in the Park With George*, and irresistable is this couplet from Cole Porter's 'But In the Morning, No': 'When my pet Pekinese / Starts to cross his Q's and P's.'

Sad Note: Too large a copyright permission fee was asked for Arthur Bryant, Michael Meyer and Jessica Mitford, so their work has been regretfully omitted.

HOMER

Brief Reunion

Thus, near the gates conferring as they drew,
Argus the dog, his ancient master knew:
He not unconscious of the voice and tread,
Lifts to the sound his ear, and rears his head;
Bred by Ulysses, nourish'd at his board,
But, ah! not fated long to please his lord;
To him, his swiftness and his strength were vain;
The voice of glory call'd him o'er the main.
Till then in every sylvan chase renown'd,
With Argus, Argus, rung the woods around;
With him the youth pursued the goat or fawn,
Or traced the mazy leveret o'er the lawn.
Now left to man's ingratitude he lay,
Unhoused, neglected in the public way;
And where on heaps the rich manure was spread,
Obscene with reptiles, took his sordid bed.

He knew his lord; he knew, and strove to meet;
In vain he strove to crawl and kiss his feet;
Yet (all he could) his tail, his ears, his eyes,
Salute his master, and confess his joys.
Soft pity touch'd the mighty master's soul;
Adown his cheek a tear unbidden stole,
Stole unperceived: he turn'd his head and dried
The drop humane: then thus impassion'd cried:
    'What noble beast in this abandon'd state
Lies here all helpless at Ulysses' gate?
His bulk and beauty speak no vulgar praise:
If, as he seems, he was in better days,
Some care his age deserves; or was he prized
For worthless beauty? therefore now despised;
Such dogs and men there are, mere things of state;

And always cherish'd by their friends, the great.'
　'Not Argus so, (Eumæus thus rejoin'd,)
But served a master of a nobler kind,
Who never, never shall behold him more!
Long, long since perish'd on a distant shore!
Oh had you seen him, vigorous, bold, and young,
Swift as a stag, and as a lion strong:
Him no fell savage on the plain withstood,
None 'scaped him bosom'd in the gloomy wood;
His eye how piercing, and his scent how true.
To wind the vapour in the tainted dew!
Such, when Ulysses left his natal coast;
Now years unnerve him, and his lord is lost!
The women keep the generous creature bare,
A sleek and idle race is all their care:
The master gone, the servants what restrains?
Or dwells humanity where riot reigns?
Jove fix'd it certain, that whatever day
Makes man a slave, takes half his worth away?
　This said, the honest herdsman strode before;
The musing monarch pauses at the door:
The dog, whom Fate had granted to behold
His lord, when twenty tedious years had roll'd,
Takes a last look, and, having seen him, dies;
So closed for ever faithful Argus' eyes!

From *Odyssey XVII*
Trans. Alexander Pope

HESIOD

Investment

. . . look after your dog with the sharp teeth,
   do not spare feeding him.
So the Man Who Sleeps in the Daytime won't be
   getting at your goods

From *Works and Days*
Trans. Richard Lattimore

THE MAHABHÁRATA

An Interrupted Journey

'O thousand eyed! O Lord of all the gods,
Give that my brothers come with me who fell,
Not without them is Swarga sweet to me.
She too, the dear and kind and queenly, – she
Whose perfect virtue Paradise must crown, –
Grant her to come with us! Dost thou grant this?'

'The God replied: "In heaven thou shalt see
Thy kinsmen and the queen – these will attain –
And Krishna. Grieve no longer for thy dead,
Thou chief of men! their mortal covering stripped,
They have their places; but to thee the gods
Allot an unknown grace: thou shalt go up
Living and in thy form, to the immortal homes."'

'But the king answered: "O thou Wisest One,
Who know'st what was, and is, and is to be,
Still one more grace! This hound hath ate with me,
Followed me, loved me: must I leave him now?" '

' "Monarch," spake Indra, "thou art now as we,
Deathless, divine; thou art become a god;
Glory and power and gifts celestial,
And all the joys of heaven are thine for aye:
What hath a beast with these? Leave here thy hound!" '

'Yet Yudhishthira answered: "O Most High
O thousand-eyed and Wisest! can it be
That one exalted should seem pitiless?
Nay, let me lose such glory: for its sake
I would not leave one living thing I loved."

'Then sternly Indra spake: "He is unclean,
And into Swarga such shall enter not.
Bethink thee, Dharmaraj! quit now this beast!
That which is seemly is not hard of heart." '

'Still he replied: "'Tis written that to spurn
A supplicant equals in offence to slay
A twice-born; wherefore, not for Swarga's bliss
Quit I Mahendra! this poor clinging dog, –
So without any hope or friend save me,
So wistful, fawning for my faithfulness,
So agonized to die, unless I help,
Who among men was called steadfast and just."

'Quoth Indra: "Nay! the altar-flame is foul
Where a dog passeth; angry angels sweep
The ascending smoke aside, and all the fruits

Of offering, and the merit of the prayer
Of him whom a hound toucheth. Leave it here
He that will enter heaven must enter pure.
Why dids't thou quit thy brethren on the way,
And Krishna, and the dear-loved Draupadi,
Attaining, firm and glorious, to this Mount
Through perfect deeds, to linger for a brute?
Hath Yudhishthira vanquished self, to melt
With one poor passion at the door of bliss?
Stay'st thou for this, who dids't not stay for them, –
Draupadi, Bhima?"'

     'But the king yet spake
"'Tis known that none can hurt or help the dead.
They, the delightful ones, who sank and died,
Following my footsteps, could not live again
Though I had turned, – therefore I did not turn;
But could help profit, I had turned to help.
There be four sins, O Sakra, grievous sins:
The first is making suppliants despair,
The second is to slay a nursing wife,
The third is spoiling Brahmans' goods by force,
The fourth is injuring an ancient friend.
These four I deem but equal to one sin,
If one, in coming forth from woe to weal,
Abandon any meanest comrade then."'

'Straight as he spake, brightly great Indra smiled;
Vanished the hound, and in its stead stood there
The Lord of Death and Justice, Dharma's self!
Sweet were the words which fell from those dread lips,
Precious the lovely praise: "O thou true king!
Thou that dost bring to harvest the good seed
Of Pandu's righteousness; thou that hast ruth

As he before, on all which lives! – O Son,
I tried thee in the Dwaita wood, what time
They smote thy brothers, bringing water; then
Thou prayed'st for Nakula's life – tender and just –
Hear thou my word! Because thou did'st not mount
This car divine, lest the poor hound be shent
Who looked to thee, lo! there is none in heaven
Shall sit above thee, King! – Bharata's son,
Enter thou now to the eternal joys,
Living and in thy form. Justice and Love
Welcome thee, Monarch! thou shalt throne with them!"'

Trans. Sir Edwin Arnold

DIODORUS

Ancient Egypt

OSIRIS WAS ACCOMPANIED on his campaign, according to the Egyptian account, by his two sons Anubis and Macedon, who were notable for their bravery. Both carried the best in armour, which was derived from animals whose character was similar to the boldness of men. Anubis wore a dog's skin and Macedon the foreparts of a wolf; these animals are therefore held in a place of honour among the Egyptians . . .

When one such animal dies it is wrapped in fine linen and then, amid wailing and beating of breasts, carried off to be embalmed; after being treated with cedar oil and pleasant-smelling spices which also act as preservative, it is laid into a consecrated tomb. Anybody that deliberately kills one of the venerated animals is put to death: the people gather in a crowd and deal with the villain forthwith – sometimes without benefit of trial. Such is the fear of this punishment that anybody who catches sight of an animal dead gives cries of lament that the animal was already dead . . . .

The dog is used both for hunting and protection, and this is why the god Anubis is represented by a dog's head, indicating that he was the bodyguard of Osiris and Isis. Some explain that dogs guided Isis during her search for Osiris, protecting her from wild beasts and others, and that, such was their affection for her, they helped by baying. For this reason, at the Festival of Isis, dogs lead the procession, a memorial of the help administered by their ancestors.

From *History of the World*
Trans. Steven Goldthorpe

ALEXANDER THE GREAT

A Memorial

AFTER THE BATTLE with Porus, too, Bucephalas died – not at once, but some time afterwards – as most writers say, from wounds for which he was under treatment, but according to Onesicritus, from old age, having become quite worn out; for he was thirty years old when he died. His death grieved Alexander mightily, who felt that he had lost nothing less than a comrade and friend; he also built a city in his memory on the banks of the Hydaspes and called it Bucephalia. It is said, too, that when he lost a dog also, named Peritas, which had been reared by him and was loved by him, he founded a city and gave it the dog's name. Sotion says he heard this from Potamon the Lesbian.

Plutarch, from *Life of Alexander*
Trans. Bernadette Perrin

ANONYMOUS

A Noble End

(1) This tomb proclaims that Indian Tauron lies dead. But his slayer saw Hades first. Like a wild beast to behold, like a relic of the Calydonian boar, it grew in the fertile plains of Arsinoe immovable, shaking from its neck the mane in masses in its lair, and dashing the froth from its jaws. Engaging the fearless dog, readily it ploughed a furrow in its breast: then immediately laid its own neck upon the ground. For Tauron, fastening upon the massive nape, with mane and all, loosed not his teeth again until he sent it down to Hades. So he saved hunter Zenon from distress, unschooled; and earned his gratitude in his tomb below the earth.

(2) A dog is buried beneath this tomb, Tauron, who did not despair in conflict with a killer. When he met a boar in battle face to face, the latter, unapproachable, puffed out its jaws and, white with froth, ploughed a furrow in his breast. The other planted two feet about its back, and fastened upon the bristling monster from the middle of its breast, and wrapped him in the earth. He gave the murderer to Hades and died, as a good Indian should. He rescued Zenon, the hunter whom he followed; and here in this light dust he is laid to rest.

D. L. Page, from *Greek Literary Papyri*

ANONYMOUS

A Warning at Pompei

Cave canem (Beware of the dog).

A surviving mosaic

PYTHAGORAS

Theology

THEY SAY THAT he passed by as a dog was being beaten, and
pitying it, spoke these words: 'Stop, and do not beat it; the animal
has the soul of a friend; I know this, for I heard it speak.'

Xenophanes, from *The Greek Anthology*
Trans. D. Chamberlain

ISLAMIC LEGEND

An Adultress

Hast seen
The record written of Salah-ud-Deen,
The Sultan? How he met upon a day,
In his own city on the public way,
A woman whom they led to die. The veil
Was stripped from off her weeping face, and pale
Her shamed cheeks were, and wild her dark fixed eye,
And her lips drawn with terror at the cry
Of the harsh people and the rugged stones
Borne in their hands to break her flesh and bones,
For the law stood that sinners such as she
Perish by stoning, and this doom must be;
So went the wan adultress to her death.
High noon it was, and the hot Khamseen's breath
Blew from the desert sands and parched the town.
The crows gasped, and the kine went up and down

With lolling tongues; the camels moaned; a crowd
Pressed with their pitchers, wrangling high and loud
About the tank; and one dog by a well,
Nigh dead with thirst, lay where he yelped and fell,
Glaring upon the water out of reach,
And praying succour in a silent speech,
So piteous were its eyes. Which, when she saw
This woman from her foot her shoe did draw,
Albeit death-sorrowful; and looping up
The long silk of her girdle, made a cup
Of the heel's hollow, and thus let it sink
Until it touched the cool black water's brink;
So filled th' embroidered shoe, and gave a draught
To the spent beast, which whined and fawned and quaffed
Her kind gift to the dregs; next licked her hand
With such glad looks that all might understand
He held his life from her; then, at her feet
He followed close all down the cruel street.
Her one friend in that city.

                          But the King,
Riding within his litter, marked this thing,
And how the woman on her way to die,
Had such compassion for the misery
Of that parched hound: 'Take off her chain, and place
The veil once more above the sinner's face,
And lead her to her house in peace!' he said,
'The law is that the people stone thee dead,
For that which thou has wrought; but there is come
Fawning around thy feet, a witness dumb,
Not heard upon thy trial; this brute beast
Testifies for thee, sister! whose weak breast
Death could not make ungentle. I hold rule
In Allah's stead, who is the Merciful,

And hope for Mercy; therefore go thou free –
I dare not show less pity unto thee.'

Sir Edwin Arnold,
from *Pearls of the Faith*

XANTHIPPUS

Dog-Stroke

WHEN THE ENTIRE city was thus putting out to sea, the sight provoked pity in some, and in others astonishment at the hardihood of the step; for they were sending off their families in one direction, while they themselves, unmoved by the lamentations and tears and embraces of their loved ones, were crossing over to the island where the enemy was to be fought. Besides, many who were left behind on account of their great age invited pity also, and much affecting fondness was shown by the tame domestic animals, which ran along with yearning cries of distress by the side of their masters as they embarked. A story is told of one of these, the dog of Xanthippus the father of Pericles, how he could not endure to be abandoned by his master, and so sprang into the sea, swam across the strait by the side of his master's trireme, and staggered out on Salamis, only to faint and die straightway. They say that the spot which is pointed out to this day as 'Dog's Mound' is his tomb.

Plutarch, from his *Life of Themistocles*
Trans. Bernadette Perrin

XENOPHON

An Owner's Manual

OF DOGS THERE are two kinds; the ones called Castorian, the other of the fox breed. The Castorian have this appellation, because Castor, who delighted in the amusement of hunting, had most regard for them; those of the fox breed were so termed because they are bred from a dog and a fox, and through length of time the natures of the two animals are completely amalgamated.

The inferior animals of these two species, which are also the more numerous, are of the following sorts: such as are small, or have turned-up noses, are blue-eyed, near-sighted, ill-shaped, stiff, weak, have thin hair, are long-legged, not well proportioned, deficient in spirit or power of scent, or have bad feet. The small, from their diminutiveness, often find their efforts in the chase fruitless; those that have turned-up noses are weak in the mouth, and are unable, for this reason, to hold the hare; the near-sighted and blue-eyed are imperfect in sight, as well as ill-shaped and unpleasing to the eye; such as are stiff in the frame come off ill in the pursuit; such as are weak, and have thin hair, are unfit to endure fatigue; such as are long-legged, and ill-proportioned, have incompact frames, and run heavily; such as are deficient in spirit quit their work, shrink away from the heat of the sun into the shade and lie down; such as are wanting in scent hardly ever find the hare; and such as have bad feet are unable, even if they are ever so spirited, to endure the exertion, but faint away from pain in the feet.

Of tracking the hare there are many different modes among the same dogs; for some, when they have found the track, proceed onwards without giving any indication, so that it is not known that they are on the track; others merely move their ears, and keep their tail perfectly still; others keep their ears unmoved, but make a motion with the end of their tail. Some, again, contract their ears, and, looking solemnly down on the track, pursue their way along it with their tails lowered and drawn between their legs; many do none of these things, but run madly about the track when they have fallen upon it, barking and trampling out the scent in the most senseless manner. Others, after making many turnings and windings, and getting an inkling of the scent in advance of the hare, leave her behind; whenever they run upon the track, they are never certain; and, when they see the hare before them, they give signs of fear, and do not advance upon her until they see her start. Whatever dogs, again, in tracking and pursuing, run forward and watch frequently, at the same time, for what other dogs discover, have no confidence in themselves. Some, on the other hand, are so rash that they do not allow the experienced dogs of the pack to precede them, but keep them back with a disturbing noise. Others pounce on false scents, and, exulting in whatever they find, take the lead at once, though conscious that they are deceiving the rest; others do the same without being conscious of it. Such dogs are worthless, too, as never leave beaten tracks, and do not know the tracks proper to be followed. Such dogs also as do not know the footsteps that lead to the hare's resting-place, and such as pass hastily over those which she makes in running, are not of a good breed.

Some start in pursuit of the hare with great speed, but relax for want of spirit; some run on, and then miss the scent; others run senselessly into the public roads, and so lose it, and show the utmost reluctance to be recalled. Many, abandoning the pursuit, turn back through dislike of the hare; many, from longing for the society of their master. Some try to draw the other dogs from the track by yelping, making a false scent appear to be true. There are some also, which, though they do not act thus, yet if, while they are running on, they hear a noise on any side, quit their own course, and start off foolishly towards it; for some run after anything in uncertainty, others fancying strongly that they are getting on a track, others imagining they have found one; some making a feint, while other maliciously quit the scent, though they are continually straying about close to it.

Dogs that have such faults, most of them perhaps from nature, but some from having been unskilfully trained, are of little service. Such dogs, indeed, may disgust people with hunting who have a strong turn for it. But of what description dogs of this species ought to be, as to their shapes and other qualities, I will now proceed to show.

In the first place, then, they ought to be large; and, in the next, they should have their heads light, short, and sinewy; the lower jaw muscular; the eyes up-raised, black, and bright; the face large and broad; the line dividing the eyes deep; the ears small, thin, and without hair on the back; the neck long, flexible, and round; the breast broad and not without flesh; the shoulder-blades standing out a little apart from the shoulders; the fore-legs small, straight, round, wiry; the knees straight; the sides should not hang down very deep, but run along obliquely; the loins should be fleshy, their size a medium between long and short, and not too soft or too hard; the upper flanks something between large and small; the hips should be round, fleshy towards the hinder part, not drawn together at the upper, but closely joined within; the part below the flank, and the lower flank itself, should be loose; the tail long, straight, sharp-pointed; the thighs firm; the lower part of the thighs long, full, compact; the hinder legs much longer than those in front, and somewhat lean; the feet round.

                              *   *   *

As to the colour of dogs, it should not be altogether red, or black, or white; for such colours are not the signs of a good breed, but of a common and wild sort. Such as are red or black should have white hair, and such as are white, red hair, growing about the face. On the upper part of the thighs they should have hair growing straight and long, as well as on the loins and at the extremity of the tail; at the upper part of the tail they should have but a moderate quantity of hair.

                              *   *   *

Next vowing to Apollo and to Diana the Huntress to offer them a share of what is captured, let him loose that one of his dogs which is most skilful in tracking; and let this be done, if it is winter, at sunrise; if summer, before daybreak; and at other seasons between the two. When the dog, out of all the tracks that intersect one another, has found the right one, let the hunter set loose another dog, and when this one has gained the track, let him loose the others one by one at no long intervals, and follow them, not urging them, but calling each by name, yet not frequently, lest they should be excited before the proper time. The dogs will hasten forward with joy and spirit, discovering two or three tracks, as the case may be, proceeding along and over them, as they intersect, form circles, run straight or winding, are strong or weak, recognised or unrecognised; the animals passing by one another waving their tails about incessantly, hanging down their ears, and casting bright gleams from their eyes. When they are near the hare, they will make it known to the huntsman by shaking not only their tails but their whole bodies, advancing as it were with hostile ardour, hastening emulously past each other, running resolutely in concert, coming quickly together, separating, and again advancing, till at last they will hit upon the hare's hiding-place, and rush towards her. She, starting up suddenly, will raise behind her, as she flees, a loud barking and clamour from the dogs; and then let the men call after her, as she is pursued, 'Forward, dogs, forward! Right, dogs! Well done, dogs!' and then let the huntsman, wrapping his cloak round his hand, and taking his staff, run along the track of the dogs toward the hare, taking care not to come in the teeth of them, for that would perplex them. The hare, retreating and soon getting out of sight, will in general come round again to the place from which she was started. The hunstman must cry, 'Upon her, boy, upon her! Now boy, now boy!' and the boy must intimate whether she is caught or not. If she is caught in the first run, he must call in the dogs, and seek for another; if not, he must still run on with the dogs with all possible speed, not relaxing, but hurrying forward with the utmost exertion. If the dogs, as they pursue, fall in with her again, he must shout, 'Well done, well done, dogs! Follow, dogs!' and if the dogs get far before him, and he is unable, pursuing their track, to come up with them, but misses the way which they have taken, or cannot see them, though they are straying about somewhere near, or yelping, or keeping on the scent, he may, as he runs on, call out to any one that he meets, and ask, 'Have you seen my dogs anywhere?' When he has discovered where they are, he may, if they are on the track, go up to them and encourage them, repeating, as often as he can, the name of each dog, and varying the tones of his voice, making it sharp or grave, or gentle or strong. In addition to other exhortations, he may, if the pursuit is on a hill, call out thus, 'Well done, dogs! Well done!' but if they are not on the track, but have gone beyond it, he must call to them, 'Come back, come back, dogs!'

*   *   *

In the winter it is proper to let the females rest from labour, and to attend to breeding, that, from enjoying repose, they may produce a stout offspring towards the spring; for that season is particularly favourable for the growth of dogs. During fourteen days the want of the male affects them.

It is proper to take them to vigorous dogs after their ardour is somewhat remitted, that they may conceive the sooner, and, while they are pregnant, not to take them out to hunt constantly, but only at intervals, lest they should miscarry from too much exertion. They go with young sixty days.

When the puppies are born, we must leave them with the mother, and not put them to another dog; for the nurture of strange dogs does not sufficiently contribute to growth; but the milk and breath of their mothers is good for them, and their caresses pleasing.

After the puppies are able to run about, we must give them milk for a year, with those sorts of food on which they are to live always, and nothing else; for much over-feeding of puppies distorts their legs, and produces diseases in their bodies; and their interior parts are thus rendered unsound.

We should give them short names, that it may be easy to call them. They ought to be such as these: Psyche,[1] Thymus,[2] Porpax,[3] Styrax,[4] Lonche,[5] Lochos,[6] Phrura,[7] Phylax,[8] Taxis,[9] Xiphon,[10] Phonax,[11] Phlegon,[12] Alce,[13] Teuchon,[14] Hyleus,[15] Medas,[16] Porthon,[17] Sperchon,[18] Orge,[19] Bremon,[20] Hybris,[21] Thalion,[22] Rhome,[23] Antheus,[24] Hebe,[25] Getheus,[26] Chara,[27] Leusson,[28] Augo,[29] Polys,[30] Bia,[31] Stichon,[32] Speude,[33] Bryas,[34] Œnas,[35] Sterrhos,[36] Crauge,[37] Cænon,[38] Tyrbas,[39] Sthenon,[40] Æther,[41] Actis,[42] Æchme,[43] Noes,[44] Gnome,[45] Stibon,[46] Horme.[47]

[1] Spirit. [2] Courage. [3] Shield-hasp. [4] Spike (at the lower end of a spear-handle). [5] Lance. [6] Ambush. [7] Guard. [8] Keeper. [9] Order. [10] Darter. [11] Barker. [12] Fiery. [13] Strength. [14] Active. [15] Search-wood. [16] Plotter. [17] Ravager. [18] Speed. [19] Passion. [20] Roarer. [21] Audacious. [22] Cheerful. [23] Might. [24] Flowery. [25] Youth. [26] Joyous. [27] Gladness. [28] Looker. [29] Bright-eyes. [30] Stout. [31] Force. [32] Goer. [33] Swift. [34] Lively. [35] Reveller. [36] Stubborn. [37] Yelper. [38] Killer. [39] Bustler. [40] Vigorous. [41] Sky. [42] Ray. [43] Spear. [44] Marker. [45] Prudence [46] Tracker. [47] Eager.

From *Cynegeticus*
Trans. J. S. Watson

ARISTOTLE

Veterinary Advice

THERE ARE SEVERAL breeds of dog. Laconian hounds of both sexes copulate at the age of eight months; at about this time some kinds of dog raise the leg for voiding urine. The bitch conceives at one copulation; this is plainly shown in cases where a dog covers a bitch by stealth: impregnation is effected by one mounting. The Laconian bitch is pregnant for a sixth of a year (*i.e.*, sixty days) – perhaps one, two, or three days more than this, or even one day less; the puppies are born blind and remain so for twelve days. After giving birth the bitch will be mounted again in six months, but not sooner. Some bitches are pregnant for a fifth of a year (*i.e.*, seventy-two days), and the puppies of these are blind for fourteen days. Others are pregnant for a quarter of a year (*i.e.*, three whole months); their puppies are blind for seventeen days. The bitch, so it appears, is in heat for an equal length of time. Menstruation in bitches lasts for seven days; simultaneously the generative organ rises. During this time the bitch does not permit the dog to have sexual intercourse, but in the seven days following: in fact it appears to be a general rule for all bitches that they are in heat for fourteen days; nevertheless, this condition lasts for sixteen days in some. The birth-discharge takes place simultaneously with the delivery of the young: it is thick and phlegm-like, and the quantity, once they have whelped, thins off less than in proportion to the body. Bitches usually have milk five days before parturition; some however seven days before, some four only. The milk is fit for use immediately after their delivery. The Laconian bitch has milk thirty days after copulation. The milk at first is thick, but gets thinner as time proceeds. A bitch's milk is thicker than that of any other animal apart from the sow and the hare. When bitches are of an age for sexual intercourse, an indication of it shows itself, as in women: a swelling occurs in the teats on the breasts and cartilage develops. It is, however, difficult for anyone who is not thoroughly acquainted with the subject to detect this, because the indication is quite small. This occurs in the female; none of these things occur in the male. The males normally lift the leg for passing urine at the age of six months, though some do it later, at eight months, others before six months: as a general statement, we may say they do it when entering on the period of exercising their full powers. Bitches all pass urine in a sitting position, though some have been known to raise the leg. The bitch produces twelve puppies at the most, but usually five or six; a case is known of a single puppy being born. Laconian bitches usually produce eight. Both sexes have intercourse throughout their lives. An unusual thing occurs in the case of the Laconian hounds: they are more vigorous in mounting the bitch after hard work than if they stay idle. The dog of this breed lives about ten years, the bitch about twelve; bitches of other breeds for the most part live about fourteen or fifteen years, some as many as twenty, which is why some people think Homer was correct in his statement that Odysseus' dog died in its twentieth year. As for the Laconian hounds, the females tend to live longer than the males, because the latter are worked harder. In other breeds this difference is not very noticeable, though males nevertheless tend to be longer-lived than females.

A dog sheds no teeth other than the 'canines' as they are called; these are shed by both sexes at the age of four months. As these are the only teeth dog shed, some people are in doubt about the facts. Since they shed only two, and as it is difficult to detect this, there are some who maintain that dogs shed none at all; others, when they see two shed, suppose that all the rest must be shed as well. A dog's age is told by inspecting its teeth: young dogs have sharp, white teeth, older dogs black blunt ones.

* * *

Other animals too are produced from the mixing of different breeds, as in Cyrene the wolves mate with the dogs and generate young, and from fox and dog came the Laconian hounds. They say too that the Indian hounds come from tiger and dog, not immediately but after the third mating; for they say the first offspring is like a savage beast. They take the bitches to deserted places and tie them up; and many are devoured, if the wild animal does not happen to be excited for mating.

From *Historia Animalium*

TYMNES

Epitaph

THE STONE RECORDS that it contains the white Maltese dog, Emmelus' faithful guardian. They called him Bull while he was alive, but now the silent paths of the night have taken his voice.

From *The Greek Anthology*
Trans. D. Chamberlain

MACEDONIUS THE CONSUL

Life and Art

THIS DOG, TRAINED in all manner of hunting, was carved by
Leucan, and dedicated by Alcimenes, who had no fault to find –
but when he saw that the statue resembled the dog in every characteristic he came up with a collar and asked Leucan to make the dog walk:
indeed, it did so much appear to be barking that he assumed it could
also walk.

From *The Greek Anthology*
Trans. D. Chamberlain

CICERO

Pragmatism

MEN DO NOT STORE up corn for the sake of mice and ants but
for their wives and children and households; so the animals share
these fruits of the earth only by stealth as I have said, whereas their
masters enjoy them openly and freely. It must therefore be admitted
that all this abundance was provided for the sake of men, unless
perchance the bounteous plenty and variety of our orchard fruit and the
delightfulness not only of its flavour but also of its scent and appearance
lead us to doubt whether nature intended this gift for man alone! So far
is it from being true that the fruits of the earth were provided for the
sake of animals as well as men, that the animals themselves, as we may
see, were created for the benefit of men. What other use have sheep
save that their fleeces are dressed and woven into clothing for men? and
in fact they could not have been reared nor sustained nor have produced
anything of value without man's care and tendance. Then think of the
dog, with its trusty watchfulness, its fawning affection for its master and
hatred of strangers, its incredible keenness of scent in following a trail

and its eagerness in hunting – what do these qualities imply except that
they were created to serve the conveniences of men?

From *De Natura Deorum*
Trans. H. Rackham

VIRGIL

Watchdogs

Nor last, forget thy faithful Dogs: but feed
With fatning Whey the Mastiff's Generous breed;
And *Spartan* Race; who for the Folds relief
Will prosecute with Cries the Nightly Thief:
Repulse the prouling Woolf, and hold at Bay
The Mountain Robbers, rushing to the Prey.
With cries of Hounds, thou may'st pursue the fear
Of flying Hares, and chace the fallow Deer;
Rouze from their desart Dens, the brisl'd rage
Of Boars, and beamy Stags in toyls engage.

From *Georgics*
Trans. Dryden

A Watchdog Foiled

If neither Piety, nor Heav'n's Command,
Can gain his Passage to the *Stygian* Strand,
This fatal Present shall prevail, at least;
Then shew'd the shining bough, conceal'd within her Vest.
No more was needful: for the gloomy God

Stood mute with Awe, to see the Golden Rod:
Admir'd the destin'd Off'ring to his Queen;
(A venerable Gift so rarely seen.)
His Fury thus appeas'd, he puts to Land:
The Ghosts forsake their Seats, at his Command:
He clears the Deck, receives the mighty Freight,
The leaky Vessel groans beneath the weight.
Slowly he sails; and scarcely stems the Tides:
The pressing Water pours within her sides.
His passengers at length are wafted o're;
Expos'd in muddy Weeds, upon the miry Shore.
No sooner landed, in his Den they found
The triple Porter of the *Stygian* Sound:
Grim *Cerberus;* who soon began to rear
His crested Snakes, and arm'd his bristling Hair.
The prudent Sibyl had before prepar'd
A Sop, in Honey steep'd, to charm the Guard:
Which, mix'd with pow'rful Drugs, she cast before
His greedy grinning Jaws, just op'd to roar:
With three enormous Mouths he gapes; and streight,
With Hunger prest, devours the pleasing Bait.
Long draughts of Sleep his monstrous Limbs enslave;
He reels, and falling, fills the spacious Cave.
The Keeper charm'd, the Chief without Delay
Pass'd on, and took th' irremeable way.

From *The Aeneid*
Trans. Dryden

COLUMELLA

Dogs on the Farm

IT SHOULD BE THE same colour all over, white being the colour which should rather be chosen for a sheep-dog and black for a farm-yard dog; for a dog of varied colouring is not to be recommended for either purpose. The shepherd prefers a white dog because it is unlike a wild beast, and sometimes a plain means of distinction is required in the dogs when one is driving off wolves in the obscurity of early morning or even at dusk, lest one strike a dog instead of a wild beast. The farmyard dog, which is pitted against the wicked wiles of men, if the thief approaches in the clear light of day, has a more alarming appearance if it is black, whereas at night it is not even seen because it resembles the shadow and so, under the cover of darkness, the dog can approach the crafty thief in greater security . . . .

Practically the same food should be given to both types of dog. If the farm is extensive enough to support herds of cattle, barley-flour with whey is a suitable food for all dogs without distinction; but if the land is closely planted with young shoots and affords no pasture, they must be given their fill of bread made with flour of emmer or bread-wheat, mixed, however, with the liquid of boiled beans, which must be lukewarm, for, if it is boiling, it causes madness.

Neither dogs nor bitches must be allowed to have sexual intercourse until they are a year old; for if they are allowed to do so when they are quite young, it enfeebles their bodies and their strength, and causes them to degenerate mentally. The first puppies which a bitch produces must be taken from her, because at the first attempt she does not nourish them properly and the rearing of them hinders her general bodily growth. Dogs procreate vigorously up to ten years of age, but beyond that they do not seem suitable for covering bitches, for the offspring of an elderly dog turns out to be slow and lazy. Bitches conceive up to nine years of age, but are not serviceable after the tenth year . . . .

Dogs should be called by names which are not very long, so that each may obey more quickly when he is called, but they should not have shorter names than those which are pronounced in two syllables, such as the Greek Σκύλαξ (puppy) and the Latin *Ferox* (savage), the Greek Λάκων (Spartan) and the Latin *Celer* (speedy) or, for a bitch, the Greek

Σπουδή (zeal), ᾿Αλκή (Valour), ῾Ρωμή (strength) or the Latin *Lupa* (she-wolf), *Cerva* (hind) and *Tigris* (tigress). It will be found best to cut the tails of puppies forty days after birth in the following manner: there is a nerve, which passes along through the joints of the spine down to the extremity of the tail; this is taken between the teeth and drawn out a little way and then broken. As a result, the tail never grows to an ugly length and (so many shepherds declare) rabies, a disease which is fatal to this animal, is prevented.

It commonly happens that in the summer the ears of dogs are so full of sores caused by flies, that they often lose their ears altogether. To prevent this, the ears should be rubbed with crushed bitter almonds. If, however, the ears are already covered with sores, it will be found a good plan to drip boiled liquid pitch mixed with lard on the wounds. Ticks also fall off if they are touched with this same preparation; for they ought not to be plucked off by hand, lest, as we have remarked also before, they cause sores. A dog which is infested with fleas should be treated either with crushed cumin mixed in water with the same weight of hellebore and smeared on, or else with the juice of the snake-like cucumber, or if these are unobtainable, with stale oil-lees poured over the whole body. If a dog is attacked by the scab, gypsum and sesame should be ground together in equal quantities and mixed with liquid pitch and smeared on the part affected; this remedy is reported to be suitable also for human beings. If this plague has become rather violent, it is got rid of by the juice of the juniper.

From *De Re Rustica*
Trans. E. S. Forster

PETRONIUS

A Debauch

TRIMALCHIO, AFTER IMITATING a man with a trumpet, looked round for his favourite, whom he called Croesus. The creature had blear eyes and very bad teeth, and was tying up an unnaturally obese black puppy in a green handkerchief, and then putting a broken piece of bread on a chair, and cramming it down the throat of the dog, who did not want it and was sick. This reminded Trimalchio of his duties, and he ordered them to bring in Scylax, 'the guardian of the house and the slaves.' An enormous dog on a chain was at once led in, and on receiving a kick from the porter as a hint to lie down, he curled up in front of the table. Then Trimalchio threw him a bit of white bread and said, 'No one in the house loves me better than Scylax.' The favourite took offence at his lavish praise of the dog, and put down the puppy, and encouraged him to attack Scylax. Scylax, after the manner of dogs, filled the dining-room with a most hideous barking, and nearly tore Croesus's little Pearl to pieces. And the uproar did not end with a dog-fight, for a lamp upset over the table, and broke all the glass to pieces, and sprinkled some of the guests with hot oil. Trimalchio did not want to seem hurt at his loss, so he kissed his favourite, and told him to jump on his back. He mounted his horse at once and went on smacking Trimalchio's shoulders with his open hand, saying, 'How many are we, blind man's cheek?' After some time Trimalchio calmed himself, and ordered a great bowl of wine to be mixed, and drinks to be served round to all the slaves who were sitting at our feet, adding this provision: 'If anyone refuses to take it, pour it over his head; business in the daytime and pleasure at night.'

*   *   *

I had even begun to lift up my voice myself, when Trimalchio said, 'Well, well, if we know we must die, why should we not live? As I hope for your happiness, let us jump into a bath. My life on it, you will never regret it. It is as hot as a furnace.' 'Very true, very true,' said Habinnas, 'making two days out of one is my chief delight.' And he got up with bare feet and began to follow Trimalchio, who was clapping his hands.

I looked at Ascyltos and said, 'What do you think? I shall die on the spot at the very sight of a bath.' 'Oh! let us say yes,' he replied, 'and we will slip away in the crowd while they are looking for the bath.' This was agreed, and Giton led us through the gallery to the door, where the dog on the chain welcomed us with such a noise that Ascyltos fell straight into the fish-pond. As I, who had been terrified even of a painted dog, was drunk too, I fell into the same abyss while I was helping him in his struggles to swim. But the porter saved us by intervening to pacify the dog, and pulled us shivering on to dry land. Giton had ransomed himself from the dog some time before by a very cunning plan; when it barked he threw it all the pieces we had given him at dinner, and food distracted the beast from his anger. But when, chilled to the bone, we asked the porter at least to let us out of the door, he replied, 'You are wrong if you suppose you can go out at the door you came in by. None of the guests are ever let out by the same door; they come in at one and go out by another.'

From *Satyricon*
Trans. Michael Heseltine

PLINY

Not Entirely Accurate

AMONG THE ANIMALS, also, that are domesticated with mankind, there are many circumstances that are far from undeserving of being known: among these, there are more particularly that most faithful friend of man, the dog, and the horse. We have an account of a dog that fought against a band of robbers, in defending its master; and although it was pierced with wounds, still it would not leave the body, from which it drove away all birds and beasts. Another dog, again, in Epirus, recognized the murderer of its master, in the midst of an assemblage of people, and, by biting and barking at him, extorted from him a confession of his crime. A king of the Garamantes also was brought back from exile by two hundred dogs, which maintained the combat against all his opponents. The people of Colophon and Castabala kept troops of dogs, for the purposes of war; and these used to fight in the front rank, and never retreat; they were the most faithful of auxiliaries, and yet required no pay. After the defeat of the Cimbri, their dogs defended their moveable houses, which were carried upon waggons. Jason, the Lycian, having been slain, his dog refused to take food, and died of famine. A dog, to which Darius gives the name of Hyrcanus, upon the funeral pile of King Lysimachus being lighted, threw itself into the flames, and the dog of King Hiero did the same. Philistus also give us a similar account of Pyrrhus, the dog of the tyrant

Gelon: and it is said, also, that the dog of Nicomedes, king of Bithynia, tore Consingis, the wife of that king, in consequence of her wanton behaviour, when toying with her husband.

Among ourselves, Volcatius, a man of rank, who instructed Cascellius in the civil law, as he was riding on his Asturian jennet, towards evening, from his country-house, was attacked by a robber, and was only saved by his dog. The senator Cælius, too, while lying sick at Placentia, was surprised by armed men, but received not a wound from them until they had first killed his dog. But a more extraordinary fact than all, is what took place in our own times, and is testified by the public register of the Roman people. In the consulship of Appius Junius and P. Silius, when Titius Sabinus was put to death, together with his slaves, for the affair of Nero, the son of Germanicus, it was found impossible to drive away a dog which belonged to one of them from the prison; nor could it be forced away from the body, which had been cast down the Gemitorian steps; but there it stood howling, in the presence of vast multitudes of people; and when some one threw a piece of bread to it, the animal carried it to the mouth of its master. Afterwards, when the body was thrown into the Tiber, the dog swam into the river, and endeavoured to raise it out of the water; quite a throng of people being collected to witness this instance of an animal's fidelity.

Dogs are the only animals that are sure to know their masters; and if they suddenly meet him as a stranger, they will instantly recognize him. They are the only animals that will answer to their names, and recognize the voices of the family. They recollect a road along which they have passed, however long it may be. Next to man, there is no living creature whose memory is so retentive. By sitting down on the ground, we may arrest their most impetuous attack, even when prompted by the most violent rage.

In daily life we have discovered many other valuable qualities in this animal; but its intelligence and sagacity are more especially shown in the chase. It discovers and traces out the tracks of the animal, leading by the leash the sportsman who accompanies it straight up to the prey; and as soon as ever it has perceived it, how silent it is, and how secret but significant is the indication which it gives, first by the tail and afterwards by the nose! Hence it is, that even when worn out with old age, blind, and feeble, they are carried by the huntsman in his arms, being still able to point out the coverts where the game is concealed, by snuffing with their muzzles at the wind. The Indians raise a breed between the dog and the tiger, and for this purpose tie up the females in the forests when in heat. The first two litters they look upon as too savage to be reared, but they bring up the third.

The Gauls do the same with the wolf and the dog; and their packs of hounds have, each of them, one of these dogs, which acts as their guide and leader. This dog they follow in the chase, and him they carefully obey; for these animals have even a notion of subordination among themselves. It is asserted that the dogs keep running when they drink at the Nile, for fear of becoming a prey to the voracity of the crocodile. When Alexander the Great was on his Indian expedition, he was presented by the king of Albania with a dog of unusual size; being greatly delighted with its noble appearance, he ordered bears, and after them wild boars, and then deer, to be let loose before it; but the dog lay down, and regarded them with a kind of immoveable contempt. The noble spirit of the general became irritated by the sluggishness thus manifested by an animal of such vast bulk, and he ordered it to be killed. The report of this reached the king, who accordingly sent another dog, and at the same time sent word that its powers were to be tried, not upon small animals, but upon the lion or the elephant; adding, that he had originally but two and that if this one were put to death, the race would be extinct. Alexander, without delay, procured a lion, which in his presence was instantly torn to pieces. He then ordered an elephant to be brought, and never was he more delighted with any spectacle; for the dog, bristling up its hair all over the body, began by thundering forth a loud barking, and then attacked the animal, leaping at it first on one side and then on the other, attacking it in the most skilful manner, and then again retreating at the opportune moment, until at last the elephant, being rendered quite giddy by turning round and round, fell to the earth, and made it quite re-echo with his fall.

This animal brings forth twice in the year; it is capable of bearing young when a year old, and gestation continues for sixty days. The young ones are born blind, and the greater the supply of nourishment from the mother's milk, the more slowly do they acquire their sight; still, however, this never takes place later than the twentieth day, or earlier than the seventh. It is said by some writers, that if only one is born, it is able to see on the ninth day; and that if there are two, they begin to see on the tenth, every additional one causing the power of seeing to come a day later. It is said, too, that the females which are produced by the mother in her first litter, are subject to the night-mare. The best dog of the litter is the one which is last in obtaining its sight, or else the one which the mother carries first into her bed.

Canine madness is fatal to man during the heat of Sirius, and, as we have already said, it proves so in consequence of those who are bitten having a deadly horror of water. For this reason, during the thirty days that this star exerts its influence, we try to prevent the disease by mixing dung from the poultry-yard with the dog's food; or else, if they are already attacked by the disease, by giving them hellebore.

We have a single remedy against the bite, which has been but lately discovered, by a kind of oracle, as it were – the root of the wild rose, which is called cynorrhodos, or dog-rose. Columella informs us, that if, on the fortieth day after the birth of the pup, the last bone of the tail is bitten off, the sinew will follow with it; after which, the tail will not grow, and the dog will never become rabid. It is mentioned, among the other prodigies, and this I take to be one indeed, that a dog once spoke; and that when Tarquin was expelled from the kingdom, a serpent barked.

From *Natural History*
Trans. J. Bostock and M. T. Riley

PLUTARCH

Compassion

THE EXCELLENT *Plutarch* (who has more Strokes of Good-nature in his Writings than I remember in any Author) cites a Saying of *Cato* to this effect, *That 'tis no easie Task to preach to the Belly which has no Ears.* 'Yet if (says he) we are ashamed to be so out of Fashion as not to Offend, let us at least Offend with some Discretion and Measure. If we kill an Animal for our Provision, let us do it with the Meltings of Compassion, and without tormenting it. Let us consider, that 'tis in its own Nature Cruelty to put a living Creature to Death; we at least destroy a Soul that has Sense and Perception' – In the life of *Cato* the Censor, he takes occasion from the Severe Disposition of that Man to Discourse in this manner. 'It ought to be esteemed a Happiness to Mankind, that our Humanity has a wider Sphere to exert itself in, than bare Justice. It is no more than the Obligation of our very Birth to practise Equity to our own kind, but Humanity may be extended thro' the whole order of Creatures, even to the meanest: Such Actions of Charity are the Over-flowings of a mild Good nature on all below us. It is certainly the part of a well-natured Man to take care of his Horses and Dogs, not only in expectation of their labour while they are Foals and Whelps, but even when their old Age has made them incapable of Service.'

Alexander Pope, from *The Guardian* 61: 21 May 1713

MARTIAL

Issa

Issa's more of a rogue than Lesbia's sparrow,
Issa's purer by far than kiss of ring-dove,
Issa's more of a coax than all the maidens,
Issa's worth all the costly pearls of India,
Issa's Publius' darling lady puppy.
If she whimpers you'll think that she is speaking,
Sorrow and joy she feels as much as he does,
Snuggling close to his neck she sleeps so softly
That you'd scarcely believe the pet was breathing.
If in the night she finds that Nature's calling,
Never a spot she'd leave on master's bedspread,
But with her paw a gentle tap she gives him,
'Please put me down' – and then, 'Please pick me up now'.
Modest and chaste a little lap-dog is she,
One who knows naught of love, nor could we ever
Find for this tender maid a spouse to match her.
So, lest death should bear off the whole of Issa,
Master has had a portrait of her painted,

Where you will see so true a likeness of her
That Issa's self is not more truly like her;
Place side by side the real and painted Issas:
Either you'll think that both are living Issas
Or you'll believe that both are in a picture.

Trans. J. M. C. Toynbee

Diverse Thoughts

Your face and lips, Manneia, your little dog licks;
I don't wonder, for a dog likes to eat filth

*   *   *

Whenever you come along we assume Cosmus [perfumer] is on the move, and that oil of cinnamon is flowing in a stream from a shaken glass-bottle. But I would not have you, Gellia, take pride in such trumpery, for, let me tell you, I think that my dog smells as sweet in much the same way.

From *Epigrams*
Trans. J. Learmonth

LUCIAN

Honour Bound

I MAKE NO BONES of telling you a story that I was told by our friend Thesmopolis, the Stoic, of something that happened to him which was very comical, and it is not beyond the bounds of possibility that the same thing may happen to someone else. He was in the household of a rich and self-indulgent woman who belonged to a distinguished family in the city. Having to go into the country one time, in the first place he underwent, he said, this highly ridiculous experience, that he, a philosopher, was given a favourite to sit by, one of those fellows who have their legs depilated and their beards shaved off; the mistress held him in high honour, no doubt. He gave the fellow's name; it was Dovey! Now what a thing that was, to begin with, for a stern old man with a grey beard (you know what a long, venerable beard Thesmopolis used to have) to sit beside a fellow with rouged cheeks, underlined eyelids, an unsteady glance, and a skinny neck – no dove, by Zeus, but a plucked vulture! Indeed, had it not been for repeated entreaties, he would have worn a hair-net on his head. In other ways too Thesmopolis suffered numerous annoyances from him all the way, for he hummed and whistled and no doubt would even have danced in the carriage if Thesmopolis had not held him in check.

Then too, something else of a similar nature was required of him. The woman sent for him and said: 'Thesmopolis, I am asking a great favour of you; please do it for me without making any objections or waiting to be asked repeatedly.' He promised, as was natural, that he would do anything, and she went on: 'I ask this of you because I see that you are kind and thoughtful and sympathetic – take my dog Myrrhina (you know her) into your carriage and look after her for me, taking care that she does not want for anything. The poor thing is unwell and is almost ready to have puppies, and these abominable, disobedient servants do not pay much attention even to me on journeys, let alone to her. So do not think that you will be rendering me a trivial service if you take good care of my precious, sweet doggie.' Thesmopolis promised, for she plied him with many entreaties and almost wept. The situation was as funny as could be: a little dog peeping out of his cloak just below his beard, wetting him often, even if Thesmopolis did not add that detail, barking in a squeaky voice (that is the way with Maltese dogs, you know), and licking the philosopher's beard, especially if any suggestion of yesterday's gravy was in it! The favourite who had sat by him was joking rather wittily one day at the expense of the company in the dining-room, and when in due course his banter reached Thesmopolis, he remarked: 'As to Thesmopolis, I can only say that our Stoic has finally gone to the dogs!' [become a Cynic]. I was told, too, that the doggie actually had her puppies in the cloak of Thesmopolis.

From *On Salaried Posts in Great Houses*
Trans. A. M. Harman

NONNUS

Devotion

BUT THE GIRL awaking tore her rose-red cheeks, and mourning scored her firm breasts with her finger-nails, and tore long locks of hair from the roots; then seeing the cattle still standing by her on the rock, the sorrowful maiden cried in a voice of lamentation:

'Where is the body of Icarios? Tell me, beloved hills! Tell me my father's fate, ye bulls that knew him well! Who were the murderers of my father slain? Where has my darling father gone? Is he wandering over the countryside, staying with the countrymen and teaching a neighbour to plant the young shoots of his fair vintage, or is he the guest of some pastoral gardener and sharing his feast? Tell his mourning daughter, and I will endure till he come. If my father is still alive, I will live with my parent again and water the plants of his garden: but if my father is dead and plants trees no more, I will face death like his over his dead body.'

So she spoke, and ran with swift knee up into the mountain forest, seeking the tracks of her father newly slain. But to her questions no goatherd was bold to reply, no herdsman of cattle in the woodlands pitied the maiden or pointed to a faint trace of her father still unheard-of, no ancient shepherd showed her the body of Icarios, but she wandered in vain. At last a gardener found her and told the sad news in a sorrowful voice, and showed the tomb to her father lately slain.

When the maiden heard it, she was distracted but with sober madness: she plucked the hair from her head and laid it upon the beloved tomb, a maiden unveiled, unshod, drenching her clothes with selfshed showers of ever-flowing tears. Speechless for a time, Erigone kept her lips sealed with silence; the dog the companion of Erigone shared her feelings, he whimpered and howled by the side of his mourning mistress, sorrowing with her sorrow. Wildly she ran up to a tall tree: she tied upon it a rope with a noose fast about her neck and hung herself high in the air, twisting in self-sought agonies with her two twitching feet. So she died, and had a willing fate; her dog ran round and round the girl with sorrowful howls, a dumb animal dropping tears of sympathy from his eyes.

The dog would not leave his mistress alone, unguarded, but there he stayed by the tree, and chased off the preying beasts, panther or lion.

Then wayfarers passed, and he showed with mute gestures the unwedded maid hanging in the tree with a noose about her neck. Full of pity they came up to the tree on tiptoe, and took down the chaste maiden from the leafy branches; then hollowed a grave close by with earthdigging shovels. The sorrowing dog knew what they did, and helped them, scratching and scattering the surface of the soil with sharp claws and grubbing with clever feet. So the wayfarers buried the body but lately dead, and they went away on their business quickfoot with a weight of sorrow under their hearts one and all. But the dog remained near the tomb alone, for love of Erigone, and there he died of his own free will.

Father Zeus had pity, and he placed Erigone in the company of the stars near the Lion's back. The rustic maid holds an ear of corn; for she did not wish to carry the red grapes which had been her father's death. And Zeus brought old Icarios into the starspangled sky to move beside his daughter, and called him Boötes, the Plowman, shining bright, and touching the Wain of the Arcadian Bear. The Dog he made also a fiery constellation chasing the Hare, in that part where the starry image of sea-faring Argo voyages round the circle of Olympos.

Such is the fiction of the Achaian story, mingling as usual persuasion with falsehood: but the truth is: Zeus our Lord on high joined the soul of Erigone with the star of the heavenly Virgin holding an ear of corn, and near the heavenly Dog he placed a dog like him in shape, Seirios of the autumn as they call him, and the soul of Icarios he combined with Boötes in the heavens. These are the gifts of Cronides to the vinelands of Attica, offering one honour to Pallas and Dionysos together.

From *Dionysiaca*
Trans. by W. H. D. Rouse

ALCIPHRON

A Trap

I SET A TRAP FOR those cursèd foxes, with a bit of meat tied to the trigger. They were raiding the vines, not only chewing at the grapes but going so far as to bite off from the vines their clusters entire; and it was reported that my master was about to arrive – he is a harsh and bitter man, who is continually proposing trifling decrees and resolutions to the Athenians on the Pnyx and who, by his rough ways and his skilful oratory, has before now sent many a man to the Eleven. So, since I was afraid, especially considering what sort of man my master is, that something might happen to me too, I wanted to catch the thieving fox and turn it over to him. But the fox never came near the trap. Little Plangon, however, the Maltese puppy that we were raising as a pet to please my mistress, rushed over-greedily at the bait, and now, as you see, it lies outstretched, a mouldering corpse already, two days dead. So, unawares, I heaped trouble on trouble. And what mercy will be found in the old churl's heart for such offences? I will run away as fast as my feet can carry me. Good-bye to the farm and to all my possessions! It's high time to save my own skin, and, instead of waiting for trouble, to take measures before trouble comes.

From *Letters of Farmers*
Trans. A. R. Beane and Francis Forbes

THE BIBLE

Research

MY AUNT PUT DOWN her glass and asked the woman behind the bar, 'Did you ever hear of the doggies' church?'

'I seem to remember hearing something, but it was donkey's years ago, wasn't it? Long before my time. Somewere in Hove, wasn't it?'

'No, dear. Not a hundred yards from where you are standing now. We used to come to the Cricketers' after the service. The Rev. Curran and me.'

'Didn't the police interfere or something?'

'They tried to make out that he had no right to the title of Rev. But we pointed out that it stood for Revered and not Reverend in *our* church, and we didn't belong to the established. They couldn't touch us, we were breakaways like Wesley, and we had all the dog-owners of Brighton and Hove behind us – they even came over from as far as Hastings. The police tried to get us once under the Blasphemy Act, but nobody could find any blasphemy in our services. They were very very solemn. Curran wanted to start the churching of bitches after the puppies came, but I said that was going too far – even the Church of England had abandoned churching. Then there was the question of marrying divorced couples – I thought it would treble our income, but there it was Curran who stood firm. "We don't recognize divorce," he said, and he was quite right – it would have sullied the sentiment.'

'Did the police win in the end?' I asked.

'They always do. They had him up for speaking to girls on the front, and a lot was said in court that wasn't apropos. I was young and angry and uncomprehending, and I wouldn't help him any more. No wonder he abandoned me and went to look for Hannibal. No one can stand not being forgiven. That's God's privilege.'

We left the Cricketers' and my aunt took a turning this way and a turning that until we came to a shuttered hall and a sign which read: 'Text for the Week. "If thou has run with the footmen, and they have wearied thee, Then how canst thou contend with horses? Jeremiah 12"' I can't say that I understood the meaning very well, unless it was a warning against Brighton races, but perhaps the ambiguity was the attraction. The sect, I noticed, was called The Children of Jeremiah.

'This was where we held our services,' Aunt Augusta said. 'Sometimes you could hardly hear the words for the barking. "It's their form of prayer," Curran would say, "let each pray after his own fashion," and sometimes they lay quite peacefully licking their parts. "Cleansing themselves for the House of the Lord," Curran would say. It makes me a little sad to see strangers here now. And I never much cared for the prophet Jeremiah.'

'I know little about Jeremiah.'

'They sank him in the mud,' Aunt Augusta said. 'I studied the Bible very carefully in those days, but there was little that was favourable to dogs in the Old Testament. Tobias took his dog with him on his journey with the angel, but it played no part in the story at all, not even when a fish tried to eat Tobias. A dog was an unclean beast, of course, in those times. He only came into his own with Christianity. It was the Christians who began to carve dogs in stone in the cathedrals, and even while they were still doubtful about women's souls they were beginning to think that maybe a dog had one, though they couldn't get the Pope to

pronounce one way or the other, not even the Archbishop of Canterbury. It was left to Curran.'

'A big responsibility,' I said. I couldn't make out whether she was
serious about Curran or not.

'It was Curran who set me reading theology,' Aunt Augusta said. 'He
wanted references to dogs. It wasn't easy to find any – even in St
Francis de Sales. I found lots about fleas and butterflies and stags and
elephants and spiders and crocodiles in St Francis but a strange neglect
of dogs. Once I had a terrible shock. I said to Curran, "It's no good.
We can't go on. Look what I've just found in the Apocalypse. Jesus is
saying who can enter the city of God. Just listen to this – 'Without are
dogs and sorcerers and whoremongers and murderers and idolaters,
and whosoever loveth or maketh a lie.' You see the company dogs are
supposed to keep?"

"It proves our point", Curran said. "Whoremongers and murderers
and the rest – they all have souls, don't they? They only have to repent,
and it's the same with dogs. The dogs who come to our church have
repented. They don't consort any more with whoremongers and
sorcerers. They live with respectable people in Brunswick Square or
Royal Crescent." Do you know that Curran was so little put off by the
Apocalypse he actually preached a sermon on that very text, telling
people that it was their responsibility to see that their dogs didn't back-
slide? "Loose the lead and spoil the dog," he said. "There are only too
many murderers in Brighton and whoremongers at the Metropole all
ready to pick up what you loose. And as for sorcerers – " Luckily Hatty,
who was with us by that time, had not yet become a fortune-teller. It
would have spoilt the image.'

'He was a good preacher?'

'It was music to hear him,' she said with happy regret, and we began
to walk back towards the front; we could hear the shingle turning over
from a long way away. 'He was not exclusive,' my aunt said. 'For him
dogs were like the House of Israel, but he was an apostle also to the
Gentiles – and the Gentiles, to Curran, included sparrows and parrots
and white mice – not cats, cats he always regarded as Pharisees. Of
course no cat dared to come into the church with all those dogs around,
but there was one who used to sit in the window of a house opposite
and sneer when the congregation came out. Curran excluded fish too –
it would be too shocking to eat something with a soul, he said. Elephants
he had a great feeling for, which was generous of him considering

Hannibal had trodden on his toe. Let's sit down here, Henry. I always find Guinness a little tiring.'

Graham Greene, from *Travels with My Aunt*

IRISH LEGEND

The Slaying of the Smith's Hound by Cuchulain, and the Reason he is Called Cuchulain

THEN IT WAS that Cormac Conlongas son of Conchobar spake: 'Again that little lad performed a second deed in the following year.' 'What deed was that?' asked Ailill.

'A goodly smith there was in the land of Ulster, Culann the Smith, by name. He made ready a feast for Conchobar and set out for Emain to invite him. He made known to him that only a few should come with him, that he should bring none but a true guest along, forasmuch as it was not a domain or lands of his own that he had, but the fruit of his two hands, his sledges and anvils, his fists and his tongs. Conchobar replied that only a few would go to him.

'Culann went back to the stithy to prepare and make ready meat and drink in readiness for the king. Conchobar sat in Emain till it was time to set out for the feast, till came the close of the day. The king put his fine, light travelling apparel about him, and went with fifty chariot-chiefs of those that were noblest and most illustrious of the heroes, and betook him to the boys before starting, to bid them farewell. It was always his custom to visit and revisit them when going and coming, to seek his blessing of the boys. Conchobar came on to the fair-green, and he saw a thing that astounded him: Thrice fifty boys at one end of the green and a single boy at the other, and the single boy won the victory at the goal and at hurling from the thrice fifty boys. When it was at hole-play they were – a game of hole that used to be played on the fair-green of Emain – and it was their turn to drive and his to keep guard, he would catch the thrice fifty balls just outside of the hole, and not one went by him into the hole. When it was their turn to keep guard and his to drive, he would send the thrice fifty balls into the hole without fail, and the boys were unable to ward them off. When it was at tearing off each other's garments they played, he would strip off them their thrice fifty suits so that they were quite naked, and they were not able all of them to take as much as the brooch from his mantle. When it was at wrestling they were, he would throw those same thrice fifty boys to the ground under him, and they did not succeed all of them around him in lifting him up. Conchobar looked with wonder at the little lad. "O, ye youths," cried Conchobar. "Hail to the land whence cometh the lad ye see, if the deeds of his manhood shall be such as are those of his boyhood!" "'Tis not just to speak thus," exclaimed Fergus; "e'en as the little lad grows, so will his deeds of manhood grow with him." "The little lad shall be called to us, that he may come with us to enjoy the feast to which we go." The little lad was summoned to Conchobar. "Good, my lad," said Conchobar. "Come thou with us to enjoy the feast whereto we go, for thou art a guest." "Nay, but I will not go," the little boy answered. "How so?" asked Conchobar. "Forasmuch as the boys have not yet had their fill of games and of sport, and I will not leave them till they have had enough play." "It is too long for us to await thee till then, little boy, and by no means shall we wait." "Go then before us," said the little boy, "and I will follow after ye." "Thou knowest naught of the way, little boy," said Conchobar. "I will follow the trail of the company and of the horses and chariots."

'Thereafter Conchobar came to the house of Culann the Smith. The king was waited upon and all were shown honour, as befitted their rank and calling and privileges, nobility and gentle accomplishment. Straw and fresh rushes were spread out under them. They commenced to carouse and make merry. Culann inquired of Conchobar: "Hast thou, O king, appointed any to come after thee this night to this dûn?" "No, I appointed no one," replied Conchobar, for he had forgotten the little lad whom he had charged to come after him. "Why so?" asked Culann. "An excellent bloodhound have I, that was brought from Spain. There are three chains upon him, and three men at each chain. Because of our goods and our cattle he is slipped and the liss is closed. When his dog-chain is loosed from him, no one dares approach the same cantred with him to make a course or a circuit, and he knows no one but myself. The power of hundreds is in him for strength." Then spake Conchobar, "Let the dûn be opened for the ban-dog, that he may guard the cantred." The dog-chain is taken off the ban-dog, and he makes a swift round of the cantred. And he comes to the mound whereon he was wont to keep guard of the stead, and there he was, his head couched on his paws, and wild, untameable, furious, savage, ferocious, ready for fight was the dog that was there.

'As for the boys: They were in Emain until the time came for them to disperse. Each of them went to the house of his father and mother, of his foster-mother and foster-father. Then the little lad went on the trail of the party, till he reached the house of Culann the Smith. He began to shorten the way as he went with his play-things. He threw his ball and threw his club after it, so that it hit the ball. The one throw was no greater than the other. Then he threw his staff after them both, so that it reached the ball and the club before ever they fell. Soon the lad came up. When he was nigh to the green of the fort wherein were Culann and Conchobar, he threw all his play-things before him except only the ball. The watch-dog descried the lad and bayed at him, so that in all the countryside was heard the howl of the watch-hound. And not a division of feasting was what he was inclined to make of him, but to swallow him down at one gulp past the cavity of his chest and the width of his throat and the pipe of his breast. And it interfered not with the lad's play, although the hound made for him. And the lad had not with him any means of defence, but he hurled an unerring cast of the ball, so that it passed through the gullet of the watch-dog's neck and carried the guts within him out through his back door, and he laid hold of the hound by the two legs and dashed him against a pillar-stone that was near him, so that every limb of him sprang apart, so that he broke into bits all over the ground. Conchobar heard the yelp of the ban-dog. Conchobar and his people could not move; they weened they would not find the lad alive before them. "Alas, O warriors," cried Conchobar; "in no good luck have we come to enjoy this feast." "How so?" asked all. "The little lad who has come to meet me, my sister's son, Setanta son of Sualtaim, is undone through the hound." As one man, arose all the renowned men of Ulster. Though a door of the hostel was thrown wide open, they all rushed in the other direction out over the palings of the fortress. But fast as they all got there, faster than all arrived Fergus, and he lifted the little lad from the ground on the slope of his shoulder and bore him into the presence of Conchobar. They put him on Conchobar's knee. A great alarm arose amongst them that the king's sister's son should have been all but killed. And Culann came out, and he saw his slaughter-hound in many pieces. He felt his heart beating against his breast. Whereupon he went into the dûn. "Welcome thy coming, little lad," said Culann, "because of thy mother and father, but not welcome is thy coming for thine own sake. Yet would that I had not made a feast." "What hast thou against the lad?" queried Conchobar. "Not luckily for me hast thou come to quaff my ale and to eat my food; for my substance is now a wealth gone to waste, and my livelihood is a livelihood lost now after my dog. He hath kept honour and life for me. Good was the friend thou hast robbed me of, even my dog, in that he tended my herds and flocks and stock for me; he was the protection of all our cattle, both afield and at home." "Be not angered thereat, O Culann my master," said the little boy. "It is no great matter, for I will pass a just judgement upon it." "What judgement thereon wilt thou pass, lad?" Conchobar asked. "If there is a whelp of the breed of that dog in Erin, he shall be reared by me till he be fit to do business as was his sire. Till then myself will be the hound to protect his flocks and his cattle and his land and even himself in the meanwhile. And I will safeguard the whole plain of Murthemne, and no one will carry off flock nor herd without that I know it."

' "Well hast thou given judgement, little lad," said Conchobar. "In sooth, we ourselves could not give one that would be better," said Cathba. "Why should it not be from this that thou shouldst take the name Cuchulain, ('Wolfhound of Culann')?" "Nay, then," answered the lad; "dearer to me mine own name, Setanta son of Sualtaim." "Say not so, lad," Cathba continued; "for the men of Erin and Alba shall hear that name and the mouths of the men of Erin and Alba shall be full of that name!" "It pleaseth me so, whatever the name that is given me," quoth the little lad. Hence the famous name that stuck to him, namely Cuchulain, after he had killed the hound that was Culann's the Smith's.

'A little lad did that deed,' added Cormac Conlongas son of Conchobar, 'when he had completed six years after his birth, when he slew the watch-dog that hosts nor companies dared not approach in the same cantred. No need would there be of wonder or of surprise if he should come to the edge of the marches, if he should cut off the four-pronged fork, if he should slay one man or two men or three men or four men, now when his seventeen years are completed on the Cattle-driving of Cualnge!'

From *Taín Bó Cúalnge*

ST BERNARD

Eternal Truth

Qui me amat, amat et canem meum (Love me, love my dog)

EDWARD, DUKE OF YORK

The Dog of Montargis

I SHALL TELL YOU a tale of a greyhound that was Auberie's of Moundydier, of which men may see the painting in the realm of France in many places. Aubery was a squire of the king's house of France, and upon a day that he was going from the court to his own house, and as he passed by the woods of Bondis, the which is nigh Paris, and led with him a well good and a fair greyhound that he had brought up. A man that hated him for great envy without any other reason, who was called Makarie, ran upon him within the wood and slew him without warning, for Auberie was not aware of him. And when the greyhound sought his master and found him he covered him with earth and with leaves with his claws and his muzzle in the best way that he could. And when he had been there three days and could no longer abide for hunger, he turned again to the king's court. There he found Makarie, who was a great gentleman, who had slain his master, and as soon as the greyhound perceived Makarie, he ran upon him, and would have maimed him, unless men had hindered him. The King of France, who was wise and a man of perception, asked what it was, and men told him the truth. The greyhound took from the boards what he could, and brought to his master and put meat in his mouth, and the same wise the greyhound did three days or four. And then the King made men follow the greyhound, for to see where he bare the meat that he took in the court. And then they found Auberie dead and buried. And then the King, as I have said, made come many of the men of his court, and made them stroke the greyhound's side, and cherish him and made his men lead him by the collar towards the house, but he never stirred. And then the King commanded Makarie to take a small piece of flesh and give it to the greyhound. And as soon as the greyhound saw Makarie, he left the flesh, and would have run upon him. And when the King saw that, he had great suspicions about Makarie, and said to him that he must needs fight against the greyhound. And Makarie began to laugh, but anon the King made him do the deed, and one of the kinsmen of Auberie saw the great marvel of the greyhound and said that he would swear upon the sacrament as is the custom in such a case for the greyhound, and Makarie swore on the other side, and then they were led into our Lady's Isle at Paris, and there fought the greyhound and Makarie. For which Makarie had a great two-handed staff, and they fought so that Makarie was discomfitted, and then the king commanded that the greyhound the which had Makarie under him should be taken up, and then the King made enquiry of the truth of Makarie, the which acknowledged he had slain Aubrey in treason, and therefore he was hanged and drawn.

From *The Master of Game*

KING ARTHUR

Ancient Manners

PEOPLE IN THOSE days had rather different ideas about the training of dogs to what we have today. They did it more by love than strictness. Imagine a modern M. F. H. going to bed with his hounds, and yet Flavius Arrianus says that it is 'Best of all if they can sleep with a person because it makes them more human and because they rejoice in the company of human beings: also if they have had a restless night or been internally upset, you will know of it and will not use them to hunt next day.' In Sir Ector's kennel there was a special boy, called the Dog Boy, who lived with the hounds day and night. He was a sort of head hound, and it was his business to take them out every day for walks, to pull thorns out of their feet, keep cankers out of their ears, bind the smaller bones that got dislocated, dose them for worms, isolate and nurse them in distemper, arbitrate in their quarrels and sleep curled up among them at night. If one more learned quotation may be excused, this is how the Duke of York who was killed at Agincourt described such a boy in his *Master of Game:* 'Also I will teach the child to lead out the hounds to scombre twice in the day in the morning and in the evening, so that the sun be up, especially in winter. Then should he let them run and play long in a meadow in the sun, and them comb every hound after the other, and wipe them with a great wisp of straw, and this he shall do every morning. And then he shall lead them into some fair place where tender grass grows as corn and other things, that therewith they may feed themselves as if it is medicine for them.' Thus, since the boy's 'heart and his business be with the hounds,' the hounds themselves become 'goodly and kindly and clean, glad and joyful and playful, and goodly to all manner of folks save to the wild beasts to whom they should be fierce, eager and spiteful.'

Sir Ector's dog-boy was none other than the one who had had his nose bitten off by the terrible Wat. Not having a nose like a human, and being, moreover, subjected to stone-throwing by the other village children, he had become more comfortable with animals. He talked to them, not in baby-talk like a maiden lady, but correctly in their own growls and barks. They all loved him very much, and revered him for taking thorns out of their toes, and came to him with their little troubles at once. He always understood immediately what was wrong, and generally he could put it right. It was nice for the dogs to have their god with them, in visible form.

The Wart was fond of the Dog Boy, and thought him very clever to be able to do all these things with animals – for he could make them do almost anything just by moving his hands – while the Dog Boy loved the Wart in much the same way as his dogs loved him, and thought the Wart was almost holy because he could read and write. They spent much of their time together, rolling about with the dogs in the kennel.

The kennel was on the ground floor, near the mews, with a loft above it, so that it should be cool in summer and warm in winter. The hounds were alaunts, gazehounds, lymers and braches. They were called Clumsy, Trowneer, Phoebe, Colle, Gerland, Talbot, Luath, Luffra, Apollon, Orthros, Bran, Gelert, Bounce, Boy, Lion, Bungey, Toby and Diamond. The Wart's own special one was called Cavall, and he happened to be licking Cavall's nose – not the other way about – when Merlyn came in and found him.

'That will come to be regarded as an insanitary habit,' said Merlyn, 'though I can't see it myself. After all, God made the creature's nose just as well as he made your tongue.'

'If not better,' added the philosopher pensively.

T. H. White, from *The Sword in the Stone*

GEOFFREY CHAUCER
The Prioress

But, for to speken of hire conscience,
She was so charitable and so pitous
She wolde wepe, if that she saugh a mous
Kaught in a trappe, if it were deed or bledde.
Of smale houndes hadde she that she fedde
With rosted flessh, or milk and wastel-breed.
But soore wepte she if oon of hem were deed,
Of if men smoot it with a yerde smerte;
And al was conscience and tendre herte.

From *The Canterbury Tales*: General Prologue

GELERT
Pilgrimage

BETHGELERT IS SITUATED in a valley surrounded by huge hills, the most remarkable of which are Moel Hebog and Cerrig Llan; the former fences it on the south, and the latter, which is quite black and nearly perpendicular, on the east. A small stream rushes through the valley, and sallies forth by a pass at its south-eastern end. The valley is said by some to derive its name of Beddgelert, which signifies the grave of Celert, from being the burial-place of Celert, a British saint of the sixth century, to wholm Llangeler in Carmarthenshire is believed to have been consecrated; but the popular and most universally received tradition is that it has its name from being the resting-place of a faithful dog called Celert, or Gelert, killed by his master, the warlike and celebrated Llywelyn ab Jorwerth, from an unlucky misapprehension. Though the legend is known to most people, I shall take the liberty of relating it.

Llywelyn, during his contests with the English, had encamped with a few followers in the valley, and one day departed with his men on an expedition, leaving his infant son in a cradle in his tent, under the care of his hound Gelert, after giving the child its fill of goat's milk. Whilst he was absent, a wolf from the neighbouring mountains, in quest of prey, found its way into the tent, and was about to devour the child, when the watchful dog interfered, and after a desperate conflict, in which the tent was torn down, succeeded in destroying the monster. Llywelyn, returning at evening, found the tent on the ground, and the dog, covered with blood, sitting beside it. Imagining that the blood with which Gelert was besmeared was that of his own son, devoured by the animal to whose care he had confided him, Llywelyn, in a paroxysm of natural indignation, forthwith transfixed the faithful creature with his spear. Scarcely, however, had he done so, when his ears were startled by the cry of a child from beneath the fallen tent, and hastily removing the canvas, he found the child in its cradle quite uninjured, and the body of an enormous wolf, frightfully torn and mangled, lying near. His breast was now filled with conflicting emotions; joy for the preservation of his son, and grief for the fate of his dog, to whom he forthwith hastened. The poor animal was not quite dead, but presently expired, in the act of licking its master's hand. Llywelyn mourned over him as over a brother, buried him with funeral honours in the valley, and erected a tomb over him as over a hero. From that time the valley was called Bethgelert.

Such is the legend, which, whether true or fictitious, is singularly beautiful and affecting.

The tomb, or what is said to be the tomb, of Gelert, stands in a beautiful meadow just below the precipitous side of Cerrig Llan; it consists of a large slab lying on its side, and two upright stones. It is shaded by a weeping willow, and is surrounded by a hexagonal paling. Who is there acquainted with the legend, whether he believes that the dog lies beneath those stones or not, can visit them without exclaiming, with a sigh, 'Poor Gelert!'

George Borrow, from *Wild Wales*

Beth-Gelert

The spearman heard the bugle sound,
   And cheerily smiled the morn;
And many a brach and many a hound,
   Obeyed Llewlyn's horn.

And still he blew a louder blast,
   And gave a lustier cheer:
'Come, Gelert, come, wert never last
   Llewelyn's horn to hear – '

'Oh, where does faithful Gelert roam,
   The flower of all his race;
So true, so brave, a lamb at home,
   A lion in the chase?'

'Twas only at Llewelyn's board
   The faithful Gelert fed;
He watched, he served, he cheered his lord,
   And sentinelled his bed.

In sooth he was a peerless hound,
   The gift of royal John;
But now no Gelert could be found,
   And all the chase rode on.

And now, as o'er the rocks and dells
   The gallant chidings rise,
All Snowdon's craggy chaos yells,
   The many mingled cries.

That day Llewelyn little loved
   The chase of hart and hare;
And scant and small the booty proved,
   For Gelert was not there.

Unpleased Llewelyn homeward hied,
   When, near the portal seat,
His truant Gelert he espied,
   Bounding his lord to greet.

But when he gained his castle door,
   Aghast the chieftain stood;
The hound all o'er was smeared with gore,
   His lips, his fangs, ran blood.

Llewelyn gazed with fierce surprise;
   Unused such looks to meet,
His favourite checked his joyful guise,
   And crouched and licked his feet.

Onward in haste, Llewelyn passed,
   And on went Gelert too,
And still, where'er his eye he cast,
   Fresh blood gouts shocked his view.

O'erturned his infants bed he found,
   With blood-stained covert rent;
And all around the walls and ground
   With recent blood besprent.

He called his child – no voice replied –
  He reached with terror wild;
Blood, blood, he found on every side,
  But nowhere found his child.

'Hell-hound! my child's by thee devoured!'
  The frantic father cried;
And to the hilt his vengeful sword
  He plunged in Gelert's side.

His suppliant looks as prone he fell,
  No pity could impart;
But still his Gelert's dying yell
  Passed heavy o'er his heart.

Aroused by Gelert's dying yell,
  Some slumberer wakened nigh –
What words the parents joy could tell
  To hear his infant's cry!

Concealed beneath a tumbled heap
  His hurried search had missed,
All glowing from his rosy sleep,
  The cherub boy he kissed.

Nor scathe had he, nor harm, nor dread,
  But the same couch beneath
Lay a gaunt wolf, all torn and dead,
  Tremendous still in death.

Ah, what was then Llewelyn's pain,
  For now the truth was clear:
His gallant hound the wolf had slain,
  To save Llewelyn's heir.

Vain, vain, was all Llewelyn's woe:
  'Best of thy kind, adieu.
The frantic blow which laid thee low
  This heart shall ever rue.'

And now a gallant tomb they raise,
  With costly sculpture decked;
And marbles storied with his praise
  Poor Gelert's bones protect.

There never could the spearman pass
  Or forester, unmoved;
There oft the tear-besprinkled grass
  Llewelyn's sorrow proved.

And there he hung his horn and spear;
  And there, as evening fell,
In fancy's ear he oft would hear
  Poor Gelert's dying yell.

And, till great Snowdon's rocks grow old,
  And cease the storms to brave,
The consecrated spot shall hold
  The name of Gelert's grave.

W. R. Spencer

STEPHEN OF BOURBON

St Guinefort

I SHOULD SPEAK OF offensive superstitions, some of which are offensive to God, others to our fellow men. Offensive to God are those which honour demons or other creatures as if they were divine: it is what idolatry does, and it is what the wretched women who cast lots do, who seek salvation by worshipping elder trees or making offerings to them; scorning churches and holy relics, they take their children to these elder trees, or to anthills, or to other things in order that a cure may be effected.

This recently happened in the diocese of Lyons where, when I preached against the reading of oracles, and was hearing confession, numerous women confessed that they had taken their children to Saint Guinefort. As I thought that this was some holy person, I continued with my enquiry and finally learned that this was actually a greyhound, which had been killed in the following manner.

In the diocese of Lyons, near the enclosed nuns' village called Neuville, on the estate of the Lord of Villars, was a castle, the lord of which and his wife had a baby boy. One day, when the lord and lady had gone out of the house, and the nurse had done likewise, leaving the baby alone in the cradle, a huge serpent entered the house and approached the baby's cradle. Seeing this, the greyhound, which had remained behind, chased the serpent and, attacking it beneath the cradle, upset the cradle and bit the serpent all over, which defended itself, biting the dog equally severely. Finally, the dog killed it and threw it well away from the cradle. The cradle, the floor, the dog's mouth and head were all drenched in the serpent's blood. Although badly hurt by the serpent, the dog remained on guard beside the cradle. When the nurse came back and saw all this she thought that the dog had devoured the child, and let out a scream of misery. Hearing it the child's mother also ran up, looked, thought the same thing and screamed too. Likewise the knight, when he arrived, thought the same thing and drew his sword and killed the dog. Then, when they went close to the baby they found it safe and sound, sleeping peacefully. Casting around for some explanation, they discovered the serpent, torn to pieces by the dog's bites, and now dead. Realising then the true facts of the matter, and deeply regretting having unjustly killed so useful a dog they threw it into a well in front of the manor door, threw a great pile of stones on top of it, and planted trees beside it, in memory of the event. Now, by divine will, the manor was destroyed and the estate, reduced to a desert, was abandoned by its inhabitants. But the peasants, hearing of the dog's conduct and of how it had been killed, although innocent, and for a deed for which it might have expected praise, visited the place, honoured the dog as a martyr, prayed to it when they were sick or in need of something, and many there fell victim to the enticements and illusions of the devil, who in this way used to lead men into error. Above all, though, it was women with sick or weak children who took them to this place. They would go and seek out an old woman in a fortified town a league distant, and she taught them the rituals they should enact in order to make offerings to demons, and in order to invoke them, and she led them to the place. When they arrived, they would make offerings of salt and other things; they would hang their babies' swaddling-clothes on the bushes roundabout; they would drive nails into the trees which had grown in this place; they would pass the naked babies between the trunks of two trees – the mother, on one side, held the baby and threw it nine times to the old woman, who was on the other side. Invoking the demons, they called upon the fauns in the forest of Rimite to take the sick, feeble child which, they said, was theirs, and to return their child that the fauns had taken away, fat and well, safe and sound.

Having done this, the infanticidal mothers took their children and laid them naked at the foot of the tree on straw from the cradle; then, using the light they had brought with them, they lit two candles, each an inch long, one on each side of the child's head and fixed them in the trunk above it. Then they withdrew until the candles had burnt out, so as not to see the child or hear him crying. Several people have told us that while the candles were burning like this they burnt and killed several babies. One woman also told me that she had just invoked the fauns and was withdrawing from the scene when she saw a wolf come out of the forest towards the baby. If maternal love had not made her feel pity and go back for him, the wolf, or as she put it, the devil in the shape of a wolf, would have devoured the baby.

When a mother returned to her child and found it still alive, she carried it out into the fast-flowing waters of a nearby river, called the Chalaronne [a tributary of the Saône], and plunged it in nine times; if it came through without dying on the spot, or shortly afterwards, it had a very strong constitution.

We went to this place, we called together all the people on the estate, and we preached against everything that had been said. We had the dead dog disinterred, and the sacred wood cut down and burnt, along with the remains of the dog. And I had an edict passed by the lords of the estate, warning that anyone going thenceforth to that place for any such reason would be liable to have his possessions seized and then sold.

Trans. Martin Thom

LOUIS XI

By Royal Appointment

ALWAYS THERE REMAINED dogs at his side, in the wilds or within his chamber. Smart in their collars of Lombardy leather with gilt studs, the greyhounds were much pampered – their feet washed in warm wine, their ailments tended by apothecaries, their welfare safe-guarded by offerings to St Hubert. The current favourite, Mistodin, wore robes and slept in a bed. It was now well known to many European princes that there was no better way to please Louis XI than to make him a present of hunting dogs. The passage of years had but refined his exacting standards.

So did Christopher da Bollate disover when, in June of 1473, he informed the King that the Duke of Milan's dog keeper, Antonio, had arrived with two hunting dogs, a bitch and a castrated male, for His Majesty. The King at once 'had Antonio and the dogs conducted to his own chamber. With what kindness and pleasure His Majesty asked about the qualities and points of the dogs – he always speaking Lombard – I will let Antonio report on his return. But I inform Your Excellency that the bitch pleased him, he told us, and would have pleased him much more if it had been younger and a male. I replied that Your Excellency had not been able to find male dogs so obedient and affectionate and with the kind of coat His Majesty prefers and so absolutely perfect at hawking as this bitch – her sagacity and skill, if one has not seen her hunt, cannot be appreciated ... As for the castrated male, His Majesty told me that he did not wish a castrated animal but a big handsome young male with a coat like Stella's [the bitch] and passionate about hawking. I replied that His Majesty had not previously explained to me the particular qualities he liked in dogs and that, in fact, Your Excellency had sent this dogkeeper in order to understand more fully the King's desires so that another time he could better satisfy them. The King then questioned Antonio at length about the kind of greyhounds Your Excellency likes best. Antonio answered – the biggest and handsomest.

'The following day His Majesty told me that Antonio had been here once before and that he had given him about a dozen good dogs to take to Your Excellency, but that Antonio had let some of them die on the road. The King added that this time Antonio had brought the two dogs all the way from Milan with iron collars around their necks. His Majesty then had two most handsome greyhounds brought in, telling me that if Your Excellency wished, he would like to have a servant of his bring them to you – and without collars so that their necks would not be injured. . . .' Having rubbed in his point, Louis went on to say 'that he was taking good care of the two dogs [brought by Antonio] and that one day he would go hawking with them.' A few days later, the King told Bollate that he had tried out the dogs and found them good, the bitch much better than the castrated male, 'but that, since he does not care for castrated dogs [or bitches], perhaps Your Excellency would wish to have them returned to him. . . . In then thanking Your Excellency for the dogs, His Majesty said that if possible he would like a male of Stella's breed, of the sort I described in my last dispatch, a dog that was expressly trained for hawking and, above all, affectionate.' Doggedly upholding the honour of the Duke of Milan, Bollate replied that the Duke would be most unhappy that the greyhounds were not to His Majesty's liking, that he would do everything to satisfy the King's desires; as for sending the two dogs back, Bollate had no doubt that the Duke would be very glad to have them again since they were the best and most attractive dogs that he had!

Paul Murray Kendal, from *Louis XI*

DAME JULIANA BERNERS
The Greyhounde

A greyhounde should be headed lyke a snake,
And neckyd lyke a drake.
Fotyd lyke a cat,
Tayled lyke a ratte,
Syded lyke a teme,
And chyned lyke a bream,
The fyrste yere he must lerne to fede,
The seconde yere to feld him lede,
The thyrde yere he is felow lyke.
The fourth yere there is non syke,
The fifth yere he is good ynough.
The syxth yere he shall hold the plough,
The seventh yere he will avaylle
Grete bytches for assayle.
But when he is come to the ninth yere
Have him then to the tannere.
For the best hounde that ever bytch had
At the ninth yere is full bad.

I AM JUST RETURNING from a most delightful Highland tour in which we have scarcely encountered a single shower of rain. The night before we set forth the Lady Juliana Berners arrived in custody of a skillful skipper (or schip-fere) who had taken the greatest care of her during her voyage. She is a great beauty and promises to be the envy of all our forest Lairds. I hope to tell you next year that she has won the silver collar which we contend for annually. If her action answers her appearance of which I have no doubt she will be quite invaluable to me as my present favourites are arrived at that time when the prioress of St Albans says a greyhound should be

> — a stale
> Gret biches to assaile.

Sir Walter Scott to George Ellis, 29 July 1810

JOACHIM DU BELLAY

Epitaphe d'un petit Chien

Dessous ceste motte verte
De lis et roses couverte
Gist le petit Peloton
De qui le poil foleton
Frisoit d'une toyson blanche
Le doz, le ventre, et la hanche.
  Son nez camard, ses gros yeux
Qui n'estoient pas chassieux,
Sa longue oreille velue
D'une soyë crespelue,
Sa queue au petit floquet,
Semblant un petit bouquet,
Sa gembe gresle, et sa patte
Plus mignarde qu'une chatte
Avec ses petits chattons
Ses quatre petits tetons,
Ses dentelettes d'ivoyre,
Et la barbelette noyre
De son musequin friand:
Bref, tout son maintien riand
Des pieds jusques à la teste,
Digne d'une telle beste,
Meritoient qu'un chien si beau
Eust un plus riche tumbeau.
  Son exercice ordinaire
Estoit de japper et braire,
Courir en hault et en bas,
Et faire cent mille esbas,
Tous estranges et farouches,
Et n'avoit guerre qu'aux mousches,
Qui luy faisoient maint torment.

Mais Peloton dextrement
Leur rendoit bien la pareille:
Car se couchant sur l'oreille,
Finement il aguignoit
Quand quelqu'une le poingnoit:
Lors d'une habile soupplesse
Happant la mouche traistresse,
La serroit bien fort dedans,
Faisant accorder ses dens
Au tintin de sa sonnette
Comme un clavier d'espinette.

Peloton ne caressoit
Sinon ceulx qu'il cognoissoit,
Et n'eust pas voulu repaistre
D'autre main que de son maistre,
Qu'il alloit tousjours suyvant;
Quelquefois marchoit devant,
Faisant ne sçay quelle feste
D'un gay branlement de teste.

Peloton tousjours veilloit
Quand son maistre sommeilloit,
Et ne souilloit point sa couche
Du ventre ny de la bouche,
Car sans cesse il gratignoit
Quand ce desir le poingnoit:
Tant fut la petite beste
En toutes choses honneste.

Le plus grand mal, ce dict-on,
Que feist nostre Peloton,
(Si mal appellé doit estre)
C'estoit d'esveiller son maistre,
Jappant quelquefois la nuict,
Quand il sentoit quelque bruit,
Ou bien le voyant escrire,

Sauter, pour le faire rire,
Sur la table, et trepigner,
Follastrer, et gratigner,
Et faire tumber sa plume,
Comme il avoit de coustume
Mais quoy? nature ne faict
En ce monde rien parfaict:
Et n'y a chose si belle,
Qui n'ait quelque vice en elle.
    Peloton ne mangeoit pas
De la chair à son repas:
Ses viandes plus prisées
C'estoient miettes brisées
Que celuy qui le paissoit
De ses doigts amollissoit:
Aussi sa bouche estoit pleine
Tousjours d'une doulce haleine.
    Mon-dieu, quel plaisir c'estoit
Quand Peloton se grattoit,
Faisant tinter sa sonnette
Avec sa teste folette!
Quel plaisir, quand Peloton
Cheminoit sur un baston,
Ou coifé d'un petit linge,
Assis comme un petit singe,
Se tenoit mignardelet
D'un maintien damoiselet!
    Ou sur les pieds de derriere
Portant la pique guerriere
Marchoit d'un front asseuré,
Avec un pas mesuré:
Ou couché dessus l'eschine,
Avec ne sçay quelle mine
Il contrefaisoit le mort!

Ou quand il couroit si fort,
Il tournoit comme une boule,
Ou un peloton, qui roule!
  Bref, le petit Peloton
Sembloit un petit mouton:
Et ne feut onc creature
De si benigne nature.
  Las, mais ce doulx passetemps
Ne nous dura pas longtemps:
Car la mort ayant envie
Sur l'ayse de nostre vie,
Envoya devers Pluton
Nostre petit Peloton,
Qui maintenant se pourmeine
Parmi ceste umbreuse plaine,
Dont nul ne revient vers nous.
Que mauldictes soyez-vous,
Filandieres de la vie,
D'avoir ainsi par envie
Envoyé devers Pluton
Nostre petit Peloton:
Peloton qui estoit digne
D'estre au ciel un nouveau signe,
Temperant le Chien cruel
D'un printemps perpetuel.

LOUIS XII

A Vanished Book

YOU MUST NOT BE surprised if I should send you a collection of Tonton's *bon mots:* I have found a precedent for such a work. A grave author [Jacques de Brézé] wrote a book on the hunt of the Grand Sénéchal of Normandy, and of *les DITS du bon chien SOUILLARD, qui fut au Roi Loy de France onzième du nom.* Louis XII, the reverse of his predecessor of the same name, did not leave to his historian to celebrate his dog, *Relais,* but did him the honour of being his biographer himself – and for a reason that was becoming so excellent a king. It was, *pour animer les descendants d'un si brave chien à se rendre aussi bons que lui, et encore meilleurs.* It was great pity that the Cardinal d'Amboise had no bastard puppies, or to be sure his Majesty would have written his prime minister's life too for a model to his successors.

Horace Walpole to Lady Ossory, 8 February 1783

HENRY VII

Presumption

OUR ENGLISHE MEN (to th' intent that theyr dogges might be the more fell and fearce) assist nature with arte, use, and custome, for they teach theyr dogges to baite the Beare, to baite the Bull and other such like cruell and bloudy beastes (appointing an ouerseer of the game) without any collar to defend theyr throtes, and oftentimes they traine them up in fighting and wrestling with a man having for the safegarde of his lyfe, eyther a Pikestaffe, a clubbe, or a sworde and by using them to such exercises as these, theyr dogges become more sturdy and strong. The force which is in them surmounteth all beleefe, the fast holde which they take with their teeth exceedeth all credit, three of them against a Beare, fowre against a Lyon are sufficient, both to try masteryes with them and utterly to overmatch them. Which *Henry* the seventh of that name, King of England (a prince both politique &

warlike) perceaving on a certaine time (as the report runneth) commaunded all such dogges (how many soever they were in number) should be hanged, beyng deeply displeased, and conceaving great disdaine that an yll favred rascall curre should with such violent villany, assault the valiaunt Lyon king of all beastes.

John Caius, from *A Short Treatise of English Dogges*
Trans. Abraham Fleming

ST THOMAS MORE

A Soothing Sound

WHAT DELIGHT CAN there be, and not rather displeasure in hearing the barking and howling of dogs? Or what greater pleasure is there felt when a dog followeth a hare than when a dog followeth a dog?

From *Utopia*

MARTIN LUTHER

Expediency

I SAW A DOG at Lintz in Austria, that was taught to go with a handbasket to the butcher's shambles for meat; when other dogs came about him, and sought to take the meat out of the basket, he set it down, and fought lustily with them; but when he saw they were too strong for him, he himself would snatch out the first piece of meat, lest he should lose all.

From *Table Talk*
Trans. W. Hazlitt

ANNE BOLEYN

A Short Life

I BESEECH YOUR lordship, after my most hearty recommendations made unto my very good lady your wife – unto whom and to your lordship, because ye be both but one soul though ye be two bodies, I write but one letter – that it may please your lordship to give her hearty thanks on my behalf for her little dog, which was so proper and so well liked by the Queen that it remained not above an hour in my hands but that her Grace took it from me. Nevertheless, her ladyship and any friend of hers, for the same, and her kindness therein, shall be assured of such pleasure as in me at any time shall be. As our Lord God knoweth, who have your lordship, with my said good lady, in his blessed preservation.

Sir Francis Bryan to Lord Lisle, 20 January 1534

A LSO SHE SAITH that the Queen's Grace setteth much store by a pretty dog, and her Grace delighted so much in little Purkoy that after he was dead of a fall there durst nobody tell her Grace of it, till it pleased the King's Highness to tell her Grace of it. But her Grace setteth more store by a dog than by a bitch, she saith.

Thomas Broke to Lady Lisle, 18 December 1534

BENVENUTO CELLINI

Barruco

I HAD IN THE HOUSE a fine large shock-dog, which Duke Alessandro had made me a present of; it was an admirable good retriever, for it would bring me all sorts of birds, and other animals that I shot with my gun; and it was an excellent house-dog besides.

It happened one night that a thief, who had been at my house pretending to be a goldsmith, and had laid a plan to rob me of my jewels, watched his opportunity and broke into my shop, where he found several small wares in gold and silver, but as he was breaking open the caskets, in order to come at the jewels, the dog flew at him, and the thief found it a difficult matter to defend himself with a sword. The faithful animal ran several times about the house, entering the journeymen's rooms, which were open, it being then summer-time; but as they did not seem to hear him barking, he drew away the bed-clothes, and pulling the men alternately by the arms, forcibly awakened them; then barking very loud, he showed the way to the thief, and went on before; but they would not follow him. The scoundrels, being quite provoked with the noise of the dog, began to throw stones and sticks at him (which they found an easy matter, as I had given them orders to keep a light in their room the whole night), and at last locked their door. The dog, having lost all hopes of the assistance of these rascals, undertook the task alone, and ran downstairs. He could not find the villain in the shop, but came up with him in the street, and tearing off his cloak, would certainly have treated him according to his deserts, if the fellow had not called to some tailors in the neighbourhood, and begged, for the love of God, they would assist him against a mad dog. The tailors, giving credit to what he said, came to his assistance, and with great difficulty drove away the poor animal. Next morning, when my young men went down into the shop, they saw it broken open, and all the caskets rifled; upon which they began to make a loud outcry, and I coming to them quite terrified, they said: 'Alas, we are undone: the shop has been plundered and robbed by a villain, who has carried off everything valuable, and broken all the caskets' . . .

Happening just about this time to pass by the square of Navona with my fine shock-dog, as soon as I came to the door of the city marshall, the dog barked very loudly and flew at a young man, who had been arrested by one Donnino, a goldsmith of Parma, formerly a pupil of Caradosso, upon suspicion of having committed a robbery. My dog made such efforts to tear this young fellow to pieces that he roused the city-guards. The prisoner asserted his innocence boldly, and Donnino did not say so much as he ought to have done, especially as I was present. There happened likewise to be by one of the chief officers of the city-guard, who was a Genoese, and well acquainted with the prisoner's father; insomuch that on account of the violence offered by the dog, and for other reasons, they were for dismissing the youth, as if he had been innocent. As soon as I came up, the dog, which dreaded neither swords nor sticks, again flew at the young man. The guards told me that if I did not keep off my dog they would kill it. I called off the dog with some difficulty, and as the young man was retiring, certain little paper bundles fell from under the cape of his cloak, which Donnino immediately discovered to belong to him. Amongst them I perceived a little ring which I knew to be my property: whereupon I said: 'This is the villain that broke open my shop, and my dog knows him again.' I therefore let the dog loose, and he once more seized the thief, who then implored mercy, and told me he would restore me whatever he had of mine. On this I again called off my dog, and the fellow returned me all the gold, silver, and rings that he had robbed me of, and gave me five-and-twenty crowns over, imploring my forgiveness.

From *Memoirs*
Trans. Thomas Roscoe

WILLIAM OF ORANGE

Saved by a Dog at Jémappes in 1572

HERE HE [Julian Romero] entered divers tents; among the rest his men killed two of the Prince's secretaries hard by the Prince's tent, and the Prince himself escaped very narrowly. I heard the Prince say often, that he thought but for a dog [Kuntze] he had been taken. The camisado was given with such resolution, that the place of armes tooke no alarme until their fellowes were running in with the enemies in their tailes; whereupon this dogge, hearing a great noyse, fell to scratching and crying, and withall leapt upon the Prince's face, awaking him being asleepe, before any of his men. And albeit the Prince lay in his armes with a lackey alwaies holding one of his horses ready bridled, yet at the going out of his tent, with much adoe hee recovered his horse before the enemie arrived. Nevertheless one of his squires was slain taking horse presently after him, and divers of his servants were forced to escape amongst the guardes of foote, which could not recover their horses; for, in troth, ever since, untill the Prince's dying day, he kept one of that dog's race, so did many of his friends and followers. The most or all of these dogs were white little hounds with crooked noses called Camuses (*i.e.* flat-nosed).

Sir Roger Williams, from *Actions of the Low Countries*

WILLIAM HARRISON
Lap-Dogs

THEY ARE LITTLE AND prettie, proper and fine, and sought out far and neere to satisfie the nice delicacie of daintie dames, and wanton womens willes; instruments of follie to plaie and dallie withall, in trifling away the treasure of time, to withdrawe their minds from more commendable exercises, and to content their corrupt concupiscences with vain disport, a sillie poore shift to shun their irksome idleness. These Sybariticall puppies, the smaller they be the better they are accepted, the more pleasure also they provoke, as meet plaiefellowes for minsing mistresses to beare in their bosoms, to keep companie withall in their chambers, to succour with sleepe in bed, and nourish with meat at bord, to lie in their laps, and licke their lips as they lie in their wagons and coches.

From *Description of England*

MARY QUEEN OF SCOTS

A report of the manner of the execution of the Scottish Queen performed the eighth day of February anno 1586 in the great hall within the castle of Fotheringham with relation of speeches uttered and actions happening in the said execution from the delivery of the said Scottish Queen unto Mr Thomas Andrewes, Esq., Sheriff of the county of Northampton unto the end of the same execution.

THEN SHE BEING stripped of all her apparell saving her petticoat and kertell, her two women beholding her made great lamentation and crying and crossed themselves prayed in Latin. Then she turning herself to them embracing them, said these words in French, 'Ne criez vous, j'ay promis pour vous'; and so crossing and kissing them, bade them pray for her, and rejoice and not mourn, for that now they should see an end of all their mistress's troubles.

Then she with a smiling countenance, turning to her men-servants, as Melvin and the rest standing upon a bench nigh the scaffold, who sometimes weeping, sometimes crying out, and loudly and continually crossing themselves, prayed in Latin, crossing them with her hand, bade them farewell, and wishing them to pray for her even until the last hour.

This done one of her women, having a Corpus Christi cloth lapt up the corner ways, kissing it, put it over the Queen of Scot's face and pinned it fast to the caul of her head. Then the two women departed from her, and she kneeling down upon a cushion most resolutely and without any token or fear of death, she spake aloud this Psalm in Latin, 'In te Domine confido, non confundat in eternum,' etc. Then groping for the block she laid down her head, putting her chin on the block with both her hands, which holding there still had been cut off had they been not espied. Then lying upon the block most quietly, and stretched out her arms and legs, cryed, 'In manus tuas, Domine,' etc., three or four times.

Then she lying very still on the block, one of the executioners holding of her slightly with one of his hands, she endured two strokes of the other executioner with an axe, she making very small noise or none at all, and not stirring any part of her from the place where she lay; and so the executioners cut off her head saving one little gristle, which being cut asunder he lifted up her head to the view of all the assembly and bade God save the Queen. Then her dressing of lawn falling off from her head it appeared as grey as one of threescore and ten years old, and polled very short, her face in a moment being so much altered from the form she had when she was alive as few could remember her by her dead face. Her lips stirred up and down almost a quarter of an hour after her head was cut off. Then Mr Dean said with a loud voice, 'So perish all the Queen's enemies,' and afterwards the Earl of Kent came to the dead body, and standing over it with a loud voice said, 'Such be the end of all the Queen's and the Gospel's enemies.'

Then one of the executioners pulling off her garters espied her little dog, which was crept under her clothes, which could not be gotten forth but by force. It afterwards would not depart from the dead corpse, but came and laid between her head and her shoulders, which being imbrued with her blood was carried away and washed, as all things else were, that had any blood, was either burned or clean washed, and the executioners sent away with money for their fees; not having any one thing that belonged unto her. And so every man being commanded out of the hall except the Sheriff and his men she was carried by them up into a great chamber lying ready for the surgeons to embalm her.

From Tanner MS, 78 f.129, Bodleian Library

JOHN CAIUS
The First Dog Book

THERE IS, BESIDE THOSE which wee haue already deliuered, another sort of gentle dogges in this our Englishe soyle but exempted from the order of the residue, the Dogges of this kinde doth Callimachus call *Melitæos*, of the Iseland Melita, in the sea of *Sicily*, (what at this day is named *Malta;* an Iseland in deede famous and renoumed, with couragious and puisaunt souldiours valliauntly fighting under the banner of Christ their unconquerable captaine) where this kind of dogges had their principall beginning.

These dogges are litle, pretty, proper, and fyne, and sought for to satisfie the delicatenesse of daintie dames, and wanton womens wills, instrumentes of folly for them to play and dally withall, to tryfle away the treasure of time, to withdraw their mindes from more commendable exercises, and to content their corrupted concupiscences with vaine disport. (A selly shift to shunne yrcksome ydlnesse.) These puppies the smaller they be, the more pleasure they provoke, as more meete play fellowes for minsing mistrisses to beare in their bosoms, to keepe company withal in their chambers, to succour with sleepe in bed, and nourishe with meate at bourde, to lay in their lappes, and licke their lippes as they ryde in their waggons, and good reason it should be so, for coursenesse with fynenesse hath no fellowship, but featnesse with neatenesse hath neighbourhood enough. That plausible proverbe verified upon a Tyraunt, namely that he loved his sowe better then his sonne, may well be applyed to these kinde of people, who delight more in dogges that are deprived of all possibility of reason, then they doe in children that be capeable of wisedome and iudgement. But this abuse peraduenture raigneth where there hath bene long lacke of issue, or else where barrennes is the best blossome of bewty.

*   *   *

Some Dogges there be, which will not suffer fyery coales to lye skattered about the hearthe, but with their pawes will rake up the burnyng coales, musying and studying fyrst with themselues how it might be conueniently be done. And if so bee that the coales caste to great a heate then will they buyry them in ashes and so remove them forwarde to a fyt place wyth theyr noses.

*   *   *

Of such dogges as keep not their kinde, of such as are mingled out of sundry sortes not imitating the conditions of some one certaine spice, because they reseble no notable shape, nor exercise any worthy property of the true perfect and gentle kind, it is not necessarye that I write any more of them, but to banishe them as unprofitable implements, out of the boundes of my Booke, unprofitable I say for any use that is commendable, except to intertaine straūgers with their barcking in the day time, giving warnyng to them of the house, that such & such be newly come, whereupon wee call them admonishing Dogges, because in that point they performe theyr office.

From *A Short Treatise of English Dogges*
Trans. Abraham Fleming

RICHARD HAKLUYT

An Early Sled

THE MICHAEL MORED ancker upon this great yce, and roade under the lee thereof: but about midnight, by the weight of it selfe, and the setting of the Tydes, the yce brake within halfe the Barkes length, and made unto the companie within boord a sodaine and fearefull noyse. The next flood toward the morning we weyed ancker, and went further up the straights, and leaving our Ore behind us which we had digged, for hast left the place by the name of Beares sound after the Masters name of the Michael, and named the Iland Lecesters Iland. In one of the small Ilands here we found a Tombe, wherein the bones of a dead man lay together, and our savage Captive being with us, & being demanded by signes whether his countreymen had not slaine this man and eat his flesh so from the bones, he made signes to the contrary, and that he was slaine with Wolves and wild beasts. Here also was found hid under stones good store of fish, and sundry other things of the inhabitants; as sleddes, bridles, kettels of fish-skinnes, knives of bone, and such other like. And our Savage declared unto us the use of all those things. And taking in his hand one of those countrey bridles, he caught one of our dogges and hampred him handsomely therein, as we doe our horses, and with a whip in his hand, he taught the dogge to drawe in a sled as we doe horses in a coach, setting himselfe thereupon like a guide: so that we might see they use dogges for that purpose that we do our horses. And we found since by experience, that the lesser sort of dogges they feede fatte, and keepe them as domesticall cattell in their tents for their eating, and the greater sort serve for the use of drawing their sleds.

From *Martin Frobisher's second voyage
in search of the North-west Passage*, 1577

SIR HENRY LEE

A Hero

A PICTURE ONCE at Ditchley represents Lee with a dog, which Lord Dillon says is a mastiff of a breed still known in Cheshire, and on it are the following verses:

> Reason in Man cannot effect such love,
>   As nature doth in them that reason wante;
> Ulisses true and kinde his dog did prove,
>   When Faith in better Frendes was very scante.
> My travailes for my frendes have been as true,
>   Tho not so far as fortune did him beare;
> No frendes my love and faith devided knew,
>   Tho neither this nor that once equall'd were.
> But in my Dog whereof I made no store,
> I find more love then them I trusted more.

Hearne preserves a report that the picture was painted on an occasion when Sir Henry was saved by his dog. Sir Walter Scott, who drew upon the history of Lee for *Woodstock*, may be responsible for calling the dog Bevis.

E. K. Chambers, from *Sir Henry Lee*

SIR PHILIP SIDNEY

Envy

> Deare, why make you more of a dog then me?
>   If he do love, I burne, I burne in love;
>   If he waite well, I never thence would move:
> If he be faire, yet but a dog can be.
> Litle he is, so litle worth is he;

He barks, my songs thine owne voyce oft doth prove:
   Bid'n, perhaps he fetcheth thee a glove,
But I unbid, fetch even my soule to thee.
   Yet while I languish, him that bosome clips,
That lap doth lap, nay lets, in spite of spite,
This sowre-breath'd mate tast of those sugred lips.
   Alas, if you graunt ony such delight
     To witlesse things, then *Love* I hope (since wit
     Becomes a clog) will soone ease me of it.

ANONYMOUS

Yolp, Yolp, Yolp, Yolp

Hark! They Cry! I hear by that
The dogs have put the hare from quat:
Then woe be unto little Wat!
    Yolp, yolp, yolp, yolp.

Hollo in the hind dogs, hollo!
So come on then – solla! solla! –
And let us so blithely follow.
    Yolp, yolp, yolp, yolp.

Oh, the dogs are out of sight,
But the cry is my delight:
Hark how Jumball hits it right!
    Yolp, yolp, yolp, yolp.

Over briars, over bushes!
Who's affeard of pricks and pushes

He's no hunter worth two rushes.
Yolp, yolp, yolp, yolp.

But how long thus shall we wander?
Oh, the hare's a lusty stander!
Follow apace! The dogs are yonder!
Yolp, yolp, yolp, yolp.

THOMAS NASHE

Disagreement

ORION: Sirrah, was't thou that call'd us from our game?
  How durst thou (being but a petty god)
  Disturb me in the entrance of my sports?
SUMMER: Twas I, Orion, caus'd thee to be call'd.
ORION: Tis I, dread Lord, that humbly will obey.
SUMMER: How haps't thou leftst the heavens, to hunt below?
  As I remember, thou wert Hireus' son,
  Whom of a huntsman Jove chose for a star,
  And thou art call'd the dog-star, art thou not?
AUTUMN: Pleaseth your honour, heaven's circumference
  Is not enough for him to hunt and range,
  But with those venom-breathed curs he leads,
  He comes to chase health from our earthly bounds.
  Each one of those foul-mouthed mangy dogs
  Governs a day (no dog but hath his day),
  And all the days by them so governed,
  The dog-days hight. Infectious fosterers
  Of meteors from carrion that arise,
  And putrefied bodies of dead men,
  Are they engender'd to that ugly shape,
  Being nought else but preserv'd corruption.

'Tis these that, in the entrance of their reign,
The plague and dangerous agues have brought in.
They arre and bark at night against the moon,
For fetching in fresh tides to cleanse the streets.
They vomit flames, and blast the ripen'd fruits:
They are Death's messengers unto all those
That sicken while their malice beareth sway.

ORION: A tedious discourse, built on no ground;
  A silly fancy, Autumn, hast thou told,
  Which no philosophy doth warrantize,
  No old received poetry confirms.
  I will not grace thee by confuting thee;
  Yet in a jest (since thou railest so gainst dogs)
  I'll speak a word or two in their defence.
  That creature's best that comes most near to men:
  That dogs of all come nearest, thus I prove.
  First, they excel us in all outward sense,
  Which no one of experience will deny;
  They hear, they smell, they see better than we.
  To come to speech, they have it questionless,
  Although we understand them not so well.
  They bark as good old Saxon as may be,
  And that in more variety than we;
  For they have one voice when they are in chase,
  Another, when they wrangle for their meat,
  Another, when we beat them out of doors.
  That they have reason, this I will allege:
  They choose those things that are most fit for them,
  And shun the contrary all that they may;
  They know what is for their own diet best,
  And seek about for't very carefully;
  At sight of any whip they run away,
  As runs a thief from noise of hue and cry;
  Nor live they on the sweat of others' brows,
  But have their trades to get their living with,
  Hunting and coney-catching, two fine arts.
  Yea, there be of them, as there be of men,
  Of every occupation more or less:
  Some carriers, and they fetch; some watermen,

And they dive and swim when you bid them;
Some butchers, and they do worry sheep by night;
Some cooks, and they do nothing but turn spits.
Chrysippus holds dogs are logicians,
In that, by study and by canvassing,
They can distinguish twixt three several things:
As when he cometh where three broad ways meet,
And of those three hath stay'd at two of them,
By which he guesseth that the game went not,
Without more pause he runneth on the third;
Which, as Chrysippus saith, insinuates
As if he reason'd thus within himself:
'Either he went this, that, or yonder way,
But neither that, nor yonder, therefore this.'
But whether they logicians be or no,
Cynics they are, for they will snarl and bite;
Right courtiers to flatter and to fawn;
Valiant to set upon the enemies,
Most faithful and constant to their friends;
Nay, they are wise, as Homer witnesseth,
Who, talking of Ulysses coming home,
Saith all his household but Argus, his dog,
Had quite forgot him. Ay, and his deep insight
Nor Pallas' art in altering of his shape,
Nor his base weeds, nor absence twenty years,
Could go beyond, or any way delude.
That dogs physicians are, thus I infer:
They are ne'er sick, but they know their disease,
And find out means to ease them of their grief;
Special good surgeons to cure dangerous wounds
For, strucken with a stake into the flesh,
This policy they use to get it out:
They trail one of their feet upon the ground,
And gnaw the flesh about, where the wound is,
Till it be clean drawn out; and then, because
Ulcers and sores kept foul are hardly cur'd,
They lick and purify it with their tongue,
And well observe Hippocrates' old rule;
'The only medicine for the foot is rest,'
For if they have the least hurt in their feet,

They bear them up and look they be not stirr'd
When humours rise, they eat a sovereign herb,
Whereby what cloys their stomachs they cast up,
And, as some writers of experience tell,
They were the first invented vomiting.
Sham'st thou not, Autumn, unadvisedly
To slander such rare creatures as they be?
SUMMER: We call'd thee not, Orion, to this end,
To tell a story of dogs' qualitites.

From *Summer's Last Will and Testament*

FRANCIS BACON

Man and God

THEY THAT DENY A God destroy man's nobility; for certainly man is of kin to the beasts by his body; and if he be not of kin to God by his spirit, he is a base and ignoble creature. It destroys likewise magnanimity, and the raising of human nature; for take an example of a dog, and mark what a generosity and courage he will put on when he finds himself maintained by a man, who to him is in stead of a god, or *melior natura;* which courage is manifestly such as that creature, without that confidence of a better nature than his own, could never attain. So man, when he resteth and assureth himself upon divine protection and favour, gathereth a force and faith which human nature in itself could not obtain. Therefore, as atheism is in all respects hateful, so in this, that it depriveth human nature of the means to exalt itself above human frailty.

From *Essays*: 'Of Atheism'

Detection

I T IS A common experience that dogs know the dog-killer; when as in times of infection some petty fellow is sent out to kill the dogs; and that though they have never seene him before, yet they will all come forth and barke and flie at him.

From *Sylva Sylvarum*

MIGUEL DE CERVANTES

The Job Market

BERGANZA: Have patience and listen to the recital of my adventures in the order they occurred, for they will afford you more pleasure in that way.

SCIPIO: Very well; tell me what you will and how you will, but be brief.

BERGANZA: I say, then, that I was pleased with my duty as a guardian of the flock, for it seemed to me that in that way I ate the bread of industry, and that sloth, the root and mother of all vices, came not nigh me; for if I rested by day, I never slept at night, the wolves continually assailing us and calling us to arms. The instant the shepherds said to me, 'The wolf! the wolf! at him, Barcino,' I dashed forward before all the other dogs, in the direction pointed out to me by the shepherds. I scoured the valleys, searched the mountains, beat the thickets, leaped the gullies, crossed the roads, and on the morning returned to the fold without having caught the wolf or seen a glimpse of him, panting, weary, all scratched and torn, and my feet cut with splinters; and I found in the fold either a ewe or a wether slaughtered and half eaten by the wolf. It vexed me desperately to see of what little avail were all my care and diligence. Then the owner of the flock would come; the shepherds would go out to meet him with the skin of the slaughtered animal: the owner would scold the shepherds for their negligence, and order the dogs to be punished for cowardice. Down would come upon us a shower of sticks and revilings; and so, finding myself punished without fault, and that my care, alertness, and courage were of no avail to keep off the wolf, I resolved to change my manner of proceeding, and not to go out to seek him, as I had been used to do, but to remain close to the fold; for since the wolf came to it, that would be the surest place to catch him. Every week we had an alarm; and one dark night I contrived to get a sight of the wolves, from which it was so impossible to guard the fold. I crouched behind a bank; the rest of the dogs ran forward; and from my lurking-place I saw and heard how two shepherds picked out one of the fattest wethers, and slaughtered it in such a manner, that it really appeared next morning as if the executioner had been a wolf. I was horror-struck, when I saw that the shepherds themselves were the wolves, and that the flock was plundered by the very men who had the keeping of it. As usual, they made known to their master the mischief done by the wolf, gave him the skin and part of the carcase, and ate the rest, and that the choicest part, themselves. As usual, they had a scolding, and the dogs a beating. Thus there were no wolves, yet the flock dwindled away, and I was dumb, all which filled me with amazement and anguish. O Lord! said I to myself, who can ever remedy this villany? Who will have the power to make known that the defence is offensive, the sentinels sleep, the trustees rob, and those who guard you kill you?

SCIPIO: You say very true, Berganza; for there is no worse or more subtle thief than the domestic thief; and accordingly there die many more of those who are trustful than of those who are wary. But the misfortune is, that it is impossible for people to get on in the world in any tolerable way without mutual confidence. However, let us drop this subject: there is no need that we should be evermore preaching. Go on.

BERGANZA: I determined then to quit that service, though it seemed so good a one, and to choose another, in which well-doing, if not rewarded, was at least not punished. I went back to Seville, and entered the service of a very rich merchant.

SCIPIO: How did you set about getting yourself a master? As things are now-a-days, an honest man has great difficulty in finding an employer. Very different are the lords of the earth from the Lord of Heaven; the former, before they will accept a servant, first scrutinise his birth and parentage, examine into his qualifications, and even require to know what clothes he has got: but for entering the service of God, the poorest is the richest, the humblest is the best born; and whoso is but disposed to serve him in purity of heart is at once entered in his book of wages, and has such assigned to him as his utmost desire can hardly compass, so ample are they.

BERGANZA: All this is preaching, Scipio.

SCIPIO: Well, it strikes me that it is. So go on.

BERGANZA: With respect to your question, how I set about getting a master: you are aware that humility is the base and foundation of all virtues, and that without it there are none. It smooths inconveniences, overcomes difficulties, and is a means which always conducts us to glorious ends; it makes friends of enemies, tempers the wrath of the choleric, and abates the arrogance of the proud: it is the mother of modesty, and sister of temperance. I availed myself of this virtue whenever I wanted to get a place in any house, after having first considered and carefully ascertained that it was one which could maintain a great dog. I then placed myself near the door; and whenever any one entered whom I guessed to be a stranger, I barked at him; and when the master entered, I went up to him with my head down, my tail wagging, and licked his shoes. If they drove me out with sticks, I took it patiently, and turned with the same gentleness to fawn in the same way on the person who beat me. The rest let me alone, seeing my perseverance and my generous behaviour; and after one or two turns of this kind, I got a footing in the house. I was a good servant: they took a liking to me immediately; and I was never turned out, but dismissed myself, or, to speak more properly, I ran away; and sometimes I met with such a master, that but for the persecution of fortune I should have remained with him to this day.

SCIPIO: It was just in the same way that I got into the house of the masters I served. It seems that we read men's thoughts.

'Dialogue Between Two Dogs', from *Exemplary Novels*
Trans. Walter Kelly

MONTAIGNE

Intelligence

CHRYSIPPUS, ALBEIT IN other things as disdainfull a judge of the condition of beasts as any other Philosopher, considering the earnest movings of the dog, who comming into a path that led three severall wayes in search or quest of his Master, whom he had lost, or in pursuit of some prey that hath escaped him, goeth senting first one way and then another, and having assured himself of two, because he findeth not the tracke of what he hunteth for, without more adoe furiously betakes himselfe to the third; he is enforced to confesse that such a dog must necessarily discourse thus with himsclfc, 'I have followed my Masters footing hitherto, hee must of necessity pass by one of these three wayes; it is neither this nor that, then consequently hee is gone this other.' And by this conclusion or discourse assuring himselfe, comming to the third path, hee useth his sense no more, nor sounds it any longer, but by the power of reason suffers himselfe violently to be carried through it. This meere logicall tricke, and this use of divided and conjoyned propositions, and of the sufficient numbring of parts: is it not as good that the dog know it by himselfe, as by Trapezuntius his logicke? Yet are not beasts altogether unapt to be instructed after our manner. We teach Blacke-birds, Starlins, Ravens, Piots, and Parots to chat; and that facilitie we perceive in them to lend us their voyce so supple and their wind so tractable, that so wee may frame and bring it to a certaine number of letters and silables, witnesseth they have a kinde of inward reason which makes them so docile and willing to learne. I think every man is cloied and wearied with seeing so many apish and mimmike trickes that juglers teach their Dogges, as the dances, where they misse not one cadence of the sounds or notes they heare: Marke but the divers turnings and severall kinds of motions which by the commandement of their bare words they make them performe: But I wonder not a little at the effect, which is ordinary amongst us; and that is, the dogs which blind men use, both in Citie and Country: I have observed how sodainly they will stop when they come before some doores where they are wont to receive almes: how carefully they will avoyd the shocke of Carts and Coaches, even when they have roome enough to passe by them selves. I have seene some going along a Towne-ditch leave a plaine and even path and take a worse, that so they might draw their Master from the ditch. How could a man make the dog conceive his charge was only to looke to his masters safetie, and for his service to despise his owne commoditie and good? And how should he have the knowledge that such a path would be broade enough for him, but not for a blind man? Can all this be conceived without reason? We must not forget what Plutarke affirmeth to have seene a dog in Rome doe before the Emperor Vespasian the father in the Theatre of Marcellus. This Dog served a jugler, who was to play a fiction of many faces and sundry countenances, where he also was to act a part. Amongst other things he was for a long while to counterfeit and faine himself dead, because he had eaten of a certain drugge: having swallowed a piece of bread, which was supposed to be the drug, he began sodainly to stagger and shake as if he had beene giddie, then stretching and laying himselfe along as stiffe as if hee were starke dead, suffered himself to be dragged and haled from one place to another, according to the subject and plot of the play, and when he knew his time, first he began faire and softly to stirre, as if he were roused out of a dead slumber, then lifting up his head hee looked and stared so gastly that all the by-standers were amazed.

From *Essays*: 'An Apologie to Raymond Sebond'
Trans. John Florio

SIR JOHN HARINGTON

To Prince Henry, son to King James I, concerninge his Dogge

MAY IT PLEASE YOUR Highnesse to accepte in as goode sorte what I nowe offer, as hath been done aforetyme; and I may saie, *I pede fausto:* but, havinge goode reason to thinke your Highnesse had goode will and likinge to reade what others have tolde of my rare dogge, I will even give a brief historie of his good deedes and straunge feats; and herein will I not plaie the curr myselfe, but in goode soothe relate what is not more nor lesse than bare verity. Althowgh I mean not to disparage the deeds of Alexander's horse [Bucephalus], I will match my dogge [Bungey] against him for good carriage, for, if he did not bear a great *Prince* on his back, I am bolde to saie he did often bear the sweet wordes of a greater *Princesse* on his necke.

I did once relate to your Highnesse after what sorte his tacklinge was wherewithe he did sojourn from my house at the Bathe to Greenwiche Palace, and deliver up to the cowrte there such matters as were entrusted to his care. This he hathe often done, and came safe to the Bathe, or my house here at Kelstone, with goodlie returnes from such nobilitie as were pleasede to emploie him; nor was it ever tolde our Ladie Queene, that this messenger did ever blab ought concerninge his highe truste, as others have done in more special matters. Neither must it be forgotten, as how he once was sente with two charges of sack wine from the Bathe to my howse, by my man Combe; and on his way the cordage did slackene; but my trustie bearer did now bear himselfe so wisely as to covertly hide one flasket in the rushes, and take the other in his teethe to the howse; after whiche he wente forthe, and returnede with the other parte of his burden to dinner. Hereat your Highnesse may perchance marvele and doubte; but we have livinge testimonie of those who wroughte in the fieldes, and espiede his worke, and now live to tell they did muche longe to plaie the dogge, and give stowage to the wine themselves; but they did refrain, and watchede the passinge of this whole business.

I neede not saie how muche I did once grieve at missinge this dogge; for, on my journie towardes Londonne, some idle pastimers did diverte themselves with huntinge mallards in a ponde, and conveyd him to the Spanish ambassadors, where (in a happie houre) after six weeks I did heare of him; but suche was the cowrte he did pay to the Don, that he was no lesse in good likinge there then at home. Nor did the householde listen to my claim, or challenge, till I rested my suite on the dogges own proofes, and made him performe such feats before the nobles assembled, as put it past doubt that I was his master. I did send him to the hall in the time of dinner, and made him bring thence a pheasant out of the dish, which created much mirthe; but much more, when he returnede at my commandment to the table, and put it again in the same cover. Herewith the companie was well content to allow me my claim, and we bothe were well content to accepte it, and came homewardes. I could dwell more on this matter, but *jubes renovare dolorem;* I will now saie in what manner he died. As we traveld towardes the Bathe, he leapede on my horses necke, and was more earneste in fawninge and courtinge my notice, than what I had observed for time backe; and, after my chidinge his disturbinge my passinge forwardes, he gave me some glances of such affection as moved me to cajole him; but, alas! he crept suddenly into a thorny brake, and died in a short time.

Thus I have strove to rehearse such of his deedes as maie suggest much more to your Highnesse thought of this dogge. But having saide so much of him in prose, I will say somewhat too in verse, as you may finde hereafter at the close of this historie. Now let Ulysses praise his dogge Argus, or Tobite be led by that dogge whose name doth not appear; yet could I say such things of my *Bungey*, (for so was he styled,) as might shame them both, either for good faith, clear wit, or wonderful deedes; to say no more than I have said, of his bearing letters to London and Greenwiche, more than an hundred miles. As I doubt not but your Highnesse would love my dogge, if not myselfe, I have been thus tedious in his storie; and again saie, that of all the dogges near your father's courte not one hathe more love, more diligence to please, or less pay for pleasinge, than him I write of; for verily a bone would contente my servante, when some expecte greater matters, or will knavishly find oute a bone of contention.

I nowe rest your Highnesse friend, in all service that maye suite him,
JOHN HARINGTON

P.S. The verses above spoke of, are in my book of Epigrams in praise of my dogge Bungey to Momus. And I have an excellente picture, curiously limned, to remaine in my posterity.
Kelstone, June 14, 1608.

From *Nugae Antiquae*

WILLIAM SHAKESPEARE

Disillusion and Joy

LAUNCE: Nay, 'twill be this hour ere I have done weeping. All the kind of the Launces have this very fault. I have received my proportion, like the prodigious son, and am going with Sir Proteus to the Imperial's court. I think Crab my dog be the sourest-natured dog that lives: my mother weeping; my father wailing; my sister crying; our maid howling; our cat wringing her hands, and all our house in a great perplexity; yet did not this cruel-hearted cur shed one tear. He is a stone, a very pebble stone, and has no more pity in him than a dog. A Jew would have wept to have seen our parting. Why, my grandam, having no eyes, look you, wept herself blind at my parting.

*   *   *

When a man's servant shall play the cur with him, look you, it goes hard: one that I brought up of a puppy; one that I saved from drowning, when three or four of his blind brothers and sisters went to it. I have taught him, even as one would say precisely 'Thus I would teach a dog'. I was sent to deliver him as a present to Mistress Silvia, from my master; and I came no sooner into the dining-chamber, but he steps me to her trencher, and steals her capon's leg. O, 'tis a foul thing, when a cur cannot keep himself in all companies: I would have (as one should say) one that takes upon him to be a dog indeed, to be, as it were, a dog at all things. If I had not had more wit than he, to take a fault upon me that he did, I think verily he had been hanged for 't; sure as I live he had suffered for 't. You shall judge: he thrusts me himself into the company of three or four gentleman-like dogs, under the Duke's table; he had not been there (bless the mark) a pissing while, but all the chamber smelt him. 'Out with the dog', says one; 'What cur is that?' says another; 'Whip him out', says the third; 'Hang him up', says the Duke. I, having been acquainted with the smell before, knew it was Crab; and goes me to the fellow that whips the dogs: 'Friend,' quoth I, 'you mean to whip the dog?' 'Ay, marry do I,' quoth he. 'You do him the more wrong,' quoth I; ''twas I did the thing you wot of.' He makes me no more ado, but whips me out of the chamber. How many masters would do this for his servant? Nay, I'll be sworn I have sat in the stocks, for puddings he hath stolen, otherwise he had been executed; I have stood on the pillory for geese he hath killed, otherwise he had suffered for 't. Thou think'st not of this now. Nay, I remember the trick you served me, when I took my leave of Madam Silvia: did not I bid thee still mark me, and do as I do? When didst thou see me heave up my leg, and make water against a gentlewoman's farthingale? Didst thou ever see me do such a trick?

From *The Two Gentlemen of Verona*

LEAR: And here's another, whose warped looks proclaim
What stone her heart is made on. Stop her there!
Arms, arms, sword, fire! Corruption in the place!
False justicer, why hast thou let her scape?

EDGAR: Bless thy five wits!

KENT: O pity! Sir, where is the patience now
That you so oft have boasted to retain?

EDGAR: My tears begin to take his part so much
They mar my counterfeiting.

LEAR: The little dogs and all,
Tray, Blanche, and Sweetheart; see, they bark at me.

EDGAR: Tom will throw his head at them. Avaunt, you curs!
Be thy mouth or black or white,
Tooth that poisons if it bite;
Mastiff, greyhound, mongrel grim,
Hound or spaniel, brach or lym,
Or bobtail tyke or trundle-tail,
Tom will make him weep and wail;
For, with throwing thus my head,
Dogs leaped the hatch, and all are fled.

From *King Lear*

HIPPOLYTA: I was with Hercules and Cadmus once
When in a wood of Crete they bay'd the boar
With hounds of Sparta: never did I hear
Such gallant chiding; for besides the groves,

The skies, the fountains, every region near,
Seem'd all one mutual cry: I never heard
So musical a discord, such sweet thunder.

THESEUS: My hounds are bred out of the Spartan kind,
So flew'd, so sanded; and their heads are hung
With ears that sweep away the morning dew;
Crook'd-knee'd, and dew-lapt like Thessalian bulls;
Slow in pursuit, but match'd in mouth like bells,
Each under each. A cry more tuneable
Was never holla'd to, nor cheer'd with horn,
In Crete, in Sparta, nor in Thessaly;
Judge when you hear.

From *A Midsummer Night's Dream*

HELENA: I am your spaniel; and, Demetrius,
The more you beat me I will fawn on you.
Use me but as your spaniel: spurn me, strike me,
Neglect me, lose me; only give me leave,
Unworthy as I am, to follow you.
What worser place can I beg in your love –
And yet a place of high respect with me –
Than to be usèd as you use your dog?

From *A Midsummer Night's Dream*

AEMELIA: The venom clamours of a jealous woman
Poisons more deadly than a mad dog's tooth.

From *The Comedy of Errors*

I MURDERER: We are men, my liege.

MACBETH: Ay, in the catalogue ye go for men,
As hounds and greyhounds, mongrels, spaniels, curs,
Shoughs, water-rugs, and demi-wolves, are clept
All by the name of dogs: the valued file
Distinguishes the swift, the slow, the subtle,
The housekeeper, the hunter, every one

According to the gift which bounteous nature
Hath in him closed, whereby he does receive
Particular addition, from the bill
That writes them all alike: and so of men.

From *Macbeth*

PAGE: I am glad to see you, good Master Slender.

SLENDER: How does your fallow greyhound, sir? I heard say he was outrun on Cotsall.

PAGE: It could not be judg'd, sir.

SLENDER: You'll not confess, you'll not confess.

SHALLOW: That he will not. 'Tis your fault; 'tis your fault; 'tis a good dog.

PAGE: A cur, sir.

SHALLOW: Sir, he's a good dog, and a fair dog. Can there be more said? He is good, and fair.

From *The Merry Wives of Windsor*

SIR TOBY: Good night, Penthesilea.

SIR ANDREW: Before me, she's a good wench.

SIR TOBY: She's a beagle true-bred, and one that adores me. What o' that?

SIR ANDREW: I was ador'd once too.

From *Twelfth Night*

ANTONY: All come to this? The hearts
That spaniel'd me at heels, to whom I gave
Their wishes, do discandy, melt their sweets
On blossoming Cæsar.

From *Antony and Cleopatra*

JAMES I

A Message Tied to the Collar of his Dog Jowler

GOOD MR JOWLER, WE pray you speake to the king for he hears you every day and so doth he not us, that it will His Majestee to goe back to London, for els the country will be undoon, all our provision is spent already, and we are not able to intertaine him longe.

GEORGE HERBERT

Proverbs

The scalded dog fears cold water

Looke not for muske in a dogges kennell

A bad dog never sees the Wolfe

When a dog is drowning, every one offers him drink

Who hath no more bread than neede, must not keepe a dog

Though the Mastiffe be gentle, yet bite him not by the lippe

If the old dog barke he gives counsell

A gentlemans grayhound, and a salt-box; seeke them at the fire

Hee that lies with the dogs, riseth with fleas

The dog that licks ashes, trust not with meale

The dog gnawes the bone because he cannot swallow it

Little dogs start the Hare, the great get her

In every country dogges bite

Beate the dog before the Lyon

Dogs are fine in the field

From *Outlandish Proverbs*

SIR JOHN DAVIES

In Cineam

Thou dogged Cineas, hated like a dogge,
For still thou grumblest like a Mastie dogge,
Comparst thy selfe to nothing but a dogge:
Thou saist thou art as weary as a dogge,
As angry, sick, and hungry as a dogge,
As dull and melancholy as a dogge,
As lazie, sleepie, idle as a dogge.
But why dost thou compare thee to a dogge?
In that, for which all men despise a dogge,
I will compare thee better to a dogge.

Thou art as faire and comely as a dogge,
Thou art as true and honest as a dogge,
Thou art as kinde and liberall as a dogge,
Thou art as wise and valiant as a dogge.
  But Cineas, I have often heard thee tell,
  Thou art as like thy father as may be,
  Tis like inough, and faith I like it well,
  But I am glad thou art not like to me.

KATHERINE PHILIPS

The Irish Greyhound

Behold this Creature's Form and state,
Which Nature therefore did create,
That to the World might be exprest
What meen there can be in a Beast;
And that we in this shape may find
A Lion of another kind.
For this Heroick beast does seem
In Majesty to Rival him;
And yet vouchsafes to Man, to shew
Both service and submission too.
From whence we this distinction have,
That Beast is fierce, but this is brave.
This Dog hath so himself subdued,
That hunger cannot make him rude:
And his behaviour doth confess
True Courage dwells with Gentleness.
With sternest Wolves he dares engage,
And acts on them successful rage.
Yet too much courtesie may chance
To put him out of countenance.
When in his opposer's blood,
Fortune hath made his vertue good;
This Creature from an act so brave
Grows not more sullen, but more grave.
Man's Guard he would be, not his sport,
Believing he hath ventur'd for't;
But yet no blood or shed or spent
Can ever make him insolent.
    Few Men, of him, to do great things have learn'd
    And when th'are done to be so unconcerned.

IZAAK WALTON

An Attempt at Persuasion

VENATOR: And I am a lover of Hounds; I have followed many a pack of
dogs many a mile, and heard many merry Huntsmen make sport and
scoff at Anglers.

*   *   *

Hunting is a game for princes and noble persons; it hath been highly
prized in all ages; it was one of the qualifications that Xenophon
bestowed on his Cyrus, that he was a hunter of wild beasts. Hunting
trains up the younger nobility to the use of manly exercises in their
riper age. What more manly exercise than hunting the Wild Boar, the
Stag, the Buck, the Fox, or the Hare? How doth it preserve health,
and increase strength and activity!

And for the dogs that we use, who can commend their excellency
to that height which they deserve? How perfect is the hound at
smelling, who never leaves or forsakes his first scent, but follows it
through so many changes and varieties of other scents, even over,
and in, the water, and into the earth! What music doth a pack of dogs
then make to any man, whose heart and ears are so happy as to be set
to the tune of such instruments! How will a right Greyhound fix his
eye on the best Buck in a herd, single him out, and follow him, and
him only, through a whole herd of rascal game, and still know and
then kill him! For my hounds, I know the language of them, and they
know the language and meaning of one another, as perfectly as we
know the voices of those with whom we discourse daily.

I might enlarge myself in the commendation of Hunting, and of
the noble Hound especially, as also of the docibleness of dogs in
general . . .

From *The Compleat Angler*

DOROTHY OSBORNE

Mail Order

W HEN YOUR FATHER goe's into Ireland, Lay your Commands upon some of his Servant's to gett you an Ireish Greyhound. I have one that was the Generalls but tis a bitch and those are alway's much lesse then the dog's, I gott it in the time of my favour there and it was all they had, H. C. undertook to write to his Brother Fleetwood for an other for mee, but I have lost my hopes there. whomsoever it is that you imploy hee will need noe other instructions but to gett the biggest hee can meet with, 'tis all the beauty of those dogs or of any indeed I think, a Masty is handsomer to mee then the most exact litle dog that ever Lady playde withall. You will not offer to take it ill that I imploy you in such a comission, since I have tolde you that the generals Sonne did not refuse it, but I shall take it ill if you doe not take the same fredom whensoever I am capable of serving you.

11 June 1653

I GIVE YOU many thanks for your care of my Irish dog, but I am Extreamly out of countenance your father should bee troubled with it. Sure hee will think I have a most Extravagant fancy but doe mee the right as to let him know I am not soe possest with it, as to consent hee should bee imployed in such a comission.

5 August 1653

I MUST TELL you what a present I had made mee to day, two the finest Young Ireish Greyhounds that ere I saw, a Gentleman that serv's the Generall sent them mee; they are newly come over and sent for by H. C. hee tels mee, but not how hee gott them for mee. however I am glad I have them and much the more because it dispenses wth a very unfitt imployment that your father out of his kindenesse to you & his Civility to mee was content to take upon him.

September 1653

YOUR DOG IS come too, and I have received him with all the Kindenesse that is due to any thinge you sende, have deffended him from the Envy and Mallice of a troupe of greyhounds that used to bee in favour with mee, and hee is soe sencible of my care over him that hee is pleased with nobody else and follow's mee as if wee had bin of longe acquaintance.

25 February 1654

LA FONTAINE

The Dog and his Bone

Mankind is but a race of dupes:
Uncountable the nincompoops
That chase each empty shade in turn!
Send 'em from Aesop's Dog to learn
The difference of *be* and *seem*;
Who, seeing his bone reflected in a stream,
Dropt it to grab the copy, and almost sank;
For as he splashed, the water seethed and tossed,
And with long toil he spluttered to the bank,
The substance and the shade both lost.

Trans. Edward Marsh

RALPH JOSSELIN
A Vicar's Perils in Essex

MY NAVEL WELL THOUGH mercy to sight as if never ill. My sonne tho escaped a great danger from a great mastive bitch, who runne mad, and snapt at him, and a little grated his flesh, his stocken being down.

From *Diary*, 5 March 1650

A hog I had died, bit with Burtons mad dog, blessed bee god it was not a child.

4 April 1655

Escaped a danger from Colemans dog flying upon mee.

5 May 1657

Mr Clokes dog flew on mee and rent my coate very much, it was gods mercy so much was not done to my selfe.

16 September 1658

This morning my dogs kild a lambe, and a sheep died: often on Sabbath mornings I have these losse lord lett me see why.

22 August 1680

CHARLES II

Missing

WE MUST CALL UPON you again for a Black Dog, between a Greyhound and a Spaniel, no white about him, only a streak on his Breast, and his Tayl a little bobbed. It is His Majesty's own Dog, and doubtless was stoln, for the Dog was not born nor bred in England, and would never forsake His master. Whoever finds him may acquaint any at Whitehall, for the Dog was better known at Court than those who stole him. Will they never leave robbing his Majesty? Must he not keep a Dog? This Dog's place at Court (though better than some imagine) is the only place which nobody offers to beg.

Notice in Whitehall, 1660

JOHN EVELYN

Sacrifice

THIS MOUNTAINE IS exceedingly fruitefull in Vines, & there is nothing so rare & exotic, which will not grow in these invirons: Now we came to a lake of about two miles in circumference, inviron'd with hills: The Water of it, is fresh & swete on the surface, and salt at botome, some mineral-salt conjectur'd to be the cause; and 'tis reported of that profunditude in the middle, as that it has no botome soundable: The People call it Lago di Agnano, from the multitude of Serpents, which involv'd together about the Spring fall downe from the cliffy hills into it: & besides these it has no fish, neither will any live in it: The first thing we did here, was, the old experiment on a Dog, which we lead from that so mortal Cave commonly nam'd Grotto del Cane or Charons Cave: It is not above three, or four paces deepe, and about the height of a man, nor is it very broad: In this Cave whatever has life presently expires; of this we made tryal with two Doggs: which we bound with a Cord to a short pole to guide him the more directly into the farther part of the Den, where he was no soner enter'd, but without the least noyse or so much as strugling, except that he panted for breath, lolling out his tongue, his eyes being fixt, we drew him out dead, to all appearance; but then immediately plunging him into the adjoyning lake, within lesse space then halfe an houre, he recoverd againe, and swimming to shore ran away from us: Another Dog, on whom we try'd the former experiment of the Cave, without the application of the Water, we left starke dead upon the shore: It seemes this has also been try'd on men, as well as beasts, as on that poore Creature which Peter of Toledo caus'd to go in; likewise on some Turkish Slaves, two Souldiers: & other foolehardy persons, who all perished, & could never be recover'd againe by the Water of the Lake, as are doggs, for which many learned reasons have ben offer'd . . .

From *Diary*, 8 February 1645

Crash Landing

I WAS FORC'D to accompanie some friends to the Bear-garden &c: Where was Cock *fighting*, Beare, *Dog-fighting*, Beare & *Bull baiting*, it being a famous day for all these butcherly Sports, or rather barbarous cruelties: The Bulls did exceedingly well but the Irish Wolfe dog exceeded, which was a tall Gray-hound, a stately creature in deede, who beate a cruell Mastife: One of the Bulls tossd a Dog full into a Ladys lap, as she sate in one of the boxes at a Considerable height from the *Arena*: There were two poore dogs killed; & so all ended with the Ape on horse-back, & I most heartily weary, of the rude & dirty passetime, which I had not seene I think in twenty yeares before.

16 June 1670

And So to Bed

THUS DIED K. Charles the 2d, of a Vigorous & robust constitution, & in all appearance capable of a longer life. A prince of many Virtues, & many greate Imperfections, Debonaire, Easy of accesse, not bloudy or Cruel: his Countenance fierce, his voice greate, proper of person, every motion became him, a lover of the sea, & skillfull in shipping, not affecting other studys, yet he had a laboratory and knew of many Empyrical Medicines, & the easier Mechanical Mathematics: Loved Planting, building, & brought in a politer way of living, which passed to Luxurie & intollerable expense: He had a particular Talent in telling stories & facetious passages of which he had innumerable, which made some bouffoones and vitious wretches too presumptuous, & familiar, not worthy the favours they abused: He tooke delight to have a number of little spaniels follow him, & lie in his bed-Chamber, where often times he suffered the bitches to puppy & give suck, which rendred it very offensive, & indeede made the whole Court nasty & stinking . . .

6 February 1685

ROBERT HERRICK

Upon his Spaniell Tracie

Now thou art dead, no eye shall ever see,
For shape and service, *Spaniell* like to thee.
This shall my love doe, give thy sad death one
Teare, that deserves of me a million.

SAMUEL PEPYS

Dogs at Home

AT HOME, MY wife's brother brought her a pretty black dog [Fancy] which I liked very well, and went away again.

From *Diary*, 8 February 1660

S O TO BED, where my wife and I had some high words upon my telling her that I would fling the dog which her brother gave her out at the window if he pissed the house any more.

12 February 1660

I N THE MORNING my wife tell me that the bich hath whelped four young ones and is very well after it, my wife having had a great fear that she would die thereof, the dog that got them being very big.

19 February 1660

A T NIGHT TO bed; and my wife and I did fall out about the dog's being put down into the Sellar, which I have a mind to have done because of his fouling the house; and I would have my will. And so we went to bed and lay all night in a Quarrell. This night I was troubled all night with a dream that my wife was dead, which made me that I slept ill all night.

6 November 1660

H OME BY WATER to dinner; and with my father, wife, and Ashwell after dinner, by water toward Woolwich; and in our way I bethought myself that we had left our poor little dog, that fallowed us out a-doors, at the waterside and God knows whether he be not lost; which did not only strike my wife into a great passion, but I must confess, myself also, more then was becoming me. We immediately returned, I taking another boat, and with my father went to Woolwich while they went back to find the dog.

I took my father on board the King's pleasure-boat – and down to Woolwich and walked to Greenwich thence; and turning into the parke to show my father the steps up the hill, we find my wife, her woman, and dog attending us, which made us all merry again.

8 April 1663

Attack

U P BETIMES AND by water to Woolwich on board the *Royall James* to see in what dispatch she is to be carried about to Chatham. So to the yard a little and thence on foot to Greenewich; where going, I was set upon by a great dog, who got hold of my garters and might have done me hurt; but Lord, to see in what a maze I was, that having a sword about me, I never thought of it or had the heart to make use of it, but might for want of that courage have been worried.

11 May 1663

Assistance

U P, AND SPENT the whole morning and afternoon at my office. Only in the evening, my wife being at my aunt Wights, I went thither; calling at my own house, going out found the parlour curtains drawn; and enquiring the reason of it, they told me that their mistress had got Mrs Buggin's fine little dog and our little bitch – which is proud at this time – and I am apt to think that she was helping him to lime her – for going afterwards to my uncle Wights and supping there with her, where very merry with Mr Woolly's drollery, and going home, I found the little dog so little that of himself he could not reach our bitch; which I am sorry for – for it is the finest dog that ever I saw in my life – as if he were painted, the colours are so finely mixed and shaded. God forgive me, it went against me to have my wife and servants look upon them while they endeavoured to do something, and yet it provoked me to pleasure with my wife more then usual tonight.

Up; and going out saw Mrs Buggins's dog, which proves, as I thought last night, so pretty that I took him and the bitch into my closet below and, by holding down the bitch, help him to lime her; which he did very stoutly, so as I hope it will take – for it is the prettiest dog that ever I saw.

22/23 March 1664

Experiments

FORCED TO RISE because of going to the Duke to St James, where we did our usual business; and thence by invitation to Mr Pierce's the surgeon, where I saw his wife, whom I had not seen in many months before. She holds her complexion still; but in everything else, even in this her new house and the best rooms in it and her closet, which her husband with some vainglory took me to show me, she continues the veriest slattern that ever I knew in my life. By and by we to see an experiment of killing a dog by letting opium into his hind leg. He and Dr Clerke did fail mightily in hitting the vein, and in effect did not do the business after many trials; but with the little they got in, the dog did presently fall asleep and so lay till we cut him up. And a little dog also, which they put it down his throate; he also staggered first, and then fell asleep and so continued; whether he recovered or no after I was gone, I know not – but it is a strange and sudden effect.

16 May 1664

Fancy's Decline

AT NIGHT IS brought home our poor Fancy, which to my great grief continues lame still, so that I wish she had not been brought ever home again, for it troubles me to see her.

12 August 1664

Further Attempts

I WAS VEXED to have a dog brought to my house to lime our little bitch, which they make him do in all their sights; which God forgive me, doth stir my Jealousy again, though of itself the thing is a very immodest sight.

2 January 1665

I DINED ALONE. And after dinner to the office and anon to Gresham College; where among other good discourse, there was tried the great Poyson of Maccassa upon a Dogg, but it had no effect all the time we sat there.

16 March 1665

Fear

AT BRANFORD I LIGHT, having need to shit; and went into an Inne doore that stood open, found the house of office, and used it, but saw no people: only after I was in the house, heard a great dog bark and so was afeared how I should get safe back again, and therefore drew my sword and scabbard out of my belt to have ready in my hand – but did not need to use it, but got safe into the coach again. But lost my belt by that shift, not missing it till I came to Hampton Court.

19 April 1665

Sad Jest

AFTER AN HOUR'S talk, we to bed – the lady [Mrs Penington] mightily troubled about a little pretty bitch she hath, which is very sick and will eat nothing. And the jest was, I could hear her in her chamber bemoaning the bitch; and by and by taking her to bed with her, the bitch pissed and shit abed, and she was fain to rise and had coals out of my chamber to dry the bed again.

5 November 1665

AND SO TO my lodging and there spent the evening till midnight talking with Mrs Penington, who is a very discreet, understanding lady; and very pretty discourse we had, and great variety. And she tells me, with great sorrow, her bitch is dead this morning – died in her bed. So broke up, and to bed.

7 November 1665

Further Experiments

Dr Croone told me that at the meeting at Gresham College tonight (which it seems they now have every Wednesday again) there was a pretty experiment, of the blood of one Dogg let out (till he died) into the body of another on one side, while all his own run out on the other side. The first died upon the place, and the other very well, and likely to do well. This did give occasion to many pretty wishes, as of the blood of a Quaker to be let into an Archbishop, and such like. But, as Dr Croone says, may if it takes be of mighty use to man's health, for the amending of bad blood by borrowing from a better body.

14 November 1666

This noon I met with Mr Hooke, and he tells me the Dogg which was filled with another dog's blood at the College the other day, is very well, and like to be so as ever. And doubts not its being found of great use to men; and so doth Dr Whistler, who dined with us at the tavern.

16 November 1666

Fancy's End

This night our poor little Dogg Fancy was in a strange fit of madness through age, of which she hath had five or six.

2 December 1667

This day, my father's letters tell me of the death of poor Fancy in the country, big with puppies, which troubles me, as being one of my oldest acquaintances and servants.

16 September 1668

LING PO

Fate

See, that fine dog there –
How proudly he marches on those legs, but little
Does he know:
These we shall first discard
When he lies belly uppermost at our feast.

Trans. Jean Du Halde

JOHN BUNYAN

Of Saints and Kennels

OBSERVE THAT THE ungodly world do love their dogs better than the children of God. You will say that is strange. It is so indeed, yet it is true, as will be clearly manifested; as, for instance, how many pounds do some men spend in a year on their dogs, when in the meanwhile the poor saints of God may starve for hunger? They will build houses for their dogs, when the saints must be glad to wander, and lodge in dens and caves of the earth. And if they be in any of their houses for the hire therof, they will warn them out or eject them, or pull down the house over their heads, rather than not rid themselves of such tenants. Again, some men cannot go half a mile from home but they must have dogs at their heels, but they can very willingly go half a score miles without the society of a Christian. Nay, if when they are busy with their dogs they should chance to meet a Christian, they would willingly shift him if they could. They will go on the other side the hedge or the way rather than they will have any society with him; and if at any time a child of God should come into a house where there are but two or three ungodly wretches, they do commonly wish either themselves or the saint out of doors; and why so? because they cannot down with the society of a Christian; though if there come in at the same time a dog, or a drunken swearing wretch, which is worse than a dog, they will make him welcome; he shall sit down with them and partake of their dainties.

From *A Few Sighs From Hell, or The Groans of a Damned Soul*

ANTHONY À WOOD
In Death Divided

IN THE BEGINNING of this month a maid and a dog were hang'd at Tyburne for that the dog laid with her severall times.

From *Life and Times*, July 1677

SETH, LORD BISHOP OF SALISBURY
For Lack of a Chamberpot

TO THIS I WILL ADD another Accident, which befel him in *England*, it being of the like nature: He was at a Gentlemans House in the Country, if I mistake not in *Cambridgeshire*, where the Necessary House was at the end of a long Garden, and consequently at a great distance from the Room where he lodgd, as he was going to it very early, even before Day, for, as I shall shew hereafter, he was sparing of sleep, and an early riser, a fierce Mastiff, who used to be chaind up all Day, and let loose late at Night for the security of the House, perceiving a strange Person in the Garden at that unseasonable time, set upon him with great fury. The Dr catchd him by the Throat, threw him, and lay upon him, and whilst he kept him down, considered what he should do in that Exigent; once he had a mind to kill him, but he quite alterd this resolution, judging it would be an unjust Action, for the Dog did his duty, and he himself was in fault for rambling out of his Lodgings before twas light. At length he calld out so loud, that he was heard by some of the House, who came presently out, and freed both the Doctor and the Dog, from the eminent danger they were both in.

Walter Pope, from his *Life of the Right Reverend Seth Lord Bishop of Salisbury*

THE EARLS OF PEMBROKE
Peace – and War

IT WAS THE RIGHT hon. Philip (1st) Earle of Pembroke, that was the great Hunter. It was in his Lordship's time (*cs. tempore Jacobi I and Caroli I*) a serene calme of Peace, that Hunting was at its greatest Heighth that ever was in this Nation. The Roman Governours had not (I thinke) the leisure; the Saxons were never at quiet; and the Baron's Warres, and these of Yorke and Lancaster, took up the greatest part of the time since the Conquest: So that the Glory of the English Hunting breath'd its last with this Earle: who deceased about 1644, and shortly after the Forests and Parkes were sold, and converted into Arable.

'Twas after his Lordship's Decease, that I was a Hunter: that is to say with the right Honble William, Lord Herbert of Cardiff, the aforesaid Philip's Grandson.

This present Earl of Pembroke (1680) has at Wilton, 52 Mastives and 30 Grey-hounds, some Bears, and a Lyon, and a matter of 60 fellowes more bestial then they.

John Aubrey, from *Brief Lives*

JAMES II

Future King and Dogs First

A S HE WAS GOING back to bring the duchess [6 May 1682], the Gloucester frigate, that carried him, struck on a bank of sand. The duke [i.e. James II-to-be] got into a boat: and took care of his dogs, and some unknown persons who were taken from that earnest care of his to be his priests: the long boat went off with very few in her, though she might have carried off above eighty more than she did. One hundred and fifty persons perished: some of them men of great quality. But the duke took no notice of this cruel neglect, which was laid chiefly to Leg's charge.

Bishop Burnet, from *A History of His Own Times*

SIR ISAAC NEWTON

Experiments Lost: An Apocryphal Report

W HILE HE WAS attending divine service in a winter morning, he had left in his study a favourite little dog called Diamond. Upon returning from chapel he found that it had overturned a lighted taper on his desk, which set fire to several papers on which he had recorded the results of some optical experiments. These papers are said to have contained the labours of many years, and it has been stated, that when Mr Newton perceived the magnitude of his loss, he exclaimed, 'Oh Diamond, Diamond, little do you know the mischief you have done me!' It is a curious circumstance that Newton never refers to the experiments which he is said to have lost on this occasion, and his nephew, Mr Conduit, makes no allusion to the event itself. The distress, however, which it occasioned is said to have been so deep as to affect even the powers of his understanding.

David Brewster, from his *Life of Newton*

DANIEL DEFOE

Not Alone

A ND I MUST NOT forget that we had in the ship a dog and two cats, of whose eminent history I may have occasion to say something in its place; for I carry'd both the cats with me, and as for the dog, he jumped out of the ship of himself, and swam on shore to me the day after I went on shore with my first cargo, and was a trusty servant to me many years; I wanted nothing that he could fetch me, nor any company that he could make up to me, I only wanted to have him talk to me, but that would not do.

From *Robinson Crusoe*

JOSEPH ADDISON

Chastity

I SHALL HERE PUBLISH the Contents of a little Manuscript lately fallen into my Hands, and which pretends to great Antiquity, tho' by Reason of some modern Phrases and other Particulars in it, I can by no means allow it to be genuine, but rather the Production of a Modern Sophist.

It is well known by the Learned, that there was a Temple upon Mount *Ætna* dedicated to *Vulcan*, which was guarded by Dogs of so exquisite a Smell, (say the Historians [Aelianus, *De natura animalium*]) that they could discern whether the Persons who came thither were chast or otherwise. They used to meet and faun upon such as were chast, caressing them as the Friends of their Master *Vulcan*; but flew at those who were polluted, and never ceased barking at them till they had driven them from the Temple.

My Manuscript gives the following Account of these Dogs, and was probably designed as a Comment upon this Story.

'These Dogs were given to *Vulcan* by his Sister *Diana*, the Goddess of Hunting and of Chastity, having bred them out of some of her Hounds, in which she had observed this natural Instinct and Sagacity. It was thought she did it in Spight to *Venus*, who, upon her Return home, always found her Husband in a good or bad Humour, according to the Reception which she met with from his Dogs. They lived in the Temple several Years, but were such snappish Curs that they frighted away most of the Votaries. The Women of *Sicily* made a solemn Deputation to the Priest, by which they acquainted him, that they would not come up to the Temple with their annual Offerings unless he muzzled his Mastiffs; and at last compromised the Matter with him, that the Offering should always be brought by a Chorus of young Girls, who were none of them above seven Years old. It was wonderful (says the Author) to see how different the Treatment was which the Dogs gave to these little Misses, from that which they had shown to their Mothers. It is said that a Prince of *Syracuse*, having married a young Lady, and being naturally of a jealous Temper, made such an Interest with the Priests of this Temple, that he procured a Whelp from them of this famous Breed. The young Puppy was very troublesome to the fair Lady at first, insomuch that she sollicited her Husband to send him away, but the good Man cut her short with the old *Sicilian* [sic] Proverb, *Love me, love my Dog.* From which Time she lived very peaceably with both of them. The Ladies of *Syracuse* were very much annoyed with him, and several of very good Reputation refused to come to Court till he was discarded. There were indeed some of them that defied his Sagacity, but it was observed tho' he did not actually bite them, he would growle at them most confoundedly. To return to the Dogs of the Temple: After they had lived here in great Repute for several Years, it so happened, that as one of the Priests, who had been making a charitable Visit to a Widow who lived on the Promontory of *Lilybeum*, returned home pretty late in the Evening, the Dogs flew at him with so much Fury, that they would have worried him if his Brethren had not come in to his Assistance: Upon which, says my Author, the Dogs were all of them hanged, as having lost their original Instinct.'

I cannot conclude this Paper without wishing, that we had some of this Breed of Dogs in *Great Britain*, which would certainly do *Justice*, I should say *Honour*, to the Ladies of our Country, and shew the World the difference between Pagan Women and those who are instructed in sounder Principles of Virtue and Religion.

From the *Spectator* 579, 11 August 1714

ALEXANDER POPE
My Dog – and Ulysses's

NOW I TALK OF my Dog, that I may not treat of a worse Subject which my Spleen tempts me to, I will give you some account of him; a thing not wholly unpresidented, since Montaigne (to whom I am but a Dog in comparison) has done the very same thing of his Catt. *Dic mihi quid melius desidiosus agam?* You are to know then, that as 'tis Likeness that begets Affection, so my Favorite Dog is a Little one, a lean one, and none of the finest Shap'd. He is not much a Spaniell in his fawning; but has (what might be worth many a Man's while to imitate from him) a dumb surly sort of Kindness, that rather shows itself when he thinks me ill-us'd by others, than when we Walk quietly & peaceably by ourselves. If it be the chief point of Friendship to comply with [a] Friend's Motions & Inclinations, he possesses this in an eminent degree; he lyes down when I sitt, & walks where I walk, which Is more than many very good Friends can pretend to, Witness Our Walk a year ago in St James's Park – Histories are more full of Examples of the Fidelity of Dogs than of Friends, but I will not insist upon many of 'em, because It is possible some may be almost as fabulous as those of Pylades & Orestes, &c. I will only say for the honour of Dogs that the Two most ancient and esteemable Books, Sacred and prophane, extant, (viz: the Scripture and Homer) have shown a particular Regard to these Animals. That of Toby is the more remarkable, because there was no manner of reason to take notice of the Dog besides the great humanity of the Author. And Homer's Account of Ulysses's Dog Argus, is the most pathetic imaginable, all the Circumstances consider'd, and an excellent Proof of the Old Bards Goodnature. Ulysses had left him at Ithaca when he embarkd for Troy, & found him on his return after 20 years, (which by the way is not unnatural, as some Criticks have said, since I remember the Dam of my Dog who was 22 years old when she dy'd: May the Omen of Longevity prove fortunate to her Successour!) You shall have it in Verse.

ARGUS.

When wise Ulysses from his native Coast
Long kept by Wars, and long by Tempests tost,
Arrivd at last, poor, old, disguis'd, alone,
To all his Friends & ev'n his Queen unknown,

Chang'd as he was, with Age, & Toils, & Cares,
Furrowd his rev'rend Face, & white his hairs,
In his own Palace forc'd to ask his Bread,
Scornd by those Slaves his former Bounty fed,
Forgot of all his own Domestic Crew;
His faithful Dog his rightful Master knew!
Unfed, unhousd, neglected, on the Clay,
Like an old Servant, now cashier'd, he lay,
And tho' ev'n then expiring on the Plain,
Touch'd with Resentment of ungrateful Man,
And longing to behold his Ancient Lord again.
Him when he Saw – he rose, & crawld to meet,
(Twas all he cou'd) and fawn'd, and kist his feet,
Seiz'd with dumb Joy – then falling by his Side,
Own'd his returning Lord, Look'd up, & Dy'd.

Plutarch (who if I have any Taste, is the greatest of Moral Philos-
ophers) relating how the Athenians were obligd to abandon Athens in
the time of Themistocles, steps back again, out of the way of his
History, to describe the lamentable Cries [&] Howlings of the poor
Dogs, when left behind. He makes mention of one that follow'd his
Master across the Sea to Salamis, where he dy'd & was honord with a
Tomb by the Athenians, who gave the name of the Dogs Tomb to that
part of the Iland where he was buried: This Respect to a Dog from the
most polite people of the World is very observable. A Modern Instance
of Gratitude to a Dog (tho' we have but few such) is that the Chief
Order of Denmark (now call'd the Order of the Elephant) was instituted
in memory of the fidelity of a Dog nam'd Wild-brat, by one of their
Kings who had been deserted by his Subjects, & gave [his Order] this
Motto, or to this effect, which still remains; Wild-Brat was faithful. Sir
William Trumbull has told me a Story which he heard from one that
was present when our King Charls I. being with some of his Court,
during his Troubles, and a Discourse arising what Sort of Dogs deservd
Pre-eminence, & it being on all hands agreed to belong either to a
Spaniell or Greyhound, the King gave his opinion on the Part of the
Greyhound, because (said he) it has all the Good-nature of the other,
without the fawning. A fine piece of Satire upon his Courtiers, with
which I will conclude my Discourse of Dogs. Call me a Cynick or what
you please, in revenge for all this Impertinence, I will be contented
provided You will but believe me, when I say a bold Word for a

Christian, that, of all Dogs, you shall find none more faithfull than Dear sir, Your most Affectionate humble Servant, A: Pope:

Letter to H. Cromwell, 19 October 1709

A Proposed Grave

WHEN MY BROTHER'S faithful Danish dog and companion in those walks died, he [Pope] had some thoughts of burying him in his garden, and putting a piece of marble over his grave with this epitaph: O RARE BOUNCE! and he would have done it I believe, had not he apprehended that some people might take it to have been meant as a ridicule upon Ben Jonson.   MRS. RACKETT

From Joseph Spence, *Anecdotes*

Against Experiments

'I SHALL BE VERY glad to see Dr Hales, and always love to see him; he is so worthy and good a man' [said Spence].

Yes he is a very good man, only – I'm sorry – he has his hands imbrued with blood [Pope replied].

'What, he cuts up rats?'

Aye, and dogs too! (and with what emphasis and concern he spoke it.) Indeed, he commits most of these barbarities with the thought of its being of use to man. But how do we know that we have a right to kill creatures that we are so little above as dogs, for our curiosity, or even for some use to us?

ibid

Epigram. Engraved on the Collar of a Dog which I gave to his Royal Highness

I am his Highness' Dog at *Kew*;
Pray tell me Sir, whose Dog are you?

How many Bounces?

ALTHOUGH READERS OF Pope's poetry or of books about him have been familiar with the fact that he had a dog named Bounce, until Norman Ault wrote his sympathetic chapter on 'Pope and his Dogs' no one had realized that there must have been at least two with this name. The first is the Bounce of 1728 described by Mrs Rackett, which on meagre evidence Ault decided was a male. The second Bounce was a bitch whose puppies Pope distributed among his friends in 1736, one of the recipients being the Prince of Wales.

We now know, however, that Pope had a dog named Bounce before he left Binfield early in 1716. A letter from Gay to Parnell written in March of that year reports, '... when I took my leave of Pope I recommended Bounce to his care as he was a f[riend of mine?] and yours' (*RES*, x, 1959, 380). Whether this dog was a Great Dane we cannot be certain, though the name suggests a creature 'big rather than elegant or graceful', thumping vigorously with ungainly movement (*OED*). If this Bounce was two years old when Gay wrote about him or her, we have a span of thirty years until the last Bounce expired in April 1744 at the Somersetshire seat of the Earl of Orrery, only a few weeks before Pope's own death. In fact, the epitaph Pope wrote may be the last verses he penned:

Ah Bounce! ah gentle Beast! why wouldst thou dye,
When thou hadst Meat enough, and Orrery?
(*Corresp.* iv. 517.)

In pondering the question of how many dogs of this name Pope may have had it is necessary to consider the life expectancy of the Danish breed. True to the rule that 'the larger the dog, the shorter the life span', Great Danes live to an average of only eight or nine years, with eleven or twelve being quite exceptional. However, this estimate holds true only under the conditions of modern veterinary science and proper feeding procedures, which have lengthened animals' lives just as medical and dietary science have altered human life expectancy. Specialists consider that any of the Bounces in Pope's day would have been lucky to reach a seventh birthday.

In July 1742 Pope gave up keeping a dog and sent his last Bounce to Lord Orrery at Marston in Somersetshire. A letter from Lady Orrery written the following spring reveals that this Bounce was a male (*Corresp.* iv. 508). Although she reported that Bounce had been bitten by a mad dog, he survived for another year.

Thus we can be certain that Pope had at least four dogs named Bounce from the evidence of 1716, 1728, 1736, and 1742–4. Because Pope had grown up in a dog-loving family and evidently found solace in their company it is likely that he was never without one for long. They may even have been descendants of one line, though not of pedigree stock ('whatever their Father's Race', *Bounce to Fop*, l. 53).

A portrait of an early Bounce has been preserved, for Jonathan Richardson included him in the picture now owned by Lord Cobham. It is reproduced as the frontispiece of Ault's *New Light*. Another occurs in the sketch of Pope in his garden by Richardson, but beyond the dog's size little can be seen which might determine the breed.

James Osborn in his edition of Spence's *Anecdotes*

DR JOHN ARBUTHNOT

An Epitaph

To the memory of
SIGNOR FIDO,
an Italian of good extraction:
who came into England,

not to bite us, like most of his countrymen,
but to gain an honest livelihood.
He hunted not after fame,
yet acquired it:
regardless of the praise of his friends,
but most sensible of their love:
though he lived amongst the great,
he neither learned nor flattered any vice:
he was no bigot,
though he doubted none of the Thirty-Nine Articles:
and if to follow nature,
and to respect the laws of society,
be philosophy,
he was a perfect philosopher,
a faithful friend,
an agreeable companion,
a loving husband,
distinguished by a numerous offspring,
all of which he lived to see take good courses:
in his old age he retired
to the house of a clergyman in the country,
where he finished his earthly race,
and died an honour and example to the whole species.
Reader,
this stone is guiltless of flattery,
for he to whom it is inscribed
was not a man,
but a
GREYHOUND.

Jonathan Swift

On the Collar of Mrs Dingley's Lap-Dog

Pray steal me not, I'm Mrs *Dingley's*
Whose Heart in this Four-footed Thing lies.

Disgruntlement in Wales

THOUGHTS UPON BEING confin'd at Holyhead. If this were to be my settlement, during life, I could amuse my self a while by forming some conveniencyes to be easy; and should not be frighted either by the solitude, or the meaness of lodging, eating or drinking. . . . I am afraid of joyning with passengers for fear of getting acquaintance with Irish. The Days are short, and I have five hours at night to spend by my self before I go to bed. I should be glad to converse with Farmers or shop-keepers, but none of them speak English. A Dog is better company than the Vicar, for I rememb^r him of old. What can I do but write every thing that comes into my head. Watt is a Booby of that Species which I dare not suffer to be familiar with me, for he would ramp on my shoulders in half an hour. . . . In short: I come from being used like an Emperor to be used worse than a Dog at Holyhead. Yet my hat is worn to pieces by answering the civilityes of the poor inhabitants as they pass by. The women might be safe enough, who all wear hats yet never pull them off, if the dirty streets did not foul their petticoats by courtisying so low. Look you; be not impatient, for I onely wait till my watch marks 10, and then I will give you ease, and my self sleep, if I can. On my conscience you may know a Welch dog as well as a Welch man or woman by its peevish passionate way of barking.

From *Holyhead Journal*: 26 September 1727

WILLIAM SOMERVILLE

Advice

First let the kennel be the huntsman's care,
Upon some little eminence erect,
And fronting to the ruddy dawn; its courts
On either hand wide op'ning to receive
The sun's all cheering beams, when mild he shines,
And gilds the mountain tops. For much the pack
(Rous'd from their dark alcoves) delight to stretch,
And bask, in his invigorating ray:
Warn'd by the streaming light and merry lark,
Forth rush the jolly clan; with tuneful throats
They carol loud, and in grand chorus join'd
Salute the new-born day. For not alone
The vegetable world, but men and brutes
Own his reviving influence, and joy
At his approach. Fountain of light! if chance
Some envious cloud veil thy refulgent brow,
In vain the Muses aid; untouch'd, unstrung,
Lies my mute harp, and thy desponding bard
Sits darkly musing o'er th' unfinish'd lay.
   Let no Corinthian pillars prop the dome,
A vain expense, on charitable deeds
Better dispos'd, to clothe the tatter'd wretch
Who shrinks beneath the blast, to feed the poor
Pinch'd with afflictive want: for use, not state,
Gracefully plain, let each apartment rise.
O'er all let cleanliness preside, no scraps
Bestrew the pavement, and no half-pick'd bones,
To kindle fierce debate, or to disgust
That nicer sense, on which the sportsman's hope
And all his future triumphs must depend.
Soon as the growling pack with eager joy

Have lapp'd their smoking viands, morn or eve,
From the full cistern lead the ductile streams,
To wash thy court well-pav'd; nor spare thy pains,
For much to health will cleanliness avail.
Seek'st thou for hounds to climb the rocky steep,
And brush th' entangled covert, whose nice scent
O'er greasy fallows and frequented roads
Can pick the dubious way? Banish far off
Each noisome stench, let no offensive smell
Invade thy wide enclosure, but admit
The nitrous air and purifying breeze.
   Water and shade no less demand thy care:
In a large square th' adjacent field enclose,
There plant in equal ranks the spreading elm,
Or fragrant lime; most happy thy design,
If, at the bottom of thy spacious court,
A large canal, fed by the crystal brook,
From its transparent bosom shall reflect
Thy downward structure and inverted grove.
Here, when the sun's too potent gleams annoy
The crowded kennel, and the drooping pack,
Restless and faint, loll their unmoisten'd tongues,
And drop their feeble tails, to cooler shades
Lead forth the panting tribe; soon shalt thou find
The cordial breeze their fainting hearts revive:
Tumultuous soon they plunge into the stream
There lave their reeking sides, with greedy joy
Gulp down the flying wave, this way and that
From shore to shore they swim, while clamour loud
And wild uproar torments the troubled flood:
Then on the sunny bank they roll and stretch
Their dripping limbs, or else in wanton rings
Coursing around, pursuing and pursued,
The merry multitude disporting play.

But here with watchful and observant eye
Attend their frolics, which too often end
In bloody broils and death. High o'er thy head
Wave thy resounding whip, and with a voice
Fierce-menacing o'er-rule the stern debate,
And quench their kindling rage; for oft in sport
Begun, combat ensues, growling they snarl,
Then, on their haunches rear'd, rampant they seize
Each other's throats, with teeth and claws, in gore
Besmear'd, they wound, they tear, till on the ground,
Panting, half dead the conquer'd champion lies:
Then sudden all the base, ignoble crowd
Loud clam'ring seize the helpless worried wretch,
And, thirsting for his blood, drag diff'rent ways
His mangled carcass on th' ensanguin'd plain.
O! breasts of pity void! t' oppress the weak,
To point your vengeance at the friendless head,
And with one mutual cry insult the fallen!
Emblem too just of man's degen'rate race.
　　Others apart by native instinct led,
Knowing instructor! 'mong the ranker grass
Cull each salubrious plant, with bitter juice
Concoctive stor'd, and potent to allay
Each vitious ferment. Thus the hand divine
Of Providence, beneficent and kind
To all his creatures, for the brutes prescribes
A ready remedy, and is himself
Their great physician. Now grown stiff with age,
And many a painful chace, the wise old hound,
Regardless of the frolic pack, attends
His master's side, or slumbers at his ease
Beneath the bending shade; there many a ring
Runs o'er in dreams; now on the doubtful soil
Puzzles perplex'd, or doubles intricate

Cautious unfolds; then wing'd with all his speed
Bounds o'er the lawn to seize his panting prey,
And in imperfect whimp'rings speaks his joy.

From *The Chase*

CAPTAIN COOK

In the South Seas

THE CHIEF FOOD OF the natives of Otaheite consists of vegetables.
They have no tame animals, except poultry, hogs, and dogs, and
these are not numerous. Captain Cook and his associates agreed that a
South Sea dog was little inferior to a British lamb, which is probably
occasioned by their being kept up, and fed solely upon vegetables.

William Smellie, from *The Philosophy of Natural History*

MATTHEW PRIOR

Reason

The lonely *Fox* roams far abroad,
On secret Rapin bent, and Midnight Fraud;
Now haunts the Cliff, now traverses the Lawn;
And flies the hated Neighborhood of Man:
While the kind *Spaniel*, and the faithful *Hound*,
Likest that *Fox* in Shape and Species found,
Refuses thro' these Cliffs and Lawns to roam;

Pursues the noted Path, and covets home;
Does with kind Joy Domestic Faces meet;
Takes what the glutted Child denies to eat;
And dying, licks his long-lov'd Master's Feet.

By what immediate Cause They are inclin'd,
In many Acts, 'tis hard, I own, to find.
I see in others, or I think I see,
That strict their Principles, and our's agree.
Evil like Us they shun, and covet Good;
Abhor the Poison, and receive the Food.
Like Us they love or hate: like Us they know,
To joy the Friend, or grapple with the Foe.
With seeming Thought their Action they intend,
And use the Means proportion'd to the End.
Then vainly the Philosopher avers,
That Reason guides our Deed, and Instinct their's.
How can We justly diff'rent Causes frame,
When the Effects entirely are the same?
Instinct and Reason how can we divide?
'Tis the Fool's Ign'rance, and the Pedant's Pride.

From *Solomon*

FRANCIS COVENTRY

High and Low

WHEN OUR HERO waked the next morning, and found himself in new apartments, the first thing he did was to piss on a pair of velvet breeches, which lay in a chair by his lordship's bedside; after which, the door being open, he travelled forth, and performed a much more disreputable action on a rich *Turkey* carpet in my lady's dining-room. Having thus taken possession of his new house by these two acts of *seisin*, he returned to the bed-side, and reposed himself again to sleep till his lord should please to be stirring.

About ten o'clock lord *Marmazet* raised himself up in his bed, and rang his bell for servants to assist him in the fatigue of putting on his cloaths. The valet in chief immediately attended, undrew the curtains, and respectfully enquired his master's pleasure. In answer to which his lordship signifying that he would get up, *Guillaume* folded his stockings, placed his slippers by the bed-side, and was going to present him with his breeches – when lo! the crime our hero had been guilty of stared him full in the face, and gave such an air of surprize to his features, that his lordship could not help asking what was the matter. *Guillaume* then related the misdemeanor, at which his master was so far from being angry, that he only laughed at the astonishment of his valet, and calling the dog upon the bed, caressed him with as much tenderness, as if he had performed the most meritorious action in the world. Then turning again to his servant, 'What does the booby stare at,' cries he, 'with such amazement? I wish to G – d the dog had pissed in thy mouth. Prythee get a fresh pair of breeches, and let me rise – or am I to lie a-bed till midnight?'

As soon as he was dressed in his morning dishabille, he went down stairs to breakfast; in which our hero bore him company, and had the honour of eating roll and butter in great magnificence. When breakfast was over, he recollected that it might now be time to send up compliments to his lady, which he generally performed every morning; and imagining that she would not be displeased with the present of so pretty a dog, 'Here, *Guillaume*,' said he, 'take this little dog, and carry him up stairs to your lady. My compliments, and desire to know how her ladyship does this morning. Tell her I found him – pox take him, I don't know where I found him, but he's a pretty little fellow, and I am sure she must be pleased with him.'

Tho' the reader must from hence conclude that lord and lady *Marmazet* reposed themselves in different beds at night, he will not, I imagine, be surprised at such a circumstance in this accomplished and fashionable age. Her ladyship was a woman of great wit, pleasure and amour, as well as her husband, only with a little more reserve and caution, to save appearances with the world. Her familiarity with a sharper at *Bath*, may have already given the reader some little sketch of her character; and for the rest it will be only necessary to inform him, that she had spent the greatest part of her life in St *James*'s parish. Her husband had married her without the temptation of love, because she was a rich heiress of a noble family; and she had consented to the match, with an equal indifference, only because it preserved her rank and station in the world. In consequence they soon grew totally unconcerned about each other; but then, being both of easy chearful tempers, their indifference did not sour into hatred; on the contrary, they made it a topic of wit, when they met, to railly one another on their mutual amours. These meetings indeed were not very frequent, once or twice a week perhaps at dinner, at which times they behaved with the utmost politeness and complaisance; or if they railled, it was done with so much gaiety and good-humour, that they only parted with the greater spirits to their evening amusements. In short, his lordship pursued his pleasures without any domestic expostulations, and her ladyship in return was permitted to live in all respects, as *Juvenal* expresses it, *tanquam vicina mariti*, more like her husband's neighbour than his wife.

Her ladyship was now just awake, and taking her morning tea in bed, when *Guillaume* ascended the stairs, and knocked at her chamber-door. The waiting gentlewoman being ordered out to see who it was, returned immediately to the bed-side with a dog in her arms, and delivered the message that accompanied him. As her ladyship had never in her life discovered any fondness for these four-footed animals, she could not conceive the meaning of such a present, and with some disdain in her countenance ordered 'the fellow to carry back his puppies again to his master.' But when the servant was gone down stairs, bethinking herself that there might be some joke in it, which she did not perceive, and resolving not to be out-done by her husband in wit, she asked her maid eagerly, if there was any such thing as a cat in the house. 'A cat, my lady!' cries the waiting gentlewoman, 'yes, my lady, I believe there is such a thing to be found.' 'Well then,' said her ladyship, 'go and catch it directly, and carry it with my compliments to his lordship. Let him know I am infinitely obliged to him for his present, and have sent him a cat in return for his dog.'

The maid simpered without offering to stir, as not indeed conceiving her mistress to be in earnest; but having the orders repeated to her, she set out immediately to fulfil them. After much laughter below stairs among the servants, a cat at length was catched, and the waiting-maid went with it in her arms to his lordship's dressing room. Having rapped at the door, and being ordered to enter, with a face half-blushing and half-smiling, she delivered her message in the following terms. 'My lady desires her compliments to your lordship, and begs the favour of you to accept of THIS, in return for your dog.' After which dropping the grave mouser on the floor, she was preparing to run away with all haste, being ready to burst with laughter. But his lordship, who was no less diverted, called her back, and having entertained himself with many jokes on the occasion, sent her up-stairs with a fresh message to her mistress. This was immediately returned on the part of her ladyship, and many little pieces of raillery were carried backwards and forwards, which perhaps might not be unentertaining: but as we are sensible with what contempt these little incidents will be received by the reader, if he happens to be a judge, a politician, or an alderman, we shall dwell no longer on them, and here put an end to the chapter.

From *Pompey the Little*

JOHN GAY
An Elegy on a Lap-Dog

Shock's fate I mourn; poor *Shock* is now no more,
Ye Muses mourn, ye chamber-maids deplore.
Unhappy *Shock*! yet more unhappy Fair,
Doom'd to survive thy joy and only care!
Thy wretched fingers now no more shall deck,
And tye the fav'rite ribband round his neck;
No more thy hand shall smooth his glossy hair,
And comb the wavings of his pendent ear.
Yet cease thy flowing grief, forsaken maid;
All mortal pleasures in a moment fade:
Our surest hope is in an hour destroy'd,
And love, best gift of heav'n, not long enjoy'd.
Methinks I see her frantick with despair,
Her streaming eyes, wrung hands, and flowing hair;

Her *Mechlen* pinners rent the floor bestrow,
And her torn fan gives real signs of woe.
Hence Superstition, that tormenting guest,
That haunts with fancy'd fears the coward breast;
No dread events upon this fate attend,
Stream eyes no more, no more thy tresses rend.
Tho' certain omens oft' forewarn a state,
And dying lyons show the monarch's fate;
Why should such fears bid *Celia*'s sorrow rise?
For when a Lap-dog falls, no lover dyes.

  Cease, *Celia*, cease; restrain thy flowing tears,
Some warmer passion will dispell thy cares.
In man you'll find a more substantial bliss,
More grateful toying, and a sweeter kiss.

  He's dead. Oh lay him gently in the ground!
And may his tomb be by this verse renown'd.
Here Shock, *the pride of all his kind, is laid;*
Who fawn'd like man, but ne'er like man betray'd.

JEAN-JACQUES ROUSSEAU

Deference

M. LE DUC DE VILLEROY'S kindness towards me showed no alteration. His nephew and heir, the young Marquis de Villeroy, did not share the kindly feelings with which his uncle honoured me, nor, I must confess, did I entertain the same respect for him. His frivolous behaviour made him unendurable to me, and my coldness brought upon me his dislike. One evening, at table, he wantonly insulted me; I came out very badly, because I am a fool and utterly without presence of mind, and anger, instead of sharpening the little ready wit I may possess, entirely deprives me of it. I had a dog which had been given to me when it was quite a puppy, almost immediately after my arrival at the Hermitage, and which I had named 'Duke.' This dog, which, although no beauty, was of an uncommon breed, I had made my friend and companion; and it certainly deserved the name better than the majority of those who have assumed it. It had become a favourite at the château of Montmorency, owing to its sensible and affectionate disposition, and the attachment which we felt for each other; but, in a moment of foolish weakness, I had changed its name to 'Turk,' as if there had not been hundreds of dogs called 'Marquis,' without any Marquis being offended at it. The Marquis de Villeroy, who knew of this change of name, pressed me so hard upon the point that I was obliged to relate, in the presence of the company, what I had done. What gave offence in the story was, not so much that I had given the dog the name of 'Duke,' as that I had afterwards altered it. The worst thing was, that there were several dukes present, amongst others, M. de Luxembourg and his son. The Marquis de Villeroy, who was a duke presumptive, and bears that title at the present day, cruelly enjoyed the embarrassing position in which he had placed me, and the effect produced by it. I was assured, the next day, that his aunt had severely scolded him.

From *The Confessions*
Trans. by anon for Everyman's Library

THE GENTLEMAN'S MAGAZINE

Matters Arising in 1770

IN A VILLAGE SITUATED between Caen and Vire, on the borders of the district called the *Grove*, there dwelt a peasant of a surly untoward temper, who frequently beat and abused his wife, insomuch that the neighbours were sometimes obliged by her outcries to interfere in order to prevent farther mischief. Being at length weary of living always with one whom he hated, he resolved to get rid of her. He pretended to be reconciled, altered his behaviour, and on holidays invited her to walk out with him into the fields for pleasure and recreation. One summer evening, after a very hot day, he carried her to cool and refresh herself on the borders of a spring, in a place very shady and solitary. He pretended to be very thirsty. The clearness of the water tempted them to drink. He laid himself down all along upon his belly, and swilled large draughts of it, highly commending the sweetness of the water, and urging her to refresh herself in like manner. She believed him, and followed his example. As soon as he saw her in that posture, he threw himself upon her, and plunged her head in to the water, in order to drown her. She struggled hard for her life, but could not have prevailed without the assistance of the dog, who used to follow, was fond of her, and never left her. He immediately flew at the husband, seized him by the throat, made him let go his hold, and saved the life of his mistress.

April

THE SECRETARY OF the Society of Agriculture of Leon hath drawn up a memorial wherein he proves that the great number of useless dogs in the kingdom annually consume of aliments proper for the human species to the amount of sixteen millions, which would furnish subsistance for upwards of 300,000 men.

September

ON THE ROAD from Delft to the Hague our observers saw a large black and white dog following a coach. As he seemed to them somewhat remarkable, M. Van der Hoeven, who accompanied them, told them, that he was the Offspring of a bear and a bitch, which could not be doubted, as he was whelped at the end of a long voyage, in which the bitch and the bear were the only animals on board.

M. de Courtenvaux's Voyages in the Aurora Frigate; *September*

OLIVER GOLDSMITH
Mad-Dog Scare

A DREAD OF MAD DOGS is the *epidemic terror* which now prevails, and the whole nation is at present actually groaning under the malignity of its influence. The people sally from their houses with that circumspection which is prudent in such as expect a mad dog at every turning. The physician publishes his prescription, the beadle prepares his halter, and a few of unusual bravery arm themselves with boots and buff gloves, in order to face the enemy if he should offer to attack them. In short, the whole people stand bravely upon their defence, and seem by their present spirit to show a resolution of not being tamely bit by mad dogs any longer.

Their manner of knowing whether a dog be mad or no, somewhat resembles the ancient European custom of trying witches. The old woman suspected was tied hand and foot and thrown into the water. If she swam, then she was instantly carried off to be burnt for a witch, if she sunk, then indeed she was acquitted of the charge, but drowned in the experiment. In the same manner a crowd gather round a dog suspected of madness, and they begin by teasing the devoted animal on every side; if he attempts to stand upon the defensive and bite, then is he unanimously found guilty, for *a mad dog always snaps at every thing*; if, on the contrary, he strives to escape by running away, then he can expect no compassion, *for mad dogs always run straight forward before them*.

It is pleasant enough for a neutral being like me, who have no share in those ideal calamities, to mark the stages of this national disease. The terror at first feebly enters with a disregarded story of a little dog, that had gone through a neighbouring village, that was thought to be mad by several that had seen him. The next account comes, that a mastiff ran through a certain town, and had bit five geese, which immediately run mad, foamed at the bill, and died in great agonies soon after. Then comes an affecting history of a little boy bit in the leg, and gone down to be dipt in the salt water; when the people have sufficiently shuddered at that, they are the next congealed with a frightful account of a man who was said lately to have died from a bite he had received some years before. This relation only prepares the way for another, still more hideous, as how the master of a family, with seven small children, were all bit by a mad lap dog, and how the poor father first perceived the infection by calling for a draught of water, where he saw the lap dog swimming in the cup.

When epidemic terror is thus once excited, every morning comes loaded with some new disaster; as in stories of ghosts each loves to hear the account, though it only serves to make him uneasy, so here each listens with eagerness, and adds to the tidings with new circumstances of peculiar horror. A lady for instance, in the country, of very weak nerves has been frighted by the barking of a dog; and this, alas! too frequently happens. The story soon is improved and spreads, that a mad dog had frighted a lady of distinction. These circumstances begin to grow terrible before they have reached the neighbouring village, and there the report is that a lady of quality was *bit* by a mad mastiff. This account every moment gathers new strength and grows more dismal as it approaches the capital, and by the time it has arrived in town the lady is described, with wild eyes, foaming mouth, running mad upon all four, barking like a dog, biting her servants, and at last smothered between two beds by the advice of her doctors: while the mad mastiff is in the mean time ranging the whole country over, slavering at the mouth, and seeking whom he may devour.

My landlady, a good-natured woman, but a little credulous, waked me some mornings ago before the usual hour with horror and astonishment in her looks; she desired me if I had any regard for my safety, to keep within; for a few days ago so dismal an accident had happened, as to put all the world upon their guard. A mad dog down in the country, she assured me, had bit a farmer, who soon becoming mad ran into his own yard, and bit a fine brindled cow; the cow quickly became as mad as the man, began to foam at the mouth, and raising herself up, walked about on her hind legs, sometimes barking like a dog, and sometimes attempting to talk like the farmer. Upon examining the grounds of this story, I found my landlady had it from one neighbour, who had it from another neighbour, who heard it from very good authority.

Were most stories of this nature thoroughly examined, it would be found that numbers of such as have been said to suffer were no way injured, and that of those who have been actually bitten, not one in a hundred was bit by a mad dog. Such accounts in general therefore only serve to make the people miserable by false terrors, and sometimes fright the patient into actual frenzy, by creating those very symptoms they pretended to deplore.

But even allowing three or four to die in a season of this terrible death (and four is probably too large a concession), yet still it is not considered, how many are preserved in their health and in their property by this devoted animal's services. The midnight robber is kept at a distance, the insidious thief is often detected, the healthful chase repairs many a worn constitution, and the poor man finds in his dog a willing assistant, eager to lessen his toil, and content with the smallest retribution.

A dog, says one of the English poets, 'is an honest creature, and I am a friend to dogs.' Of all the beasts that graze the lawn or hunt the forest, a dog is the only animal, that leaving his fellows, attempts to cultivate the friendship of man; to man he looks in all his necessities with a speaking eye for assistance; exerts for him all the little service in his power with cheerfulness and pleasure; for him bears famine and fatigue with patience and resignation; no injuries can abate his fidelity, no distress induce him to forsake his benefactor; studious to please, and fearing to offend, he is still an humble stedfast dependent, and in him alone fawning is not flattery. How unkind then to torture this faithful creature who has left the forest, to claim the protection of man; how ungrateful a return to the trusty animal for all its services.

From *The Citizen of the World*, Letter CXIX

Elegy on the Death of a Mad Dog

Good people all, of every sort,
    Give ear unto my song;
And if you find it wond'rous short,
    It cannot hold you long.

In Islington there was a man,
    Of whom the world might say,
That still a godly race he ran,
    Whene'er he went to pray.

A kind and gentle heart he had,
    To comfort friends and foes;

The naked every day he clad,
    When he put on his clothes.

And in that town a dog was found,
    As many dogs there be,
Both mongrel, puppy, whelp, and hound,
    And curs of low degree.

This dog and man at first were friends;
    But when a pique began,
The dog, to gain some private ends,
    Went mad and bit the man.

Around from all the neighbouring streets
    The wond'ring neighbours ran,
And swore the dog had lost his wits,
    To bite so good a man.

The wound it seem'd both sore and sad
    To every Christian eye;
And while they swore the dog was mad,
    They swore the man would die.

But soon a wonder came to light,
    That show'd the rogues they lied:
The man recover'd of the bite,
    The dog it was that died.

FREDERICK THE GREAT

THE MORE I SEE of men, the better I like dogs

The Emperor's Death

HE DRANK ONCE, grasping the goblet with both hands, a draught of fennel-water, his customary drink; and seemed relieved by it – his last refection in this world. Towards nine in the evening, there had come on a continual short cough, and a rattling in the breast, breath more and more difficult. Why continue? Friedrich is making exit, on the common terms; you may *hear* the curtain rustling down. For most part he was unconscious, never more than half-conscious. As the wall-clock above his head struck 11 he asked: 'What o'clock?' 'Eleven,' answered they. 'At 4,' murmured he, 'I will rise.' One of his dogs sat on its stool near him; about midnight he noticed it shivering for cold: 'Throw a quilt over it,' said or beckoned he; that, I think, was his last completely-conscious utterance.

Thomas Carlyle from his *Life of Frederick the Great*

HORACE WALPOLE

Another Scare

IN LONDON THERE is a more cruel campaign than that waged by the Russians: the streets are a very picture of the murder of the innocents – one drives over nothing but poor dead dogs! The dear, good-natured, honest, sensible creatures! Christ! how can anybody hurt them? Nobody could but those Cherokees the English, who desire no better than to be halloo'd to blood: – one day Admiral Byng, the next Lord George Sackville, and today the poor dogs!

To Lord Strafford, 4 September 1770

On Heat

Y OU KNOW I have always some favourite, some successor of
Patapan. The present is a tanned black spaniel, called Rosette. She
saved my life last Saturday night, so I am sure you will love her too. I
was undressing for bed. She barked and was so restless, that there was
no quieting her. I fancied there was somebody under the bed, but there
was not. As she looked at the chimney which roared much, I thought it
was the wind, yet wondered, as she had heard it so often. At last, not
being able to quiet her, I looked to see what she barked at, and
perceived sparks of fire falling from the chimney, and on searching
farther perceived it in flames. It had not gone far, and we easily
extinguished it. I wish I had as much power over the nation's chimney.
Adieu!

To Sir Horace Mann, 23 March 1770

Dogmanity

L ONDON IS A desert, and nobody asks but if there is any mail from
Ireland? There is not a new book, play, wedding or funeral.
Duchess Hervey is already forgotten. My life is passed alone here, or in
going to London to talk with lawyers and stewards, and writing letters
to Norfolk about farms – So that your Lordship is not singular in being
out of your element. The rest of my time has been employed in nursing
Rosette – alas! to no purpose. After suffering dreadfully for a fortnight
from the time she was seized at Nuneham, she has only languished till
about ten days ago. As I have nothing to fill my letter, I will send you
her epitaph – it has no merit, for it is an imitation, but in coming from
the heart, if ever epitaph did, and therefore your Dogmanity will not
dislike it.

> Sweetest roses of the year
> Strew around my Rose's bier.
> Calmly may the dust repose
> Of my pretty faithful Rose!
> And if yon cloud-topt hill behind,
> This frame dissolv'd, this breath resign'd,

Some happier Isle, some humbler Heav'n
Be to my trembling Wishes giv'n,
Admitted to that equal sky
May sweet Rose bear me company!

To Lord Nuneham, 6 November 1773

Blasphemy

I SAW CHARMING Lady Sarah [Bunbury], who is a little fatter, but as fresh and beautiful as ever: her little girl is sweetly pretty and lively. We had much billiards, music, loo and company; I could take no part in the two first; I love most of the last that I know, and as there were two or three children and two- or three-and-forty dogs, I could not want amusement, for I generally prefer both to what the common people call *Christians*.

To Lady Ossory, 29 August 1774

A Servant's Sensitivities

I TOLD YOU in my last, that Tonton [bequeathed by Madame du Deffand] was arrived. I brought him this morning to take possession of his new villa; but his inauguration has not been at all pacific. As he has already found out that he may be as despotic as at Saint-Joseph's, he began with exiling my beautiful little cat; – upon which, however, we shall not quite agree. He then flew at one of my dogs, who returned it, by biting his foot till it bled; but was severely beaten for it. I immediately rung for Margaret [housekeeper] to dress his foot; but in the midst of my tribulation could not keep my countenance; for she cried, 'Poor little thing, he does not understand my language!' – I hope she will not recollect too that he is a papist!

To Henrietta Seymour Conway, 6 May 1781

Growing Affection

Y OU WILL FIND that I have gotten a new idol, in a word, a successor to Rosette and almost as great a favourite, nor is this a breach of vows and constancy, but an act of piety. In a word, my poor dear old friend Madame du Deffand had a little dog of which she was extremely fond, and the last time I saw her she made me promise if I should survive her to take charge of it. I did. It is arrived and I was going to say, it is incredible how fond I am of it, but I have no occasion to brag of my dogmanity. I dined at Richmond House t'other day, and mentioning whither I was going, the Duke said, 'Own the truth, shall not you call at home first and see Tonton?' He guessed rightly. He is now sitting on my paper as I write – not the Duke, but Tonton.

To Rev. William Mason, 22 May 1781

The Library [by George Crabbe] I have read. There are some pretty lines, and easy verses; but it is too long. One thought is charming, *that a dog though a flatterer, is still a friend.* It made me give Tonton a warm kiss, and swear it was true.

To Lady Ossory, 4 September 1781

WILLIAM HAMILTON

Bonny Heck

Alas, alas, quo' bonny Heck
On former days which I reflect!
I was a dog much in respect
  For doughty deed:
But now I must hing by the neck
  Without remeed.

O fy, sirs, for black burning shame,
Ye'll bring a blunder on your name
Pray tell me wherein I'm to blame?
        Is't, in effect,
Because I'm cripple, auld and lame?
        Quo' bonny Heck.

What great feats I have done my sell
Within clink of Kilrenny Bell,
When I was souple, young and fell
        But fear or dread:
John, Ness, and Paterson can tell,
        Whose hearts may bleid.

They'll witness that I was the vier
Of all the dogs within the shire,
I'd run all day and never tire:
        But now my neck,
It must be stretchèd for my hire,
        Quo' bonny Heck.

How nimbly could I turn the hare,
Then serve myself, that was right fair!
For still it was my constant care
        The van to lead.
Now, what could sery Heck do mair,
        Syne kill her dead?

At the King's-Muir, and Kelly-law,
Where good stout hares gang fast awa',
So cliverly I did it claw,
        With pith and speed:
I bure the bell before them
        As clear's a beid.

I ran alike on a'kind grounds,
Yea in the midst of Ardry Whines,
I grip't the mackings be the bunns,
      Or be the neck:
Where nathing could slay them but guns,
      Save bonny Heck:

I wily, witty was, and gash,
With my auld felni packy pash,
Nae man might anes buy me for cash
      In some respect.
Are they not then confounded rash,
      That hangs poor Heck?

I was a bardy tyke and bauld,
Tho' my beard's grey, I'm not so auld.
Can any man to me unfald
      What is the feid,
To stane me ere I be well cauld?
      A cruel deed!

Now honesty was ay my drift,
An innocent and harmless shift,
A kaill-pot-lid gently to lift,
      Or amry-sneck.
Shame fa the chafts, dare call that thift,
      Quo' bonny Heck.

So well's I cou'd play hocus pocus,
And of the servants mack jodocus,
And this I did in every locus
      Throw their neglect.
And was not this a merry jocus,
      Quo' bonny Heck?

But now, good sirs, this day is lost,
The best dog in the east-nook coast:
For never ane durst brag nor boast
　　Me, for their neck.
But now I must yield up the ghost,
　　Quo' bonny Heck.

And put a period to my talking,
For I'm unto my exit making:
Sirs, ye may a' gae to the hawking,
　　And there reflect,
Ye'll ne'er get sick a dog for makin'
　　As bonny Heck.

But if my puppies ance were ready,
Which I gat on a bonny lady:
They'll be baith cliver, keen, and beddy,
　　And ne'er neglect,
To clink it like their ancient deddy,
　　The famous Heck.

SAMUEL JOHNSON

On the Air

THE CUSTOM OF EATING dogs at Otaheite being mentioned, Goldsmith observed, that this was also a custom in China; that a dog-butcher is as common there as any other butcher; and that when he walks abroad all the dogs fall on him. JOHNSON: 'That is not owing to his killing dogs, Sir. I remember a butcher at Lichfield, whom a dog that was in the house where I lived, always attacked. It is the smell of carnage which provokes this, let the animals he has killed be what they may.'

James Boswell, from his Life of Johnson, 29 April 1773

Cast in Marble

F: 'I HAVE been looking at this famous antique marble dog of Mr Jennings, valued at a thousand guineas, said to be Alcibiades's dog.' JOHNSON: 'His tail then must be docked. That was the mark of Alcibiades's dog.' E: 'A thousand guineas! The representation of no animal whatever is worth so much. At this rate a dead dog would indeed be better than a living lion.' JOHNSON: 'Sir, it is not the worth of the thing, but of the skill in forming it which is so highly estimated. Every thing that enlarges the sphere of human powers, that shows man he can do what he thought he could not do, is valuable. The first man who balanced a straw upon his nose; Johnson, who rode upon three horses at a time; in short, all such men deserved the applause of mankind, not on account of the use of what they did, but of the dexterity which they exhibited.'

ibid, 3 April 1778

EDWARD GIBBON

A Gift

I ACCEPT THE Pomeranian Lady with gratitude and pleasure, and shall be impatient to form an acquaintance with her.

To Dorothea Gibbon, 2 May 1775

TODAY DEYVERDUN MYSELF and and another Gentleman dined at home. After drinking Coffee in the Library we went down stairs again and as we entered the Parlour, our ears were saluted with a very harmonious barking, and our eyes gratified by the sight of one of the prettiest animals I ever saw. Her figure and coat are perfect, her manners Genteel and lively, and her teeth (as a pair of ruffles have already experienced) most remarkably sharp. She is not in the least fatigued with her Voyage, and compleatly at home in Bentick Street. I call her *Bath*. Gibbon would be ambiguous and Dorothea disrespectful.

16 July 1775

PARSON WOODFORDE

Various Calamities

I BREAKFASTED, DINED, supped and slept again at Weston. Very much disturbed in the night by our dog which was kept within doors tonight, was obliged to get out of bed naked twice or thrice to make him quiet, had him into my room, and there he emptied himself all over the room.

Diary: 5 June 1776

IN THE AFTERNOON my dog Pompey came home shot terribly, so bad that I had her hanged directly out of her Misery. My greyhound Minx who was with her did not come and we suppose she has met with the same fate. It is supposed that Mr Townshend's gamekeeper who goes by the name of black Jack, shot Pompey.

21 September 1777

BEN WENT TO help Stephen Andrew's Men at Harvest, came home in the evening in Liquor, and at 11 o'clock after I got up to my Room to go to bed, I heard my little Puppy cry much and therefore I went down to see what was the matter with him and he had got his Head between the Pales by the garden gate and could not get back again, I released him and carried him towards the back door and there I saw a light burning in Ben's Room, upon that I walked up into his Room, and there saw him laying flat upon his back on the bed asleep with his Cloaths on and the candle burning on the Table. I waked him, made him put out the candle and talked with him a little on it, but not much as he was not in a capacity of answering but little. I was very uneasy to see matters go on so badly.

25 August 1778

ABOUT 10 THIS morning took a ride to Mr Townshend's Clumps, there met Du Quesne by appointment, and went acoursing. . . . We coursed till 2 o'clock, had a number of courses, saw at least 12 brace of Hares, and killed only 1 Hare. My Bitch Dutchess went with me, and she had not begun coursing before she was caught in a Rabbitt Gin, by one of her forefeet. She did not perform at all well after, being very shy and her foot painful.

22 February 1781

GILBERT WHITE

Chinese Dogs

MY NEAR NEIGHBOUR, a young gentleman in the service of the East-India Company, has brought home a dog and a bitch of the Chinese breed from Canton; such as are fattened in the country for the purpose of being eaten: they are about the size of a moderate spaniel; of a pale yellow colour, with coarse bristling hairs on their backs; sharp upright ears, and peaked head, which give them a very fox-like appearance. Their hind legs are unusually straight, without any bend at the hock or ham, to such a degree as to give them an awkward gait when they trot. When they are in motion their tails are curved high over their backs like those of some hounds, and have a bare place each on the outside from the tip midway, that does not seem to be matter of accident, but somewhat singular. Their eyes are jet black, small, and piercing; the insides of their lips and mouths of the same colour, and their tongues blue. The bitch has a dew-claw on each hind leg; the dog has none. When taken out into a field the bitch showed some disposition for hunting, and dwelt on the scent of a covey of partridges till she sprung them, giving her tongue all the time. The dogs in South America are dumb; but these bark much in a short thick manner, like foxes; and have a surly, savage demeanour like their ancestors, which are not domesticated, but bred up in sties, where they are fed for the table with rice-meal and other farinaceous food. These dogs, having been taken on board as soon as weaned, could not learn much from their dam; yet they did not relish flesh when they came to England. In the islands of the Pacific Ocean the dogs are bred up on vegetables, and would not eat flesh when offered them by our circumnavigators.

We believe that all dogs, in a state of nature, have sharp, upright fox-like ears; and that hanging ears, which are esteemed so graceful, are the effect of choice breeding and cultivation. Thus, in the Travels of Ysbrandt Ides from Muscovy to China, the dogs which draw the Tartars on snow-sledges near the river Oby are engraved with prick-ears, like those from Canton. The Kamschatdales also train the same sort of sharp-eared peak-nosed dogs to draw their sledges; as may be seen in an elegant print engraved for Captain Cook's last voyage round the world.

Now we are upon the subject of dogs it may not be impertinent to add, that spaniels, as all sportsmen know, though they hunt partridges and pheasants as it were by instinct, and with much delight and alacrity, yet will hardly touch their bones when offered as food; nor will a mongrel dog of my own, though he is remarkable for finding that sort of game. But, when we came to offer the bones of patridges to the two Chinese dogs, they devoured them with much greediness, and licked the platter clean.

No sporting dogs will flush woodcocks till inured to the scent and trained to the sport, which they then pursue with vehemence and transport; but then they will not touch their bones, but turn from them with abhorrence, even when they are hungry.

Now, that dogs should not be fond of the bones of such birds as they are not disposed to hunt is no wonder; but why they reject and do not care to eat their natural game is not so easily accounted for, since the end of hunting seems to be, that the chase pursued should be eaten. Dogs again will not devour the more rancid water-fowls, nor indeed the bones of any wild-fowls; nor will they touch the fœtid bodies of birds that feed on offal and garbage: and indeed there may be somewhat of providential instinct in this circumstance of dislike; for vultures and kites, and ravens, and crows, etc., were intended to be messmates with dogs over their carrion; and seem to be appointed by nature as fellow-scavengers to remove all cadaverous nuisances from the face of the earth.

From *The Natural History of Selbourne*: Letter LVIII

WILLIAM COWPER

Dog and Hare

B ESS [HARE], I HAVE SAID, died young; Tiney [hare] lived to be nine years old, and died at last, I have reason to think, of some hurt in his loins by a fall. Puss [hare] is still living, and has just completed his tenth year, discovering no signs of decay nor even of age, except that he is grown more discreet and less frolicksome than he was. I cannot conclude, Sir, without informing you that I have lately introduced a dog to his acquaintance, a spaniel that had never seen a hare to a hare that had never seen a spaniel. I did it with great caution, but there was no real need of it. Puss discovered no token of fear, nor Marquis the least symptom of hostility. There is therefore, it should seem, no natural antipathy between dog and hare, but the pursuit of the one occasions the flight of the other, and the dog pursues because he is trained to it: they eat bread at the same time out of the same hand, and are in all respects sociable and friendly.

Letter to the *Gentleman's Magazine*, June 1784

Thunderstorms

YOU HAD BEEN gone two days when a violent thunder storm came over us. I was passing out of the parlour into the hall with Mungo at my heels when a flash seem'd to fill the rooom with fire. In the same instant came the clap, so that the explosion was, I suppose, perpendicular to the roof. Mungo's courage upon the tremendous occasion constrained me to smile in spite of the solemn impression that such an event never fails to affect me with. The moment that he heard the thunder, which was like the burst of a great gun, with a wrinkled forehead and with eyes directed to ceiling whence the sound seemed to proceed, he barked. But he barked exactly in concert with the thunder. It thunder'd once, and he bark'd once, and so precisely in the very instant when the thunder happen'd, that both sounds seemed to begin and to end together. – Some dogs will clap their tails close and sneak into a corner at such a time, but Mungo it seems is of a more fearless family.

To William Unwin, 28 July 1785

On Beau

HAD I KNOWN or could I have suspected that poor Jockey was dead, my dog should have borne his name. But it is now too late to Christen him again. Beau is his second name, and should I give him a third, he might possibly never answer to any at all. It is an old maxim of mine that he who multiplies connexions multiplies troubles. If this be true, it is consequently impolitic to keep a dog. Dogs as they are, they have yet good qualities that recommend them to our affections, and we cannot lose them without regret. Yet being myself a friend to the species, I cannot but wish *you* to keep one of them; because *that one* will be an individual added to the number of happy ones: a small number compared with the thousands whom it would be mercy to poison or drown or knock on the head. While he lives he will entertain you, and when he dies, the loss is easily repaired.

To Lady Hesketh, 10 December 1787

M Y DOG, MY dear is a spaniel. Till Miss Gunning begged him, he
was the property of a farmer, and while he was their property had
been accustomed to lie in the chimney corner, among the embers, till
the hair was singed from his back, and till nothing was left of his tail
but the gristle. Allowing for these disadvantages, he is really handsome;
and when nature shall have furnished him with a new coat, a gift which,
in consideration of the ragged condition of his old one, it is hoped she
will not long delay, he will then be unrivalled in personal endowments
by any dog in this country. He and my cat are excessively fond of each
other, and play a thousand gambols together that it is impossible not to
admire.

To Lady Hesketh, 17 December 1787

I FORGOT TO tell you that my dog is spotted liver-colour and white,
or rather white and chestnut. He is at present my pupil as well as
dog, and just before I sat down to write I gave him a lesson in the
science of fetch and carry. He performs with an animation past all
conception, except your own, whose poor head will never forget Tinker.
But I am now grown more reasonable, and never make such a dreadful
din but when Beau and I are together. To teach him is necessary, in
order that he may take the water, and *that* is necessary in order that he
may be sweet in summer.

To Lady Hesketh, 24 December 1787

The Hunt

O NE DAY LAST Week, Mrs Unwin and I having taken our morning
walk, and returning homeward through the wilderness, met the
three Throckmortons. A minute after we had met them, we heard the
cry of hounds at no great distance, and mounting the broad stump of
an Elm which had been felled, & by the aid of which we were enabled
to look over the Wall, we saw them. They were at that time in our
Orchard. Presently we heard a Terrier belonging to Mrs Throg, which
you may remember by the name of Fury, yelping with much vehemence,
and saw her running through the thickets within few yards of us at her

utmost speed as if in pursuit of something which we doubted not was the Fox. Before we could reach the other end of the wilderness, the hounds enter'd also; and when we arrived at the Gate which opens into the grove, there we found the whole dirty and weary cavalcade assembled. The Huntsman dismounting begg'd leave to follow his hounds on foot, for he was sure, he said, that they had killed him. A conclusion which I suppose he drew from their profound silence. He was accordingly admitted, and with a sagacity that would not have dishonour'd the best hound in the world, pursuing precisely the track which the Fox and the dogs had taken, though he had never had a glimpse of either after their first entrance through the rails, soon arrived where he found the slaughter'd prey, videlicet in the Pit of a certain place called Jessamy Hall, into which both the Fox and the dogs had enter'd by a large aperture in the Brick-work at the bottom of it. Being himself by far too staunch to boggle at a little filth contracted in so honourable a cause, he soon produced dead Reynard, and rejoined us in the grove with all his dogs about him. Having an opportunity to see a ceremony which I was pretty sure would never fall in my way again, I determined to stay and to notice all that passed with the most minute attention. The Fox's tail, or brush as I ought to call it, was given to one of the Hall Foot-boys, who bearing it in his hat-band, ran with it to his mistress, and in the height of his transport offer'd it to her fair hand, neither so clean nor so sweet as it had been while the Fox possess'd it. Happily however for Mrs Throg, not being quite so entraptured, she had the presence of mind to decline the offer. The boy therefore for aught I know, remains to this hour in possession both of the tail and the stink that belongs to it. The Huntsman having by the aid of a Pitchfork lodged Reynard on the arm of an Elm at the height of about 9 feet from the ground, there left him for a considerable time. The Gentlemen sat on their horses contemplating the Fox for which they had toiled so hard, and the hounds assembled at the foot of the tree with faces not at all less expressive of the most rational delight, contemplated the same object. The Huntsman remounted. He cut off a foot and threw it to the hounds. One of them swallow'd it whole like a Bolus. He then once more alighted, and drawing down the fox by his hinder legs, desired the people who were by this time rather numerous to open a lane for him to the right and left. He was instantly obey'd, when throwing the fox to the distance of some yards, and screaming like a fiend as he is – Tear him in pieces – at least six times repeatedly, he consign'd him over absolutely to the pack, who in a few minutes devour'd him completely.

Thus, my Dear, as Virgil says, What none of the Gods could have ventured to promise me, time itself pursuing its accustom'd course has of its own accord presented me with. – I have been In at the death of a Fox – and you now know as much of that matter as I, who am as well inform'd as any Sportsman in England.

* * *

My Dog turns out a most beautiful creature but is at present apt to lift up his leg in the house, on which subject he and I had a terrible quarrel this morning. My Cat is the most affectionate of all her kind, and in my eyes a beauty also.

To Lady Hesketh, 3 March 1788

Transplant Denied

I NOT ONLY performed these two excursions without injury to my health, but have by means of them gained indisputable proof that my ambulatory faculty is not yet impaired. A discovery which, considering that to my feet alone I am likely, as I have ever been, to be indebted always for my transportation from place to place, I find very delectable. My little dog was on the point of killing a most beautiful pheasant there, but fortunately the Gardener caught him in his arms time enough to prevent it. Beau, the handsomest creature in the world were it not for the extreme brevity of his tail, observing the pheasant's felicity in that respect whose tail was of a length unexampled, conceived envy at the sight and would have slain him. Foolish creature, could he by killing him have made that tail his own, who would not have laughed at a dog's rump adorned with a pheasant's tail! So little do we sometimes understand our own true advantage.

To Lady Hesketh, 12 May 1788

Beau's Feat

I MUST TELL you a feat of my Dog Beau. Walking by the River-side I observed some Water-Lilies floating at a little distance from the Bank. They are a large white flower with an Orange colour'd Eye, and extremely beautiful. I had a desire to gather one, and having your long Cane in my hand, by the help of it endeavor'd to bring one of them within my reach. But the attempt proved vain and I walked forward. Beau had all the while observed me very attentively. Returning soon after toward the same place, I observed him plunge into the river while I was about 40 yards distant from him, and when I had nearly reached the spot, he swam to land with a Lily in his mouth, which he came and lay'd at my foot.

To Lady Hesketh, 27 June 1788

BEAU'S PERFORMANCE WAS exactly such as I represented it, without any embellishment. I may now add that the next time we walk'd to the same place together, he repeated it. With respect to his diet it is always of the most salutary kind; Lights he never eats, and liver, having observed that it makes him sick, we never give him now. Bread he eats in abundance, and it is the only thing for which he begs with much importunity. He is regularly comb'd, and his Ears which are remarkably handsome, are my own particular care. They gather burrs while he threads all the thickets in his way, from which I deliver them myself as soon as we get home. But having taught him to take the water and even to delight in it, I never give him a forced washing, lest he should contract an Hydrophobia and refuse the river. I have observed too that dogs often washed get Rheumatisms, because they do not dry themselves by exercise, but lie down in their damp coats which is hurtful to every thing but a Highlander.

To Lady Hesketh, 5 July 1788

The Dog and the Water-Lily
NO FABLE

The noon was shady, and soft airs
    Swept Ouse's silent tide,
When, 'scap'd from literary cares,
    I wander'd on his side.

My spaniel, prettiest of his race,
    And high in pedigree,
(Two nymphs, adorn'd with ev'ry grace,
    That spaniel found for me)

Now wanton'd lost in flags and reeds,
    Now starting into sight
Pursued the swallow o'er the meads
    With scarce a slower flight.

It was the time when Ouse display'd
    His lilies newly blown;
Their beauties I intent survey'd;
    And one I wish'd my own.

With cane extended far I sought
    To steer it close to land;
But still the prize, though nearly caught,
    Escap'd my eager hand.

Beau marked my unsuccessful pains
    With fixt consid'rate face,
And puzzling sat his puppy brains
    To comprehend the case.

But with a chirrup clear and strong,
    Dispersing all his dream,

I thence withdrew, and follow'd long
   The windings of the stream.

My ramble finish'd, I return'd.
   Beau trotting far before
The floating wreath again discern'd,
   And plunging left the shore.

I saw him with that lily cropp'd
   Impatient swim to meet
My quick approach, and soon he dropp'd
   The treasure at my feet.

Charm'd with the sight, the world, I cried,
   Shall hear of this thy deed,
My dog shall mortify the pride
   Of man's superior breed;

But, chief, myself I will enjoin,
   Awake at duty's call,
To show a love as prompt as thine
   To Him who gives me all.

Epitaph on Fop

A Dog Belonging to Lady Throckmorton

Though once a puppy, and though Fop by name,
Here moulders one, whose bones some honour claim;
No sycophant, although of spaniel race!
And though no hound, a martyr to the chase!

Ye squirrels, rabbits, leverets, rejoice!
Your haunts no longer echo to his voice.

This record of his fate exulting view,
He died worn out with vain pursuit of you.
  'Yes!' the indignant shade of Fop replies,
'And worn with vain pursuit, man also dies.'

On A Spaniel Called Beau
Killing a Young Bird

A Spaniel, Beau, that fares like you,
  Well-fed, and at his ease,
Should wiser be, than to pursue
  Each trifle that he sees.

But you have kill'd a tiny bird,
  Which flew not till to-day,
Against my orders, whom you heard
  Forbidding you the prey.

Nor did you kill, that you might eat,
  And ease a doggish pain,
For him, though chas'd with furious heat,
  You left where he was slain.

Nor was he of the thievish sort,
  Or one whom blood allures,
But innocent was all his sport,
  Whom you have torn for yours.

My dog! what remedy remains,
  Since, teach you all I can,
I see you, after all my pains,
  So much resemble man!

Beau's Reply

Sir! when I flew to seize the bird,
In spite of your command,
A louder voice than yours I heard,
And harder to withstand:

You cried – Forbear! – but in my breast
A mightier cried – Proceed!
'Twas nature, Sir, whose strong behest
Impell'd me to the deed.

Yet much as nature I respect,
I ventur'd once to break
(As you perhaps may recollect)
Her precept, for your sake;

And when your linnet, on a day,
Passing his prison-door,
Had flutter'd all his strength away,
And panting press'd the floor,

Well knowing him a sacred thing,
Not destin'd to my tooth,
I only kiss'd his ruffled wing,
And lick'd the feathers smooth.

Let my obedience then excuse
My disobedience now,
Nor some reproof yourself refuse
From your aggriev'd Bow-wow!

If killing birds be such a crime,
(Which I can hardly see)
What think you, Sir, of killing Time
With verse address'd to me?

ROBERT BURNS
The Twa Dogs

A Tale

'Twas in that place o' Scotland's isle,
That bears the name o' Auld King Coil,
Upon a bonie day in June,
When wearing thro' the afternoon,
Twa dogs, that were na thrang at hame,   busy
Forgather'd ance upon a time.   Met

    The first I'll name, they ca'd him Cæsar,
Was keepit for his Honor's pleasure;
His hair, his size, his mouth, his lugs,   ears
Shew'd he was nane o' Scotland's dogs,
But whalpit some place far abroad,
Whare sailors gang to fish for Cod.

    His locked, letter'd, braw brass collar   handsome
Shew'd him the gentleman and scholar;
But tho' he was o' high degree,
The fient a pride, na pride had he,   devil
But wad hae spent an hour caressin,
Ev'n wi' a tinkler-gypsey's messin: mongrel, cur
At kirk or market, mill or smiddie,   smithy
Nae tawted tyke, tho' e'er sae duddie,   matted cur; ragged
But he wad stan't, as glad to see him,   would have stood
And stroan't on stanes an' hillocks wi' him.   watered

    The tither was a ploughman's collie,   The other
A rhyming, ranting, raving billie,   Rollicking; young fellow
Wha for his friend and comrade had him,
And in his freaks had Luath ca'd him,

After some dog in Highland sang,
Was made lang syne, Lord knows how lang.   long ago

He was a gash an' faithful tyke,   wise
As ever lap a sheugh or dyke.   leapt; ditch; wall
His honest, sonsie, baws'nt face   pleasant, white-striped
Ay gat him friends in ilka place;   every
His breast was white, his touzie back   shaggy
Weel clad wi' coat o' glossy black;
His gawcie tail, wi' upward curl,   ample
Hung owre his hurdies wi' a swirl.   buttocks

Nae doubt but they were fain o' ither,   fond of each other
An' unco pack an' thick thegither;   very intimate
Wi' social nose whyles snuff'd an' snowkit,   sometimes; scented
Whyles mice an' moudieworts they howkit;   moles; dug up
Whyles scour'd awa in lang excursion,
An' worry'd ither in diversion;
Till tir'd at last wi' mony a farce,
They sat them down upon their arse,
And there began a lang digression
About the *lord o' the creation*.

Cæsar
I've aften wonder'd, honest Luath,
What sort o' life poor dogs like you have;
An' when the gentry's life I saw,
What way poor bodies liv'd ava.   at all

Our Laird gets in his racked rents,
His coals, his kain, and a' his stents: rents in kind; dues
He rises when he likes himsel;
His flunkies answer at the bell;
He ca's his coach; he ca's his horse;

He draws a bonie, silken purse
As lang's my tail, whare thro the steeks,   stitches
The yellow letter'd Geordie keeks.   guinea; peeps

    Frae morn to e'en it's nought but toiling,
At baking, roasting, frying, boiling;
An' tho' the gentry first are stechin,   stuffing
Yet ev'n the ha' folk fill their pechan   servants; stomach
Wi' sauce, ragouts, and siclike trashtrie,
That's little short o' downright wastrie.
Our Whipper-in, wee, blastit wonner,   wonder
Poor, worthless elf, it eats a dinner,
Better than ony tenant man
His Honour has in a' the lan':
An' what poor cot-folk pit their painch in,   put; paunch
I own it's past my comprehension.

Luath
    Trowth, Cæsar, whyles they're fash't enough;   bothered
A cotter howkin in a sheugh,   digging
Wi' dirty stanes biggin a dyke,   building
Baring a quarry, and siclike,   Clearing
Himsel, a wife, he thus sustains,
A smytrie o' wee duddie weans,   swarm; little ragged children
An' nought but his han' darg to keep   hands' labour
Them right an' tight in thack an' rape.   thatch and rope

    An' when they meet wi' sair disasters,
Like loss o' health or want o' masters,
Ye maist wad think, a wee touch langer,
An' they maun starve o' cauld and hunger:
But how it comes, I never kend yet,
They're maistly wonderfu' contented;
An' buirdly chiels, an' clever hizzies,   stout lads; young women
Are bred in sic a way as this is.

Cæsar

But then to see how ye're negleckit,
How huff'd, and cuff'd, and disrespeckit!
Lord, man, our gentry care as little
For delvers, ditchers, an' sic cattle;
They gang as saucy by poor folk,
As I wad by a stinking brock.   badger

I've notic'd, on our Laird's court-day,   rent-
An' mony a time my heart's been wae,   sad
Poor tenant bodies, scant o' cash,
How they maun thole a factor's snash   endure; abuse
He'll stamp an' threaten, curse an' swear,
He'll apprehend them, poind their gear: seize
While they maun stan', wi' aspect humble,
An' hear it a', an' fear an' tremble!

I see how folk live that hae riches;
But surely poor folk maun be wretches!

Luath

They're nae sae wretched's ane wad think;
Tho' constantly on poortith's brink,   poverty's
They're sae accustom'd wi' the sight,
The view o't gies them little fright.

Then chance an' fortune are sae guided,
They're ay in less or mair provided;
An' tho' fatigu'd wi' close employment,
A blink o' rest's a sweet enjoyment.   moment

The dearest comfort o' their lives,
Their grushie weans an' faithfu' wives   thriving
The prattling things are just their pride,
That sweetens a' their fire-side.

An' whyles twalpennie worth o' nappy   ale
Can mak the bodies unco happy;
They lay aside their private cares,
To mind the Kirk and State affairs;
They'll talk o' patronage and priests,
Wi' kindling fury in their breasts,
Or tell what new taxation's comin,
An' ferlie at the folk in Lon'on.   marvel

As bleak-fac'd Hallowmass returns,
They get the jovial, ranting Kirns,   harvest-homes
When rural life, o' ev'ry station,
Unite in common recreation;
Love blinks, Wit slaps, an' social Mirth   glances
Forgets there's Care upo' the earth.

That merry day the year begins,
They bar the door on frosty win's;
The nappy reeks wi' mantling ream,   smokes; froth
An' sheds a heart-inspiring steam;
The luntin pipe, an' sneeshin mill,   smoking; snuff-box
Are handed round wi' right guid will;
The cantie, auld folks, crackin crouse,   cheery; talking
The young anes ranting thro' the house –   merrily romping
My heart has been sae fain to see them,
That I for joy hae barkit wi' them.

Still it's owre true that ye hae said,
Sic game is now owre aften play'd;   tøo often
There's monie a creditable stock
O' decent, honest fawsont folk,   seemly
Are riven out baith root and branch,
Some rascal's pridefu' greed to quench,
Wha thinks to knit himsel the faster

In favor wi' some gentle Master,
Wha ablins thrang a parliamentin   perhaps busy
For Britain's guid his saul indentin –

Cæsar

Haith, lad, ye little ken about it;   Faith
For Britain's guid! guid faith! I doubt it.
Say rather, gaun as Premiers lead him,   going
An' saying *aye* or *no*'s they bid him:
At operas an' plays parading,
Mortgaging, gambling, masquerading:
Or maybe, in a frolic daft,
To Hague or Calais taks a waft,
To mak a tour, an' tak a whirl,
To learn *bon ton* an' see the worl'.

There, at Vienna or Versailles,
He rives his father's auld entails;
Or by Madrid he taks the rout,
To thrum guitars an' fecht wi' nowt;   fight; cattle
Or down Italian vista startles,
Whore hunting amang groves o' myrtles:
Then bouses drumly German water,   muddy
To mak himsel look fair and fatter,
An' clear the consequential sorrows,
Love-gifts of Carnival Signoras.

For Britain's guid! for her destruction!
Wi' dissipation, feud an' faction.

Luath

Hech man! dear sirs! is that the gate   way
They waste sae mony a braw estate!

Are we sae foughten an' harass'd   *worn out*
For gear to gang that gate at last!   *wealth to go*

O would they stay aback frae courts,
An' please themsels wi' countra sports,
It wad for ev'ry ane be better,
The Laird, the Tenant, an' the Cotter!
For thae frank, rantin, ramblin billies,   *those; roistering*
Fient haet o' them's ill hearted fellows;   *devil a one*
Except for breakin o' their timmer,   *timber*
Or speakin lightly o' their Limmer,   *Mistress*
Or shootin o' a hare or moorcock,
The ne'er-a-bit they're ill to poor folk.

But will ye tell me, master Cæsar,
Sure great folk's life's a life o' pleasure?
Nae cauld nor hunger e'er can steer them,   *disturb*
The vera thought o't need na fear them.

Cæsar

Lord, man, were ye but whyles whare I am,
The gentles ye wad ne'er envy 'em.

It's true, they need na starve or sweat,
Thro' winter's cauld, or Simmer's heat;
They've nae sair wark to craze their banes,   *hard*
An' fill auld age wi' grips an' granes;   *gripes and groans*
But human bodies are sic fools,
For a' their colleges and schools,
That when nae real ills perplex them,
They mak enow themsels to vex them;
An' ay the less they hae to sturt them,   *annoy*
In like proportion, less will hurt them.
A country fellow at the pleugh,

His acre's till'd, he's right eneugh;
A country girl at her wheel,
Her dizzen's done, she's unco weel: dozen
But Gentlemen, an' Ladies warst,
Wi ev'n down want o' wark are curst.   utter
They loiter, lounging, lank, an' lazy;
Tho' deil haet ails them, yet uneasy;   devil a thing
Their days, insipid, dull an' tasteless,
Their nights, unquiet, lang, and restless,
An' ev'n their sports, their balls an' races,
Their galloping thro' public places,
There's sic parade, sic pomp an' art,
The joy can scarcely reach the heart.
The Men cast out in party matches,
Then sowther a' in deep debauches,   solder
Ae night, they're mad wi' drink an' whoring,
Niest day their life is past enduring.
The Ladies arm-in-arm in clusters,
As great an' gracious a' as sisters;
But hear their absent thoughts o' ither,
They're a' run deils an' jads thegither.   downright
Whyles, owre the wee bit cup an' platie,
They sip the scandal potion pretty;
Or lee-lang nights, wi' crabbit leuks,   live-long
Pore owre the devil's pictur'd beuks   playing-cards
Stake on a chance a farmer's stackyard,
An' cheat like ony unhang'd blackguard.

    There's some exception, man an' woman;
But this is Gentry's life in common.

    By this, the sun was out o' sight,
An' darker gloamin brought the night:
The bum-clock humm'd wi' lazy drone,   beetle

The kye stood rowtin i' the loan   cattle; lowing; pasture
When up they gat an' shook their lugs,
Rejoic'd they were na *men*, but *dogs*;
An' each took aff his several way,
Resolv'd to meet some ither day.

On the Death of Echo, a Lap-Dog

In wood and wild, ye warbling throng,
    Your heavy loss deplore;
Now half extinct your powers of song,
    Sweet Echo is no more.

Ye jarring, screeching things around,
    Scream your discordant joys;
Now half your din of tuneless sound
    With Echo silent lies.

Another Version

Ye warblers of the vocal grove,
    Your heavy loss deplore;
Now half your melody is lost,
    Sweet Echo is no more.

Each shrieking, screaming bird and beast,
    Exalt your tuneless voice;
Half your deformity is hid,
    Here Echo silent lies.

THOMAS BEWICK

Gourmet

IN DECEMBER, 1784, A Dog was left by a smuggling vessel, near Boomer, on the coast of Northumberland. Finding himself deserted, he began to worry sheep; and did so much damage, that he became the terror of the country within a circuit of about twenty miles. We are assured, that when he caught a sheep, he bit a hole in its right side, and after eating the tallow about the kidneys, left it: several of them, thus lacerated, were found alive by the shepherds; and being taken proper care of, some of them recovered, and afterwards had lambs. From his delicacy in this respect, the destruction he made may in some measure be conceived; as it may be supposed, that the fat of one sheep in a day would hardly satisfy his hunger. The farmers were so much alarmed by his depredations, that various means were used for his destruction. They frequently pursued him with Hounds, Greyhounds, &c.; but when the Dogs came up with him, he laid down on his back, as if supplicating for mercy; and in this position they never hurt him: he therefore laid quietly, taking his rest till the hunters approached, when he made off without being followed by the Hounds, till they were again excited to the pursuit, which always terminated unsuccessfully. It is worthy of notice, that he was one day pursued from Howick to upwards of thirty miles distance: but returned thither and killed sheep the same evening. His constant residence, during the day, was upon a rock on the Heugh-hill, near Howick, where he had a view of four roads that approached it; and in March, 1785, after many fruitless attempts, he was at last shot there.

The Comforter

IS A MOST elegant little animal, and is generally kept by the ladies as an attendant of the toilette or the drawing-room. It is very snappish, ill-natured, and noisy; and does not readily admit the familiarity of strangers.

From *The History of Quadrupeds*

ROUSHAM HOUSE

In Front of this Stone lie the Remains of
RINGWOOD
an *OTTER-HOUND* of extraordinary Sagacity

Tyrant of the Cherwell's Flood
Come not near this tarred Gloom
Nor, with thy insulting Brood,
Dare pollute my *RINGWOOD'S* Tomb.

What tho Death has laid him low,
Long the terror of thy Race,
Couples taught by him to Know,
Taught to force thy lurking place.

Hark how STUBBORN'S airy Tongue
Warns the time to point the Spear,
RUFFUN loud thy Knell has rung,
RULER echoes Death is near.

All the Skies in Consort rend,
BUTLER chears with highest glee
Still thy Master and thy friend
RINGWOOD ever think on thee

ADMIRAL COLLINGWOOD

Trafalgar – and After

HOW HAPPY SHOULD I be, could I but hear from home, and know how my dear girls are going on! Bounce is my only pet now, and he is indeed a good fellow: he sleeps by the side of my cot, whenever I lie in one, until near the time of tacking, and then marches off, to be out of the hearing of the guns, for he is not reconciled to them yet. . . . What I look to as the first and great object, is to defeat the projects of this combined fleet, of whom I can get little information; but I watch them narrowly, and if they come out will fight them merrily; for on their discomfiture depends the safety of England, and it shall not fail in my hands if I can help it.

Off Cadiz, September 1805

I AM OUT of all patience with Bounce. The consequential airs he gives himself since he became a right honourable dog are insufferable. He considers it beneath his dignity to play with commoners' dogs, and truly thinks that he does them grace when he condescends to lift up his leg against them. This, I think, is carrying the insolence of rank to the extreme; but he is a dog that does it.

Off Carthagena, December 1805

ADELBERT VON CHAMISSO

The Beggar and his Dog

'Pay down three dollars for my hound!
May lightning strike me to the ground!
What mean the Messieurs of Police?
And when and where shall this mockery cease?

'I am a poor, old, sickly man,
And earn a penny I nowise can;
I have no money, I have no bread,
And live upon hunger and want instead.

'Who pitied me when I grew sick and poor
And neighbours turned me from their door?
And who, when I was left alone
In God's wide world made my fortunes his own?

'Who loved me when I was weak and old?
And warmed me when I was numb with cold?
And who, when I in poverty pined,
Has shared my hunger and never whined?

'Here is the noose, and here the stone,
And there the water – it must be done!
Come hither, poor Pomp, and look not on me,
One kick – it is over – and thou art free!'

As over his head he lifted the band,
The fawning dog licked his master's hand;
Back in an instant the noose he drew,
And round his own neck in a twinkling threw.

The dog sprang after him into the deep,
His howlings started the sailors from sleep;
Moaning and twitching, he showed them the spot:
They found the beggar, but life was not!

They laid him silently in the ground,
His only mourner the whimpering hound,

Who stretched himself out on the grave and cried
Like an orphan child – and so he died.

Trans. C. T. Brooks

WILLIAM TAPLIN

Ancestry

THE SOULS OF DECEASED bailliffs and common constables are in the bodies of setting dogs and pointers; the terriers are inhabited by trading justices: the bloodhounds were formerly a set of informers, thief takers, and false evidences; the spaniels were heretofore courtiers, hangers-on of administration and hack-journal writers, all of whom preserve their primitive qualities of fawning on their feeders, licking their hands, and snarling and snapping at all who offer to offend their masters. A former train of gamblers and blacklegs are now embodied in that particular species denominated lurchers; bulldogs and mastiffs were once butchers and drovers; grey-hounds and hounds owe their animation to country squires and foxhounds; while whistling, useless lap-dogs draw their existence from the quondam beau; macaronies and gentlemen of the tiffy, still being the playthings of the ladies, and used for their diversion. There are also a set of sad dogs derived from attornies; and puppies who were in past times attornies' clerks, shopmen to retail haberdashers, men-milliners, etc., etc. Turnspits are animated by old aldermen who still enjoy the smell of roast meat; that droning, snarling species stiled Dutch pugs have been fellows of colleges; and that faithful, useful tribe of shepherds' dogs were in days of yore, members of parliament who guarded the flock, and protected the sheep from the wolves and thieves, although indeed, of late, some have turned sheep-biters, and worried those they ought to have defended.

From *The Sportsman's Cabinet*

JAMES HOGG

The Author's Address to his Auld Dog Hector

Come, my auld, towzy, trusty friend,
    What gars ye look sae dung wi' wae?
D'ye think my favour's at an end,
    Because thy head is turnin' gray?

Although thy strength begins to fail,
    Its best was spent in serving me;
An' can I grudge thy wee bit meal,
    Some comfort in thy age to gie?

For mony a day, frae sun to sun,
    We've toiled fu' hard wi' ane anither;
An' mony a thousand mile thou'st run,
    To keep my thraward flocks thegither.

To nae thrawn boy nor naughty wife,
    Shall thy auld banes become a drudge;
At cats an' callans a' thy life,
    Thou ever bor'st a mortal grudge.

An' whiles thy surly look declared,
    Thou loe'd the women warst of a';
Because my love wi' thee they shared,
    A matter out o' right or law.

When sittin' wi' my bonnie Meg,
    Mair happy than a prince could be,
Thou placed'st thee by her other leg,
    An' watched her wi' a jealous ee.

An' then at ony start or flare,
  Thou wad'st hae worried furiouslye;
While I was forced to curse an' swear,
  Afore thou wad'st forbidden be.

Yet wad she clasp thy towzy paw;
  Thy gruesome grips were never skaithly;
An' thou than her hast been mair true,
  An' truer than the friend that gae thee.

Ah me! o' fashion, self, an' pride,
  Mankind hae read me sic a lecture!
But yet it's a' in part repaid
  By thee, my faithful, grateful Hector!

O'er past imprudence, oft alane
  I've shed the saut an' silent tear;
The sharin' a' my grief an' pain,
  My poor auld friend came snoovin' near.

For a' the days we've sojourned here,
  An' they've been neither fine nor few,
That thought possest thee year to year,
  That a' my grief arase frae you.

Wi' waesome face an' hingin head,
  Thou wad'st hae pressed thee to my knee;
While I thy looks as weel could read,
  As thou had'st said in words to me; –

'O my dear master, dinna greet;
  What hae I ever done to vex thee?
See here I'm cowrin' at your feet;
  Just take my life, if I perplex thee.

'For a' my toil, my wee drap meat
    Is a' the wage I ask of thee;
For whilk I'm oft obliged to wait
    Wi' hungry wame an' patient ee.

'Whatever wayward course ye steer;
    Whatever sad mischance o'ertake ye;
Man, here is ane will hald ye dear!
    Man, here is ane will ne'er forsake ye!'

Yes, my puir beast, though friends me scorn,
    Whom mair than life I valued dear;
An' thraw me out to fight forlorn,
    Wi' ills my heart dow hardly bear,

While I hae thee to bear a part –
    My health, my plaid, an' heezle rung, –
I'll scorn th' unfeeling haughty heart,
    The saucy look, and slanderous tongue.

Some friends, by pop'lar envy swayed,
    Are ten times waur than ony fae!
My heart was theirs: an' to them laid
    As open as the light o' day.

I feared my ain; but had nae dread,
    That I for loss o' their should mourn;
Or that when luck an' favour fled,
    Their friendship wad injurious turn.

But He who feeds the ravens young,
    Lets naething pass he disna see;
He'll sometime judge o' right an' wrang,
    An' aye provide for you an' me.

An' hear me, Hector, thee I'll trust,
   As far as thou hast wit an' skill;
Sae will I ae sweet lovely breast,
   To me a balm for every ill.

To these my trust shall ever turn,
   While I have reason truth to scan;
But ne'er beyond my mother's son,
   To aught that bears the shape o' man. –

I ne'er could thole thy cravin' face,
   Nor when ye pattit on my knee;
Though in a far an' unco place,
   I've whiles been forced to beg for thee.

Even now I'm in my master's power,
   Where my regard may scarce be shown;
But ere I'm forced to gie thee o'er,
   When thou art auld an' senseless grown,

I'll get a cottage o' my ain,
   Some wee bit cannie, lonely biel',
Where thy auld heart shall rest fu' fain,
   An' share wi' me my humble meal.

Thy post shall be to guard the door
   Wi' gousty bark, whate'er betides;
Of cats an' hens to clear the floor,
   An' bite the flaes that vex thy sides.

When my last bannocks's on the hearth,
   Of that thou sanna want thy share;
While I hae house or hauld on earth,
   My Hector shall hae shelter there.

An' should grim death thy noddle save,
  Till he has made an end o' me;
Ye'll lye a wee while on the grave
  O' ane whae aye was kind to thee.

There's nane alive will miss me mair;
  An' though in words thou can'st not wail,
On a' the claes thy master ware,
  I ken thou'lt smell an' wag thy tail.

If e'er I'm forced wi' thee to part,
  Which will be sair against my will;
I'll sometimes mind thy honest heart,
  As lang as I can climb a hill.

Come, my auld, towzy, trusty friend,
  Let's speel to Queensb'ry's lofty height;
All warldly cares we'll leave behind,
  An' onward look to days more bright.

While gazing o'er the Lawland dales,
  Despondence on the breeze shall flee;
An' muses leave their native vales
  To scale the clouds wi' you an' me.

SAMUEL WHITBREAD

On a Monument at Southill

The good, the faithful and the just
Are honoured in the silent dust.
Near his beloved mistress' seat

Departed Jock such honours meet.
Ye dogs who in succession share
Your kindest lady's tender care,
Drink at this font, for see above
A model of the truest love
That ever warmed your faithful race;
This living form you there may trace,
Drink at this font and humbly vie
With him in matchless constancy.

SIR WALTER SCOTT

Home Life

O N HIS RETURN FROM the Abbey, [Washington] Irving found
Scott ready for a ramble. I cannot refuse myself the pleasure of
extracting some parts of his description of it.

'As we sallied forth, every dog in the establishment turned out to
attend us. There was the old staghound, Maida, that I have already
mentioned, a noble animal, and Hamlet, the black greyhound, a wild
thoughtless youngster, not yet arrived at the years of discretion; and
Finette, a beautiful setter, with soft, silken hair, long pendant ears, and
a mild eye, the parlour favourite. When in front of the house, we were
joined by a superannuated greyhound, who came from the kitchen
wagging his tail; and was cheered by Scott as an old friend and comrade.
In our walks, he would frequently pause in conversation, to notice his
dogs, and speak to them as if rational companions; and, indeed, there
appears to be a vast deal of rationality in these faithful attendants on
man, derived from their close intimacy with him. Maida deported
himself with a gravity becoming his age and size, and seemed to
consider himself called upon to preserve a great degree of dignity and
decorum in our society. As he jogged along a little distance ahead of us,
the young dogs would gambol about him, leap on his neck, worry at his

ears, and endeavour to tease him into a gambol. The old dog would keep on for a long time with imperturbable solemnity, now and then seeming to rebuke the wantonness of his young companions. At length he would make a sudden turn, seize one of them, and tumble him in the dust, then giving a glance at us, as much as to say, "You see, gentlemen, I can't help giving way to this nonsense," would resume his gravity, and jog on as before. Scott amused himself with these peculiarities. "I make no doubt," said he, "when Maida is alone with these young dogs, he throws gravity aside, and plays the boy as much as any of them; but he is ashamed to do so in our company, and seems to say – Ha' done with your nonsense, youngsters: what will the laird and that other gentleman think of me if I give way to such foolery?"

'Scott amused himself with the peculiarities of another of his dogs, a little shamefaced terrier, with large glassy eyes, one of the most sensitive little bodies to insult and indignity in the world. "If ever he whipped him," he said, "the little fellow would sneak off and hide himself from the light of day in a lumber garret, from whence there was no drawing him forth but by the sound of the chopping-knife, as if chopping up his victuals, when he would steal forth with humiliated and downcast look, but would skulk away again if any one regarded him."

'While we were discussing the humours and peculiarities of our canine companions, some object provoked their spleen, and produced a sharp and petulant barking from the smaller fry; but it was some time before Maida was sufficiently roused to ramp forward two or three bounds, and join the chorus with a deep-mouthed *bow wow*. It was but a transient outbreak, and he returned instantly, wagging his tail, and looking up dubiously in his master's face, uncertain whether he would receive censure or applause. "Ay, ay, old boy!" cried Scott, "you have done wonders; you have shaken the Eildon hills with your roaring: you may now lay by your artillery for the rest of the day. Maida," continued he, "is like the great gun at Constantinople; it takes so long to get it ready, that the smaller guns can fire off a dozen times first: but when it does go off, it plays the very devil."

'These simple anecdotes may serve to show the delightful play of Scott's humours and feelings in private life. His domestic animals were his friends. Everything about him seemed to rejoice in the light of his countenance.

Lockhart, from his *Life of Scott*

Bankruptcy

M EN WILL THINK pride has had a fall. Let them indulge their own pride in thinking that my fall makes them higher or seem so at least. I have the satisfaction to recollect that my prosperity has been of advantage to many and that some at least will forgive my transient wealth on account of the innocence of my intentions and my real wish to do good to the poor. This news will make sad hearts at Darnick and in the cottages of Abbotsford which I do not nourish the least hope of preserving. It has been my Dalilah and so I have often termd it – and now – the recollection of the extensive woods I have planted and the walks I have formed from which strangers must derive both the pleasure and profit will excit feelings likely to sober my gayest moments. I have half resolved never to see the place again – how could I tread my hall with such a diminishd crest? How live a poor indebted man where I was once the wealthy – the honourd? My children are provided – thank God for that. I was to have gone there on Saturday in joy and prosperity to receive my friends – my dogs will wait for me in vain – it is foolish – but the thoughts of parting from these dumb creatures have moved me more than any of the painful reflections I have put down – poor things I must get them kind masters. There may be yet those who loving me may love my dog because it has been mine. I must end this or I shall lose the tone of mind with which men should meet distress. I find my dogs' feet on my knees – I hear them whining and seeking me everywhere – this is nonsense but it is what they would do could they know how things are.

From his *Journal*: 18 December 1825

A Frequent Sitter

M AIDA MY GREAT dog has been sitting at Mr Blores instance to Mr Nasmyth who admires him very much. I was obliged to attend the sittings myself for the subject though regularly supplied with a cold beef bone was apt to grow impatient.

To Daniel Terry, 25 December 1816

THERE IS A certain old proverb which saith Love me love my dog and I feel very much flattered indeed to judge of your regard by the honour which you have done Maida. The picture is most beautiful and expresses the form and character of the animal perfectly. I need not add how much I am gratified by possessing it as a most interesting piece in itself rendered still more valuable as the gift of an artist so justly distinguished.

To Sir David Wilkie, 6 November 1817

THE KING HAS commanded me to sit to Sir Thomas Lawrence for a portrait for his most sacred apartment. I want to have in Maida that there may be one handsome fellow of the party. Will you take the picture in the little room adjoining the armoury (I mean the oil picture with Maida & Panick) out of the frame, cause Swanstoun make a box to its size, wedge it neatly in, cover it with flax or cotton, & send it by the mail. With that and one or two sketches which are here the honest gentleman may be introduced.

To William Laidlaw, 28 February 1821

I REMEMBER WELL sitting to him [Edward Berens] and Heber reading Milton all the while – Since that time my block has been traced by many a brush of eminence and at this very *now* while I am writing to you Mr Landseer who has drawn every dog in the House but myself is at work upon me under all the disadvantages which my employment puts him to. He has drawn old Maida in particular with much spirit indeed and it is odd enough that though I sincerely wish old Mai had been younger I never thought of wishing the same advantage for myself.

To Mrs Thomas Hughes, 6 October 1824

OLD MAIDA DIED quietly on his straw last week after a good supper. This considering his weak state was rather a deliverance. He is buried below his monument on which the following epitaph is engraved: though it is great audacity to send Teviotdale Latin to Brazen nose

Maidæ marmorea dormis sub imagine Maida
Ad januam domini sit tibi terra levis.

Thus Englishd by an eminent hand

Beneath the sculptured form which late you wore
Sleep soundly Maida at the masters door.

To Charles Scott, 22 October 1824

I MUST TELL your Lordship about Maida that a friend picked up at
Mun[i]ch a tin snuffbox such as is sold for a franc a piece bearing
the effigy of poor Mai obviously taken from your beautiful picture but
with a different background and two or three words of a motto signifying
in german the favourite dog of Walter Scott. Poor Maida was sitting
bobbishly the man said though he knew but little about the subject. It
was however *fame* both to Landseer and me, as Goldsmith said when
he found a volume of his writing in a remote ale-house.

To the Lord Chief Commissioner, Blair Adam, 15 May 1831

Hellvellyn

I climb'd the dark brow of the mighty Hellvellyn,
    Lakes and mountains beneath me gleam'd misty and wide;
All was still, save by fits, when the eagle was yelling,
    And starting around me the echoes replied.
On the right, Striden-edge round the Red-tarn was bending,
And Catchedicam its left verge was defending,
One huge nameless rock in the front was ascending,
    When I mark'd the sad spot where the wanderer had died.

Dark green was that spot 'mid the brown mountain-heather,
    Where the Pilgrim of Nature lay stretch'd in decay,
Like the corpse of an outcast abandon'd to weather,
    Till the mountain winds wasted the tenantless clay.

Nor yet quite deserted, though lonely extended,
For, faithful in death, his mute favourite attended,
The much-loved remains of her master defended,
    And chased the hill-fox and the raven away.

How long didst thou think that his silence was slumber?
    When the wind waved his garment, how oft didst thou start?
How many long days and long weeks didst thou number,
    Ere he faded before thee, the friend of thy heart?
And, oh, was it meet, that – no requiem read o'er him –
No mother to weep, and no friend to deplore him,
And thou, little guardian, alone stretch'd before him –
    Unhonour'd the Pilgrim from life should depart?

When a Prince to the fate of the Peasant has yielded,
    The tapestry waves dark round the dim-lighted hall;
With scutcheons of silver the coffin is shielded,
    And pages stand mute by the canopied pall:
Through the courts, at deep midnight, the torches are gleaming;
In the proudly-arch'd chapel the banners are beaming,
Far adown the long aisle sacred music is streaming,
    Lamenting a Chief of the people should fall.

But meeter for thee, gentle lover of nature,
    To lay down thy head like the meek mountain lamb,
When, wilder'd, he drops from some cliff huge in stature,
    And draws his last sob by the side of his dam.
And more stately thy couch by this desert lake lying,
Thy obsequies sung by the grey plover flying,
With one faithful friend but to witness thy dying,
    In the arms of Hellvellyn and Catchedicam.

WILLIAM WORDSWORTH
Fidelity

A barking sound the Shepherd hears,
A cry as of a dog or fox;
He halts – and searches with his eyes
Among the scattered rocks:
And now at distance can discern
A stirring in a brake of fern;
And instantly a dog is seen,
Glancing through that covert green.

The Dog is not of mountain breed;
Its motions, too, are wild and shy;
With something, as the Shepherd thinks,
Unusual in its cry:
Nor is there anyone in sight
All round, in hollow or on height;
Nor shout, nor whistle strikes his ear;
What is the creature doing here?

It was a cove, a huge recess,
That keeps, till June, December's snow;
A lofty precipice in front,
A silent tarn below!
Far in the bosom of Helvellyn,
Remote from public road or dwelling,
Pathway, or cultivated land;
From trace of human foot or hand.

There sometimes doth a leaping fish
Send through the tarn a lonely cheer;
The crags repeat the raven's croak,
In symphony austere;

Thither the rainbow comes – the cloud –
And mists that spread the flying shroud;
And sunbeams; and the sounding blast,
That, if it could, would hurry past;
But that enormous barrier holds it fast.

Not free from boding thoughts, a while
The Shepherd stood; then makes his way
O'er rocks and stones, following the Dog
As quickly as he may;
Nor far had gone before he found
A human skeleton on the ground;
The appalled Discoverer with a sigh
Looks round, to learn the history.

From those abrupt and perilous rocks
The Man had fallen, that place of fear!
At length upon the Shepherd's mind
It breaks, and all is clear:
He instantly recalled the name,
And who he was, and whence he came;
Remembered, too, the very day
On which the Traveller passed this way.

But hear a wonder, for whose sake
This lamentable tale I tell!
A lasting monument of words
This wonder merits well.
The Dog, which still was hovering nigh,
Repeating the same timid cry,
This Dog, had been through three months' space
A dweller in that savage place.

Yes, proof was plain that, since the day
When this ill-fated Traveller died,

The Dog had watched about the spot,
Or by his master's side:
How nourished here through such long time
He knows, Who gave that love sublime;
And gave that strength of feeling, great
Above all human estimate!

Incident Characteristic of a Favourite Dog

On his morning rounds the Master
Goes to learn how all things fare;
Searches pasture after pasture,
Sheep and cattle eyes with care;
And, for silence or for talk,
He hath comrades in his walk;
Four dogs, each pair of different breed,
Distinguished two for scent, and two for speed.

See a hare before him started!
– Off they fly in earnest chase;
Every dog is eager-hearted,
All the four are in the race:
And the hare whom they pursue,
Knows from instinct what to do;
Her hope is near: no turn she makes;
But, like an arrow, to the river takes.

Deep the river was, and crusted
Thinly by a one night's frost;
But the nimble Hare hath trusted
To the ice, and safely crost;
She hath crost, and without heed
All are following at full speed,

When, lo! the ice, so thinly spread,
Breaks – and the greyhound, DART, is over-head!

Better fate have PRINCE and SWALLOW –
See them cleaving to the sport!
MUSIC has no heart to follow,
Little MUSIC, she stops short.
She hath neither wish nor heart,
Hers is now another part:
A loving creature she, and brave!
And fondly strives her struggling friend to save.

From the brink her paws she stretches,
Very hands as you would say!
And afflicting moans she fetches,
As he breaks the ice away.
For herself she hath no fears, –
Him alone she sees and hears, –
Makes efforts with complainings; nor gives o'er
Until her fellow sinks to re-appear no more.

Tribute to the Memory of the Same Dog

Lie here, without a record of thy worth,
Beneath a covering of the common earth!
It is not from unwillingness to praise,
Or want of love, that here no Stone we raise;
More thou deserv'st; but *this* man gives to man,
Brother to brother, *this* is all we can.
Yet they to whom thy virtues made thee dear
Shall find thee through all changes of the year:
This Oak points out thy grave; the silent tree
Will gladly stand a monument of thee.

We grieved for thee, and wished thy end were past;
And willingly have laid thee here at last:
For thou hadst lived till everything that cheers
In thee had yielded to the weight of years;
Extreme old age had wasted thee away,
And left thee but a glimmering of the day;
Thy ears were deaf, and feeble were thy knees, –
I saw thee stagger in the summer breeze,
Too weak to stand against its sportive breath,
And ready for the gentlest stroke of death.
It came, and we were glad; yet tears were shed;
Both man and woman wept when thou wert dead;
Not only for a thousand thoughts that were,
Old household thoughts, in which thou hadst thy share;
But for some precious boons vouchsafed to thee,
Found scarcely anywhere in like degree!
For love, that comes wherever life and sense
Are given by God, in thee was most intense;
A chain of heart, a feeling of the mind,
A tender sympathy, which did thee bind
Not only to us Men, but to thy Kind:
Yea, for thy fellow-brutes in thee we saw
A soul of love, love's intellectual law: –
Hence, if we wept, it was not done in shame;
Our tears from passion and from reason came,
And, therefore, shalt thou be an honoured name!

LORD BYRON

Boatswain

M Y DEAR HODGSON – Boatswain is dead! he expired in a state of madness on the 10th after suffering much, yet retaining all the gentleness of his nature to the last, never attempting to do the least injury to any one near him.

To Francis Hodgson, 18 November 1808

M Y DEAR SIR – Boatswain is to be buried in a vault waiting for myself. I have also written an epitaph, which I would send, were it not for two reasons: one is, that it is too long for a letter; and the other, that I hope you will some day read it on the spot where it will be engraved.

To Francis Hodgson, 27 November 1808

Inscription on the Monument of a Newfoundland Dog

When some proud son of man returns to earth,
Unknown to glory, but upheld by birth,
The sculptor's art exhausts the pomp of woe,
And storied urns record who rest below:
When all is done, upon the tomb is seen,
Not what he was, but what he should have been:
But the poor dog, in life the firmest friend,
The first to welcome, foremost to defend,
Whose honest heart is still his master's own,
Who labours, fights, lives, breathes for him alone,
Unhonour'd falls, unnoticed all his worth,
Denied in heaven the soul he held on earth,
While man, vain insect! hopes to be forgiven,

And claims himself a sole exclusive heaven.
Oh man! thou feeble tenant of an hour,
Debased by slavery, or corrupt by power,
Who knows thee well must quit thee with disgust,
Degraded mass of animated dust!
Thy love is lust, thy friendship all a cheat,
Thy smiles hypocrisy, thy words deceit!
By nature vile, ennobled but by name,
Each kindred brute might bid thee blush for shame.
Ye! who perchance behold this simple urn,
Pass on – it honours none you wish to mourn:
To mark a friend's remains these stones arise;
I never knew but one, – and here he lies.

Newstead Abbey, 30 November 1808

T HIS IS THE last will and testament of me the Rt. Honble. George
Gordon Lord Byron, Baron Byron of Rochdale in the county of
Lancaster. I desire that my body may be buried in the vault of the
garden at Newstead without any ceremony or burial-service whatever,
and that no inscription, save my name and age, be written on the tomb
or tablet; and it is my will that my faithful dog may not be removed
from the said vault. To the performance of this my particular desire, I
rely on the attention of my executors hereinafter named.

[Bolton's comment] 'It is submitted to Lord Byron whether this
clause relative to the funeral had not better be omitted. The substance
of it can be given in a letter from his lordship to the executors, and
accompany the will; and the will may state that the funeral shall be
performed in such manner as his lordship may by letter direct, and, in
default of any such letter, then at the discretion of his executors.'

It must stand.   B.

1811

T O YOUR QUESTION about the 'dog' – Umph! – my 'mother,' I
won't say anything against – that is, about her; but how long a
'mistress' or friend may recollect paramours or competitors (lust and

thirst being the two great and only bonds between the amatory or the amicable), I can't say, – or, rather, you know as well as I could tell you. But as for canine recollections, as far as I could judge by a cur of mine own (always bating Boatswain, the dearest and, alas! the maddest of dogs), I had one (half a *wolf* by the she side) that doted on me at ten years old, and very nearly ate me at twenty. When I thought he was going to enact Argus, he bit away the backside of my breeches, and never would consent to any kind of recognition, in despite of all kinds of bones which I offered him. So, let Southey blush and Homer too, as far as I can decide upon quadruped memories.

I humbly take it, the mother knows the son that pays her jointure – a mistress her mate, till he * * and refuses salary – a friend his fellow, till he loses cash and character, and a dog his master, till he changes him.

To Thomas Moore, 19 January 1815

Later Dogs

BEING OUT OF the mountains my journal must be as flat as my journey. – – From Thoun to Bern good road – hedges – villages – industry – prosperity – and all sorts of tokens of insipid civilization. – – From Bern to Fribourg. – Different Canton – Catholics – passed a field of Battle – Swiss beat the French – in one of the late wars against the French Republic. – Bought a dog – a very ugly dog – but '*tres mechant*'. This was his great recommendation in the owner's eyes & mine – for I mean him to watch the carriage – he hath no tail – & is called 'Mutz' – which signifies '*Short-tail*' – he is apparently of the Shepherd dog genus! – The greater part of this tour has been on horseback – on foot – and on mule; – the Filly (which is one of two young horses I bought of the Baron de Vincy) carried me very well – she is young and as quiet as anything of her sex can be – very goodtempered – and perpetually neighing – when she wants any thing – which is every five minutes – I have called her *Biche* – because her manners are not unlike a little dog's – but she is a very tame – pretty childish quadruped. –

From *Journal*, 26 September 1816

P.S. – I forgot to tell you that my dog (Mutz by name & Swiss by nation) shuts a door when he is told – there – that's more than Tip can do. – Remember me to the child*er* – and to Georgiana – who I suppose is grown a prodigious penwoman. – I hope she likes her seals and all her share of Mont Blanc. – I have had so much of mountains that I am not yet reconciled to the plains – but they improve. Verona seems a fine city.

To Augusta Leigh, 6 November 1816

I BELIEVE MURRAY has by this time published the new Canto & Chillon &c. but I know nothing for certain. – – The man of learning is still a prosperous gentleman – Berger amuses himself with making love to some Harlotry on the other side of the street – out of the hall window – at least this is the household scandal – Stevens slumbers – and Mutz is learning to obey the word of command with a piece of bread upon his nose until permission is accorded to eat it – he has stolen some more legs of mutton – and I detected him myself in the street the other day investigating a barrel of tripe – whereupon I cuffed him soundly. – – I have (to use young A's phrase) 'done' some more 'acquaintance' since you went but have mostly lived pleasant & sulky. I like Venice and it's marine melancholy – and rather – wish to *have seen* Rome than to *see* it – though to be sure having 'done' Constantinople I must also do 't'other place.

To John Cam Hobhouse, 19 December 1816

FROM PADOVA I diverged to Arqua to Petrarch's present & former habitation – the present is in the best repair – but both are rather ragged & somewhat poetical. – – The old Castle of Ferrara has the actual court as heretofore where Parisina and Hugo lost their heads – according to Gibbon – I wonder where he got his authority? – Mutz is here – he was promoted into a *Bear* in the natural History of the Bolognese (who might have learned better at the Institute) a character which he has by no means sustained in point of valour – he having been defeated with loss of honour – hair – & almost the small remains of tail which the Docker had left him – by a moderate-sized Pig on the top of the Pennine Alps – the Pig was first thrown into confusion & compelled to retire with great disorder over a steep stone wall but somehow he faced about in a damned hollow way or defile & drove Mutz from all his positions – with such slaughter that nothing but night prevented a total defeat. – – Recollect – I shall do my best to be up with you soon – I am called to a *warm bath* – & to bed – having been up since 4 – I set off Thursday – in great haste –

To John Cam Hobhouse, 22 April 1817

T HE BULLDOGS WILL be very agreeable – I have only those of this
   country who though good – & ready to fly at any thing – yet have not the tenacity of tooth and Stoicism in endurance of my canine fellow citizens, then pray send them – by the readiest conveyance, perhaps best by Sea.

To John Murray, 21 February 1820

S IR – I HAVE received with great gratitude yr. present of the
   Newfoundland Dog. – Few gifts could have been more gratifying – as I have ever been partial to the breed. – – He shall be taken the greatest care of – and I would not part with him for any consideration; – he is already a chief favourite with the whole house.

To Edward Le Mesurier, 5 May 1823

Verse – From the Life

The approach of home to husbands and to sires,
    After long travelling by land or water,
Most naturally some small doubt inspires.
    A female family's a serious matter
(None trusts the sex more or so much admires,
    But they hate flattery, so I never flatter).
Wives in their husbands' absences grow subtler,
And daughters sometimes run off with the butler.

An honest gentleman at his return
  May not have the good fortune of Ulysses;
Not all lone matrons for their husbands mourn,
  Or show the same dislike to suitors' kisses.
The odds are that he finds a handsome urn
  To his memory, and two or three young misses
Born to some friend, who holds his wife and riches,
And that his Argus bites him by the breeches.

From *Don Juan* III 21–23

Faithful to the End

LORD BYRON HAD taken a small corps of Suliotes into his own pay, and kept them about him as a body-guard. They consisted altogether of fifty-six men, and of these a certain number were always on duty. A large outer room in his lordship's house was appropriated to them, and their carbines were suspended against the walls. Like other soldiers, they found various means to amuse themselves when on guard. While some were walking about, discoursing violently and eagerly, with animated gestures, others were lying or sitting on the floor, playing at cards.

In this room, and among these rude soldiers, Lord Byron was accustomed to walk a great deal, particularly in wet weather. On such occasions he was almost always accompanied by his favourite dog Lyon, who was perhaps his dearest and most affectionate friend. They were, indeed, very seldom separated. Riding or walking, sitting or standing, Lyon was his constant attendant. He can scarcely be said to have forsaken him even in his sleep. Every evening did he go to see that his master was safe, before he lay down himself, and then he took his station close to his door, a guard certainly as faithful, though not so efficient, as Lord Byron's corps of Suliotes. This valuable and affectionate animal was brought to England after Lord Byron's death, and is now, I believe, in the possession of Mrs Leigh, his Lordship's sister.

With Lyon Lord Byron was accustomed, not only to associate, but to commune very much, and very often. His most usual phrase was, 'Lyon, you are no rogue, Lyon;' or 'Lyon,' his Lordship would say, 'thou art an honest fellow, Lyon.' The dog's eyes sparkled, and his tail swept the floor, as he sat with his haunches on the ground. 'Thou art more faithful than men, Lyon; I trust thee more.' Lyon sprang up, and barked and bounded round his master, as much as to say, 'You may trust me, I will watch actively on every side.' 'Lyon, I love thee, thou art my faithful dog!' and Lyon jumped and kissed his master's hand, as an acknowledgement of his homage. In this sort of mingled talk and gambol Lord Byron passed a good deal of time, and seemed more contented, more calmly self-satisfied, on such occasions, than almost on any other. In conversation and in company he was animated and brilliant; but with Lyon and in stillness he was pleased and perfectly happy.

William Parry, from *The Last Days of Lord Byron*

GEORGE CRABBE

Lord Byron's Inscription upon a Newfoundland Dog

FROM whence, Lord Byron, did your Lordship find
This horrid Picture of undone Mankind?
What to thy Muse the colours could impart,
Thy Dogs? thy friends? or thine own Head and Heart?
Thy Dog could nothing of the matter tell,
But his poor Master could have done as well.
If Friends, thy friends can make th' assertions true
The Friends of Satan are a nobler crew.
If your own Heart inspir'd your angry Pen,
No Wonder you exclaim: 'What Brutes are men!'
But if your Head alone, your Wit and Spleen,
Have drawn mankind so wretched and so mean,
If these have sketched for you th' abandonn'd Race,
So worse than brutal and so more than base,

Recant, my Lord, and learn what numbers live
Thy Powers t'admire, thyne error to forgive.
Ten thousand minds in either sex agree
To prove thy falshood and to pity thee,
And many a fervent Prayer to Heav'n is sent
Thou migh'st thy Verses or thy Life repent –
That like thy Friend, the Dog, thou wouldst be mute,
Or mourn and be above the Brute.

JOHANN WOLFGANG VON GOETHE

Man versus Dog

THERE WAS AT that period, 1817, a comedian named Karsten, whose poodle performed the leading part in that well-known melodrama of the Duke of Montargis with such perfection that he carried the public everywhere with him, in Paris as in Germany. It may be imagined with what sorrowing scorn Goethe [then in charge of Weimar's State Theatre] heard of this. The dramatic art to give place to a poodle! He, who detested dogs, to hear of a dog performing on all the stages of Germany with greater success than the best of actors! The occasion was not one to be lost. The Duke, whose fondness for dogs was as kindly as Goethe's aversion to them, was craftily assailed, from various sides, to invite Karsten and his poodle to Weimar. When Goethe heard of this, he haughtily answered, 'In our Theatre regulations stand: NO DOGS ADMITTED ON THE STAGE' – and paid no more attention to it. As the Duke had already written to invite Karsten and his dog, Goethe's opposition was set down to systematic arbitrariness, and people artfully 'wondered' how a prince's wishes could be opposed for such trifles. The dog came. After the first rehearsal, Goethe declared that he would have nothing more to do with a theatre on which a dog was allowed to perform; and at once started for Jena. Princes ill brook opposition; and the Duke, after all, was a Duke. In an unworthy moment, he wrote the following, which was posted in the theatre, and forwarded to Goethe: 'From the expressed opinions which have reached me, I have come to the conviction that the Herr Geheimrath von Goethe wishes to be released from his functions as Intendant, which I hereby accord.'

G. H. Lewes, from his *Life of Goethe*

An Unexpected Visitor

(*Outside the city gate.*)

FAUST: D'you see a jet-black dog now scampering wide
　Through corn and stubble?

WAGNER: Him I have espied
　Some time ago, but gave him not a thought.

FAUST: Look closer now, with care, and say what sort
　Of beast you think he is.

WAGNER: Why, Sir, a hound
　Of poodle breed who snuffs his way around
　To find his master.

FAUST: Mark the spiral trail
　With which he comes from far, yet ever nigher
　Encircling us: unless my senses fail
　His track is traced with little tongues of fire.

WAGNER: Some optical illusion, Sir, maybe:
　He's nothing but a poodle-dog to me.

FAUST: It seems like magic tracing of a snare,
　Or meshes in our future pathway spread.

WAGNER: I'm sure he seeks his master everywhere,
　And frets to find two strangers here instead.

FAUST: The circle narrows, brings him near.

WAGNER: A dog, Sir – see, no phantom have we here!
　He growls, misdoubts, and settles on his hocks,
　And wags his tail: all canine orthodox.

FAUST: Come here then, sirrah, come with us!

WAGNER: The animal has all the poodle's fuss,
   For if you stop he stays expectant, too;
   You speak, and he'll come jumping up at you.
   Try him: he'll know the good retriever's trick,
   Or dash into the water for your stick.
FAUST: Friend, you are right: this cunning quaint result
   Is due to training, nothing here occult!
WAGNER: A dog that hears his trainer, and complies,
   Can win affection even from the wise.
   And this one earns your grace with his discerning:
   He, scholar-like, looks up to men of learning.

Faust's Study

FAUST: O sirrah, down! Why snuffle at the door?
   You restless dog, here's not the place to rove.
   My cushion – there! Don't wander any more
   As if you're lost: lie down behind the stove.
   Out there you showed a poodle's pedigree,
   And played your tricks upon the hilly crest;
   But if I give you hospitality,
   Lie down, and be my welcome quiet guest.
     Within this little room again
   The lamp burns peacefully and kind,
   And light has steady, soft domain
   Upon my bosom and my mind.
   The heart comes to itself, and clear
   The voice of hope and reason speaks,
   Again the wells of life grow dear,
   Whose water-springs our spirit seeks.
     Cease growling, sir! That puppy sound
   Comes jarring on the hallowed tone
   With which my soul would dwell alone.
   True, human beings may abound
   Who growl at things beyond their ken,
   Mocking the beautiful and good,
   And all they haven't understood:

Let dogs not join these gentlemen.
   Ay me, though humbly I entreat for rest,
No more comes sweet contentment to my breast.
Must we then find so soon the fountain dry,
And man in thirsty torment left to lie?
That is the truth that long experience brings,
Yet may these sorrows bear a compensation:
We learn to cherish here immortal things,
And look with longing hearts for revelation,
Whose high inspired and wonder-bearing word
Most clear in the New Testament is heard.
My mind is moved this hour to consecrate,
In simple, honest will to understand
The sacred codex, and its truth translate
In the loved accents of my native land.
        (He opens a volume and sets to work.)
'Tis writ, 'In the beginning was the Word.'
I pause, to wonder what is here inferred.
The Word I cannot set supremely high:
A new translation I will try.
I read, if by the spirit I am taught,
This sense: 'In the beginning was the Thought.'
This opening I need to weigh again.
Or sense may suffer from a hasty pen.
Does Thought create, and work, and rule the hour?
'Twere best: 'In the beginning was the Power.'
Yet, while the pen is urged with willing fingers,
A sense of doubt and hesitancy lingers.
The spirit comes to guide me in my need,
I write, 'In the beginning was the Deed.'
   If in my room you wish to share,
Stop whining, poodle, and forbear
Your yelps. I pray you, cease!
You thoroughly destroy my peace.
I can't have such a comrade near me,
One of us two must go, I fear me.
As host, I am reluctant to withdraw;
But you are free, good poodle, there's the door!
Yet – what must my eyes behold!
Has nature such enigmas to unfold?

The dog assumes a stature strange to see:
Is it a phantom, or reality?
He rises up in might,
No canine form has such a height.
What spectre have I harboured here,
That like a hippopotamus comes near,
With fearful fangs and fiery, staring brow?

From *Faust, Part One*
[Trans. Philip Wayne]

THOMAS HOOD

Lament of a Poor Blind

Oh what shall I do for a dog?
Of sight I have not a particle,
    Globe Standard, or Sun,
    Times, Chronicle – none
Can give me a good leading article.

A Mastiff once led me about,
But people appeared so to fear him –
    I might have got pence
    Without his defence,
But Charity would not come near him.

A Bloodhound was not much amiss,
But instinct at last got the upper;
    And tracking Bill Soames
    And thieves to their homes,
I never could get home to supper.

A Foxhound once served me as guide,
A good one at hill, and at valley;
 But day after day
 He led me astray,
To follow a milk-woman's tally.

A Turnspit once did me good turns
At going and crossing and stopping;
 Till one day his breed
 Went off at full speed
To spit at a great fire in Wapping.

A Pointer once pointed my way,
But did not turn out quite so pleasant,
 Each hour I'd stop
 At a poulterer's shop
To point at a very high pheasant.

A Pug did not suit me at all;
The feature unluckily rose up,
 And folks took offence
 When offering pence
Because of his turning his nose up.

A butcher once gave me a dog,
That turn'd out the worst one of any;
 A Bull-dog's own pup,
 I got a toss up,
Before he had brought me a penny.

My next was a Westminster dog,
From Aistop the regular cadger;
 But, sightless, I saw

He never would draw
A blind man as well as a badger.

A Greyhound I got by a swop,
But Lord, we soon came to divorces;
  He treated my strip
  Of cord, like a slip,
And left me to go my own courses.

A Poodle once towed me along,
But always we came to one harbour,
  To keep his curls smart,
  And shave his hind part,
He constantly called on a barber.

My next was a Newfoundland brute,
As big as a calf fit for slaughter;
  But my old cataract
  So truly he backed
I always fell into the water.

I once had a Sheep-dog for guide,
His worth did not value a button;
  I found it no go,
  A Smithfield Ducrow,
To stand on four saddles of mutton.

My next was an Esquimaux dog,
A dog that my bones ache to talk on,
  For picking his ways
  On cold frosty days
He picked out the slides for a walk on.

Bijou was a lady-like dog,
But vexed me at night not a little,

When tea-time was come
She would not go home –
    Her tail had once trailed a tin kettle.

I once had a sort of a Shock,
And kissed a street post like a brother,
        And lost every tooth
        In learning this truth –
One blind cannot well lead another.

A Terrier was far from a trump,
He had one defect, and a thorough,
        I never could stir,
        'Od rabbit the cur!
Without going into the Borough.

My next was Dalmatian, the dog!
And led me in danger, oh crikey!
        By chasing horse heels,
        Between carriage wheels,
Till I came upon boards that were spiky.

The next that I had was from Cross,
And once was a favourite Spaniel
        With Nero, now dead,
        And so I was led
Right up to his den like a Daniel.

A Mongrel I tried, and he did,
As far as the profit and lossing;
        Except that the kind
        Endangers the blind,
The breed is so fond of a crossing.

A Setter was quite to my taste,
In alleys or streets, broad or narrow.
 Till one day I met
 A very dead set
At a very dead horse in a barrow.

I once had a dog that went mad,
And sorry I was that I got him;
 I came to a run,
 And a man with a gun,
Peppered me when he ought to have shot him.

My profits have gone to the dogs,
My trade has been such a deceiver,
 I fear that my aim
 Is a mere losing game –
Unless I can find a Retriever.

Love Me, Love my Dog,

SEEMS, AT FIRST sight, an unreasonable demand. May I profess no tenderness for Belinda without vowing an attachment to Shock? Must I feel an equal warmth towards my bosom friend and his greyhound? Some country gentlemen keep a pack of dogs. Am I expected to divide my personal regard for my Lord D. amongst all his celebrated fox-hounds?

I may be constitutionally averse to the whole canine species; I have been bitten, perhaps, in my infancy by a mastiff, or pinned by a bull-dog. There are harrowing tales on record of hydrophobia, of human barkings, and inhuman smotherings. A dog may be my bugbear. Again, there are differences in taste. One man may like to have his hand licked all over by a grateful spaniel; but I would not have *my* extremity served so – even by the human tongue.

But the proverb, so arrogant and absolute in spirit, becomes harmless in its common application. The terms are seldom enforced, except by persons that a gentleman is not likely to embrace in his affection – rat-catchers, butchers and bull-baiters, tinkers and blind mendicants, beldames and witches. A slaughterman's tulip-eared puppy is as likely to engage one's liking as his chuckle-headed master. When a courtier makes friends with a drover, he will not be likely to object to a sheep-dog as a third party in the alliance. 'Love me,' says Mother Sawyer, 'love my dog.' Who careth to dote on either a witch or her familiar? The proverb thus loses half of its oppression; in other cases, it may become a pleasant fiction, an agreeable confession. I forget what pretty Countess it was, who made confession of her tenderness for a certain sea-captain, by her abundant caresses of his Esquimaux wolf-dog. The shame of the avowal became milder (as the virulence of the small-pox is abated after passing through the constitution of a cow) by its transmission through the animal.

In like manner, a formal young Quaker and Quakeress – perfect strangers to each other, and who might otherwise have sat mum-chance together for many hours – fell suddenly to romping, merely through the maiden's playfulness with Obadiah's terrier. The dog broke the ice of formality, – and, as a third party, took off the painful awkwardness of self-introduction.

Sir Ulic Mackilligut, when he wished to break handsomely with Mistress Tabitha Bramble, kicked her cur. The dog broke the force of the affront, and the knight's gallantry was spared the reproach of a direct confession of disgust towards the spinster; as the lady took the aversion to herself only as the brute's ally.

My stepmother Hubbard and myself were not on visiting terms for many years. Not, we flattered ourselves, through any hatred or unchari-tableness, disgraceful between relations, but from a constitutional antipathy on the one side, and a doting affection on the other – to a dog. My breach of duty and decent respect was softened down into my dread of hydrophobia: my second-hand parent even persuaded herself that I was jealous of her regard for Bijou. It was a comfortable self-delusion on both sides, – but the scapegoat died, and then, having no reasonable reason to excuse my visits, we came to an open rupture. There was no hope of another favourite. My stepmother had no general affection for the race, but only for that particular cur. It was one of those incongruous attachments, not accountable to reason, but seem-ingly predestined by fate. The dog was no keepsake – no favourite of a dear deceased friend; – ugly as the brute was, she loved him for his own sake, – not for any fondness and fidelity, for he was the most ungrateful dog, under kindness, that I ever knew, – not for his vigilance, for he was never wakeful. He was not useful, like a turnspit; nor accomplished, for he could not dance. He had not personal beauty even, to make him a welcome object; and yet, if my relation had been requested to display her jewels, she would have pointed to the dog, and have answered, in the very spirit of Cornelia, – 'There is my Bijou.'

Conceive, Reader, under this endearing title, a hideous dwarf-mongrel, half pug and half terrier, with a face like a frog's – his goggle-eyes squeezing out of his head: – a body like a barrel-churn, on four short bandy legs, – as if, in his puppyhood, he had been ill-nursed, – terminating in a tail like a rabbit's. There is only one sound in nature similar to his barking: – to hear his voice, you would have looked, not for a dog, but for a duck. He was fat, and scant of breath. It might have been said, that he was stuffed alive; – but his loving mistress, in mournful anticipation of his death, kept a handsome glass case to hold his mummy. She intended, like Queen Constance, to 'stuff out his vacant garment with his form;' – to have him ever before her, 'in his habit as he lived;' – but that hope was never realized.

In those days there were dog-stealers, as well as slave-dealers, – the kidnapping of the canine, as of the Negro victim, being attributable to his skin.

One evening, Bijou disappeared. A fruitless search was made for him at all his accustomed haunts, – but at daybreak the next morning, – stripped naked of his skin, – with a mock paper frill, – and the stump of a tobacco-pipe, stuck in his nether jaw, – he was discovered, set upright against a post!

My stepmother's grief was ungovernable. Tears, which she had not wasted on her deceased step-children, were shed then. In her first transport, a reward of £100 was offered for the apprehension of the murderers, but in vain.

The remains of Bijou, such as they were, she caused to be deposited under the lawn.

I forget what popular poet was gratified with ten guineas for writing his epitaph; but it was in the measure of the 'Pleasures of Hope.'

CHARLES LAMB

A Complaint of the Decay of Beggars
in the Metropolis

IF I WERE NOT the independent gentleman that I am, rather than I
would be a retainer to the great, a led captain, or a poor relation, I
would choose, out of the delicacy and true greatness of my mind, to be
a Beggar.

Rags, which are the reproach of poverty, are the Beggar's robes, and
graceful *insignia* of his profession, his tenure, his full dress, the suit in
which he is expected to show himself in public. He is never out of the
fashion, or limpeth awkwardly behind it. He is not required to put on
court mourning. He weareth all colours, fearing none. His costume
hath undergone less change than the Quaker's. He is the only man in
the universe who is not obliged to study appearances. The ups and
downs of the world concern him no longer. He alone continueth in one
stay. The price of stock or land affecteth him not. The fluctuations of
agricultural or commercial prosperity touch him not, or at worst but
change his customers. He is not expected to become bail or surety for
any one. No man troubleth him with questioning his religion or politics.
He is the only free man in the universe.

The Mendicants of this great city were so many of her sights, her
lions. I can no more spare them than I could the Cries of London. No
corner of a street is complete without them. They are as indispensable
as the Ballad Singer; and in their picturesque attire as ornamental as
the Signs of old London. They were the standing morals, emblems,
mementos, dial-mottos, the spital sermons, the books for children, the
salutary checks and pauses to the high and rushing tide of greasy
citizenry – 'Look/Upon that poor and broken bankrupt there.' Above
all, those old blind Tobits that used to line the wall of Lincoln's Inn
Garden, before modern fastidiousness had expelled them, casting up
their ruined orbs to catch a ray of pity, and (if possible) of light, with
their faithful Dog Guide at their feet, – whither are they fled? or into
what corners, blind as themselves, have they been driven, out of the
wholesome air and sun-warmth? immersed between four walls, in what
withering poor-house do they endure the penalty of double darkness,
where the chink of the dropt half-penny no more consoles their forlorn
bereavement, far from the sound of the cheerful and hope-stirring tread

of the passenger? Where hang their useless staves? and who will farm their dogs? – Have the overseers of St. L – caused them to be shot? or were they tied up in sacks, and dropt into the Thames, at the suggestion of B – , the mild Rector of – ?

Well fare the soul of unfastidious Vincent Bourne, most classical, and at the same time, most English, of the Latinists! – who has treated of this human and quadrupedal alliance, this dog and man friendship, it the sweetest of his poems, the *Epitaphium in Canem,* or, *Dog's Epitaph.* Reader, peruse it; and say, if customary sights, which could call up such gentle poetry as this, were of a nature to do more harm or good to the moral sense of the passengers through the daily thoroughfares of a vast and busy metropolis.

> Poor Irus' faithful wolf-dog here I lie,
> That wont to tend my old blind master's steps,
> His guide and guard: nor, while my service lasted,
> Had he occasion for that staff, with which
> He now goes picking out his path in fear
> Over the highways and crossings; but would plant,
> Safe in the conduct of my friendly string,
> A firm foot forward still, till he had reach'd
> His poor seat on some stone, nigh where the tide
> Of passers by in thickest confluence flow'd:
> To whom with loud and passionate laments
> From morn to eve his dark estate he wail'd.
> Nor wail'd to all in vain: some here and there,
> The well-disposed and good, their pennies gave.
> I meantime at his feet obsequious slept;
> Not all-asleep in sleep, but heart and ear
> Prick'd up at his least motion; to receive
> At his kind hand my customary crums,
> And common portion in his feast of scraps;
> Or when night warn'd us homeward, tired and spent
> With our long day and tedious beggary.
> These were my manners, this my way of life,
> Till age and slow disease me overtook,
> And sever'd from my sightless master's side.
> But lest the grace of so good deeds should die,
> Through tract of years in mute oblivion lost,
> This slender tomb of turf hath Irus reared,
> Cheap monument of no ungrudging hand,
> And with short verse inscribed it, to attest,

> In long and lasting union to attest,
> The virtues of the Beggar and his Dog.

A Diagnosis of Dash

Dear [P.G.] Patmore,

Excuse my anxiety – but how is Dash? [previously owned by Hood] (I should have asked if Mrs Patmore kept her rules, and was improving – but Dash came uppermost. The order of our thoughts should be the order of our writing.) Goes he muzzled, or *aperto ore?* Are his intellects sound, or does he wander a little in *his* conversation? You cannot be too careful to watch the first symptoms of incoherence. The first illogical snarl he makes, to St Luke's with him! All the dogs here are going mad, if you believe the overseers; but I protest they seem to me very rational and collected. But nothing is so deceitful as mad people to those who are not used to them. Try him with hot water. If he won't lick it up, it is a sign he does not like it. Does his tail wag horizontally or perpendicularly? That has decided the fate of many dogs in Enfield. Is his general deportment cheerful? I mean when he is pleased – for otherwise there is no judging. You can't be too careful. Has he bit any of the children yet? If he has, have them shot, and keep *him* for curiosity, to see if it was the hydrophobia. They say all our army in India had it at one time – but that was in the *Hyder*-Ally's time. Do you get paunch for him? Take care the sheep was sane. You might pull out his teeth (if he would let you), and then you need not mind if he were as mad as a Bedlamite. It would be rather fun to see his odd ways. It might amuse Mrs Patmore and the children. They'd have more sense than he! He'd be like a Fool kept in the family, to keep the household in good humour with their own understanding. You might teach him the mad dance set to the mad howl. *Madge Owl-et* would be nothing to him. 'My, how he capers!' [*In the margin is written:*] One of the children speaks this.

[*Three lines here are erased.*] What I scratch out is a German quotation from Lessing on the bite of rabid animals; but, I remember, you don't read German. But Mrs Patmore may, so I wish I had let it stand. The meaning in English is – 'Avoid to approach an animal suspected of madness, as you would avoid fire or a precipice:' – which I think is a sensible observation. The Germans are certainly profounder than we.

If the slightest suspicion arises in your breast, that all is not right with him (Dash), muzzle him, and lead him in a string (common pack-thread will do; he don't care for twist) to Hood's, his quondam master, and he'll take him in at any time. You may mention your suspicion or not, as you like, or as you think it may wound or not Mr H.'s feelings. Hood, I know, will wink at a few follies in Dash, in consideration of his former sense. Besides, Hood is deaf, and if you hinted anything, ten to one he would not hear you. Besides, you will have discharged your conscience, and laid the child at the right door, as they say.

June 1827

Dear Lamb,

Dash is very mad indeed. As I knew you would be shocked to hear it, I did not volunteer to trouble your peaceful retreat by the sad information, thinking it could do no good, either to you, to Dash, to us, or to the innocent creature that he has already bitten, or to those he may (please God) bite hereafter. But when you ask it of me as a friend, I cannot withhold the truth from you. The poor little patient has resolutely refused to touch *water* (either hot or cold) ever since, and if we attempt to force it down her throat, she scratches, grins, fights, makes faces, and utters strange noises, showing every recognised symptom of being very mad indeed . . . .

As for your panacea (of shooting the bitten one), we utterly set our faces against it, not thinking death 'a happy release' under any given circumstances, and being specially averse to it under circumstances given by our own neglect.

By the bye, it has just occurred to me, that the fact of the poor little sufferer making a noise more like a cat's than a dog's, may possibly indicate that she is not quite so mad as we first feared. Still there is no saying but the symptom may be one of aggravation. Indeed I shouldn't wonder if the 'faculty' preferred the *bark*, as that (under the queer name of *quinine*) has been getting very fashionable among them of late.

I wish you could have seen the poor little patient before we got rid of her, – how she scoured round the kitchen among the pots and pans, scampered about the garden, and clambered to the top of the highest trees. (No symptoms of *high*-drophobia, you will say, in that) . . . .

By the bye again, I have entirely forgotten to tell you, that the injured innocent is not one of *our* children, but of the cat's; and this reminds me to tell you that, putting cats out of the question (to which, like some of his so-called 'betters,' Dash has evidently a 'natural antipathy'), he comports himself in all other respects as a sane and well-bred dog should do. In fact, his distemper, I am happy to tell you, is clearly not insanity, but only a temporary hallucination or monomania in regard (want of regard, you will say) to one particular species of his fellow-creatures – videlicet, cats. (For the delicate distinctions in these cases, see Hazlem *passim*; or pass him, if you prefer it) . . . .

Talking of being stopped on the King's Highway, reminds me of Dash's last exploit. He was out at near dusk, down the lane, a few nights ago, with his mistress (who is as fond of him as his master – please to be careful how you construe this last equivocally expressed phrase, and don't make the 'master' an accusative case), when Dash attacked a carpenter armed with a large saw – not Dash but the carpenter – and a 'wise saw' it turned out, for its teeth protected him from Dash's, and a battle royal ensued, worthy the Surrey theatre. Mrs Patmore says that it was really frightful to see the saw, and the way in which it and Dash gnashed their teeth at each other . . . .

THOMAS LOVELL BEDDOES

To Tartar, a Terrier Beauty

> Snowdrop of dogs, with ear of brownest dye,
> Like the last orphan leaf of naked tree
> Which shudders in bleak autumn; though by thee,
> Of hearing careless and untutored eye,
> Not understood articulate speech of men,
> Nor marked the artificial mind of books,
> – The mortal's voice eternized by the pen, –
> Yet hast thou thought and language all unknown
> To Babel's scholars; oft intensest looks,
> Long scrutiny o'er some dark-veined stone
> Dost thou bestow, learning dead mysteries

Of the world's birth-day, oft in eager tone
With quick-tailed fellows bandiest prompt replies,
Solicitudes canine, four-footed amities.

W. S. LANDOR

Hat

ONCE A WEEK I USED to go into Bath, to dine with my father's old friend Walter Savage Landor, who had been driven away from his Florentine home by his wife's violent temper. Mr Landor's rooms were entirely covered with pictures, the frames fitting close to one another, leaving not the smallest space of wall visible. One or two of these pictures were real works of art, but as a rule he had bought them at Bath, quite willing to imagine that the little shops of the Bath dealers could be storehouses of Titians, Giorgiones, and Vandycks. The Bath picture-dealers never had such a time; for some years almost all their ware made their way to Mr Landor's walls. Mr Landor lived alone with his beautiful white Spitz dog Pomero, which he allowed to do whatever it liked, and frequently to sit in the oddest way on the bald top of his head. He would talk to Pomero by the hour together, poetry, philosophy, whatever he was thinking of, all of it imbued with his own powerful personality, and would often roar with laughter till the whole house seemed to shake. I have never heard a laugh like that of Mr Landor – 'deep-mouthed Beotian Savage Landor,' as Byron called him – such a regular cannonade. He was 'the sanest madman and the maddest reasonable man in the world,' as Cervantes says of Don Quixote.

Augustus Hare, from *The Years with Mother*

To a Spaniel

No, Daisy! lift not up thy ear,
It is not she whose steps draw near.
Tuck under thee that leg, for she
Continues yet beyond the sea,
And thou may'st whimper in thy sleep
These many days, and start and weep.

A Dispute

LA FONTAINE: Sad doings! sad oversight! The other two chairs were
sent yesterday evening to be scoured and mended. But that dog is the
best-tempered dog, an angel of a dog, I do assure you: he would have
gone down in a moment, at a word. I am quite ashamed of myself for
such inattention. With your sentiments of friendship for me, why
could you not have taken the liberty to shove him gently off, rather
than give me this uneasiness?

ROCHEFOUCAULT: My true and kind friend! we authors are too sedentary; we are heartily glad of standing to converse, whenever we can
do it without any restraint on our acquaintance.

LA FONTAINE: I must reprove that animal when he uncurls his body.
He seems to be dreaming of Paradise and Houris. Ay, twitch thy ear,
my child! I wish at my heart there were as troublesome a fly about
the other: God forgive me! The rogue covers all my clean linen! –
shirt and cravat!

ROCHEFOUCAULT: Dogs are not very modest.

LA FONTAINE: Never say that, M. de la Rochefoucault! The most
modest people upon earth! Look at a dog's eyes; and he half-closes
them, or gently turns them away, with a motion of the lips, which he
licks languidly, and of the tail, which he stirs tremulously, begging
your forbearance. I am neither blind nor indifferent to the defects of
these good and generous creatures. They are subject to many such
as men are subject to: among the rest, they disturb the neighborhood
in the discussion of their private causes; they quarrel and fight on

small motives, such as a little bad food, or a little vain-glory, or the sex. But it must be something present or near that excites them; and they calculate not the extent of evil they may do or suffer.

ROCHEFOUCAULT: Certainly not: how should dogs calculate?

LA FONTAINE: I know nothing of the process. I am unable to inform you how they leap over hedges and brooks, with exertion just sufficient, and no more. In regard to honor and a sense of dignity, let me tell you, a dog accepts the subsidies of his friends, but never claims them. A dog would not take the field to obtain power for a son, but would leave the son to obtain it by his own activity and prowess. He conducts his visitor or inmate out a-hunting, and makes a present of the game to him as freely as an emperor to an elector. Fond as he is of slumber, – which is indeed one of the pleasantest and best things in the universe, particularly after dinner, – he shakes it off as willingly as he would a gadfly, in order to defend his master from theft or violence. Let the robber or assailant speak as courteously as he may, he waives your diplomatical terms, gives his reasons in plain language, and makes war. I could say many other things to his advantage; but I never was malicious, and would rather let both parties plead for themselves: give me the dog, however.

ROCHFOUCAULT: Faith! I will give you both, and never boast of my largess in so doing.

From *Imaginary Conversations*

JOHN WILSON (CHRISTOPHER NORTH)

Curs and Dowgs

TICKLER: I hate curs.

SHEPHERD: A man ca'in himsel a Christian, and hatin poetry and dowgs!

TICKLER: Hang the brutes.

SHEPHERD: There's nae sic perfeck happiness, I supeck, sir, as that o' the brutes. No that I wuss I had been born a brute – yet aften hae I been tempted to envy a dowg. What gladness in the cretur's een, gin ye but speak a single word to him, when you and him's sittin thegither by your twa sels on the hill. Pat him on the head and say 'Hector, ma man!' and he whines wi' joy – snap your thooms, and he gangs dancin round you like a whirlwind – gie a whusslin hiss, and he loups frantic ower your heid – cry halloo, and he's aff like a shot, chasing naething, as if he were mad.

NORTH: Alas! poor Bronte!

SHEPHERD: Whisht, dinna think o' him, but in general o' dowgs. Love is the element a dowg leeves in, and a' that's necessary for his enjoyment o' life is the presence o' his master.

REGISTRAR: 'With thee conversing he forgets all time.'

SHEPHERD: Yet, wi' a' his sense, he has nae idea o' death. True, he will lie upon his master's grave, and even howk wi' his paws in an affeckin manner, but for a' that, believe me, he has nae idea o' death. He snokes wi' his nose into the hole his paws are howkin, just as if he were after a moudie-warp.

NORTH: God is the soul of the brute creatures.

SHEPHERD: Ay, sir – instinct wi' them's the same's reason wi' us, – only we ken what what we intend – they do not; we reflect in a mathematical problem, for example, how best to big a house; they reflect nane, but what a house they big!

From *Noctes Ambrosinae*

SYDNEY SMITH

Good Nick

Here lies poor Nick, an honest creature,
    Of faithful, gentle, courteous nature;
A parlour pet unspoiled by favour,
A pattern of good dog behaviour.

Without a wish, without a dream,
Beyond his home and friends at Cheam,
Contentedly through life he trotted
Along the path that fate allotted;
Till Time, his aged body wearing,
Bereaved him of his sight and hearing,
Then laid them down without a pain
To sleep, and never wake again.

A Biblical Allusion

THE FAMOUS PAINTER of animals, Landseer, asked Scott's biographer, Lockhart, in a patronising manner, whether he would like to sit for his portrait. Lockhart replied: 'Is thy servant a dog that he should do this thing?' Sydney was delighted when he heard this, and, meeting Landseer some days later, said, 'I think I shall take it.' He did take it, repeated it everywhere, and it became known as one of his wittiest sayings.

Hesketh Pearson, from *The Smith of Smiths*

GRANTLEY BERKELEY

Poachers

THE FIRST DOG I could call my own was a black one, of a cross between the bull and mastiff, and with some other stain in the blood of his progenitors that I do not know, indicated by the appearance of the puppy. His name was 'Grumbo,' and he became attached to me with an affection that a dog only can exhibit. He was my constant companion – and was the brother of the much handsomer sort of large bull bitch so well known at Cheltenham as the pet of Colonel Berkeley.

Grumbo and myself very soon came to a most extraordinary understanding in all matters, whether of sport or war, and to a mutual understanding to back each other up, let the impending danger be of any kind whatever. He was a capital retriever, and soon began to exert that gift which all dogs are more or less in possession of, a nose; and when objects intervened between me and the possession of anything I wanted, Grumbo would fetch it, or use his best exertions to do so, at once. If, while out shooting, there was no obstacle between me and the dead game, the dog displayed no predilection in the matter, but left me to pick it up myself. In short, Grumbo seemed to reason in all he did, and on that account became to me a most valuable companion. It mattered not to him what the understood duty was; if I threw a brick into the artificial water in the park at Cranford, where it was not too deep, and told him to recover it, he would with his paws feel where it lay at the bottom, and duck his head and neck after it till he brought it up. Bulls and cows he tried to bring to me by the nose, pigs by the ears, and men or boys by any part of their persons which seemed to him to be at the moment most convenient for his hold.

It was on one of those lovely days, about the middle of May, I was walking about the cover rides at Cranford, to places where, from within the high palings, I could command views of the common fields that lay between the park and the sweet cherry orchards of what was then the pretty little rural village of Harlington. In the orchard at home, then blooming, and in its richest promise of fruit, I had paused beneath each apple tree to study the interesting and beautiful ornithological and entomological lesson afforded me by the mass of lovely blossom ornamenting every bough. Each tree was a hive for happy, busy bees of every kind, and for tinier insects attracted by the honied cells so liberally provided for them, that everywhere glowed under the brilliant sunshine, and were redolent of perfume. There was not a breath of air, and yet as I stood by the grateful bouquet spread above and around, the soft flakes fell to the grass, and snow-spotted the herbage. What makes these showers of bloom drop from the budding fruit and fall before their time, it would take too long to dwell on; my attention would be attracted by other objects, the graceful summer visitors, the willow wren, and lesser fly-catchers. How smoothly and noiselessly they glide through that rich world of sweets, with sharp and graceful head and taper bill, scaring the bees, but not hurting them, for they seek their proper prey in a totally different insect! The rustic, if he glances up as the blossom falls, and observes the bird on its beneficial duty, in all probability would believe that it spoilt the promise of his apples. In that conviction he fires at, and probably destroys his friend, the enemy of the smaller grub, the pest of every fruit tree. The blooming orchard is a glorious place for study, or for the enjoyment of that *dolce far niente* which can be experienced only in the society of the one loved companion of our youth or manhood; but at boyhood's less discriminating age we are too restless to appreciate such pleasant indolence. In later life a new taste is acquired, a filled cup is presented to our lips, and very few can resist its temptation – more frequently it is drained to the dregs.

On the day to which I refer, accompanied by my faithful dog, I left the orchard for the more exciting amusement of watching the preserve of game, or catching, if I could, any of the poachers who were known to commit depredations whenever they could find a chance.

Grumbo and myself were standing within and beneath the high palings at the bottom of the 'Ash cover'; I was extending my vigil over the open cornfields through a chink made for the purpose, when I observed two men come along the headland towards the park, searching the long grass, young nettles, and scrubby bushes, evidently for pheasants' eggs. When about a hundred yards from me, a hen pheasant, with her peculiar cry, flew from beneath their feet, and I saw them stoop and rob her nest. I had not the key to unlock the gate, and a hundred yards was a long start, particularly when I had to help a heavy dog over the palings it was impossible for him to jump, and the space to be accomplished not over three or four times the distance, to the Cherry Orchards and village, and the fellows, if they reached the latter, would soon be screened from sight. So, waiting till the men turned to retreat with their booty, in the hope of their not becoming aware of pursuit, I made a sign to Grumbo that he was wanted, and to try to jump the pales. He comprehended that I would aid him. When he had sprung as high as he could, I was ready, and pushed him up from behind until he got his paws over the top, then he climbed on, and fell outside the park.

I was not long after him, and together we set off, but before we had gone ten yards, the egg stealers discovered us, and commenced running at full speed. Grumbo gathered from my manner that he was to catch and hold something, but whether it was a man, a horse, a dog, or cow, as yet he knew not, nor did he much care. I gave the well-known word and sign, pointing to the objects in advance, when he dashed on, and soon took up the running at the only thing he at first saw, the distant figures of two men. By this time they had reached and turned up the orchard hedge and headland by its side, on which was tethered with a rope a grazing cow. They passed the cow, and then I dreaded the interposition of her tempting nose as the dog came up upon her traces. We were now on that long headland in full sight of each other, and I had seen the men, as they ran, throw the pheasants' eggs away. At that moment Grumbo came up to the cow, and stopping close beneath her nose, with an ominous lick of his lip, looked back at me for confirmation of his idea. A wave of my hand, and a shout, 'Go on,' disclosed to him that it was a man and not a cow on whom I wished him to fix his hold, so to make up for this erroneous pause he dashed away on the now well-assured chase, more furiously than ever.

The vagabonds had had time to turn short to the right down a little grass lane leading at once to the cottages of the village, and were lost to my sight; but gaining on them fast, my dear companion turned that corner too, and I felt almost sure that before they could reach the village, one or the other would be caught. It was in breathless anxiety that I turned the corner, and got into the last bit of straight running that yet remained, along which I had a full view. Never shall I forget my joy, when, about three parts of the way down the path, I saw the back of one of the men, his figure stationary, his hands held high above his head, and Grumbo, my faithful, sagacious dog, a yard in front of him, barring his path, couched like a lion in the act to spring, his eyes, not his teeth, fixed on the fellow's throat. The menace sufficed, he stood in terror of the result of any further attempt to run, and in this position I presently seized him by the collar.

There was a good deal of difference in our muscular proportions, though he was not a big man; I was only a boy, but he was aware that if a struggle between us began, I had a resolute assistant at hand, that would give me sufficient odds against him; so he at once surrendered, praying that I would call off my dog. I could see that Grumbo very much wanted a fight, but understanding at once the surrender and a sign from my hand, he calmed down to what was to the prisoner a horrible and close inspection of his leg, and walked back with us to the park, close at his heels, with his broad muzzle occasionally nudging the limb, as if to remind the man of the close approximation of teeth, ever ready, at a sign from me, to meet in some part of his person. It was with much boyish triumph that I led my prisoner into the great stone courtyard at Cranford House, and thence into the servants' hall; and leaving him under the surveillance of the servants, went to call my brother to come and look at the first poacher I had caught.

From *Recollections*

CAPTAIN MARRYAT

Loyal Villains

B UT THERE WAS ANOTHER personage on the deck, a personage of no small importance, as he was all in all to Mr Vanslyperken, and Mr Vanslyperken was all in all to him; moreover, we may say, that he is the hero of the TAIL. This was one of the ugliest and most ill-conditioned curs which had ever been produced: ugly in colour; for he was of a dirty yellow, like the paint served out to decorate our men-of-war by his Majesty's dockyards: ugly in face; for he had one wall-eye, and was so far under-jawed as to prove that a bull-dog had had something to do with his creation: ugly in shape; for although larger than a pointer, and strongly built, he was coarse and shambling in his make, with his forelegs bowed out. His ears and tail had never been docked, which was a pity, as the more you curtailed his proportions, the better looking the cur would have been. But his ears, although not cut, were torn to ribbons by the various encounters with dogs on shore, arising from the acidity of his temper. His tail had lost its hair from an inveterate mange, and reminded you of the same appendage to a rat. Many parts of his body were bared from the same disease. He carried his head and tail low, and had a villanous sour look. To the eye of a casual observer, there was not one redeeming quality that would warrant his keep; to those who knew him well, there were a thousand reasons why he should be hanged. He followed his master with the greatest precision and exactitude, walking aft as he walked aft, and walking forward with the same regular motion, turning when his master turned, and moreover, turning in the same direction; and, like his master, he appeared to be not a little nipped with the cold, and, as well as he, in a state of profound meditation. The name of this uncouth animal was very appropriate to his appearance, and to his temper. It was Snarleyyow.

At last, Mr Vanslyperken gave vent to his pent-up feelings. 'I can't, I won't stand this any longer,' muttered the lieutenant, as he took his six strides forward. At this first sound of his master's voice the dog pricked up the remnants of his ears, and they both turned aft. 'She has been now fooling me for six years;' and as he concluded this sentence, Mr Vanslyperken and Snarleyyow had reached the taffrail, and the dog raised his tail to the half cock.

They turned, and Mr Vanslyperken paused a moment or two, and compressed his thin lips – the dog did the same. 'I will have an answer, by all that's blue!' was the ejaculation of the next six strides. The lieutenant stopped again, and the dog looked up in his master's face; but it appeared as if the current of his master's thoughts was changed, for the current of keen air reminded Mr Vanslyperken that he had not yet had his breakfast.

The lieutenant leant over the hatchway, took his battered speaking-trumpet from under his arm, and putting it to his mouth, the deck reverberated with, 'Pass the word for Smallbones forward.' The dog put himself in a baying attitude, with his forefeet on the coamings of the hatchway, and enforced his master's orders with a deep-toned and measured bow, wow, wow.

From *Snarleyyow*

SAMUEL TAYLOR COLERIDGE

Stray Thoughts

THE DOG ALONE, OF all brute animals, has στοργη or affection *upwards* to man.

* * *

There seems a sort of sympathy between the more generous dogs and little children. I believe an instance of a little child being attacked by a large dog is very rare indeed.

From *Table Talk*

H E SPOKE OF the effect of different sounds upon his sensations; said, of all the pains the sense of hearing ever brought to him, that of the effect made by a dog belonging to some German conjuror was the greatest. The man pretended that the dog could answer '*Ich bedanke mein herr*' when anything was given to it; and the effort and contortion made by the dog to produce the required sound, proved that the scourge, or some similar punishment, had been applied to effect it.

Sarah Flower Adams, from 'An Evening with Charles Lamb and Coleridge', *Monthly Repository*, IX 1835

M AN'S UNDERSTANDING HAS likewise an organ of inward sense, and therefore the power of acquainting itself with invisible realities or spiritual objects. This organ is his Reason. Again, the Understanding and Experience may exist without Reason. Of this no one would feel inclined to doubt, who had seen the poodle dog, whom the celebrated Blumenbach, a name so dear to science, as a physiologist and Comparative Anatomist, and not less dear as a man, to all Englishmen who have ever resided at Gottingen in the course of their education, trained up not only to hatch the eggs of the hen with all the mother's care and patience, but to attend to the children afterwards, and find the food for them. I have myself known a Newfoundland dog, who watched and guarded a family of young children with all the intelligence of a nurse, during their walks.

From the *Friend*: The Loading Place, Essay Five: 'Reason and Understanding'

CHARLES DARWIN

Shepherd-Dogs

W HILE STAYING AT this estancia, I was amused with what I saw
and heard of the shepherd-dogs of the country. When riding, it
is a common thing to meet a large flock of sheep guarded by one or two
dogs, at the distance of some miles from any house or man. I often
wondered how so firm a friendship had been established. The method
of education consists in separating the puppy, while very young, from
the bitch, and in accustoming it to its future companions. An ewe is
held three or four times a day for the little thing to suck, and a nest of
wool is made for it in the sheep-pen; at no time is it allowed to associate
with other dogs, or with the children of the family. The puppy is,
moreover, generally castrated; so that, when grown up, it can scarcely
have any feelings in common with the rest of its kind. From this
education it has no wish to leave the flock, and just as another dog will
defend its master, man, so will these the sheep. It is amusing to observe,
when approaching a flock, how the dog immediately advances barking,
and the sheep all close in his rear, as if round the oldest ram. These
dogs are also easily taught to bring home the flock, at a certain hour in
the evening. Their most troublesome fault, when young, is their desire
of playing with the sheep; for in their sport they sometimes gallop their
poor subjects most unmercifully.

The shepherd-dog comes to the house every day for some meat, and
as soon as it is given him, he skulks away as if ashamed of himself. On
these occasions the house-dogs are very tyrannical, and the least of
them will attack and pursue the stranger. The minute, however, the
latter has reached the flock, he turns round and begins to bark, and
then all the house-dogs take very quickly to their heels. In a similar
manner a whole pack of the hungry wild dogs will scarcely ever (and I
was told by some never) venture to attack a flock guarded by even one
of these faithful shepherds. The whole account appears to me a curious
instance of the pliability of the affections in the dog; and yet, whether
wild or however educated, he has a feeling of respect or fear for those
that are fulfilling their instinct of association. For we can understand on
no principle the wild dogs being driven away by the single one with its
flock, except that they consider, from some confused notion, that the
one thus associated gains power, as if in company with its own kind. F.

Cuvier has observed, that all animals that readily enter into domestication, consider man as a member of their own society, and thus fulfil their instinct of association. In the above case the shepherd-dog ranks the sheep as its fellow-brethren, and thus gains confidence; and the wild dogs, though knowing that the individual sheep are not dogs, but are good to eat, yet partly consent to this view when seeing them in a flock with a shepherd-dog at their head.

From *Voyages of a Naturalist*

ROBERT SOUTHEY

On the Death of a Favourite Old Spaniel

And they have drown'd thee then at last! poor Phillis!
The burden of old age was heavy on thee,
And yet thou should'st have lived! What though thine eye
Was dim, and watch'd no more with eager joy
The wonted call that on thy dull sense sunk
With fruitless repetition, the warm Sun
Might still have cheer'd thy slumbers; thou didst love
To lick the hand that fed thee, and though past
Youth's active season, even Life itself
Was comfort. Poor old friend, how earnestly
Would I have pleaded for thee! thou hadst been
Still the companion of my boyish sports;
And as I roam'd o'er Avon's woody cliffs,
From many a day-dream has thy short quick bark
Recall'd my wandering soul. I have beguiled
Often the melancholy hours at school,
Sour'd by some little tyrant, with the thought
Of distant home, and I remember'd then

Thy faithful fondness; for not mean the joy,
Returning at the happy holydays,
I felt from thy dumb welcome. Pensively
Sometimes have I remark'd thy slow decay,
Feeling myself changed too, and musing much
On many a sad vicissitude of Life.
Ah, poor companion! when thou followedst last
Thy master's parting footsteps to the gate
Which closed for ever on him, thou didst lose
Thy truest friend, and none was left to plead
For the old age of brute fidelity.
But fare thee well! Mine is no narrow creed;
And HE who gave thee being did not frame
The mystery of life to be the sport
Of merciless Man. There is another world
For all that live and move . . . a better one!
Where the proud bipeds, who would fain confine
INFINITE GOODNESS to the little bounds
Of their own charity, may envy thee.

Diligence

A BOAST BEING made of the obedience of a dog in fetching and carrying (a Newfoundland) the master put a marked shilling under a large square stone by the road side, and having ridden on three miles ordered the dog to go back and fetch it. The dog set off, but did not return the whole day. He had gone to the place, and being unable to turn the stone, sat howling by it. Two horsemen came by and saw her distress, and one of them alighting removed the stone, and finding the shilling, put it in his pocket, not supposing that the dog could possibly be looking for that. The dog followed the horses for upwards of twenty miles, stayed in the room where they supped, got into the bedroom, got the breeches in which the fatal shilling had been put, made his escape with them, and dragged them through mud and mire, hedge and ditch, to his master's house.

Remedy for Dogs Supposed to be Mad

'To about six grains of calomel add thirty of powdered jalap and ten of scammony; make them into a pill with honey, or any other convenient vehicle, and give it to the dog immediately. In all probability an abundant evacuation will succeed, from which alone the cure sometimes results. This medicine, however, should not be solely relied on, but should be followed up by pills of about the size of a very large marrow-fat pea, given half-hourly. These pills are to be made of pure camphor, dissolved sufficiently to be worked into a mass, by means of a few drops of spirit of wine, which should be added drop by drop, as it is very easy to render the camphor too liquid. A short time will decide the case: if the medicine take proper effect, the jaws will be freed from that slimy, ropy excretion occasioned by the disease, and in its stead, a free discharge of saliva will appear, rather inclined to froth like soap-suds. I can only assure the reader, that I have more than once saved the life of dogs by these means, although they were so far gone as to snap at me whilst administering the medicine.'

From *Commonplace Book*

THE BRONTËS

Keeper

THE HELPLESSNESS OF AN animal was its passport to Charlotte's heart; the fierce, wild, intractability of its nature was what often recommended it to Emily. Speaking of her dead sister, the former told me that from her many traits in Shirley's character were taken; her way of sitting on the rug reading, with her arm round her rough bull-dog's neck; her calling to a strange dog, running past, with hanging head and lolling tongue, to give it a merciful draught of water, its maddened snap at her, her nobly stern presence of mind, going right into the kitchen, and taking up one of Tabby's red-hot Italian irons to sear the bitten place, and telling no one, till the danger was well-nigh over, for fear of the terrors that might beset their weaker minds. All this, looked upon as a well-invented fiction in *Shirley*, was written down by Charlotte with streaming eyes; it was the literal true account of what Emily had done. The same tawny bulldog (with his 'strangled whistle'), called 'Tartar' in *Shirley*, was 'Keeper' in Haworth parsonage; a gift to Emily. With the gift came the warning. Keeper was faithful to the depths of his nature as long as he was with friends; but he who struck him with a stick or whip, roused the relentless nature of the brute, who flew at his throat forthwith, and held him there till one or the other was at the point of death. Now Keeper's household fault was this. He loved to steal up-stairs, and stretch his square, tawny limbs, on the comfortable beds, covered over with delicate white counterpanes. But the cleanliness of the parsonage arrangements was perfect; and this habit of Keeper's was so objectionable, that Emily, in reply to Tabby's remonstrances, declared that, if he was found again transgressing, she herself, in defiance of warning and his well-known ferocity of nature, would beat him so severely that he would never offend again. In the gathering dusk of an autumn evening, Tabby came, half triumphantly, half tremblingly, but in great wrath, to tell Emily that Keeper was lying on the best bed, in drowsy voluptuousness. Charlotte saw Emily's whitening face, and set mouth, but dared not speak to interfere; no one dared when Emily's eyes glowed in that manner out of the paleness of her face, and when her lips were so compressed into stone. She went up-stairs, and Tabby and Charlotte stood in the gloomy passage below, full of the dark shadows of coming night. Down-stairs came Emily, dragging after her the unwilling Keeper, his hind legs set in a heavy attitude of resistance, held by the 'scuft of his neck,' but growling low and savagely all the time. The watchers would fain have spoken, but durst not, for fear of taking off Emily's attention, and causing her to avert her head for a moment from the enraged brute. She let him go, planted in a dark corner at the bottom of the stairs; no time was there to fetch stick or rod, for fear of the strangling clutch at her throat – her bare clenched fist struck against his red fierce eyes, before he had time to make his spring, and, in the language of the turf, she 'punished him' till his eyes were swelled up, and the half-blind, stupified beast was led to his accustomed lair, to have his swelled head fomented and cared for by the very Emily herself. The generous dog owed her no grudge; he loved her dearly ever after; he walked first among the mourners to her funeral; he slept moaning for nights at the door of her empty room, and never, so to speak, rejoiced, dog fashion, after her death. He, in his turn, was mourned over by the surviving sister. Let us somehow hope, in half Red Indian creed, that he follows Emily now; and, when he rests, sleeps on some soft white bed of dreams, unpunished when he awakens to the life of the land of shadows.

Mrs Gaskell, from her *Life of Charlotte Brontë*

First Meeting

ABOVE THE CHIMNEY were sundry villainous old guns, and a couple of horse-pistols, and, by way of ornament, three gaudily painted canisters disposed along its ledge. The floor was of smooth, white stone: the chairs, high-backed, primitive structures, painted green: one or two heavy black ones lurking in the shade. In an arch, under the dresser, reposed a huge, liver-coloured bitch pointer surrounded by a swarm of squealing puppies; and other dogs, haunted other recesses . . . .

I took a seat at the end of the hearthstone opposite that towards which my landlord advanced, and filled up an interval of silence by attempting to caress the canine mother, who had left her nursery, and was sneaking wolfishly to the back of my legs, her lip curled up, and her white teeth watering for a snatch.

My caress provoked a long, guttural gnarl.

'You'd better let the dog alone,' growled Mr Heathcliff, in unison, checking fiercer demonstrations with a punch of his foot. 'She's not accustomed to be spoiled – not kept for a pet.'

Then, striding to a side-door, he shouted again.

'Joseph!'

Joseph mumbled indistinctly in the depths of the cellar; but, gave no intimation of ascending; so, his master dived down to him, leaving me *vis-à-vis* the ruffianly bitch, and a pair of grim, shaggy sheep dogs, who shared with her a jealous guardianship over all my movements.

Not anxious to come in contact with their fangs, I sat still – but, imagining they would scarcely understand tacit insults, I unfortunately indulged in winking and making faces at the trio, and some turn of my physiognomy so irritated madam, than she suddenly broke into a fury, and leapt on my knees. I flung her back, and hastened to interpose the table between us. This proceeding roused the whole hive. Half-a-dozen four-footed fiends, of various sizes, and ages, issued from hidden dens to the common centre. I felt my heels, and coat-laps peculiar subjects of assault; and, parrying off the larger combatants, as effectually as I could, with the poker, I was constrained to demand, aloud, assistance from some of the household, in re-establishing peace.

Mr Heathcliff and his man climbed the cellar steps with vexatious phlegm. I don't think they moved one second faster than usual, though the hearth was an absolute tempest of worrying and yelping.

Happily, an inhabitant of the kitchen made more dispatch; a lusty dame, with tucked-up gown, bare arms, and fire-flushed cheeks, rushed into the midst of us flourishing a fryingpan; and used that weapon, and her tongue to such purpose, that the storm subsided magically, and she only remained, heaving like a sea after a high wind, when her master entered on the scene.

'What the devil is the matter?' he asked, eyeing me in a manner that I could ill endure after this inhospitable treatment.

'What the devil, indeed!' I muttered. 'The herd of possessed swine could have had no worse spirits in them than those animals of yours, sir. You might as well leave a stranger with a brood of tigers!'

'They won't meddle with persons who touch nothing,' he remarked, putting the bottle before me, and restoring the displaced table. 'The dogs do right to be vigilant. Take a glass of wine?'

'No, thank you.'

'Not bitten, are you?'

'If I had been, I would have set my signet on the biter.'

Heathcliff's countenance relaxed into a grin.

'Come, come,' he said, 'you are flurried, Mr Lockwood. Here, take a little wine. Guests are so exceedingly rare in this house that I and my dogs, I am willing to own, hardly know how to receive them. Your health, sir.'

I bowed and returned the pledge; beginning to perceive that it would be foolish to sit sulking for the misbehaviour of a pack of curs: besides, I felt loth to yield the fellow further amusement, at my expense; since his humour took that turn.

Emily Brontë, from *Wuthering Heights*

Mr Donne's Exodus

'HERE HE COMES!' suddenly exclaimed Shirley, breaking off, starting up and running to the window. 'Here comes a diversion. I never told you of a superb conquest I have made lately – made at those parties to which I can never persuade you to accompany me; and the thing has been done without effort or intention on my part: that I aver. There is the bell – and, by all that's delicious! there are two of them. Do they never hunt, then, except in couples? You may have one, Lina, and you may take your choice: I hope I am generous enough. Listen to Tartar!'

The black-muzzled, tawny dog, a glimpse of which was seen in the chapter which first introduced its mistress to the reader, here gave tongue in the hall, amidst whose hollow space the deep bark resounded formidably. A growl, more terrible than the bark – menacing as muttered thunder – succeeded.

'Listen!' again cried Shirley, laughing. 'You would think that the prelude to a bloody onslaught: they will be frightened: they don't know old Tartar as I do: they are not aware his uproars are all sound and fury, signifying nothing.'

Some bustle was heard. 'Down, sir! – down!' exclaimed a high-toned, imperious voice, and then came a crack of a cane or whip. Immediately there was a yell – a scutter – a run – a positive tumult.

'Oh! Malone! Malone!'

'Down! down! down!' cried the high voice.

'He really is worrying them!' exclaimed Shirley. 'They have struck him: a blow is what he is not used to, and will not take.'

Out she ran – a gentleman was fleeing up the oak staircase, making for refuge in the gallery or chambers in hot haste; another was backing fast to the stair-foot, wildly flourishing a knotty stick, at the same time reiterating, 'Down! down! down!' while the tawny dog bayed, bellowed, howled at him, and a group of servants came bundling from the kitchen. The dog made a spring: the second gentleman turned tail and rushed after his comrade: the first was already safe in a bed-room: he held the door against his fellow; – nothing so merciless as terror; – but the other fugitive struggled hard: the door was about to yield to his strength.

'Gentlemen,' was uttered in Miss Keeldar's silvery but vibrating tones, 'spare my locks, if you please. Calm yourselves! – come down! Look at Tartar, – he won't harm a cat.'

She was caressing the said Tartar: he lay crouched at her feet, his fore-paws stretched out, his tail still in threatening agitation, his nostrils snorting, his bulldog eyes conscious of a dull fire. He was an honest, phlegmatic, stupid, but stubborn canine character: he loved his mistress, and John – the man who fed him – but was mostly indifferent to the rest of the world: quiet enough he was, unless struck or threatened with a stick, and that put a demon into him at once.

'Mr Malone, how do you do?' continued Shirley, lifting up her mirth-lit face to the gallery. 'That is not the way to the oak-parlour: that is Mrs Pryor's apartment. Request your friend Mr Donne to evacuate: I shall have the greatest pleasure in receiving him in a lower room.'

'Ha! ha!' cried Malone, in hollow laughter, quitting the door, and leaning over the massive balustrade. 'Really that animal alarmed Donne. He is a little timid,' he proceeded, stiffening himself, and walking trimly to the stairhead. 'I thought it better to follow, in order to reassure him.'

'It appears you did: well, come down, if you please. John' (turning to her manservant), 'go upstairs and liberate Mr Donne. Take care, Mr Malone, the stairs are slippery.'

In truth they were; being of polished oak. The caution came a little late for Malone: he had slipped already in his stately descent, and was only saved from falling by a clutch at the banisters, which made the whole structure creak again.

Tartar seemed to think the visitor's descent effected with unwarranted éclat, and accordingly he growled once more. Malone, however, was no coward: the spring of the dog had taken him by surprise: but he passed him now in suppressed fury rather than fear: if a look could have strangled Tartar, he would have breathed no more. Forgetting politeness, in his sullen rage, Malone pushed into the parlour before Miss Keeldar. He glanced at Miss Helstone; he could scarcely bring himself to bend to her. He glared on both the ladies: he looked as if, had either of them been his wife, he would have made a glorious husband at the moment: in each hand he seemed as if he would have liked to clutch one and gripe her to death.

However, Shirley took pity: she ceased to laugh; and Caroline was too true a lady to smile even at any one under mortification. Tartar was dismissed; Peter Augustus was soothed: for Shirley had looks and tones that might soothe a very bull: he had sense to feel that, since he could not challenge the owner of the dog, he had better be civil; and civil he tried to be; and his attempts being well received, he grew presently *very* civil and quite himself again. He had come, indeed, for the express purpose of making himself charming and fascinating: rough portents had met him on his first admission to Fieldhead; but that passage got over, charming and fascinating he resolved to be. Like March, having come in like a lion, he purposed to go out like a lamb.

For the sake of air, as it appeared, or perhaps for that of ready exit in case of some new emergency arising, he took his seat – not on the sofa, where Miss Keeldar offered him enthronisation, not yet near the fireside, to which Caroline, by a friendly sign, gently invited him, – but on a chair close to the door. Being no longer sullen or furious, he grew, after his fashion, constrained and embarrassed. He talked to the ladies by fits and starts, choosing for topics whatever was most intensely commonplace: he sighed deeply, significantly, at the close of every sentence; he sighed in each pause; he sighed ere he opened his mouth. At last, finding it desirable to add ease to his other charms, he drew forth to aid him an ample silk pocket-handkerchief. This was to be the graceful toy with which his unoccupied hands were to trifle. He went to work with a certain energy: he folded the red and yellow square cornerwise; he whipped it open with a waft: again he folded it in narrower compass: he made of it a handsome band. To what purpose would he proceed to apply the ligature? Would he wrap it about his throat – his head? Should it be a comforter or a turban? Neither. Peter Augustus had an inventive – an original genius: he was about to show the ladies graces of action possessing at least the charm of novelty. He sat on the chair with his athletic Irish legs crossed, and these legs, in that attitude, he circled with the bandanna and bound firmly together. It was evident he felt this device to be worth an encore: he repeated it more than once. The second performance sent Shirley to the window to laugh her silent but irrepressible laugh unseen: it turned Caroline's head aside, that her long curls might screen the smile mantling on her features. Miss Helstone, indeed, was amused by more than one point in Peter's demeanour: she was edified at the complete though abrupt diversion of his homage from herself to the heiress: the £5000 he supposed her likely one day to inherit, were not to be weighed in the balance against Miss Keeldar's estate and hall. He took no pains to conceal his calculations and tactics: he pretended to no gradual change of views: he wheeled about at once: the pursuit of the lesser fortune was openly relinquished for that of the greater. On what grounds he expected to succeed in his chase, himself best knew: certainly not by skilful management.

From the length of time that elapsed, it appeared that John had some difficulty in persuading Mr Donne to descend. At length, however, that gentleman appeared: nor, as he presented himself at the oak-parlour door, did he seem in the slightest degree ashamed or confused – not a whit. Donne, indeed, was of that coldly phlegmatic, immovably complacent, densely self-satisfied nature which is insensible to shame. He had never blushed in his life: no humiliation could abash him: his nerves were not capable of sensation enough to stir his life, and make colour mount to his cheek: he had no fire in his blood, and no modesty in his soul: he was a frontless, arrogant, decorous slip of the commonplace; conceited, inane, insipid: and this gentleman had a notion of wooing Miss Keeldar! He knew no more, however, how to set about the business than if he had been an image carved in wood: he had no idea of a taste to be pleased, a heart to be reached in courtship: his notion was, when he should have formally visited her a few times, to write a letter proposing marriage; then he calculated she would accept him for love of his office, then they would be married, then he should be master of Fieldhead, and he should live very comfortably, have servants at his command, eat and drink of the best, and be a great man. You would not have suspected his intentions when he addressed his intended bride in an impertinent, injured tone – 'A very dangerous dog that, Miss Keeldar. I wonder you should keep such an animal.'

'Do you, Mr Donne? Perhaps you will wonder more than I tell you I am very fond of him.'

'I should say you are not serious in the assertion. Can't fancy a lady fond of that brute – 'tis so ugly – a mere carter's dog – pray hang him.'

'Hang what I am fond of!'

'And purchase in his stead some sweetly pooty pug or poodle: something appropriate to the fair sex: ladies generally like lapdogs.'

'Perhaps I am an exception.'

'Oh! you can't be, you know. All ladies are alike in those matters: that is universally allowed.'

'Tartar frightened you terribly, Mr Donne. I hope you won't take any harm.'

'That I shall, no doubt. He gave me a turn I shall not soon forget. When I *sor* him' (such was Mr Donne's pronunciation) 'about to spring, I thought I should have fainted.'

'Perhaps you did faint in the bed-room – you were a long time there?'

'No; I bore up that I might hold the door fast: I was determined not to let any one enter: I thought I would keep a barrier between me and the enemy.'

'But what if your friend Mr Malone had been worried?'

'Malone must take care of himself. Your man persuaded me to come out at last by saying the dog was chained up in his kennel: if I had not been assured of this, I would have remained all day in the chamber. But what is that? I declare the man has told a falsehood! The dog is there!'

And indeed Tartar walked past the glass-door opening to the garden, stiff, tawny, and black-muzzled as ever. He still seemed in bad humour; he was growling again, and whistling a half-strangled whistle, being an inheritance from the bull-dog side of his ancestry.

'There are other visitors coming,' observed Shirley, with that provoking coolness which the owners of formidable-looking dogs are apt to show while their animals are all bristle and bay. Tartar sprang down the pavement towards the gate, bellowing 'avec explosion'. His mistress quietly opened the glass-door, and stepped out chirruping to him. His bellow was already silenced, and he was lifting up his huge, blunt, stupid head to the new callers to be patted.

'What – Tartar, Tartar!' said a cheery, rather boyish voice, 'don't you know us? Good-morning, old boy!'

And little Mr Sweeting, whose conscious good-nature made him comparatively fearless of man, woman, child, or brute, came through the gate, caressing the guardian. His vicar, Mr Hall, followed: he had no fear of Tartar either, and Tartar had no ill-will to him: he snuffed both the gentlemen round, and then, as if concluding that they were harmless, and might be allowed to pass, he withdrew to the sunny front of the hall, leaving the archway free. Mr Sweeting followed, and would have played with him, but Tartar took no notice of his caresses: it was only his mistress's hand whose touch gave him pleasure; to all others he showed himself obstinately insensible.

Shirley advanced to meet Messrs Hall and Sweeting, shaking hands with them cordially: they were come to tell her of certain successes they had achieved that morning in applications for subscriptions to the fund. Mr Hall's eyes beamed benignantly through his spectacles: his plain face looked positively handsome with goodness, and when Caroline, seeing who was come, ran out to meet him, and put both her hands into his, he gazed down on her with a gentle, serene, affectionate expression, that gave him the aspect of a smiling Melanchthon.

Instead of re-entering the house, they strayed through the garden, the ladies walking one on each side of Mr Hall. It was a breezy sunny day; the air freshened the girls' cheeks, and gracefully dishevelled their ringlets: both of them looked pretty, – one, gay: Mr Hall spoke oftenest to his brilliant companion, looked most frequently at the quiet one. Miss Keeldar gathered handfuls of the profusely blooming flowers, whose perfume filled the enclosure; she gave some to Caroline, telling her to choose a nosegay for Mr Hall; and with her lap filled with delicate and splendid blossoms, Caroline sat down on the steps of a summer-house: the Vicar stood near her, leaning on his cane.

Shirley, who could not be inhospitable, now called out the neglected pair in the oak-parlour: she convoyed Donne past his dread enemy Tartar, who, with his nose on his fore-paws, lay snoring under the meridian sun. Donne was not grateful: he never *was* grateful for kindness and attention; but he was glad of the safeguard.

Charlotte Brontë, from *Shirley*

Snap

THE FOLLOWING DAY was as fine as the preceding one. Soon after breakfast, Miss Matilda, having galloped and blundered through a few unprofitable lessons, and vengibly thumped the piano for an hour, in a terrible humour with both me and it, because her mamma would not give her a holiday, had betaken herself to her favorite places of resort, the yards, the stables, and the dog-kennels: and Miss Murray was gone forth to enjoy a quiet ramble with a new fashionable novel for her companion, leaving me in the school-room, hard at work upon a water-colour drawing I had promised to do for her, and which she insisted upon my finishing that day.

At my feet lay a little rough terrier. It was the property of Miss Matilda; but she hated the animal, and intended to sell it, alleging that it was quite spoiled. It was really an excellent dog of its kind; but she affirmed it was fit for nothing, and had not even the sense to know its own mistress.

The fact is, she had purchased it when but a small puppy, insisting, at first, that no one should touch it but herself; but, soon becoming tired of so helpless and troublesome a nursling, she had gladly yielded to my entreaties to be allowed to take charge of it; and I, by carefully nursing the little creature from infancy to adolescence, of course, had obtained its affections; a reward I should have greatly valued and looked upon as far outweighing all the trouble I had had with it, had not poor

Snap's grateful feelings exposed him to many a harsh word and many a spiteful kick and pinch from his owner, and were he not now in danger of being 'put away,' in consequence, or transferred to some rough, stony-hearted master. But how could I help it? I could not make the dog hate me by cruel treatment; and she would not propitiate him by kindness.

However, while I thus sat, working away with my pencil, Mrs Murray came, half-sailing, half-bustling, into the room.

'Miss Grey,' she began, – 'Dear! how can you sit at your drawing such a day as this?' (she thought I was doing it for my own pleasure). 'I *wonder* you don't put on your bonnet and go out with the young ladies.'

'I think, ma'am, Miss Murray is reading; and Miss Matilda is amusing herself with her dogs.'

'If you would try to amuse Miss Matilda yourself a little more, I think she would not be *driven* to seek amusement in the companionship of dogs and horses, and grooms, so much as she is; and if you would be a little more cheerful and conversable with Miss Murray, she would not often go wandering in the fields with a book in her hand. However, I don't want to vex you,' added she, seeing, I suppose, that my cheeks burned and my hand trembled with some unamiable emotion. 'Do, pray, try not to be so touchy! – there's no speaking to you else. And tell me if you know where Rosalie is gone: and why she likes to be so much alone?'

'She says she likes to be alone when she has a new book to read.'

Anne Brontë, from *Agnes Grey*

LORD BROUGHAM

A Conversation

B: THE CUNNING OF a Dog, which Serjeant Wilde tells me of, as known to him, is at least equal. He used to be tied up as a precaution against hunting sheep. At night he slipped his head out of the collar, and returning before dawn, put on the collar again, in order to conceal his nocturnal excursion. Nobody has more familiarity with various animals (beside his great knowledge of his own species) than my excellent, learned, and ingenious friend, the Serjeant; and he possesses many curious ones himself. His anecdote of a drover's dog is striking, as he gave it me, when we happened, near this place, to meet a drove. The man had brought seventeen out of twenty oxen from a field, leaving the remaining three there mixed with another herd. He then said to the dog 'Go, fetch them;' and he went and singled out those very three. The Serjeant's brother, however, a highly respectable man, lately Sheriff of London, has a dog that distinguishes Saturday night, from the practice of tying him up for the Sunday, which he dislikes. He will escape on Saturday night and return on Monday morning. The Serjeant himself had a gander which was at a distance from the goose, and hearing her make an extraordinary noise, ran back and put his head into the cage – then brought back all the goslings one by one and put them into it with the mother, whose separation from her brood had occasioned her clamour. He then returned to the place whence her cries had called him. I must however add, that I often have conversed with Scotch shepherds coming up from the Border country to our great fairs, and have found them deny many of the stories of the miraculous feats of sheep-dogs.

* * *

B: We find in it a curious passage from an old Spanish author of the seventeenth century, giving a quaint and lively account of the sagacity of the beggars' dogs at Rome; and we also find the titles of some German works on the faculties of brutes, which are truly curious, and show how great a degree of attention that laborious people have paid to the subject, but, at the same time, betray not a little of the characteristic boldness and enthusiasm of their speculations.

A: I conclude you have never seen more than these titles in this book?

B: Never; and I really should wish to see the works themselves. One is *Mayer de peccatis et pœnis Brutorum*, 1686, in quarto. Another, in 1725, *Hermansen de peccatis Brutorum;* this, however, is printed at Upsal. A third is *Schrœder de Simulacris virtutam in Brutis Animantibus*, 1691; and a fourth, *Schrœder de Brutorum Religione*, 1702. Then, it appears that one Drechsler wrote, in 1672, a *Dissertation on the Speech of Animals*, and Meyer and Martin, not to be outdone, followed this up a few years after, the one with a *Treatise on the Logic of Animals*, and another with one *De Animalium Syllogismo*.

A: Does the Spaniard give any curious particulars of dogs?

B: Not perhaps any that surpass what we have been stating from facts known among ourselves. But his account is diverting enough. 'The blindman's dog,' says he, 'will take him to the places where he may best hope to get his alms, and bring him thither through the crowd by the shortest way and the safest; nay, he will take him out of the city some miles to the great church of St Paul, as you go to Ostia. When in the town he cometh to a place where several ways meet, and with the sharpness of ear that the blind have, guided by some sound of a fountain, he gives the string a jerk by either hand, straightway will the poor dog turn and guide him to the very church where he knows his master would beg. In the street, too, knoweth he the charitable-disposed houses that be therein, and will lead thither the beggar-man, who, stopping at one, saith his pater-noster; then down lieth the dog till he hear the last word of the beadsman, when straight he riseth and away to another house. I have seen myself, to my great joy, mingled with admiration, when a piece of money was thrown down from some window, the dog would run and pick it up and fetch it to the master's hat; nor, when bread is flung down, will he touch it be he ever so hungry, but bring it to his master, and wait till he may have his share given him. A friend of mine was wont to come to my dwelling with a great mastiff, which he left by the door on entering; but he, seeing that his master had entered after drawing the string of the bell, would needs do likewise, and so made those within open the door, as though some one should have rung thereat.'

From *Dialogues on Instinct*

FLORENCE NIGHTINGALE

Reprieve

EVERY BOOK ABOUT the heroine of the Crimea contains, too, a tale of 'first aid to the wounded' when Florence [aged 16] administered to Cap, the shepherd's collie, whom she found with a broken leg on the downs near Embley. 'I wonder,' wrote her 'old pastor' to her in 1858, 'whether you remember how 20 years ago, you and I together averted the intended hanging of poor old Shepherd Smither's dog, Cap? How many times I have told the story since! I well recollect the pleasure with which the saving of a poor dog then gave to your young mind. I was delighted to witness it; it was to me not indeed an omen of what you were about to do and be (for of that I never dreamed), but it was an index of that kind and benevolent disposition, of that 1 Cor xiii Charity, which has been at the root of it.'

Sir Edward Cook, from his *Life of Florence Nightingale*

Dog Aid

A SMALL PET IS often an excellent companion for the sick, for long chronic cases especially ... an invalid in giving an account of his nursing by a nurse and a dog, infinitely preferred that of the dog. 'Above all,' he said, 'it did not talk.'

From *Notes on Nursing*

NIKOLAI GOGOL

Return to Sender

HER LITTLE DOG WASN'T quite quick enough to nip in after her and had to stay out in the street. I'd seen that dog before. She's called Medji. I hadn't been there more than a minute when I heard a faint little voice: 'Hello, Medji!' Well, I never! Who was that talking? I looked around and saw two ladies walking along under an umbrella: one was old, but her companion was quite young. They'd already gone past when I heard that voice again: 'Shame on you, Medji!' What was going on, for heaven's sake? Then I saw Medji sniffing round a little dog following the two ladies. 'Aha,' I said to myself, 'It can't be true, I must be drunk.' But I hardly ever drink. 'No Fidèle,' I told myself, 'you're quite mistaken.' With my own eyes I actually saw Medji mouth these words: 'I've been, bow wow, very ill, bow wow.' Ah, you nasty little dog!

I must confess I was staggered to hear it speak just like a human being. But afterwards, when I'd time to think about it, my amazement wore off. In fact, several similar cases have already been reported. It's said that in England a fish swam to the surface and said two words in such a strange language the professors have been racking their brains for three years now to discover what it was, so far without success. What's more, I read somewhere in the papers about two cows going into a shop to ask for a pound of tea. Honestly, I was much more startled when I heard Medji say: 'I *did* write to you, Fidèle. Polkan couldn't have delivered my letter.' I'd stake a month's salary that that was what the dog said. Never in my life have I heard of a dog that could write. Only noblemen know how to write correctly. Of course, you'll always find some traders or shopkeepers, even serfs, who can scribble away: but they write like machines – no commas or full stops, and simply no idea of style.

*   *   *

Today something suddenly dawned on me which made everything clear: I recalled the conversation I'd heard between the two dogs on Nevsky Avenue. I thought to myself 'Good, now I'll find out what it's all about. Somehow I must get hold of the letters that passed between those two filthy little dogs. There's sure to be something there.' To be frank, once I very nearly called Medji and said: 'Listen, Medji, we're alone now. If you want I'll shut the door so no one can see. Tell me everything you know about the young lady, who she is and what she's like. I swear I won't tell a soul.'

But that crafty dog put her tail between her legs, seemed to shrink to half her size, and went quietly out through the door, as though she had heard nothing. I'd suspected for a long time that dogs are cleverer than human beings. I was even convinced she could speak if she wanted to, but didn't, merely out of sheer cussedness. Dogs are extraordinarily shrewd, and notice everything, every step you take.

From *Diary of a Madman*

R. S. SURTEES

A Startled Dog

'I THOUGHT YOU TOLD me you were going to get me a hare,' observed Mrs Jog; adding, 'I'm sure shooting is a much more rational amusement than tearing your clothes going after the hounds,' eyeing the much-dilapidated moleskins as she spoke.

Mrs Jog found shooting more useful than hunting.

'Oh, if a (puff) hare comes in my (gasp) way, I'll turn her over,' replied Jog, carelessly, as if turning them over was quite a matter of course with him; adding, 'but I'm not (wheezing) out for the express purpose of shooting one.'

'Ah, well,' observed Sponge, 'I'll go with you, all the same.'

'But I've only got one gun,' gasped Jog, thinking it would be worse to have Sponge laughing at his shooting than even leaving him at home.

'Then, we'll shoot turn and turn about,' replied the pertinacious guest.

Jog did his best to dissuade him, observing that the birds were (puff) scarce and (wheeze) wild, and the (gasp) hares much troubled with poachers; but Mr Sponge wanted a walk, and moreover had a fancy for seeing Jog handle his gun.

Having cut himself some extremely substantial sandwiches, and filled his 'monkey' full of sherry, our friend Jog slipped out the back way to loosen old Ponto, who acted the triple part of pointer, house-dog, and horse to Gustavus James. He was a great fat, black-and-white brute, with a head like a hat-box, a tail like a clothes'-peg, and a back as broad as a well-fed sheep's. The old brute was so frantic at the sight of his master in his green coat, and wide-awake to match, that he jumped and bounced, and barked, and rattled his chain, and set up such yells, that his noise sounded all over the house, and soon brought Mr Sponge to the scene of action, where stood our friend, loading his gun and looking as consequential as possible.

'I shall only just take a (puff) stroll over moy (wheeze) ter-ri-to-ry,' observed Jog, as Mr Sponge emerged at the back door.

Jog's pace was about two miles and a half an hour, stoppages included, and he thought it advisable to prepare Mr Sponge for the trial. He then shouldered his gun and waddled away, first over the stile into Farmers Stiffland's stubble, round which Ponto ranged in the most riotous, independent way, regardless of Jog's whistles and rates, and the crack of his little knotty whip. Jog then crossed the old pasture into Mr Lowland's turnips, into which Ponto dashed in the same energetic way, but these impediments to travelling soon told on his great buttermilk carcass, and brought him to a more subdued pace; still, the dog had a good deal more energy than his master. Round he went, sniffing and hunting, then dashing right through the middle of the field, as if he was out on his own account alone, and had nothing whatever to do with a master.

'Why, your dog'll spring all the birds out of shot,' observed Mr Sponge; and, just as he spoke, *whirr!* rose a covey of partridges, eleven in number, quite at an impossible distance, but Jog blazed away all the same.

'Ord rot it, man! if you'd only held your (something) tongue,' growled Jog, as he shaded the sun from his eyes to mark them down, 'I'd have (wheezed) half of them over.'

'Nonsense, man!' replied Mr Sponge. 'They were a mile out of shot.'

'I think I should know my (puff) gun better than (wheeze) you,' replied Jog, bringing it down to load.

* * *

They now got through a well-established cattle-gap into a very rushy, squashy, gorse-grown pasture, at the bottom of the rising ground on which Mr Sponge had marked the birds. Ponto, whose energetic exertions had been gradually relaxing, until he had settled down to a leisurely hunting-dog, suddenly stood transfixed, with the right foot up, and his gaze settled on a rushy tuft.

'*P-o-o-n-to!*' ejaculated Jog, expecting every minute to see him dash at it. '*P-o-o-n-to!*' repeated he, raising his hand.

Mr Sponge stood on the tip-toe of expectation; Jog raised his wide-awake hat from his eyes, and advanced cautiously with the engine of destruction cocked. Up started a great hare; *bang!* went the gun with the hare none the worse. *Bang!* went the other barrel, which the hare acknowledged by two or three stotting bounds and an increase of pace.

'*Well missed!*' exclaimed Mr Sponge.

Away went Ponto in pursuit.

'*P-o-o-n-to!*' shrieked Jog, stamping with rage.

'I could have wiped your nose,' exclaimed Mr Sponge, covering the hare with a hedge-stake placed to his shoulder like a gun.

'Could you?' growled Jog; ''spose you wipe your own,' added he not understanding the meaning of the term.

Meanwhile, old Ponto went rolling away most energetically, the farther he went the farther he was left behind, till the hare having scuttled out of sight, he wheeled about and came leisurely back, as if he was doing all right.

Jog was very wrath, and vented his anger on the dog, which, he declared, had caused him to miss, vowing, as he rammed away at the charge, that he never missed such a shot before. Mr Sponge stood eyeing him with a look of incredulity, thinking that a man who could miss such a shot could miss anything. They were now all ready for a fresh start, and Ponto, having pocketed his objurgation, dashed forward again up the rising ground over which the covey had dropped.

Jog's thick wind was a serious impediment to the expeditious mounting of the hill, and the dog seemed aware of his infirmity, and to take pleasure in aggravating him.

'*P-o-o-n-to!*' gasped Jog, as he slipped, and scrambled, and toiled, sorely impeded by the incumbrance of his gun.

But P-o-o-n-to heeded him not. He knew his master couldn't catch him, and if he did, that he durstn't flog him.

'*P-o-o-n-to!*' gasped Jog again, still louder, catching at a bush to prevent his slipping back. '*T-o-o-h-o-o! P-o-o-n-to!*' wheezed he; but the dog just rolled his great stern, and bustled about more actively than ever.

'Hang ye! but I'd cut you in two if I had you!' exclaimed Mr Sponge, eyeing his independent proceedings.

'He's not a bad (puff) dog,' observed Jog, mopping the perspiration from his brow.

'He's not a good 'un,' retorted Mr Sponge.

'D'ye think not (wheeze)?' asked Jog.

'*Sure* of it,' replied Sponge.

'Serves me,' growled Jog, labouring up the hill.

'Easy served,' replied Mr Sponge, whistling, and eyeing the independent animal.

'*T-o-o-h-o-o! P-o-o-n-to!*' gasped Jog, as he dashed forward on reaching level ground more eagerly then ever.

'*P-o-o-n-to! T-o-o-h-o-o!*' repeated he, in a still louder tone, with the same success.

'You'd better get up to him,' observed Mr Sponge, 'or he'll spring all the birds.'

Jog, however, blundered on at his own pace, growling –

'Most (puff) haste, least (wheeze) speed.'

The dog was now fast drawing upon where the birds lit; and Mr Sponge and Jog having reached the top of the hill, Mr Sponge stood still to watch the result.

Up whirred four birds out of a patch of gorse behind the dog, all presenting most beautiful shots. Jog blazed a barrel at them without touching a feather, and the report of the gun immediately raised three brace more, into the thick of which he fired with similar success. They all skimmed away unhurt.

'Well missed!' exclaimed Mr Sponge again. 'You're what they call a good shooter but a bad hitter.'

'You're what they call a (wheeze) fellow,' growled Jog.

He meant to say 'saucy' but the word wouldn't rise. He then commenced re-loading his gun, and lecturing P-o-o-n-to, who still continued his exertions, and inwardly anathematising Mr Sponge. He wished he had left him at home. Then recollecting Mrs Jog, he thought perhaps he was as well where he was. Still his presence made him shoot worse than usual, and there was no occasion for that.

'Let *me* have a shot now,' said Mr Sponge.

'Shot (puff) – shot (wheeze); well, take a shot if you choose,' replied he.

Just as Mr Sponge got the gun, up rose the eleventh bird, and he knocked it over.

'*That's* the way to do it!' exclaimed Mr Sponge, as the bird fell dead before Ponto.

The excited dog, unused to such descents, snatched it up and ran off. Just as he was getting out of shot, Mr Sponge fired the other barrel at him, causing him to drop the bird and run yelping and howling away. Jog was furious. He stamped, and gasped, and fumed, and wheezed, and seemed like to burst with anger and indignation. Though the dog ran away as hard as he could lick, Jog insisted that he was mortally wounded, and would die. 'He never saw so (wheeze) a thing done. He wouldn't have taken twenty pounds for the dog. No, he wouldn't have taken thirty. Forty wouldn't have bought him. He was worth fifty of anybody's money,' and so he went on, fuming and advancing his value as he spoke.

Mr Sponge stole away to where the dog had dropped the bird; and Mr Jog, availing himself of his absence, retraced his steps down the hill, and struck off home at a much faster pace than he came. Arrived there, he found the dog in the kitchen, somewhat sore from the visitation of the shot, but not sufficiently injured to prevent his enjoying a most liberal plate of stick-jaw pudding, supplied by a general contribution of the servants. Jog's wrath was then turned in another direction, and he blew up for the waste and extravagance of the act, hinting pretty freely that he knew who it was that had set them against it. Altogether he was full of troubles, vexations, and annoyances; and after spending another most disagreeable evening with our friend Sponge, went to bed more determined than ever to get rid of him.

From *Mr Sponge's Sporting Tour*

Elizabeth Barrett Browning

Flush or Faunus

You see this dog. It was but yesterday
I mused forgetful of his presence here
Till thought on thought drew downward tear on tear,
When from the pillow where wet-cheeked I lay,
A head as hairy as Faunus thrust its way
Right sudden against my face, – two golden-clear
Great eyes astonished mine, – a drooping ear
Did flap me on either cheek to dry the spray!
I started first as some Arcadian
Amazed by goatly god in twilight grove,
But as the bearded vision closelier ran
My tears off, I knew Flush, and rose above
Surprise and sadness, – thanking the true Pan
Who, by low creatures, leads to heights of love.

Scenes in the Life

T HE FIRST MONTHS OF his life were passed at Three Mile Cross, a working man's cottage near Reading. Since the Mitfords had fallen on evil days – Kerenhappock was the only servant – the chair-covers were made by Miss Mitford herself and of the cheapest material; the most important article of furniture seems to have been a large table; the most important room a large greenhouse – it is unlikely that Flush was surrounded by any of those luxuries, rain-proof kennels, cement walks, a maid or boy attached to his person, that would now be accorded a dog of his rank. But he throve; he enjoyed with all the vivacity of his temperament most of the pleasures and some of the licences natural to his youth and sex. Miss Mitford, it is true, was much confined to the cottage. She had to read aloud to her father hour after hour; then to play cribbage; then, when at last he slumbered, to write and write and write at the table in the greenhouse in the attempt to pay their bills and settle their debts. But at last the longed-for moment would come. She thrust her papers aside, clapped a hat on her head, took her umbrella and set off for a walk across the fields with her dogs. Spaniels are by nature sympathetic; Flush, as his story proves, had an even excessive appreciation of human emotions. The sight of his dear mistress snuffing the fresh air at last, letting it ruffle her white hair and redden the natural freshness of her face, while the lines on her huge brow smoothed themselves out, excited him to gambols whose wildness was half sympathy with her own delight. As she strode through the long grass so he leapt hither and thither, parting its green curtain. The cool globes of dew or rain broke in showers of iridescent spray about his nose; the earth, here hard, here soft, here hot, here cold, stung, teased and tickled the soft pads of his feet. Then what a variety of smells interwoven in subtlest combination thrilled his nostrils; strong smells of earth, sweet smells of flowers; nameless smells of leaf and bramble; sour smells as they crossed the road; pungent smells as they entered bean-fields. But suddenly down the wind came tearing a smell sharper, stronger, more lacerating than any – a smell that ripped across his brain stirring a thousand instincts, releasing a million memories – the smell of hare, the smell of fox. Off he flashed like a fish drawn in a rush through water further and further. He forgot his mistress; he forgot all human kind. He heard dark men cry 'Span! Span!' He heard whips crack. He raced; he rushed. At last he stopped bewildered; the incantation faded;

very slowly, wagging his tail sheepishly, he trotted back across the fields
to where Miss Mitford stood shouting 'Flush! Flush! Flush!' and waving
her umbrella. And once at least the call was even more imperious: the
hunting horn roused deeper instincts, summoned wilder and stronger
emotions that transcended memory and obliterated grass, trees, hare,
rabbit, fox in one wild shout of ecstasy. Love blazed her torch in his
eyes; he heard the hunting horn of Venus. Before he was well out of his
puppyhood, Flush was a father.

Such conduct in a man even, in the year 1842, would have called for
some excuse from a biographer; in a woman no excuse could have
availed; her name must have been blotted in ignominy from the page.
But the moral code of dogs, whether better or worse, is certainly
different from ours, and there was nothing in Flush's conduct in this
respect that requires a veil now, or unfitted him for the society of the
purest and the chastest in the land then.

*   *   *

At Three Mile Cross Flush had mixed impartially with tap-room dogs
and the Squire's greyhounds; he had known no difference between the
tinker's dog and himself. Indeed it is probable that the mother of his
child though by courtesy called Spaniel, was nothing but a mongrel,
eared in one way, tailed in another. But the dogs of London, Flush
soon discovered, are strictly divided into different classes. Some are
chained dogs; some run wild. Some take their airings in carriages and
drink from purple jars; others are unkempt and uncollared and pick up
a living in the gutter. Dogs therefore, Flush began to suspect, differ;
some are high, others low; and his suspicions were confirmed by
snatches of talk held in passing with the dogs of Wimpole Street. 'See
that scallywag? A mere mongrel! . . . By gad, that's a fine Spaniel. One
of the best blood in Britain! . . . Pity his ears aren't a shade more curly
. . . There's a topknot for you!'

From such phrases, from the accent of praise or derision in which
they were spoken, at the pillar-box or outside the public-house where
the footmen were exchanging racing tips, Flush knew before the
summer had passed that there is no equality among dogs: some dogs
are high dogs; some are low. Which, then, was he? No sooner had
Flush got home than he examined himself carefully in the looking-
glass. Heaven be praised, he was a dog of birth and breeding! His head
was smooth; his eyes were prominent but not gozzled; his feet were
feathered; he was the equal of the best-bred cocker in Wimpole Street.

He noted with approval the purple jar from which he drank – such are the privileges of rank; he bent his head quietly to have the chain fixed to his collar – such are its penalties. When about this time Miss Barrett observed him staring in the glass, she was mistaken. He was a philosopher, she thought, meditating the difference between appearance and reality. On the contrary, he was an aristocrat considering his points.

But the fine summer days were soon over; the autumn winds began to blow; and Miss Barrett settled down to a life of complete seclusion in her bedroom. Flush's life was also changed. His outdoor education was supplemented by that of the bedroom, and this, to a dog of Flush's temperament, was the most drastic that could have been invented. His only airings, and these were brief and perfunctory, were taken in the company of Wilson, Miss Barrett's maid. For the rest of the day he kept his station on the sofa at Miss Barrett's feet. All his natural instincts were thwarted and contradicted. When the autumn winds had blown last year in Berkshire he had run in wild scampering across the stubble; now at the sound of the ivy tapping on the pane Miss Barrett asked Wilson to see to the fastenings of the window. When the leaves of the scarlet runners and nasturtiums in the window-box yellowed and fell she drew her Indian shawl more closely round her. When the October rain lashed the window Wilson lit the fire and heaped up the coals. Autumn deepened into winter and the first fogs jaundiced the air. Wilson and Flush could scarcely grope their way to the pillar-box or to the chemist. When they came back, nothing could be seen in the room but the pale busts glimmering wanly on the tops of the wardrobes; the peasants and the castle had vanished on the blind; blank yellow filled the pane. Flush felt that he and Miss Barrett lived alone together in a cushioned and firelit cave.

* * *

In Whitechapel, or in a triangular space of ground at the bottom of the Tottenham Court Road, poverty and vice and misery had bred and seethed and propagated their kind for centuries without interference. A dense mass of aged buildings in St Giles's was 'wellnigh a penal settlement, a pauper metropolis in itself'. Aptly enough, where the poor conglomerated thus, the settlement was called a Rookery. For there human beings swarmed on top of each other as rooks swarm and blacken tree-tops. Only the buildings here were not trees; they were hardly any longer buildings. They were cells of brick intersected by lanes which ran with filth. All day the lanes buzzed with half-dressed human beings; at night there poured back again into the stream the thieves, beggars and prostitutes who had been plying their trade all day in the West End. The police could do nothing. No single wayfarer could do anything except hurry through as fast as he could and perhaps drop a hint, as Mr Beames did, with many quotations, evasions and euphemisms, that all was not quite as it should be. Cholera would come, and perhaps the hint that cholera would give would not be quite so evasive.

But in the summer of 1846 that hint had not yet been given; and the only safe course for those who lived in Wimpole Street and its neighbourhood was to keep strictly within the respectable area and to lead your dog on a chain. If one forgot, as Miss Barrett forgot, one paid the penalty, as Miss Barrett was now to pay it. The terms upon which Wimpole Street lived cheek by jowl with St Giles's were well known. St Giles's stole what St Giles's could; Wimpole Street paid what Wimpole Street must. Thus Arabel at once 'began to comfort me by showing how certain it was that I should recover him for ten pounds at most'. Ten pounds, it was reckoned, was about the price that Mr Taylor would ask for a cocker spaniel. Mr Taylor was the head of the gang. As soon as a lady in Wimpole Street lost her dog she went to Mr Taylor; he named his price, and it was paid; or if not, a brown paper parcel was delivered in Wimpole Street a few days later containing the head and paws of the dog. Such, at least, had been the experience of a lady in the neighbourhood who had tried to make terms with Mr Taylor. But Miss Barrett of course intended to pay. Therefore when she got home she told her brother Henry, and Henry went to see Mr Taylor that afternoon. He found him 'smoking a cigar in a room with pictures' – Mr Taylor was said to make an income of two or three thousand a year out of the dogs of Wimpole Street – and Mr Taylor promised that he would confer with his 'Society' and that the dog would be returned next day. Vexatious as it was, and especially annoying at a moment when Miss Barrett needed all her money, such were the inevitable consequences of forgetting in 1846 to keep one's dog on a chain.

But for Flush things were very different. Flush, Miss Barrett reflected, 'doesn't know that we can recover him'; Flush had never mastered the principles of human societies. 'All this night he will howl and lament, I know perfectly,' Miss Barrett wrote to Mr Browning on the afternoon of Tuesday, the 1st September. But while Miss Barrett wrote to Mr Browning, Flush was going through the most terrible experience of his life. He was bewildered in the extreme. One moment he was in Vere Street, among ribbons and laces; the next he was tumbled head over heels into a bag; jolted rapidly across streets, and at length was tumbled out – here. He found himself in complete darkness. He found himself in chillness and dampness. As his giddiness left him he made out a few shapes in a low dark room – broken chairs, a tumbled mattress. Then he was seized and tied tightly by the leg to some obstacle. Something sprawled on the floor – whether beast or human being, he could not tell. Great boots and draggled skirts kept stumbling in and out. Flies buzzed on scraps of old meat that were decaying on the floor. Children crawled out from dark corners and pinched his ears. He whined, and a heavy hand beat him over the head. He cowered down on the few inches of damp brick against the wall. Now he could see that the floor was crowded with animals of different kinds. Dogs tore and worried a festering bone that they had got between them. Their ribs stood out from their coats – they were half famished, dirty, diseased, uncombed, unbrushed; yet all of them, Flush could see, were dogs of the highest breeding, chained dogs, footmen's dogs, like himself.

He lay, not daring even to whimper, hour after hour. Thirst was his worst suffering; but one sip of the thick greenish water that stood in a pail near him disgusted him; he would rather die than drink another. Yet a majestic greyhound was drinking greedily. Whenever the door was kicked open he looked up. Miss Barrett – was it Miss Barrett? Had she come at last? But it was only a hairy ruffian, who kicked them all aside and stumbled to a broken chair upon which he flung himself. Then gradually the darkness thickened. He could scarcely make out what shapes those were on the floor, on the mattress, on the broken chairs. A stump of candle was stuck on the ledge over the fireplace. A flare burnt in the gutter outside. By its flickering, coarse light Flush could see terrible faces passing outside, leering at the window. Then in they came, until the small crowded room became so crowded that he had to shrink back and lie even closer against the wall. These horrible monsters – some were ragged, others were flaring with paint and feathers – squatted on the floor; hunched themselves over the table. They began to drink; they cursed and struck each other. Out tumbled, from the bags that were dropped on the floor, more dogs – lapdogs, setters, pointers, with their collars still on them; and a giant cockatoo that flustered and fluttered its way from corner to corner, shrieking 'Pretty Poll', 'Pretty Poll', with an accent that would have terrified its mistress, a widow in Maida Vale. Then the women's bags were opened, and out were tossed on to the table bracelets and rings and brooches such as Flush had seen Miss Barrett wear and Miss Henrietta. The demons pawed and clawed them; cursed and quarrelled over them. The dogs barked. The children shrieked, and the splendid cockatoo – such a bird as Flush had often seen pendant in a Wimpole Street window – shrieked 'Pretty Poll! Pretty Poll!' faster and faster until a slipper was thrown at it and it flapped its great yellow-stained dove-grey wings in frenzy. Then the candle toppled over and fell. The room was dark. It grew steadily hotter and hotter; the smell, the heat, were unbearable. Flush's nose burnt; his coat twitched. And still Miss Barrett did not come.

*   *   *

But soon Flush became aware of the more profound differences that distinguish Pisa – for it was in Pisa that they were now settled – from London. The dogs were different. In London he could scarcely trot round to the pillar-box without meeting some pug dog, retriever, bull-dog, mastiff, collie, Newfoundland, St Bernard, fox terrier or one of the seven famous families of the Spaniel tribe. To each he gave a different name, and to each a different rank. But here in Pisa, though dogs abounded, there were no ranks; all – could it be possible? – were mongrels. As far as he could see, they were dogs merely – grey dogs, yellow dogs, brindled dogs, spotted dogs; but it was impossible to detect a single spaniel, collie, retriever or mastiff among them. Had the Kennel Club, then, no jurisdiction in Italy? Was the Spaniel Club unknown? Was there no law which decreed death to the topknot, which cherished the curled ear, protected the feathered foot, and insisted absolutely that the brow must be domed but not pointed? Apparently not. Flush felt himself like a prince in exile. He was the sole aristocrat among a crowd of *canaille*. He was the only pure-bred cocker spaniel in the whole of Pisa.

For many years now Flush had been taught to consider himself an aristocrat. The law of the purple jar and of the chain had sunk deep into his soul. It is scarcely surprising that he was thrown off his balance. A Howard or a Cavendish set down among a swarm of natives in mud huts can hardly be blamed if now and again he remembers Chatsworth and muses regretfully over red carpets and galleries daubed with coronets as the sunset blazes down through painted windows. There was an element, it must be admitted, of the snob in Flush; Miss Mitford had detected it years ago; and the sentiment, subdued in London among equals and superiors, returned to him now that he felt himself unique. He became overbearing and impudent. 'Flush has grown an absolute monarch and barks one distracted when he wants a door opened,' Mrs Browning wrote. 'Robert', she continued, 'declares that the said Flush considers him, my husband, to be created for the especial purpose of doing him service, and really it looks rather like it.'

'Robert', 'my husband' – if Flush had changed, so had Miss Barrett. It was not merely that she called herself Mrs Browning now; that she flashed the gold ring on her hand in the sun; she was changed, as much as Flush was changed. Flush heard her say 'Robert', 'my husband', fifty times a day, and always with a ring of pride that made his hackles rise and his heart jump. But it was not her language only that had changed. She was a different person altogether. Now, for instance, instead of sipping a thimbleful of port and complaining of the headache, she tossed off a tumbler of Chianti and slept the sounder. There was a flowering branch of oranges on the dinner-table instead of one denuded, sour, yellow fruit. Then instead of driving in a barouche landau to Regent's Park she pulled on her thick boots and scrambled over rocks. Instead of sitting in a carriage and rumbling along Oxford Street, they rattled off in a ramshackle fly to the borders of a lake and looked at mountains; and when she was tired she did not hail another cab; she sat on a stone and watched the lizards. She delighted in the sun; she delighted in the cold. She threw pine logs from the Duke's forest on to the fire if it froze. They sat together in the crackling blaze and snuffed up the sharp, aromatic scent. She was never tired of praising Italy at the expense of England. '. . . our poor English', she exclaimed, 'want educating into gladness. They want refining not in the fire but in the sunshine.' Here in Italy was freedom and life and the joy that the sun breeds. One never saw men fighting, or heard them swearing; one never saw the Italians drunk; – 'the faces of those men' in Shoreditch came again before her eyes. She was always comparing Pisa with London and saying how much she preferred Pisa. In the streets of Pisa pretty women could walk alone; great ladies first emptied their own slops and then went to Court 'in a blaze of undeniable glory'. Pisa with all its bells, its mongrels, its camels, its pine woods, was infinitely preferable to Wimpole Street and its mahogany doors and its shoulders of mutton. So Mrs Browning every day, as she tossed off her Chianti and broke another orange from the branch, praised Italy and lamented poor, dull, damp, sunless, joyless, expensive, conventional England.

Virginia Woolf, from *Flush*

THE CARLYLES

The Emperor of Chelsea

TELLING THIS YOUNG man of the loss of her cat, she had said, idly, that she thought a dog would be better company – a little, well-behaved dog, she added, remembering her mother's little dog Shandy, who had been so much loved. To her surprise, Dilberoglue took her seriously: a small dog, he wrote, would shortly arrive at Cheyne Row. A little taken aback, she set about preparing the way.

'My dear,' she told Carylyle, 'it's borne in upon my mind that I am to have a dog!' She made a joke of it, but she was nervous of the dog's reception.

One evening a small fluffy black and white object was delivered at the front door by a railway guard.

'He is about the size of Shandy,' wrote Jane, 'but has long white silky hair hanging all about him – and over his eyes which are very large and black.' For the first few days Jane was on tenterhooks. 'I was afraid Mr Carlyle would have found him a plague and ordered him about his business – and so he would if the dog had been noisy – but he is as good as dumb – *never* barks unless I make him do it in play – and then when Mr C. comes in in bad humour the little beast never troubles its head but dances round him on its hind legs – till he comes *to* and feels quite grateful for his confidence in his good will. So he gives it raisins, of which it is very fond, one by one, and blows tobacco smoke in its face which it does not like so well – and calls it "you little villain" in a tone of great kindness.'

Jane was immensely relieved. Her delight in owning Nero had to be shared with all her friends.

'Oh, Lord! I forgot to tell you I have got a little dog,' she told Forster, 'and Mr C. has accepted it with an amiability! To be sure, when he comes down gloomy in the morning, or comes in wearied from his walk, the infatuated little beast dances round him on its hind legs as I ought to do and can't; and he feels flattered and surprised by such unwonted capers to his honour and glory.'

And to her sympathetic friend Mary Russell she confided:

'*The* pleasantest fact of my life for a good while is, that I have got a beautiful little dog.' She hopes that she will not make a fool of herself with the creature, and repeats firmly that 'he is not of course, either so pretty or so clever as Shandy'. But 'I like him better,' she admits, 'than I should choose to show publicly.'

Nero's conquest of Carlyle pleased her: 'Not only has Mr C. no temptation to "kick his foot thro' it", but seems getting quite fond of it and looks flattered when it musters the hardihood to leap on *his* knee.'

'My fear now,' she continues, 'is not that Mr C. will put it away, but that I shall become the envy of surrounding dog-stealers! . . . Well! I can but get a chain to fasten it to my arm, and keep a sharp look out.'

One morning, only a week or two after his arrival, Nero disappeared.

'Yesterday, O heavens! I made my first experience of the strange, suddenly-struck-solitary, altogether ruined feeling of having lost one's dog,' wrote Jane. She had missed him, she said, just opposite the Wine Cooper's in Justice Walk, and the Cooper's apprentices, whom she employed from time to time on odd jobs, rushed off in search of the little dog. A man was caught, leading Nero by his collar: 'He said he had *found* the dog who was *losing* himself, and was bringing him after me!! and I would surely "give him a trifle for his *trouble*!" And I was coward enough to give him two pence,' she admitted, 'to rid Nero and myself of his dangerous proximity.'

This was only the first of several alarms. The following February, Nero was stolen 'for a whole day', wrote Jane; 'but escaped back to me on its own four legs. Mr C. asked while it was a-missing: "What will you be inclined to give the dog-stealers, for bringing it back to you?" (dog-stealing being a regular trade here); and I answered passionately with a flood of tears "my whole half-year's allowance!"'

These calamities served to strengthen the bond between Jane and Nero. 'I have a little dog that I make more fuss about than beseems a sensible woman,' she told her sister-in-law. 'He walks with me, this creature, and sleeps with me and sits with me, so I am no longer alone any more than you are with your bairns. . . .'

Nero slept at the foot of her bed, and never disturbed her, she said, till she was ready to get up. 'It follows me like my shadow, and lies in my lap; and at meals, when animals are apt to be so troublesome, it makes no sort of demonstration beyond standing on its hind legs!'

When Nero arrived at Cheyne Row the black cat imported to get rid of the mice was already installed. It accepted Nero as a friend, and the two animals became allies. 'Directly on the dining-room door opening', wrote Carlyle, Nero and the cat 'used to come waltzing in . . . in the height of joy, like Harlequin and Columbine, as I once heard remarked and did not forget.' From then, the little cat became known as Columbine.

Carlyle, staying at The Grange with the Ashburtons in January 1850, received the following missive:

'Dear Master, – I take the liberty to write to you myself (my mistress being out of the way of writing to you she says) that you may know Columbine and I are quite well, and play about as usual. There was no dinner yesterday to speak of; I had for my share only a piece of biscuit that might have been round the world; and if Columbine got anything at all, I didn't see it. I made a grab at one or two of the "small beings" on my mistress's plate; she called them "heralds of the morn"; but my mistress said, "Don't you wish you may get it?" and boxed my ears. I wasn't taken to walk on account of its being wet. And nobody came, but a man for "burial rate"; and my mistress gave him a rowing because she wasn't going to be buried here at all. Columbine and I don't mind where we are buried.'

The letter was continued later in the day:

'Dear Master, – My mistress brought my chain, and said "come along with me, while it shined and I could finish after". But she kept me so long in the London Library and other places, that I had to miss the post. An old gentleman in the omnibus took such notice of me! He looked at me a long time, and then turned to my mistress and said "Sharp, isn't he?" and my mistress was so good as to say "Oh yes!" And the old gentleman said again, "I knew it; easy to see that!" And he put his hand in his hind-pocket, and took out a whole biscuit, a sweet one, and gave it me in bits. I was quite sorry to part from him, he was such a good judge of dogs.'

The letter breaks off again, to be finished next morning.

'I left off last night, dear master, to be washed. This morning I have seen a note from you, which says you will come to-morrow. Columbine and I are extremely happy to hear it; for then there will be some dinner to come and go on. Being to see you so soon, no more at present from your

Obedient little dog
Nero.'

Nero had not been at Cheyne Row two months, but already he was one of the family. Part Maltese terrier and part mongrel, he was, as the old gentleman noticed, 'sharp'; and 'in spite of Carlyle's disbelief,' said Jane, he was 'capable of a profound sentiment of affection'. He was very lively, and enjoyed long night walks with his master.

'Nero ran with me through the Brompton solitudes last night, merry as a maltman', wrote Carlyle; and on a long country walk, 'I took the little dog with me, which amused me by its happy gambollings.'

'The dog Nero,' he told his brother, 'goes out with (Jane) in the forenoon, out with *me* towards midnight (often about eleven) . . . and is the happiest of little dogs, poor wretch!' When Jane was unwell, Carlyle took him out in the mornings: 'The poor little *tatty* wretch, coursing after sparrows which he never catches – eager as a Californian *Digger*, and probably about as successful, often makes me reflect, and rather entertains me, in the Kensington field-lanes.'

But walks with Nero were not always so pleasantly philosophical.

'He lost me yesternight, the intolerable messin that he is. I was hurrying home from a long walk, full of reflections not pleasant. At the bottom of Cadogan Place eleven o'clock struck: time to hurry home for porridge. But the vermin was wanting; no whistle would bring him. I had to go back as far as Wilton Crescent. There the miserable quadruped appeared, and I nearly bullied the life out of him.'

But his master's wrath left Nero unmoved. 'He licked my milk-dish at home,' said Carlyle, 'with the same relish.' 'On the whole,' he continues angrily, 'he is a real nuisance and absurdity in this house.'

'Ach! we could have better spared a better dog,' cried Jane after another of these episodes: Carlyle returning from the walk and shouting 'Is that vermin come back?' 'Having received my horrified "No!"' said Jane, 'he hurried off again, and for twenty minutes I was in the agonies of one's dog lost, my heart beating up into my ears. At last I heard Mr C's feet in he street; and, oh joy! heard him gollaring at something, and one knew what the little bad something was . . .'

* * *

Nero's welcomes after a parting always warmed Jane's heart and she was unashamedly disappointed when her reception was not enthusiastic.

'Nero was awoke out of a sound sleep by my rap', she wrote on coming home from Addiscombe; 'and came to the door yawning and stretching himself, and did not give even one bark; just looked, as much as to say, "Oh, you are there again, are you? well, I was doing quite nicely with Ann". So there was not even "a dog glad at my home-coming!"'

In the summer of 1857 she went to Scotland, leaving Nero at Cheyne Row with his master. Her letters contain messages to him – 'a kiss to Nero'; 'Be kind to Nero'; and when she announced the time of her return, 'Tell Nero'. But when he arrived, 'I am shocked', she wrote, 'to have to confess that Nero was far from showing the enthusiasm "England expected" of him! He knew me quite well, but took me very coolly indeed. Ann said he had just been sleeping. Let us hope he was in a state of indigestion, in which dogs are not capable of being more amiable than their owners.'

In a household where indigestion was synonymous with bad temper it was natural that Nero's 'interior' should be thought to influence his state of mind. Jane watched over his health with as much care as if he were a child. Just as she raged at Carlyle for eating crystallized greengages at Lady Ashburton's she inveighed against 'everyone stuffing (Nero) with dainties, out of kindness'.

'When I say I am well, it means also Nero is well; he is part and parcel of myself', she wrote. He was her constant companion – 'the chief comfort of my life – night and day he never leaves me, and it is something, I can tell you, to have such a bit of live cheerfulness always beside one'.

She flattered herself that Nero returned her affection.

'Going down into the kitchen the morning after my return from Sherborne, I spoke to the white cat, in common politeness, and even stroked her', she wrote to Carlyle in 1852; 'whereupon the jealousy of Nero rose to a pitch. He snapped and barked at me, then flew at the cat quite savage. I "felt it my duty" to box his ears. He stood a moment as if taking his resolution; then rushed up the kitchen stairs; and, as it afterward appeared, out of the house! For, in ten minutes or so, a woman came to the front door with master Nero in her arms; and said she had met him running up Cook's grounds, and was afraid he "would go and lose himself!" He would take no notice of *me* for several hours after!' 'And yet,' she added, 'he had never read "George-Sand Novels", that dog, or any sort of Novels!'

To Jane this display of jealousy was entrancing; often she was to write of Nero as if he were human.

'The clock struck twelve', she wrote to Carlyle, 'and Nero, with his usual good sense, insisted on my going to bed; he had gone half an hour before by himself, and established himself under the bedclothes; but he returned at twelve and jumped till I rose and followed him.'

'I could stand the creature's loss now less than ever', she wrote in 1852, after Nero had disappeared while his mistress was in the nursery-man's buying plants. 'After looking all about for him, I hurried back home and when the door was opened he bounded into my arms. Ann said "he got a lady to knock at the door for him!" 'The half hour's fright', she added, 'had given me what Ann called "quite a turn".'

Her feelings for Nero made her sympathetic to other dog-lovers. 'By the way, how is Mary's blessed Tearem?' she asked Helen Welsh. 'Her attachment to that I must say not very lovely dog was quite beautiful, so superior to both abuse and ridicule.' But she could not bear to see a dog spoiled. Though it pleased her to invest Nero with human characteristics, he was treated as a dog; his diet was scraps and biscuit. She was shocked, when lunching at a restaurant called Grange's, to see a dog seated on a chair at the next table, devouring plateful after plateful of cakes. 'His companion, who was treating him, finally snatched up a large pound-cake, cut it into junks, and handed him one after another on the point of a knife, till that also had gone *ad plura*.'

'By the way,' she continued, 'it must have been a curious sight for the starved beggars, who hang about the doors of such places, to see a dog make away with as much cake in five minutes as would have kept them in bread for a week, or weeks!' 'I should like to know the name of the "gentleman as belonged to that dog",' she said. 'Should one find him some other day maintaining in Parliament that "all goes well", it would throw some light on the worth of his opinion to know that his dog may have as much pound-cake at Grange's as it likes to eat!'

Dogs are said to reflect the characteristics of their owners, and something of Jane may perhaps have found its way into Nero, who was an original and intrepid character. Carlyle might lose his temper, declare 'that vermin' to be 'a real nuisance and absurdity in this house'; but there was something disarming about the little beast whch always made him relent.

Nero seemed to bear a charmed life. 'He has had another escape, that dog!' wrote Jane in March 1850. She had been in bed with a cold, and Nero, missing his morning walk, was at a loose end. 'Imagine', wrote his fond mistress, 'Imagine his taking it into his head that he could *fly* – like the birds – if he tried! and actually trying it – out at the Library window! For a first attempt his success was not so bad; for he fairly cleared the area spikes – and tho' he *did* plash down on the pavement at the feet of an astonished Boy he broke no bones, was only quite *stunned*. He gave us a horrid fright however.' It was after breakfast, and he had been standing in the open window, watching the birds – one of his chief delights – while Elizabeth was 'dusting out' for Mr C. 'Lying in my bed', wrote Jane, 'I heard thro' the deal partition Elizabeth scream; "Oh God ! oh Nero!" and rush downstairs like a strong wind out at the street door. I sat up in bed aghast – waiting with a feeling as of the Heavens falling till I heard her reascending the stairs and then I sprang to meet her in my night shift. She was white as a sheet, ready to faint – could just say; "Oh *take* him!" the dog's *body* lay on her arm! "Is he killed?" I asked with terrible self-possession. "Not quite – I think, all *but*!'

'Mr C. came down from his bedroom with his chin all over soap and asked "has anything happened to Nero?" "Oh Sir he *must* have broken *all* his legs, he leapt out at *your* window!" "God bless me!" said Mr C. and returned to his shaving. I sat down on the floor and laid my insensible dog over my knees, but could see no *breakage* – only a stun. So I took him to bed with me – *under* the clothes – and in an hour's time he was as brisk and active as ever.'

Some nine years later she had to face a worse disaster. The maid, Charlotte, had taken Nero out shopping. Charlotte was devoted to Jane's dog, who had kept her company the summer before when the Carlyles were at Bay House. She was young and lively, and played with Nero whenever Jane was ill; and if she ran to the shops Nero ran with her. On this fateful evening Jane opened the door to find Charlotte in floods of tears with Nero in her arms, "all crumpled together like a crushed spider, and his poor little eyes protruding and fixedly staring in his head!' He had been run over. 'A butcher's cart, driving furiously round a sharp corner', had passed over his throat. He was not dead; but when Jane placed him gently on the floor he toppled over 'quite stiff and unconscious'. Once again she mastered her feelings – 'Charlotte was so distressed,' she said, 'and really could not have helped it.'

'I put him in a warm bath,' she said, 'and afterwards wrapped him warmly and laid him on a pillow, and left him, without much hope of finding him alive in the morning. But in the morning he still breathed, though incapable of any movement; but he swallowed some warm milk I put into his mouth. About midday I was saying aloud "Poor dog! poor little Nero!" when I saw the bit tail trying to wag itself! and after that, I had good hopes.'

Nero recovered, 'but it was ten days before he was able to raise a bark, his first attempt was like the scream of an infant'. His recovery seemed miraculous – 'a revelation,' said Jane, 'of the strength of the throat of a dog.'

But the recovery was not complete: Nero was never the same. He grew languid and asthmatic. 'I have made him a little red cloak', Jane wrote later that autumn, 'and he keeps the house with me.' The Carlyles spent Christmas at The Grange, and Jane returned 'with sickening apprehension'. For the first time in eleven years there was no welcoming bark. 'Was he really dead then? No! strange to say, he was actually a little better and had run up the kitchen stairs to welcome me as usual; but there he had been arrested by a paroxysm of coughing, and the more he tried to show his joy the more he could not do it.'

This pathetic picture is the last: Nero had not much longer to live. 'Mr C.,' said Jane, 'keeps insisting on "a little prussic acid" for him!' She could not bear the thought; and even Carlyle had his moments of sentiment. 'Poor little fellow!' Jane heard him saying in the garden, 'I declare I am heartily sorry for you! If I could make you young again, upon my soul I would!'

In the end, Jane gave way: on 1 February 1860, she called on her doctor, Mr Barnes, and asked him with tears streaming down her face, to come and put an end to Nero's sufferings.

'My dear good Mr Barnes,' she wrote next day, 'I cannot put into words how much I feel your kindness. It was such a kind thing to do! and so kindly done! My gratitude to you will be as long as my life, for shall I not, as long as I live, remember that poor little Dog?

'Oh don't think me absurd – *you* – for caring so much about a dog! Nobody but myself can have any idea what that little creature has been in my life! My inseparable Companion during eleven years, ever doing *his* little best to keep me from feeling sad and lonely! Docile, affection-ate, loyal up to his last hour, when weak and full of pain he *offered to go with me*, seeing my bonnet on; and came panting to welcome me on my return! and the reward I gave him – the only reward I *could* or *ought* to give him – to such a pass had things come – was, ten minutes after, to give him up to be poisoned!

'I thought it not unlikely you would call today – because your coming today would be of a piece with the rest of your goodness to me. Nevertheless I went out for a lonely drive. I couldn't bear myself in the house, where everything I looked at reminded me of yesterday. And I wouldn't be at home for visitors, to criticise my swollen eyes and smile at grief "about a dog!" and besides, suppose *you* came, I wished to *not* treat you to more tears, of which you had had too much – and today I couldn't for my life have seen you without crying dreadfully.'

The death of Nero shook the whole household. 'Mr C.,' said Jane, 'couldn't have reproached me (for wasting so much feeling on a dog), for he himself was in tears at the poor little thing's end! and his own heart was (as he phrased it) "unexpectedly and distractedly torn to pieces with it!" As for Charlotte, she went about for three days after with her face all swollen and red with weeping. But on the fourth day,' Jane was obliged to add, 'she got back her good looks and gay spirits; and much sooner, Mr C. had got to speak of "poor Nero" composedly enough.'

For Jane, the grief was not so quickly overcome. She spoke of 'a constantly recurring blank'; she even speculated about Nero's immortality. 'What is become of that little, beautiful, graceful *Life*, so full of love and loyalty and sense of duty, up to the last minute that it animated the body of that little dog?' And she was grateful to her aunt Grace Welsh, who 'actually gave me a reference to certain verses in *Romans* which *seemed* to warrant my belief in the immortality of animal life as well as human.' 'One thing is sure, however,' she concluded, 'my little dog is buried at the top of our garden; and I grieve for him as if he had been my little human child.'

Thea Holme, from *The Carlyles at Home*

LORD MACAULAY

To No Avail

AFTER LUNCH I went to walk alone in the pleasure ground, but was pestered by a most sociable cur who would not be got rid of. I went into a plantation, railed off with gates at each end, and shut the brute out; but he perfectly understood my tactics, – curse his intelligence! – and waited for me at the other gate. After vainly trying to escape him in this way, I shut him in, and stayed outside myself. When I walked away, he saw that he had been out-generalled by human reason, and set up the most ludicrous howl that I ever heard in my life.

From his *Journal*: 31 January 1857

I FIND THAT I must have a dog, or rather a bitch, a little, sharp, yelping terrier, to deter those whom my old master Preston used, in his evening prayer, to describe as 'the Sons of Violence and Plunder'.

To Thomas Flower Ellis, 29 March 1856

CHARLOTTE WILLIAMS-WYNN

A Literary Companion

MY DOG HAS BEEN made nearly as much of as his mistress [in Berlin]; and when they found that whenever he goes out with Miles, he trots into every bookseller's shop, expecting to find me, the astonishment was great. It is funny. One has heard of dogs going into each tavern, in hopes of their master being there; but I should not have thought Moey had seen me go in much.

To Mrs Milnes Gaskell, September 1852

THE OTHER DAY, WE went into an enormous crowd to see the blessing of the animals [in Rome]. All the horses and mules were brought up, our horses as well, and Moey duly received a benediction. Some dogs are regularly blessed every year here; but I do not hear they are much the better for it.

November 1853

FEODOR DOSTOEVSKY

Sharik

WHEN I RETURNED to the prison, weary and worn out, in the evening, when the after-dinner work was finished, a terrible anguish again took possession of me. 'How many thousands of days like this one still lie before me,' I thought, 'and all alike, all exactly alike!' Silent and alone, I wandered in the already gathering twilight behind the barracks, along the outer palisade, and suddenly saw our Sharik bounding straight towards me. We had a prison dog, Sharik, just as they have company, battery, or squadron dogs. He had been in the prison from time immemorial and lived on scraps from the kitchen. He was a fairly big dog, black with white markings, a mongrel, not very old, with wise eyes and a bushy tail. Nobody ever made a fuss of him, nobody ever paid the slightest attention to him. From my very first day I had stroked him and given him bread from my hand. When I stroked him he stood quietly, looking lovingly at me and gently wagging his tail in token of pleasure. Now, when he had not seen me for some time – me, the first for years who had ever thought of petting him – he would run and look for me among the others, and this time, having found me behind the barracks, he yelped and ran to meet me. I don't know what came over me, but I flung my arms round his head and kissed him; he jumped up with his front paws on my shoulders and began to lick my face. 'So this is the friend fate sends me!' thought I, and after this, every time I returned from work during that first heavy and grievous period, before I went anywhere else I hurried first of all behind the barracks, with Sharik bounding along before me with yelps of joy, put my arms round his head and kissed him again and again, and my heart ached with a feeling that was at once somehow sweet and agonizingly bitter. And I remember that I even took pleasure, as though I were boasting to myself of my own misery, in thinking that here was the only creature now remaining in the whole world who loved me and was attached to me, my sole friend – my faithful dog Sharik.

*   *   *

As I have already said, our regular prison dog was Sharik, a wise and good-natured animal with whom I was always the best of friends. But since dogs in general are regarded by all peasants as unclean animals to whom no attention ought to be paid, hardly anybody among us took any notice of Sharik. The dog simply existed, slept in the yard, lived on scraps from the kitchen, and aroused no particular interest in anybody, but he knew everybody and regarded everybody in the prison as his master. When the prisoners were returning from work, as soon as the cry of 'Corporals!' sounded from the guardroom, he ran to the gates, affectionately welcomed every party, wagged his tail, and looked invitingly into the face of everybody who came in, in the hope of some sort of caress. But for many years all his efforts did not bring him a single pat from anybody except me. Because of this, he loved me best of all. I don't remember how it happened that another dog, Belka, afterwards turned up in the prison. The third, though, Kultyapka, I brought in myself, carrying him back with me from work when he was a puppy. Belka was a strange creature. Somebody had run over him in a cart, and his back was bent downwards, so that when he ran it used to look from a distance as though two animals joined into one were running. Besides this, he was all mangy, with suppurating eyes; his tail was almost denuded of hair and always carried between his legs. Thus abused by fate, he had plainly made up his mind to submit. He never barked or growled at anybody, as though he did not dare. He lived for the most part behind the barracks, on scraps; if ever he saw one of us he would immediately, while we were still some paces distant, turn over on his back in token of submission, as if to say, 'Do what you please with me; you can see I will not even think of offering resistance.' And every prisoner before whom he squirmed on his back would aim a blow at him with his boot, as though considering it his bounden duty. 'Look at that miserable cur!' the convicts used to say. But Belka dared not even howl, and if he felt the pain too much to be silent, would only utter a pitiful stifled yelp. In just the same way he would squirm before Sharik or any other dog whenever he ran out of the prison on his own affairs. He used to turn over on his back and lie there submissively whenever a big lop-eared mongrel rushed at him, barking wildly. But dogs like other dogs to be humble and submissive. The savage cur would be appeased at once, and would stand in a thoughtful kind of way over the humble animal lying there with his legs in the air and slowly and with immense curiosity begin to sniff him all over. What did the wriggling Belka think of during this time? 'Well, what now? Is this ruffian going to tear me to pieces?'; this was probably what came into his mind. But, after sniffing him carefully all over, the other dog, finding nothing particularly remarkable, would give it up. Belka would jump up at once and again, limping, attach himself to the end of a long string of dogs escorting some pampered bitch. And though he knew for certain that he would never be allowed to be on an intimate footing with the bitch, nevertheless to hobble along with them, although only at a distance – even that was some comfort to him in his misery. He had plainly long ago ceased to worry about honour. Having lost all chance of a career in the future, he lived only for food and was fully aware of it. Once I tried to stroke him; this was something so new and unexpected that he suddenly squatted close to the ground, began to tremble all over, and whined loudly with emotion. Out of pity I stroked him many times. After that he could not see me without whining. He would see me from a distance and give a plaintive and pitiable whine. The end came when he was torn to pieces by other dogs on the rampart outside the prison.

Kultyapka was of a quite different character. Why I carried him to the prison from the workshop, when he was still a blind puppy, I do not know. I enjoyed feeding and rearing him. Sharik at once took Kultyapka under his wing and slept with him. When Kultyapka grew a little bigger he allowed him to bite his ears and pull his hair, and played with him in the way full-grown dogs usually do play with puppies. It was strange, but Kultyapka grew hardly at all in height, but only in length and breadth. He had curly hair, of a mousy light-brown colour; one of his ears hung down and the other was pricked. He had an excitable and high-spirited disposition, like every puppy, who is usually so glad to see his master that he squeals, yelps, and clambers up to lick his face, and is ready to parade all his other feelings on the spot: 'Only let my enthusiasm be seen; decorum doesn't matter!' Wherever I might be, as soon as I shouted 'Kultyapka!' he would appear suddenly round some corner, as if he had shot out of a trapdoor, and rush towards me, squealing rapturously, bounding along like a little ball and tumbling head over heels as he came. I was terribly fond of this little monster. It looked as though fate had nothing in store for him but a life of contentment and happiness. But one fine day the prisoner Neustroev, whose occupation was tanning skins and making women's shoes, began to take particular notice of Kultyapka. Some idea had struck him. He called Kultyapka to him, felt his coat, and rolled him gently over on his back. Kultyapka, quite unsuspicious, squealed with pleasure. But next morning he had disappeared. I looked for him for a long time, but there was no sign of him anywhere; it was not until two months later that it was all explained: Neustroev had taken a great fancy to Kultyapka's coat. He had skinned him, tanned the skin, and used it to line a pair of velvet winter bootees, which the judge's wife had ordered from him. He even showed me the boots when they were finished. The lining was wonderful. Poor Kultyapka!

Many of our prisoners tanned skins, and they often used to bring in with them dogs with good coats, who immediately disappeared. Some had been stolen, some were even bought. I remember seeing two prisoners once behind the kitchen. They were laying their heads together and seemed very busy about something. One of them held on a rope a magnificent large black dog, evidently of an expensive breed. Some good-for-nothing manservant had stolen it from his master and sold it to our shoemakers for thirty copecks in silver. The convicts were preparing to hang it. This was a very convenient procedure: they stripped off the skin and flung the body into a big, deep cess-pit which was situated in the remotest corner of the prison yard, and which stank horribly in the heat of summer. It was rarely cleaned out. The poor animal seemed to understand the fate in store for it. It looked searchingly and uneasily from one to another of us three, and occasionally ventured on a slight wave of the bushy tail hanging between its legs, as if trying to soften our hearts by this sign of its trust in us. I moved away as quickly as I could and they, of course, brought their business to a successful conclusion.

From *Memoirs From the House of the Dead*

W. M. THACKERAY

Marrowbones and Cleavers

WAS THERE EVER SUCH confounded ill-luck? My whole life has been a tissue of ill-luck: although I have laboured perhaps harder than any man to make a fortune, something always tumbled it down. In love and in war I was not like others. In my marriages, I had an eye to the main chance; and you see how some unlucky blow would come and throw them over. In the army I was just as prudent, and just as unfortunate. What with judicious betting, and horse-swapping, good luck at billiards, and economy, I do believe I put up my pay ever year, – and that is what few can say who have but an allowance of a hundred a year.

I'll tell you how it was. I used to be very kind to the young men: I chose their horses for them, and their wine; and showed them how to play billiards, or écarté, of long mornings, when there was nothing better to do. I didn't cheat: I'd rather die than cheat; – but if fellows *will* play, I wasn't the man to say no – why should I? There was one young chap in our regiment off whom I really think I cleared three hundred a year.

His name was Dobble. He was a tailor's son, and wanted to be a gentleman. A poor weak young creature; easy to be made tipsy; easy to be cheated; and easy to be frightened. It was a blessing for him that I found him; for if anybody else had, they would have plucked him of every shilling.

Ensign Dobble and I were sworn friends. I rode his horses for him, and chose his champagne, and did everything, in fact, that a superior mind does for an inferior, – when the inferior has got the money. We were inseparables, – hunting everywhere in couples. We even managed to fall in love with two sisters, as young soldiers will do, you know; for the dogs fall in love with every change of quarters.

Well, once, in the year 1793 (it was just when the French had chopped poor Louis's head off), Dobble and I, gay young chaps as ever wore sword by side, had cast our eyes upon two young ladies by the name of Brisket, daughters of a butcher in the town where we were quartered. The dear girls fell in love with us, of course. And many a pleasant walk in the country, many a treat to a tea-garden, many a smart riband and brooch used Dobble and I (for his father allowed him six hundred pounds, and our purses were in common) to present to these young ladies. One day, fancy our pleasure at receiving a note couched thus:-

'DEER CAPTING STUBBS AND DOBBLE – Miss Briskets presents their compliments, and as it is probble that our papa will be till twelve at the corprayshun dinner, we request the pleasure of their company to tea.'

Didn't we go! Punctually at six we were in the little back-parlour; we quaffed more Bohea, and made more love than half-a-dozen ordinary men could. At nine, a little punch-bowl succeeded to the little teapot; and, bless the girls! a nice fresh steak was frizzling on the gridiron for our supper. Butchers were butchers then, and their parlour was their kitchen too; at least old Brisket's was – one door leading into the shop, and one into the yard, on the other side of which was the slaughter-house.

Fancy, then, our horror when, just at this critical time, we heard the shop-door open, a heavy staggering step on the flags, and a loud husky voice from the shop, shouting, 'Hallo, Susan; hallo, Betsy! show a light!' Dobble turned as white as a sheet; the two girls each as red as a lobster; I alone preserved my presence of mind. 'The back-door,' says I. – 'The dog's in the court,' say they. 'He's not so bad as the man,' said I. 'Stop!' cries Susan, flinging open the door and rushing to the fire. 'Take *this*, and perhaps it will quiet him.'

What do you think 'this' was? I'm blest if it was not the *steak*!

She pushed us out, patted and hushed the dog, and was in again in a minute. The moon was shining on the court, and on the slaughter-house, where there hung the white ghastly-looking carcasses of a couple of sheep; a great gutter ran down the court – a gutter of *blood*! The dog was devouring his beef-steak (*our* beef-steak) in silence; and we could see through the little window the girls bustling about to pack up the supper-things, and presently the shop-door being opened, old Brisket entering, staggering, angry, and drunk. What's more, we could see, perched on a high stool, and nodding politely, as if to salute old Brisket, the *feather of Dobble's cocked hat*! When Dobble saw it, he turned white, and deadly sick; and the poor fellow, in an agony of fright, sank shivering down upon one of the butcher's cutting-blocks, which was in the yard.

We saw old Brisket look steadily (as steadily as he could) at the confounded, impudent, pert, waggling feather; and then an idea began to dawn upon his mind, that there was a head to the hat; and then he slowly rose up – he was a man of six feet, and fifteen stone – he rose up, put on his apron and sleeves, and *took down his cleaver*.

'Betsy,' says he, 'open the yard door.' But the poor girls screamed, and flung on their knees, and begged, and wept, and did their very best to prevent him. 'OPEN THE YARD DOOR!' says he, with a thundering loud voice; and the great bulldog, hearing it, started up and uttered a yell which sent me flying to the other end of the court. – Dobble couldn't move; he was sitting on the block, blubbering like a baby.

The door opened, and out Mr Brisket came.

'*To him, Jowler!*' says he. '*Keep him, Jowler!*' – and the horrid dog flew at me, and I flew back into the corner, and drew my sword, determining to sell my life dearly.

'That's it,' says Brisket. 'Keep him there, – good dog, – good dog! And now, sir,' says he, turning round to Dobble, 'is this your hat?'

'Yes,' says Dobble, fit to choke with fright.

'Well, then,' says Brisket, 'it's my – (hic) – my painful duty to – (hic) – to tell you, that as I've got your hat, I must have your head; – it's painful, but it must be done. You'd better – (hic) – settle yourself com – comfumarably against that – (hic) – that block, and I'll chop it off before you can say Jack – (hic) – no, I mean Jack Robinson.'

Dobble went down on his knees and shrieked out, 'I'm an only son, Mr Brisket! I'll marry her, sir; I will, upon my honour, sir. – Consider my mother, sir; consider my mother.'

'That's it, sir,' says Brisket – 'that's a good – (hic) – a good boy; –

just put your head down quietly – and I'll have it off – yes, off – as if you were Louis the Six – the Sixtix – the Siktickleteenth. – I'll chop the other *chap afterwards*.'

When I heard this, I made a sudden bound back, and gave such a cry as any man might who was in such a way. The ferocious Jowler, thinking I was going to escape, flew at my throat; screaming furious; I flung out my arms in a kind of desperation, – and, to my wonder, down fell the dog, dead, and run through the body!

At this moment a posse of people rushed in upon old Brisket, – one of his daughters had had the sense to summon them, – and Dobble's head was saved. And when they saw the dog lying dead at my feet, my ghastly look, my bloody sword, they gave me no small credit for my bravery. 'A terrible fellow that Stubbs,' said they; and so the mess said, the next day.

I didn't tell them that the dog had committed *suicide* – why should I? and I didn't say a word about Dobble's cowardice. I said he was a brave fellow, and fought like a tiger; and this prevented *him* from telling tales. I had the dogskin made into a pair of pistol-holsters, and looked so fierce, and got such a name for courage in our regiment, that when we had to meet the regulars, Bob Stubbs was always the man put forward to support the honour of the corps. The women, you know, adore courage; and such was my reputation at this time, that I might have had my pick out of half-a-dozen, with three, four, or five thousand pounds apiece, who were dying for love of me and my red coat. But I wasn't such a fool. I had been twice on the point of marriage, and twice disappointed; and I vowed by all the Saints to have a wife, and a rich one. Depend upon this, as an infallible maxim to guide you through life: *It's as easy to get a rich wife as a poor one*; – the same bait that will hook a trout will hook a salmon.

From *The Fatal Boots*

GUSTAVE FLAUBERT

Dogs

1 *The Dog Romantic.* This was a large Newfoundland, the property of Elisa Schlesinger. If we believe Du Camp, he was called Nero; if we believe Goncourt, he was called Thabor. Gustave met Mme Schlesinger at Trouville: he was fourteen and a half, she twenty-six. She was beautiful, her husband was rich; she wore an immense straw hat, and her well-modelled shoulders could be glimpsed through her muslin dress. Nero, or Thabor, went everywhere with her. Gustave often followed at a discreet distance. Once, on the dunes, she opened her dress and suckled her baby. He was lost, helpless, tortured, fallen. Ever afterwards he would maintain that the brief summer of 1836 had cauterised his heart. (We are at liberty, of course, to disbelieve him. What did the Goncourts say? 'Though perfectly frank by nature, he is never wholly sincere in what he says he feels and suffers and loves.') And whom did he first tell of this passion? His schoolfriends? His mother? Mme Schlesinger herself? No: he told Nero (or Thabor). He would take the Newfoundland for walks across the Trouville sands, and in the soft secrecy of a dune he would drop down on his knees and wrap his arms around the dog. Then he would kiss it where he knew its mistress's lips had been not long before (the location of the kiss remains a matter of debate: some say on the muzzle, some say on the top of the head); he would whisper in the shaggy ear of Nero (or Thabor) the secrets he longed to whisper in the ear that lay between the muslin dress and the straw hat; and he would burst into tears.

The memory of Mme Schlesinger, and her presence too, pursued Flaubert for the rest of his life. What happened to the dog is not recorded.

2 *The Dog Practical.* Not sufficient study, to my mind, has been made of the pets which were kept at Croisset. They flicker into brief existence, sometimes with a name attached, sometimes not; we rarely know when or how they were acquired, and when or how they died. Let us assemble them:

In 1840 Gustave's sister Caroline had a goat called Souvit.
In 1840 the family had a black Newfoundlnd bitch called Néo (perhaps this

name influenced Du Camp's memory of Mme Schlesinger's
Newfoundland).

In 1853 Gustave dines alone at Croisset with an unnamed dog.

In 1854 Gustave dines with a dog named Dakno; probably the same animal
as above.

In 1856–7 his niece Caroline has a pet rabbit.

In 1856 he exhibits on his lawn a stuffed crocodile he has brought back
from the East: enabling it to bask in the sun again for the first time in
3,000 years.

In 1858 a wild rabbit takes up residence in the garden; Gustave forbids its
slaughter.

In 1866 Gustave dines alone with a bowl of goldfish.

In 1867 the pet dog (no name, no breed) is killed by poison which has been
laid down for rats.

In 1872 Gustave acquires Julio, a greyhound.

Note: If we are to complete the list of known domestic creatures to which
Gustave played host, we must record that in October 1842 he suffered
an infestation of crab-lice.

Of the pets listed above, the only one about which we have proper
information is Julio. In April 1872 Mme Flaubert died; Gustave was
left alone in the big house, having meals at a large table 'tête-à-tête
with myself'. In September his friend Edmond Laporte offered him a
greyhound. Flaubert hesitated, being frightened of rabies; but eventually
accepted it. He named the dog Julio (in honour of Juliet Herbert? – if
you wish) and quickly grew fond of it. By the end of the month he was
writing to his niece that his sole distraction (thirty-six years after casting
his arms round Mme Schlesinger's Newfoundland) was to embrace his
'*pauvre chien*'. 'His calm and his beauty make one jealous.'

The greyhound became his final companion at Croisset. An unlikely
couple: the stout, sedentary novelist and the sleek racing dog. Julio's
own private life began to feature in Flaubert's correspondence: he
announced that the dog had become 'morganatically united' with 'a
young person' of the neighbourhood. Owner and pet even got ill
together: in the spring of 1879 Flaubert had rheumatism and a swollen
foot, while Julio had an unspecified canine disease. 'He is exactly like a
person,' Gustave wrote. 'He makes little gestures that are profoundly
human.' Both of them recovered, and staggered on through the year.
The winter of 1879–80 was exceptionally cold. Flaubert's housekeeper
made Julio a coat out of an old pair of trousers. They got through the
winter together. Flaubert died in the spring.

What happened to the dog is not recorded.

3 *The Dog Figurative.* Madame Bovary has a dog, given to her by a game-keeper whose chest infection has been cured by her husband. It is *une petite levrette d'Italie*: a small Italian greyhound bitch. Nabokov, who is exceedingly peremptory with all translators of Flaubert, renders this as whippet. Whether he is zoologically correct or not, he certainly loses the sex of the animal, which seems to me important. This dog is given a passing significance as ... less than a symbol, not exactly a metaphor; call it a figure. Emma acquires the greyhound while she and Charles are still living at Tostes: the time of early, inchoate stirrings of dissatisfaction within her; the time of boredom and discontent, but not yet of corruption. She takes her greyhound for walks, and the animal becomes, tactfully, briefly, for half a paragraph or so, something more than just a dog. 'At first her thoughts would wander aimlessly, like her greyhound, which ran in circles, yapping after yellow butterflies, chasing field-mice and nibbling at poppies on the edge of a cornfield. Then, gradually, her ideas would come together until, sitting on a stretch of grass and stabbing at it with the end of her parasol, she would repeat to herself, "Oh God, why did I get married?"'

That is the first appearance of the dog, a delicate insertion; afterwards, Emma holds its head and kisses it (as Gustave had done to Nero/Thabor): the dog has a melancholy expression, and she talks to it as if to someone in need of consolation. She is talking, in other words (and in both senses), to herself. The dog's second appearance is also its last. Charles and Emma move from Tostes to Yonville – a journey which marks Emma's shift from dreams and fantasies to reality and corruption. Note also the traveller who shares the coach with them: the ironically named Monsieur Lheureux, the fancy-goods dealer and part-time usurer who finally ensnares Emma (financial corruption marks her fall as much as sexual corruption). On the journey, Emma's greyhound escapes. They spend a good quarter of an hour whistling for it, and then give up. M. Lheureux plies Emma with a foretaste of false comfort: he tells her consoling stories of lost dogs which have returned to their masters despite great distances; why, there was even one that made it all the way back to Paris from Constantinople. Emma's reaction to these stories is not recorded.

What happened to the dog is also not recorded.

4 *The Dog Drowned and the Dog Fantastical.* In January 1851 Flaubert and Du Camp were in Greece. They visited Marathón, Eleusis and Salamís. They met General Morandi, a soldier of fortune who had

fought at Missolonghi, and who indignantly denied to them the calumy put about by the British aristocracy that Byron had deteriorated morally while in Greece: 'He was magnificent,' the General told them. 'He looked like Achilles.' Du Camp records how they visited Thermopylae and re-read their Plutarch on the battlefield. On January 12th they were heading towards Eleuthera – the two friends, a dragoman, and an armed policeman they employed as a guard – when the weather worsened. Rain fell heavily; the plain they were crossing became inundated; the policeman's Scotch terrier was suddenly carried away and drowned in a swollen torrent. The rain turned to snow, and darkness closed in. Clouds shut out the stars; their solitude was complete.

An hour passed, then another; snow gathered thickly in the folds of their clothes; they missed their road. The policeman fired some pistol shots in the air, but there was no answer. Saturated, and very cold, they faced the prospect of a night in the saddle amid inhospitable terrain. The policeman was grieving for his Scotch terrier, while the dragoman – a fellow with big, prominent eyes like a lobster's – had proved singularly incompetent throughout the trip; even his cooking had been a failure. They were riding cautiously, straining their eyes for a distant light, when the policeman shouted, 'Halt!' A dog was barking somewhere in the far distance. It was then that the dragoman displayed his sole talent: the ability to bark like a dog. He began to do so with a desperate vigour. When he stopped, they listened, and heard answering barks. The dragoman howled again. Slowly they advanced, stopping every so often to bark and be barked back at, then reorienting themselves. After half an hour of marching towards the ever-loudening village dog, they eventually found shelter for the night.

What happened to the dragoman is not recorded.

Note: Is it fair to add that Gustave's journal offers a different version of the story? He agrees about the weather; he agrees about the date; he agrees that the dragoman couldn't cook (a constant offering of lamb and hard-boiled eggs drove him to lunch on dry bread). Strangely, though, he doesn't mention reading Plutarch on the battlefield. The policeman's dog (breed unidentified in Flaubert's version) wasn't carried away by a torrent; it just drowned in deep water. As for the barking dragoman, Gustave merely records that when they heard the village dog in the distance, he ordered the policeman to fire his pistol in the air. The dog barked its reply; the policeman fired again; and by this more ordinary means they progressed towards shelter.

What happened to the truth is not recorded.

Julian Barnes, from *Flaubert's Parrot*

CHARLES ALLSTON COLLINS

Mazard

AND WHERE WAS Mr Pinchbold all this time? Mr Pinchbold had gone to pay a visit to Mazard.

And who or what was Mazard?

It happened that one evening, some time after their arrival at Paris, and about the period of the events narrated in the last chapter, our two friends were taking an after-dinner walk about the town, when, as they were passing down one of its smaller thoroughfares, they happened to notice a dog of the same kind as that which we have seen in the sketch of M. Morve, the veterinary surgeon of Malaise, though somewhat different in colour from that faithful ally of their medical acquaintance. The dog was standing on the extreme edge of the pavement with his back to the houses – the shop behind him being, it should be stated, a pastrycook's. Our friends were walking in the road and not on the pavement, in deference to an earnest request of Mr Pinchbold, for whom the midnight assassin lurked in every dark-looking doorway; so, as they were in the middle of the road, and the dog was standing with his face turned in that direction, he was rather a conspicuous object, and Mr Fudge, whose partiality for animals verged on insanity, instantly uttered the masonic signal, which consists, as everybody knows, of three words spoken in the minor key or falsetto.

'Good little dog!' said Mr Fudge.

The dog instantly responded to Mr Fudge's salutation, and signalized his appreciation of the attention paid to him by executing a kind of dance peculiar to dogs of the species to which he belonged – a dance almost entirely executed by the fore-legs, the hinder extremities remaining almost stationary.

'What a sociable beast!' said Mr Fudge.

He was a very odd dog to look at. His colour was in the main dirty white, but his two upright ears were of a tan or yellowish tint, and there were one or two spots of the same colour on other parts of his body. He was very fat, his fur was very thick and soft, his brush of a tail tightly curled up upon his back, and his eyes of the most eloquent description conceivable. There was a curious expression about his mouth, caused by the projection of one of his under teeth, which made him appear as if he was always smiling.

Mr Fudge having engaged in a brief conversation with this animal, having asked him how he was, whether he was not a very nice dog, and a few other questions, to all of which he received satisfactory replies, tore himself away from the society of this fascinating animal, and went on his way, accompanied by his companion. The dog seemed, however, singularly unwilling to part from his new friends. He jumped about them, followed them, barked about their heels, and then ran on in front of them and looked back with the strangest expression of interest conceivable. In fact, he followed them in this way to the end of the street, and stood there till they were out of sight, looking wistfully after them.

'What a very singular animal!' said Mr Fudge; 'one would say that he wanted something.'

'I trust he is not insane,' remarked Mr Pinchbold, gloomily.

It so happened that, on the evening of which we are now speaking, our two friends were, contrary to their usual custom, returning by the way by which they came. They had no sooner entered the by-street in which their interview with the sociable dog had taken place, than this strange animal burst out upon them again, and began dancing and barking round them precisely as before.

An old woman looked out of an upper window, and addressing the dog by the name of 'Mazard,' said something to him in a semi-reproachful tone. Neither Mr Fudge nor his friend heard what she said, though it seemed to both of them that the expression 'un sous' occurred more than once in the course of her address. 'Mazard,' which was evidently the dog's name, became less importunate in his attentions after the old lady's expostulation, but he still followed them at a little distance, and still looked wistfully after them till they disappeared.

'What a *very* singular dog!' said Mr Fudge, again.

'I begin to think that he is insane,' answered Mr Pinchbold.

The next day the mystery became still more complicated. Our travellers, passing down the street in which Mazard resided, found that remarkable animal in a violent state of excitement, caused apparently by the proceedings of an old gentleman in a military dress, who kept chinking a piece of money of some kind upon the pavement, alternately letting it go and then snatching it up again just when Mazard, who followed all his movements, was advancing his paw towards it. Two or three bystanders appeared to be enjoying the joke, whatever it was, in no way surprised, however, at the peculiar nature of the pastime in which Mazard and the old officer were engaged. The military gentleman presently restored the piece of money to his pocket, the bystanders walked off, and Mazard was left looking rather disconsolate in the middle of the road. He had now leisure to observe the presence of the two Englishmen, which he had no sooner done than he came capering up to them, and stood staring in their faces with the same inquiring expression which they had taken note of before.

'Do you know,' said Mr Fudge, looking steadily at his companion with the air of a man who is about to propound a theory which he does not expect to be believed – 'do you know that I actually believe that this dog is asking for a sous.'

'Nonsense,' said Mr Pinchbold; 'what could he do with a sous if he had it? The sons of men alone tear each other to pieces for these rascal counters. The sons of men – '

'Never mind about the sons of men,' said Mr Fudge, 'but mark the result of an experiment I am going to make. The old woman at the window last night said something about a sous. The old officer this evening was tantalizing the dog by alternately offering him one of those coins and withdrawing it just as Mazard was going to seize it. From all this I draw my own inferences.'

Mr Fudge now proceeded to put his hypothesis to a practical test. First of all he unbuttoned his coat. Mazard became intensely excited, and shifted his fore-legs from side to side. Mr Fudge put his hand into his left trousers pocket. Mazard began to jump backwards and forwards. Mr Fudge rattled half-a-dozen sous that were in his pocket. Mazard jumped more buoyantly than ever, uttering at intervals a short bark of delight. Mr Fudge looked at Mr Pinchbold in triumph, and Mr Pinchbold looked at Mr Fudge in consternation.

'You see there is no doubt about it,' said Mr Fudge, as he took a sous out of his pocket and extended it towards the dog. Mazard instantly took the coin into his mouth, and to all appearance swallowed it.

Directly that Mazard had got the sous, which he had been soliciting so eagerly, into his mouth, his whole appearance and conduct underwent a great change, and, from being violently and unreasonably excited, he instantly became the most perfectly calm, and even apathetic animal that ever was seen. He took no more notice of the two friends, and began moving about, snuffing and smelling hither and thither, just like other and less gifted dogs. So that our two Englishmen, after lingering and watching him some time, concluded that there was an end of the entertainment, and began to move off. It happened, however, that as they did so Mr Pinchbold looked back.

'Mazard is going back into the shop,' said he, arresting his companion. Mr Fudge looked round just in time to see this eccentric animal pushing violently at the shop door with his nose. He at last managed to get the door open, and entering immediately, was lost to sight. Our two friends immediately retracing their steps, and looking through the glass door of the shop, beheld the explanation of the mystery about which they had been so much troubled.

The extraordinary and gifted animal, as showmen say, whose proceedings we have thus minutely described, was now trotting up and down the interior of the shop, which the reader will remember was a pastry-cook's, and was endeavouring apparently to attract the attention of a young woman behind the counter engaged in serving a customer. The whole carriage and demeanour of the dog was sufficiently remarkable. His head was thrown back, his tail was in the air, and his movements were characterized by a peculiar kind of strut of great and conscious importance. At times, too, he would utter a peculiar crowing sound, such as one does not usually identify with the lungs of the canine species. It was some time before the woman behind the counter was able to pay any attention to the dog; but when her customer was at length disposed of, she came round at once to where the dog was, in the central part of the shop between the two counters.

'What, Mazard,' she said, 'hast thou got a sous?' and she stooped down and held her hand open under the dog's mouth. This seemed to be, however, only an established form understood by both parties. Messrs Fudge and Pinchbold, gazing into the shop with eager curiosity, saw the dog deliberately shake his head with an air that said plainly, 'No, no, I'm not going to give it up like that, and you know that as well as I do.' After which he recommenced his course up and down the shop, crowing away more vain-gloriously than ever. 'Very well,' said the young woman, 'delivery before payment is your rule, isn't it?' and she took a peculiar sort of sponge-cake, of which there were several upon a tray on the counter, holding it out towards the dog with her right hand, and placing as before her left hand under his mouth.

The dog instantly dropped Mr Fudge's sous into her palm, and snatching the cake out of her hand, trotted off in high glee into the back shop to enjoy it by himself.

Messrs Fudge and Pinchbold turned themselves about, and gazed mutely in each other's countenances in speechless astonishment. They remained thus for the space of two minutes, at the expiration of which time they faced about once more and rushed tumultuously, and by common consent, into the pastry-cook's shop.

'The history of that dog!' shrieked Mr Fudge, who was the first to enter.

'That dog and his history!' yelled Mr Pinchbold from the steps outside.

The woman behind the counter was obviously not unaccustomed to inquiries relating to her dog, but she seemed a little taken aback by the extremely energetic nature of the curiosity of the two Englishmen.

'Ah, Monsieur,' she said, 'Mazard is the apple of our eyes, and the astonishment of all who behold him. The talent of which you have just been a witness has only however recently been developed in him, and what is more extraordinary, the trick was a thing of his own discovery, and was not taught him, as far as we know, by a living soul.'

'And how did it originate, then?' inquired Mr Fudge.

'It originated thus,' answered the woman. 'One of our customers, a lady who lives close by, was making some purchases here, and in paying for what she had, she happened to drop a sous out of her change. When she stooped down to look for it, it was nowhere to be found. "It is singular, too," she said; "I am certain I dropped it, and yet I can nowhere see it." We all helped to look for it, and Mazard even, who was standing by, snuffed about as dogs will, as if he too were assisting in the search. "It is only a sous lost," said the lady; "so much the worse for the beggars."

'Well, sir, a little time after the lady was gone, our attention was attracted by the peculiar behaviour of Mazard, who was trotting up and down the shop in a state of great excitement, and uttering a peculiar kind of cry, such as a cat will make over a kitten, as you heard to-day.

'For some time we did not take much notice of him, but at last my mother, who happened to be in the shop, and who is very fond of the dog, went to him and began talking to him, "What is the matter, Mazard?" she said; "what ails thee, my dog?" and then she took one of those sponge cakes from the counter, it being her habit now and then, on rare occasions, to give one of them, when it had got quite stale and was no longer saleable, to her favourite.

'What was her astonishment, when Mazard instantly dropped a sous out of his mouth as if in payment for the cake, and then began romping and tearing round the shop as you have seen him to-day, as if in a state of ecstasy at his own cleverness.

'This, gentlemen, is all,' the woman said, in conclusion, 'positively all that we know about the matter. After that day, when the thing came to be talked about, our friends and customers would give the dog a sous to try him, and by and by it got known out of doors, and all sorts of people would give Mazard a five-centime piece to see what he would do with it. Always with the same result. He always goes through exactly the same performance that you have seen, and has never altered a bit since the first day when he showed his accomplishment.

'But oh, sir,' the woman said, interrupting herself in her admiration of her favourite, 'if you knew what that dog is as I do! If you knew his honesty. Why, we have left those cakes which he is so fond of about on the floor to try him, and he will not touch one of them. He will not accept a two-sous cake either, if we offer it to him in exchange for his sous; nor will he take one of those which he always buys as a gift, unless he has the money to pay for it. See,' she continued, 'Mazard – Mazard,' and she held out to him one of his favourite cakes.

The dog, who had been listening attentively to the recent conversation, and who appeared to have derived much gratification from the honourable mention of his name which had occurred in it, instantly obeyed his mistress's call, but declined to take the proffered cake. Of course, Mr Pinchbold gave him a sous on the spot, and of course he laid it out instantly in his chosen delicacy.

'And has he ever been known to go through this performance elsewhere?' inquired Mr Fudge.

'Never,' answered the woman; 'and I am persuaded' (she always spoke of the dog as if he was a customer) 'that he would rather starve than deal at any other shop than his own.'

Of course Mazard and his extraordinary performance were the subject of much conversation between Mr Fudge and his companion;

and of course there was much speculation as to how far the statement of his mistress was to be relied on.

'I see no reason,' said Mr Fudge, 'to doubt it; there seems to me nothing beyond canine intellect in the process of thought implied by what we have just seen. This dog passes his whole time in a certain place, where he sees, all day long, certain articles of food handed over to those who apply for them, whilst in every case he sees also that a certain circular piece of metal is given in exchange for those articles of food. Is it too much to suppose that the dog would learn at last to think that if he could become possessed of one of those pieces of metal, he would have a right to one of those cakes in which his inmost heart delighted?'

Mr Pinchbold shook his head, and intimated vaguely, that he was disposed to take a supernatural view of the whole affair. The fact is, that this worthy gentleman was ruminating in his own mind over a project which kept him silent throughout the whole evening which succeeded the visit of the two friends to the pastrycook's shop. The next morning he could contain it no longer.

'Fudge,' he said, smiting the breakfast table with his fist, 'I must have him.'

'Have who?' asked Mr Fudge.

'Mazard,' replied Mr Pinchbold, and with that he proceeded to develop to his astonished companion, all the advantages that would accrue to them from such an addition to the travelling party. 'Think,' he said, 'what a safeguard he would be in times of danger, and what an amusement in moments of ennui.'

From *A Cruise Upon Wheels*

ALEXANDRE DUMAS

Pritchard's Hospitality

I LEFT SAINT-GERMAIN, therefore, to go and live at the Porte-Marly, in the much-discussed house which was subsequently christened Monte Cristo by Madame Mélingue, and which later on made such a noise in the world.

Michel had long before this made all his arrangements for the accommodation of my animals. I am bound to say he paid far less attention to my comfort, or, for the matter of that, to his own.

I do not know what is the condition of Monte Cristo nowadays; but I do know that, in the time of my occupancy, there was neither wall nor ditch nor hedge nor enclosure of any sort about the place. Consequently men as well as animals could enter at their own sweet will, walk about where they pleased, pluck the flowers and gather the fruits, without any fear of being charged with trespass or burglary. As for the animals – and it is to the dogs I would specially refer, – Pritchard, who was naturally of a very hospitable disposition, did the honours of the house with an agreeable and disinterested freedom from formality quite Highland in its character.

This hospitality was practised by Pritchard in the most simple and antique fashion. He would squat well in the middle of the Marly road, go up to every dog that passed with that low growling that is half a threat and half a family greeting, and is the canine manner of saying 'How d'ye do?' – smell the new-comer in the orthodox way, and submit to the same ceremony himself.

Then, as soon as a proper understanding had been reached by dint of these little familiarities, conversation would begin on something like the following lines –

'Have you a good master?' the strange dog would ask.

'Oh, not bad,' Pritchard would say.

'And are you well fed at your place?'

'Why, we have pie twice a day, bones for breakfast and dinner, and all through the day anything we can prig from the kitchen.'

The strange dog would lick his chops at the mere thought.

'Plague on't!' he would say, 'you've nothing to complain of!'

'I'm not complaining,' Pritchard would declare.

Then, seeing the strange dog looking pensive –

'Would you like to dine with me?' Pritchard would invite him.

Dogs never have the silly habit men are prone to of waiting to be pressed.

The guest always accepted eagerly, and at dinner-time I was greatly surpised to see an animal I knew nothing about walk in under Pritchard's escort, sit down on my right, if Pritchard took the left, and paw my knee coaxingly in a fashion that told me plainly what flattering accounts he had received of my kindly and Christian disposition.

No doubt invited by his host to spend the evening with him, as he had spent the day, the dog stayed on, and presently, finding it was too late for him to get home, found a comfortable place for himself somewhere about the premises, and there slept off his heavy meal.

Next morning, when the time came to go, the dog would stroll once or twice in the direction of the outer gate, then, thinking better of it, would remark to Pritchard –

'Would it be making very bold if I stayed on in the house?'

To which Pritchard would reply –

'With a little care and ingenuity you can very easily make them think you are the dog from next-door. Then in a day or two nobody will think any more about you, and you will be one of the household, every bit the same as those lazy apes that do nothing whatever all day long, and that greedy vulture that does nothing but gobble guts, and that squalling macaw that shouts all the time without ever knowing what it's talking about.'

So the dog would stay where it was, hiding itself a bit the first day, wagging its tail at me the second, gambolling at my heels the third, and there would be an inmate the more of my establishment.

This sort of thing went on. Michel asked me one day –

'Does Monsieur know how many dogs we have on the premises?'

'No, Michel, I don't.'

'Sir, there are thirteen of them.'

'It is an unlucky number, Michel, and we must take care they don't all sit down to table together; there would infallibly be one that would die first.'

'But that's not the point, sir,' insisted Michel.

'Well, what is it, then?'

'Why, these fine chaps would eat up an ox a day, horns and all.'

'Do you really think they would eat the horns, Michel? I cannot believe it myself.'

'Oh! if Monsieur takes it like that, I've no more to say.'

'You are wrong, Michel; speak out, and I will take it exactly as you prefer.'

'Well, sir, if you give me a free hand, I'll just take a good whip and I'll turn the whole crew out of doors this very morning.'

'Come, Michel, let us be reasonable. All these dogs, after all, are paying a compliment to the house by staying here. Give them a grand dinner to-day and tell them it's a farewell feast; then at dessert you will put them all out at the door.'

'How does Monsieur think I am going to put them out at the door? There *is* no door.'

'Michel,' I replied gravely, 'we must put up with certain conditions of locality and social position and inherited disposition, such as we have unfortunately been endowed with by fate. The dogs are in the house, and, by the Lord! they must just stay there, I don't suppose, anyhow, it's the dogs will ever ruin me, Michel. Only, for their own welfare, see to it they are not thirteen for the future.'

'Well, sir, I'll drive one away, and make them a dozen.'

'No, Michel, let another one come in, so as to make fourteen.'

Michel heaved a sigh.

'If it were a pack, that would be something,' he muttered.

Well, it was a pack – and a very strange pack at that. There was a wolf-dog, a poodle, a water-spaniel, a mastiff, a basset-hound with twisty legs, a mongrel terrier, a mongrel King Charles, – there was even a Turkey dog with never a hair on his body except a tuft on the top of the head and a plume at tip of his tail.

Well, all this crew lived together on the very best of terms, and might have given an example of brotherly love to a philanstery or a community of Moravian brethren. True, at meal times there would be a snap now and then to right or left; there would be some love quarrels between rivals, in which, as always, the weaker would go to the wall; but the most touching harmony would be instantly restored the moment I appeared in the garden. Not an animal, no matter how lazily stretched in the sun, no matter how luxuriously curled up on the soft turf, no matter how amorously engaged in conversation with a canine mistress, but would break off his sleep or love-making to sidle up to me with affectionate eye and waving tail. All did their best to manifest their gratitude, each in his own way, – some by slipping familiarly between my legs, others by getting up on their hind paws and begging, others again by jumping over the stick I held for them, whether for the Czar of Russia or the Queen of Spain, but positively refusing to leap for the poor King of Prussia, the humblest and most hackneyed of all monarchs, not only at home but among the canine population of all Europe.

We recruited a little spaniel bitch named Lisette, and the number of our pack was duly raised to fourteen.

Well, these fourteen dogs, when all was said and done, cost me say fifty or sixty francs a month. A single dinner to five or six of my literary brethren would have demanded three times the sum, and then they would have left my house, saying, it may be, my wine was decent stuff, but there was no doubt my books were rubbish.

Among all the pack Pritchard had chosen out a comrade and Michel a favourite. This was a basset-hound with twisty legs, a short, thickset animal, that seemed to walk on his stomach, and at utmost speed might perhaps have covered a league in an hour and a half, but, as Michel was never tired of saying, the finest organ in all the department of the Seine-et-Oise.

It was quite true; Portugo – that was the basset's name – had one of the finest bass voices ever uttered by dog in pursuit of rabbit, hare, or roebuck. Sometimes at night, as I sat at work, these majestic tones would make themselves heard about the neighbourhood, and it was a sound to rejoice the heart of St Hubert in his grave. Now, what was Portugo after at this hour of the night, and why was he up and about when the rest of the pack were sleeping? The mystery was resolved one morning.

'Would Monsieur like,' Michel asked me, 'would Monsieur like to have a nice dish of stewed rabbit for his breakfast?'

'Very good,' I said; 'has Vatrin sent us some rabbits, then?'

'Oh, M. Vatrin! why it's over a year since I've set eyes on him.'

'Well, where did they come from, then?'

'Monsieur doesn't need to know where the rabbit came from, provided the stew is all right.'

'Take care, Michel, take care; you will get yourself caught one of these days.'

'Why, what *do* you mean, sir? I have not so much as touched my gun since the end of the shooting season.'

I could see that Michel had made up his mind to tell me nothing that time; but I knew him well enough to be quite sure he would open his lips one day or another.

'Why, yes, Michel,' I told him, answering his original question, 'I should be very glad to eat a good dish of stewed rabbit.'

'Does Monsieur prefer to cook it himself or to let Augustine see to it?'

'Let Augustine attend to it, Michel; I have work to do this morning.'

It was Michel waited at breakfast that morning instead of Paul; he wished to see how much I liked his stew.

The much-talked-of dish appeared in due course, and I finished it to the last scrap.

'So Monsieur liked it?' Michel asked, beaming with satisfaction.

'Excellent, excellent!'

'Well, Monsieur can have one like that every morning, if he so pleases.'

'What, Michel, every morning? It seems to me you are going ahead pretty fast, my friend.'

'I know what I'm talking about.'

'Well, Michel, we shall see. Stewed rabbit is very good; but there is a certain tale entitled *Eel-pie*, the moral of which is we must never abuse a good thing – not even stewed rabbit. Besides, before consuming such a lot of rabbits, I should like to know where they come from?'

'Sir, you shall know this very night, if you will condescend to come with me.'

'Did not I say you were a poacher, Michel?'

'Oh no, sir! I'm as innocent as a new-born babe. As I said before, if only Monsieur will come with me to-night . . .'

'Is is far, Michel?'

'Only a hundred yards from this spot, sir.'

'What time?'

'When Monsieur hears Portugo's first bark.'

'Well, so be it, Michel; if you see a light in my room when Portugo first gives cry, I am your man.'

I had almost forgotten I had pledged my word to Michel, and was working away as usual, when about eleven o'clock of a magnificent moonlight night Michel walked into my room.

'Well,' said I, 'I don't think Portugo has given voice, has he?'

'No,' he told me; 'but it struck me that, if Monsieur waited till then, he would miss the most curious part of all.'

'Why, what should I miss, Michel?'

'Monsieur would not see the Council of War.'

'Council of War! What Council of War?'

'The Council of War beween Pritchard and Portugo.'

'You are quite right; it must be a curious sight.'

'If Monsieur will come down now, he can see it.'

I followed Michel, and presently, as he had led me to expect, I saw in the midst of the encampment of the fourteen dogs, lying each as he found most comfortable, Portugo and Pritchard sitting up solemnly on their tails and apparently debating some question of the last importance.

This point decided, the pair separated. Portugo darted out of the gate, struck into the upper Marly road, which bounded the property on that side, and disappeared.

As for Pritchard, he showed every sign of having time to spare, and started off at a leisurely pace to follow the by-path that, after passing alongside the island in the river, mounted the hill behind the quarry.

We in turn set off after Pritchard, who appeared to pay no attention to us, though he had evidently scented our presence.

The dog climbed to the top of the quarry, which was planted with vines extending as far as the Marly road above. There he examined the ground with the utmost care, keeping to the line of the quarry, lighted on a scent, sniffed and found it fresh, advanced a few yards along a furrow formed by a double line of vine-sticks, crouched flat on his belly and waited.

Almost at the same moment Portugo's first bark could be heard five hundred yards away. The plan of campaign was now clear. At nightfall the rabbits always quitted the quarry and scattered to feed. Pritchard would then nose out the scent of one of them, while Portugo, making a wide detour, chased the rabbit. Now rabbits and hares invariably hark back on their own track, and Pritchard, enscreened treacherously in ambush, awaited the creature's return.

And so it was; the nearer Portugo's barks approached, the more brilliantly we saw Pritchard's yellow eyes gleam. Then suddenly, using all four paws as a sort of quadruple spring, he gave a leap, and we heard a little scream of surprise and distress from the victim.

'The trick's done!' exclaimed Michel and going up to Pritchard, he took a very fine rabbit out of his jaws, and finished it with a sharp blow on the back of the neck. He disembowelled it there and then, dividing the entrails beween the two dogs, who shared them amicably, feeling presumably only one regret, that Michel's interference, backed by my authority, robbed them of the whole to leave them only a part. As Michel said, I might, if I had so desired, have had every morning for breakfast a nice dish of stewed rabbit.

*   *   *

The day before that on which I was to return to Saint-Germain, I wrote to tell Michel, and found my factotum waiting for me at the bottom of the hill of Marly.

'Sir,' he shouted directly I was within hail, 'two great events have happened in the house.'

'What are they, Michel?'

'To begin with, Pritchard caught his hind paw in a *trarp*, and going mad with rage and pain, instead of staying caught as any other dog would have done, he gnawed off his foot with his teeth, sir, and came back home on three pins.'

'But the poor beast died, I suppose, after it all?'

'Died! why should he die, sir? Wasn't *I* there?'

'And how did you treat him, Michel?'

'I amputated the paw neatly at the joint, with a pruning-knife; I sewed up the skin over the place, and there's no sign of a wound. Look! the scoundrel, he's scented you and here he comes!'

Yes, there was Pritchard, dashing up on three legs, and at such a pace that, as Michel said, he really looked as if he had never lost the fourth.

The greetings between Pritchard and his master were very tender, as you may suppose, on both sides. I commiserated the poor fellow very much on his mutilation.

'Pooh, sir,' said Michel, 'it only means that out shooting he won't be so fond of pointing now.'

From *Histoire de mes Bêtes*
Trans. Alfred Allinson

Historical Researches into the Origins of the Peculiar Fashion of Greeting Among Dogs

'MONSIEUR,' SAID MICHEL to me when Flora and Pritchard had made mutual acquaintance in the usual canine fashion – that is to say, by a reciprocal exploration of each other's rear quarters – 'Monsieur, do you know why dogs greet one another in that way?'

Michel put the question to me in the tone of voice a man who counts on a negative answer in the hope of airing his knowledge.

'No, Michel,' I replied.

'Well, it's like this, Monsieur. Once upon a time the canine race came to the conclusion that they should do as we did in 1848, and make themselves into a republic. But the older dogs, when consulted, declared that before any change of government was brought about, the sanction of the supreme Ruler should be sought and obtained. The rest agreed. They resolved, therefore, to send a petition to Jupiter by messenger, and chose the swiftest greyhound they could find.

'The greyhound was summoned, and the purpose of the petition explained to him. Although highly flattered at being chosen as their representative, he observed that it was no mere stone's throw from there to the summit of Mount Olympus, and that it would take him at least three months to get there and back. It appears, Monsieur,' remarked Michel parenthetically, 'that Mount Olympus is in Greece.'

'Between Thessaly and Macedonia, in fact,' I replied.

'Well,' Michel went on, 'a learned dog was found to draft the petition, after which it was drawn up and signed by the committee of dogs and handed over to the greyhound.

'It was decided to send an escort with the greyhound so far on his journey, to give him moral support and good advice on how best to succeed in his capacity as ambassador.

'But after proceeding a few miles, they came to a river.'

'The Eurotas, Michel.'

'Yes, I believe it is, Monsieur – the Eurotas. I'd forgotten it. Well, it seems that for the greater part of the year the Eurotas is no deeper than the Arno I've heard you tell of.'

'It's even shallower, Michel. I've crossed it jumping from stone to stone.'

'Yes, but apparently there'd been a storm the previous night, just to make things awkward, and when the dogs got there they found the Eurotas as deep and wide as the Seine.'

'But surely it's not beyond a dog to swim the Seine?'

'Possibly not, Monsieur. But the petition – what about that?'

'That's true, Michel. I'd forgotten the all-important petition.'

'What would you have done with it in similar circumstances, Monsieur? Tell me that.'

'I haven't the least idea, Michel.'

'Well, the dogs weren't so hard up for ideas as you, Monsieur. They took the petition, folded it up small, rolled it like a cigarette and stuck it . . . you understand, Monsieur?'

'I take my hat off to your dogs, Michel. I should never have thought of that!'

'The greyhound, at ease about the safety of the petition, took to the water, swam across, waved a farewell paw to his comrades on the other bank, and disappeared . . .

'They never saw him again, Monsieur, with the result that ever since, whenever dogs meet, they look to see whether any of them has got Jupiter's reply.'

'Now I come to think about it, I believe I've heard the story, before Michel, but I'd forgotten it; and in any case, your narration of it gives it all the flavour of originality. But keep an eye on Pritchard. He's being rather too curious as to the possibility of Flora's having that reply.'

Pritchard, in fact, regardless of his infirmities, or perhaps telling himself that, like their human counterparts, the females of the canine race have their caprices, Pritchard with his three legs and one eye was playing the *galant*, and triumphantly waving the brush which served him for a tail.

From *Histoire de mes Bêtes*
Trans. A. Craig Bell

HARRIET BEECHER STOWE

Of Sheep, the Pope and Thomas Henry

'ROVER, YOU NAUGHTY dog! Don't you know you mustn't chase the sheep? You'll be killed some of these days.' Admonitions of this kind, well shaken and thumped in, at last seemed to reform him thoroughly. He grew so conscientious that, when a flock of sheep appeared on the side of the road, he would immediately go to the other side of the carriage, and turn away his head, rolling up his eyes meanwhile to us for praise at his extraordinary good conduct. 'Good dog, Rove! nice dog! good fellow! he doesn't touch the sheep, – no, he doesn't.' Such were the rewards of virtue which sweetened his self-denial; hearing which, he would plume up his feathery tail, and loll out his tongue, with an air of virtuous assurance quite edifying to behold.

Another of Rover's dangers was a habit he had of running races and cutting capers with the railroad engines as they passed near our dwelling. We lived in plain sight of the track, and three or four times a day the old, puffing, smoky iron horse thundered by, dragging his trains of cars, and making the very ground shake under him. Rover never could resist the temptation to run and bark, and race with so lively an antagonist; and, to say the truth, John and Willy were somewhat of his mind – so that, though they were directed to catch and hinder him, they entered so warmly into his own feelings that they never succeeded in breaking up the habit. Every day, when the distant whistle was heard, away would go Rover, out of the door or through the window – no matter which – race down to meet the cars, couch down on the track in front of them, barking with all his might, as if it were only a fellow-dog, and when they came so near that escape seemed utterly impossible, he would lie flat down between the rails and suffer the whole train to pass over him, and then jump up and bark, full of glee, in the rear. Sometimes he varied this performance more dangerously by jumping out full tilt between two middle cars when the train had passed half-way over him. Everybody predicted, of course, that he would be killed or maimed, and the loss of a paw, or of his fine saucy tail, was the least of the dreadful things which were prophesied about him. But Rover lived and throve in his imprudent courses notwithstanding.

The engineers and firemen, who began by throwing pieces of wood and bits of coal at him, at last were quite subdued by his successful impudence, and came to consider him as a regular institution of the railroad, and, if any family excursion took him off for a day, they would inquire with interest, 'Where's our dog? what's become of Rover?' As to the female part of our family, we had so often anticipated piteous scenes when poor Rover would be brought home with broken paws or without his pretty tail, that we quite used up our sensibilities, and concluded that some kind angel, such as is appointed to watch over little children's pets, must take special care of our Rover.

Rover had very tender domestic affections. His attachment to his little playfellows was most intense; and one time, when all of them were taken off together on a week's excursion, and Rover was left alone at home, his low spirits were really pitiful. He refused entirely to eat for the first day, and finally could only be coaxed to take nourishment, with many strokings and caresses, by being fed out of Miss Anna's own hand. What perfectly boisterous joy he showed when the children came back! – careering round and round, picking up chips and bits of sticks, and coming and offering them to one and another, in the fulness of his doggish heart, to show how much he wanted to give them something.

This mode of signifying his love by bringing something in his mouth was one of his most characteristic tricks. At one time he followed the carriage from Brunswick to Bath, and in the streets of the city somehow lost his way, so that he was gone all night. Many a little heart went to bed anxious and sorrowful for the loss of its shaggy playfellow that night, and Rover doubtless was remembered in many little prayers. What, therefore, was the joy of being awakened by a joyful barking under the window the next morning, when his little friends rushed in their night-gowns to behold Rover back again, fresh and frisky, bearing in his mouth a branch of a tree about six feet long, as his offering of joy.

When the family removed to Zion Hill, Rover went with them, the trusty and established family friend. Age had somewhat matured his early friskiness. Perhaps the grave neighbourhood of a theological seminary and the responsibility of being a professor's dog might have something to do with it, but Rover gained an established character as a dog of respectable habits, and used to march to the post-office at the heels of his master twice a day as regularly as any theological student.

*   *   *

One day we had been riding outside of the walls of the city, and just as we were returning home we saw coming towards us quite a number of splendid carriages with prancing black horses. It was the Pope and several of his cardinals coming out for an afternoon airing. The carriages stopped, and the Pope and cardinals all got out to take a little exercise on foot, and immediately all carriages that were in the way drew to one side, and those of the people in them who were Roman Catholics got out and knelt down to wait for the Pope's blessing as he went by. As for us, we were contented to wait sitting in the carriage.

On came the Pope, looking like a fat, mild, kind-hearted old gentleman, smiling and blessing the people as he went on, and the cardinals scuffing along in the dust behind him. He walked very near to our carriage, and Miss Florence, notwithstanding all our attempts to keep her decent, would give a smart little bow-wow right in his face just as he was passing. He smiled benignly, and put out his hand in sign of blessing toward our carriage, and Florence doubtless got what she had been asking for.

From Rome we travelled to Naples, and Miss Flo went with us through our various adventures there – up Mount Vesuvius, where she half choked herself with sulphurous smoke. There is a place near Naples called the Solfatara, which is thought to be the crater of the extinct volcano, where there is a cave that hisses, and roars, and puffs out scalding steam like a perpetual locomotive, and all the ground around shakes and quivers as if it were only a crust over some terrible abyss. The pools of water are all white with sulphur; the ground is made of sulphur and arsenic and all such sort of uncanny matters; and we were in a fine fright lest Miss Florence, being in one of her wildest and most indiscreet moods, should tumble into some burning hole, or choke herself with sulphur; and in fact she rolled over and over in a sulphur puddle, and then, scampering off, rolled in ashes by way of cleaning herself. We could not, however, leave her at home during any of our excursions, and so had to make the best of these imprudences.

*   *   *

Great was the sensation. Grandma tottered with trembling steps to the door, and asked, with hesitating tones, what sort of a creature that might be; and being saluted with the jubilant proclamation, 'Why, grandma, it's my dog – a real, genuine Scotch terrier; he'll never grow any larger, and he's a perfect beauty! don't you think so?' – grandma could only tremblingly reply, 'Oh, there is not any danger of his going mad, is there? Is he generally so playful?'

Playful was certainly a mild term for the tempest of excitement in which Master Wix flew round and round in giddy circles, springing over ottomans, diving under sofas, barking from beneath chairs, and resisting every effort to recapture the slipper with bristling hair and blazing eyes, as if the whole of his dog-life consisted in keeping his prize; till at length he caught a glimpse of pussy's tail – at which, dropping the slipper, he precipitated himself after the flying meteor, tumbling, rolling, and scratching down the kitchen stairs, and standing on his hind legs barking distractedly at poor Tom, who had taken refuge in the sink, and sat with his tail magnified to the size of a small bolster.

This cat, the most reputable and steady individual of his species, the darling of the most respectable of cooks, had received the name of Thomas Henry, by which somewhat lengthy appellation he was gener-ally designated in the family circle, as a mark of the respect which his serious and contemplative manner commonly excited. Thomas had but one trick of popularity. With much painstaking and care the cook had taught him the act of performing a somerset over our hands when held at a decent height from the floor; and for this one elegant accomplish-ment, added to great success in his calling of rat-catching, he was held in great consideration in the family, and had meandered his decorous way about the house, slept in the sun, and otherwise conducted himself with the innocent and tranquil freedom which became a family cat of correct habits and a good conscience.

The irruption of Wix into our establishment was like the bursting of a bomb at the feet of some respectable citizen going tranquilly to market. Thomas was a cat of courage, and rats of the largest size shrunk appalled at the very sight of his whiskers; but now he sat in the sink quite cowed, consulting with great, anxious yellow eyes the throng of faces that followed Wix down the stairs, and watching anxiously the efforts Miss Jenny was making to subdue and quiet him.

'Wix, you naughty little rascal, you mustn't bark at Thomas Henry; be still!' Whereat Wix, understanding himself to be blamed, brought forth his trump card of accomplishments, which he always offered by way of pacification whenever he was scolded. He reared himself up on his hind legs, hung his head languishingly on one side, lolled out his tongue, and made a series of supplicatory gestures with his fore paws – a trick which never failed to bring down the house in a storm of applause, and carry him out of any scrape with flying colours.

Poor Thomas Henry, from his desolate sink, saw his terrible rival carried off in Miss Jenny's arms amid the applause of the whole circle, and had abundance of time to reflect on the unsubstantial nature of popularity. After that he grew dejected and misanthropic – a real Cardinal Wolsey in furs – for Wix was possessed with a perfect cat-hunting mania, and, whenever he was not employed in other mischief, was always ready for a bout with Thomas Henry.

It is true, he sometimes came back from these encounters with a scratched and bloody nose, for Thomas Henry was a cat of no mean claw, and would turn to bay at times; but generally he felt the exertion too much for his advanced years and quiet habits, and so for safety he passed much of his time in the sink, over the battlements of which he would leisurely survey the efforts of the enemy to get at him. The cook hinted strongly of the danger of rheumatism to her favourite from these damp quarters; but Wix at present was the reigning favourite, and it was vain to dispute his sway.

Next to Thomas Henry, Wix directed his principal efforts to teasing grandmamma. Something or other about her black dress and quiet movements seemed to suggest to him suspicions. He viewed her as something to be narrowly watched; he would lie down under some chair or table, and watch her motions with his head on his fore paws as if he were watching at a rat-hole.

From *Our Dogs*

FRANK DALBY DAVISON

Cross Breed

For the better part of an hour a small boring sound in the night told of the pleasant contact of teeth on green bone, and an occasional small growl of the satisfaction this afforded. Only when the bone gave him back nothing more than the taste of his own mouth did he give it a final lick. He quickly gulped down what remained of the soft food; licked his chops with satisfaction, hollowed his back in a contented stretch, then trotted past the side of the house toward the farm outbuildings, wagging his tail a little in gratitude which he felt a need to express even though not expecting acknowledgement.

He settled himself on the old bag lying just inside the entrance to the cart shed, which was his nightly resting place; and after some yawning and chop-licking, began to draw himself together for sleep. It was at this moment that he heard, far in the distance, miles up the valley and among the hills on the far side, a thin thread of sound winding through the night. Only a dog's ear would have heard it so far away. He recognized it as the cry of a dingo, a hunting dog, a thief, a plunderer of small stock belonging to the human creatures with whom dogs of his kind identified themselves, a free dog against one happy in servitude, therefore, for some reason deeply felt and unquestioned, a mortal foe. The sound was too far off to trouble him; he pricked his ears and growled softly, but didn't stir.

It was repeated a while later, somewhat closer. He had dozed off, but it penetrated his light sleep, and he lifted his head. The moon was shining in on him now. It was clear of the tree-tops and lit the homestead and its surroundings. He looked around at as much of the familiar scene as was framed between the edges of the open-sided shed. He did it as if reassuring himself, something as a man of property might look over his possessions, or one waking from a troubled sleep might look about a room; then he dropped his head again.

The next time the dingo's call sounded it came from only a mile or so up the valley, as clear as notes winding from a bugle. The kelpie came awake and leaped to his feet and was out of the shed in an instant, tensed and staring across the valley. He barked in reply, challenging, and then stood staring in the direction from which the sound had come, lifting his head to smell the air.

In the bedroom of the darkened homestead the kelpie's owner and his wife heard the dingo's call and their dog's answering bark, and each thought, 'He is a good dog, barking at the dingoes!'

At the corner of the cart shed the kelpie was still looking across the valley. Two things about the call had come to his notice. It was the call of a solitary dog, and it was the call of a female. The hair bristled on his neck. He was disturbed that he had not heard the call of a male. He recognized an irregularity. He suspected evil; a trap. He scratched the ground with his hind legs and waited. He barked challengingly again, but there was no reply.

When the call came again it sounded from directly across the valley, and he became even more disturbed. The dingo was travelling alone. She was in search of a mate. There was something in the call that was intended for him. He whimpered. He barked threateningly, but somewhat perfunctorily; then he turned and trotted toward the house. He sat on his tail by the corner-post of the garden for a few seconds; but he sat with his back to the house and he was looking across the valley. He got up and trotted acoss to the cow bails and sat again facing the slope down to the valley. From there he shifted to the farther side of the cart shed, and now the whole homestead was at his back.

The call came from quite near by when it came again. The dingo had left the shelter of the timber and was in the middle of the paddock. He barked again, but it was a false threat, convincing neither to himself nor to the one for whom it was intended. For some time he stood staring into the misty valley, outwardly as still as a dog carved from wood, but with every sense alert, and inwardly heedful of strong promptings. The homestead, so close behind him, had receded to the very margin of his awareness. He was a young, strong creature, beckoned from without and challenged from within. He whined softly and took a few steps forward, almost as if he were impatient for the dingo to call again.

He glanced swiftly behind him as if he had remembered something, then looked to his front again, with his tail wagging just a little, as if while he looked he was thinking a little of that which had caused him to turn his head; then his tail steadied and stiffened and again he went forward a little. Nature was crooking a sure finger at him, and presently he was trotting down the hill, the homestead quite forgotten. He was wholly his own dog now, intent upon his own errand; still wary, as his tensed and watchful bearing indicated, but the vessel of high expectancy.

At the foot of the slope he crossed the sandy bed of the creek, scampered up the farther bank, and stood looking toward the timbered knoll, sniffing the air. He broke into a run across the grass and steadied again to a walk as he came to the margin of the timber. He halted within the edge of the shadows.

The dingo had understood the changing tone of his bark from the hill. She was in the shadows of the trees, and had watched him cross the grass from the creek. As he came among the timber of the knoll she crouched and remained still, knowing she would be found. The dog discerned her, by scent and then by sight. That was she, lying between the butts of two tall trees, as light in colour almost as a lump of bleached wood. He advanced a step at a time, while she lay waiting and watching; each with every step looming larger in both the outer and inner vision of the other. At the distance of a foot or so the dog froze, and for a long while neither moved; then the necks of both stretched forward slowly. For one ecstatic moment their noses touched, then the dingo leaped to her feet and was off through the timber and across the open valley, with the kelpie following hard behind as though drawn by a string.

In the late morning of the following day they lay facing each other at a few yards distance among the bushes in the mouth of a remote gully of the lower slopes of the range. Their tongues were lolling and they were panting. They were dusty from travel and hollow-flanked from fatigue. The dingo had led the kelpie a long chase through the night. Perhaps this was from a hunting creature's need to assure herself of the speed and endurance of her mate and the prospective father of her young. It was also an instinctive retreat from the dangers of his environment to the security of her own. Perhaps, again, it was to ensure, by the drawing out of desire, that their union should come to complete and effective fulfilment. The chase had often been broken while they rested and made sure by means other than flight and pursuit of their acceptability to each other; while they struck at each other's faces with playful paws; while they stood side by side in happy contact, or advanced their courtship with gentle pretences before she led off again on the long run.

They had coupled at mid-morning; and the sun, the earth and the trees, and all the being of each that was not of the moment, were lost in their mutual preoccupation and gratified flesh. Their love and intent awareness of each other mounted with the duration of their union, though the purpose of it was achieved in a moment when they were of a sudden lost from each other, and each within itself was lost to everything but the tumult of its own pleasure. They uncoupled after this, as soon as the mechanism of their bodies permitted, and lay apart, breathless; and the sun, the earth and the trees returned to their places. They were at rest and fulfilled, and regarded each other companionably.

From *Dusty*

RICHARD WAGNER

An Extra Burden

H OW HE MANAGED to work at all under the load of anxieties and annoyances laid on him by Minna and others at this time is a mystery to be explained only on the theory of the almost complete insulation of the creative instinct in an artist from his outward circumstances; but work he did for a time. By the third week in April the score of the *Meistersinger* overture was complete, precisely as it stands to-day, although he appears to have made little progress as yet with the first act of the opera. By the third week in July he had got as far with this as the scene where Pogner introduces Walther to the Mastersingers; then an accident occurred that stopped all work upon the score. The architect who owned the house of which Wagner's three rooms formed a part had a bull-dog whose verminous and generally neglected condition aroused Wagner's sympathy. As he had made friends with the animal he thought it safe to hold its head while a servant washed it, only to meet with the fate that so often attends benefactors in this imperfect world – the helping hand was bitten. His right thumb soon swelled to such an extent that work upon the *Meistersinger* score became impossible, and remained so for a good two months. The dog played a larger part in determining Wagner's future fortunes than he could have foreseen when he snapped at him: the enforced delay in the delivery of the score of the opera led to a temporary drying up of supplies from Schott, so that Wagner was compelled, later in the year, to plunge once more into the wearisome business of concert-conducting: and this in its turn threw him into still further arrears with his composition.

Ernest Newman, from his *Life of Wagner*

Tales of Woe

I HAD A TERRIBLE shock during our walk; not far from the railroad R. was reading out loud to me a letter from Pohl ('This letter resembles not exactly a bad apple, but at any rate a baked one,' said R.); suddenly we see Kos in the middle of the track fighting with another dog, the train almost on top of him! R. seemed to shoot off like an arrow, and through his running and shouting he rescues Kos, himself escaping only by a miracle – but the sight!

Cosima Wagner, from her Diary: 30 March 1869

A DRIVE IN THE afternoon; when we remark on Kos's intelligence, I ask, 'Where does the soul of such an animal go?' 'We must think of that as a really friendly place,' R. replies. 'It is only Death itself of which we must think solemnly, as a test of life; what comes after, however, in as friendly a light as possible.'

ibid, 28 May 1870

K OS VERY BAD. 'The way inanimate forces, chemical forces, fight over such a poor creature and destroy it truly demonstrates that life is just a condition, an agony.' R. says.

ibid, 26 June 1870

A T LUNCH – FOR what reason I do not know – R. told me that in his youth the worst thing he could imagine was to take leave of somebody forever, and he knew now that he could never have had Fritz and Kos put to death if he had had to say goodbye to them. I understand that; I once had to take leave of somebody, and from that hour, which also brought me my first gray hairs, I realized the true meaning of life; up till then everything I had read in the poets about the dreadfulness and blameworthiness of life I could feel only intuitively; but when I gave Hans my hand in farewell, I felt it all inside myself, and the veil of illusion was torn forever. From then on I understood life and death, and from then on I have wished for nothing more.

ibid, 16 September 1871

TERRIBLE DAY! MY children walk into town with Anna, take Fitzo with them, return home weeping, and tell me that Fitzo has been run over by the locomotive. I run to the spot and bury our poor little dog. It is a holiday, people come and go, the sun shines, and I feel as if I were to blame for his death. Today, when the bell rang and I did not hear his barking, I felt so desolate; I cannot help thinking that recently Kos was calling Fitzo; Fitzo heard the knocking and wanted to fly to me for protection. I feel as if I had lost Kos twice, and the terrible sight of that poor, mangled body will never leave me.

Went sadly to bed; rose despondent! A new snowfall, which covers poor Fitzo. The children do not seem to be thinking about him, I shall probably be the only one in whom the poor creature will live on.

ibid, 2/3 February 1872

An Incompetent Vet

BECAUSE THE WEATHER is fine, we drive home via the Eremitage road. We are alone at supper, the children tell us that our dear good dog Molly is ill, the veterinary surgeon is sent for and says it is just a slight chill. Some time ago, since her face was looking much changed, I asked Dr Landgraf, and he told me that she was quite well but was eating too much and must get a lot of exercise.

ibid, 13 July 1873

R. FEELS WEAK AND takes medicine. At around 10 o'clock Georg brings me the news that our lovely dear dog has died – and you know, my children, what she meant to us! ... After paying my final respects to the good creature, who suffered in such silence, I drive up to the theater to inspect the Flower costumes; then back home, to the Jägers', to do what I can to raise the poor offended man's spirits. At lunch we have 3 Flowers and 2 concertmasters. There is a rehearsal in the afternoon, I tell R. that the children have caught cold; they stay at home (the younger ones), and after the dissection they bury our dear Molly.

ibid, 14 July 1873

R. ASKS AFTER MOLLE, Georg tells him that we must be prepared for the worst, he goes into the garden around lunchtime, sits down in the arbor, notices Marke sniffing at the grave! At table, where we are alone, he utters the name, and we burst into tears, realizing that he knows all. He thanks us for not having told him. . . . Toward two o'clock my father arrives, met by the children and looking well – we are overjoyed to see him! While the children and I are keeping him company during his meal, R. joins us, stands for a while unnoticed behind my father's chair, and whispers to me, '*Die Mutter!*' – Our dog came into my mind, too, yesterday when I heard those words! – When I return to my room as my father is resting, I hear R. calling out 'Molle!' in the garden and sobbing. I rush to him, and we weep together in the arbor.

ibid, 15 July 1873

CHARLES DICKENS

A Daughter Remembers

FOR A SHORT TIME I had the care of a mongrel called 'Gipsy.' She was not allowed to enter any of the family rooms, and used to spend her time lying contentedly on the rug outside the drawing-room. One afternoon a friend came from Chatham bringing with him a wonderful poodle who had been specially invited to perform all his tricks for my father's enjoyment. On his arrival, 'Mrs Bouncer' became furious, and when he began his tricks she went deliberately into the hall and escorted 'Gipsy' into the drawing-room, as much as to say: 'I can't stand this. If strange dogs are to be made much of, surely the dogs in the house may be at least permitted to enter the room.' She would not look at 'Fosco,' the poodle, but sat throughout his performance with her back toward him, the picture of offended dignity. Just as soon however, as he was fairly out of the house, and not until then, she escorted 'Gipsy' back to her rug. My father was intensely amused by this behaviour of 'Bouncer's' and delighted in telling this story about her.

'Mrs Bouncer' was honored by many messages from her master during his absences from home. Here is one written as I was convalescing from a serious illness: 'In my mind's eye I behold "Mrs Bouncer", still with some traces of anxiety on her faithful countenance, balancing herself a little unequally on her forelegs, pricking up her ears with her head on one side, and slightly opening her intellectual nostrils. I send my loving and respectful duty to her.' Again: 'Think of my dreaming of "Mrs Bouncer," each night!!!'

My father's love for dogs led him into a strange friendship during our stay at Boulogne. There lived in a cottage on the street which led from our house to the town, a cobbler who used to sit at his window working all day with his dog – a Pomeranian – on the table beside him. The cobbler, in whom my father became very much interested because of the intelligence of his Pomeranian companion, was taken ill, and for many months was unable to work. My father writes: 'The cobbler has been ill these many months. The little dog sits at the door so unhappy and anxious to help that I every day expect to see him beginning a pair of top boots.' Another time father writes in telling the history of this little animal: 'A cobbler at Boulogne, who had the nicest of little dogs that always sat in his sunny window watching him at his work, asked me if I would bring the dog home as he couldn't afford to pay the tax for him. The cobbler and the dog being both my particular friends I complied. The cobbler parted with the dog heartbroken. When the dog got home here, my man, like an idiot as he is, tied him up and then untied him. The moment the gate was open, the dog (on the very day after his arrival) ran out. Next day Gregory and I saw him lying all covered with mud, dead, outside the neighbouring church. How am I ever to tell the cobbler? He is too poor to come to England, so I feel that I must lie to him for life, and say that the dog is fat and happy.'

Mamie Dickens, from *My Father As I Recall Him*

Shy Neighbourhoods

THE DOGS OF shy neighbourhoods, I observe to avoid play, and to be conscious of poverty. They avoid work, too, if they can, of course; that is in the nature of all animals. I have the pleasure to know a dog in a back street in the neighbourhood of Walworth, who has greatly distinguished himself in the minor drama, and who takes his portrait with him when he makes an engagement, for the illustration of the play-bill. His portrait (which is not at all like him) represents him in the act of dragging to the earth a recreant Indian, who is supposed to have tomahawked, or essayed to tomahawk, a British officer. The design is pure poetry, for there is no such Indian in the piece, and no such incident. He is a dog of the newfoundland breed, for whose honesty I would be bail to any amount; but whose intellectual qualities in association with dramatic fiction, I cannot rate high. Indeed, he is too honest for the profession he had entered. Being at a town in Yorkshire last summer, and seeing him posted in the bill of the night, I attended the performance. His first scene was eminently successful; but, as it occupied a second in its representation (and five lines in the bill), it scarcely afforded ground for a cool and deliberate judgement of his powers. He had merely to bark, run on, and jump through an inn window, after a comic fugitive. The next scene of importance to the fable was a little marred in its interest by his over-anxiety; forasmuch as while his master (a belated soldier in a den of robbers on a tempestuous night) was feelingly lamenting the absence of his faithful dog, and laying great stress on the fact that he was thirty leagues away, the faithful dog was barking furiously in the prompter's box, and clearly choking himself against his collar. But it was in his greatest scene of all, that his honesty got the better of him. He had to enter a dense and trackless forest, on the trail of the murderer, and there to fly at the murderer when he had found him resting at the foot of a tree, with his victim bound ready for slaughter. It was a hot night, and he came into the forest from an altogether unexpected direction, in the sweetest temper, at a very deliberate trot, not in the least excited; trotted to the foot-lights with his tongue out; and there sat down, panting, and amiably surveying the audience, with his tail beating on the boards, like a Dutch clock. Meanwhile the murderer, impatient to receive his doom, was audibly calling to him 'CO-O-OME here!' while the victim, struggling with his bonds, assailed him with the most injurious expressions. It happened through these means, that when he was in course of time persuaded to trot up and rend the murderer limb from limb, he made it (for dramatic purposes) a little too obvious that he worked out that awful retribution by licking butter of his blood-stained hands.

In a shy street, behind Long-acre, two honest dogs live, who perform in Punch's shows. I may venture to say that I am on terms of intimacy with both, and that I never saw either guilty of the falsehood of failing to look down at the man inside the show, during the whole performance. The difficulty other dogs have in satisfying their minds about these dogs appears to be never overcome by time. The same dogs must encounter them over and over again, as they trudge along in their off-minutes behind the legs of the show and beside the drum; but all dogs seem to suspect their frills and jackets, and to sniff at them as if they thought those articles of personal adornment, an eruption – a something in the nature of mange, perhaps. From this Covent-garden window of mine I noticed a country dog, only the other day, who had come up to Covent-garden Market under a cart, and had broken his cord, an end of which he still trailed along with him. He loitered about the corners of the four streets commanded by my window; and bad London dogs came up, and told him lies that he didn't believe; and worse London dogs came up, and made proposals to him to go and steal in the market, which his principles rejected; and the ways of the town confused him, and he crept aside and lay down in a doorway. He had scarcely got a wink of sleep, when up comes Punch with Toby. He was darting to Toby for consolation and advice, when he saw the frill, and stopped, in the middle of the street, appalled. The show was pitched, Toby retired behind the drapery, the audience formed, the drum and pipes struck up. My country dog remained immovable, intently staring at these strange appearances, until Toby opened the drama by appearing on his ledge, and to him entered Punch, who put a tobacco-pipe into Toby's mouth. At this spectacle, the country dog threw up his head, gave one terrible howl, and fled due west.

We talk of men keeping dogs, but we might often talk more expressively of dogs keeping men. I know a bull-dog in a shy corner of Hammersmith who keeps a man. He keeps him up a yard, and makes him go to public-houses and lay wagers on him, and obliges him to lean against posts and look at him, and forces him to neglect work for him, and keeps him under rigid coercion. I once knew a fancy terrier who kept a gentleman – a gentleman who had been brought up at Oxford, too. The dog kept the gentleman entirely for his glorification, and the gentleman never talked about anything but the terrier. This, however, was not in a shy neighbourhood, and is a digression consequently.

There are a great many dogs in shy neighbourhoods, who keep boys. I have my eye on a mongrel in Somerstown who keeps three boys. He feigns that he can bring down sparrows, and unburrow rats (he can do neither), and he takes the boys out on sporting pretences into all sorts of suburban fields. He has likewise made them believe that he possesses some mysterious knowledge of the art of fishing, and they consider themselves incompletely equipped for the Hampstead ponds, with a pickle-jar and wide-mouthed bottle, unless he is with them and barking tremendously. There is a dog residing in the Borough of Southwark who keeps a blind man. He may be seen, most days, in Oxford-Street, hauling the blind man away on expeditions wholly uncontemplated by, and unintelligible to, the man: wholly of the dog's conception and execution. Contrariwise, when the man has projects, the dog will sit down in a crowded thoroughfare and meditate. I saw him yesterday, wearing the money-tray like an easy collar, instead of offering it to the public, taking the man against his will, on the invitation of a disreputable cur, apparently to visit a dog at Harrow – he was so intent on that direction. The north wall of Burlington House Gardens, between the Arcade and the Albany, offers a shy spot for appointments among blind men at about two or three o'clock in the afternoon. They sit (very uncomfortably) on a sloping stone there, and compare notes. Their dogs may always be observed at the same time, openly disparaging the men they keep, to one another, and settling where they shall respectively take their men when they begin to move again. At a small butcher's, in a shy neighbourhood (there is no reason for suppressing the name; it is by Notting-Hill, and gives upon the district called the Potteries), I know a shaggy black and white dog who keeps a drover. He is a dog of an easy disposition, and too frequently allows this drover to get drunk. On these occasions, it is the dog's custom to sit outside the public-house, keeping his eye on a few sheep, and thinking. I have seen him with six sheep, plainly casting up in his mind how many he began with when he left the market, and at what places he has left the rest. I have seen him perplexed by not being able to account to himself for certain particular sheep. A light has gradually broken on him, he has remembered at what butcher's he left them, and in a burst of grave satisfaction has caught a fly off his nose, and shown himself much relieved. If I could at any time have doubted the fact that it was he who kept the drover, and not the drover who kept him, it would have been abundantly proved by his way of taking undivided charge of the six sheep, when the drover came out besmeared with red ochre and beer, and gave him wrong directions, which he calmly disregarded. He has taken the sheep entirely in to his own hands, has merely remarked with respectful firmness, 'That instruction would place them under an omnibus; you had better confine your attention to yourself – you will want it all;' and has driven his charge away, with an intelligence of ears and tail, and a knowledge of business, that has left his lout of a man very, very far behind.

From *The Uncommercial Traveller*

Dancing Dogs

'I,' REPEATED SHORT emphatically and slowly, 'am not a going to stand it. I am not a going to see this fair young child a falling into bad hands, and getting among people that she's no more fit for, than they are to get among angels as their ordinary chums. Therefore when they dewelope an intention of parting company from us, I shall take measures for detaining of 'em, and restoring 'em to their friends, who I dare say have had their disconsolation pasted up on every wall in London by this time.'

'Short,' said Mr Codlin, who with his head upon his hands and his elbows on his knees, had been shaking himself impatiently from side to side up to this point and occasionally stamping on the ground, but who now looked up with eager eyes; 'it's possible that there may be uncommon good sense in what you've said. If there is, and there should be a reward, Short, remember that we're partners in everything!'

His companion had only time to nod a brief assent to this position, for the child awoke at the instant. They had drawn close together during the previous whispering, and now hastily separated and were rather awkwardly endeavouring to exchange some casual remarks in their usual tone, when strange footsteps were heard without, and fresh company entered.

These were no other than four very dismal dogs, who came pattering in one after the other, headed by an old bandy dog of particularly mournful aspect, who, stopping when the last of his followers had got as far as the door, erected himself upon his hind legs and looked round at his companions, who immediately stood upon their hind legs, in a grave and melancholy row. Nor was this the only remarkable circumstance about these dogs, for each of them wore a kind of little coat of some gaudy colour trimmed with tarnished spangles, and one of them had a cap upon his head, tied very carefully under his chin, which had fallen down upon his nose and completely obscured one eye; add to this, that the gaudy coats were all wet through and discoloured with rain, and that the wearers were splashed and dirty, and some idea may be formed of the unusual appearance of these new visitors to the Jolly Sandboys.

Neither Short nor the landlord nor Thomas Codlin, however, were the least surprised, merely remarking that these were Jerry's dogs and that Jerry could not be far behind. So there the dogs stood, patiently winking and gaping and looking extremely hard at the boiling pot, until Jerry himself appeared, when they all dropped down at once and walked about the room in their natural manner. This posture it must be confessed did not much improve their appearance, as their own personal tails and their coat tails – both capital things in their way – did not agree together.

Jerry, the manager of these dancing dogs, was a tall black-whiskered man in a velveteen coat, who seemed well known to the landlord and his guests and accosted them with great cordiality. Disencumbering himself of a barrel-organ which he placed upon a chair, and retaining in his hand a small whip wherewith to awe his company of comedians, he came up to the fire to dry himself, and entered into conversation.

'Your people don't usually travel in character, do they?' said Short, pointing to the dresses of the dogs. 'It must come expensive if they do?'

'No', replied Jerry, 'no, it's not the custom with us. But we've been playing a little on the road to-day, and we come out with a new wardrobe at the races, so I didn't think it worth while to stop to undress. Down, Pedro!'

This was addressed to the dog with the cap on, who being a new member of the company and not quite certain of his duty, kept his unobscured eye anxiously on his master, and was perpetually starting upon his hind legs when there was no occasion, and falling down again.

'I've got a animal here,' said Jerry, putting his hand into the capacious pocket of his coat, and diving into one corner as if he were feeling for a small orange or an apple or some such article, 'a animal here, wot I think you know something of, Short.'

'Ah!' cried Short, 'let's have a look at him.'

'Here he is,' said Jerry, producing a little terrier from his pocket. 'He was once a Toby of yours, warn't he!'

In some versions of the great drama of Punch there is a small dog – a modern innovation – supposed to be the private property of that gentleman, whose name is always Toby. This Toby has been stolen in youth from another gentleman, and fraudulently sold to the confiding hero, who having no guile himself has no suspicion that it lurks in others; but Toby, entertaining a grateful recollection of his old master, and scorning to attach himself to any new patrons, not only refuses to smoke a pipe at the bidding of Punch, but to mark his old fidelity more strongly, seizes him by the nose and wrings the same with violence, at which instance of canine attachment the spectators are deeply affected. This was the character which the little terrier in question has once sustained; if there had been any doubt upon the subject he would speedily have resolved it by his conduct; for not only did he, on seeing Short, give the strongest tokens of recognition, but catching sight of the flat box he barked so furiously at the pasteboard nose which he knew as inside, that his master was obliged to gather him up and put him into his pocket again, to the great relief of the whole company.

The landlord now busied himself in laying the cloth, in which process Mr Codlin obligingly assisted by setting forth his own knife and fork in the most convenient place and establishing himself behind them. When everything was ready, the landlord took off the cover for the last time, and then indeed there burst forth such a goodly promise of supper, that if he had offered to put it on again or had hinted at postponement, he would certainly have been sacrificed on his own hearth.

However, he did nothing of the kind, but instead thereof assisted a stout servant girl in turning the contents of the cauldron into a large tureen; a proceeding which the dogs, proof against various hot splashes which fell upon their noses, watched with terrible eagerness. At length the dish was lifted on the table, and mugs of ale having been previously set round, little Nell ventured to say grace, and supper began.

At this juncture the poor dogs were standing on their hind legs quite surprisingly; the child, having pity on them, was about to cast some morsels of food to them before she tasted it herself, hungry though she was, when their master interposed.

'No, my dear, no, not an atom from anybody's hand but mine if you please. That dog,' said Jerry, pointing out the old leader of the troop, and speaking in a terrible voice, 'lost a halfpenny to-day. *He* goes without his supper.'

The unfortunate creature dropped upon his fore-legs directly, wagged his tail, and looked imploringly at his master.

'You must be more careful, sir,' said Jerry, walking coolly to the chair where he had placed the organ, and setting the stop. 'Come here. Now, sir, you play away at that, while we have supper, and leave off if you dare.'

The dog immediately began to grind most mournful music. His

master having shown him the whip resumed his seat and called up the others, who, at his directions, formed in a row, standing upright as a file of soldiers.

'Now gentlemen,' said Jerry, looking at them attentively. 'The dog whose name's called eats. The dogs whose names an't called, keep quiet. Carlo!'

The lucky individual whose name was called, snapped up the morsel thrown towards him, but none of the others moved a muscle. In this manner they were fed at the discretion of their master. Meanwhile the dog in disgrace ground hard at the organ, sometimes in quick time, sometimes in slow, but never leaving off for an instant. When the knives and forks rattled very much, or any of his fellows got an unusually large piece of fat, he accompanied the music with a short howl, but he immediately checked it on his master looking round, and applied himself with increasing diligence to the Old Hundredth.

From *The Old Curiosity Shop*

Diogenes

'DON'T BE AFRAID to speak to me,' said Florence, with a quiet smile. 'I should be very glad if you would talk about my brother.'

'Would you, though,' retorted Mr Toots, with sympathy in every fibre of his otherwise expressionless face. 'Poor Dombey! I'm sure I never thought that Burgess & Co – fash'nable tailors (but very dear), that we used to talk about – would make this suit of clothes for such a purpose.' Mr Toots was dressed in mourning. 'Poor Dombey! I say! Miss Dombey!' blubbered Toots.

'Yes,' said Florence.

'There's a friend he took to very much at last. I thought you'd like to have him, perhaps, as a sort of keepsake. You remember his remembering Diogenes?'

'Oh yes! oh yes!' cried Florence.

'Poor Dombey! So do I,' said Mr Toots.

Mr Toots, seeing Florence in tears, had great difficulty in getting beyond this point, and had nearly tumbled into the well again. But a chuckle saved him on the brink.

'I say,' he proceeded, 'Miss Dombey! I could have had him stolen for ten shillings, if they hadn't given him up: and I would: but they were glad to get rid of him, I think. If you'd like to have him, he's at the door. I brought him here on purpose for you. He ain't a lady's dog, you know,' said Mr Toots, 'but you won't mind that, will you?'

In fact, Diogenes was at that moment, as they presently ascertained from looking down into the street, staring through the window of a hackney cabriolet, into which, for conveyance to that spot, he had been ensnared, on a false pretence of rats among the straw. Sooth to say, he was as unlike a lady's dog as dog might be; and in his gruff anxiety to get out presented an appearance sufficiently unpromising, as he gave short yelps out of one side of his mouth, and overbalancing himself by the intensity of every one of those efforts, tumbled down into the straw, and then sprung panting up again, putting out his tongue, as if he had come express to a Dispensary to be examined for his health.

But though Diogenes was as ridiculous a dog as one would meet with on a summer's day; a blundering, ill-favoured, clumsy, bullet-headed dog, continually acting on a wrong idea that there was an enemy in the neighbourhood, whom it was meritorious to bark at; and though he was far from good-tempered, and certainly was not clever, and had hair all over his eyes, and a comic nose, and an inconsistent tail, and a gruff voice; he was dearer to Florence, in virtue of that parting remembrance of him and that request that he might be taken care of, than the most valuable and beautiful of his kind. So dear, indeed, was this same ugly Diogenes, and so welcome to her, that she took the jewelled hand of Mr Toots and kissed it in her gratitude. And when Diogenes, released, came tearing up the stairs and bouncing into the room (such a business as there was, first, to get him out of the cabriolet!), dived under all the furniture, and wound a long iron chain, that dangled from his neck, round legs of chairs and tables, and then tugged at it until his eyes became unnaturally visible, in consequence of their nearly starting out of his head; and when he growled at Mr Toots, who affected familiarity; and went pell-mell at Towlinson, morally convinced that he was the enemy whom he had barked at round the corner all his life and had never seen yet; Florence was as pleased with him as if he had been a miracle of discretion.

Mr Toots was so overjoyed by the success of his present, and was so delighted to see Florence lovingly bending down over Diogenes, smoothing his coarse back with her little delicate hand – Diogenes graciously allowing it from the first moment of their acquaintance – that he felt it difficult to take leave, and would, no doubt, have been a much longer time in making up his mind to do so, if he had not been assisted by Diogenes himself, who suddenly took it into his head to bay Mr Toots, and to make short runs at him with his mouth open. Not exactly seeing his way to the end of these demonstrations, and sensible that they placed the pantaloons constructed by the art of Burgess & Co. in jeopardy, Mr Toots, with chuckles, lapsed out at the door: by which, after looking in again two or three times without any object at all, and being on each occasion greeted with a fresh run from Diogenes, he finally took himself off and got away.

'Come then, Di! Dear Di! Make friends with your new mistress. Let us love each other, Di!' said Florence, fondling his shaggy head. And Di, the rough and gruff, as if his hairy hide were pervious to the tear that dropped from it, and his dog's heart melted as it fell, put his nose up to her face, and swore fidelity.

Diogenes the man did not speak plainer to Alexander the Great than Diogenes the dog spoke to Florence. He subscribed to the offer of his little mistress cheerfully, and devoted himself to her service. A banquet was immediately provided for him in a corner; and when he had eaten and drunk his fill, he went to the window where Florence was sitting, looking on, rose up on his hind legs, with his awkward fore paws on her shoulders, licked her face and hands, nestled his great head against her heart, and wagged his tail till he was tired. Finally, Diogenes coiled himself up at her feet, and went to sleep.

Although Miss Nipper was nervous in regard to dogs, and felt it necessary to come into the room with her skirts carefully collected about her, as if she were crossing a brook on stepping-stones; also to utter little screams and stand up on chairs when Diogenes stretched himself; she was in her own manner affected by the kindness of Mr Toots, and could not see Florence so alive to the attachment and society of this rude friend of little Paul's, without some mental comments thereupon that brought the water to her eyes. Mr Dombey, as a part of her reflections, may have been, in the association of ideas, connected with the dog; but, at any rate, after observing Diogenes and his mistress all the evening, and after exerting herself with much good will to provide Diogenes a bed in an ante-chamber outside his mistress's door, she said hurriedly to Florence, before leaving her for the night: 'Your Pa's a-going off, Miss Floy, tomorrow morning.'

From *Dombey and Son*

Jip

I T WAS A FINE morning, and early, and I thought I would go and take a stroll down one of those wire-arched walks, and indulge my passion by dwelling on her image. On my way through the hall, I encountered her little dog, who was called Jip – short for Gipsy. I approached him tenderly, for I loved even him; but he showed his whole set of teeth, got under a chair expressly to snarl, and wouldn't hear of the least familiarity.

The garden was cool and solitary. I walked about, wondering what my feelings of happiness would be, if I could ever become engaged to this dear wonder. As to marriage, and fortune, and all that, I believe I was almost as innocently undesigning then, as when I loved little Em'ly. To be allowed to call her 'Dora,' to write to her, to dote upon and worship her, to have reason to think that when she was with other people she was yet mindful of me, seemed to me the summit of human ambition – I am sure it was the summit of mine. There is no doubt whatever that I was a lackadaisical young spooney; but there was a purity of heart in all this still, that prevents my having quite a contemptuous recollection of it, let me laugh as I may.

I had not been walking long, when I turned a corner, and met her. I tingle again from head to foot as my recollection turns that corner, and my pen shakes in my hand.

'You – are – out early, Miss Spenlow,' said I.

'It's so stupid at home,' she replied, 'and Miss Murdstone is so absurd! She talks such nonsense about its being necessary for the day to be aired, before I come out. Aired!' (She laughed, here, in the most melodious manner). 'On a Sunday morning, when I don't practise, I must do something. So I told papa last night I *must* come out. Besides, it's the brightest time of the whole day. Don't you think so?'

I hazarded a bold flight, and said (not without stammering) that it was very bright to me then, though it had been very dark to me a minute before.

'Do you mean a compliment?' said Dora, 'or that the weather has really changed?'

I stammered worse than before, in replying that I meant no compliment, but the plain truth; though I was not aware of any change having taken place in the weather. It was in the state of my own feelings, I added bashfully: to clench the explanation.

I never saw such curls – how could I, for there never were such curls! – as those she shook out to hide her blushes. As to the straw hat and blue ribbons which was on top of the curls, if I could only have hung it up in my room in Buckingham Street, what a priceless possession it would have been!

'You have just come home from Paris,' said I.

'Yes,' said she. 'Have you ever been there?'

'No.'

'Oh! I hope you'll go soon. You would like it so much!'

Traces of deep-seated anguish appeared in my countenance. That she should hope I would go, that she should think it possible I *could* go, was insupportable. I depreciated Paris; I depreciated France. I said I wouldn't leave England, under existing circumstances, for any earthly consideration. Nothing should induce me. In short, she was shaking the curls again, when the little dog came running along the walk to our relief.

He was mortally jealous of me, and persisted in barking at me. She took him up in her arms – oh my goodness! – and caressed him, but he insisted upon barking still. He wouldn't let me touch him, when I tried; and then she beat him. It increased my sufferings greatly to see the pats she gave him for punishment on the bridge of his blunt nose, while he winked his eyes, and licked her hand, and still growled within himself like a little double-bass. At length he was quiet – well he might be with her dimpled chin upon his head! – and we walked away to look at a greenhouse.

'You are not very intimate with Miss Murdstone, are you?' said Dora. – 'My pet!'

(The two last words were to the dog. Oh if they had only been to me!)

'No,' I replied. 'Not at all so.'

'She is a tiresome creature,' said Dora pouting. 'I can't think what papa can have been about, when he chose such a vexatious thing to be my companion. Who wants a protector! I am sure *I* don't want a protector. Jip can protect me a great deal better than Miss Murdstone, – can't you Jip dear?'

He only winked lazily, when she kissed his ball of a head.

'Papa calls her my confidential friend, but I am sure she is no such thing – is she, Jip? We are not going to confide in such cross people, Jip and I. We mean to bestow our confidence where we like, and to find out our own friends, instead of having them found for us – don't we, Jip?'

Jip made a comfortable noise, in answer, a little like a tea-kettle when it sings. As for me, every word was a new heap of fetters, rivetted above the last.

'It is very hard, because we have not a kind Mama, that we are to have, instead, a sulky, gloomy old thing like Miss Murdstone, always following us about – isn't it, Jip? Never mind, Jip. We won't be confidential, and we'll make ourselves as happy as we can in spite of her, and we'll teaze her, and not please her, – won't we, Jip?'

If it had lasted any longer, I think I must have gone down on my knees on the gravel, with the probability before me of grazing them, and of being presently ejected from the premises besides. But, by good fortune the greenhouse was not far off, and these words brought us to it.

It contained quite a show of beautiful geraniums. We loitered along in front of them, and Dora often stopped to admire this one or that one, and I stopped to admire the same one, and Dora, laughing, held the dog up childishly, to smell the flowers; and if we were not all three in Fairyland, certainly *I* was. The scent of a geranium leaf, at this day, strikes me with a half comical half serious wonder as to what change has come over me in a moment; and then I see a straw hat and blue ribbons, and a quantity of curls, and a little black dog being held up, in two slender arms, against a bank of blossoms and bright leaves.

Miss Murdstone had been looking for us. She found us here; and presented her uncongenial cheek, the little wrinkles in it filled with hair-powder, to Dora to be kissed. Then she took Dora's arm in hers, and marched us in to breakfast as if it were a soldier's funeral.

*   *   *

I fatigued myself as much as I possibly could in the Commons all day, by a variety of devices, and at the appointed time in the evening repaired to Mr Mills's street. Mr Mills, who was a terrible fellow to fall asleep after dinner, had not yet gone out, and there was no birdcage in the middle window.

He kept me waiting so long, that I fervently hoped the Club would fine him for being late. At last he came out; and then I saw my own Dora hang up the birdcage, and peep into the balcony to look for me, and run in again when she saw I was there, while Jip remained behind, to bark injuriously at an immense butcher's dog in the street, who could have taken him like a pill.

Dora came to the drawing-room door to meet me; and Jip came scrambling out, tumbling over his own growls, under the impression that I was a Bandit; and we all three went in, as happy and loving as could be. I soon carried desolation into the bosom of our joys – not that I meant to do it, but that I was so full of the subject – by asking Dora, without the smallest preparation, if she could love a beggar?

My pretty, little, startled Dora! Her only association with the word was a yellow face and a nightcap, or a pair of crutches, or a wooden leg, or a dog with a decanter-stand in his mouth, or something of that kind; and she stared at me with the most delightful wonder.

'How can you ask me anything so foolish!' pouted Dora. 'Love a beggar!'

'Dora, my own dearest!' said I. '*I* am a beggar!'

'How can you be such a silly thing,' replied Dora, slapping my hand, 'as to sit there, telling such stories? I'll make Jip bite you!'

Her childish way was the most delicious way in the world to me, but it was necessary to be explicit, and I solemnly repeated:

'Dora, my own life, I am your ruined David!'

'I declare I'll make Jip bite you!' said Dora, shaking her curls, 'if you are so ridiculous.'

But I looked so serious, that Dora left off shaking her curls, and laid her trembling little hand upon my shoulder, and first looked scared and anxious, then began to cry. That was dreadful. I fell upon my knees before the sofa, caressing her, and imploring her not to rend my heart; but, for some time, poor little Dora did nothing but exclaim Oh dear! oh dear! And oh, she was so frightened! And where was Julia Mills! And oh, take her to Julia Mills, and go away, please! until I was almost beside myself.

At last, after an agony of supplication and protestation, I got Dora to look at me, with a horrified expression of face, which I gradually soothed until it was only loving, and her soft, pretty cheek was lying against mine. Then I told her, with my arms clasped round her, how I loved her, so dearly, and so dearly; how I felt it right to offer to release her from her engagement, because now I was poor; how I never could bear it, or recover it, if I lost her; how I had no fears of poverty, if she had none, my arm being nerved and my heart inspired by her; how I was already working with a courage such as none but lovers knew; how I had begun to be practical, and to look into the future; how a crust well-earned was sweeter far than a feast inherited; and much more to the same purpose, which I delivered in a burst of passionate eloquence quite surprising to myself, though I had been thinking about it, day and night, ever since my aunt had astonished me.

'Is your heart mine still, dear Dora?' said I, rapturously, for I knew by her clinging to me that it was.

'Oh, yes!' cried Dora. 'Oh, yes, it's all yours. Oh, don't be dreadful!'

I dreadful! To Dora!

'Don't talk about being poor, and working hard!' said Dora, nestling closer to me. 'Oh, don't, don't!'

'My dearest love,' said I, 'the crust well-earned – '

'Oh, yes; but I don't want to hear any more about crusts!' said Dora. 'And Jip must have a mutton-chop every day at twelve, or he'll die!'

I was charmed with her childish, winning way. I fondly explained to Dora that Jip should have his mutton-chop with his accustomed regularity. I drew a picture of our frugal home, made independent by my labor – sketching-in the little house I had seen at Highgate, and my aunt in her room up-stairs.

'I am not dreadful now, Dora?' said I, tenderly.

'Oh, no, no!' cried Dora. 'But I hope your aunt will keep in her own room a good deal! And I hope she's not a scolding old thing!'

If it were possible for me to love Dora more than ever, I am sure I did. But I felt she was a little impracticable. It damped my new-born ardor, to find that ardor so difficult of communication to her. I made another trial. When she was quite herself again, and was curling Jip's ears, as he lay upon her lap, I became grave, and said:

'My own! May I mention something?'

'Oh, please don't be practical!' said Dora, coaxingly. 'Because it frightens me so!'

'Sweet heart!' I returned; 'there is nothing to alarm you in all this. I want you to think of it quite differently. I want to make it nerve you, and inspire you, Dora!'

'Oh, but that's so shocking!' cried Dora.

'My love, no. Perseverance and strength of character will enable us to bear much worse things.'

'But I haven't got any strength at all,' said Dora, shaking her curls. 'Have I, Jip? Oh, do kiss Jip, and be agreeable!'

It was impossible to resist kissing Jip, when she held him up to me for that purpose, putting her own bright rosy little mouth into kissing form, as she directed the operation, which she insisted should be performed symmetrically, on the centre of his nose. I did as she bade me – rewarding myself afterwards for my obedience – and she charmed me out of my graver character for I don't know how long.

'But, Dora, my beloved!' said I, at last resuming it; 'I was going to mention something.'

The Judge of the Prerogative Court might have fallen in love with her, to see her fold her little hands and hold them up, begging and praying me not to be dreadful any more.

'Indeed I am not going to be, my darling!' I assured her. 'But, Dora, my love, if you will sometimes think, – not despondently, you know; far from that! – but if you will sometimes think – just to encourage yourself – that you are engaged to a poor man – '

'Don't, don't! Pray don't!' cried Dora. 'It's so very dreadful!'

From *David Copperfield*

Hunger

J O COMES OUT of Tom-All-Alone's, meeting the tardy morning which is always late in getting down there, and munches his dirty bit of bread as he comes along. His way lying through many streets, and the houses not yet being open, he sits down to breakfast on the door-step of the Society for the Propagation of the Gospel in Foreign Parts, and gives it a brush when he has finished, as an acknowledgment of the accommodation. He admires the size of the edifice, and wonders what it's all about. He has no idea, poor wretch, of the spiritual destitution of a coral reef in the Pacific, or what it costs to look up the precious souls among the cocoa-nuts and bread-fruit.

He goes to his crossing, and begins to lay it out for the day. The town awakes; the great tee-totum is set up for its daily spin and whirl; all that unaccountable reading and writing, which has been suspended for a few hours, recommences. Jo, and the other lower animals, get on in the unintelligible mess as they can. It is market-day. The blinded oxen, over-goaded, over-driven, never guided, run into wrong places and are beaten out; and plunge, red-eyed and foaming, at stone walls; and often sorely hurt the innocent, and often sorely hurt themselves. Very like Jo and his order; very, very like!

A band of music comes and plays. Jo listens to it. So does a dog – a drover's dog, waiting for his master outside a butcher's shop, and evidently thinking about those sheep he has had upon his mind for some hours, and is happily rid of. He seems perplexed respecting three or four; can't remember where he left them; looks up and down the street, as half expecting to see them astray; suddenly pricks up his ears and remembers all about it. A thoroughly vagabond dog, accustomed to low company and public-houses; a terrific dog to sheep; ready at a whistle to scamper over their backs, and tear out mouthfuls of their wool; but an educated, improved, developed dog, who has been taught his duties and knows how to discharge them. He and Jo listen to the music, probably with much the same amount of animal satisfaction; likewise, as to awakened association, aspiration or regret, melancholy or joyful reference to things beyond the senses, they are probably upon a par. But, otherwise, how far above the human listener is the brute!

Turn that dog's descendants wild, like Jo, and in a very few years they will so degenerate that they will lose even their bark – but not their bite.

From *Bleak House*

At the Easel

BEFORE BREAKFAST IN the morning, Arthur walked out to look about him. As the morning was fine, and he had an hour on his hands, he crossed the river by the ferry, and strolled along a footpath through some meadows. When he came back to the towing-path, he found the ferry-boat on the opposite side, and a gentleman hailing it and waiting to be taken over.

This gentleman looked barely thirty. He was well dressed, of a sprightly and gay appearance, a well-knit figure, and a rich dark complexion. As Arthur came over the stile and down to the water's edge, the lounger glanced at him for a moment, and then resumed his occupation of idly tossing stones into the water with his foot. There was something in his way of spurning them out of their places with his heel, and getting them into the required position, that Clennam thought had an air of cruelty in it. Most of us have more or less frequently derived a similar impression, from a man's manner of doing some very little thing:

plucking a flower, clearing away an obstacle, or even destroying an insentient object.

The gentleman's thoughts were preoccupied, as his face showed, and he took no notice of a fine Newfoundland dog, who watched him attentively, and watched every stone too, in its turn, eager to spring into the river on receiving his master's sign. The ferry-boat came over, however, without his receiving any sign, and when it grounded his master took him by the collar and walked him into it.

'Not this morning,' he said to the dog. 'You won't do for ladies' company, dripping wet. Lie down.'

Clennam followed the man and the dog into the boat, and took his seat. The dog did as he was ordered. The man remained standing, with his hands in his pockets, and towered between Clennam and the prospect. Man and dog both jumped lightly out as soon as they touched the other side, and went away. Clennam was glad to be rid of them.

The church clock struck the breakfast hour, as he walked up the little lane by which the garden-gate was approached. The moment he pulled the bell, a deep barking assailed him from within the wall.

'I heard no dog last night,' thought Clennam. The gate was opened by one of the rosy maids, and on the lawn were the Newfoundland dog and the man.

'Miss Minnie is not down yet, gentlemen,' said the blushing portress, as they all came together in the garden. Then she said to the master of the dog, 'Mr Clennam, sir,' and tripped away.

'Odd enough, Mr Clennam, that we should have met just now,' said the man. Upon which the dog became mute. 'Allow me to introduce myself – Henry Gowan. A pretty place this, and looks wonderfully well this morning!'

The manner was easy, and the voice agreeable; but still Clennam thought, that if he had not made that decided resolution to avoid falling in love with Pet, he would have taken a dislike to this Henry Gowan.

'It's new to you, I believe?' said this Gowan, when Arthur had extolled the place.

'Quite new. I made acquaintance with it only yesterday afternoon.'

'Ah! Of course this is not its best aspect. It used to look charming in the spring, before they went away last time. I should like you to have seen it then.'

But for that resolution so often recalled, Clennam might have wished him in the crater of Mount Etna, in return for this civility.

'I have had the pleasure of seeing it under many circumstances during the last three years, and it's – a Paradise.'

It was (at least it might have been, always excepting for that wise resolution) like his dexterous impudence to call it a Paradise. He only called it a Paradise because he first saw her coming, and so made her out within her hearing to be an angel, Confusion to him!

And ah, how beaming she looked, and how glad! How she caressed the dog, and how the dog knew her! How expressive that heightened color in her face, that fluttered manner, her downcast eyes, her irresolute happiness! When had Clennam seen her look like this? Not that there was any reason why he might, could, would, or should have ever seen her look like this, or that he had ever hoped for himself to see her look like this; but still – when had he ever known her do it!

He stood at a little distance from them. This Gowan, when he had talked about a Paradise, had gone up to her and taken her hand. The dog had put his great paws on her arm and laid his head against her dear bosom. She had laughed and welcomed them, and made far too much of the dog, far, far, too much – that is to say, supposing there had been any third person looking on who loved her.

*   *   *

There was no reason for her faltering and breaking off, other than that Mrs Gowan had touched her hand in speaking to her, and their looks had met. Something thoughtfully apprehensive in the large, soft eyes, had checked Little Dorrit in an instant.

'You don't know that you are a favorite of my husband's, and that I am almost bound to be jealous of you?' said Mrs Gowan.

Little Dorrit, blushing, shook her head.

'He will tell you, if he tells you what he tells me, that you are quieter, and quicker of resource, than any one he ever saw.'

'He speaks far too well of me,' said Little Dorrit.

'I doubt that; but I don't at all doubt that I must tell him you are here. I should never be forgiven, if I were to let you – and Miss Dorrit – go, without doing so. May I? You can excuse the disorder and discomfort of a painter's studio?'

The enquiries were addressed to Miss Fanny, who graciously replied that she would be beyond anything interested and enchanted. Mrs Gowan went to a door, looked in beyond it, and came back. 'Do Henry the favor to come in,' said she. 'I knew he would be pleased!'

The first object that confronted Little Dorrit, entering first, was

Blandois of Paris in a great cloak and a furtive slouched hat, standing on a throne-platform in a corner, as he had stood on the Great Saint Bernard, when the warning arms seemed to be all pointing up at him. She recoiled from this figure, as it smiled at her.

'Don't be alarmed,' said Gowan, coming from his easel behind the door. 'It's only Blandois. He is doing duty as a model to-day. I am making a study of him. It saves me money to turn him to some use. We poor painters have none to spare.'

Blandois of Paris pulled off his slouched hat, and saluted the ladies without coming out of his corner.

'A thousand pardons!' said he. 'But the Professore here, is so inexorable with me, that I am afraid to stir.'

'Don't stir, then,' said Gowan, coolly, as the sisters approached the easel. 'Let the ladies at least see the original of the daub, that they may know what it's meant for. There he stands, you see. A bravo waiting for his prey, a distinguished noble waiting to save his country, the common enemy waiting to do somebody a bad turn, an angelic messenger waiting to do somebody a good turn – whatever you think he looks most like!'

'Say, Professore Mio, a poor gentleman waiting to do homage to elegance and beauty,' remarked Blandois.

'Or say, Cattivo Soggetto Mio,' returned Gowan, touching the painted face with his brush in the part where the real face had moved, 'a murderer after the fact. Show that white hand of yours, Blandois. Put it outside the cloak. Keep it still.'

Blandois' hand was unsteady; but he laughed, and that would naturally shake it.

'He was formerly in some scuffle with another murderer, or with a victim, you observe,' said Gowan, putting in the markings of the hand with a quick, impatient, unskilful touch, 'and these are the tokens of it. Outside the cloak, man! – Corpo di San Marco, what are you thinking of!'

Blandois of Paris shook with a laugh again, so that his hand shook more; now he raised it to twist his moustache, which had a damp appearance; and now he stood in the required position, with a little new swagger.

His face was so directed in reference to the spot where Little Dorrit stood by the easel, that throughout he looked at her. Once attracted by his peculiar eyes, she could not remove her own, and they had looked at each other all the time. She trembled now; Gowan, feeling it, and supposing her to be alarmed by the large dog beside him, whose head she caressed in her hand, and who had just uttered a low growl, glanced at her to say, 'He won't hurt you, Miss Dorrit.'

'I am not afraid of him,' she returned, in the same breath; 'but will you look at him?'

In a moment Gowan had thrown down his brush, and seized the dog with both hands by the collar.

'Blandois! How can you be such a fool as to provoke him! By Heaven, and the other place too, he'll tear you to bits! Lie down! Lion! Do you hear my voice, you rebel!'

The great dog, regardless of being half-choked by his collar, was obdurately pulling with his dead weight against his master, resolved to get across the room. He had been crouching for a spring, at the moment when his master caught him.

'Lion! Lion!' He was up on his hind legs, and it was a wrestle between master and dog. 'Get back! Down, Lion! Get out of his sight, Blandois! What devil have you conjured into the dog?'

'I have done nothing to him.'

'Get out of his sight, or I can't hold the wild beast! Get out of the room! By my soul, he'll kill you!'

The dog, with a ferocious bark, made one other struggle, as Blandois vanished; then, in the moment of the dog's submission, the master, little less angry than the dog, felled him with a blow on the head, and standing over him, struck him many times severely with the heel of his boot, so that his mouth was presently bloody.

'Now get you into that corner and lie down,' said Gowan, 'or I'll take you out and shoot you!'

Lion did as he was ordered, and lay down licking his mouth and chest. Lion's master stopped for a moment to take breath, and then, recovering his usual coolness of manner, turned to speak to his frightened wife and her visitors. Probably the whole occurrence had not occupied two minutes.

'Come, come, Minnie! You know he is always good-humoured and tractable. Blandois must have irritated him, – made faces at him. The dog has his likings and dislikings, and Blandois is no great favorite of his; but I am sure you'll give him a character, Minnie, for never having been like this before.'

Minnie was too much disturbed to say anything connected in reply; Little Dorrit was already occupied in soothing her; Fanny, who had cried out twice or thrice, held Gowan's arm for protection; Lion, deeply ashamed of having caused them this alarm, came trailing himself along the ground, to the feet of his mistress.

'You furious brute,' said Gowan, striking him with his foot again. 'You shall do penance for this.' And he struck him again, and yet again.

'O, pray don't punish him any more,' cried Little Dorrit. 'Don't hurt him. See how gentle he is!' At her entreaty, Gowan spared him; and he deserved her intercession, for truly he was as submissive, and as sorry, and as wretched as a dog could be.

From *Little Dorrit*

A Born Devil

IN THE OBSCURE parlour of a low public-house, situate in the filthiest part of Little Saffron-Hill; a dark and gloomy den, where a flaring gas-light burnt all day in the winter-time: and where no ray of sun ever shone in the summer; there sat: brooding over a little pewter measure and a small glass, strongly impregnated with the smell of liquor: a man in a velveteen coat, drab shorts, half-boots, and stockings, whom, even by that dim light, no experienced agent of police would have hesitated for one instant to recognise as Mr William Sikes. At his feet, sat a white-coated, red-eyed dog; who occupied himself, alternately, in winking at his master with both eyes at the same time; and in licking a large, fresh cut on one side of his mouth, which appeared to be the result of some recent conflict.

'Keep quiet, you warmint! keep quiet!' said Mr Sikes, suddenly breaking silence. Whether his meditations were so intense as to be disturbed by the dog's winking, or whether his feelings were so wrought upon by his reflections that they required all the relief derivable from kicking an unoffending animal to allay them, is matter for argument and consideration. Whatever was the cause, the effect was a kick and a curse bestowed upon the dog simultaneously.

Dogs are not generally apt to revenge injuries inflicted upon them by their masters; but Mr Sikes's dog, having faults of temper in common with his owner: and labouring, perhaps, at this moment, under a powerful sense of injury: made no more ado but at once fixed his teeth in one of the half-boots. Having given it a hearty shake, he retired, growling, under a form; thereby just escaping the pewter measure which Mr Sikes levelled at his head.

'You would, would you?' said Sikes, seizing the poker in one hand, and deliberately opening with the other a large clasp-knife, which he drew from his pocket. 'Come here, you born devil! Come here! D'ye hear?'

The dog no doubt heard; because Mr Sikes spoke in the very harshest key of a very harsh voice; but, appearing to entertain some unaccountable objecting to having his throat cut, he remained where he was, and growled more fiercely than before: at the same time grasping the end of the poker between his teeth, and biting at it like a wild beast.

This resistance only infuriated Mr Sikes the more; who, dropping on his knees, began to assail the animal most furiously. The dog jumped from right to left, and from left to right: snapping, growling, and barking; the man, thrust and swore, and struck and blasphemed; and the struggle was reaching a most critical point for one or other, when, the door suddenly opening, the dog darted out: leaving Bill Sikes with the poker and the clasp-knife in his hands.

There must always be two parties to a quarrel, says the old adage. Mr Sikes, being disappointed of the dog's participation, at once transferred his share in the quarrel to the new-comer.

'What the devil do you come in between me and my dog for?' said Sikes, with a fierce gesture.

'I didn't know, my dear, I didn't know,' replied Fagin, humbly – for the Jew was the new-comer.

'Didn't know, you white-livered thief!' growled Sikes. 'Couldn't you hear the noise?'

'Not a sound of it, as I'm a living man, Bill,' replied the Jew.

'Oh no! You hear nothing, you don't,' retorted Sikes with a fierce sneer. 'Sneaking in and out, so as nobody hears how you come or go! I wish you had been the dog, Fagin, half a minute ago.'

'Why?' inquired the Jew with a forced smile.

''Cause the government, as cares for the lives of such men as you, as haven't half the pluck of curs, lets a man kill a dog how he likes,' replied Sikes, shutting up the knife with a very expressive look; 'that's why.'

From *Oliver Twist*

'. . . DOGS, SIR?'

'Not just now,' said Mr Winkle.

'Ah! you should keep dogs – fine animals – sagacious creatures – dog of my own once – Pointer – surprising instinct – out shooting one day – entering enclosure – whistled – dog stopped – whistled again – Ponto – no go; stock still – called him – Ponto, Ponto – wouldn't move – dog transfixed – staring at a board – looked up, saw an inscription – "Gamekeeper has orders to shoot all dogs found in the enclosure" – wouldn't pass it – wonderful dog – valuable dog that – very.'

'Singular circumstance, that,' said Mr Pickwick. 'Will you allow me to make a note of it?'

'Certainly, sir, certainly – hundred more anecdotes of the same animal.'

From *The Pickwick Papers*

'THQUIRE, YOU DON'T need to be told that dogth ith wonderful animalth.'

'Their instinct,' said Mr Gradgrind, 'is surprising.'

'Whatever you call it – and I'm bletht if *I* know what to call it,' said Sleary, 'it ith athtonithing. The way in whith a dog'll find you – the dithtanthe he'll come!'

'His scent,' said Mr Gradgrind, 'being so fine.'

'I'm bletht if I know what to call it,' repeated Sleary, shaking his head, 'but I have had dogth find me, Thquire, in a way that made me think whether that dog hadn't gone to another dog, and thed, "You don't happen to know a perthon of the name of Thleary, do you? Perthon of the name of Thleary, in the Horthe-Riding way – thout man – game eye?" And whether that dog mightn't have thed, "Well, I can't thay I know him mythelf, but I know a dog that I think would be likely to be acquainted with him." And whether that dog mightn't have thought it over, and thed, "Thleary, Thleary! O yeth, to be thure! A friend of mine mentioned him to me at one time. I can get you hith addreth directly." In consequenth of my being afore the public, and going about tho muth, you thee, there might be a number of dogth acquainted with me, Thquire, that *I* don't know!'

From *Hard Times*

HANS CHRISTIAN ANDERSEN
The Tinder-Box

LEFT, RIGHT! LEFT, RIGHT! ... Down the country-road came a
soldier marching. Left, right! Left, right! ... He had his knapsack
on his back and a sword at his side, for he had been at the war, and
now he was on his way home. But then he met an old witch on the road.
Oh! she was ugly – her lower lip hung right down on her chest. 'Good
evening, soldier,' she said, 'What a nice sword you've got, and what a
big knapsack! You're a proper soldier! Now I'll show you how to get as
much money as you want!' 'Thank you very much, old dame!' said the
soldier.

'Do you see that big tree over there?' said the witch, pointing to a
tree near by. 'It's quite hollow inside. Now, you must climb right up it,
and then you'll see a hole; slip through this, and you'll come deep down
into the tree. I will tie a rope round your waist, so that I can haul you
up again, as soon as you give me a shout.'

'But what am I to do down in the tree?' asked the soldier.

'Fetch money!' answered the witch. 'For, mind you, when you get
down to the bottom of the tree, you will find yourself in a large passage.
It's quite light there, because hundreds of lamps are burning there.
Next, you will see three doors; you can open them all right, for the key's
in the lock. If you go into the first room, you will see in the middle of
the floor a big chest, with a dog sitting on it which has got eyes as big
as tea-cups; but never you mind about that! I'll give you my blue-check
apron, and you can spread it out on the floor. Then go along quickly
and lift off the dog and put it on my apron; open the lid of the chest
and take just as many pennies as you like. They are all copper, but if
you would rather have silver, then you must go into the next room.
There sits a dog with eyes as large as mill-wheels, but never you mind
about that! Put the dog down on my apron, and help yourself to the
money! And yet, if it's gold you want, you can get that too – as much as
ever you can carry – if only you go into the third room. But this time
the dog which is sitting on the money-chest has two eyes each one as
big as the Round Tower ... Something like a dog, I can tell you! But
never you mind a bit about that! Just put the dog down on my apron,
and then it won't do you any harm, and you can take as much gold out
of the chest as you like.'

'That doesn't sound at all bad,' said the soldier. 'But tell me, old witch, what am I to give you? Because I expect you'll be wanting your share!'

'No,' said the witch, 'not a single penny will I take. You've simply got to bring me an old tinder-box that my grandmother forgot, when she was last down there.'

'Oh, come on, then! let me get that rope round my middle!' said the soldier.

'Here it is,' said the witch, 'and here's my blue-check apron.'

Then the soldier crawled up the tree, let himself down, plump! through the hole, and now he was standing, as the witch had said, down in the great passage where the hundreds of lamps were burning.

Then he unlocked the first door. Ugh! there sat the dog with eyes as big as tea-cups and glared at him.

'You are a nice chap, you are!' said the soldier. He put it down on the witch's apron and took just as many copper pennies as he could stuff into his pocket. Then he shut the chest, put the dog up again and went into the second room. Bless my soul! there sat the dog with eyes as big as mill-wheels.

'You shouldn't stare at me so!' said the soldier; 'you'll strain your eyes.' And then he put the dog down on the witch's apron; but when he saw such piles of silver in the chest, he threw away all the coppers he had got and filled his pockets and his knapsack with nothing but silver. And now he went into the third room! . . . Oh, but it was horrible! The dog in there had actually got two great eyes as big as the Round Tower, and they were going round and round in its head like wheels!

'Good evening!' said the soldier; and he touched his cap, because never in his life had he seen such a dog. But after he had looked at it for a bit, he thought to himself, 'Enough of that!' and went and lifted the dog down on to the floor and opened the chest – why, goodness gracious, what a lot of gold there was! There was enough for him to buy the whole of Copenhagen, all the sugar-pigs that the cake-women sell, and all the tins-soldiers and whips and rocking-horses in the world. Yes, yes, plenty of money in there – my word, there was!

So at once the soldier emptied out all the silver coins from his pockets and his knapsack and put in gold instead; yes, and he filled up everything with gold, his pockets, his knapsack, his cap and even his boots, so that he could hardly walk. Now he had got some money! He put the dog back on the chest, slammed the door, and then shouted up through the tree, 'Hi, mother! haul me up again, will you?'

'Have you got the tinder-box?' asked the witch.

'Oh no! that's true, I had clean forgotten it,' said the soldier; and he went straight back and fetched it. The witch hauled him up out of the tree, and there he was again, standing on the road with his pockets, boots, cap and knapsack bulging with money.

'What are you going to do with this tinder-box?' asked the soldier.

'That's no business of yours!' answered the witch. 'You've got your money; now just give me my tinder-box!'

'Rubbish!' said the soldier. 'Tell me at once what you want to do with it – or I'll have out my sword and cut your head off.'

'No,' said the witch.

So he cut off her head . . . . There she lay!

But the soldier tied up all his money in her apron and made a bundle of it, to go on his back. He put the tinder-box in his pocket and went straight on into the town.

It was a fine town, and he put up at the finest inn. He ordered the very best rooms and the food he was most fond of; for, now that he had all that money, he was a rich man. The servant who had to clean his boots thought, well, this was a funny old pair of boots for such a rich gentleman to have; but he hadn't yet brought any new ones. The next day he went out and got some good boots and some really smart clothes. And now the soldier had become quite a fashionable gentleman, and they told him all about the sights of their town, and about their King, and what a pretty Princess his daughter was.

'Where is she to be seen?' asked the soldier.

'She just isn't to be seen,' they all answered. 'She lives in a big copper castle with lots of walls and towers all round it. No one but the king is allowed to go to her there, because a fortune-teller once said that she is to marry a common soldier, and the king doesn't like that at all.'

'My word! I should like to see her'; thought the soldier; but of course he couldn't possibly get leave to.

And now he lived a merry life.

He was always going to the theatre, or driving in the Park; and he gave away lots of money to the poor. That was very nice of him; you see, he remembered so well from the old days how awful it was to be absolutely penniless. But now he was rich and well-dressed, and so he made lots of friends who all said what a fine fellow he was – a real gentleman – and the soldier liked that very much. But as he was spending money every day and never getting any back, at last he had only got twopence left; and so he had to move from the fine rooms he had been living in and go and live in a little poky attic right under the roof. He had to clean his own boots and mend them with a darning-needle, and none of his friends ever came to see him, for there were such a lot of stairs to climb.

One evening, when it was quite dark and he couldn't even buy himself a candle, he suddenly remembered that there was a little bit of candle left in the tinder-box that he had got for the old witch out of the hollow tree. So he fetched out the tinder-box and the bit of candle; but just as he was striking a light and the sparks flew up from the flint, the door sprang open, and the dog he had seen down in the tree with eyes as big as tea-cups stood before him and said 'What are my lord's commands?'

'I say!' said the soldier. 'This must be a queer sort of tinder-box, if I can get whatever I want like that.' 'Bring me some money', he said to the dog; then flick! and away it went, and flick! here it was back again, with a large bagful of pennies in its mouth.

And now the soldier realised what a splendid tinder-box it was. One stroke brought before him the dog which sat on the chest with the copper money; two strokes, the dog with the silver; and three strokes, the dog with the gold. The soldier lost no time in changing back into the fine rooms and the smart clothes, and of course all his friends remembered him again at once and were tremendously fond of him.

And then one day he thought to himself 'There's something queer about this, that no one's allowed to see the Princess. She's supposed to be so very lovely, according to all these people; but what's the good of that, if she has to sit the whole time inside the copper castle, the one that has all those towers? Can't I possibly manage to see her somehow? Now then, where's my tinder-box?' So he struck a light and flick! there stood the dog with the eyes as big as tea-cups.

'Of course I know it's the middle of the night,' said the soldier, 'but all the same I would like to see the Princess, that I would! Just for half a jiffy!'

The dog was out of the door in a flash and, before the soldier had time to think about it, there was the dog again with the Princess lying asleep on his back; and she looked so lovely that anyone could see she was a real princess; and the soldier simply couldn't resist, he had to kiss her – he was a soldier all over.

The the dog scuttled back again with the Princess, but in the morning, when the King and Queen were at breakfast, the Princess said she had had such a curious dream in the night, about a dog and a soldier. She had ridden on the dog's back, and the soldier had kissed her.

'That's a pretty tale, if you like!' said the Queen.

And so one of the old ladies-in-waiting was told to sit up the following night by the Princess's bed and see if it was really a dream or not.

The soldier did so long for another look at the pretty Princess; and so up came the dog by night and took her and dashed off at full speed. But the old lady-in-waiting put on her overboots and ran just as fast after them, and when she saw them disappear into a big house she thought to herself, 'Now I know where it is', and chalked up a big cross on the door. Then she went home to bed, and the dog came back too with the Princess. But when it saw a cross had been chalked on the door where the soldier was living, the dog also took a bit of chalk and put a cross on every door in the town. That was a clever idea, because now, you see, the lady-in-waiting couldn't find the right door, as there were crosses on the whole lot of them.

Early in the morning the King and Queen, the old lady-in-waiting and all the Court officials sallied forth in order to see where it was the Princess had been.

'Here's the house!' said the King, when he saw the first door with a cross on it.

'No, it's there, darling!' said the Queen, catching sight of the second door with a cross on it.

'But here's another – and there's another!' they all kept saying. Whichever way they turned, there were crosses on the doors. So then they soon realised that it was no good searching any longer.

But the Queen, you know, was a very clever woman, who could do more than just drive out in a coach. She took her great golden scissors and cut up a large piece of silk and sewed the pieces together into a pretty little bag, which she filled with the finest buckwheat flour. She fastened the little bag to the Princess's back, and then she snipped a little hole in the bag, so as to sprinkle the flour wherever the Princess went.

At night, up came the dog once more, took the Princess on his back and ran off with her to the soldier, who loved her so dearly and did so wish he were a prince and could marry her.

The dog never noticed how the flour kept leaking out all the way from the castle to the soldier's window, where it ran up the wall with the Princess. The next morning it was quite plain to the King and

Queen where their daughter had been going; so they took the soldier and put him in prison.

There he sat. Ugh! how dark and dreary his cell was! And, besides, they kept saying to him 'To-morrow you're going to be hanged!' That didn't sound at all cheerful, and the worst of it was he had left his tinder-box at the inn. In the morning, through the iron bars of his little window, he watched people hurrying out of the town to see him hanged. He heard the drums and saw the soldiers marching past. Everyone was afoot. Among them was a cobbler's boy in leather apron and slippers; he was trotting along so fast that one of his slippers came of and flew right against the wall where the soldier sat peeping out between the iron bars.

'I say! you young cobbler, you don't need to hurry like that,' the soldier said to him, 'they can't begin without me. But look here – if you will kindly run along to where I've been living and fetch me my tinder-box, you shall have twopence for your trouble; but mind you get a move on!' The cobbler's boy was very glad to earn twopence, so he sprinted off for the tinder-box, brought it to the soldier, and – well, now listen to what happened!

Outside the town a high gallows had been built, and round about it stood the soldiers and thousands and thousands of people. The King and Queen sat on a beautiful throne opposite the judge and all his councillors.

Already the soldier had climbed the ladder; but just as they were going to put the rope round his neck he reminded them that, before being executed, a criminal always had the right to ask for one harmless favour. He said he would so like to smoke a pipe of tobacco – after all, it would be the last pipe he could smoke in this world.

Now, the King didn't like to say no to that; so the soldier took his tinder-box and struck a light – one, two, three! – and there stood all three dogs: the one with eyes as big as tea-cups, the one with eyes like mill-wheels, and the one which had eyes as big as the Round Tower.

'Save me now from being hanged!' said the soldier; and then the dogs flew at the judges and all the councillors, and seized some by their legs and others by their noses, and tossed them so high into the air that when they came down they were dashed to pieces.

'I won't be tossed!' said the King; but the biggest dog picked them both up, King and Queen, and sent them hurtling after the others. Then the soldiers got frightened, and the people all shouted out 'Soldier boy, you shall be our King and have the pretty Princess'. And they put the soldier into the King's coach, and all three dogs went dancing in front of it and cried out, 'Hurrah!' And the boys whistled on their fingers, and the soldiers presented arms. The Princess came out of the copper castle and was made Queen, and how pleased she was! The wedding-feast lasted for a week, and the dogs sat at table with everyone else and kept rolling their great big eyes.

Trans. R. P. Keigwin

GREYFRIARS BOBBY

The First Report

NEARLY SIX YEARS ago a terrier dog was found lying under a horizontal grave-stone in Old Greyfriar's grave-yard in Edinburgh. The poor brute had evidently been there some days, and, although exhausted with hunger and thirst, viciously refused to be removed. It was coaxed with milk and other canine luxuries, and through the kindness and attention of the gravediggers was soon in a position to run about; but it resolutely refused to leave the kirkyard. There had been a number of funerals from the country for some days prior to that on which the dog was observed, and it was believed that the dog's master had been among the number laid under the sod; but whither it came no one could tell. From that day to this 'Bob', for such is the name he gets, has remained in Greyfriar's Kirkyard. He sleeps in it every night, and spend most of his time in it during the day. During the inclement winter the year before last, Sergeant Scott, of the Royal Engineers, one of Bob's best friends, got him coaxed into his house for a night or two; but the dog was evidently unhappy, and soon returned to his quiet quarters under the tombstone. Bob got to know Sergeant's dinner hours to a minute. With military precision he would meet him at George IV Bridge at a certain hour each day, go home with him, and share his dinner. In the afternoon, when Sergeant Scott prepared to return to the office, Bob would give him a 'Scotch convoy' a short distance past Greyfriars, give a farewell wag or two with his tail, and trot away back to the graveyard.

From the *Ayrshire Express*, 1865

FRED GIPSON

Battles Lost and Won

A BOY, BEFORE HE really grows up, is pretty much like a wild animal. He can get the wits scared clear out of him today and by tomorrow have forgotten all about it.

At least, that's the way it was with me. I was plenty scared of the hydrophobia plague that Burn Sanderson told me about. I could hardly sleep that night. I kept picturing in my mind mad dogs and mad wolves reeling about with the blind staggers, drooling slobbers and snapping and biting at everything in sight. Maybe biting Mama and Little Arliss, so that they got the sickness and went mad, too. I lay in bed and shuddered and shivered and dreamed all sorts of nightmare happenings.

Then, the next day, I went to rounding up and marking hogs and forgot all about the plague.

Our hogs ran loose on the range in those days, the same as our cattle. We fenced them out of the fields, but never into a pasture; we had no pastures. We never fed them, unless maybe it was a little corn that we threw to them during a bad spell in the winter. The rest of the time, they rustled for themselves.

They slept out and ate out. In the summer-time, they slept in the cool places around the water holes, sometimes in the water. In the winter, they could always tell at least a day ahead of time when a blizzard was on the way; then they'd gang up and pack tons of leaves and dry grass and sticks into some dense thicket or cave. They'd pile all this into a huge bed and sleep on until the cold spell blew over.

They ranged all over the hills and down into the canyons. In season, they fed on acorns, berries, wild plums, prickly-pear apples, grass, weeds, and bulb plants which they rooted out of the ground. They especially liked the wild black persimmons that the Mexicans called *chapotes*.

Sometimes, too, they'd eat a newborn calf if the mama cow couldn't keep them horned away. Or a baby fawn that the doe had left hidden in the tall grass. Once, in a real dry time, Papa and I saw an old sow standing belly deep in a drying up pothole of water, catching and eating perch that were trapped in there and couldn't get away.

Most of these meat eaters were old hogs, however. Starvation, during some bad drought or extra cold winter had forced them to eat anything they could get hold of. Papa said they generally started out by feeding on the carcass of some deer or cow that had died, then going from there to catching and killing live meat. He told a tale about how one old range hog had caught him when he was a baby and his folks got there just barely in time to save him.

It was that sort of thing, I guess, that always made Mama so afraid of wild hogs. The least little old biting shoat could make her take cover. She didn't like it a bit when I started out to catch and mark all the pigs that our sows had raised that year. She knew we had it to do, else we couldn't tell our hogs from those of the neighbours. But she didn't like the idea of my doing in alone.

'But I'm not working hogs alone, Mama,' I pointed out. 'I've got Old Yeller, and Burn Sanderson says he's a real good hog dog.'

'That doesn't mean a thing,' Mama said. 'All hog dogs are good ones. A good one is the only kind that can work hogs and live. But the best dog in the world won't keep you from getting cut all to pieces if you ever make a slip.'

Well, Mama was right. I'd worked with Papa enough to know that any time you messed with a wild hog, you were asking for trouble. Let him alone, and he'll generally snort and run from you on sight, the same as a deer. But once you corner him, he's the most dangerous animal that ever lived in Texas. Catch a squealing pig out of the bunch, and you've got a battle on your hands. All of them will turn on you at one time and here they'll come, roaring and popping their teeth, cutting high and fast with gleaming white tushes that they keep whetted to the sharpness of knife points. And there's no bluff to them, either. They mean business. They'll kill you if they can get to you; and if you're not fast footed and don't keep a close watch, they'll get to you.

They had to be that way to live in a country where the wolves, bobcats, panther, and bear were always after them, trying for a bait of fresh hog meat. And it was because of this that nearly all hog owners usually left four or five old barrows, or 'bar' hogs,' as we called them, to run with each bunch of sows. The bar' hogs weren't any more vicious than the boars, but they'd hang with the sows and help them protect the pigs and shoats, when generally the boars pulled off to range alone.

I knew all this about range hogs, and plenty more; yet I still wasn't bothered about the job facing me. In fact, I sort of looked forward to it. Working wild hogs was always exciting and generally proved to be a lot of fun.

I guess the main reason I felt this way was because Papa and I had figured out a quick and nearly fool-proof way of doing it. We could catch most of the pigs we needed to mark and castrate without ever getting in reach of the old hogs. It took a good hog dog to pull off the trick; but the way Burn Sanderson talked about Old Yeller, I was willing to bet that he was that good.

He was, too. He caught on right away.

We located our first bunch of hogs at a seep spring at the head of a shallow dry wash that led back toward Birdsong Creek. There were seven sows, two long-tushed old bar' hogs, and fourteen small shoats.

They'd come there to drink and to wallow around in the potholes of soft cool mud.

They caught wind of us about the same time I saw them. The old hogs threw up their snouts and said 'Woo-oof!' Then they all tore out for the hills, running through the rocks and brush almost as swiftly and silently as deer.

'Head 'em, Yeller,' I hollered. 'Go get 'em, boy!'

But it was a waste of words. Old Yeller was done gone.

He streaked down the slant, crossed the draw, and had the tail-end pig caught by the hind leg before the others knew he was after them.

The pig set up a loud squeal. Instantly, all the old hogs wheeled. They came at Old Yeller with their bristles up, roaring and popping their teeth. Yeller held on to his pig until I thought for a second they had him. Then he let go and whirled away, running toward me, but running slow. Slow enough that the old hogs kept chasing him, thinking every second that they were going to catch him the next.

When they finally saw that they couldn't, the old hogs stopped and formed a tight circle. They faced outward around the ring, their rumps to the centre, where all the squealing pigs were gathered. That way, they were ready to battle anything that wanted to jump on them. That's the way they were used to fighting bear and panther off from their young, and that's the way they aimed to fight us off.

But we were too smart, Old Yeller and I. We knew better than to try to break into that tight ring of threatening tushes. Anyhow, we didn't need to. All we needed was just to move the hogs along to where we wanted them, and Old Yeller already knew how to do this.

Back he went, right up into their faces, where he pestered them with yelling bays and false rushes till they couldn't stand it. With an angry roar, one of the barrows broke the ring to charge him. Instantly, all the others charged, too.

They were right on Old Yeller again. They were just about to get him. Just let them get a few inches closer, and one of them would slam a four-inch tush into his soft belly.

The thing was, Old Yeller never would let them gain that last few inches on him. They cut and slashed at him from behind and both sides, yet he never was quite there. Always he was just a little bit beyond their reach, yet still so close that they couldn't help thinking that the next try was sure to get him.

It was a blood-chilling game Old Yeller played with the hogs, but one that you could see he enjoyed by the way he went at it. Give him time, and he'd take that bunch of angry hogs clear down out of the hills and into the pens at home if that's where I wanted them – never driving them, just leading them along.

But that's where Papa and I had other hog hunters out-figured. We almost never took our hogs to the pens to work them any more. That took too much time. Also, after we got them penned, there was still the dangerous job of catching the pigs away from the old ones.

I hollered at Old Yeller. 'Bring 'em on, Yeller,' I said. Then I turned and headed for a big gnarled live-oak tree that stood in a clear patch of ground down the draw a piece.

I'd picked out that tree because it had a huge branch that stuck out to one side. I went and looked the branch over and saw that it was just right. It was low, yet still far enough above the ground to be out of reach of the highest-cutting hog.

I climbed up the tree and squatted on the branch. I unwound my rope from where I'd packed it coiled around my waist and shook out a loop. Then I hollered for Old Yeller to bring the hogs to me.

He did what I told him. He brought the fighting hogs to the tree and rallied them in a ring around it. Then he stood back, holding them there while he cocked his head sideways at me, wanting to know what came next.

I soon showed him. I waited till one of the pigs came trotting under my limb. I dropped my loop around him, gave it a quick yank, and lifted him, squealing and kicking, up out of the shuffling and roaring mass of hogs below. I clamped him between my knees, pulled out my knife, and went to work on him. First I folded his right ear and sliced out a three-cornered gap in the top side, a mark that we called an overbit. Then, from the under side of his left ear, I slashed off a long strip that ran clear to the point. This is what we called an underslope. That had him marked for me. Our mark was overbit the right and underslope the left.

Other settlers had other marks, like crop the right and underbit the left, or two underbits in the right ear, or an overslope in the left and an overbit in the right. Everybody knew the hog mark of everybody else and we all respected them. We never butchered or sold a hog that didn't belong to us or mark a pig following a sow that didn't wear our mark.

Cutting marks in a pig's ear is bloody work, and the scared pig kicks and squeals like he's dying; but he's not really hurt. What hurts him is the castration, and I never did like that part of the job. But it had to be done, and still does if you want to eat hog meat. Let a boar hog get grown without cutting his seeds out, and his meat is too tough and rank smelling to eat.

The squealing of the pig and the scent of his blood made the hogs beneath me go nearly wild with anger. You never heard such roaring and teeth-popping, as they kept circling the tree and rearing up on its trunk, trying to get to me. The noise they made and the hate and anger that showed in their eyes was enough to chill your blood. Only, I was used to the feeling and didn't let it bother me. That is, not much. Sometimes I'd let my mind slip for a minute and get to thinking how they'd slash me to pieces if I happened to fall out of the tree, and I'd feel a sort of cold shudder run all through me. But Papa had told me right from the start that fear was a right and natural feeling for anybody, and nothing to be ashamed of.

'It's a thing of your mind,' he said, 'and you can train your mind to handle it just like you can train your arm to throw a rock.'

Put that way, it made sense to be afraid; so I hadn't bothered about that. I'd put in all my time trying to train my mind not to let fear stampede me. Sometimes it did yet, of course, but not when I was working hogs. I'd had enough experience at working hogs that now I could generally look down and laugh at them.

I finished with the first pig and dropped it to the ground. Then, one after another, I roped the others, dragged them up into the tree, and worked them over.

A couple of times, the old hogs on the ground got so mad that they broke ranks and charged Old Yeller. But right from the start, Old Yeller had caught on to what I wanted. Every time they chased him from the tree, he'd just run off a little way and circle back, then stand off far enough away that they'd rally around my tree again.

In less than an hour, I was done with the job, and the only trouble we had was getting the hogs to leave the tree after I was finished. After going to so much trouble to hold the hogs under the tree, Old Yeller had a hard time understanding that I finally wanted them out of the way. And even after I got him to leave, the hogs were so mad and so suspicious that I had to squat there in the tree for nearly an hour longer before they finally drifted away into the brush, making it safe for me to come down.

From *Old Yeller*

LEO TOLSTOY

An Extra Traveller

UNTIL THE LAST minute, Aunt Toinette kept expecting another about-face. Once before, he [Tolstoy] had taken it into his head to follow Valerian when he was leaving for Siberia on business, and instantly had gone racing after the tarantass like a madman; then, noticing that he had come off without his hat, he turned back to the house and, suddenly deflated, began thinking of something else.... What if he forgot his hat again this time? But he forgot nothing. On 20 April 1851 the two brothers, one in civilian dress and the other in uniform, said their good-byes to the old lady, who tried not to cry as she blessed them, and jumped into the coach. Tragic barking resounded through the house until the horses moved off: Leo had locked up his dog Bulka to prevent him from following them. At the first relay, as he was climbing back into the tarantass, he saw a black ball rolling down the road – it was Bulka, without his brass collar. 'He came running like the wind and threw himself upon me, licked my hands, and then went to lie down in the shadow of the coach,' Tolstoy wrote. 'Afterwards I learned he had pushed out the windowpanes, jumped out and, following my scent, covered the twelve miles at a dead run in the suffocating heat.' He could not bring himself to send the dog back, so he settled him on his knees and they pursued their journey with an additional passenger, who had heaving flanks, a lolling tongue and blissful eyes.

Henri Troyat, from his *Life of Tolstoy*

Out of Town

WAKING AT DAYBREAK Levin tried to rouse his companions. Vasenka was lying face downwards, one stockinged leg out-stretched, and sleeping so soundly that he could not wake him. Oblonsky sleepily declined to budge so early. Even Laska, who had slept curled round in the hay, got up reluctantly, and lazily stretched and settled one hind leg and then the other. Levin put on his boots and stockings, took his gun, cautiously opened the creaking door of the barn, and went out into the open air. The coachmen were asleep beside the vehicles, the horses were dozing. Only one was lazily eating oats, scattering and blowing them about in the trough. The outside world was still grey.

'Why are you up so early, my dear?' the old woman of the hut asked from the doorway, addressing him in a friendly tone as a good acquaintance of long standing.

'I'm off shooting, Granny. Can I get to the marsh this way?'

'Straight along at the back; past our threshing-floors, my dear, and then by the hemp-patches. You'll find the footpath.'

Treading carefully with her bare, sunburnt feet, the old woman conducted him to the threshing-floor and moved back the fence for him.

'Go straight on and you'll come upon the marsh. Our lads took the horses that way last night.'

Laska bounded gaily ahead along the footpath. Levin followed with a light, brisk step, continually glancing up at the sky. He was anxious to get to the marsh before sunrise. But the sun would not wait. The moon, which had been bright when he first came out, now only gleamed like quicksilver. The pink flush of dawn, which one could not help seeing before, now had to be sought to be discerned at all. What had been vague smudges in the distant countryside were now quite distinct. They were shocks of rye. The dew, not visible till the sun was up, on the tall fragrant hemp which had already shed its pollen, drenched Levin's legs and his blouse even above the belt. In the translucent stillness of the morning the minutest sounds were audible. A bee flew past Levin's ear like the whizz of a bullet. He looked close, and saw another, and then a third. They all came from behind the wattle-fence of an apiary, and disappeared over the hemp-field in the direction of the marsh. The path led straight to the marsh, which was recognizable by the vapours rising from it, thicker in one place and thinner in another, so that the reeds and willow-bushes swayed like little islands in the mist. At the edge of the marsh by the road the peasant boys and men, who had pastured their horses in the night, were lying under their coats, having fallen asleep at daybreak. Near by three hobbled horses were moving about, one of them clattering its chain. Laska trotted beside her master, beseeching to be allowed to run forward, and looking around. Passing the sleeping peasants and reaching the first bog, Levin examined his percussion caps and let the dog go. One of the horses, a sleek, chestnut three-year-old, shied at the sight of Laska, switched its tail and snorted. The other horses were also startled, and splashed through the water with their hobbled feet, making a sucking sound as they drew their hooves out of the thick, clayey mud and began floundering their way out of the marsh. Laska stopped, looking derisively at the horses and inquiringly at Levin. Levin patted her, and gave a whistle to tell her she might begin.

Joyful and intent, Laska started through the bog, which gave beneath her feet.

Running into the marsh, Laska at once detected all over the place, mingled with the familiar smells of roots, marsh grass, slime, and the extraneous odour of horse dung, the scent of birds – of that strong-smelling bird that always excited her more than any other. Here and there among the moss and swamp-sage this scent was very strong, but it was impossible to be sure in which direction it grew stronger or fainter. To find this out it was necessary to get farther to the lee of the wind. Scarcely aware of her legs under her, Laska bounded on with a stiff gallop, so that at each bound she could stop short, going to the right, away from the morning breeze blowing from the east, and turned to face the wind. Sniffing in the air with dilated nostrils, she knew at once that not their scent only but they themselves were here before her, and not only one but a great many of them. Laska slackened her pace. They were here, but precisely where she could not yet decide. To find the exact spot, she began circling round, when suddenly her master's voice drew her off. 'Laska! Here!' he called, pointing to the other side. She stood still, asking him if it would not be better to let her go on as she had begun. But he repeated his command in an angry voice, pointing to a tufty place under water, where there could not be anything. She obeyed, pretending to search, and to please him went over the whole place and then returned to the first spot, and was at once on the scent again. Now, when he was not hindering her, she knew what to do, and without looking where she was stepping, stumbling impatiently over hummocks and falling into water, but righting herself with her strong, supple legs, she began the circle that was to make everything clear. *Their* scent came to her more and more pungently, more and more distinctly, until all at once it became quite plain that one of them was here, on the other side of this tuft of reeds, five paces in front of her. She stopped and her whole body grew rigid. Her short legs prevented her from seeing ahead, but by the scent she was certain it was there, not five paces off. More and more conscious of its presence, she stood still, in the joy of anticipation. Her tail was stretched straight and tense, only the very tip twitching. Her mouth was slightly open, her ears pricked. One ear had got folded back when she was running. She breathed heavily but warily, and still more warily looked round, more with her eyes than her head, to her master. He was coming along, with his familiar face but ever terrible eyes, stumbling over the hummocks and taking to her an unusually long time. She thought he came slowly but in reality he was running.

From Laska's peculiar posture – her mouth half open and her body crouched down as if dragging her hind legs along the ground – Levin knew she was pointing at snipe, and with an inward prayer for success, especially with his first bird, he ran towards her. When he came up close to her and looked beyond, he saw from his height what she had perceived with her nose. In a little space between two hummocks he caught sight of a snipe. It had turned its head and was listening. Then lightly preening and folding its wings, it disappeared round a corner with an awkward jerk of its tail.

'Go, Laska, go!' shouted Levin, giving her a shove from behind.

'But I can't go,' thought Laska. 'Where am I to go? I can scent them from here, but if I move I shan't know where they are or what they are.' But now he pushed her with his knee, and in an excited whisper said, 'Go, Laska, good dog, go!'

'All right, if that's what he wants, but I can't answer for myself now,' thought Laska, and rushed forward at full tilt between the hummocks. She was no longer on the scent, but only saw and heard, without understanding anything.

Ten paces from her former place a snipe rose with a guttural cry, its wings making the hollow sound peculiar to snipe. And immediately following the report it fell heavily on its white breast in the wet bog. Another rose behind Levin, without waiting to be put up by the dog. By the time Levin had turned towards it, it was already some way off. But his shot caught it. It flew on about twenty feet, rose sharply, and then, turning over and over like a ball, dropped heavily to the ground, on a dry spot.

'This looks like business!' thought Levin, stowing the warm fat snipe into his game-bag. 'Eh, Laska, what do you think?'

From *Anna Karenin*
Trans. Rosemary Edmonds

EMILY DICKINSON

Wisdom

YOU ASK OF my companions. Hills, sir, and the sundown, and a dog as large as myself, that my father bought me. They are better than beings, because they know, but do not tell.

To Col. T. W. Higginson, 25 April 1862

CHRISTINA ROSSETTI

A Poor Old Dog

Pity the sorrows of a poor old dog
   Who wags his tail a-begging in his need;
Despise not even the sorrows of a frog,
   God's creature too, and that's enough to plead;
Spare puss who trusts us dozing on our hearth;
   Spare bunny, once so frisky and so free;
Spare all the harmless creatures of the earth:
   Spare, and be spared – or who shall plead for thee?

GEORGE ELIOT

Research

'Fuck off, Hiram.'
   'Always promises, my sweet.' Quickly he poured himself more gin; from long experience he knew that his time with us would be short. 'You do make a pretty couple, no doubt of that, like two boys in the sort of vulgar fiction you-know-who writes.'

'Get your ass out of here.' Any attack on *The City and the Pillar* always sends V.'s blood pressure up. I suppose because he knows it isn't very good.

'Temper, temper!' Hiram's green teeth flashed. 'You really should work harder, and read more. I'll lend you my Ph.D. thesis if you like. It was much admired at Northwestern – so was I until I was rusticated, or urbinated as it turned out. The subject was "How The Spaniel Figures in the Novels of George Eliot". Of course, you've never read her – too busy writing when you should've been reading – but it was I who made the discovery that in each book not only is there a spaniel but the angel dog – they are all glorified such was her vision – invariably turns the plot at a crucial moment, as in *Silas Marner* when the dog is *not* petted by the young squire at the start of the novel, demonstrating to both dog and us that the young man's nature is unloving. In *Felix Holt the Radical*, however, it is a different story . . . oh dear, I'm boring you. I can tell. You don't like dogs, do you? or literature. I should've known. . . .'

Gore Vidal, from *Two Sisters*

Dogs in the Life

I ENJOY VERY MUCH the great expanse of blue and clouds that make a great arch over us when we are walking on Wimbledon Common, which is really worthy to be called a 'plain' – it is such a grand stretch of heath-clad level ground. This fine Common is the chief thing we have to make amends for the loss of the Richmond walks, which are so various and so beautiful. We have had a long, long walk today – Pug being with us of course; and I wish you had seen that young gentleman's interview with a brood of small pigs. Pug goes up to every animal with an apparent intention of making their acquaintance, but no sooner do they put out their noses in an inspecting or threatening manner, than he runs to a distance, and like the South Sea Islanders, dances his war dance at a safe remoteness from hoofs and noses. Yet the next minute he forgets his fear and runs up again: clearly a dog to whom experience is not a successful teacher!

(To Charles Lewes, 7 October 1859)

Y OU MUST NO longer believe in Pug's portrait – he is so much handsomer, to say nothing of the new 'mind, the music breathing from his face.' Considering that when he came, he was a sort of crétin, fit for Dr Guggenbühl's establishment, I am proud of the advance he has made in three months of our intellectual society.

To John Blackwood, 16 October 1859

Y OU HAVE NEVER sent us a word of news about Pug! I hope no tragedy awaits us on our return. We have seen a pair of puppies – brother and sister – here at Venice that made us long to carry them home as companions for our very slow child.

To Mrs Bell, 8 June 1860

A GREAT DOMESTIC EVENT for us has been the arrival of a new dog [Dash] who has all Ben's virtues, with more intelligence, and a begging attitude of irresistible charm. He is a dark-brown spaniel. You see what infantine innocence we live in!

To Mrs Congreve, 22 January 1872

D ASH LOST.

From G. H. Lewes, *Diary*, 5 February 1872

W ILL YOU TELL Dr John Brown that when I read an account of 'Rab and his Friends' in a newspaper, I wished I had the story to read at full length and I thought to myself, the writer of 'Rab' would perhaps like 'Adam Bede.'

When you have told him this, he will understand the peculiar pleasure I had on opening the little parcel with 'Rab' inside and a kind word from Rab's friend. I have read the story twice – once aloud, and once to myself, very slowly, that I might dwell on the pictures of Rab and Ailie, and carry them about with me more distinctly. I will not say any commonplace words of admiration about what has touched me so deeply: there is no adjective of that sort left undefiled by the newspapers. The writer of 'Rab' *knows* that I must love the grim old mastiff with the short tail and the long dewlaps – that I must have felt present at the scenes of Ailie's last trial.

To John Blackwood, 13 February 1859

DR JOHN BROWN

Ailie

O NE FINE OCTOBER afternoon, I was leaving the hospital, when I saw the large gate open, and in walked Rab, with that great and easy saunter of his. He looked as if taking general possession of the place; like the Duke of Wellington entering a subdued city, satiated with victory and peace. After him came Jess, now white from age, with her cart; and in it a woman, carefully wrapped up, – the carrier leading the horse anxiously, and looking back. When he saw me, James (for his name was James Noble) made a curt and grotesque 'boo' and said, 'Maister John, this is the mistress; she's got a trouble in her breast – some kind o' an income we're thinkin'.'

By this time I saw the woman's face; she was sitting on a sack filled with straw, her husband's plaid round her, and his big-coat, with its large white metal buttons, over her feet. I never saw a more unforgetable face – pale, serious, *lonely*, delicate, sweet, without being what we call fine. She looked sixty, and had on a mutch, white as snow, with its black ribbon; her silvery smooth hair setting off her dark-grey eyes – eyes such as one sees only twice or thrice in a lifetime, full of suffering, but full also of the overcoming of it; her eye-brows black and delicate, and her mouth firm, patient, and contented, which few mouths ever are.

As I have said, I never saw a more beautiful countenance, or one more subdued to settled quiet. 'Ailie,' said James, 'this is Maister John, the young doctor; Rab's freend, ye ken. We often speak aboot you, doctor.' She smiled, and made a movement, but said nothing; and prepared to come down, putting her plaid aside and rising. Had Solomon, in all his glory, been handing down the Queen of Sheba at his palace gate, he could not have done it more daintily, more tenderly, more like a gentleman, than did James the Howgate carrier, when he lifted down Ailie, his wife. The contrast of his small, swarthy, weather-beaten, keen, worldly face to hers – pale, subdued, and beautiful – was something wonderful. Rab looked on concerned and puzzled, but ready for anything that might turn up, – were it to strangle the nurse, the porter, or even me. Ailie and he seemed great friends.

'As I was sayin', she's got a kind o' trouble in her breast, doctor; wull ye tak' a look at it?' We walked into the consulting room, all four; Rab grim and comic, willing to be happy and confidential if cause could be shown, willing also to be quite the reverse, on the same terms. Ailie sat down, undid her open gown and her lawn handkerchief round her neck, and, without a word, showed me her right breast. I looked at and examined it carefully, – she and James watching me, and Rab eyeing all three. What could I say? there it was, that had once been so soft, so shapely, so white, so gracious and bountiful, 'so full of all blessed conditions,' – hard as a stone, a centre of horrid pain, making that pale face, with its grey, lucid, reasonable eyes, and its sweet resolved mouth, express the full measure of suffering overcome. Why was that gentle, modest, sweet woman, clean and lovable, condemned by God to bear such a burden?

I got her away to bed. 'May Rab and me bide?' said James. '*You* may; and Rab, if he will behave himself.' 'I'se warrant he's do that, doctor;' and in slunk the faithful beast. I wish you could have seen him. There are no such dogs now: he belonged to a lost tribe. As I have said, he was brindled, and grey like Aberdeen granite; his hair short, hard, and close, like a lion's; his body thick set, like a little bull – a sort of compressed Hercules of a dog. He must have been ninety pounds' weight, at the least; he had a large blunt head; his muzzle black as night; his mouth blacker than any night, a tooth or two – being all he had – gleaming out of his jaws of darkness. His head was scarred with the records of old wounds, a sort of series of fields of battle all over it; one eye out, one ear cropped as close as was Archbishop Leighton's father's – but for different reasons, – the remaining eye had the power of two; and above it, and in constant communication with it, was a tattered rag of an ear, which was for ever unfurling itself, like an old flag; and then that bud of a tail, about one inch long, if it could in any sense be said to be long, being as broad as long – the mobility, the instantaneousness of that bud was very funny and surprising, and its expressive twinklings and winkings, the intercommunications between the eye, the ear, and it, were of the subtlest and swiftest. Rab had the dignity and simplicity of great size; and having fought his way all along the road to absolute supremacy, he was as mighty in his own line as Julius Cæsar or the Duke of Wellington; and he had the gravity of all great fighters.

You must have often observed the likeness of certain men to certain animals, and of certain dogs to men. Now, I never looked at Rab without thinking of the great Baptist preacher, Andrew Fuller. The same large, heavy, menacing, combative, sombre, honest countenance, the same inevitable eye, the same look, – as of thunder asleep, but ready, – neither a dog nor a man to be trifled with.

Next day, my master, the surgeon, examined Ailie. There was no doubt it must kill her, and soon. It could be removed – it might never return – it would give her speedy relief – she should have it done. She curtsied, looked at James, and said, 'When?' 'Tomorrow,' said the kind surgeon, a man of few words. She and James and Rab and I retired. I noticed that he and she spoke little, but seemed to anticipate everything in each other. The following day, at noon, the students came in, hurrying up the great stair. At the first landing-place, on a small well-known black board, was a bit of paper fastened by wafers, and many remains of old wafers beside it. On the paper were the words, 'An operation to-day. J B *Clerk.*'

Up ran the youths, eager to secure good places: in they crowded, full of interest and talk. 'What's the case?' 'Which side is it?'

Don't think them heartless; they are neither better nor worse than you or I: they get over their professional horrors, and into their proper work; and in them pity – as an *emotion*, ending in itself or at best in tears and a long-drawn breath, lessens, while pity as a *motive*, is quickened, and gains power and purpose. It is well for poor human nature that it is so.

The operating theatre is crowded; much talk and fun, and all the cordiality and stir of youth. The surgeon with his staff of assistants is there. In comes Ailie: one look at her quiets and abates the eager students. That beautiful old woman is too much for them; they sit down, and are dumb, and gaze at her. These rough boys feel the power of her presence. She walks in quickly, but without haste; dressed in her mutch, her neckerchief, her white dimity shortgown, her black bomba-zeen petticoat, showing her white worsted stockings and her carpet-shoes. Behind her was James, with Rab. James sat down in the distance, and took that huge and noble head between his knees. Rab looked perplexed and dangerous; for ever cocking his ear and dropping it as fast.

Ailie stepped up on a seat, and laid herself on the table, as her friend the surgeon told her; arranged herself, gave a rapid look at James, shut her eyes, rested herself on me, and took my hand. The operation was at once begun; it was necessarily slow; and chloroform – one of God's best gifts to his suffering children – was then unknown. The surgeon did his work. The pale face showed its pain, but was still and silent. Rab's soul was working within him; he saw that something strange was going on, – blood flowing from his mistress, and she suffering; his ragged ear was up, and importunate; he growled and gave now and then a sharp impatient yelp; he would have liked to have done something to that man. But James had him firm, and gave him a glower from time to time, and an intimation of a possible kick; – all the better for James, it kept his eye and his mind off Ailie.

It is over: she is dressed, steps gently and decently down from the table, looks for James; then, turning to the surgeon and the students, she curtsies, – and in a low, clear voice, begs their pardon if she has behaved ill. The students – all of us – wept like children; the surgeon happed her up carefully, – and, resting on James and me, Ailie went to her room, Rab following. We put her to bed. James took off his heavy shoes, crammed with tackets, heel-capt and toe-capt, and putting them carefully under the table, saying, 'Maister John, I'm for nane o' yer strynge nurse bodies for Ailie. I'll be her nurse, and on my stockin' soles I'll gang about as canny as pussy.' And so he did; and handy and clever, and swift and tender as any woman, was that horny-handed, snell, peremptory little man. Everything she got he gave her: he seldom slept; and often I saw his small, shrewd eyes out of the darkness, fixed on her. As before, they spoke little.

Rab behaved well, never moving, showing us how meek and gentle he could be, and occasionally, in his sleep, letting us know that he was demolishing some adversary. He took a walk with me every day, generally to the Candlemaker Row; but he was sombre and mild; declined doing battle, though some fit cases offered, and indeed submitted to sundry indignities; and was always very ready to turn, and came faster back, and trotted up the stair with much lightness, and went straight to *that* door.

Jess, the mare – now white – had been sent, with her weather-worn cart, to Howgate, and had doubtless her own dim and placid meditations and confusions, on the absence of her master and Rab, and her unnatural freedom from the road and her cart.

For some days Ailie did well. The wound healed 'by the first intention;' as James said, 'Oor Ailie's skin's ower clean to beil.' The students came in quiet and anxious, and surrounded her bed. She said she liked to see their young, honest faces. The surgeon dressed her, and spoke to her in his own short kind way, pitying her through his eyes, Rab and James outside the circle, – Rab being now reconciled, and even cordial, and having made up his mind that as yet nobody required worrying, but, as you may suppose *semper paratus*.

So far well: but, four days after the operation, my patient had a sudden and long shivering, a 'groofin',' as she called it. I saw her soon after; her eyes were too bright, her cheek coloured; she was restless, and ashamed of being so; the balance was lost; mischief had begun. On looking at the wound, a blush of red told the secret: her pulse was rapid, her breathing anxious and quick, she wasn't herself, as she said, and was vexed at her restlessness. We tried what we could. James did everything, was everywhere; never in the way, never out of it; Rab subsided under the table into a dark place, and was motionless, all but his eye, which followed every one. Ailie got worse; began to wander in her mind, gently; was more demonstrative in her ways to James, rapid in her questions, and sharp at times. He was vexed, and said, 'She was never that way afore; no, never.' For a time she knew her head was wrong, and was always asking our pardon – the dear, gentle old woman: then delirium set in strong, without pause. Her brain gave way, and that terrible spectacle,

> 'The intellectual power, through words and things,
>   Went sounding on its dim and perilous way;'

she sang bits of old songs and Psalms, stopping suddenly, mingling the Psalms of David, and the diviner words of his Son and Lord, with homely odds and ends and scraps of ballads.

Nothing more touching, or in a sense more strangely beautiful, did I ever witness. Her tremulous, rapid, affectionate, eager Scotch voice, – the swift, aimless, bewildered mind, the baffled utterance, the bright and perilous eye; some wild words, some household cares, something for James, the names of the dead, Rab called rapidly and in a 'fremyt' voice, and he starting up, surprised, and slinking off as if he were to blame somehow, or had been dreaming he heard. Many eager questions and beseechings which James and I could make nothing of, and on which she seemed to set her all and then sink back ununderstood. It was very sad, but better than many things that are not called sad. James hovered about, put out and miserable, but active and exact as ever; read to her, when there was a lull, short bits from the Psalms, prose and metre, chanting the latter in his own rude and serious way, showing great knowledge of the fit words, bearing up like a man, and doating over her as his 'ain Ailie.' 'Ailie, ma woman!' 'Ma ain bonnie wee dawtie!'

The end was drawing on: the golden bowl was breaking; the silver cord was fast being loosed – that *animula, blandula, vagula, hospes, comesque*, was about to flee. The body and the soul – companions for sixty years – were being sundered, and taking leave. She was walking, alone, through the valley of that shadow, into which one day we all must enter – and yet she was not alone, for we know whose rod and staff were comforting her.

One night she had fallen quiet, and as we hoped, asleep; her eyes were shut. We put down the gas, and sat watching her. Suddenly she sat up in bed, and taking a bedgown which was lying on it rolled up, she held it eagerly to her breast, – to the right side. We could see her eyes bright with a surprising tenderness and joy, bending over this bundle of clothes. She held it as a woman holds her sucking child; opening out her night-gown impatiently, and holding it close, and brooding over it, and murmuring foolish little words, as over one whom his mother comforteth, and who is sucking, and being satisfied. It was pitiful and strange to see her wasted dying look, keen and yet vague – her immense love. 'Preserve me!' groaned James, giving way. And then she rocked back and forward, as if to make it sleep, hushing it, and wasting on it her infinite fondness. 'Wae's me, doctor; I declare she's thinkin' its that bairn.' 'What bairn?' 'The only bairn we ever had; our wee Mysie, and she's in the the Kingdom, forty years and mair.' It was plainly true: the pain in the breast, telling its urgent story to a bewildered, ruined brain; it was misread and mistaken; it suggested to her the uneasiness of a breast full of milk, and then the child; and so again once more they were together, and she had her ain wee Mysie in her bosom.

This was the close. She sunk rapidly; the delirium left her; but as she whispered, she was clean silly; it was the lightening before the final darkness. After having for some time lain still – her eyes shut, she said 'James!' He came close to her, and lifting up her calm, clear, beautiful eyes, she gave him a long look, turned to me kindly but shortly, looked for Rab but could not see him, then turned to her husband again, as if she would never leave off looking, shut her eyes, and composed herself. She lay for some time breathing quick, and passed away so gently, that when we thought she was gone, James, in his old-fashioned way, held the mirror to her face. After a long pause, one small spot of dimness was breathed out; it vanished away, and never returned, leaving the blank clear darkness of the mirror without a stain. 'What is our life? it is even a vapour, which appeareth for a little time, and then vanisheth away.'

Rab all this time had been full awake and motionless: he came forward beside us: Ailie's hand, which James had held, was hanging down; it was soaked with his tears; Rab licked it all over carefully, looked at her, and returned to his place under the table.

James and I sat, I don't know how long, but for some time, – saying nothing: he started up abruptly, and with some noise went to the table, and putting his right fore and middle fingers each into a shoe, pulled them out, and put them on, breaking one of the leather latchets, and muttering in anger, 'I never did the like o' that afore!'

I believe he never did; nor after either. 'Rab!' he said roughly, and pointing with his thumb to the bottom of the bed. Rab leapt up, and settled himself; his head and eye to the dead face. 'Maister John, ye'll wait for me,' said the carrier; and disappeared in the darkness, thundering down stairs in his heavy shoes. I ran to a front window: there he was, already round the house, and out at the gate, fleeing like a shadow.

I was afraid about him, and yet not afraid; so I sat down beside Rab, and being wearied, fell asleep. I awoke from a sudden noise outside. It was November, and there had been a heavy fall of snow. Rab was in *statu quo*; he heard the noise too, and plainly knew it, but never moved. I looked out; and there, at the gate, in the dim morning – for the sun was not up, was Jess and the cart, – a cloud of steam rising from the old mare. I did not see James; he was already at the door, and came up the stairs, and met me. It was less than three hours since he left, and he must have posted out – who knows how? – to Howgate, full nine miles off; yoked Jess, and driven her astonished into town. He had an armful of blankets, and was streaming with perspiration. He nodded to me, spread out on the floor two pairs of old clean blankets, having at their corners, 'A. G., 1794,' in large letters in red worsted. These were the initials of Alison Græme, and James may have looked in at her from without – unseen but not unthought of – when he was 'wat, wat, and weary,' and had walked many a mile over the hills, and seen her sitting, while 'a' the lave were sleepin';' and by the firelight putting her name on the blankets for her ain James's bed. He motioned Rab down, and taking his wife in his arms, laid her in the blankets, and happed her carefully and firmly up, leaving the face uncovered; and then lifting her, he nodded again sharply to me, and with a resolved but utterly miserable face, strode along the passage, and down stairs, followed by Rab. I also followed, with a light; but he didn't need it. I went out, holding stupidly the light in my hand in the frosty air; we were soon at the gate. I could have helped him, but I saw he was not to be meddled with, and he was strong, and did not need it. He laid her down as tenderly, as safely, as he had lifted her out ten days before – as tenderly as when he had her first in his arms when she was only 'A. G.,' – sorted her, leaving that beautiful sealed face open to the heavens; and then taking Jess by the head, he moved away. He did not notice me, neither did Rab, who presided alone behind the cart.

I stood till they passed through the long shadow of the College, and turned up Nicolson Street. I heard the solitary cart sound through the streets, and die away and come again; and I returned, thinking of that company going up Libberton brae, then along Roslin muir, the morning light touching the Pentlands and making them like on-looking ghosts; then down the hill through Auchindinny woods, past 'haunted Wood-houselee;' and as daybreak came sweeping up the bleak Lammermuirs, and fell on his own door, the company would stop, and James would take the key, and lift Ailie up again, laying her on her own bed, and, having put Jess up, would return with Rab and shut the door.

James buried his wife, with his neighbours mourning, Rab inspecting the solemnity from a distance. It was snow, and that black ragged hole would look strange in the midst of the swelling spotless cushion of white. James looked after everything; then rather suddenly fell ill, and took to bed; was insensible when the doctor came, and soon died. A sort of low fever was prevailing in the village, and his want of sleep, his exhaustion, and his misery, made him apt to take it. The grave was not difficult to re-open. A fresh fall of snow had again made all things white and smooth; Rab once more looked on, and slunk home to the stable.

And what of Rab? I asked for him next week at the new carrier's who got the goodwill of James's business, and was now master of Jess and her cart. 'How's Rab?' He put me off, and said rather rudely, 'What's *your* business wi' the dowg?' I was not to be so put off. 'Where's Rab?' He, getting confused and red, and intermeddling with his hair, said, ''Deed, sir, Rab's died.' 'Dead! what did he die of?' 'Weel, sir,' said he, getting redder, 'he didna exactly die; he was killed. I had to brain him wi' a rack-pin; there was nae doin' wi' him. He lay in the treviss wi' the mear, and wadna come oot. I tempit him wi' kail and meat, but he wad tak' naething, and keepit me frae feedin' the beast, and he was aye gur gurrin', and grup gruppin' me by the legs. I was laith to mak' awa wi' the auld dowg, his like wasna atween this and Thornhill, – but 'deed, sir, I could do naething else.' I believed him. Fit end for Rab, quick and

complete. His teeth and his friends gone, why should he keep the peace
and be civil?

From *Horae Subsecivae*

A. C. SWINBURNE
To Dr John Brown

Beyond the north wind lay the land of old
   Where men dwelt blithe and blameless, clothed and fed
   With joy's bright raiment and with love's sweet bread,
The whitest flock of earth's maternal fold.
None there might wear about his brows enrolled
   A light of lovelier fame than rings your head,
   Whose lovesome love of children and the dead
All men give thanks for: I far off behold
A dear dead hand that links us, and a light
The blithest and benignest of the night,
   The night of death's sweet sleep, wherein may be
A star to show your spirit in present sight
   Some happier island in the Elysian sea
   Where Rab may lick the hand of Marjorie.

At a Dog's Grave

I

Good night, we say, when comes the time to win
The daily death divine that shuts up sight,
Sleep, that assures for all who dwell therein
      Good night.

The shadow shed round those we love shines bright
As love's own face, when death sleep's gentler twin,
From them divides us even as night from light.

Shall friends born lower in life, though pure of sin,
Though clothed with love and faith to usward plight,
Perish and pass unbidden of us, their kin,
      Good night?

II

To die a dog's death once was held for shame.
Not all men so beloved and mourned shall lie
As many of these, whose time untimely came
      To die.

His years were full: his years were joyous: why
Must love be sorrow, when his gracious name
Recalls his lovely life of limb and eye?

If aught of blameless life on earth may claim
Life higher than death, though death's dark wave rise high,
Such life was this among us never came
      To die.

III

White violets, there by hands more sweet than they
Planted, shall sweeten April's flowerful air
About a grave that shows to night and day
    White violets there.

A child's light hands, whose touch makes flowers more fair,
Keep fair as these for many a March and May
The light of days that are because they were.

It shall not like a blossom pass away;
It broods and brightens with the days that bear
Fresh fruits of love, but leave, as love might pray,
    White violets there.

ALFRED, LORD TENNYSON
Owd Roä

NAÄY, noä mander o' use to be callin' 'im Roä, Roä, Roä,
Fur the dog's stoän-deäf, an' e's blind, 'e can naither stan' nor goä.

But I meäns fur to maäke 'is owd aäge as 'appy as iver I can,
Fur I owäs owd Roäver moor nor I iver owäd mottal man.

Thou's rode of 'is back when a babby, afoor thou was gotten too owd,
Fur 'e'd fetch an' carry like owt, 'e was allus as good as gowd.

Eh, but 'e'd fight wi' a will *when* 'e fowt; 'e could howd 'is oan,
An' Roä was the dog as knaw'd when an' wheere to bury his boane.

An' 'e kep his heäd hoop like a king, an' 'e'd niver not down wi' 'is
taäil,
Fur 'e'd niver done nowt to be shaämed on, when we was i' Howlaby
Daäle.

An' 'e sarved me sa well when 'e lived, that, Dick, when 'e cooms to be
deäd,
I thinks as I'd like fur to hev soom soort of a sarvice reäd.

Fur 'e's moor good sense na the Parliament man 'at stans fur us 'ere,
An' I'd voät fur 'im, my oän sen, if 'e could but stan fur the Shere.

'Faäithful an' True' – them words be 'i Scriptur – an' Faäithful an'
True
Ull be fun' upo' four short legs ten times fur one upo' two.

An' maäybe they'll walk upo' two but I knaws they runs upo' four, –
Bedtime, Dicky! but waäit till tha 'eärs it be strikin' the hour.

Fur I wants to tell tha o' Roä when we lived i' Howlaby Daäle,
Ten year sin – Naäy – naäy! tha mun nob but hev' one glass of aäle.

Straänge an' owd-farran'd the 'ouse, an' belt long afoor my daäy
Wi' haäfe o' the chimleys a-twizzen'd an' twined like a band o' haäy.

The fellers as maäkes them picturs, 'ud coom at the fall o' the year,
An' sattle their ends upo stools to pictur the door-poorch theere,

An' the Heagle 'as hed two heäds stannin' theere o' the brokken stick;
An' they niver 'ed seed sich ivin' as graw'd hall ower the brick;

An' theere i' the 'ouse one night – but it's down, an' all on it now
Goan into mangles an' tonups, an, raäved slick thruf by the plow –

Theere, when the 'ouse wur a house, one night I wur sittin' aloän,
Wi Roäver athurt my feeät, an' sleeäpin still as a stoän,

Of a Christmas Eäve, an' as cowd as this, an' the midders as white,
An' the fences all on 'em bolster'd oop wi' the windle that night;

An' the cat wur a sleeäpin alongside Roäver, but I wur awaäke,
An' smoäkin' an' thinkin' o' things – Doänt maäke thysen sick wi' the
caäke.

Fur the men ater supper 'ed sung their songs an' 'ed 'ed their beer,
An' 'ed goän their waäys; ther was nobbut three, an' noän on 'em
theere.

They was all on 'em fear'd o' the Ghoäst an' dussn't not sleeäp i' the
'ouse,
But Dicky, the Ghoäst moästlins was nobbut a rat or a mouse.

An' I looökt out wonst at the night, an' the daäle was all of a thaw,
Fur I seed the beck coomin' down like a long black snaäke i' the snaw,

An' I heärd greät heäps o' the snaw slushin' down fro' the bank to the
beck,
An' then as I stood i' the doorwaäy, I feeäld it drip o' my neck.

Saw I turn'd in ageän, an' I thowt o' the good owd times 'at was goan,
An' the munney they maäde by the war, an' the times 'at was coomin'
on;

Fur I thowt if the Staäte was a gawin' to let in furriners' wheät,
Howiver was British farmers to stan' ageän o' their feeät.

Howiver was I fur to find my rent an' to paäy my men?
An' all along o' the feller as turn'd 'is back of hissen.

Thou slep i' the chaumber above us, we couldn't ha' 'eärd tha call,
So Moother 'ed tell'd ma to bring tha down, an' thy craädle an' all;

Fur the gell o' the farm 'at slep wi' tha then 'ed gotten wer leäve,
Fur to goä that night to 'er foälk by cause o' the Christmas Eäve;

But I cleän forgot tha, my lad, when Moother 'ed gotten to bed,
An' I slep i' my chair hup-on-end, an' the Freeä Traäde runn'd i'
my 'ead,

Till I dreäm'd 'at Squire walkt in, an' I says to him 'Squire, ya're
laäte,'
Then I seed at 'is faäce wur was red as the Yule-block theer i' the
graäte.

An' 'e says 'can ya paäy me the rent To-night?' an' I says to 'im 'Noä,'
An' 'e cotch'd howd hard o' my hairm, 'Then hout to-night tha shall
goä.'

'Tha'll niver,' says I, 'be a-turnin ma hout upo' Christmas Eäve'?
Then I waäked an' I fun it was Roäver a-tuggin' an' teärin' my slieäve.

An' I thowt as 'e'd goän cleän-wud, fur I noäwaäys knaw'd 'is intent;
An' I says 'Git awaäy, ya beäst,' an' I fetcht 'im a kick an' 'e went.

Then 'e tummled up stairs, fur I 'eärd 'im, as if 'e'd 'a brokken 'is
neck,
An' I'd cleär forgot, little Dicky, thy chaumber door wouldn't sneck;

An' I slep' i' my chair ageän wi' my hairm hingin' down to the floor,
An' I thowt it was Roäver a-tuggin' an' teärin' me wuss nor afoor,

An' I thowt 'at I kick'd 'im ageän, but I kick'd thy Moother istead.
'What arta snorin' theere fur? the house is afire,' she said.

Thy Moother 'ed beän a-naggin' about the gell o' the farm,
She offens 'ud spy summut wrong when there warn't not a mossel o'
                                                                harm;

An' she didn't not solidly meän I wur gnawin' that waäy to the bad,
Fur the gell was as howry a trollope as iver traäpes'd i' the squad.

But Moother was free of 'er tongue, as I offens 'ev tell'd 'er mysen,
Sa I kep i' my chair, fur I thowt she was nobbut a-rilin' ma then.

An' I says 'I'd be good to tha, Bess, if tha'd onywaäys let ma be good,'
But she skelpt ma haäfe ower i' the chair, an' screeäd like a Howl gone
                                                                wud –

'Ya mun run fur the lether. Git oop, if ya're onywaäys good for owt.'
And I says 'If I beänt noäwaäys – not nowadaäys – good fur nowt –

Yit I beänt sich a Nowt of all Nowts as 'ull hallus do as 'e's bid.'
'But the stairs is afire,' she said; then I seed 'er a-cryin', I did.

An' she beäld 'Ya mun saäve little Dick, an' be sharp about it an' all,'
Sa I runs to the yard fur a lether, an' sets 'im ageän the wall,

An' I claumns an' I mashes the winder hin, when I gits to the top,
But the heät druv hout i' my heyes till I feäld mysen ready to drop.

Thy Moother was howdin' the lether, an' tellin' me not to be skeärd,
An' I wasn't afeärd, or I thinks leästwaäys as I wasn't afeärd;

But I couldn't see fur the smoäke wheere thou was a-liggin, my lad,
An' Roäver was theere i' the chaumber a-yowlin' an' yaupin' like mad;

An' thou was a-beälin' likewise, an' a- squeälin', as if tha was bit,
An' it wasn't a bite but a burn, fur the merk's o' thy shou'der yit;

Then I call'd out Roä, Roä, Roä, thaw I didn't haäfe think as'e'd 'ear,
But 'e coom'd thruf the fire wi' my bairn i' is mouth to the winder theere!

He coom'd like a Hangel o' marcy as soon as 'e 'eärd 'is naäme,
Or like tother Hangel i' Scriptur 'at sum mun seed i' the flaäme,

When summun 'ed hax'd fur a son, an' 'e promised a son to she,
An' Roä was as good as the Hangel i' saävin' a son fur me.

Sa I browt that down, an' I says 'I mun gaw up ageän fur Roä.'
'Gaw up ageän fur the varmint?' I tell'd 'er 'Yeäs I mun goä.'

An' I claumb'd up agean to the winder, an' clemm'd owd Roä by the
'eäd,
An' 'is 'air coom'd off i' my 'ands an' I taäked 'im at fust fur deäd;

Fur 'e smell'd like a herse a-singein', an' seeäm'd as blind as a poop,
An' haäfe on 'im bare as a bublin', I couldn't wakken 'im oop,

But I browt 'im down, an' we got to the barn, fur the barn wouldn't
burn
Wi' the wind blawin' hard tother waäy, an' the wind wasn't like to turn.

An' *I* kept a-callin' o' Roä til 'e waggled 'is taäil fur a bit,
But the cocks kep a-crawin' an crawin' all night, an' I 'ears 'em yit;

An' the dogs was a-yowlin' all round, and thou was a-squealin' thysen,
An' Moother was naggin' an' groänin' an' moänin' an' naggin' ageän;

An' I 'eärd the bricks an' the baulks rummle down when the roof gev
waäy,
Fur the fire was a-raägin' an' raävin' an' roarin' like judgment daäy.

Warm enew theere sewer-ly, but the barn was as cowd as owt,
An' we cuddled and huddled togither, an' happt wersens oop as we
                                                          mowt.

An' I browt Roä round, but Moother 'ed beän sa soäk'd wi' the thaw
'At she cotch'd 'er death o' cowd that night, poor soul, i' the straw.

Haäfe o' the parish runn'd oop when the rigtree was tummlin' in –
Too laäte – but it's all ower now – hall hower – an' ten year sin;

Too laäte, tha mun git tha to bed, but I'll coom an' I'll squench the
                                                          light,
Fur we moänt 'ev naw moor fires – and soa little Dick, good-night.

OWEN WISTER

Em'ly the Demented Hen

I N HER NEW choice of offspring, this hen had at length encountered
an unworthy parent. The setter was bored by her own puppies. She
found the hole under the house an obscure and monotonous residence
compared with the dining room, and our company more stimulating
and sympathetic than that of her children. A much-petted contact with
our superior race had developed her dog intelligence above its natural
level, and turned her into an unnatural, neglectful mother, who was
constantly forgetting her nursery for worldly pleasures.

At certain periods of the day she repaired to the puppies and fed
them, but came away when this perfunctory ceremony was accomplished; and she was glad enough to have a governess bring them up.
She made no quarrel with Em'ly, and the two understood each other
perfectly. I have never seen among animals any arrangement so civilized
and so perverted. It made Em'ly perfectly happy. To see her sitting all

day jealously spreading her wings over some blind puppies was sufficiently curious; but when they became large enough to come out from under the house and toddle about in the proud hen's wake, I longed for some distinguished naturalist. I felt that our ignorance made us inappropriate spectators of such a phenomenon. Em'ly scratched and clucked, and the puppies ran to her, pawed her with their fat limp little legs, and retreated beneath her feathers in their games of hide and seek. Conceive, if you can, what confusion must have reigned in their infant minds as to who the setter was!

'I reckon they think she's the wet-nurse,' said the Virginian.

When the puppies grew to be boisterous, I perceived that Em'ly's mission was approaching its end. They were too heavy for her, and their increasing scope of playfulness was not in her line. Once or twice they knocked her over, upon which she arose and pecked them severely, and they retired to a safe distance, and sitting in a circle, yapped at her. I think they began to suspect that she was only a hen after all.

From *The Virginian*

JACK MOSES

You're a Good Old Dog

I'm sorry Bluey for what I did
    To put the boot in you.
Often I've been in a fix
    And you have pulled me through.

I remember well the 'ninety' flood
    (How it rushed across the ground!)
You saved a thousand head of stock
    That must have all been drowned.

Remember when you killed that snake
    Beside this very log?
You saved my life that day as well,
    You are a good old dog.

Remember when I smashed my leg
    Against a fallen tree?
You streaked off twenty miles for help
    And brought it back to me.

I am a selfish sort of chap,
    I forget the good you do,
And the least thing that annoys me:
    I put the boot in you,

But, Bluey, that's the world always,
    You'll find where'er you go
You've got to take your gruel, mate,
It's part of this 'ere show.

I wonder when we leave this earth
    Will we meet by the way
A-droving mobs of cattle,
    I wonder will we – eh?

We don't know much of what may come;
    But we'll be on the square.
I hope we'll meet and share a bone
    Around the billy flare.

We can't stop pitching here now;
    We've got some graft to do.
We have to take those ballys on
    To Kooleamingaroo.

So let us be pals again –
   I'm sorry what I did.
You're a good old dog,
   So help me Gawd – no kid.

JOHN RUSKIN

Dash

I have a dog of Blenheim birth,
With fine long ears and full of mirth;
and sometimes, running o'er the plain,
He tumbles on his nose:
But quickly jumping up again
Like lightning on he goes.

Memories

WHEN I WAS about five years old, having been on amicable terms
for a while with a black Newfoundland, then on probation for
watch dog at Herne Hill; after one of our long summer journeys my first
thought on getting home was to go to see Lion. My mother trusted me to
go to the stable with our one serving-man, Thomas, giving him strict
orders that I was not to be allowed within stretch of the dog's chain.
Thomas, for better security, carried me in his arms. Lion was at his
dinner, and took no notice of either of us; on which I besought leave to
pat him. Foolish Thomas stooped towards him that I might, when the
dog instantly flew at me, and bit a piece clean out of the corner of my lip
on the left side. I was brought up the back stairs, bleeding fast, but not a
whit frightened, except lest Lion should be sent away. Lion indeed had
to go; but not Thomas: my mother was sure he was sorry, and I think

blamed herself the most. The bitten side of the (then really pretty) mouth, was spoiled for evermore, but the wound, drawn close, healed quickly; the last use I made of my moveable lips before Dr Aveline drew them into ordered silence for a while, was to observe, 'Mama, though I can't speak, I can play upon the fiddle.' But the house was of another opinion, and I never attained any proficiency upon that instrument worthy of my genius. Not the slightest diminution of my love of dogs, nor the slightest nervousness in managing them, was induced by the accident.

*   *   *

And my dog Wisie, was he dead too? It seems wholly wonderful to me at this moment that he should ever have died. He was a white Spitz, exactly like Carpaccio's dog in the picture of St Jerome; and he came to me from a young Austrian officer, who had got tired of him, – the Count Thun, who fell afterwards at Scho ferino. Before the dog was used enough to us, George and I took him to Lido to give him a little sea bath. George was holding him by his forepaws upright among the little crisp breakers. Wisie snatched them out of his hands, ran at full speed – into Fairyland, like Frederick the Great at Mollwitz. He was lost on Lido for three days and nights, living by petty larceny, the fishermen and cottagers doing all they could to catch him; but they told me he 'ran liked a hare and leaped like a horse.'

At last, either overcome by hunger, or having made up his mind that even *my* service was preferable to liberty on Lido, he took the deep water in broad daylight, and swam straight for Venice. A fisherman saw him from a distance, rowed after him, took him, tired among the weeds, and brought him to me – the Madonna della Salute having been propitious to his repentant striving with the sea.

From that time he became an obedient and affectionate dog, though of extremely self-willed and self-possessed character. I was then living on the north side of St Mark's Place, and he used to sit outside the window on the ledge at the base of its pillars greater part of the day, observant of the manners and customs of Venice. Returning to England, I took him over the St Gothard, but found him entirely unappalled by any of the work of Devils on it – big or little. He saw nothing to trouble himself about in precipices, if they were wide enough to put his paws on; and the dog who had fled madly from a crisp sea wave, trotted beside the fall of the Reuss just as if it had been another White Dog, a little bigger, created out of foam.

Reaching Paris, he considered it incumbent upon him to appear unconscious of the existence of that city, of the Tuileries gardens and Rue Rivoli, since they were not St Mark's Place; but, half asleep one evening, on a sofa in the entresol at Meurice's, and hearing a bark in the street which sounded Venetian, – sprang through the window in expectation of finding himself on the usual ledge – and fell fifteen feet[1] to the pavement. As I ran down, I met him rushing up the hotel stairs, (he had gathered himself from the stones in an instant), bleeding and giddy; he staggered round and round two or three times, and fell helpless on the floor. I don't know if young ladies' dogs faint, really, when they are hurt. He, Wisie, did not faint, nor even moan, but he could not stir, except in cramped starts and shivers. I sent for what veterinary help was within reach, and heard that the dog might recover, if he could be kept quiet for a day or two in a dog-hospital. But my omnibus was at the door – for the London train. In the very turn and niche of time I heard that Macdonald of St Martin's was in the hotel, and would take charge of Wisie for the time necessary. The poor little speechless, luckless, wistfully gazing doggie was tenderly put in a pretty basket, (going to be taken where? thinks the beating heart,) looks at his master to read what he can in the sad face – can make out nothing, is hurried out of the inexorable door, downstairs; finds himself more nearly dead next day, and among strangers. (*Two miles* away from Meurice's, along the Boulevard, it was.)

He takes and keeps counsel with himself on that matter. Drinks and eats what he is given, gratefully; swallows his medicine obediently; stretches his limbs from time to time. There was only a wicket gate, he saw, between the Boulevard and him. Silently, in the early dawn of the fourth or fifth day – I think – he leaped it, and along two miles of Parisian Boulevard came back to Meurice's.

I do not believe there was ever a more wonderful piece of instinct certified. For Macdonald received him, in astonishment, – and Wisie trusted Macdonald to bring him to his lost master again. The Schehallien chief brought him to Denmark Hill; where of course Wisie did not know whether something still worse might not befall him, or whether he would be allowed to stay. But he was allowed, and became a bright part of my mother's day, as well as of mine, from 1852 to 1858, or perhaps longer.

From *Praeterita*

---

[1] Thirteen feet nine, I find, on exact measurement – coming back to Meurice's to make sure. It is the height of the capitals of the piers in the Rue Rivoli.

Dogs in Art

A T VENICE ALL this was reversed, and so boldly as at first to shock, with its seeming irreverence, a spectator accustomed to the formalities and abstractions of the so-called sacred schools. The madonnas are no more seated apart on their thrones, the saints no more breathe celestial air. They are on our own plain ground – nay, here in our houses with us. All kind of worldly business going on in their presence, fearlessly; our own friends and respected acquaintances, with all their mortal faults, and in their mortal flesh, looking at them face to face unalarmed: nay, our dearest children playing with their pet dogs at Christ's very feet.

I once myself thought this irreverent. How foolishly! As if children whom He loved *could* play anywhere else.

The picture most illustrative of this feeling is perhaps that at Dresden, of Veronese's family, painted by himself.

He wishes to represent them as happy and honoured. The best happiness and highest honour he can imagine for them is that they should be presented to the Madonna, to whom, therefore, they are being brought by the three virtues – Faith, Hope, and Charity. . . . The youngest child, perhaps about three years old, is neither frightened nor interested, but finds the ceremony tedious, and is trying to coax the dog to play with him; but the dog, which is one of the little curly, short-nosed, fringy-pawed things, which all Venetian ladies petted, will not now be coaxed. For the dog is the last link in the chain of lowering feeling, and takes his doggish views of the matter. He cannot understand, first, how the Madonna got into the house; nor, secondly, why she is allowed to stay, disturbing the family, and taking all their attention from his dogship. And he is walking away, much offended.

The dog is thus constantly introduced by the Venetians in order to give the fullest contrast to the highest tones of human thought and feeling. I shall examine this point presently farther, in speaking of pastoral landscape and animal painting.

*   *   *

And first of the animals which have had more influence over the human soul, in its modern life, than ever Apis or the crocodile had over Egyptian – the dog and horse. I stated, in speaking of Venetian religion, that the Venetians always introduced the dog as a contrast to the high aspects of humanity. They do this, not because they consider him the basest of animals, but the highest – the connecting link between men and animals; in whom the lower forms of really human feeling may be best exemplified, such as conceit, gluttony, indolence, petulance. But they saw the noble qualities of the dog, too; – all his patience, love, and faithfulness; therefore Veronese, hard as he is often on lap-dogs, has painted one great heroic poem on the dog.

Two mighty brindled mastiffs, and beyond them, darkness. You scarcely see them at first, against the gloomy green. No other sky for them – poor things. They are gray themselves, spotted with black all over; their multitudinous doggish vices may not be washed out of them, – are in grain of nature. Strong thewed and sinewed, however, – no blame on them as far as bodily strength may reach: their heads coal-black, with drooping ears and fierce eyes, bloodshot a little. Wildest of beasts perhaps they would have been, by nature. But between them stands the spirit of their human love, dove-winged and beautiful, the resistless Greek boy, golden quivered; his glowing breast and limbs the only light upon the sky, – purple and pure. He has cast his chain about the dogs' necks, and holds it in his strong right hand, leaning proudly a little back from them. They will never break loose.

This is Veronese's highest, or spiritual view of the dog's nature. He can only give this when looking at the creature alone. When he sees it in company with men, he subdues it, like an inferior light in presence of the sky; and generally then gives it a merely brutal nature, not insisting even on its affection. It is thus used in the Marriage in Cana to symbolize gluttony. That great picture I have not yet had time to examine in all its bearings of thought; but the chief purpose of it is, I believe, to express the pomp and pleasure of the world, pursued without thought of the presence of Christ; therefore the Fool with the bells is put in the centre, immediately underneath the Christ; and in front are the couple of dogs in leash, one gnawing a bone. A cat lying on her back scratches at one of the vases which hold the wine of the miracle.

In the picture of Susannah, her little pet dog is merely doing his duty, barking at the Elders. But in that of the Magdalen (at Turin) a noble piece of bye-meaning is brought out by a dog's help. On one side is the principle figure, the Mary washing Christ's feet; on the other, a dog has just come out from beneath the table (the dog under the table eating of the crumbs), and in doing so, has touched the robe of one of the Pharisees, thus making it unclean. The Pharisee gathers up his robe in a passion, and shows the hem of it to a bystander, pointing to the dog at the same time.

In the Supper at Emmaus, the dog's affection is, however, fully dwelt upon. Veronese's own two little daughters are playing, on the hither side of the table, with a great wolf-hound, larger than either of them. One with her head down, nearly touching his nose, is talking to him – asking him questions it seems, nearly pushing him over at the same time:–the other raising her eyes, half archly, half dreamily, – some far-away thought coming over her, – leans against him on the other side, propping him with her little hand, laid slightly on his neck. He, all passive, and glad at heart, yielding himself to the pushing or sustaining hand, looks earnestly into the face of the child close to his; would answer her with the gravity of a senator, if so it might be: – can only look at her, and love her.

To Velasquez and Titian dogs seem less interesting than to Veronese; they paint them simply as noble brown beasts, but without any special character; perhaps Velasquez' dogs are sterner and more threatening than the Venetian's, as are also his kings and admirals. This fierceness in the animal increases, as the spiritual power of the artist declines; and, with the fierceness, another character. One great and infallible sign of the absence of spiritual power is the presence of the slightest taint of obscenity. Dante marked this strongly in all his representations of demons, and as we pass from the Venetians and Florentines to the Dutch, the passing away of the soul-power is indicated by every animal becoming savage or foul. The dog is used by Teniers, and many other Hollanders, merely to obtain unclean jest; while by the more powerful men, Rubens, Snyders, Rembrandt, it is painted only in savage chase, or butchered agony. I know no pictures more shameful to humanity than the boar and lion hunts of Rubens and Snyders, signs of disgrace all the deeper, because the powers desecrated are so great. The painter of the village ale-house sign may, not dishonourably, paint the fox-hunt for the village squire; but the occupation of magnificent art-power in giving semblance of perpetuity to those bodily pangs which Nature has mercifully ordained to be transient, and in forcing us, by the fascination of its stormy skill, to dwell on that from which eyes of merciful men should instinctively turn away, and eyes of high-minded men scornfully, is dishonourable, alike in the power which it degrades, and the joy to which it betrays.

In our modern treatment of the dog, of which the prevailing tendency is marked by Landseer, the interest taken in him is disproportionate to that taken in man, and leds to a somewhat trivial mingling of sentiment, or warping by caricature; giving up the true nature of the animal for the sake of a pretty thought or pleasant jest. Neither Titian nor Velasquez ever jests; and though Veronese jests gracefully and tenderly, he never for an instant oversteps the absolute facts of nature. But the English painter looks for sentiment or jest primarily, and reaches both by a feebly romantic taint of fallacy, except in one or two simple and touching pictures, such as the Shepherd's Chief Mourner.

I was pleased by a little unpretending modern German picture at Düsseldorf, by E. Bosch, representing a boy carving a model of his sheep-dog in wood; the dog sitting on its haunches in front of him, watches the progress of the sculpture with a grave interest and curiosity, not in the least caricatured, but highly humorous. Another small picture, by the same artist, of a forester's boy being taught to shoot by his father, – the dog critically and eagerly watching the raising of the gun, – shows equally true sympathy.

I suppose the Greek artists always to have fully appreciated the horse's fineness of temper and nervous constitution. They seem, by the way, hardly to have done justice to the dog. My pleasure in the entire *Odyssey* is diminished because Ulysses gives not a word of kindness or of regret to Argus.

From *Modern Painters*

I AM GOING TO put in the Rudimentary Series, where you can always get at it, this much more delightful, though not in all points standard, picture by Reynolds, of an infant daughter of George the Third's, with her Skye terrier.

I have no doubt these dogs are the authentic pets, given in as true portraiture as their mistresses; and that the little Princess of Florence and Princess of England were both shown in the company which, at that age, they best liked; – the elder feeding her favourite, and the baby with her arms about the neck of hers.

But the custom of putting either the dog, or some inferior animal, to be either in contrast, or modest companionship, with the nobleness of human form and thought, is a piece of what may be called mental comparative anatomy, which has its beginning very far back in art indeed. One of quite the most interesting Greek vases in the British Museum is that of which the painting long went under the title of 'Anacreon and his Dog.' It is a Greek lyric poet, singing with lifted head, in the action given to Orpheus and Philammon in their moments of highest inspiration; while, entirely unaffected by and superior to the music, there walks beside him a sharp-nosed and curly-tailed dog, painted in what the exclusive admirers of Greek art would, I suppose, call an ideal manner; that is to say, his tail is more like a display of fireworks than a tail; but the ideal evidently founded on the material existence of a charming, though supercilious animal, not unlike the one which is at present the chief solace of my labours in Oxford, Dr Acland's dog Bustle. I might go much farther back than this; but at all events, from the time of the golden dog of Pandareos, the fawn of Diana, and the eagle, owl, and peacock of the great Greek gods, you find a succession of animal types – centralized in the Middle Ages, of course, by the hound and the falcon – used in art either to symbolize, or contrast with, dignity in human persons. In modern portraiture, the custom has become vulgarized by the anxiety of everybody who sends their picture, or their children's, to the Royal Academy, to have it demonstrated to the public by the exhibition of a pony, and a dog with a whip in its mouth, that they live, at the proper season, in a country house. But by the greater masters the thing is done always with a deep sense of the mystery of the comparative existences of living creatures, and of the methods of vice and virtue exhibited by them. Albert Dürer scarcely ever draws a scene in the life of the Virgin, without putting into the foreground some idle cherubs at play with rabbits or kittens; and sometimes lets his love of the grotesque get entirely the better of him, as in the engraving of the Madonna with the monkey. Veronese disturbs the interview of the Queen of Sheba with Solomon, by the petulance of the Queen of Sheba's Blenheim spaniel, whom Solomon had not treated with sufficient respect; and when Veronese is introduced himself, with all his family, to the Madonna, I am sorry to say that his own pet dog turns its back to the Madonna, and walks out of the room.

But among all these symbolic playfulnesses of the higher masters, there is not one more perfect than this study by Reynolds of the infant English Princess with her wire-haired terrier. He has put out his whole strength to show the infinite differences, yet the blessed harmonies, between the human and the lower nature. First, having a blue-eyed,[1]

---

[1] I have not seen the picture: in the engraving the tint of the eyes would properly represent grey or blue.

soft baby to paint, he gives its full face, as round as may be, and rounds its eyes to complete openness, because somebody is coming whom it does not know. But it opens its eyes in quiet wonder, and is not disturbed, but behaves as a princess should. Beside this soft, serenely-minded baby, Reynolds has put the roughest and roughest-minded dog he could think of. Instead of the full round eyes, you have only the dark places in the hair where you know the terrier's eyes must be – sharp enough, if you could see them – and very certainly seeing you, but not at all wondering at you, like the baby's. For the terrier has instantly made up his mind about you; and above all, that you have no business there; and is growling and snarling in his fiercest manner, though without moving from his mistress's side, or from under her arm. You have thus the full contrast between the grace and true charm of the child, who 'thinketh no evil' of you, and the uncharitable narrowness of nature in the grown-up dog of the world, who thinks nothing but evil of you. But the dog's virtue and faithfulness are not told less clearly; the baby evidently uses the creature just as much for a pillow as a playmate; – buries its arm in the rough hair of it with a loving confidence, half already converting itself to protection: and baby will take care of dog, and dog of baby, through all chances of time and fortune.

Now the exquisiteness with which the painter has applied all his skill in composition, all his dexterity in touch of pencil, and all his experience of the sources of expression, to complete the rendering of his comparison, cannot, in any of the finest subtleties of it, be explained; but the first steps of its science may be easily traced; and with little pains you may see how a simple and large mass of white is opposed to a rugged one of grey; how the child's face is put in front light, that no shadow may detract from the brightness which makes her, as in Arabian legends, 'a princess like to the full moon' – how, in this halo, the lips and eyes are brought out in deep and rich colour, while scarcely a gleam of reflection is allowed to disturb the quietness of the eyes; – (the terrier's you feel, would glitter enough, if you could see them, and flash back in shallow fire; but the princess's eyes are thinking, and do not flash;) – how the quaint cap surrounds, with its not wholly painless formalism, the courtly and patient face, opposed to the rugged and undressed wild one; and how the easy grace of soft limb and rounded neck is cast, in repose, against the uneasily gathered up crouching of the short legs, and petulant shrug of the eager shoulders, in the ignobler creature.

Now, in his doing of all this, Sir Joshua was thinking of, and seeing, whatever was best in the creatures, within and without. Whatever was most perfectly doggish – perfectly childish – in soul and body. The absolute truth of outer aspect, and of inner mind, he seizes infallibly; but there is one part of the creatures which he never, for an instant, thinks of, or cares for, – their bones. Do you suppose that, from first to last, in painting such a picture, it would ever enter Sir Joshua's mind to think what a dog's skull would look like, beside a baby's? The quite essential facts to him are those of which the skull gives no information – that the baby has a flattish pink nose, and the dog a bossy black one. You might dissect all the dead dogs in the water supply of London without finding out, what, as a painter, it is here your only business precisely to know, – what sort of shininess there is on the end of a terrier's nose; and for the position and action of the creatures, all the four doctors together, who set Bustle's leg for him the other day, when he jumped out of a two-pair-of-stairs window to bark at the volunteers, could not have told Sir Joshua how to make his crouching terrier look ready to snap, nor how to throw the child's arm over its neck in complete, yet not languid, rest.

From *The Eagle's Nest*

OTTO VON BISMARCK

Brushes With Authority

WHEN BISMARCK CAME to Göttingen, as we have said, he had not the remotest notion of student life; its customs were all unknown to him, nor did he learn anything of them immediately, as he there found no friend of any degree of intimacy. By a certain Herr von Drenckhahn, whom he had formerly seen for a short time, he was introduced to a circle of Mecklenburgers, who belonged to no academical body, but passed a tolerably jolly life. With these he travelled into the Harz, and on his return it was agreed that the glories of real student life should be opened to him. Bismarck gave his fellow travellers a breakfast in celebration of the journey, and here matters went on somewhat madly. At length somebody threw a bottle out of the window. Next morning the Dominus de Bismarck was cited to the Deanery and, obedient to his academical superiors, he set forth on the way. He came in a tall hat, a gay Berlin dressing-gown, and riding boots, accompanied by his enormous dog. The Dean stared at this fantastic garb, and only dared to pass the huge creature when Bismarck had called him in. On account of this illegal dog, his fortunate possessor was at once fined five thalers – then came a painful investigation in the bottle-throwing matter.

J. G. L. Hesekiel, from his *Life of Bismarck*

A BELL SASH HANGING over the desk was used for summoning clerks, and a hole in the wall connected with an adjoining room which contained a telegraph to keep the Prince informed of what was happening in the Reichstag. Every ten minutes, while the Reichstag was in session, a length of tape was pushed through the aperture in the wall. Bismarck took it, read it, and threw it aside. While the Chancellor worked, his giant dog, Tiras, lay on the carpet, staring fixedly at his master. Tiras, known as the *Reichshund* (dog of the empire), terrorized the Chancellory staff, and people speaking to Bismarck were advised to make no unusual gestures which Tiras might interpret as threatening. Prince Alexander Gorchakov, the elderly Russian Foreign Minister, once raised an arm to make a point and found himself pinned to the floor, staring up at Tiras' bared teeth.

Robert Massie, from *Dreadnought*

W. H. WHITE

An Unliterary Companion

S O I WAS MARRIED, and I went to live in a dark manufacturing town, away from all my friends. I awoke to my misery by degrees, but still rapidly. I had my books sent down to me. I unpacked them in

Mr Hexton's presence, and I kindled at the thought of ranging my old favourites in my sitting-room. He saw my delight as I put them on some empty shelves, but the next day he said that he wanted a stuffed dog there, and that he thought my books, especially as they were shabby, had better go upstairs.

From *The Autobiography of Mark Rutherford*

IVAN TURGENEV
Pégas

SPORTSMEN OFTEN LOVE to boast about their dogs and to extol their qualities: this also is a sort of indirect self-glorification. But there is no doubt that among dogs, as among men, there are clever and foolish ones, talented and untalented ones, and there are among them even animals of genius, even eccentrics,[1] and the diversity of their qualities, both 'physical and mental', their temperament and habits, will not yield anything to the diversity observed in the human race. Indeed, it can be said without fear of contradiction that as a result of his long companionship with man, a companionship that goes back to prehistoric times, the dog has become infected with him, both in the good and the bad sense of the word: his own normal order of life has certainly been disturbed and undergone a change, as his appearance itself has been disturbed and changed. The dog has become more subject to disease, more nervous, and his expectation of life has decreased; but he has become more intelligent, more impressionable and more quick-witted; his mental outlook has widened. Envy, jealousy and – a capacity for friendship; desperate bravery, devotion to the point of self-sacrifice and – ignominious cowardice and fickleness; suspiciousness, spitefulness and – good nature, cunning and straightforwardness – all these qualities manifest themselves – sometimes with astonishing force – in the dog that has been re-educated by man and that deserves more than the

---

[1] In the spring of 1871 I saw in a circus in London a dog performing the part of a clown, showing quite an undoubted flair for comedy.

horse to be called the noblest of all man's conquests, according to the well-known expression of Buffon.

But enough of philosophizing: let the facts speak for themselves.

Like many another 'inveterate' sportsman, I've had many dogs, bad, good and excellent – I even had one that was positively mad and that committed suicide by jumping out of the dormer window of a drying-room on the fourth floor of a paper mill. But the best hound that I ever possessed was undoubtedly a long-haired, black woolly dog with yellow spots, called 'Pégas'. I bought him near Karlsruhe from a gamekeeper (*Jagdhüter*) for 120 gulden, about eighty silver roubles. I was several times offered a thousand francs for him. Pégas – (he is still alive, though at the beginning of the present year he suddenly lost almost all of his scent, his hearing, his eyesight and is altogether in a sorry state) – Pégas is a big dog with a wavy coat of hair, and an astonishingly intelligent and proud face. He is not of an entirely pure breed: he is a mixture of an English setter and a German sheepdog; his tail is thick, his fore legs too fleshy and his hind legs a little too skinny. He was quite extraordinarily strong and a mighty fighter: he must have several canine souls on his conscience, not to mention cats . . . .

To start with his faults in hunting: there are not many of them and it will not take me long to enumerate them. He was afraid of heat, and when there was no water near he got into the state when a dog is said to be 'dying for a drop'; he was also a little slow and heavy in search of game; but as he had a simply fabulous scent – I have never seen or met anything like it – he still found the game quicker and oftener than any other dog. His pointing used to astonish everyone – and never, *never* did he make a mistake. 'If Pégas points, there must be game,' was a generally accepted axiom among all our fellow-sportsmen. He never chased after a hare or any other game; but not having received a correct and strict English training, he rushed to pick up the game immediately after a shot was fired without waiting for the word of command – a bad fault! He immediately recognized by its flight whether a bird was wounded or not and if, after following it with his eyes, he ran after it, raising his head in a special way, it was a sure sign that he would find it and bring it. At the height of his powers and abilities not one bird that had been hit escaped him: he was the most wonderful retriever one could imagine. It is difficult to enumerate the pheasants he had retrieved from the bramble thickets which abound in almost all German woods, or partridges who had run almost half a mile from the spot where they had fallen or hares, wild goats, foxes. Sometimes he would pick up the scent two, three or four hours after the animal had been wounded. One had only to say to him *Cherche, verloren!* (search, lost!) and he at once went loping first to one side, then another and, coming across the track of the animal, followed it at a spanking pace. One minute, two minutes passed and the hare or wild goat was already screeching between his teeth, or he would be running back with the booty in his mouth.

Once, at a hare chase, Pégas performed such a wonderful trick that I would have hesitated to tell about it if I had not a dozen witnesses to back me up. The chase through the woods had come to an end and the huntsmen gathered in a clearing near the edge of the wood. 'I have wounded a hare just at this spot,' one of my fellow-huntsmen told me and he put the usual request to me: to let Pégas follow its scent. I must observe that no dog except mine, *l'illustre Pégas*, was taken on these hunting expeditions. In such cases, dogs are only a nuisance: they get excited themselves and excite their owners – and by their own movements give warning to the game and drive it away. The beaters keep *their* dogs on a leash. As soon as the chase started and the cries were heard, my Pégas was transformed into a statue; he looked attentively in the direction of the thicket in the woods, raising and dropping his ears imperceptibly. He even stopped breathing; the animal might run across under his very nose and his sides would just quiver or he would lick his nose – that was all. Once a hare ran literally over his paws. All Pégas did was to pretend to bite it. But to return to my story.

I gave the order: *Cherche, verloren!* and he went off. A few minutes later we heard the scream of the caught hare – and there was the beautiful figure of my dog rushing back straight towards me. (He never gave up his booty to anyone else.) Suddenly, twenty feet from me, he stopped, put the hare on the ground, and off he went again! We all exchanged astonished glances. 'What's the meaning of this?' I was asked. 'Why did Pégas not bring the hare up to you? He has never done anything like that before.' I did not know what to say, for I could not understand it myself – when suddenly there was another scream of a hare in the woods – and Pégas again came running through the thicket with *another* hare between his teeth! He was greeted with loud and unanimous applause.

Ony a huntsman can appreciate how keen must be the scent of a dog and how great his intelligence and perspicacity if he is able – with a killed and still warm hare in his mouth – to scent, while running at full speed and in the sight of his master, another wounded hare and to grasp the fact that it is the scent of *another* one and not of the hare he held between his teeth.

Another time he was taken to pick up the scent of a wounded wild goat. The hunt was taking place on the bank of the Rhine. He ran up to the bank, rushed off to the right, then to the left and, probably realizing that a wild goat could not be lost though he had lost its scent, jumped into the water, swam across the Rhine (which, opposite the Grand Duchy of Baden is divided into many branches) and, getting out on a little island overgrown with reeds, lying opposite, caught the wild goat there.

I can also remember a winter hunt on the summits of the Schwarz-wald. There was deep snow everywhere, the trees were covered with hoar-frost, a thick mist hung over everything, concealing the contours of objects. The huntsman next to me fired and when, after the beaters had done their work, I went up to him, he told me that he had fired at a fox and probably wounded it, because it waved its brush. We let Pégas follow its trail and he at once disappeared in the white haze which surrounded us. Five, ten, fifteen minutes passed. . . . Pégas did not come back. My friend must have hit the fox, for if it had not been wounded and Pégas had been sent off on a wild goose chase, he would have returned at once. Suddenly we heard an indistinct barking in the distance: it seemed to reach us from another world. We at once went in the direction of the barking: we knew that if Pégas was not able to bring back the game, he stood barking over it. Led by the infrequent, desultory sounds of his bass voice, we moved carefully through the mist, as though in a dream, hardly seeing where we put down our feet. We were going up hill and down dale, walking through the damp, cold mist with snow up to our knees; icicles kept falling down on us as we brushed aside the branches. . . . It was like a journey through fairy-land. Each one of us looked like a ghost to everyone else, and everything around had a ghost-like appearance. At last something dark loomed in front of us at the bottom of a hollow. It was Pégas. Sitting on his hind legs, he hung his head and, as they say, 'looked glum'; in front of his very nose, in a deep hole between two granite slabs, lay the dead fox. It had crawled there before it died and Pégas could not get it out. That was why he let us know about it by his barking. He had a bad scar over his right eye; it was from the deep wound another fox had inflicted on him after he had found it alive six hours after it had been hit by a bullet – and with whom he had fought a deadly battle.

I also remember another case. I was invited to a shooting party in

Offenburg, a town not far from Baden. The shooting rights of that particular district were owned by a whole crowd of sportsmen from Paris: there was a large amount of game, especially pheasants, in it. I, of course, took Pégas with me. There were altogether fifteen of us. Many had excellent, mostly English thoroughbred, gundogs. As we passed from one beat to another, we formed a single file on a road skirting a wood; to our left was a huge, empty field; in the middle of it – and about fifty feet away from us – was a small heap of Jerusalem artichokes (*topinambour*). Suddenly my Pégas raised his head, sniffed the air and went straight towards that distant heap of dried-up stalks standing erect in the field. I stopped and invited my fellow-sportsmen to follow my dog, for 'there's sure to be something there'. Meanwhile, the other dogs gathered round and began running round Pégas, sniffing the ground, but they scented nothing; but he, not in the least disconcerted, kept walking along as though following a straight line. 'I expect a hare must be hiding somewhere in the field,' one Parisian remarked to me. But I could see by my dog's bearing and by the way he walked that it was not a hare and invited them all again to follow him. 'Our dogs can scent nothing,' they replied in one voice, 'yours must be mistaken.' (They did not know Pégas in Offenburg at that time.) I let it pass, cocked my double-barrelled shotgun and went after Pégas, who was glancing at me from time to time over his shoulder, and at last reached the heap of Jerusalem artichokes. 'What if nothing happens?' I asked myself. 'We'll make fools of ourselves, Pégas and I.' But at that very moment a whole dozen cock-pheasants rose into the air with an ear-splitting noise, and to my great delight I shot down a brace, which did not always happen to me, for I am an indifferent shot. 'That's put you in your place, my Parisian gentlemen – you and your thoroughbred dogs!' With the dead pheasants in my hands I returned to my fellow sportsmen.... Compliments were showered on me and on Pégas. I suppose I must have looked pleased, but he – why, he just looked as if nothing had happened, he did not even put on an air of modesty.

I can state without exaggeration that Pégas again and again picked up the scent of partridges at a distance of a hundred or two hundred feet. And how well he thought everything out in spite of his somewhat lazy search! Just like an experienced strategist. He never dropped his head, sniffing at the trail, shamefully snorting and pushing down his nose; he always acted by sniffing the air, *dans le grand style*, as the French say. I did not have to budge from my place: all I had to do was to watch him. I was greatly amused when I happened to go out shooting with someone who did not know Pégas. Within hardly half an hour I would hear him exclaim: 'What a dog! Why, he's a professor!'

He caught my meaning at once; a look was enough for him. That dog was the cleverest animal I had ever come across. That on one occasion, having missed me, he left Karlsruhe, where I was spending the winter, and four hours later was discovered at my old lodgings in Baden-Baden, is perhaps nothing extraordinary; but the following incident shows what an intelligent animal he was. A mad dog happened to be at large in the environs of Baden-Baden and had bitten someone; the police at once issued an order that all dogs without exception should wear muzzles. In Germany such orders were instantly obeyed; and Pégas found himself wearing a muzzle. He resented it extremely; he kept complaining – that is, sitting down opposite me, barking or offering me his paw, but there was nothing to be done, the order had to be obeyed. One morning my landlady came into my room and told me that, taking advantage of a minute when he was free, Pégas had buried his muzzle! I could not believe it. But a few moments later my landlady again ran into my room and whispered to me to follow her quickly. I went out on the front steps – and what did I see? Pégas with the muzzle in his mouth was walking stealthily, as though on tiptoe, across the yard and, having got into the shed, began digging a hole with his paws, and then carefully buried his muzzle in it! There could be no doubt that he thought to get rid of his hateful constraint in this way.

Like almost all dogs, he could not bear beggars or badly dressed people (women and children he never touched), and the main thing was that he did not allow anyone to take anything away: the sight of a bundle over the shoulder or in the hand aroused his suspicions – and then woe to the back of the trousers of the suspicious character and – in the last resort – woe to my purse! I had to pay a lot of money in damages for him! Once I heard a terrible uproar in my front garden. I went out and saw on the other side of the gate a badly dressed man with torn 'unmentionables' and in front of the gate Pégas in the attitude of a conqueror. The man complained bitterly about Pégas and kept shouting, but the masons, who worked on the opposite side of the street, told me with a loud laugh that the man had picked an apple from a tree in the front garden – and only then had he been attacked by Pégas.

He had – why conceal it? – a dour and stern character; but he was greatly, even tenderly, devoted to me.

Pégas's mother was famous in her time, too, and she also was of a very stern character; she showed no affection even for her master. His brothers and sisters were also distinguished by their talents; but of his numerous progeny not one could even remotely compare with him.

Last year (1870) he was still at the top of his form, though he began to show signs of fatigue; but this year everything has changed suddenly. I suspect he has suffered something like the softening of the brain. Even his intelligence forsook him, and yet it was impossible to say that he was too old.

He is only nine. It was pitiful to see this truly great dog transformed into an idiot; at a shoot he would begin searching senselessly, that is to say, running forward in a straight line, with his tail and head hanging down. Or he would stop dead suddenly and look at me intently and dully, as though asking me what he should do and what had happened to him! *Sic transit gloria mundi!* He still lives with me *en pension*, but it is no longer the former Pégas – it is a pitiful wreck of his former self! I took leave of him not without a feeling of sadness. 'Good-bye,' I thought, 'my incomparable dog! I shall never forget you, and I shall never have such a friend as you!'

I don't suppose I shall go hunting any more, either.

From *Literary Reminiscences*

AUGUST STRINDBERG

Opinion

I LOATHE PEOPLE WHO keep dogs. They are cowards who haven't got the guts to bite people themselves.

From *A Madman's Discourse*

FRANCIS KILVERT

A Narrow Escape

CALLED AT PECKINGELL Farm on the Austins. Jane told me that the other night their dog who cannot endure thunder hung himself during a thunderstorm by jumping up on to the low wall from his kennel, and in his turn tumbling down the other side where he hung by his chain between earth and heaven unable to reach the ground. The family rushed from their beds just in time to prevent him expiring. Jane said they always had to 'put the dog away' during a thunderstorm. Usually they put him away in a barn.

From *Diary*, 24 July 1872

MATTHEW ARNOLD

Geist's Grave

Four years! – and didst thou stay above
The ground, which hides thee now, but four?
And all that life, and all that love,
Were crowded, Geist! into no more?

Only four years those winning ways,
Which make me for thy presence yearn,
Call'd us to pet thee or to praise,
Dear little friend! at every turn?

That loving heart, that patient soul,
Had they indeed no longer span,
To run their course, and reach their goal,
And read their homily to man?

That liquid, melancholy eye,
From whose pathetic, soul-fed springs
Seem'd surging the Virgilian cry,
The sense of tears in mortal things –

That steadfast, mournful strain, consoled
By spirits gloriously gay,
And temper of heroic mould –
What, was four years their whole short day?

Yes, only four! – and not the course
Of all the centuries yet to come,
And not the infinite resource
Of Nature, with her countless sum

Of figures, with her fulness vast
Of new creation evermore,
Can ever quite repeat the past,
Or just thy little self restore.

Stern law of every mortal lot!
Which man, proud man, finds hard to bear,
And builds himself I know not what
Of second life I know not where.

But though, when struck thine hour to go,
On us, who stood despondent by,
A meek last glance of love didst throw,
And humbly lay thee down to die.

Yet would we keep thee in our heart –
Would fix our favourite on the scene,
Nor let thee utterly depart
And be as if thou ne'er hadst been.

And so there rise these lines of verse
On lips that rarely form them now;
While to each other we rehearse:
Such ways, such arts, such looks hadst thou!

We stroke thy broad brown paws again,
We bid thee to thy vacant chair,
We greet thee by the window-pane,
We hear thy scuffle on the stair.

We see the flaps of thy large ears
Quick raised to ask which way we go;
Crossing the frozen lake, appears
Thy small black figure on the snow!

Nor to us only art thou dear
Who mourn thee in thine English home;
Thou hast thine absent master's tear,
Dropt by the far Australian foam.

Thy memory lasts both here and there,
And thou shalt live as long as we.
And after that – thou dost not care!
In us was all the world to thee.

Yet, fondly zealous for thy fame,
Even to a date beyond our own
We strive to carry down thy name,
By mounded turf, and graven stone.

We lay thee, close within our reach,
Here, where the grass is smooth and warm,
Between the holly and the beech,
Where oft we watch'd thy couchant form,

Asleep, yet lending half an ear
To travellers on the Portsmouth road; –
There build we thee, O guardian dear,
Mark'd with a stone, thy last abode!

Then some, who through this garden pass,
When we too, like thyself, are clay,
Shall see thy grave upon the grass,
And stop before the stone, and say:

People who lived here long ago
Did by this stone, it seems, intend
To name for future times to know
The dachs-hound, Geist, their little friend.

Kaiser Dead

April 6, 1887

What, Kaiser dead? The heavy news
Post-haste to Cobham calls the Muse,
From where in Farringford she brews
        The ode sublime,
Or with Pen-bryn's bold bard pursues
        A rival rhyme.

Kai's bracelet tail, Kai's busy feet,
Were known to all the village-street,
'What, poor Kai dead?' say all I meet;
        'A loss indeed!'
O for the croon pathetic, sweet,
        Of Robin's reed!

Six years ago I brought him down,
A baby dog, from London town;
Round his small throat of black and brown
    A ribbon blue,
And vouch'd by glorious renown
    A dachshound true.

His mother, most majestic dame,
Of blood-unmix'd, from Potsdam came;
And Kaiser's race we deem'd the same –
    No lineage higher.
And so he bore the imperial name.
    But ah, his sire!

Soon, soon the days conviction bring.
The collie hair, the collie swing,
The tail's indomitable ring,
    The eye's unrest –
The case was clear; a mongrel thing
    Kai stood confest.

But all those virtues, which commend
The humbler sort who serve and tend,
Were thine in store, thou faithful friend.
    What sense, what cheer!
To us, declining tow'rds our end,
    A mate how dear!

For Max, thy brother-dog, began
To flag, and feel his narrowing span.
And cold, besides, his blue blood ran,
    Since, 'gainst the classes,
He heard, of late, the Grand Old Man
    Incite the masses.

Yes, Max and we grew slow and sad;
But Kai, a tireless shepherd-lad,
Teeming with plans, alert, and glad
     In work or play,
Like sunshine went and came, and bade
     Live out the day!

Still, still I see the figure smart –
Trophy in mouth, agog to start,
Then, home return'd, once more depart;
     Or prest together
Against thy mistress, loving heart,
     In winter weather.

I see the tail, like bracelet twirl'd,
In moments of disgrace uncurl'd,
Then at a pardoning word re-furl'd,
     A conquering sign;
Crying, 'Come on, and range the world,
     And never pine.'

Thine eye was bright, thy coat it shone;
Thou hadst thine errands, off and on;
In joy thy last morn flew; anon,
     A fit! All's over;
And thou art gone where Geist hath gone,
     And Toss, and Rover.

Poor Max, with downcast, reverent head,
Regards his brother's form outspread;
Full well Max knows the friend is dead
     Whose cordial talk,
And jokes in doggish language said,
     Beguiled his walk.

And Glory, stretch'd at Burwood gate,
Thy passing by doth vainly wait;
And jealous Jock, thy only hate,
    The chiel from Skye,
Lets from his shaggy Highland pate
    Thy memory die.

Well, fetch his graven collar fine,
And rub the steel, and make it shine,
And leave it round thy neck to twine,
    Kai, in thy grave.
There of thy master keep that sign,
    And this plain stave.

SIR EDWIN LANDSEER

The Missing Glove

HE LOVED HIS old rough-haired white terrier Brutus, we are told, so consumedly that he never entirely got over its loss, never again attached himself to one favourite, but ever afterwards was usually seen surrounded with half-a-dozen dogs. There was one dog which when it wanted its walk, and when Sir Edwin tarried too long at his easel, used to bring him his hat and lay it at his feet on the floor. He had a marvellous way of ingratiating himself with dogs, which he knew as few fanciers have ever known them. At Redleaf one afternoon he and Frederick Goodall went out for a stroll, their only companion being a beautiful retriever. In frolicsome spirit the dog was running here, there, and everywhere, and whilst it was racing ahead Landseer unseen hung up one of his gloves on the bough of a tree. After they had walked on for a quarter of a mile or so, he called the dog, showed it his two hands, one ungloved. Without a word from him the creature went back, and in a couple of minutes returned with the missing glove.

His wonderful power over dogs is well-known. An illustrious lady (whom we shall venture upon identifying as Queen Victoria) asked him how it was that he gained this knowledge. 'By peeping into their hearts, ma'am,' was his answer. I remember once being wonderfully struck with the mesmeric attractions he possessed with them. A large party of his friends were with him at his house in St John's Wood; his servant opened the door; three or four dogs rushed in, one a very fierce-looking mastiff. We ladies recoiled, but there was no fear; the creature bounded up to Landseer, treated him like an old friend, with most expansive demonstrations of delight. Some one remarking 'how fond the dog seemed of him,' he said, 'I never saw it before in my life.'

James Manson, from *Sir Edwin Landseer*

QUEEN VICTORIA

An Artist's Revelations

A N ARTIST WAS seated 'close to the ridge of a noble down', the very down to which Lord Tennyson alludes, painting a group of sheep huddled in the poet's chalk-pit – an artist, around whom gambolled three charming children and a beautiful collie dog; and whom, as I drew nearer, I recognized (writes one of our representatives) to be Mr Burton-Barber, the celebrated painter of 'The Order of the Bath', 'Once Bit, Twice Shy' and many other well-known favourites of the British public. We fell into conversation at once, and at my request Mr Barber told me the story of his work.

'I have been at it all my life,' said he, 'and my mother still has pictures of dogs that I drew when I was one-and-a-half years of age. Thus is the child father to the man. Sir Edwin Landseer, to whom my father sent some of my early productions, and who was much pleased with them, urged me to study at the Royal Academy. The picture I exhibited there was called "First at the Fence", thirty years ago, when I was about sixteen.'

'Do you paint your droll incidents from life?' I asked. The artist shook his head. 'No, I make all the incidents out of my own head; I have never once got an idea from nature.'

'But,' I objected, 'don't you run a danger of *forcing* nature now and again?' – 'No,' was the reply, 'I am very fond of animals, and I am always studying them. You can't paint animals unless you fully sympathise with them. So I get throughly to know them and to guess pretty accurately how they would behave under certain circumstances. They are very like human beings, even anatomically they resemble us so much that I often go down on all fours and think how I would do such and such a thing. But I never force nature, and I would sacrifice much for exactitude. It is a regular grind with me to sit down and think of some droll situation for a dog, which yet must not caricature it or be impossible. I sit down, and think of *what might be*.

'I have the greatest difficulty in getting people to help me pose the animals. An old woman who is dead used to have a wonderful power with them. But it is curious that those who are professionally connected with animals are hopeless for my purpose. A groom is the worst man in the world to hold a horse for me. I have by now learned all sorts of dodges, and I know thoroughly how to work on their feelings. There is hardly anything a dog won't do to oblige you if you ask him in a proper way. I respect them very much. I don't keep any dogs in London because one is constantly hurting their feelings. They want to go out, but, perhaps, generally indeed, it is impossible to take them, and then how crestfallen they are. Fox-terriers are, of course, the best; they are ready for anything from pitch and toss to manslaughter. One great aim of my pictures is to help people to love and understand dogs better.'

'Pray tell me about some of your best-known pictures, Mr Barber, and how you came to paint them.' 'Well – let us take "The Order of the Bath", in which I represent a dog undergoing his Saturday night's bath and struggling in his little mistress's arms. I imagined that to myself, and knowing exactly how wretched a dog would look under such circumstances, I first of all made a rough sketch by guess; then my little girl and I coaxed the dog into that very position, and I made my sketch in full. At one time I tried instantaneous photography but I didn't find it much good. One day my little girl, three years old, rushed into my studio, dressed up in a red hunting coat, and with the black velvet cap above her golden curls, and a whip in her hand. There at once was my picture, "The New Whip", that was very popular. It was hung very badly at the Academy, but before the day was out I was besieged by dealers and people wanting to buy it.'

We then wandered into a discussion on the public taste. 'We must respect it,' said Mr Barber. 'A picture buyer often knows nothing about art in the abstract; all he asks for is a good subject and a story, and it must not be too sorrowful. I really am by nature cut out for pathos, not humour. Sometimes I try and combine the two, as I did in "In Disgrace", where the little girl and her playfellow, the little dog, are in disgrace for tearing up some papers. But after all it is an "April shower" picture, and we know it will be all right soon. You can't live with a picture of hopeless grief. People are really grateful to anyone who can make them laugh in these days of drive and worry.

'The Queen is one of my best patrons,' continued Mr Barber, 'and I have painted hundreds of pictures for her, and I have had absolutely hundreds of interviews with her. Perhaps you may like to hear a little about them. I often go to Windsor or Osborne, and Her Majesty always comes in and has long talks with me, showing a knowledge of dogs and how to pose them. She is very particular and considerate even in trifles. I remember on the first occasion of my going to Windsor I was painting a pair of her gloves – for she always stipulates that some little article of hers should appear in the picture – and suddenly she and John Brown came in. I had placed them on a chair. She watched the collie "posed", and John Brown started forwards to move the gloves and to place the dog there. At once the Queen stopped him. "Have you quite finished, Mr Burton-Barber, or would you like them left there still?" she said. Few people are so considerate as that in a studio. On another occasion I was at Osborne the very April in which Lord Beaconsfield died. The Queen had fields full of primroses, and every day she employed twenty-five people to pick them, and she would send a basket to him and to her family abroad daily. She asked me to paint a picture of these fields, which I did rather unwillingly, as flowers are not my forté. She was delighted with the result, and placed the picture in the panel of her bedroom door at Windsor, giving me a signed portrait of herself in exchange. She is a great picture collector, and I have to paint smaller and smaller, as she has scarcely room to stow away all she buys. Lately I have been painting all her grandchildren. The Duke of Connaught's little ones always play in the Queen's room before going to bed, and I have painted them in the act of kissing her old dog "good night". At the Queen's special request I have reproduced the room and all that is in it exactly. While I painted the Duchess of Albany's children in the hall, the Duchess sat on the stairs and read Hans Andersen to them. "Shep", the Queen's collie, whom I have sketched for you, is very ill-tempered to everyone but the Queen, whose exact position he knows, and recognizes as fully as you and I would do. I give you also my collie "Lassie", of whom I was very fond, and who had an extravagant affection for me; a famous bulldog, whose ferocious appearance quite belied his really gentle character; and "Tarquin", a notorious savage, who killed a postman among other things, and who, although quite friendly to me while I was taking his portrait, would allow no one else to enter my studio.'

From the *Pall Mall Gazette*, 18 August 1891

IT WAS MY good fortune recently to come across the 'Royal' Punch and Judy show – one beloved of the Royal children for two, if not three, generations. . . .

As regards the origin and history of Punch and Judy, there is as much dispute amongst authorities as touching the birthplace of Homer. But on one point there appears to be little, if any, doubt; and that is, that the comedy came to us from Italy, where it was popular in the Middle Ages, as Punchinello (contracted with us to simple Punch). The original characters were: Punch; his wife Judy; the Baby; Toby, the dog; Scaramouch, transmogrified later into the Clown; a Courtier; a Doctor; Constable; the Hangman, etc. In short, the four chief characters are always the same; the others change somewhat according to localities, national requirements, etc.

Mr Punch is well known nearly all over Europe, as well as wherever the English tongue is spoken. Toby always has the distinction of being performed by a living individual, if one may speak of a humble member of the canine family as an individual. It is popularly thought that a dog of breed only can be trained to take the part of Toby. This is a mistake, as I was informed by Mr Jesson, whom we may designate the 'Short' of the firm which 'runs' the Royal Punch and Judy, his son taking the part of 'Codlin', albeit nothing like the immortal 'friend' in character. Indeed, it is not at all improbable that Mr Jesson's father was the original of Mr Dickens's 'Short', he having performed with the 'dolls' for something like sixty years, while his son has been in the profession forty years. Grandpère Jesson, now, of course, defunct, chiefly frequented London and the home counties, although he made wide stretches now and again for variety's sake, and 'to see a bit of life,' as his son puts it.

But to return to Toby. The part is always taken by a mongrel; nothing else in the canine line will stand the training. The Toby of the present Royal Punch and Judy is eleven years old, and he has taken the part since he was a few months old. His father was twenty-three years old when he was born, and he too had been in the profession – on the stage so to speak – since he was a puppy.

This does away with another popular tradition, namely, that the life of a Punch and Judy dog was six years, never more. But perhaps in the 'good old times,' when there was so much tramping and rough weather to be endured, and in addition, possibly, so much hard training, six years may have been the span of life allotted to Toby. But things are changed now, and the life of the Punch and Judy man, and dog, has fallen in pleasant places compared with what was formerly the case.

There has been a general elevation of the stage – thanks to Sir Henry Irving *et autres*; and Punch and Judy has gone up with the rest. It is now one of the professions to be looked up to, and there is some talk of training younger sons for it, instead of sending them into the Church and to cattle-ranching in the Far West. There is more money to be made in it than in stock-broking, the fine arts, journalism, or gold-mining, and when you are good, you play to Royalty, and put up the Royal Arms.

Mr Jesson 'shook the dolls' before the Prince of Wales and his brothers and sisters when they were little children, and he remembers His Royal Highness laughing till the tears ran down his face when Punch rolled the baby about as though he were making a roly-poly pudding of it, in order, as he said, 'to soothe it to sleep'. The others were amused, but none laughed like the Prince of Wales.

Says Mr Jesson, with pride, 'I've played before the Prince's children, too, and they were just as pleased as their father used to be.' He adds, 'I've played at Windsor, at Marlborough House, at Buckingham Palace, at Osborne, at Frogmore, and at Sandringham.'

'You do pretty well, then?' we naturally queried.

'Oh, yes, I make enough at Christmas to keep me the year round, if I liked to be idle the rest of the year.'

It should, perhaps, be said here, lest too many of those in search of a profession should rush in, that to be a Punch and Judy showman is not so easy as might at first sight appear. Apart from the fact that there is a good deal of dialogue to commit to memory, and that, in our days, novelties must be introduced from time to time; the one who aspires to perform with the dolls must be very ready-witted, quick to get up fresh 'patter', good at repartee, and if not a Sims Reeves, at least distinctly 'Sims-Reevesy' at a song. Then he must be something of a mechanical genius into the bargain. . . .

However, if, after fairly considering the difficulties, the ambitious youth (or maiden, for, like medicine, the law, and other honourable callings, the profession is open to the fair sex) should decide to take up with the dolls, he will find the following text, with a due admixture of his own brains, all that is required in the way of dialogue:

(PUNCH *enters: and after a few preliminary squeaks he bows three times to the spectators – once in the centre, and once at each side of the stage, and then speaks as follows*):

PROLOGUE.
Ladies and gentlemen, pray, how d'ye do?
If you're all happy, I'm happy too.
Stop and hear my merry little play;
If I make you laugh, I need not make you pay.

(*After this* PUNCH *makes his bow and exit. He is then heard behind the scene singing, or rather squeaking, the song, 'Mr Punch is a Jolly Good Fellow'.*)

[Formerly the tune used to be the popular one of 'Malbrook', but nearly all performers nowadays have different tunes, generally picking up some of the popular airs of the day.]

(*After squeaking for a minute or so behind the scene,* PUNCH *makes his appearance and dances upon the stage, while he sings*)

Mr Punch is a jolly good fellow,
His dress is all scarlet and yellow;
And if now and then he gets mellow,
    It's only among his good friends.

(*He continues to dance and sing, and then calls*): Judy, my dear! Judy!
(*This constitutes the first scene of the play. The second scene opens with the entrance of dog* TOBY. PUNCH *salutes him with*): Halloa, Toby! Who call'd you? How do ye do, Mr Toby? Hope you are very well, Mr Toby?
(*To which* TOBY *answers with a snarl or a bark*): Bow-wow-wow!
PUNCH: Poor Toby! (*Putting his hand out cautiously, and trying to coax the dog, who snaps at it*): Toby, you are a nasty, cross dog. Get away with you! (*Strikes at him.*)

TOBY: Bow-wow-wow! (*seizing* PUNCH *by the nose*).

PUNCH: Oh, dear! Oh, dear! Oh, my nose! My poor nose! My beautiful nose! Get away! Get away, you nasty dog. I'll tell your master. Oh, dear! dear! Judy! Judy!
(PUNCH *shakes his nose, but cannot shake off the dog, who follows him as he retreats round the stage. He continues to call* 'Judy! Judy, my dear!' *until the dog quits his hold and exits.*)

PUNCH (*solus, and rubbing his nose with both hands*): Oh, my nose! my pretty little nose! Judy! Judy! You nasty, nasty brute, I will tell your master of you. Mr Scaramouch! (*calls*) My good friend, Mr Scaramouch! Look what your nasty brute of a dog has done!
(*Enter* SCARAMOUCH, *the clown, with a stick.*)

SCARAMOUCH: Halloa, Mr Punch! What have you been doing to my poor dog?

PUNCH (*retreating behind the scene, on observing the stick, and peeping round the corner*): Ha! my good friend, how d'y' do? Glad to see you look so well! (*Aside*) I wish you were further with your nasty great stick.

SCARAMOUCH: You have been beating and ill-using my poor dog, Mr Punch.

PUNCH: He has been biting and ill-using my poor nose, Mr Scaramouch. What have you got there, sir?

SCARAMOUCH: Where?

PUNCH: In your hand?

SCARAMOUCH: A fiddle.

PUNCH: A fiddle! What a pretty thing is a fiddle! Can you play upon that fiddle?

SCARAMOUCH: Come here, and I'll try.

PUNCH: No, thank you. I can hear the music where I am very well.

SCARAMOUCH: Then you shall try yourself. Can you play?

PUNCH (*coming in*): I do not know till I try. Let me see! (*Takes the stick and moves slowly about, singing some popular tune. He hits* SCARAMOUCH *a slight blow on his cap, as if by accident.*)

SCARAMOUCH: You play very well, Mr Punch. Now let me try. I will give you a lesson how to play the fiddle. (*Takes the stick and dances to the same tune, hitting* PUNCH *a hard blow on the back of the head.*)
There's sweet music for you!

PUNCH: I do not like your playing so well as my own. Let me play again.

Alfred Story, in the *Strand Magazine*, October 1895

ROBERT LOUIS STEVENSON

The Character of Dogs

THE CIVILISATION, THE manners, and the morals of dog-kind are to a great extent subordinated to those of his ancestral master, man. This animal, in many ways so superior, has accepted a position of inferiority, shares the domestic life, and humours the caprices of the tyrant. But the potentate, like the British in India, pays small regard to the character of his willing client, judges him with listless glances, and condemns him in a byword. Listless have been the looks of his admirers, who have exhausted idle terms of praise, and buried the poor soul below exaggerations. And yet more idle and, if possible, more unintelligent has been the attitude of his express detractors; those who are very fond of dogs 'but in their proper place'; who say 'poo' fellow, poo' fellow,' and are themselves far poorer; who whet the knife of the vivisectionist or heat his oven; who are not ashamed to admire 'the creature's instinct'; and flying far beyond folly, have dared to resuscitate the theory of animal machines. The 'dog's instinct' and the 'automaton-dog,' in this age of psychology and science, sound like strange anachronisms. An automaton he certainly is; a machine working independently of his control, the heart like the mill-wheel, keeping all in motion, and the consciousness, like a person shut in the mill garret, enjoying the view out of the window and shaken by the thunder of the stones; an automaton in one corner of which a living spirit is confined: an automaton like man. Instinct again he certainly possesses. Inherited aptitudes are his, inherited frailties. Some things he at once views and understands, as though he were awakened from a sleep, as though he came 'trailing clouds of glory.' But with him, as with man, the field of instinct is limited; its utterances are obscure and occasional; and about the far larger part of life both the dog and his master must conduct their steps by deduction and observation.

The leading distinction between dog and man, after and perhaps before the different duration of their lives, is that the one can speak and that the other cannot. The absence of the power of speech confines the dog in the development of his intellect. It hinders him from many speculations, for words are the beginning of metaphysic. At the same blow it saves him from many superstitions, and his silence has won for him a higher name for virtue than his conduct justifies. The faults of the dog are many. He is vainer than man, singularly greedy of notice, singularly intolerant of ridicule, suspicious like the deaf, jealous to the degree of frenzy, and radically devoid of truth. The day of an intelligent small dog is passed in the manufacture and the laborious communication of falsehood; he lies with his tail, he lies with his eye, he lies with his protesting paw; and when he rattles his dish or scratches at the door his purpose is other than appears. But he has some apology to offer for the vice. Many of the signs which form his dialect have come to bear an arbitrary meaning, clearly understood both by his master and himself; yet when a new want arises he must either invent a new vehicle of meaning or wrest an old one to a different purpose; and this necessity frequently recurring must tend to lessen his idea of the sanctity of symbols. Meanwhile the dog is clear in his own conscience, and draws, with a human nicety, the distinction between formal and essential truth. Of his punning perversions, his legitimate dexterity with symbols, he is even vain; but when he has told and been detected in a lie, there is not a hair upon his body but confesses guilt. To a dog of gentlemanly feeling theft and falsehood are disgraceful vices. The canine, like the human, gentleman demands in his misdemeanours Montaigne's '*je ne sais quoi de généreux.*' He is never more than half ashamed of having barked or bitten; and for those faults into which he has been led by the desire to shine before a lady of his race, he retains, even under physical correction, a share of pride. But to be caught lying, if he understands it, instantly uncurls his fleece.

Just as among dull observers he preserves a name for truth, the dog has been credited with modesty. It is amazing how the use of language blunts the faculties of man – that because vainglory finds no vent in words, creatures supplied with eyes have been unable to detect a fault so gross and obvious. If a small spoiled dog were suddenly to be endowed with speech, he would prate interminably, and still about himself; when we had friends, we should be forced to lock him in a garret; and what with his whining jealousies and his foible for falsehood, in a year's time he would have gone far to weary out our love. I was about to compare him to Sir Willoughby Patterne, but the Patternes have a manlier sense of their own merits; and the parallel, besides, is ready. Hans Christian Andersen, as we behold him in his startling memoirs, thrilling from top to toe with an excruciating vanity, and scouting even along the street for shadows of offence – here was the talking dog.

It is just this rage for consideration that has betrayed the dog into his satellite position as the friend of man. The cat, an animal of franker appetites, preserves his independence. But the dog, with one eye ever on the audience, has been wheedled into slavery, and praised and patted into the renunciation of his nature. Once he ceased hunting and became man's plate-licker, the Rubicon was crossed. Thenceforth he was a gentleman of leisure; and except the few whom we keep working, the whole race grew more and more self-conscious, mannered and affected. The number of things that a small dog does naturally is strangely small. Enjoying better spirits and not crushed under material cares, he is far more theatrical than average man. His whole life, if he be a dog of any pretension to gallantry, is spent in a vain show, and in the hot pursuit of admiration. Take out your puppy for a walk, and you will find the little ball of fur clumsy, stupid, bewildered, but natural. Let but a few months pass, and when you repeat the process you will find nature buried in convention. He will do nothing plainly; but the simplest processes of our material life will all be bent into the forms of an elaborate and mysterious etiquette. Instinct, says the fool, has awakened. But it is not so. Some dogs – some, at the very least – if they be kept separate from others, remain quite natural; and these, when at length they meet with a companion of experience, and have the game explained to them, distinguish themselves by the severity of their devotion to its rules. I wish I were allowed to tell a story which would radiantly illuminate the point; but men, like dogs, have an elaborate and mysterious etiquette. It is their bond of sympathy that both are the children of convention.

The person, man or dog, who has a conscience is eternally condemned to some degree of humbug; the sense of the law in their members fatally precipitates either towards a frozen and affected bearing. And the converse is true; and in the elaborate and conscious manners of the dog, moral opinions and the love of the ideal stand confessed. To follow for ten minutes in the street some swaggering, canine cavalier, is to receive a lesson in dramatic art and the cultured conduct of the body; in every act and gesture you see him true to a refined conception; and the dullest cur, beholding him, pricks up his ear and proceeds to imitate and parody that charming ease. For to be a high-mannered and high-minded gentleman, careless, affable, and gay, is the inborn pretension of the dog. The large dog, so much lazier, so much more weighed upon with matter, so majestic in repose, so beautiful in effort, is born with the dramatic means to wholly represent the part. And it is more pathetic and perhaps more instructive to consider the small dog in his conscientious and imperfect efforts to outdo Sir Philip Sidney. For the ideal of the dog is feudal and religious; the ever-present polytheism, the whip-bearing Olympus of mankind, rules them on the one hand; on the other, their singular difference of size and strength among themselves effectually prevents the appearance of the democratic notion. Or we might more exactly compare their society to the curious spectacle presented by a school – ushers, monitors, and big and little boys – qualified by one circumstance, the introduction of the other sex. In each, we should observe a somewhat similar tension of manner, and somewhat similar points of honour. In each the larger animal keeps a contemptuous good humour; in each the smaller annoys him with wasp-like impudence, certain of practical immunity; in each we shall find a double life producing double characters, and an excursive and noisy heroism combined with a fair amount of practical timidity. I have known dogs, and I have known school heroes that, set aside the fur, could hardly have been told apart; and if we desire to understand the chivalry of old, we must turn to the school playfields or the dungheap where the dogs are trooping.

Woman, with the dog, has been long enfranchised. Incessant massacre of female innocents has changed the proportions of the sexes and perverted their relations. Thus, when we regard the manners of the dog, we see a romantic and monogamous animal, once perhaps as delicate as the cat, at war with impossible conditions. Man has much to answer for; and the part he plays is yet more damnable and parlous than Corin's in the eyes of Touchstone. But his intervention has at least created an imperial situation for the rare surviving ladies. In that society they reign without a rival: conscious queens; and in the only instance of a canine wife-beater that has ever fallen under my notice, the criminal was somewhat excused by the circumstances of his story. He is a little, very alert, well-bred, intelligent Skye, as black as a hat, with a wet bramble for a nose and two cairngorms for eyes. To the human observer, he is decidedly well-looking; but to the ladies of his race he seems abhorrent. A thorough elaborate gentleman, of the plume and sword-knot order, he was born with a nice sense of gallantry to women. He took at their hands the most outrageous treatment; I have heard him bleating like a sheep, I have seen him streaming blood, and his ear tattered like a regimental banner; and yet he would scorn to make reprisals. Nay more, when a human lady upraised the contumelious whip against the very dame who had been so cruelly misusing him, my little great-heart gave but one hoarse cry and fell upon the tyrant tooth and nail. This is the tale of a soul's tragedy. After three years of unavailing chivalry, he suddenly, in one hour, threw off the yoke of obligation; had he been Shakespeare he would then have written *Troilus and Cressida* to brand the offending sex; but being only a little dog, he began to bite them. The surprise of the ladies whom he attacked indicated the monstrosity of his offence; but he had fairly beaten off his better angel, fairly committed moral suicide; for almost in the same hour, throwing aside the last rags of decency, he proceeded to attack the aged also. The fact is worth remark, showing, as it does, that ethical laws are common both to dogs and men; and that with both a single deliberate violation of the conscience loosens all. 'But while the lamp holds on to burn,' says the paraphrase, 'the greatest sinner may return.' I have been cheered to see symptoms of effectual penitence in my sweet ruffian; and by the handling that he accepted uncomplainingly the other day from an indignant fair one, I begin to hope the period of *Sturm und Drang* is closed.

All these little gentlemen are subtle casuists. The duty to the female dog is plain; but where competing duties rise, down they will sit and study them out, like Jesuit confessors. I knew another little Skye, somewhat plain in manner and appearance, but a creature compact of amiability and solid wisdom. His family going abroad for a winter, he was received for that period by an uncle in the same city. The winter over, his own family home again, and his own house (of which he was very proud) reopened, he found himself in a dilemma between two conflicting duties of loyalty and gratitude. His old friends were not to be neglected, but it seemed hardly decent to desert the new. This was how he solved the problem. Every morning, as soon as the door was opened, off posted Coolin to his uncle's, visited the children in the nursery, saluted the whole family, and was back at home in time for breakfast and his bit of fish. Nor was this done without a sacrifice on his part, sharply felt; for he had to forego the particular honour and jewel of his day – his morning's walk with my father. And, perhaps from this cause, he gradually wearied of and relaxed the practice, and at length returned entirely to his ancient habits. But the same decision served him in another and more distressing case of divided duty, which happened not long after. He was not at all a kitchen dog, but the cook had nursed him with unusual kindness during the distemper; and though he did not adore her as he adored my father – although (born snob) he was critically conscious of her position as 'only a servant' – he still cherished for her a special gratitude. Well, the cook left, and retired some streets away to lodgings of her own; and there was Coolin in precisely the same situation with any young gentleman who has had the inestimable benefit of a faithful nurse. The canine conscience did not solve the problem with a pound of tea at Christmas. No longer content to pay a flying visit, it was the whole forenoon that he dedicated to his solitary friend. And so, day by day, he continued to comfort her solitude until (for some reason which I could never understand and cannot approve) he was kept locked up to break him of the graceful habit. Here, it is not the similarity, it is the difference, that is worthy of remark; the clearly marked degrees of gratitude and the proportional duration of his visits. Anything further removed from instinct it were hard to fancy; and one is even stirred to a certain impatience with a character so destitute of spontancity, so passionless in justice, and so priggishly obedient to the voice of reason.

There are not many dogs like this good Coolin, and not many people. But the type is one well marked, both in the human and the canine family. Gallantry was not his aim, but a solid and somewhat oppressive respectability. He was a sworn foe to the unusual and the conspicuous, a praiser of the golden mean, a kind of city uncle modified by Cheeryble. And as he was precise and conscientious in all the steps of his own blameless course, he looked for the same precision and an even greater gravity in the bearing of his deity, my father. It was no sinecure to be Coolin's idol: he was exacting like a rigid parent; and at every sign of levity in the man whom he respected, he announced loudly the death of virtue and the proximate fall of the pillars of the earth.

I have called him a snob; but all dogs are so, though in varying degrees. It is hard to follow their snobbery among themselves; for though I think we can perceive distinctions of rank, we cannot grasp what is the criterion. Thus in Edinburgh, in a good part of the town, there were several distinct societies or clubs that met in the morning to – the phrase is technical – to 'rake the backets' in a troop. A friend of mine, the master of three dogs, was one day surprised to observe that they had left one club and joined another; but whether it was a rise or a fall, and the result of an invitation or an expulsion, was more than he could guess. And this illustrates pointedly our ignorance of the real life of dogs, their social ambitions and their social hierarchies. At least, in their dealings with men they are not only conscious of sex, but of the difference of station. And that in the most snobbish manner; for the poor man's dog is not offended by the notice of the rich, and keeps all his ugly feeling for those poorer or more ragged than his master. And again, for every station they have an ideal of behaviour, to which the master, under pain of derogation, will do wisely to conform. How often has not a cold glance of an eye informed me that my dog was disappointed; and how much more gladly would he not have taken a beating than to be thus wounded in the seat of piety!

I knew one disrespectable dog. He was far liker a cat; cared little or nothing for men, with whom he merely co-existed as we do with cattle, and was entirely devoted to the art of poaching. A house would not hold him, and to live in a town was what he refused. He led, I believe, a life of troubled but genuine pleasure, and perished beyond all question in a trap. But this was an exception, a marked reversion to the ancestral type; like the hairy human infant. The true dog of the nineteenth century, to judge by the remainder of my fairly large acquaintance, is in love with respectability. A street-dog was once adopted by a lady. While still an Arab, he had done as Arabs do, gambolling in the mud, charging into butchers' stalls, a cat-hunter, a sturdy beggar, a common rogue and vagabond; but with his rise into society he laid aside these inconsistent pleasures. He stole no more, he hunted no more cats; and conscious of his collar, he ignored his old companions. Yet the canine upper class was never brought to recognise the upstart, and from that hour, except for human countenance, he was alone. Friendless, shorn of his sports and the habits of a lifetime, he still lived in a glory of happiness, content with his acquired respectability, and with no care but to support it solemnly. Are we to condemn or praise this self-made dog? We praise his human brother. And thus to conquer vicious habits is as rare with dogs as with men. With the more part, for all their scruple-mongering and moral thought, the vices that are born with them remain invincible throughout; and they live all their years, glorying in their virtues, but still the slaves of their defects. Thus the sage Coolin was a thief to the last; among a thousand peccadilloes, a whole goose and a whole cold leg of mutton lay upon his conscience; but Woggs,[1]

[1] Walter, Watty, Woggy, Woggs, Wogg, and lastly Bogue; under which last name he fell in battle some twelve months ago. Glory was his aim and he attained it; for his icon, by the hand of Caldecott, now lies among the treasures of the nation.

whose soul's shipwreck in the matter of gallantry I have recounted above, has only twice been known to steal, and has often nobly conquered the temptation. The eighth is his favourite commandment. There is something painfully human in these unequal virtues and mortal frailties of the best. Still more painful is the bearing of those 'stammering professors' in the house of sickness and under the terror of death. It is beyond a doubt to me that, somehow or other, the dog connects together, or confounds, the uneasiness of sickness and the consciousness of guilt. To the pains of the body he often adds the tortures of the conscience; and at these times his haggard protestations form, in regard to the human deathbed, a dreadful parody or parallel.

I once supposed that I had found an inverse relation between the double etiquette which dogs obey; and that those who were most addicted to the showy street life among other dogs were less careful in the practice of home virtues for the tyrant man. But the female dog, that mass of carneying affections, shines equally in either sphere; rules her rough posse of attendant swains with unwearying tact and gusto; and with her master and mistress pushes the arts of insinuation to their crowning point. The attention of man and the regard of other dogs flatter (it would thus appear) the same sensibility; but perhaps, if we could read the canine heart, they would be found to flatter it in very different degrees. Dogs live with man as courtiers round a monarch, steeped in the flattery of his notice and enriched with sinecures. To push their favour in this world of pickings and caresses is, perhaps, the business of their lives; and their joys may lie outside. I am in despair at our persistent ignorance. I read in the lives of our companions the same processes of reason, the same antique and fatal conflicts of the right against the wrong, and of unbitted nature with too rigid custom; I see them with our weaknesses, vain, false, inconstant against appetite, and with our one stalk of virtue, devoted to the dream of an ideal; and yet, as they hurry by me on the street with tail in air, or come singly to solicit my regard, I must own the secret purport of their lives is still inscrutable to man. Is man the friend, or is he the patron only? Have they indeed forgotten nature's voice? or are those moments snatched from courtiership when they touch noses with the tinker's mongrel, the brief reward and pleasure of their artificial lives? Doubtless, when man shares with his dog the toils of a profession and the pleasures of an art, as with the shepherd or the poacher, the affection warms and strengthens till it fills the soul. But doubtless, also, the masters are, in many cases, the object of a merely interested cultus, sitting aloft like Louis

Quatorze, giving and receiving flattery and favour; and the dogs, like the majority of men, have but foregone their true existence and become the dupes of their ambition.

STEPHEN CRANE

A Dark-brown Dog

A CHILD WAS STANDING on a street-corner. He leaned with one shoulder against a high board-fence and swayed the other to and fro, the while kicking carelessly at the gravel.

Sunshine beat upon the cobbles, and a lazy summer wind raised yellow dust which trailed in clouds down the avenue. Clattering trucks moved with indistinctness through it. The child stood dreamily gazing.

After a time, a little dark-brown dog came trotting with an intent air down the sidewalk. A short rope was dragging from his neck. Occasionally he trod upon the end of it and stumbled.

He stopped opposite the child, and the two regarded each other. The dog hesitated for a moment, but presently he made some little advances with his tail. The child put out his hand and called him. In an apologetic manner the dog came close, and the two had an interchange of friendly pattings and waggles. The dog became more enthusiastic with each moment of the interview, until with his gleeful caperings he threatened to overturn the child. Whereupon the child lifted his hand and struck the dog a blow upon the head.

This thing seemed to overpower and astonish the little dark-brown dog, and wounded him to the heart. He sank down in despair at the child's feet. When the blow was repeated, together with an admonition in childish sentences, he turned over upon his back, and held his paws in a peculiar manner. At the same time with his ears and his eyes he offered a small prayer to the child.

He looked so comical on his back, and holding his paws peculiarly, that the child was greatly amused and gave him little taps repeatedly, to keep him so. But the little dark-brown dog took this chastisement in the most serious way, and no doubt considered that he had committed some grave crime, for he wriggled contritely and showed his repentance in every way that was in his power. He pleaded with the child and petitioned him, and offered more prayers.

At last the child grew weary of this amusement and turned toward home. The dog was praying at the time. He lay on his back and turned his eyes upon the retreating form.

Presently he struggled to his feet and started after the child. The latter wandered in a perfunctory way toward his home, stopping at times to investigate various matters. During one of these pauses he discovered the little dark-brown dog who was following him with the air of a footpad.

The child beat his pursuer with a small stick he had found. The dog lay down and prayed until the child had finished, and resumed his journey. Then he scrambled erect and took up the pursuit again.

On the way to his home the child turned many times and beat the dog, proclaiming with childish gestures that he held him in contempt as an unimportant dog, with no value save for a moment. For being this quality of animal the dog apologized and eloquently expressed regret, but he continued stealthily to follow the child. His manner grew so very guilty that he slunk like an assassin.

When the child reached his door-step, the dog was industriously ambling a few yards in the rear. He became so agitated with shame when he again confronted the child that he forgot the dragging rope. He tripped upon it and fell forward.

The child sat down on the step and the two had another interview. During it the dog greatly exerted himself to please the child. He performed a few gambols with such abandon that the child suddenly saw him to be a valuable thing. He made a swift, avaricious charge and seized the rope.

He dragged his captive into a hall and up many long stairways in a dark tenement. The dog made willing efforts, but he could not hobble very skilfully up the stairs because he was very small and soft, and at last the pace of the engrossed child grew so energetic that the dog became panic-stricken. In his mind he was being dragged toward a grim unknown. His eyes grew wild with the terror of it. He began to wiggle his head frantically and to brace his legs.

The child redoubled his exertions. They had a battle on the stairs. The child was victorious because he was completely absorbed in his purpose, and because the dog was very small. He dragged his acquirement to the door of his home, and finally with triumph across the threshold.

No one was in. The child sat down on the floor and made overtures to the dog. These the dog instantly accepted. He beamed with affection upon his new friend. In a short time they were firm and abiding comrades.

When the child's family appeared, they made a great row. The dog was examined and commented upon and called names. Scorn was leveled at him from all eyes, so that he became much embarrassed and drooped like a scorched plant. But the child went sturdily to the center of the floor, and, at the top of his voice, championed the dog. It happened that he was roaring protestations, with his arms clasped about the dog's neck, when the father of the family came in from work.

The parent demanded to know what the blazes they were making the kid howl for. It was explained in many words that the infernal kid wanted to introduce a disreputable dog into the family.

A family council was held. On this depended the dog's fate, but he in no way heeded, being busily engaged in chewing the end of the child's dress.

The affair was quickly ended. The father of the family, it appears, was in a particularly savage temper that evening, and when he perceived that it would amaze and anger everybody if such a dog were allowed to remain, he decided that it should be so. The child, crying softly, took his friend off to a retired part of the room to hobnob with him, while the father quelled a fierce rebellion of his wife. So it came to pass that the dog was a member of the household.

He and the child were associated together at all times save when the child slept. The child became a guardian and a friend. If the large folk kicked the dog and threw things at him, the child made loud and violent objections. Once when the child had run, protesting loudly, with tears raining down his face and his arms outstretched, to protect his friend, he had been struck in the head with a very large saucepan from the hand of his father, enraged at some seeming lack of courtesy in the dog. Ever after, the family were careful how they threw things at the dog. Moreover, the latter grew very skilful in avoiding missiles and feet. In a small room containing a stove, a table, a bureau and some chairs, he would display strategic ability of a high order, dodging, feinting and scuttling about among the furniture. He could force three or four people armed with brooms, sticks and handfuls of coal, to use all their ingenuity to get in a blow. And when they did, it was seldom that they could do him a serious injury or leave any imprint.

But when the child was present, these scenes did not occur. It came to be recognized that if the dog was molested, the child would burst into sobs, and as the child, when started, was very riotous and practically unquenchable, the dog had therein a safeguard.

However, the child could not always be near. At night, when he was asleep, his dark-brown friend would raise from some black corner a wild, wailful cry, a song of infinite lowliness and despair, that would go shuddering and sobbing among the buildings of the block and cause people to swear. At these times the singer would often be chased all over the kitchen and hit with a great variety of articles.

Sometimes, too, the child himself used to beat the dog, although it is not known that he ever had what could be truly called a just cause. The dog always accepted these thrashings with an air of admitted guilt. He was too much of a dog to try to look to be a martyr or to plot revenge. He received the blows with deep humility, and furthermore he forgave his friend the moment the child had finished, and was ready to caress the child's hand with his little red tongue.

When misfortune came upon the child, and his troubles overwhelmed him, he would often crawl under the table and lay his small distressed head on the dog's back. The dog was ever sympathetic. It is not to be supposed that at such times he took occasion to refer to the unjust beatings his friend, when provoked, had administered to him.

He did not achieve any notable degree of intimacy with the other members of the family. He had no confidence in them, and the fear that he would express at their casual approach often exasperated them exceedingly. They used to gain a certain satisfaction in underfeeding him, but finally his friend the child grew to watch the matter with some care, and when he forgot it, the dog was often successful in secret for himself.

So the dog prospered. He developed a large bark, which came wondrously from such a small rug of a dog. He ceased to howl persistently at night. Sometimes, indeed, in his sleep, he would utter little yells, as from pain, but that occurred, no doubt, when in his dreams he encountered huge flaming dogs who threatened him direfully.

His devotion to the child grew until it was a sublime thing. He wagged at his approach; he sank down in despair at his departure. He could detect the sound of the child's step among all the noises of the neighborhood. It was like a calling voice to him.

The scene of their companionship was a kingdom governed by this terrible potentate, the child; but neither criticism nor rebellion ever lived for an instant in the heart of the one subject. Down in the mystic, hidden fields of his little dog-soul bloomed flowers of love and fidelity and perfect faith.

The child was in the habit of going on many expeditions to observe strange things in the vicinity. On these occasions his friend usually jogged aimfully along behind. Perhaps, though, he went ahead. This necessitated his turning around every quarter-minute to make sure the child was coming. He was filled with a large idea of the importance of these journeys. He would carry himself with such an air! He was proud to be the retainer of so great a monarch.

One day, however, the father of the family got quite exceptionally drunk. He came home and held carnival with the cooking utensils, the furniture and his wife. He was in the midst of this recreation when the child, followed by the dark-brown dog, entered the room. They were returning from their voyages.

The child's practised eye instantly noted his father's state. He dived under the table, where experience had taught him was a rather safe place. The dog, lacking skill in such matters, was, of course, unaware of the true condition of affairs. He looked with interested eyes at his friend's sudden dive. He interpreted it to mean: Joyous gambol. He started to patter across the floor to join him. He was the picture of a little dark-brown dog en route to a friend.

The head of the family saw him at this moment. He gave a huge howl of joy, and knocked the dog down with a heavy coffee-pot. The dog, yelling in supreme astonishment and fear, writhed to his feet and ran for cover. The man kicked out with a ponderous foot. It caused the dog to swerve as if caught in a tide. A second blow of the coffee-pot laid him upon the floor.

Here the child, uttering loud cries, came valiantly forth like a knight. The father of the family paid no attention to these calls of the child, but advance with glee upon the dog. Upon being knocked down twice in swift succession, the latter apparently gave up all hope of escape. He rolled over on his back and held his paws in a peculiar manner. At the same time with his eyes and his ears he offered up a small prayer.

But the father was in a mood for having fun, and it occurred to him that it would be a fine thing to throw the dog out of the window. So he reached down and grabbing the animal by a leg, lifted him, squirming, up. He swung him two or three times hilariously about his head, and then flung him with great accuracy through the window.

The soaring dog created a surprise in the block. A woman watering plants in an opposite window gave an involuntary shout and dropped a flower-pot. A man in another window leaned perilously out to watch the flight of the dog. A woman who had been hanging out clothes in a yard, began to caper wildly. Her mouth was filled with clothes-pins, but her arms gave vent to a sort of exclamation. In appearance she was like a gagged prisoner. Children ran whooping.

The dark-brown body crashed in a heap on the roof of a shed five stories below. From thence it rolled to the pavement of an alleyway.

The child in the room far above burst into a long, dirgelike cry, and toddled hastily out of the room. It took him a long time to reach the alley, because his size compelled him to go downstairs backward, one step at a time, and holding with both hands to the step above.

When they came for him later, they found him seated by the body of his dark-brown friend.

MARK TWAIN

Chase

THE CAYOTE IS A living, breathing allegory of Want. He is *always* hungry. He is always poor, out of luck and friendless. The meanest creatures despise him, and even the fleas would desert him for a velocipede. He is so spiritless and cowardly that even while his exposed teeth are pretending a threat, the rest of his face is apologizing for it. And he is *so* homely! – so scrawny, and ribby, and coarse-haired, and pitiful. When he sees you he lifts his lip and lets a flash of his teeth out, and then turns a little out of the course he was pursuing, depresses his head a bit, and strikes a long, soft-footed trot through the sage-brush, glancing over his shoulder at you, from time to time, till he is about out of easy pistol range, and then he stops and takes a deliberate survey of you; he will trot fifty yards and stop again – another fifty and stop again;

and finally the gray of his gliding body blends with the gray of the sage-brush, and he disappears. All this is when you make no demonstration against him; but if you do, he develops a livelier interest in his journey, and instantly electrifies his heels and puts such a deal of real estate between himself and your weapon, that by the time you have raised the hammer you see that you need a minie rifle, and by the time you have got him in line you need a rifled cannon, and by the time you have 'drawn a bead' on him you see well enough that nothing, but an unusually long-winded streak of lightning could reach him where he is now. But if you start a swift-footed dog after him, you will enjoy it ever so much – especially if it is a dog that has a good opinion of himself, and has been brought up to think he knows something about speed. The cayote will go swinging gently off on that deceitful trot of his, and every little while he will smile a fraudful smile over his shoulder that will fill that dog entirely full of encouragement and worldly ambition, and make him lay his head still lower to the ground, and stretch his neck further to the front, and pant more fiercely, and stick his tail out straighter behind, and move his furious legs with a yet wilder frenzy, and leave a broader and broader, and higher and denser cloud of desert sand smoking behind, and marking his long wake across the level plain! And all this time the dog is only a short twenty feet behind the cayote, and to save the soul of him he cannot understand why it is that he cannot get perceptibly closer; and he begins to to get aggravated, and it makes him madder and madder to see how gently the cayote glides along and never pants or sweats or ceases to smile; and he grows still more and more incensed to see how shamefully he has been taken in by an entire stranger, and what an ignoble swindle that long, calm, soft-footed trot is; and next he notices that he is getting fagged, and that the cayote actually has to slacken speed a little to keep from running away from him – and *then* that town-dog is mad in earnest, and he begins to strain and weep and swear, and paw the sand higher than ever, and reach for the cayote with concentrated and desperate energy. This 'spurt' finds him six feet behind the gliding enemy, and two miles from his friends. And then, in the instant that a wild new hope is lighting up his face, the cayote turns and smiles blandly upon him once more, and with a something about it which seems to say: 'Well, I shall have to tear myself away from you, bub – business is business, and it will not do for me to be fooling along this way all day' – and forthwith there is a rushing sound, and the sudden splitting of a long crack through the atmosphere, and behold that dog is solitary and alone in the midst of a vast solitude!

It makes his head swim. He stops, and looks all around; climbs the nearest sand-mound, and gazes into the distance; shakes his head reflectively, and then, without a word, he turns and jogs along back to his train, and takes up a humble position under the hindmost wagon, and feels unspeakably mean, and looks ashamed, and hangs his tail at half-mast for a week. And for as much as a year after that, whenever there is a great hue and cry after a cayote, that dog will merely glance in that direction without emotion, and apparently observe to himself, 'I believe I do not wish any of the pie.'

A Further Chase

Mono Lake lies in a lifeless, treeless, hideous desert, eight thousand feet above the level of the sea, and is guarded by mountains two thousand feet higher, whose summits are always clothed in clouds. This solemn, silent, sailless sea – this lonely tenant of the loneliest spot on earth – is little graced with the picturesque. It is an unpretending expanse of grayish water, about a hundred miles in circumference, with two islands in its centre, mere upheavals of rent and scorched and blistered lava, snowed over with gray banks and drifts of pumice-stone and ashes, the winding sheet of the dead volcano, whose vast crater the lake has seized upon and occupied.

The lake is two hundred feet deep, and its sluggish waters are so strong with alkali that if you only dip the most hopelessly soiled garment into them once or twice, and wring it out, it will be found as clean as if it had been through the ablest of washerwomen's hands. While we camped there our laundry work was easy. We tied the week's washing astern of our boat, and sailed a quarter of a mile, and the job was complete, all to the wringing out. If we threw the water on our heads and gave them a rub or so, the white lather would pile up three inches high. This water is not good for bruised places and abrasions of the skin. We had a valuable dog. He had raw places on him. He had more raw places on him than sound ones. He was the rawest dog I almost ever saw. He jumped overboard one day to get away from the flies. But it was bad judgment. In his condition, it would have been just as comfortable to jump into the fire. The alkali water nipped him in all the raw places simultaneously, and he struck out for the shore with considerable interest. He yelped and barked and howled as he went – and by the time he got to the shore there was no bark to him – for he had barked the bark all out of his inside, and the alkali water had cleaned the bark all off his outside, and he probably wished he had never embarked in any such enterprise. He ran round and round in a circle, and pawed the earth and clawed the air, and threw double somersaults, sometimes backward and sometimes forward, in the most extraordinary manner. He was not a demonstrative dog, as a general thing, but rather of a grave and serious turn of mind, and I never saw him take so much interest in anything before. He finally struck out over the mountains, at a gait which we estimated at about two hundred and fifty miles an hour, and he is going yet. This was about nine years ago. We look for what is left of him along here every day.

From *Roughing It*

HENRY MAYHEW

On His Bike

'I'M ALWAYS AT FIRE-EATING. That's how I entirely get my living, and I perform five nights out of the six. Thursday night is the only night, as I may say, I'm idle. Thursday night everybody's fagged, that's the saying – Got no money. Friday, there's many large firms pays their men on, especially in Bermondsey.

'I was very hard up at one time – when I was living in Friar-street – and I used to frequent a house kept by a betting-man, near the St George's Surrey Riding-school. A man I knew used to supply this betting-man with rats. I was at this public-house one night when this rat-man comes up to me, and says he, "Hallo! my pippin; here, I want you: I want to make a match. Will you kill thirty rats against my dog?"

So I said, "Let me see the dog first;" and I looked at his mouth, and he was an old dog; so I says, "No, I won't go in for thirty; but I don't mind trying at twenty." He wanted to make it twenty-four, but I wouldn't. They put the twenty in the rat-pit and the dog went in first and killed his, and he took a quarter of an hour and two minutes. Then a fresh lot were put in the pit, and I began; my hands were tied behind me. They always make an allowance for a man, so the pit was made closer, for you see a man can't turn round like a dog; I had half the space of the dog. The rats lay in a cluster, and then I picked them off where I wanted 'em and bit 'em between the shoulders. It was when they came to one or two that I had the work, for they cut about. The last one made me remember him, for he gave me a bite, of which I've got the scar now. It festered, and I was obliged to have it cut out. I took Dutch drops for it, and poulticed it by day, and I was bad for three weeks. They made a subscription in the room of fifteen shillings for killing these rats. I won the match, and beat the dog by four minutes. The wager was five shillings, which I had. I was at the time so hard up, I'd do anything for some money; though, as far as that's concerned, I'd go into a pit now, if anybody would make it worth my while.'

From *London Labour and London Poor*

ANTON CHEKHOV

Rescue – and After

A LITTLE WHILE afterwards the stranger came in again, and brought a strange thing with him like a hurdle, or like the figure II. On the crosspiece on the top of this roughly made wooden frame hung a bell, and a pistol was also tied to it; there were strings from the tongue of the bell, and the trigger of the pistol. The stranger put the frame in the middle of the room, spent a long time tying and untying something, then looked at the gander and said: 'Ivan Ivanitch, if you please!'

The gander went up to him and stood in an expectant attitude.

'Now then,' said the stranger, 'let us begin at the very beginning. First of all, bow and make a curtsey! Look sharp!'

Ivan Ivanitch craned his neck, nodded in all directions, and scraped with his foot.

'Right. Bravo. . . . Now die!'

The gander lay on his back and stuck his legs in the air. After performing a few more similar, unimportant tricks, the stranger suddenly clutched at his head, and assuming an expression of horror, shouted: 'Help! Fire! We are burning!'

Ivan Ivanitch ran to the frame, took the string in his beak, and set the bell ringing.

The stranger was very much pleased. He stroked the gander's neck and said:

'Bravo, Ivan Ivanitch! Now pretend that you are a jeweller selling gold and diamonds. Imagine now that you go to your shop and find thieves there. What would you do in that case?'

The gander took the other string in his beak and pulled it, and at once a deafening report was heard. Kashtanka was highly delighted with the bell ringing, and the shot threw her into so much ecstasy that she ran round the frame barking.

'Auntie, lie down!' cried the stranger; 'be quiet!'

Ivan Ivanitch's task was not ended with the shooting. For a whole hour afterwards the stranger drove the gander round him on a cord, cracking a whip, and the gander had to jump over barriers and through hoops; he had to rear, that is, sit on his tail and wave his legs in the air. Kashtanka could not take her eyes off Ivan Ivanitch, wriggled with delight, and several times fell to running after him with shrill barks. After exhausting the gander and himself, the stranger wiped the sweat from his brow and cried:

'Marya, fetch Havronya Ivanovna here!'

A minute later there was the sound of grunting. . . . Kashtanka growled, assumed a very valiant air, and to be on the safe side, went nearer to the stranger. The door opened, an old woman looked in, and, saying something, let in a black and very ugly sow. Paying no attention to Kashtanka's growls, the sow lifted up her little hoof and grunted good-humouredly. Apparently it was very agreeable to her to see her master, the cat and Ivan Ivanitch. When she went up to the cat and gave him a light tap on the stomach with her hoof, and then made some remark to the gander, a great deal of good-nature was expressed in her movements, and the quivering of her tail. Kashtanka realised at once that to growl and bark at such a character was useless.

The master took away the frame and cried: 'Fyodor Timofeyitch, if you please!'

The cat stretched lazily, and reluctantly, as though performing a duty, went up to the sow.

'Come, let us begin with the Egyptian pyramid,' began the master.

He spent a long time explaining something, then gave the word of command, 'One . . . two . . . three!' At the word 'three' Ivan Ivanitch flapped his wings and jumped on to the sow's back. . . . When, balancing himself with his wings and his neck, he got a firm foothold on the bristly back, Fyodor Timofeyitch listlessly and lazily, with manifest disdain, and with an air of scorning his art and not caring a pin for it, climbed on to the sow's back, then reluctantly mounted on to the gander, and stood on his hind legs. The result was what the stranger called the Egyptian pyramid. Kashtanka yapped with delight, but at that moment the old cat yawned and, losing his balance, rolled off the gander. Ivan Ivanitch lurched and fell off too. The stranger shouted, waved his hands, and began explaining something again. After spending an hour over the pyramid their indefatigable master proceeded to teach Ivan Ivanitch to ride on the cat, then began to teach the cat to smoke, and so on.

The lesson ended in the stranger's wiping the sweat off his brow and going away. Fyodor Timofeyitch gave a disdainful sniff, lay down on his mattress, and closed his eyes; Ivan Ivanitch went to the trough, and the pig was taken away by the old woman. Thanks to the number of her new impressions, Kashtanka hardly noticed how the day passed, and in the evening she was installed with her mattress in the room with the dirty wallpaper, and spent the night in the society of Fyodor Timofeyitch and the gander.

A month passed.

Kashtanka had grown used to having a nice dinner every evening, and being called Auntie. She had grown used to the stranger too, and to her new companions. Life was comfortable and easy.

Every day began in the same way. As a rule, Ivan Ivanitch was the first to wake up, and at once went up to Auntie or to the cat, twisting his neck, and beginning to talk excitedly and persuasively, but, as before, unintelligibly. Sometimes he would crane up his head in the air and utter heavily, while their master became red in the face and could not mop the sweat from his brow fast enough.

The lesson and the dinner made the day very interesting, but the evenings were tedious. As a rule, their master went off somewhere in the evening and took the cat and the gander with him. Left alone, Auntie lay down on her little mattress and began to feel sad . . . .

Melancholy crept on her imperceptibly and took possession of her by degrees, as darkness does of a room. It began with the dog's losing every inclination to bark, to eat, to run about the rooms, and even to look at things; then vague figures, half dogs, half human beings, with countenances attractive, pleasant, but incomprehensible, would appear in her imagination; when they came Auntie wagged her tail, and it seemed to her that she had somewhere, at some time, seen them and loved them. . . . And as she dropped asleep, she always felt that those figures smelt of glue, shavings, and varnish.

When she had grown quite used to her new life, and from a thin, long mongrel, had changed into a sleek, well-groomed dog, her master looked at her one day before the lesson and said:

'It's high time, Auntie, to get to business. You have kicked up your heels in idleness long enough. I want to make an artiste of you. . . . Do you want to be an artiste?'

And he began teaching her various accomplishments. At the first lesson he taught her to stand and walk on her hind legs, which she liked extremely. At the second lesson she had to jump on her hind legs and catch some sugar, which her teacher held high above her head. After that, in the following lessons she danced, ran tied to a cord, howled to music, rang the bell, and fired the pistol, and in a month could successfully replace Fyodor Timofeyitch in the 'Egyptian Pyramid.' She learned very eagerly and was pleased with her own success; running with her tongue out on the cord, leaping through the hoop, and riding on old Fyodor Timofeyitch, gave her the greatest enjoyment. She accompanied every successful trick with a shrill, delighted bark, while her teacher wondered, was also delighted, and rubbed his hands.

'It's talent! It's talent!' he said. 'Unquestionable talent! You will certainly be successful!'

And Auntie grew so used to the word talent, that every time her master pronounced it, she jumped up as if it had been her name.

From 'Kashtanka'
Trans. Constance Garnett

ANONYMOUS

Dandy Dogs

WHEN YOU HEAR a man say he has 'led the life of a dog,' it is pretty safe to assume he has not been dandled in the lap of luxury for some time anterior to his plaint. But surely, after the publication of this article, the popular significance of the metaphor will lose its force – if, indeed, the meaning be not completely reversed, so that inclusion in Dandy Dog-dom will represent the Alpha and Omega of epicurean splendour.

The fact is, mere ordinary folk have not the remotest notion of the extravagant extent to which canine pets are pampered nowadays by their highly-placed mistresses; and so utterly astounding and fantastic are the details, that I propose giving chapter and verse, so to speak, for every statement made.

The Dogs' Toilet Club, in New Bond Street – an institution certainly beyond the wildest dreams of the Battersea pariahs – was started by an enterprising and cultured lady, who had noticed the righteous wrath of the average domestic on being asked to give a pampered pet its daily bath. Everything about this club is of the daintiest; the very prospectus is in blue and gold, with a delicate bow of green ribbon at one corner. The reception-room is quite a sumptuous apartment; and the ordinary man on entering it may stumble over a costly occasional table, or occasional dog, as the case may be. For many ladies leave their pets here while shopping; others bring the little creatures to be shampooed, brushed, combed, clipped, and attended to by a professional chiropod-ist. Expensive sweetmeats are provided as a temporary solatium for the absence of the mistresses.

The pictorial art of this handsome apartment is distinctly canine; so, too, are the contents of the glass-topped table. This contains an interesting – not to say surprising – collection of requisites for fashionable dogs. There are morning, afternoon, and evening coats; mourning outfits, travelling costumes, and bridal dresses – for woe unto the canine aristocrat that hath not on a wedding garment when occasion demands. But more of this hereafter. The very latest sweet thing is the dog's driving coat – the 'Lonsdale' – made to measure, in fawn cloth, lined with dark red silk; it has a cape of the same that falls upon the pet's shoulders, and a frill round the neck. This ornate garment is finished off with two gold bells; and the full collar is edged with fur to match that on the dress of the mistress.

Where did all this originate? In Paris, the city of eccentric, extravagant *modes*.

Occasionally an aristocratic mistress is dreadfully afraid her doggie will catch cold, leading to lung troubles and other dreadful things. Sometimes, too, the pet's owner will express a wish to 'see it done' – much to the disgust of the operator, be he clipper or shampooer. For the lady will often throw herself on the dirty floor near the bath (unmindful of her own eighty-guinea dress) and keep up a running fire of oral consolation. 'Now, it won't last long, Birdie.' 'Ah! 'oo's all dripping-wet, little darling; but 'oo'll soon be d'y.' 'Don't pull Birdie so, naughty man.' If only the 'naughty man' dared speak his mind!

Dentistry, of course, forms an important item in canine toilet clubs, both in London and Paris. Many a pet dog is to be seen in the Bois whose teeth are as false as its complexion – or rather colour; for fashionable dogs in the gay capital are frequently dyed to meet the exigencies of a passing *mode*.

During one of my visits to the interesting Bond Street institution, a Skye terrier was brought in to have two teeth extracted; the fee was half a guinea. And there is a special assistant retained for cleaning dogs' teeth – obviously as perilous a pastime as big-game shooting; it is done with an ordinary toothbrush and some table salt. I should mention, though, that some toy dogs *will* have a perfumed dentifrice used; they do not like salt.

We now come to an exceedingly interesting part of the toilet club – the clipping of pet poodles. The premier dog-clipper is Mr W. R. Brown, of Regent Street, whose dexterity and skill are such that he is justly entitled to lay claim (as he does) to the designation of 'artist.'

It is not high art, but it is wonderful in its way. Poor peaceful 'Mouton' can never know the true inwardness of the desperate struggle going on above him. It depicts the Corbett-Mitchell prize-fight that took place in New Orleans; and the English champion has apparently just received the knock-out blow. In the ordinary course of Nature, both pugilists gradually vanish – I mean the dog's hair grows: and at the end of every month (when Mouton is clipped) they either make their appearance in a fresh round, or they give place to another pattern – something pastoral, perhaps, with trees and things in it.

Brown is a smart man – quite a character in his way. On the morning of a certain Derby Day he cut in the hair of his own poodle an inelegant racehorse, with a suggestion of the course and crowd, leaving underneath a fine patch of woolly hair in which the winner's name might be clipped in a few minutes. This last detail Brown procured direct from the course by special telegram; the name was instantly filled in – or cut out; and then the clever clipper, dog and all, went round the town in search of the lucky owner of the winning horse, the result being that the 'pictorial' poodle – in a truly interesting condition – changed hands for £100.

The clipper, Brown, assures me he frequently has great difficulty in persuading people that these designs are actually worked in the dog's hair, or coat. Now, I have seen him at work with his battery of machine-clippers, razors, and scissors of every shape and size. I say 'shape' advisedly, because some of this 'artist's' scissors are curved in queer ways, so as to get into small corners when reproducing fine lace on the poodle's back. The man will cut anything on your dog – even elaborate crests.

Let me show you 'Zulu', a fine poodle belonging to Mrs Beer, of Chesterfield Gardens. 'Zulu' bears the crest of his master and mistress – a pelican feeding its nest of young ones with blood from its own breast. The motto is *Rien sans Peine* – probably a hint to the poodle to remain passive in the clipper's hands. By the way, the difficulty experienced in clipping a dog greatly depends on the animal's disposition. Mr Brown and his wife have done five in a single day, but three is about the average. Like ourselves, the pet poodle is cursed with a sensitive cuticle, and its least movement has to be watched during the clipping lest it should be cut – a misfortune which would also damage the operator's artistic reputation.

Some of the more intricate lace patterns take two sittings to complete, and after the design is once traced, the dog has to be clipped and shaved about once a month. The charge for working out a difficult pattern or 'set scene' is £2 2s.; the clipping of an involved monogram or coronet costs from 25s. to 30s.; and a sovereign is asked for 'plain treatment.' Brown has one canine client on his books whose owners, being Irish and rabid Home Rulers, will have nothing depicted on his back but a big shamrock; yet another poodle bears testimony to his master's patriotism by carrying about a quaint-looking thistle, the prickly part being cunningly fashioned from the animal's own stubbly bristles.

Here is a third example of Mr Brown's peculiar art; a poodle is marked with a lion rampant – presumably representing its owner's crest. As a rule, an article from a toilet case – hairbrush or scent-bottle stopper – is sent to the clipper, and from this he copies the monogram.

Mr Brown likewise trains dogs of all breeds to perform, it being quite fashionable for these little canine swells to possess such accomplishments as *skirt-dancing*, tight-rope walking, and piano playing. I need scarcely tell you that the slightest attempt at these feats suffices. And it is curious to note that the value of pet dogs is in an inverse ratio to their size. Mr Brown recently sold a black-and-tan terrier, weighing exactly 20oz., for £40; so let no one say that the lap-dog's outfit is more costly than the lap-dog himself.

An expert is putting the finishing touches to the 'Warwick'. This is a promenade costume in fine brown cloth, shot with pink, lined with rose-coloured silk, fastened with a 15-carat gold clasp, and further ornamented with a double ruching at the neck like a lady's cape. The coat on the machine is in dull red velvet, lined with white moiré. There are large scent-bottles near the seamstress; for these dainty garments *must* be perfumed, otherwise the captious canines might (and do) evince a sudden dislike to the expensive garment selected.

But the aristocratic dog's wardrobe also contains outfits for special occasions. I have seen a yellow satin coat trimmed with Honiton, and priced at ten guineas. An old favourite, seventeen years of age, was shown to me, and on being requested to examine his coat (of fine cloth lined with costly sable) I found a small electro-magnetic appliance sewn between the cloth and the fur lining. This dog was a bit of a hypochondriac – always fancying he was ill; he did, however, occasionally suffer from pneumonia and backache.

It is absurd to suppose that all kinds of dogs wear these garments; for example, no one would think of putting a coat on a Chow-Chow. On the other hand, dachshunds are sometimes provided with warm coats, and *sealskin waistcoats also*, mainly because they are apt to run through pretty long grass, and in this way, being short-legged, get their precious little stomachs wet, thus inducing various parlous canine ills. Wedding garments are always attractive; and of course, on such festive occasions, her ladyship's pet is very much *en suite*. The little animal's interest in the function may be infinitesimal – he may even regard the whole business with fierce loathing; still, he is dressed. The Maison Ledouble turns out wedding coats in white, yellow, and crimson satins trimmed with orange blossom at the neck, and with white satin leaders; these coats cost about £5 each.

Should the newly-made bride wish to take her darling with her on the honeymoon trip, the dog-maid (no sinecure, this) swiftly changes Fido's garments, replacing the gorgeous wedding outfit with a neat travelling suit of box-cloth, complete with hood and pockets for handkerchief, railway ticket, and biscuit – the latter by way of refreshment *en route*. If you think the toy dog is hustled into the guard's van, you are grievously mistaken. He is carefully placed in a travelling kennel. This is really a beautiful hand-bag of cow-hide or crocodile, silver-mounted, and costing from four to ten guineas. It is well ventilated, and supplied with lambs' wool mats. The wire grating is heavily gilt, or plated; and there is a leather flap which may be let down at the dog's bed-time, or when the sun is too powerful for his eyes.

The mistress does *not* carry her pet's handkerchief; this would be an unpardonable breach of canine etiquette. The perfumed cambric or silken square is coquettishly stuck in Fido's own coat-pocket, so that it may be available for use on wet days, when those low omnibuses, carts, and cabs splash so horribly.

In winter Dandy wears a fur coat; and I may say that these garments are usually lined with seal and sable, their cost ranging up to ten or fifteen guineas.

Dogs' bracelets or bangles cost, in gold, from two to ten guineas each; and in silver from 15s. to 30s. In Paris, these ornaments are frequently seen studded with precious stones, rendering the pet a most desirable piece of portable property. And the gems used vary according to the breed of dog.

Why, the very combs and brushes used on canine toilet-tables are as costly as choice of materials can make them. The hair-brushes are specially designed so that the hairs stand at a certain angle, thus facilitating the treatment of tangled (natural) coats. Three or four large brushes are first used; then come the finer kinds, and lastly the combs, which are made in steel, silver, buffalo-horn, and tortoise-shell. The brushes cost from 5s. to 10s. 6d. each (dog's name in gold or silver extra, of course); and the cheaper kind of combs are sold at Barrett's for 3s. 6d. and 5s. 6d.

Fastidious folk sometimes design collars in silver or gold for their own dogs; and big dogs often have solid silver collars made for them.

The fact is, money is literally no object where aristocratic pet dogs are concerned. Mr Barrett tells me he has often made *muzzles* in gold and silver – as though such would be more tolerable than the 'regulation pattern'; also leaders consisting of long chains of fine gold, and golden couples for promenading with pairs of dogs. Pretty bracelets lock on the dogs' paws, thus obviating to a certain extent the annoyance of periodical loss of valuable jewellery. By the way, anyone who has seen a lady trying to lead two playful pet dogs in the West-End will at once appreciate the use of the couples.

There are fashions in ladies' dogs just as there are in dresses and millinery. The King Charles and Blenheim spaniels, once so popular, have quite lost caste in the 'hupper suckles'. On the other hand, a Yorkshire terrier, weighing only 2¼lb., was recently sold for eighty guineas, and was considered cheap at that.

I asked how the changes in fashionable dogs came about, and was told that in this, as in other matters, Royalty leads the way. Suppose the Princess of Wales's favourite dog, for the time being, is a Chow-Chow, and in due time that exalted animal dies. Then Her Royal Highness will probably visit some big dog show and choose a new pet – perhaps a Japanese pug (a well-bred specimen will now fetch from fifty to 100 guineas); a small white Pomeranian (Princess Beatrice's favourite); a Spitz, or a small French bull-terrier. In any case, the Princess's choice decides the fashion in pet dogs; though, of course, other considerations also operate to work the change. Yorkshire terriers are very popular just now.

Baskets are now being ordered which can be attached to cycles, so that the mistress can take her own daily exercise and give her beloved pet an airing at one and the same time.

The well-being of these toy dogs is studied to a truly amazing degree. What could possibly be more comical than a fully-equipped canine dandy? One black-and-tan terrier is dressed for a morning call with his mistress, who will *leave her pet's card* as well as her own, this extraordinary custom being considered necessary if there happens to be a toy dog at the house about to be visited. The little animal has a quaint tie and collar; and a card-case, sticking out of the front of his coat. The fair Parisienne, on hearing of ordinary sober English customs, is contemptuously amused, and probably exclaims: '*Mais! c'est drôle!*' But the leaving of her dog's card on a fellow-pet during the morning drive – this she considers in no wise funny.

And yet this fashion is now fairly with us; and, absurd as it is, there are still more outrageous canine *modes* to follow. For example, there are wet weather dogs' boots: pretty little rubber goloshes, with black studs or buttons. The rubber goloshes are sometimes worn by rheumatic dogs; others wear them because, while in London, they suffer from a foot complaint caused by the metallic grit on the roads.

Now, as to diet; but in regard to this part of the article I must acknowledge my indebtedness to the well-known canine 'vet', Mr C.

Rotherham, of South Molton Street. Here is an astounding fact vouched for by my informant. There is in the West-End of London a poodle for whose consumption a prime leg of mutton is cooked regularly every day, and the dog demolishes the joint. A little less startling is the case of the greyhound, who has the first and choicest cuts off the joint below stairs!

But it is when their pets are sick that ladies of high degree cast common-sense completely overboard. The fashionable canine surgeons are not easily astonished – as you may imagine. At the same time, ladies give them infinite trouble by their innumerable questions, not to mention the demonstrative agony they suffer over the ailments of their darlings. The Earl and Countess of —— burst into the very dingy surgery of an eminent 'vet' one day and asked after the health of a sick pug, who lay there in a basket; the little brute was a monument of ugliness. 'He is dying, my lord; dying, my lady,' replied the 'vet' (a most correct man), with a sympathetic catch in his voice.

Lady —— at once became hysterical; she threw herself prostrate on the dusty floor in her superb dress and sobbed aloud, commanding the dignified surgeon to kneel down and pray for the departing pug. The noble earl, too, was deeply moved, but he controlled his emotion, merely glaring at the bottles on the shelves and sniffing audibly.

It is amusing to learn that Mr Rotherham occasionally receives letters direct from his patients; that is to say, requests for his services which purport to come from the dogs themselves. The following is a very droll example: –

> – , Belgrave Square, W.,
> 22nd January, 1896.

Dear Dr Rotherham, – As they say in America, I feel 'real sick' this morning; so mother tells me to write and ask you to call here as early as possible after receiving this. I am not at all nervous as to my not feeling well; but as poor mother is mourning the loss of my uncle 'Puck', she naturally feels anxious about me. I will tell you how I feel, so that you may in some measure be guided in your treatment of my indisposition. You must promise not to tell mother, but she gave a dinner last evening, and I *did* enjoy myself. I had *such* a lot of nice things! Do you think it is possible for them to have made me feel as I do? I was in great pain during the night, so that poor mother and myself did not have a wink of sleep. At eight o'clock this morning I was dreadfully sick, and my poor head is terribly hot, and difficult to hold up. My eyes will not keep open; and my lovely tail, which you have admired so often, is a disgrace to me; it hangs straight down, and will not curl a wee bit. I am quite ashamed of it. Do come soon, and be the good doctor you have always been.

Your grateful patient,

NIGGY.

When sick dogs 'lie up' at home, they are constantly fed with the breasts of pheasants, served on silver. Old 'Noble', the Queen's collie, was once found suffering from indigestion, brought on by a too plentiful supply of the above-named delicacy. Canine invalids in hospital are usually visited at least once a day by their mistresses, who will probably produce from the carriage whole roast partridges, hare's tongues, or sweetbreads; and Mr Rotherham knows of one little pampered brute whose jaded palate would reject everything save ptarmigan.

But could anything be more ludicrous than a coated, booted, and generally weather-protected pug? An umbrella was actually made by Messrs. Barrett in such a way that it could not be dislodged, no matter how obnoxious it became to the wearer. It opened the moment it was pressed down on to the pug's back; and it cost five guineas.

But to return to the sick pets. Some doting mistresses send their suffering dogs to the 'vet's' house to be boarded there under the surgeon's constant care. Now and then the latter is obliged to intercept the extravagant dainties brought for his patient, and substitute plain, wholesome food.

Here is a funny story in this connection. One of the leading canine specialists was sent for by a titled lady to see her poodle, who was in a bad way. The moment the animal came into the drawing-room, the dog-doctor knew it was a case of over-feeding; so 'Jacko' was sent with tremendous pomp to the surgeon's house to be treated. His anxious mistress did not neglect him, though. Twice a day, a splendid carriage drove up, and a footman brought round to the surgeon's man a massive silver dish, whereon reposed some succulent bird. 'How is Jacko to-day?' the footman would ask, according to instructions. 'Well, a little better, James; but still poorly,' the other would reply. The surgeon's man would then take the tempting meal round to the stables, eat it with immense relish, and then clean and polish the silver ready for the exchange dish, which he knew would be brought along in a few hours. For many days this went on, till at last the surgeon remarked to his man: 'I shall have to be sending Jacko home soon.' 'Don't do it yet, sir,' was the earnest and unexpected reply; 'I never lived so well in my life.'

Another really clever canine 'vet' with a lucrative practice told me he had a simple way of treating ladies' pampered pets. On receiving an over-fed toy dog, he would put him into a disused brick oven with a crust of bread, an onion, and an old boot. When the dog gnawed the bread, the surgeon wrote to the mistress that the dear little thing was 'doing nicely.' When it commenced operations on the onion, word was sent that the pet was 'decidedly better'; but when the animal tackled the boot, the lady was respectfully informed that her darling was 'ready to be removed' – a rational, if drastic, cure. Beyond question, the finest canine hospital in Europe is Spratt's Sanatorium at Beddington, which is under the supervision of Mr Alfred Sewell, the famous canine surgeon. This institution has numbered among its in-patients the *crème de la crème* of Dandy Dog-dom; and the perfection of the scientific arrangements must be seen to be believed.

It is not unusual for dogs to be ordered to Brighton, Bournemouth, and other resorts on the south coast, for a change of air – especially if the complaint is a troublesome cough. Many a canine invalid, too, has been specially taken all the way to the Riviera – Nice, Mentone, Hyères, Biarritz, Monte Carlo – solely for the benefit of its health. And, of course, it would be wrapped in swansdown *en route*, and not left out of sight, lest those horrid railway porters should treat the precious darling harshly. Mr Alfred Sewell, the eminent canine specialist, living in the vicinity of Eaton Square, was once telegraphed for from Oxford, a pet dog having broken its leg through a fall downstairs. It was, however, so late at night that Mr Sewell wired back, 'Last train gone.' The next message from the dog's mistress read, 'Take special.' He did, and it cost £20.

In large and fashionable houses the dogs (two or three is the usual number kept) have a special servant to minister unto their countless wants; and the position of dog-maid, as I have hinted elsewhere, is one of grave responsibility. Her charges must be laid to rest in their sumptuous little beds at a certain hour; they must be up early for their bath, and then taken out for a walk or a drive. Or perhaps a manservant is retained at £60 a year to perform these offices. In that case a specially fitted bath would be installed in the house, together with a complete outfit of expensive toilet articles. Thus the actual cost of the canine *ménage* – having in mind the extensive wardrobe necessary, not to speak of the jewellery – can safely be computed at hundreds of pounds a year.

And yet, with all this, dandy dogs die like their humbler brethren – probably much sooner. Then comes the funeral, with its flowers, carriages, and marble monuments. I am not jesting. An illustrated article has already appeared in the *Strand Magazine* on the Dogs' Cemetery, situated, appropriately, in Hyde Park. Mr Rotherham, the canine specialist, has an extensive burying-ground of the same kind on his property at Neasden.

Mr Kenyon, the gentle, sympathetic undertaker of Edgware Road, tells me he was sent for in hot haste one Saturday afternoon. He was out at the time, but he called on the Sunday – thinking, of course, that he was required to take an order for the burial of an ordinary Christian. It was not so. The deceased was a pet dog that had met with a tragic death in the street beneath a coal cart. The lady tearfully explained that she wanted the body embalmed and then placed in a glass coffin, so that she could have poor dear 'Friskie' with her all days – even to the consummation of her own; the two would then be interred together. Mr Kenyon thought this might be magnificent, but it was not business; so he declined the commission.

Mr Rotherham knows of dozens of cases in which toy dogs have had costly funerals. Pets that die in town are usually buried at the country seat of the family. In this surgeon's canine cemetery lies one dog that was brought from France.

But listen to Mr Rotherham's record case. 'A year or two ago I was called to the Grosvenor Hotel to see a dog. When I entered the room I saw a young man stretched on the hearth-rug. I thought I had been called to see *him*; but I found I was mistaken. The dog was dead, the circumstances being these: The gentleman had occasion to go out, so he shut his dog in the sitting room. The dog protested strongly in his absence – mainly by disfiguring the door, and driving several other visitors nearly crazy with continuous howls. When the master returned, the hotel people complained, whereupon the young gentleman proceeded to chastise his demonstrative pet – which chastisement took the form of a running kick that ended the dog's days.

'The remorseful man's reparation resolved itself into a gorgeous funeral. There was a purple velvet pall, two broughams (one for the coffin and one for the mourners), and three guineas' worth of flowers – chiefly lilies of the valley. A leaden shell was made and inclosed in a polished mahogany coffin, with silver fittings and name-plate. A touch of romance was given to this unique function when, just as the leaden shell was about to be sealed up, the impetuous young fellow was seen to put in with the dog's remains a packet of letters and a gold locket containing hair. I imagine the dog must have belonged to the chief mourner's deceased lady-love.'

This funeral, Mr Rotherham assures me, cost £30 or £40; and the funniest thing about it was that the surgeon himself was requested to 'follow'. He consented to do this, and was forthwith provided with a white silk sash and a satin rosette. Another very interesting dog's funeral was one carried out by a London undertaker, although the remains were to be interred in the tomb of the sorrowing master's ancestors in Sicily. The dog's body was, of course, embalmed; and the headstone was sent with it.

'Monkey' was a quaint little Yorkshire; and his mistress – an enormously rich woman, and a great believer in Sir Henry Thompson – had his remains cremated. 'Monkey's' cinerary urn probably represents the very highest pinnacle of (deceased) Dandy Dog-dom. It cost *six hundred guineas*, being in the form of a solid tortoise-shell sedan chair, enamelled all over the front and sides in the most costly manner, and inlaid with brilliants, rubies, emeralds, and pearls; the extremities of the handles are simply incrusted with jewels.

Inside is a gold-mounted crystal jar, with a monogram in diamonds; this contains the ashes. It is surmounted by a skull. The name of the departed pet is perpetuated by the monkey on top of the casket; and in his paw he holds a fine pearl. This casket was made by Messrs. A. Barrett and Sons, of 63 and 64, Piccadilly; of course, it was an exceptional order, but Mr H. Barrett tells me that the firm ordinarily make cinerary urns, ranging in price from £10 to £250, for holding the ashes of cremated pet dogs.

In conclusion it may be said that pet dogs are treated by their mistresses almost precisely as though they were human members of the family; the only discrepancy in the analogy being that it is horribly bad form for a lady to drive in the park with her baby by her side, while the presence of a pompous pug or a toy terrier is irreproachably correct.

From the *Strand Magazine*, 1896
(abridged)

SIR ARTHUR CONAN DOYLE

On the Trail

'ROUSE OLD SHERMAN up, and tell him with my compliments that I want Toby here at once. You will bring Toby back in the cab with you.'

'A dog, I suppose?'

'Yes, a queer mongrel, with a most amazing power of scent. I would rather have Toby's help than that of the whole detective force of London.'

From *The Sign of Four*

JEROME K. JEROME

Mayhem

WE GOT UP TOLERABLY early on the Monday morning at Marlow, and went for a bathe before breakfast; and, coming back, Montmorency made an awful ass of himself. The only subject on which Montmorency and I have any serious difference of opinion is cats. I like cats; Montmorency does not.

When I meet a cat, I say, 'Poor Pussy!' and stoop down and tickle the side of its head; and the cat sticks up its tail in a rigid, cast-iron manner, arches its back, and wipes its nose up against my trousers; and all is gentleness and peace. When Montmorency meets a cat, the whole street knows about it; and there is enough bad language wasted in ten seconds to last an ordinary respectable man all his life, with care.

I do not blame the dog (contenting myself, as a rule, with merely clouting his head or throwing stones at him), because I take it that it is his nature. Fox-terriers are born with about four times as much original sin in them as other dogs are, and it will take years and years of patient effort on the part of us Christians to bring about any appreciable reformation in the rowdiness of the fox-terrier nature.

I remember being in the lobby of the Haymarket Stores one day, and all round about me were dogs, waiting for the return of their owners, who were shopping inside. There were a mastiff, and one or two collies, and a St Bernard, a few retrievers and Newfoundlands, a boar-hound, a French poodle, with plenty of hair round its head, but mangy about the middle; a bulldog, a few Lowther Arcade sort of animals, about the size of rats, and a couple of Yorkshire tykes.

There they sat, patient, good, and thoughtful. A solemn peacefulness seemed to reign in that lobby. An air of calmness and resignation – of gentle sadness pervaded the room.

Then a sweet young lady entered, leading a meek-looking little fox-terrier, and left him, chained up there, between the bulldog and the poodle. He sat and looked about him for a minute. Then he cast up his eyes to the ceiling, and seemed, judging from his expression, to be thinking of his mother. Then he yawned. Then he looked round at the other dogs, all silent, grave, and dignified.

He looked at the bulldog, sleeping dreamlessly on his right. He looked at the poodle, erect and haughty, on his left. Then, without a word of warning, without the shadow of a provocation, he bit that poodle's near fore-leg, and a yelp of agony rang through the quiet shades of that lobby.

The result of his first experiment seemed highly satisfactory to him, and he determined to go on and make things lively all round. He sprang over the poodle and vigorously attacked a collie, and the collie woke up, and immediately commenced a fierce and noisy contest with the poodle. Then Foxey came back to his own place, and caught the bulldog by the ear, and tried to throw him away; and the bulldog, a curiously impartial animal, went for everything he could reach, including the hall-porter, which gave that dear little terrier the opportunity to enjoy an uninterrupted fight of his own with an equally willing Yorkshire tyke.

Anyone who knows canine nature need hardly be told that, by this time, all the other dogs in the place were fighting as if their hearths and homes depended on the fray. The big dogs fought each other indiscriminately; and the little dogs fought among themselves, and filled up their spare time by biting the legs of the big dogs.

The whole lobby was a perfect pandemonium, and the din was terrific. A crowd assembled outside in the Haymarket, and asked if it was a vestry meeting; or, if not, who was being murdered, and why? Men came with poles and ropes, and tried to separate the dogs, and the police were sent for.

And in the midst of the riot that sweet young lady returned, and snatched up that sweet little dog of hers (he had laid the tyke up for a month, and had on the expression, now, of a new-born lamb) into her arms, and kissed him, and asked him if he was killed, and what those great nasty brutes of dogs had been doing to him; and he nestled up against her, and gazed up into her face with a look that seemed to say: 'Oh, I'm so glad you've come to take me away from this disgraceful scene!'

She said that the people at the Stores had no right to allow great savage things like those other dogs to be put with respectable people's dogs, and that she had a great mind to summon somebody.

Such is the nature of fox-terriers; and, therefore, I do not blame Montmorency for his tendency to row with cats; but he wished he had not given way to it that morning.

We were, as I have said, returning from a dip, and half-way up the High Street a cat darted out from one of the houses in front of us, and began to trot across the road. Montmorency gave a cry of joy – the cry of a stern warrior who sees his enemy given over to his hands – the sort of cry Cromwell might have uttered when the Scots came down the hill – and flew after his prey.

His victim was a large black Tom. I never saw a larger cat, nor a more disreputable-looking cat. It had lost half its tail, one of its ears, and a fairly appreciable proportion of its nose. It was a long, sinewy-looking animal. It had a calm, contented air about it.

Montmorency went for that poor cat at the rate of twenty miles an hour; but the cat did not hurry up – did not seem to have grasped the idea that its life was in danger. It trotted quietly on until its would-be assassin was within a yard of it, and then it turned round and sat down in the middle of the road, and looked at Montmorency with a gentle, inquiring expression, that said:

'Yes! You want me?'

Montmorency does not lack pluck; but there was something about the look of that cat that might have chilled the heart of the boldest dog. He stopped abruptly, and looked back at Tom.

Neither spoke; but the conversation that one could imagine was clearly as follows:

THE CAT: 'Can I do anything for you?'

MONTMORENCY: 'No – no, thanks.'

THE CAT: 'Don't you mind speaking, if you really want anything, you know.'

MONTMORENCY (*backing down the High Street*): 'Oh, no – not at all – certainly – don't trouble. I – I am afraid I've made a mistake. I thought I knew you. Sorry I disturbed you.'

THE CAT: 'Not at all – quite a pleasure. Sure you don't want anything now?'

MONTMORENCY (*still backing*): 'Not at all, thanks – not at all – very kind of you. Good morning.'

THE CAT: 'Good morning.'

Then the cat rose, and continued his trot; and Montmorency, fitting what he calls his tail carefully into its groove, came back to us, and took up an unimportant position in the rear.

To this day, if you say the word 'Cats!' to Montmorency, he will visibly shrink and look up piteously at you, as if to say:

'Please don't.'

From Three Men in a Boat

At the Vicar's

STORIES ABOUT HORSES one listens to suspiciously, thinking to one's self: Now is this guileless anecdote, or is he hoping to lead up to a deal; and unconsciously one allows one's tone and manner to suggest a disconcerting, if not insulting disbelief. Even the weather has its dangers. One may be hurting an agricultural party's feelings by speaking disparagingly of weather that he in secret has been praying for and is pleased with now he has got it.

Cats appeal to but a limited circle. Guinea pigs and white mice, after a certain age, one loses interest in.

But the Dog is the one thing in nature that makes the whole world kin. The clergyman of a charming village in Oxfordshire told me that a week or so after his arrival his wife organized a sewing party, to which were invited all the ladies of the district for some three miles round. I use the word ladies in its conventional sense as signifying folks with sufficient leisure to indulge in social functions. The six ladies so invited punctually arrived, but on looking about them were sorry they had come. It seemed that three of them belonged to one set and three of them to another, and never before that afternoon had they found themselves together, fellow guests, under the same roof. His drawing-room was not a big one, but, fortunately, it possessed two windows, and with the help of a screen they made the most of it. Three of them sat the north side of the screen; and three of them gathered together south of the screen. And the ambition of each party was to appear to be enjoying itself more than the other party. But, as a matter of fact, neither party was enjoying itself in the least. My friend's wife, a woman of some tact, worked hard to break down the barrier dividing these good folk from one another. But all her efforts proved fruitless. The ladies on the north side of the screen had heard – gossip will filter through – that there were three other families residing somewhere in the neighbourhood – had been residing there, so it was said, for many years, and were likely to continue in residence; but they were not the sort of people that one knows. The ladies who sat working to the south side of the screen had met occasionally strange people – said to be inhabitants of the neighbourhood. But really one cannot know everybody. So matters continued till, with the tea things there entered – it would perhaps be more correct to say, there burst into the room – my friend's dog, a Newfoundland of a cheerful disposition. He was not of importance from the breeder's point of view, but commonplace people have often a deal of sense. Or maybe he had taken his views from an old sheep-dog, his boon companion. His idea is and always has been that people should be as much as possible together. I know this because even when out for a walk with a party he will never allow two or three of us to linger behind. 'I'll be losing one of them,' he says to himself, 'why can't they keep together. Just look at them – those two, philandering round that stile, all the others nearly a quarter of a mile ahead.' The two lingering by the stile may protest, may even grow indignant with him; he can't help that, his business is to chivy them up. If they will not come on fast enough, then the only thing to be done is to bark loudly to those in front till, wondering what the trouble is about, they turn and come back. When he has got the party together again he is contented. That there are those in the party who are not contented does not trouble him.

The sight of the screen annoyed him at once. 'That's not a neatly arranged drove of people,' said he to himself. 'What's the good of the fence between them; we don't want it.' He had it over promptly. When two ladies had taken their heads out of it and another lady her feet, it was not worth putting up again. What followed was confusion, mingled with laughter and apologies, and before it was over those six ladies were hopelessly herded together, the dog sitting eyeing them with contentment. He did not rest there; he went in and out among them; he literally bullied them into friendship.

From Essays

W. H. HUDSON

Dogs in London

THE SUBJECT OF this paper, for which I am unable to find a properly descriptive title, will be certain changes noticeable during recent years in the dogs of the metropolis, and, in a less degree, of the country generally. At the same time there has been an improvement in the character of the dog population, due mainly to the weeding out of the baser breeds, but this matter does not concern us here; the change with which I propose to deal is in the temper and, as to one particular, the habits of the animal. This was the result of the famous (it used to be called infamous) muzzling order of 1897, which restrained dogs throughout the country from following their ancient custom of quarrelling with and biting one another for the unprecedented period of two and a half years. Nine hundred days and over may not seem too long a period of restraint in the case of a being whose natural term runs to threescore years and ten, but in poor Tatters' or Towzer's brief existence of a dozen summers it is the equivalent of more than twenty years in the life of the human animal.

As a naturalist I was interested in the muzzling order, and after noting its effects my interest in the subject has continued ever since. It should also, I imagine, be a matter of interest and importance to all who have a special regard for the dog or who are 'devoted to dogs,' who regard them as the 'friends of man,' even holding with the canophilists of the old Youatt period of the last century that the dog was specially created to fill the place of man's servant and companion. Strange to say, I have not yet met with any person of the dog-loving kind who has himself noticed any change in the temper or habits of the dog during the last fourteen or fifteen years or has any knowledge of it. One can only suppose – and this applies not only to those who cherish a peculiar affection for the dog, but to the numerous body of London naturalists as well – that the change was unmarked on account of the very long period during which the order was in force, when dogs were deprived of the power to bite, so that when the release came the former condition of things in the animal world was no longer distinctly remembered. It was doubtless assumed that, the muzzle once removed, all things were exactly as they had been before: if a few remembered and noticed the change, they failed to record it – at all events I have seen nothing about it in print. Circumstances made it impossible for me not to notice the immediate effect of the order, and at the end of the time to forget the state of things as they existed before its imposition.

I was probably more confined to London during the years 1897–9 than most persons who are keenly interested in animal life, and being so confined, I was compelled to gratify my taste or passion by paying a great deal of attention to the only animals that there are to observe in our streets, the dog being the most important. I also took notes of what I observed – my way of remembering not to forget; and, refreshing my mind by returning to them, I am able to recover a distinct picture of the state of things in the pre-muzzling times. It is a very different state from that of to-day. One thing that was a cause of surprise to me in those days was the large number of dogs, mostly mongrels and curs, to be seen roaming masterless about the streets. These I classed as pariahs, although they all, no doubt, had their homes in mean streets and courts, just as the ownerless pariah dogs in Eastern towns have their homes – their yard or pavement or spot of waste ground where they live and bask in the sun when not roaming in quest of food and adventures. Many of these London pariahs were wretched-looking objects, full of sores and old scars, some like skeletons and others with half their hair off from mange and other skin diseases. They were to be seen all over London, always hunting for food, hanging about areas, like the bone- and bottle-buyers, looking for an open dustbin where something might be found to comfort their stomachs. They also haunted butchers' shops, where the butcher kept a jealous eye on their movements and sent them away with a kick and a curse whenever he got the chance. Most, if not all, of these poor dogs had owners who gave them shelter but no food or very little, and probably in most cases succeeded in evading the licence duty.

There is no doubt that in the past the dog population of London was always largely composed of animals of this kind – 'curs of low degree,' and a great variety of mongrels, mostly living on their wits. An account of the dogs of London of two or three or four centuries ago would have an extraordinary interest for us now, but, unfortunately, no person took the pains to write it. Caius, our oldest writer on dogs, says of 'curres of the mungrel and rascall sort' – the very animals we want to know about: 'Of such dogs as keep not their kind, of such as are mingled out of sundry sortes not imitating the conditions of some one certaine Spece, because they resemble no notable shape, nor exercise any worthy property of the true, perfect, and gentle kind, it is not necesarye that I write any more of them, but to banish them as unprofitable implements out of the boundes of my Booke.' It is regrettable that he did 'banish' them, as he appears to have been something of an observer on his own account. Had he given us a few pages on the life and habits of the 'rascall sort' of animal, his *Booke of Englishe Dogges*, which after so many centuries is still occasionally reprinted, would have been as valuable to us now as Turner's on British birds (1544) and Willughby's half a century later on the same subject, and as Gould's brilliant essay on the habits of British ants – which, by the way, has never been reprinted – and as Gilbert White's classic, which came later in the eighteenth century.

That the bond uniting man and dog in all instances when the poor brute was obliged to fend for himself in the inhospitable streets of London was an exceedingly frail one was plainly seen when the muzzling order of 1897 was made. An extraordinary number of apparently ownerless dogs, unmuzzled and collarless, were found roaming about the streets and taken by hundreds every week to the lethal chamber. In thirty months the dog population of the metropolis had decreased by about one hundred thousand. The mongrels and dogs of the 'rascall sort' had all but vanished, and this was how the improvement in the character of the dog population mentioned before came about immediately. But a far more important change had been going on at the same time – the change in the temper of our dogs; and it may here be well to remark that this change in disposition was not the result of the weeding-out process I have described. The better breeds are not more amiable than the curs of low degree. The man who has made a friend and companion of the cur will tell you that he is as nice-tempered, affectionate, faithful, and intelligent as the nobler kinds, the dogs of 'notable shape.'

Let us now go back to the muzzling time of 1897–9, and I will give here the substance of the notes I made at the time. They have among my notes on many subjects a peculiar interest to me as a naturalist because in the comments I made at the time I ventured to make a prediction which has not been fulfilled. I was astonished and delighted to find that (on this one occasion) I had proved a false prophet.

The dog-muzzling question (I wrote) does not interest me personally, since I keep no dog, nor love to see so intelligent and serviceable a beast degraded to the position of a mere pet or plaything – a creature that has lost or been robbed of its true place in the scheme of things. Looking at the matter from the outside, simply as a student of the ways of animals, I am surprised at the outcry made against Mr Long's order, especially here in London, where there is so great a multitude of quite useless animals. No doubt a large majority of the dogs of the metropolis are household pets, pure and simple, living indoors in the same rooms as their owners, in spite of their inconvenient instincts. On this subject I have had my say in an article on 'The Great Dog Superstition', for which I have been well abused; the only instinct of the dog with which I am concerned at present is that of pugnacity. This is like his love of certain smells disgusting to us, part and parcel of his being, so that for a dog to be perfectly gentle and without the temper that barks and bites must be taken as evidence of its decadence – not of the individual but of the race or breed or variety. Whether this fact is known or only dimly surmised by dog-lovers, more especially by those who set the fashion in dogs, we see that in recent years there has been a distinct reaction against the more degenerate kinds[1] – those in whose natures the jackal and wild-dog writing has quite or all but faded out – the numerous small toy terriers; the Italian greyhound, shivering like an aspen leaf; the drawing-room pug, ugliest of man's (the breeder's) many inventions; the pathetic Blenheim and King Charles spaniels, the Maltese, the Pomeranian, and all the others that have, so to speak, rubbed themselves out by acquiring a white liver to please their owners' fantastic tastes. A

[1] Alas! since these notes were made, fourteen years ago, there has been a recrudescence of the purely woman's drawing-room pet dog. The wretched griffon, looking like a mean cheap copy of the little Yorkshire – one of the few small pet animals which has not wholly lost its soul – appears to have vanished. But the country has now been flooded with the Pekinese, and one is made to loathe it from the constant sight of it in every drawing-room and railway carriage and motor-car and omnibus, clasped in a woman's arms.

more vigorous beast is now in favour, and one of the most popular is undoubtedly the fox-terrier. This is assuredly the doggiest dog we possess, the most aggressive, born to trouble as the sparks fly upward. From my own point of view it is only right that fox-terriers and all other good fighters should have liberty to go out daily into the streets in their thousands in search of shindies, to strive with and worry one another to their hearts' content; then to skulk home, smelling abominably of carrion and carnage, and, hiding under their master's sofa, or other dark place, to spend the time licking their wounds until they are well again and ready to go out in search of fresh adventures. For God hath made them so.

But this is by no means the view of the gentle ladies and mild-tempered gentlemen who own them, nor, I dare say, of any canophilist, whether the owner of a dog or not. What these people want is that their canine friends shall have the same liberty enjoyed by themselves to make use of our streets and parks without risk of injury or insult; that they shall be free to notice or not the salutations and advances of others of their kind; to graciously accept or contemptuously refuse, with nose in air, according to the mood they may happen to be in or to the state of their digestive organs, an invitation to a game of romps. This liberty and safety they do now undoubtedly enjoy, thanks to the much-abused muzzling order.

It is true that to the canine mind this may not be an ideal liberty: 'For on a knight that hath neither hardihood nor valour in himself, may not another knight that hath more force in him reasonably prove his mettle; for many a time have I heard say that one is better than other.' These words, spoken by the Best Knight in the World, exactly fit the case of the fox-terrier, or any other vigorous variety whose one desire when he goes out into the world is reasonably to prove his mettle. 'Tis an ancient and noble principle of action, conceivably advantageous in certain circumstances; but in the conditions in which we human beings find ourselves placed it is not tolerated, and the valour and hardihood of our Percivals may no longer shine in the dark forests of this modern world.

Is it, then, so monstrous a thing, so great a tyranny, that the same restraint which has this long time been put upon the best and brightest of our own kind should now, for the public good, be imposed on our four-footed companions and servants! True, we think solely of ourselves when we impose the restraint, but incidentally (and entirely apart from the question of rabies) we are at the same time giving the greatest protection to the dogs themselves. Furthermore – and here we come to the point which mainly concerns us – the reflex effect of the muzzle on the dogs themselves may now be seen to be purely beneficial. Confining ourselves to London, the change in the animals' disposition, or at all events behaviour, has been very remarkable. It has forcibly reminded me of the change of temper I have witnessed in a rude, semi-barbarous community when some one in authority has issued an order that at all festivals and other public gatherings every man shall yield up his weapons – knives, pistols, iron-handled whips, etc. – to some person appointed to receive them, or be turned back from the gates. The result of such a general disarmament has been an all-round improvement in temper, a disposition of the people to mix freely instead of separating into well-defined groups, each with some famous fighting-man, wearing a knife as long as a sword, for its centre; also instead of wild and whirling words, dust raised, and blood shed, great moderation in language, good humour, and reasonableness in argument.

In the same way we may see that our dogs grow less and less quarrelsome as they become more conscious of their powerlessness to inflict injury. Their confidence, and with it their friendliness towards one another, increases; the most masterful or truculent cease from bullying, the timid outgrow their timidity, and in their new-found glad courage dare to challenge the fiercest among them to a circular race and rough-and-tumble on the grass.

Now all this, from the point of view of those who make toys of sentient and intelligent beings, is or should be considered pure gain. Moreover, this undoubted improvement could not have come about if the muzzle had been the painful instrument that some dog-owners believe or say. It seems to me that those who cry out against torturing our dogs, as they put it, do not love their pets wisely and are bad observers. Undoubtedly every restraint is in some degree disagreeable, but it is only when an animal has been deprived of the power to exercise his first faculties and obey his most importunate impulses that the restraint can properly be described as painful. Take the case of a chained dog; he is miserable, as any one may see since there are many dogs in that condition, because eternally conscious of the restraint; and the perpetual craving for liberty, like that of the healthy energetic man immured in a cell, rises to positive torture. Again, we know that smell is the most important sense of the dog, that it is as much to him as vision to the bird; consequently, to deprive him of the use of this all-important faculty by, let us say, plugging up his nostrils, or by destroying the olfactory nerve in some devilish way known to the vivisectors, would be to make him perfectly miserable, just as the destruction of its sense of sight would make a bird miserable. By comparison the restraint of the muzzle is very slight indeed; smell, hearing, vision are unaffected, and there is no interference with free locomotion; indeed so slight is the restraint that after a while the animal is for the most part unconscious of it except when the impulse to bite or to swallow a luscious bit of carrion is excited.

We frequently see or hear of dogs that joyfully run off to fetch their muzzles when they are called to go out for a walk, or even before they are called if they but see any preparations being made for a walk: no person will contend that these are made unhappy by the muzzle, or that they deliberately weigh two evils in their mind and make choice of the lesser. The most that may be said is that these muzzle-fetchers are exceptions, though they may be somewhat numerous. For how otherwise can the fact be explained that some dogs, however ready and anxious to go for a walk they may be, will, on catching sight of the muzzle, turn away with tail between their legs and the expression of a dog that has been kicked or unjustly rebuked? My experience is that this attitude towards the muzzle of some dogs, which was quite common in the early muzzling days, is now rare and is dying out. The explanation, I think, is that as the muzzle is at first keenly felt as a restraint, imposed for no cause that the dog sees, it is in fact taken as a punishment, and resented as much as an undeserved blow or angry word would be. Every one who observes dogs must be familiar with the fact that they do very often experience the feeling of injury and resentment towards their human masters and companions. As a rule this feeling vanishes with the exciting cause; unfortunately, in some cases the sight of the muzzle becomes associated with the feeling and is slow to disappear.

But if dogs still exist in this city of dogs that show any sign of such a feeling when a muzzle is held up before them, we can see that even in these super-sensitive ones it vanishes the instant they are out of doors. Again, let any person watch the scores and hundreds of dogs that disport themselves in our grassy parks on any fine day, and he will quickly be convinced that not only are they happy but that they are far happier than any company of unmuzzled dogs thrown casually together. They are happier, madly happy, because they know – this knowledge having now filtered down into their souls – that it is perfectly safe for them to associate with their fellows, to be hail-fellow-well-met with all the dogs in the place, from the tiniest trembling lap-dog to the burliest and most truculent-looking bull-dog and the most gigantic St Bernard or Danish boarhound. It is for us a happiness to see their confidence, their mad games, the way they all chase and tumble over one another, pretending to be furious and fighting a grand battle.

I do not say that there is any radical or any permanent change in the dog's character. Like other beasts, he is morally and mentally non-progressive; that which the uninformed canophilist takes as progression is merely decadence. Remove the muzzle, and in a short time the habit which the muzzle has bred will fade away and the old bickerings and bullyings and blood-sheddings begin afresh. As it is, some dogs refuse to let their fighting temper rust in spite of the muzzle.

In Hyde Park some time ago I witnessed a sublime but bloodless battle between a Danish boarhound and a bull-dog. Neither of them lost consciousness of the muzzle which prevented them from 'washing' their teeth in one another's blood; they simply dashed themselves against each other, then drew back and dashed together again and again, with such fury that they would, no doubt, have succeeded in injuring each other had not their owners, assisted by several persons who were looking on, succeeded in drawing them apart.

One more instance of many which I have observed during the last two years. This is of a rather large and exceptionally powerful fox-terrier, who when out for a walk keeps a very sharp lookout for other dogs, and the instant he spies one not bigger than himself charges him furiously and with the impact hurls him to the ground, and, leaving him there, he dashes on in search of a fresh victim.

These are, however, exceptions, few individuals having intelligence enough to find out a new way of inflicting injury. As a rule the dog of ineradicably savage temper looks at his fellows as if saying, 'Oh, for five minutes with this cursed muzzle off!' And the others, seeing his terrible aspect, are glad that the muzzle is on – a *blessed* muzzle it is to them; and if they only knew what the doggie people were saying in the papers and could express their views on the subject, many of them would be heard to cry out, 'Save us from our friends!'

The muzzling order had thus appeared to me as a sort of Golden Age of the metropolitan dogs – and cats, for these too had incidentally been affected and strangely altered in their habits. And here I must say that all I wrote in my note-book about the dogs during and just after the muzzling period has been compressed into as short a space as possible, and all I wrote about the cats (as indirectly affected by the order) has been left out for want of space to deal with the entire subject in a single chapter.

When dog-owners were rejoicing to hear that the Board of Agriculture had come to the conclusion that rabies had been completely stamped out, and were eagerly looking forward to the day when they would be allowed to remove the hated muzzle from their pets, the prospect did not seem a very pleasant one to me and to many others who kept no pets. I was prepared once more for the old familiar but unforgotten spectacle of a big dog-fight in the streets producing a joyful excitement in a crowd, quickly sprung out of the stones of the pavement as it were, of loafers and wastrels of all kinds – keen sportsmen every one of them – a spectacle which was witnessed every day by any person who took a walk in London before the muzzling time. These scenes would be common again: in one day the dogs' (and cats') dream of perpetual peace would be ended, and all canines of a lofty spirit would go forth again like the good Arthurian knight and the Zulu warrior to wash his long-unused weapons in an adversary's blood. But I was wrong. A habit had been formed in those two and a half years of restraint which did not lose its power at once: the something new which had come into the dog's heart still held him. But it would not, it could not, hold him long.

Days followed and nothing happened – the Golden Age was still on. I walked the streets and watched and waited; then, when nearly a week had elapsed, I witnessed a fine old-fashioned dog-fight, with two dogs in a tangle on the ground biting and tearing each other with incredible fury and with all the growls and shrieks and other warlike noises appropriate to the occasion. From all parts around the 'wond'ring neighbours ran' to look on, even as in former times down to the blessed year 1897.

'Just as I thought!' I exclaimed, and heartily wished that the President of the Board of Agriculture had made the muzzling order a perpetual one.

Other days and weeks followed and I witnessed no serious quarrel, and later it was so rare to see a dog-fight in the streets and parks, fights which one used to witness every day, that I began to think the new pacific habit had got a tighter grip on the animal than I could have believed. It would, I thought, perhaps take them two or three months to outgrow it and go back to their true natures.

I was wrong again: not months only but years have gone by – fourteen to fifteen years – and the beneficent change which had been wrought in those thirty months of restraint about which so great a pother was made at the time by dog-owners has continued to the present time.

We may say that in more senses than one the dogs (and cats) of the London of to-day are not the same beings we were familiar with in the pre-muzzling days. The object of that order we have seen was gained in the brief period of thirty months. Hydrophobia for the first time in the annals of England had ceased to exist, and so long as the quarantine law is faithfully observed will perhaps never return. Rabies broke out again in this country in 1917, its first reappearance since 1897, owing to some person having succeeded in eluding the quarantine order and bringing an infected dog to Plymouth. From that centre it spread to other parts of Devon and to Cornwall, and despite the prompt action of the authorities in imposing a new muzzling order in these two counties, the infection has spread to other parts of the country, and new muzzling orders are being issued just now – April 1919. Up till the year of 1897 the average number of persons who perished annually as the result of a dog-bite was twenty-nine. 'Well, that's not many in a population of forty millions,' cried the canophilists; but for twenty-nine who actually died of dog-madness, the most horrible shape in which death can appear to a human being, there were hundreds, and probably thousands, every year who lived for weeks and months in a constant state of apprehension lest some slight bite or abrasion received from the tooth of an angry or playful dog should result in that frightful malady.

This was unquestionably a great, a very great gain; but Mr Long had builded better than he knew, and I am not sure that the accidental result, the change in the dog's habits in one particular, will not be regarded as the most important gain by those who are fond of dogs and by all who recognise that, in spite of some disgusting instincts which can't be changed, the dog is and probably always will be with us – our one and only four-footed associate.

GEORGE MEREDITH
'Islet' the Dachs

Our 'Islet' out of Helgoland, dismissed
From his quaint tenement, quits hates and loves.
There lived with us a wagging humourist
In that hound's arch dwarf-legged on boxing-gloves.

Over the Hills

The old hound wags his shaggy tail,
    And I know what he would say:
It's over the hills we'll bound, old hound,
    Over the hills, and away.

There's nought for us here save to count the clock,
    And hang the head all day:
But over the hills we'll bound, old hound,
    Over the hills and away.

Here among men we're like the deer
    That yonder is our prey:
So, over the hills we'll bound, old hound,
    Over the hills and away.

The hypocrite is master here,
    But he's the cock of clay:
So, over the hills we'll bound, old hound,
    Over the hills and away.

The women, they shall sigh and smile,
    And madden whom they may:

It's over the hills we'll bound, old hound,
Over the hills and away.

Let silly lads in couples run
To pleasure, a wicked fay:
'Tis ours on the heather to bound, old hound,
Over the hills and away.

The torrent glints under the rowan red,
And shakes the bracken spray:
What joy on the heather to bound, old hound,
Over the hills and away.

The sun bursts broad, and the heathery bed
Is purple, and orange, and gray:
Away, and away, we'll bound, old hound,
Over the hills and away.

DAME ETHEL SMYTH

A Passion for Brahms

IT IS AMAZING TO think of the tasks one took on in by-gone years without blenching! My Leipzig lodgings were on the third floor, and though, if only in the interests of her trade, the washer-woman had seen to Marco's house-manners, the digestion of very young dogs is notoriously uncertain. Many a night in that first winter I had to get up in a hurry, and seizing ulster, slippers and goloshes, hastily conduct him down to the snowy street; and we all know how maddeningly deliberate dogs can be, once the danger of an indoor-catastrophe has been avoided.

Otherwise from the very first he was as great a philosopher, as perfect a comrade as busy woman could desire, walking, skating, doing everything with me. And though in the free Germany of those days a lead was not imperative, he never strolled across the communal flower beds or paid the wrong sort of compliment to projecting flowers. In England he won all hearts, notably my mother's, even when he walked under a wicker table at one of her tea parties and marched about the room as beneath a canopy, bearing tea cups and anchovy sandwiches. He would do any mortal thing you asked him, including leaping three and a half feet up on to the six-inch ledge of the high schoolroom bookcase, snapping a glove placed on the top shelf, turning in mid-air, and descending with his back to the bookcase – a really marvellous feat for a heavy dog. Yet at one thing he absolutely drew the line – and I always thought this refusal very interesting; nothing would induce him to drag the go-carts of my small nieces and nephews, who had heard all about his past and counted on his obliging them with alacrity. I suppose he had seen enough of that sort of thing in Vienna.

Devoted to music – or at least to noise – for hours he would lie entranced, his head on the pedals of a seldom silent piano. Indeed one day he carried the musical passion to extremes, and instead of staying in the street as he was bidden, dashed up two pairs of stairs and burst into a room where Brahms and four local artists were rehearsing his divine F minor piano quintet, upsetting the 'cellist's desk in his stride. After which, to the horror of his mistress who was seated beside Brahms and turning over, he dived under the piano and pushed in between us. I have sometimes described Brahms as rather a curmudgeon, so let me add that on this occasion he laughed till he got purple in the face and said the scene took him back to the Pantomime Harlequinades of his youth.

From *Inordinate(?) Affection*

'OUIDA'

Reason and Folly

PEOPLE CALL SUCH a faculty 'instinct'. This word seems to me the silliest and most misleading that was ever used in human speech. There are in the dog, who thus finds his way through the unknown to a remembered home, many mental qualities, memory, prudence, ingenuity, tenacity, choice, and beside all these a faculty which we do not possess and cannot analyse.

In a study of *'Psychologie Positive'*, admirably written and deserving of the perusal of all thinkers and students, a friend of mine, the Marquis Bourbon del Monte, speaking of the observant intelligence and strong reasoning powers of the dog, relates how his own dog, always accompanying him in his walks, but never in his rides, looks at his feet the moment he enters the hall, and if it see spurs there, goes away sorrowful, but if it see none, leaps at him, barking with joy. He continues to relate how a priest, well-known to him, living in a village near Florence, fell one day into a pond, his hat caught in a branch above the water; a dog that was with him tried to help him for a few minutes, but finding its efforts in vain, seized the hat off the bough, and darted off with it to the priest's house, where the sight of the hat, and the disquietude of the dog, roused the alarm of the sacristan, and the household following the animal, reached the piece of water in time to save the life of the poor curate. He proceeds to ask, with justice, in what quality are these acute and accurate powers of discernment and deducation different to the mental reasonings by which human beings guide their acts? I have myself known many instances in my own dogs of a similar kind, arguing the shrewdest observation and reflections. My Newfoundland, Sulla, was the most perfectly sweet-tempered of all created creatures; once he saw a man hurling a pewter pot at a woman, and once he saw a man beating a little child; on each occasion he sprang on the man and knocked him down.

*   *   *

The effect of exhibitions on the *morale* of dogs is injurious beyond words. They are harrassed, intimidated, irritated, annoyed alike in their stalls, on the benches, and in the ring. Large dogs are either daunted or infuriated; small ones are cowed, fretted and made miserable. We are constantly told that such and such a champion dog did not show to advantage, because he was 'nervous,' or that such another only missed the first prize because he would not hold his head up, or would lie down in the sand from fright; what a piteous state of suffering to be created and renewed every time that the unhappy creature is dragged to a Show! The little toy-dogs cooped up in their cages are tortured no less; to be stared at by an ever-changing crowd of strangers, must be torment, of which we can form no idea, to the sensitive temperament of the dog, so distressed by alteration of every kind, so antagonistic to strange faces, so alarmed at every novelty and startled by every noise.

One well-known female exhibitor of the little Yorkshire terriers so fashionable now, combs their hair daily in their cages and *wraps their feet in silver paper!* Poor little martyrs to human greed, pride and folly! Their little feet should be flying joyously through grass and heather on their own moors, and their long hair should be blowing about in the wind, in their merry scampers by the brook side, and the meadow hedge. I repeat that if some check is not put upon the craze of shutting up dogs in exhibitions for the gratification of their owners' miserable vanity and love of lucre, the injury wrought to the *morale* of dogs will be incalculable and speedily irreparable; whilst if the laws, which go side by side with the increase of such exhibitions, for the muzzling and enforced inaction and suffering of the canine race be persisted in, the dog, as our companion, guard, and friend, will practically cease to exist; the active, merry, light-spirited and ever-animated creature, which the dog is *naturally*, will vanish from all countries cursed by Shows and regulations, and in his stead there will be a timid, hesitating, 'faked', artificially-created animal, *crétinisé* by inaction and worry, and dull of instinct, because instinct only exists in him to be thwarted, ignored, and suppressed by his human tyrants. He is becoming a mere gambling tool in the hands of men like his fellow-sufferer the racer, and the results to him are torture, injury and early death.

From *Dogs*

SIR EDWARD ELGAR

Battle

S CAP HAS HAD a cough during the last fortnight – I have taken him to a Vet: (a good one) and he (Scap) has had a few pills; he is all right again now. He had the mug & the beefbone on Xmas day; I have many anecdotes to tell you when we meet; if we ever do; which will not bear writing.

I hit a large dog, which was growling after Scap on Xmas eve & knocked the Handle off my walking stick which someone found; *it had my name on* & I had the owner of the cur after me; threatening police court &c, &c.; I talked to him like a man & came off with flying colours; my knowledge of the law, real & *pretended*, startled him (& well it might) – he touches his hat to me & keeps his dog tied up.

To Dr Charles Buck, 8 January 1886
From *Letters of a Lifetime*, ed. Jerrold Northrop Moore

Aural Wonder

'THEY ARE ON THE line now, Sir Edward,' announced the hall porter [at Brooks's Club], and soon [James] Lees-Milne over-heard the great Worcestershire composer admonishing, 'Don't bite the cushions', between barks at the other end of the line.

Hugh Montgomery-Massingberd in the *Daily Telegraph*,
6 August 1988, quoted *ibid*

Bars and Star

IN [*Enigma Variation*] XI, 'G.R.S.' (Dr G. R. Sinclair, organist of Hereford Cathedral) some injustice is done, for, as Elgar noted, the Variation has 'nothing to do with organs or cathedrals or, except remotely, with G. R. S. The first few bars were suggested by his great bulldog Dan (a well-known character) falling down the steep bank into the River Wye (bar 1); his paddling up stream to find a landing place (bars 2 and 3); and his rejoicing bark on landing (2nd half of bar 5). G. R. S. said "Set that to music". I did; here it is.' Suggestions that this was another of Elgar's deceptions and that the music has nothing to do with Dan are effectively refuted by the autograph sketch of the variation, in which Elgar has written the one word 'Dan'.

It has also been said that bulldogs do not like water – but, as Elgar made clear, Dan fell in, unwillingly. Nothing more needs to be said except that Dan has further claims to immortality. Inscribed by Elgar in Sinclair's visitors' book at Hereford between 1897 and 1903 were several themes representing 'The moods of Dan'. Among them, as will emerge, were themes later to be used in *Gerontius*, *In the South*, and *The Apostles*.

Michael Kennedy, from his *Portrait of Elgar*

SIR WILLIAM WATSON

An Epitaph

His friends he loved. His direst earthly foes –
    Cats – I believe he did but feign to hate
My hand will miss the insinuated nose,
    Mine eyes the tail that wagg'd contempt at Fate.

'ORIEL BILL'

THOSE WHO ARE familiar with Mr Andrew Lang's *Oxford* will readily recall in the picture of Oriel College a quaintly-gabled house just opposite the College gate. Famous as a students' lodging-house, the building is further distinguished as the principal residence of Oriel Bill, one of the greatest characters alike in university and town.

Though acquainted with the dog in a general way for some time, it was not until the necessity for interviewing him arose that I discovered all his wonderful qualities – his eccentricities, without which no dog can be great; and his virtues, which are many. For obvious reasons the interview aforesaid had to be conducted through the medium of an interpreter, but this in no way detracted from the interest of the meeting, and proved no barrier to our intercourse.

Bill, as is usual with him, received me most kindly, and did everything in his power to aid me in learning all about his own quaint personality. 'I am about eight years old,' he admitted, 'not just an old dog altogether, and I've been connected with Oriel some five years or so. My former master, on taking his degree, left me to his landlady's care at 15, Oriel Street, so my connection with the College is likely to last, especially as my master stipulated that I'm to remain in Oxford. Of this I'm glad, for I've many friends here.'

'Undergraduates chiefly, I suppose?'

'Well, not altogether. You see, College law forbids me to enter the quadrangle, though on special occasions I go to lunch in a friend's rooms sometimes; but I've friends everywhere. Children, servant-girls, cabmen – all adore me. With the last-mentioned I am on terms of the easiest familiarity, and may drive anywhere free of charge. Not to know me is a disgrace. Why, once I got into the cab of a new-comer, who tried to eject me, but failed. At length he hailed a brother of the whip, and asked him wot 'e'd do with this 'ere fare? "W'y, don't yer know '*im?*" the other roared. "That's Bill; run 'im down to *Oriel*, of course!" I was driven there accordingly, and stepped out quietly at my own abode. In the evening I often go with my friendly Jehus to their clubs and pubs, where I'm always welcome; but one evening recently on coming home my mistress was unwilling to admit me, for my coat had unluckily acquired an extraordinary taint of my chums' very ordinary tobacco. The bother was, I couldn't change it. Yes,' he added, 'I've one or two things to put up with. The other day I overheard a Member of the College declare that he never had seen the expression of the *Weltschmerz* so strong anywhere as in my face. He was a wit, so I forgave him. Another trouble I have is the undergraduate custom of discharging fireworks, about the Fifth of November chiefly. The first squib I hear, I just go off quietly to Headington, about two miles out of town, to see my old master, where I stay till the disturbance blows over. Once I stayed from the 5th to the 9th November. I go there too for my health whenever I feel the heavy air of Oxford tell on my system, or when I've received any serious shock to my nerves. But,' he added, 'you mustn't think my chums are all of the kind I've mentioned. I've distinguished acquaintances; one of the most intimate is a niece of Fenimore Cooper's, Miss Fenimore Woolson; she's putting me into a book just now. Look here' (Bill produced a small gray paper packet tied with pink ribbon), 'this was attached to my collar one evening after I'd been to see her. Open it and read the contents.'

I did so. Within was a card with the inscription: –

'William of Oriel dined this evening with Miss Fenimore Woolson, and after a hearty meal, a drink of water, and a nap before the fire, he now returns home.

                                                '8 P.M. *January 27th*, 1892

'Excuse me a moment,' said Bill as I handed back the packet. 'I've some photos I want you to see. I'll just go to fetch them.'

While he was absent I learned a host of curious and interesting things about Bill from his mistress. It appears that he indulges occasionally in warfare with other dogs, his chief enemies being collies. To dogs smaller than himself, however, Bill is a generous foe, and contents himself with bestowing merely a good shaking on such as provoke him to wrath. Once he chastised a spaniel in a street close by, and to this day, when passing the spot where the fray took place, Bill rises on his hind legs and looks over the gate in quest of his ancient adversary.

Bill's vagaries are manifold. He abhors persons carrying skates, and if he meets any in the Meadows he straightway returns home deeply depressed, and goes forth no more that day. One of his haunts, which he did not mention to me himself, is the refreshment-room at the railway station. Why he concealed this, Bill best knows himself. Perhaps it is a tender point. He is fairly regular in the hours he keeps at night, but should he find himself by any chance shut out he is in no way distressed, for he knows that if he goes to the Lodge at Merton College he will find comfortable quarters for the night. Comfort he must have, and in the morning at home, while the fires are being lighted, he follows the servant from room to room, carefully studying the fires until he finds one bright enough to suit him. There he lies down and toasts himself till breakfast is ready. In the matter of food he is most 'gentledogly' when other dogs, and even cats, are beside, for he patiently abstains from helping himself till all others are served. This kindness of heart is his most prominent characteristic, for if any of his friends feign grief in his presence, he endeavours with his paws to remove the afflicted person's hands from his face, and administers such comfort as he can. His gentleness finds its reward, especially from children, who get him out of scrapes. The other day, a little girl brought him home all the way from Osney, where he had been belated, and had found shelter for the night. On another occasion two small boys called at 15, Oriel Street, and asked, 'Does that dog with the bull's face live here? Because he's behind the big iron gates at the Wine Company's, and can't get out.'

Here Bill returned with some photos. In one he was represented as 'the Goal Keeper,' with the Oriel football costume; in another he was kicking off. The other two were more serious, portraying him as a barrister in wig, gown, and bands; for Bill is of the legal brotherhood, as most sly dogs are. 'Nonsuited' and 'Cross-examination' were the titles of the portraits, and in each, Bill looked the part to perfection. In fact, Bill always looks his part, for he's an accomplished amateur actor. Last summer he performed at the Oxford Institute in a farce entitled *A Lucky Dog*. 'Come and see Oriel Bill, the Record Protagonist!' said a notice in the Lodge. I went; and on the way had the pleasure of seeing Bill walk calmly down St Aldate's in front of me to the place of performance, his hands in his pockets like a seasoned old actor, and, to quote the Porter of Oriel, 'as orderly as could be.' Lastly, came two photographs, reminiscences of his undergraduate days. One, called 'Passed,' he showed with alacrity, but the other, 'Ploughed,' he produced with something like a sigh. 'You see,' he explained apologetically, 'I'd been ragging a bit that term, and didn't know my texts well enough; but I got through all right next time.'

Here, Bill again retired for a few minutes to put away his treasures (great numbers of which are sold in America), and I learned that he is a trifle vain; for when dressed for the photographer he won't consent to have his finery removed for the rest of the day. Dress of any sort he adores, and when very ill with influenza he was only too proud to be wrapped in a shawl, and be allowed to sit on a kitchen chair with a compress on his throat, looking for all the world like a sick old woman. Once too, after a fight, where his head had suffered, he submitted joyfully to the application of a wet sponge, which was tied upon the wound, and lent him a most grotesque appearance.

'You must feel very proud,' I said to Bill on his reappearance, 'to belong to such a college as Oriel.'

'Justly proud,' he replied, 'for was it not the great College of the Oxford Movement?'

'Undoubtedly,' I said. 'Now tell me, Bill; do you, who are surely in a position to know, consider that there is great need – not on the old issues, perhaps, but on different questions altogether – of a new Oxford Movement?'

But instead of answering, Bill slowly rose and went out. I watched him jog leisurely up Oriel Street towards the High, and disappear. They told me he was off to Headington!

James Symon in the *English Illustrated Magazine*

R. I. P.

Another Idol gone,
　　Another friend to mourn;
For Oxford's lost another son
　　In all her grief new-born.

The time has long gone by –
　　For years soon roll away –
Since first to glorify the 'High'
　　He came, and came to stay!

Majestic, gentle, grave,
　　We knew him, and we loved;
Could no kind Power avail to save
　　A life so soon removed?

Ah! old familiar friend,
   The Lord of all the 'High';
Of everything there is an end,
   But, Bill – we wonder why!

His college stands serene
   And scorns a stormy past,
But he is laid in grave of green
   Within her walls at last!

The 'High', the Parks, the 'Corn',
   Are now in grief at one;
Another friend they have to mourn –
   Another Idol gone!

                          Bernard Nunn

MAX BEERBOHM

Honour of the College

THEY PASSED TOGETHER across the vast gravelled expanse of the Front Quadrangle. In the porch of the College there were, as usual, some chained-up dogs, patiently awaiting their masters. Zuleika, of course, did not care for dogs. One has never known a good man to whom dogs were not dear; but many of the best women have no such fondness. You will find that the woman who is really kind to dogs is always one who has failed to inspire sympathy in men. For the attractive woman, dogs are mere dumb and restless brutes – possibly dangerous, certainly soulless. Yet will coquetry teach her to caress any dog in the presence of a man enslaved by her. Even Zuleika, it seems, was not above this rather obvious device for awaking envy. Be sure she did not at all like the look of the very big bulldog who was squatting outside the porter's lodge. Perhaps, but for her present anger, she would not have stooped endearingly down to him, as she did, cooing over him and trying to pat his head. Alas, her pretty act was a failure. The bulldog cowered away from her, horrifically grimacing. This was strange. Like the majority of his breed, Corker (for such was his name) had ever been wistful to be noticed by any one – effusively grateful for every word of pat, an ever-ready wagger and nuzzler, to none ineffable. No beggar, no burglar, had ever been rebuffed by this catholic beast. But he drew the line at Zuleika.

Seldom is even a fierce bulldog heard to growl. Yet Corker growled at Zuleika.

From *Zuleika Dobson*

THORSTEIN VEBLEN

A Sociologist Writes

THE DOG HAS advantages in the way of uselessness as well as in special gifts of temperament. He is often spoken of, in an eminent sense, as the friend of man, and his intelligence and fidelity are praised. The meaning of this is that the dog is man's servant and that he has the gift of an unquestioning subservience and a slave's quickness in guessing his master's mood. Coupled with these traits, which fit him well for the relation of status – and which must for the present purpose be set down as serviceable traits – the dog has some characteristics which are of a more equivocal æsthetic value. He is the filthiest of the domestic animals in his person and the nastiest in his habits. For this he makes up in a servile, fawning attitude towards his master, and a readiness to inflict damage and discomfort on all else.

And even those varieties of the dog which have been bred into grotesque deformity by the dog-fancier are in good faith accounted beautiful by many. These varieties of dogs – and the like is true of other fancy-bred animals – are rated and graded in æsthetic value somewhat in proportion to the degree of grotesqueness and instability of the particular fashion which the deformity takes in the given case. For the purpose in hand, this differential utility on the ground of grotesqueness and instability of structure is reducible to terms of a greater scarcity and consequent expense. The commercial value of canine monstrosities, such as the prevailing styles of pet dogs both for men's and women's use, rests on their high cost of production, and their value to their owners lies chiefly in their utility as items of conspicuous consumption. Indirectly, through reflection upon their honorific expensiveness, a social worth is imputed to them; and so, by an easy substitution of words and ideas, they come to be admired and reputed beautiful.

From *The Theory of the Leisure Class*

SENATOR GRAHAM VEST

Prosecuting a Dog-Killer

THE ONE ABSOLUTELY unselfish friend that a man can have in this selfish world, the one that never deserts him, the one that never proves ungrateful or treacherous, is his dog.

A man's dog stands by him in prosperity and in poverty, in health and in sickness. He will sleep on the cold ground where the wintry winds blow and the snow drives fiercely, if only he may be near his master's side. He will kiss the hand that has no food to offer, he will lick the sores and wounds that come in encounters with the roughness of the world. He guards the sleep of his pauper master as if he were a prince.

When all other friends desert, he remains. When riches take wings and reputation falls to pieces, he is as constant in his love as the sun in its journey through the heavens.

If misfortune drives the master forth an outcast in the world, friendless and homeless, the faithful dog asks no higher privilege than that of accompanying him to guard against danger, to fight against his enemies.

And when the last scene of all comes, and death takes the master in its embrace, and his body is laid away in the cold ground, no matter if all other friends pursue their way, there by the graveside will the noble dog be found, his head between his paws, his eyes sad, but open in alert watchfulness, faithful and true, even in death.

Aaron Klopstein, from *Annals of Missouri State*

EMILE ZOLA

Why I Love My Dog

I HAD A LITTLE dog, a griffon of the smallest kind, whose name was *Fanfan*. One day, at the dog show at Cours-la-Reine, I saw him in a cage, with a large cat as a companion. He regarded me with eyes so full of sadness, that I asked the attendant to let him out of his cage for a little while. As soon as he was on the ground he commenced to walk like a little toy dog. Enthusiastically I bought him. It was a little mad dog. One morning, after I had him about a week, he commenced to turn in a circle without ceasing, round and round without ever stopping. When he had fallen with fatigue, in appearance drunk, he would painfully raise himself and set to turning again. When, seized by pity, I took him in my arms, his paws would keep up the movement of the continual round, and when I placed him on the ground, he commenced turning again, turning always. I called in a veterinary, who spoke of an injury to the brain. Then he offered to poison him. I refused. All the animals who live with me die a natural death, and they all sleep in a tranquil corner of my garden. *Fanfan* appeared recovered after this first attack. During the two years that it entered into my life, it was so much to me that I cannot find words to describe it. It never quitted me, crouching near to me, in the bottom of my armchair, in the morning during my four hours of work; it had become, thus, part of my agony, part of my joys, raising its little nose at the moments of repose, and regarding me with its little clear eyes. And then it took part in all my walks, going before me with his gait of little toy dog, which used to make all the passers-by laugh, sleeping, when we returned, under my chair, passing the night upon a cushion at the foot of my bed. There was a tie so strong between us that, even at the shortest of separations, I missed him as much as he missed me.

And shortly *Fanfan* became again mad. He had two or three attacks at different intervals. Then the attacks were so frequent that our life was frightful. When the madness was upon him, he would turn and turn without ceasing. I was not able to keep him in my chair. A demon seemed to possess him. And I have seen him turn for two hours around my table. But it was in the night that I suffered the most, hearing him do this involuntary round, headstrong and savage, with the continual noise of the fall of his little paws upon the carpet. I have often risen and taken him in my arms, keeping him thus for an hour, two hours, hoping that the attack would subside, but as soon as I put him to the ground he would commence to turn.

People laughed at me, and said I was mad myself to keep the dog in my room. I could not do otherwise. My heart melted at the idea that I should not be there any more to take him and try to calm him, and that he would regard me no more, with his little clear eyes, his eyes distracted by misery, yet which thanked me.

It was thus, in my arms, one morning, that *Fanfan* died while regarding me. He had but a slight shock, and all was finished. I felt simply his little convulsed body become of the suppleness of chiffon. The tears came to my eyes, and I felt it was a loss to me. An animal, nothing but a little animal, and to suffer thus at its loss! To be haunted by its recollection to such an extent, that I wished to write of my sorrow, certain of leaving the impression of my heart on the page! To-day, all that is distant, and other sorrows have come, and I feel that the things I have said are cold. But then it seemed to me that I had so much to say, that I should have said the things profound, definite, upon this love of animals – so obscure and so powerful, at which I see people around me smile, and which pains me to the extent of troubling my life.

And why was I attached so profoundly to this little mad dog? Why have I fraternised with it as one fraternises with a human being? Why have I cried as one cries for a lost friend? Is it not that the unquenchable tenderness which I feel for everything which lives and feels is a brotherhood of suffering! A charity which inclines one towards the most humble and disinherited?

Trans. Sidney Trist

Grief

O NE EVENING LAZARE said a cruel thing. 'How lonely one is
here!' he remarked with a yawn.

She looked at him. Was this a hint? But her courage failed to ask him
outright. Her goodness of heart was being sorely tried; her life was once
again becoming a torture.

A final shock awaited Lazare. His old Mathieu was not well. The
poor dog, who had been fourteen years old the previous March, was
fast losing the power of his hind legs. When a fit of numbness seized
him he could barely walk, and would stay in the yard, stretched out in
the sunshine, watching people go by with his mournful eyes. Those old
eyes were what distressed Lazare most – eyes grown dim, clouded with
a bluish film, vacant as a blind man's. And yet he could still see, he
would drag himself along to lay his great head on his master's knee and
stare fixedly at him, sadly, as though he understood it all. And he was
no longer handsome; his curly white coat had turned yellow, his jet-
black nose had grown pale; he was a pitiful sight, grubby and dejected,
for they dared not wash him on account of his great age. He had given
up all his games, he no longer rolled on his back nor chased his tail, he
was no longer stirred by fits of compassion for Minouche's kittens when
the maid carried them off to drown them in the sea. Now he spent his
days drowsing like an old man, and he found such difficulty in standing
up, it was such a strain on his weak legs, that some member of the
household, moved with pity, would often hold him up for a minute so
that he could start walking.

Internal haemorrhages weakened him still further every day. A vet
had been sent for, but had burst out laughing when he saw the dog.
What, had he put himself out for such a creature? The best thing was
to destroy it. You had to try and keep a man alive, but what was the use
of letting an incurable animal linger on in pain? The vet had been
shown the door, with six francs for his trouble.

On Saturday, Mathieu was losing so much blood that he had to be
shut up in the coach-house. He left a trail of great red drops behind
him. As Dr Cazenove had come early, he offered Lazare to look at the
dog, who was treated as one of the family. They found him lying down,
his head held high, grown very weak, but with a spark of life in his eyes
still. The doctor examined him at great length, with the thoughtful air
that he wore at a patient's bedside. At last he said:

'Such a copious discharge of blood must come from a cancerous degeneration of the kidneys. He's done for. But he may still last a few days, unless a sudden haemorrhage finishes him off.'

Mathieu's desperate condition cast a gloom over the meal. They recalled how Madame Chanteau had loved him, and his battles with other dogs, and his youthful pranks, the cutlets he had stolen off the grill, the new-laid eggs he had devoured. However, at dessert, when Abbé Horteur brought out his pipe, their spirits rose again, and they listened to the priest telling about his pears, which promised to be splendid that year. Chanteau, in spite of the faint tingling that foretold an attack, ended by singing a merry song of his youth. They were all enjoying themselves, and even Lazare grew gay.

Suddenly, about nine o'clock, as tea had been served, Pauline exlaimed: 'Look, here he is, poor old Mathieu!'

And there was Mathieu, bleeding and emaciated, creeping unsteadily into the dining-room. Immediately, Véronique could be heard bustling after him with a cloth. She came in saying: 'I needed something out of the coach-house, and he escaped. Right up to the end he wants to be where you are; you can't take a step without having him among your skirts ... Come on now, you can't stop there.'

Gently and humbly, the dog dropped his old shaky head.

'Oh, let him stop,' begged Pauline.

But the maid was indignant. 'Good gracious no! ... I'm fed up with wiping up the blood behind him. My kitchen's been full of it for the last two days. It's disgusting ... The room'll be in a fine mess if he goes wandering about everywhere ... Come along, gee up! Hurry up now!'

'Let him stop,' Lazare repeated. 'Go away.'

Then, while Véronique slammed the door in a fury, Mathieu, as though he had understood, came to lay his head on his master's knee. Everyone wanted to make him welcome, breaking pieces of sugar for him and trying to excite him. In the old days, the favourite game of an evening was to lay a piece of sugar on the far side of the table; he would quickly run round, but the piece had already been taken away and put at the opposite end; and he kept running round, and the sugar kept escaping him, till, bewildered and stupefied by this continual sleight of hand, he would start barking furiously. This was the game that Lazare tried to revive, in the kindly hope of enlivening the poor creature's last moments. The dog wagged his tail for an instant, and turned round, only to stumble against Pauline's chair. He could not see the sugar, and his wasted body wandered off crookedly, while red drops of blood spattered the floor all round the room. Chanteau had stopped humming, and everybody's heart ached at the sight of the poor dying Mathieu groping his way as he remembered the games played by greedy Mathieu of old.

'Don't tire him,' the doctor said gently. 'You're killing him.'

The *curé*, who was smoking in silence, commented, no doubt to explain his own emotion to himself: 'These big dogs are like human beings.'

At ten o'clock, when the priest and the doctor had gone, Lazare, before going up to his room, went to shut Mathieu up in the coach-house himself. He laid the dog on some fresh straw, made sure that his bowl of water was by him, embraced him and then prepared to leave him alone. But the dog, with a painful effort, had already staggered up and was following his master. Lazare had to lay him down again three times. At last he submitted, and lay there with his head raised, watching his master go away, with such a sad gaze that Lazare, heartbroken, went back to kiss him once more.

Upstairs, Lazare tried to read till midnight. In the end he went to bed, but he could not sleep, haunted by the image of Mathieu lying there on his straw bed, with his unsteady gaze turned towards the door. By to-morrow his dog would be dead. And despite himself he kept on sitting up and listening, thinking he heard Mathieu barking outside in the yard. His watchful ear caught all sorts of imaginary noises. About two o'clock he fancied he heard moans, and leapt out of bed. Where did that weeping come from? He went on to the landing; the house was dark and silent, and not a sound came from Pauline's room. Then he could no longer resist his urge to go downstairs. His eager wish to see the dog once more spurred him on; he quickly slipped on a pair of trousers and hurried downstairs with his candle.

In the coach-house, Mathieu had got up from the straw. He had chosen rather to drag himself a little way off on to the beaten earth. When he saw his master come in he had not even strength left to raise his head. Lazare, after standing his candlestick on a pile of old planks, had bent down, surprised at the dark colour of the earth; and he fell on his knees, heartbroken, when he saw that the dog was dying in a welter of blood. His life-blood was flowing out of him, and he wagged his tail feebly, while a faint gleam lit up his deep eyes.

'Oh, my poor old dog,' muttered Lazare, 'my poor old dog!'

He was speaking out loud, saying: 'Wait, I'll move you . . . No, that would hurt you . . . But you're so wet! And I haven't even got a sponge. Would you like a drink?'

Mathieu's eyes were still fixed on him. Slowly, a gasping sound began to rattle his sides. The pool of blood grew silently wider, as though it issued from a hidden spring. Ladders and broken barrels cast great shadows, and the candle gave a feeble light. There was a rustle of straw; it was the cat, Minouche, who was lying on the straw bed prepared for Mathieu, and who had been disturbed by the light.

'D'you want a drink, old fellow?' repeated Lazare.

He had found a rag, he dipped it into the bowl of water and pressed it against the dying animal's muzzle. This seemed to give it some relief; the fever-scorched nose grew somewhat cooler. Half an hour went by, and Lazare never stopped dipping the rag in water, with that lamentable sight always before his eyes and his heart heavy with boundless grief. As beside a sick-bed, he was seized with the wildest hopes: perhaps he was about to bring back life by means of this simple process of bathing.

'What is it then?' he said suddenly. 'D'you want to stand up?'

Shaken by a violent shudder, Mathieu was striving to raise himself. He stiffened his limbs, while his neck swelled with hiccoughs that came in great waves from his sides. But the end had come, and he collapsed across his master's knees, still keeping his eyes, under their heavy lids, fixed on him in an effort to see him once more. Overwhelmed by the intelligence in this dying gaze, Lazare held the dog on his knees; and the great body, as long and heavy as a man's, endured a human being's death agony in his frantic arms. It lasted a few minutes. Then he saw real tears, great tears roll down the dim eyes, while the jaws opened convulsively to let the tongue give out one more caress.

'My poor old boy!' cried Lazare, bursting into tears himself. Mathieu was dead. A little bloodstained foam trickled from his jaws. When he lay stretched out on the ground he seemed to be sleeping.

Then Lazare felt that everything had come to an end once more. His dog was dead now, and he felt a disproportionate grief, a despair that swallowed up his whole existence. This death revived other deaths; the wound had not been more cruel when he had crossed the yard behind his mother's coffin. He had lost yet another part of her; his bereavement was complete. The months of concealed suffering revived, his nightmare-haunted nights, his walks in the little graveyard, his terror at the thought of eternally ceasing to be.

There was a sound; Lazare turned round and saw Minouche quietly preening herself on the straw. But the door had creaked as Pauline came in, impelled by the same preoccupation as her cousin. When he saw her his grief redoubled and he, who had mourned his mother in secret with a sort of fierce shyness, burst out: 'O God, O God! She loved him so much! Do you remember? She had him when he was a puppy and it was she that fed him, and he used to follow her about all over the house!'

Then he added: 'There's nothing left, we're dreadfully alone.' Tears rose to Pauline's eyes. She had bent over to look at poor Mathieu in the dim light of the candle. Without attempting to comfort Lazare, she made a despondent gesture, for she felt herself useless and powerless.

From *Zest for Life*
Trans. Jean Stewart

SAMUEL BUTLER

Observations

THE GREAT PLEASURE of a dog is that you may make a fool of yourself with him and not only will he not scold you, but he will make a fool of himself too.

*   *   *

Gogin was one day going down Cleveland Street and saw an old, lean, careworn man crying over the body of his dog which had been just run over and killed by the old man's own cart. I have no doubt it was the dog's fault, for the man was in great distress; as for the dog itself there it lay, all swelled and livid where the wheel had gone over it, its eyes protruded from their sockets and its tongue lolled out, but it was dead. The old man gazed on it helplessly weeping for some time, and then got a large piece of brown paper, in which he wrapped up the body of his favourite; he tied it neatly with a piece of string, and placing it in his cart went homeward with a heavy heart. The day was dull, the gutters were full of cabbage stalks, and the air resounded with the cry of costermongers.

On this a Japanese gentleman who had watched the scene lifted up his voice and made the bystanders a set oration; he was very yellow, he had long black hair, and was a typical Japanese, but he spoke English perfectly. He said the scene they had all just witnessed was a very sad one, and that it ought not to be passed over entirely without comment. He explained that it was very nice of the old man to be so sorry about his dog and to be so careful of its remains, and that he and all the bystanders must sympathize with this good man in his grief, to the expression of which sympathy both with the man and with the poor dog he had thought fit with all respect to make them his present speech.

I have not the man's words, but Gogin said they were like a Japanese drawing; that is to say, wonderfully charming, and showing great knowledge, but not done in the least after the manner in which a European would do them. As for the bystanders, they stood open-mouthed and could make nothing of it; they liked it, and the Japanese gentleman liked addressing them. When he left off and went away, they followed him with their eyes, speechless.

From *Notebooks*

SIR HENRY IRVING

His Mistresses' Voices

MY ONLY COMPLAINT against Brooklyn was that they would not take Fussie in at the hotel there. Fussie, during these early American tours, was still *my* dog. Later on he became Henry's. He had his affections alienated by a course of chops, tomatoes, strawberries, 'ladies' fingers' soaked in champagne, and a beautiful fur rug of his very own presented by the Baroness Burdett-Coutts!

How did I come by Fussie? I went to Newmarket with Rosa Corder, whom Whistler painted.

'How wonderfully different are the expressions on terriers' faces,' I said to her, looking at a painting of hers of a fox-terrier pup. 'That's the only sort of dog I should like to have.'

'That one belonged to Fred Archer,' Rosa Corder said. 'I daresay he could get you one like it.'

We went out to find Archer. Curiously enough I had known the famous jockey at Harpenden when he was a little boy, and I believe used to come round with vegetables.

'I'll send you a dog, Miss Terry, that won't be any trouble. He's got a very good head, a first-rate tail, stuck in splendidly, but his legs are too long. He'd follow you to America!'

Prophetic words! On one of our departures for America, Fussie was left behind by mistake at Southampton. He could not get across the Atlantic, but he did the next best thing. He found his way back from there to his own theatre in the Strand, London!

Fred Archer sent him originally to the stage-door at the Lyceum. The man who brought him out from there to my house in Earl's Court said:

'I'm afraid he gives tongue, Miss. He don't like music, anyway. There was a band at the bottom of your road, and he started hollering.'

We were at luncheon when Fussie made his début into the family circle, and I very quickly saw his *stomach* was his fault. He had a great dislike to *Charles I*; we could never make out why. Perhaps it was because Henry wore armour in one act – and Fussie may have barked his shins against it. Perhaps it was the firing off of the guns; but more probably it was because the play once got him into trouble. As a rule Fussie had the most wonderful sense of the stage, and at rehearsal would skirt the edge of it, but never cross it. But at Brooklyn one night when we were playing *Charles I* – the last act, and that most pathetic part of it where Charles is taking a last farewell of his wife and children – Fussie, perhaps excited by his run over the bridge from New York, suddenly bounded on to the stage! The good children who were playing Princess Mary and Prince Henry didn't even smile; the audience remained solemn, but Henry and I nearly went into hysterics. Fussie knew directly that he had done wrong. He lay down on his stomach, then rolled over on his back, whimpering an apology – while carpenters kept on whistling and calling to him from the wings. The children took him up to the window at the back of the scene, and he stayed there cowering between them until the end of the play.

America seems to have been always fatal to Fussie. Another time when Henry and I were playing in some charity performance in which John Drew and Maude Adams were also acting, he disgraced himself again. Henry having 'done his bit' and put on hat and coat to leave the theatre, Fussie thought the end of the performance must have come; the stage had no further sanctity for him, and he ran across it to the stage door barking! John Drew and Maude Adams were playing *A Pair of Lunatics*. Maude Adams, sitting looking into the fire, did not see Fussie, but was amazed to hear John Drew departing madly from the text:

> Is this a dog I see before me,
> His tail towards my hand?
> Come, let me clutch thee.

She began to think that he had really gone mad!

When Fussie first came, Charlie was still alive, and I have often gone into Henry's dressing-room and seen the two dogs curled up in both the available chairs, Henry *standing* while he made up, rather than disturb them!

When Charlie died, Fussie had Henry's idolatry all to himself. I have caught them often sitting quietly opposite each other at Grafton Street, just adoring each other! Occasionally Fussie would thump his tail on the ground to express his pleasure.

Wherever we went in America the hotel people wanted to get rid of the dog. In the paper they had it that Miss Terry asserted that Fussie was a little terrier, while the hotel people regarded him as a pointer, and funny caricatures were drawn of a very big me with a very tiny dog, and a very tiny me with a dog the size of an elephant; Henry often walked straight out of an hotel where an objection was made to Fussie. If he wanted to stay, he had recourse to strategy. At Detroit the manager of the hotel said that dogs were against the rules. Being very tired Henry let Fussie go to the stables for the night, and sent Walter to look after him. The next morning he sent for the manager.

'Yours is a very old-fashioned hotel, isn't it?'

'Yes, sir, very old and ancient.'

'Got a good chef? I didn't think much of the supper last night; but still – the beds are comfortable enough – I am afraid you don't like animals?'

'Yes, sir, in their proper place.'

'It's a pity,' said Henry meditatively, 'because you happen to be overrun by rats!'

'Sir, you must have made a mistake. Such a thing couldn't – '

'Well, I couldn't pass another night here without my dog,' Henry interrupted. 'But there are, I suppose, other hotels?'

'If it will be any comfort to you to have your dog with you, sir, do by all means, but I assure you that he'll catch no rat here.'

'I'll be on the safe side,' said Henry calmly.

And so it was settled. That very night Fussie supped off, not rats, but terrapin and other delicacies in Henry's private sitting-room.

It was the 1888 tour, the great blizzard year, that Fussie was left behind by mistake at Southampton. He jumped out at the station just before Southampton, where they stop to collect tickets. After this long separation, Henry naturally thought that the dog would go nearly mad with joy when he saw him again. He described to me the meeting in a letter.

> 'My dear Fussie gave me a terrible shock on Sunday night. When we got in, J——, Hatton, and I dined at the Café Royal. I told Walter to bring Fussie there. He did, and Fussie burst into the room while the waiter was cutting some mutton, when, what d'ye think – one bound at me – another instantaneous bound at the mutton, and from the mutton nothing would get him until he'd got his plateful.
>
> 'Oh, what a surprise it was indeed! He never now will leave my side, my legs, or my presence, but I cannot but think, alas, of that seductive piece of mutton!'

Poor Fussie! He met his death through the same weakness. It was at Manchester, I think [1897]. A carpenter had thrown down his coat with a ham sandwich in the pocket, over an open trap on the stage. Fussie, nosing and nudging after the sandwich, fell through and was killed instantly. When they brought up the dog after the performance, every man took his hat off . . . Henry was not told until the end of the play.

He took it so very quietly that I was frightened, and said to his son Laurence who was on that tour:

'Do let's go to his hotel and see how he is.'

We drove there and found him sitting eating his supper with the poor dead Fussie, who would never eat supper any more, curled up in his rug on the sofa. Henry was talking to the dog exactly as if it were alive. The next day he took Fussie back in the train with him to London, covered with a coat. He is buried in the dogs' cemetery, Hyde Park.

His death made an enormous difference to Henry. Fussie was his constant companion. When he died, Henry was really alone. He never spoke of what he felt about it, but it was easy to know.

We used to get hints how to get this and that from watching Fussie! His look, his way of walking! He *sang*, whispered eloquently and low – and then barked suddenly and whispered again! Such a lesson in the law of contrasts!

The first time that Henry went to the Lyceum after Fussie's death, every one was anxious and distressed, knowing how he would miss the dog in his dressing-room. Then an odd thing happened. The wardrobe cat, who had never been near the room in Fussie's lifetime, came down and sat on Fussie's cushion! No one knew how the 'Governor' would take it. But when Walter was sent out to buy some meat for it, we saw that Henry was not going to resent it! From that night onwards the cat always sat night after night in the same place, and Henry liked its companionship.

Ellen Terry, from *The Story of My Life*

FUSSIE, THE TERRIER I disliked because my soup would grow cold in its bowl while his appetite was coaxed, was our invariable follower, although retrieving sticks and stones did not improve his cough, nor ease his slight limp. Irving was devoted to the little beast and would never have another dog after he died. Laurence always declared that Fussie crept away and committed suicide through a hole in the scenery because his father spoke crossly to him during rehearsal.

Eliza Aria, from *My Sentimental Self*

MARSHALL SAUNDERS

The Cruel Milkman

I HAVE SAID that Jenkins spent most of his days in idleness. He had to start out very early in the morning, in order to supply his customers with milk for breakfast. Oh, how ugly he used to be, when he came into the stable on cold winter mornings, before the sun was up.

He would hang his lantern on a hook, and get his milking stool, and if the cows did not step aside just to suit him, he would seize a broom or fork, and beat them cruelly.

My mother and I slept on a heap of straw in the corner of the stable, and when she heard his step in the morning she always roused me, so that we could run out-doors as soon as he opened the stable door. He always aimed a kick at us as we passed, but my mother taught me how to dodge him.

After he finished milking, he took the pails of milk up to the house for Mrs Jenkins to strain and put in the cans, and he came back and harnessed his horse to the cart. His horse was called Toby, and a poor, miserable, broken-down creature he was. He was weak in the knees, and weak in the back, and weak all over, and Jenkins had to beat him all the time, to make him go. He had been a cab horse, and his mouth had been jerked, and twisted, and sawed at, till one would think there could be no feeling left in it; still I have seen him wince and curl up his lip when Jenkins thrust in the frosty bit on a winter's morning.

Poor old Toby! I used to lie on my straw sometimes and wonder he did not cry out with pain. Cold and half starved he always was in the winter time, and often with raw sores on his body that Jenkins would try to hide by putting bits of cloth under the harness. But Toby never murmured, and he never tried to kick and bite, and he minded the least word from Jenkins, and if he swore at him, Toby would start back, or step up quickly, he was so anxious to please him.

After Jenkins put him in the cart, and took in the cans, he set out on his rounds. My mother, whose name was Jess, always went with him. I used to ask her why she followed such a brute of a man, and she would hang her head, and say that sometimes she got a bone from the different houses they stopped at. But that was not the whole reason. She liked Jenkins so much, that she wanted to be with him.

I had not her sweet and patient disposition, and I would not go with her. I watched her out of sight, and then ran up to the house to see if Mrs Jenkins had any scraps for me. I nearly always got something, for she pitied me, and often gave me a kind word or look with the bits of food that she threw to me.

When Jenkins came home, I often coaxed mother to run about and see some of the neighbors' dogs with me. But she never would, and I would not leave her. So, from morning to night we had to sneak about, keeping out of Jenkins' way as much as we could, and yet trying to keep him in sight. He always sauntered about with a pipe in his mouth, and his hands in his pockets, growling first at his wife and children, and then at his dumb creatures.

I have not told what became of my brothers and sisters. One rainy day, when we were eight weeks old, Jenkins, followed by two or three of his ragged, dirty children, came into the stable and looked at us. Then he began to swear because we were so ugly, and said if we had been good-looking, he might have sold some of us. Mother watched him anxiously, and fearing some danger to her puppies, ran and jumped in the middle of us, and looked pleadingly up at him.

It only made him swear the more. He took one pup after another, and right there, before his children and my poor distracted mother, put an end to their lives. Some of them he seized by the legs and knocked against the stalls, till their brains were dashed out, others he killed with a fork. It was very terrible. My mother ran up and down the stable, screaming with pain, and I lay weak and trembling, and expecting every instant that my turn would come next. I don't know why he spared me. I was the only one left.

His children cried, and he sent them out of the stable and went out himself. Mother picked up all the puppies and brought them to our nest in the straw and licked them, and tried to bring them back to life, but it was of no use. They were quite dead. We had them in our corner of the stable for some days, till Jenkins discovered them, and swearing horribly at us, he took his stable fork and threw them out in the yard, and put some earth over them.

My mother never seemed the same after this. She was weak and miserable, and though she was only four years old, she seemed like an old dog. This was on account of the poor food she had been fed on. She could not run after Jenkins, and she lay on our heap of straw, only turning over with her nose the scraps of food I brought her to eat. One day she licked me gently, wagged her tail, and died.

As I sat by her, feeling lonely and miserable, Jenkins came into the stable. I could not bear to look at him. He had killed my mother. There she lay, a little, gaunt, scarred creature, starved and worried to death by him. Her mouth was half open, her eyes were staring. She would never again look kindly at me, or curl up to me at night to keep me warm. Oh, how I hated her murderer! But I sat quietly, even when he went up and turned her over with his foot to see if she was really dead. I think he was a little sorry, for he turned scornfully toward me and said, 'she was worth two of you; why didn't you go instead.'

Still I kept quiet till he walked up to me and kicked at me. My heart was nearly broken and I could stand no more. I flew at him and gave him a savage bite on the ankle.

'Oho,' he said, 'so you are going to be a fighter, are you? I'll fix you for that.' His face was red and furious. He seized me by the back of the neck and carried me out to the yard where a log lay on the ground. 'Bill,' he called to one of his children, 'bring me the hatchet.'

He laid my head on the log and pressed one hand on my struggling body. I was now a year old and a full-sized dog. There was a quick, dreadful pain, and he had cut off my ear, not in the way they cut puppies' ears, but close to my head, so close that he cut off some of the skin beyond it. Then he cut off the other ear, and turning me swiftly round, cut off my tail close to my body.

Then he let me go, and stood looking at me as I rolled on the ground and yelped in agony. He was in such a passion that he did not think that people passing by on the road might hear me.

From *Beautiful Joe*

L. FRANK BAUM

The Oz Trail

THERE WERE FEW birds in this part of the forest, for birds love the open country where there is plenty of sunshine; but now and then there came a deep growl from some wild animal hidden among the trees. These sounds made the little girl's heart beat fast, for she did not know what made them; but Toto knew, and he walked close to Dorothy's side, and did not even bark in return.

'How long will it be,' the child asked of the Tin Woodman, 'before we are out of the forest?'

'I cannot tell,' was the answer, 'for I have never been to the Emerald City. But my father went there once, when I was a boy, and he said it was a long journey through a dangerous country, although nearer to the city where Oz dwells the country is beautiful. But I am not afraid so long as I have my oil-can, and nothing can hurt the Scarecrow, while you bear upon your forehead the mark of the good Witch's kiss, and that will protect you from harm.'

'But Toto!' said the girl, anxiously; 'what will protect him?'

'We must protect him ourselves, if he is in danger,' replied the Tin Woodman.

Just as he spoke there came from the forest a terrible roar, and the next moment a great Lion bounded into the road. With one blow of his paw he sent the Scarecrow spinning over and over to the edge of the road, and then he struck at the Tin Woodman with his sharp claws. But, to the Lion's surprise, he could make no impression on the tin, although the Woodman fell over in the road and lay still.

Little Toto, now that he had an enemy to face, ran barking toward the Lion, and the great beast had opened his mouth to bite the dog, when Dorothy, fearing Toto would be killed, and heedless of danger, rushed forward and slapped the Lion upon his nose as hard as she could, while she cried out:

'Don't you dare to bite Toto! You ought to be ashamed of yourself, a big beast like you, to bite a poor little dog!'

'I didn't bite him,' said the Lion, as he rubbed his nose with his paw where Dorothy had hit it.

'No, but you tried to,' she retorted. 'You are nothing but a big coward.'

'I know,' said the Lion, hanging his head in shame; 'I've always known it. But how can I help it?'

'I don't know, I'm sure. To think of your striking a stuffed man, like the poor Scarecrow!'

'Is he stuffed?' asked the Lion, in surprise, as he watched her pick up the Scarecrow and set him upon his feet, while she patted him into shape again.

'Of course he's stuffed,' replied Dorothy, who was still angry.

'That's why he went over so easily,' remarked the Lion. 'It astonished me to see him whirl around so. Is the other one stuffed, also?'

'No,' said Dorothy, 'He's made of tin.' And she helped the Woodman up again.

'That's why he nearly blunted my claws,' said the Lion. 'When they scratched against the tin it made a cold shiver run down my back. What is that little animal you are so tender of?'

'He is my dog, Toto,' answered Dorothy.

'Is he made of tin, or stuffed?' asked the Lion.

'Neither. He's a – a – a meat dog,' said the girl.

'Oh! He's a curious animal, and seems remarkably small, now that I look at him. No one would think of biting such a little thing except a coward like me,' continued the Lion, sadly.

From *The Wonderful Wizard of Oz*

SIR JAMES FRAZER

Anthropology

AMONG THE HIGH mountains of Japan there is a district in which, if rain has not fallen for a long time, a party of villagers goes in procession to the bed of a mountain torrent, headed by a priest, who leads a black dog. At the chosen spot they tether the beast to a stone, and make it a target for their bullets and arrows. When its life-blood bespatters the rocks, the peasants throw down their weapons and lift up their voices in supplication to the dragon divinity of the stream, exhorting him to send down forthwith a shower to cleanse the spot from its defilement. Custom has prescribed that on these occasions the colour of the victim shall be black, as an emblem of the wished-for rain-clouds. But if fine weather is wanted, the victim must be white, without a spot.

* * *

In Kumaon a way of stopping rain is to pour hot oil in the left ear of a dog. The animal howls with pain, his howls are heard by Indra, and out of pity for the beast's suffering the god stops the rain.

From *The Golden Bough*

JOHN GALSWORTHY
To My Dog

My dear! When I leave you
I always drop a bit of me –
A holy glove or sainted shoe –
Your wistful corse I leave it to,
For all your soul has followed me –
How could I have the stony heart
So to abandon you?

My dear! When you leave me
You drop no glove, no sainted shoe;
And yet you know what humans be –
Mere blocks of dull monstrosity!
My spirit cannot follow you,
When you're away, with all its heart
As yours can follow me.

My dear! Since we must leave
(One sorry day) I you, you me;
I'll learn your wistful way to grieve;
Then through the ages we'll retrieve
Each other's scent and company;
And longing shall not pull my heart –
As now you pull my sleeve!

Death and War

JOLYON, WHO HAD crossed from Calais by night, arrived at Robin
Hill on Sunday morning. He had sent no word beforehand, so walked
up from the station, entering his domain by the coppice gate. Coming
to the log seat fashioned out of an old fallen trunk, he sat down, first

laying his overcoat on it. 'Lumbago!' he thought; 'that's what love ends in at my time of life!' And suddenly Irene seemed very near, just as she had been that day of rambling at Fontainebleau when they sat on a log to eat their lunch. Hauntingly near! Odour drawn out of fallen leaves by the pale filtering sunlight soaked his nostrils. 'I'm glad it isn't spring,' he thought. With the scent of sap, and the song of birds, and the bursting of the blossoms, it would have been unbearable! 'I hope I shall be over it by then, old fool that I am!' And picking up his coat, he walked on into the field. He passed the pond and mounted the hill slowly. Near the top a hoarse barking greeted him. Up on the lawn above the fernery he could see his old dog Balthasar. The animal, whose dim eyes took his master for a stranger, was warning the world against him. Jolyon gave his special whistle. Even at that distance of a hundred yards and more he could see the dawning recognition in the obese brown-white body. The old dog got off his haunches, and his tail, close-curled over his back, began a feeble, excited fluttering; he came waddling forward, gathered momentum, and disappeared over the edge of the fernery. Jolyon expected to meet him at the wicket gate, but Balthasar was not there, and, rather alarmed, he turned into the fernery. On his fat side, looking up with eyes already glazing, the old dog lay.

'What is it, my poor old man?' cried Jolyon. Balthasar's curled and fluffy tail just moved; his filming eyes seemed saying: 'I can't get up, master, but I'm glad to see you.'

Jolyon knelt down; his eyes, very dimmed, could hardly see the slowly ceasing heave of the dog's side. He raised the head a little – very heavy.

'What is it, dear man? Where are you hurt?' The tail fluttered once; the eyes lost the look of life. Jolyon passed his hands all over the inert warm bulk. There was nothing – the heart had simply failed in that obese body from the emotion of his master's return. Jolyon could feel the muzzle, where a few whitish bristles grew, cooling already against his lips. He stayed for some minutes kneeling, with his hand beneath the stiffening head. The body was very heavy when he bore it to the top of the field; leaves had drifted there, and he strewed it with a covering of them; there was no wind, and they would keep him from curious eyes until the afternoon. 'I'll bury him myself,' he thought. Eighteen years had gone since he first went into the St John's Wood house with that tiny puppy in his pocket. Strange that the old dog should die just now! Was it an omen? He turned at the gate to look back at that russet mound, then went slowly towards the house, very choky in the throat.

June was at home; she had come down hot-foot on hearing the news of Jolly's enlistment. His patriotism had conquered her feeling for the Boers. The atmosphere of his house was strange and pocketty when Jolyon came in and told them of the dog Balthasar's death. The news had a unifying effect. A link with the past had snapped – the dog Balthasar! Two of them could remember nothing before his day; to June he represented the last years of her grandfather; to Jolyon that life of domestic stress and æsthetic struggle before he came again into the kingdom of his father's love and wealth! And he was gone!

In the afternoon he and Jolly took picks and spades and went out to the field. They chose a spot close to the russet mound, so that they need not carry him far, and, carefully cutting off the surface turf, began to dig. They dug in silence for ten minutes and then rested.

'Well, old man,' said Jolyon, 'so you thought you ought?'

'Yes,' answered Jolly; 'I don't want to a bit, of course.'

How exactly those words represented Jolyon's own state of mind!

'I admire you for it, old boy. I don't believe I should have done it at your age – too much of a Forsyte, I'm afraid. But I suppose the type gets thinner with each generation. Your son, if you have one, may be a pure altruist; who knows?'

'He won't be like me, then, Dad; I'm beastly selfish.'

'No, my dear, that you clearly are not.' Jolly shook his head, and they dug again.

'Strange life a dog's,' said Jolyon suddenly; 'the only four-footer with rudiments of altruism and a sense of God!'

Jolly looked at his father.

'Do you believe in God, Dad? I've never known.'

At so searching a question from one to whom it was impossible to make a light reply, Jolyon stood for a moment, feeling his back tried by the digging.

'What do you mean by God?' he said; 'there are two irreconcilable ideas of God. There's the Unknowable Creative Principle – one believes in That. And there's the Sum of altruism in man – naturally one believes in That.'

'I see. That leaves out Christ, doesn't it?'

Jolyon stared. Christ, the link between the two ideas! Out of the mouths of babes! Here was orthodoxy scientifically explained at last! The sublime poem of the Christ life was man's attempt to join those two irreconcilable conceptions of God. And since the Sum of human altruism was as much a part of the Unknowable Creature Principle as anything else in Nature and the Universe, a worse link might have been chosen after all. Funny – how one went through life without seeing it in that sort of way!

'What do *you* think, old man?' he said.

Jolly frowned. 'Of course, my first year we talked a good bit about that sort of thing. But in the second year one gives it up; I don't know why – it's awfully interesting.'

Jolyon remembered that he also had talked a good deal about it in his first year at Cambridge, and given it up in his second.

'I suppose,' said Jolly, 'it's the second God, you mean, that old Balthasar had a sense of.'

'Yes, or he would never have burst his poor old heart because of something outside himself.'

'But wasn't that just selfish emotion, really?'

Jolyon shook his head. 'No, dogs are not pure Forsytes, they love something outside themselves.'

Jolly smiled.

'Well, I think I'm one,' he said. 'You know, I only enlisted because I dared Val Dartie to.'

'But why?'

'We bar each other,' said Jolly shortly.

'Ah!' muttered Jolyon. So the feud went on unto the third generation – this modern feud which had no overt expression!

'Shall I tell the boy about it?' he thought. But to what end – if he had to stop short of his own part?

And Jolly thought: 'It's for Holly to let him know about that chap. If she doesn't, it means she doesn't want him told, and I should be sneaking. Anyway, I've stopped it. I'd better leave well alone!'

So they dug on in silence, till Jolyon said:

'Now, old man, I think it's big enough.' And, resting on their spades, they gazed down into the hole where a few leaves had drifted already on a sunset wind.

'I can't bear this part of it,' said Jolyon suddenly.

'Let me do it, Dad. He never cared much for me.'

Jolyon shook his head.

'We'll lift him very gently, leaves and all. I'd rather not see him again. I'll take his head. Now!'

With extreme care they raised the old dog's body, whose faded tan and white showed here and there under the leaves stirred by the wind. They laid it, heavy, cold, and unresponsive, in the grave, and Jolly spread more leaves over it, while Jolyon, deeply afraid to show emotion before his son, began quickly shovelling the earth on to that still shape. There went the past! If only there were a joyful future to look forward to! It was like stamping down earth on one's own life. They replaced the turf carefully on the smooth little mound and, grateful that they had spared each other's feelings, returned to the house arm-in-arm.

From *The Forsyte Saga*

Looking Back

THE CALL OF the wild – Spring running – whatever it is – that besets men and dogs, seldom attained full mastery over him; but one could often see it struggling against his devotion to the scent of us, and, watching the dumb contest, I have time and again wondered how far this civilization of ours was justifiably imposed on him; how far the love for us that we had so carefully implanted could ever replace in him the satisfaction of his primitive wild yearnings. He was like a man, naturally polygamous, married to one loved woman.

It was surely not for nothing that Rover is dog's most common name, and would be ours, but for our too tenacious fear of losing something to admit, even to ourselves, that we are hankering. There was a man who said: Strange that two such queerly opposite qualities as courage and hypocrisy are the leading characteristics of the Anglo-Saxon! But is not hypocrisy just a product of tenacity, which is again the lower part of courage? Is not hypocrisy but an active sense of property in one's good name, the clutching close of respectability at any price, the feeling that one must not part, even at the cost of truth, with what he has sweated so to gain? And so we Anglo-Saxons will not answer to the name of Rover, and treat our dogs so that they, too, hardly know their natures.

The history of his one wandering, for which no respectable reason can be assigned, will never, of course, be known. It was in London, of an October evening, when we were told he had slipped out and was not anywhere. Then began those four distressful hours of searching for that black needle in that blacker bundle of hay. Hours of real dismay and suffering – for it is suffering, indeed, to feel a loved thing swallowed up in that hopeless maze of London streets. Stolen or run over? Which was worst? The neighbouring police stations visited, the Dogs' Home notified, an order for five hundred 'Lost Dog' bills placed in the printer's hands, the streets patrolled! And then, in a lull snatched for food, and still endeavouring to preserve some aspect of assurance, we heard the bark which meant: 'Here is a door I cannot open!' We hurried forth, and there he was on the top doorstep – busy, unashamed, giving no explanations, asking for his supper; and very shortly after him came his five hundred 'Lost Dog' bills. Long I sat looking at him that night after my companion had gone up, thinking of the evening, some years before, when there followed us that shadow of a spaniel who had been lost for eleven days. And my heart turned over within me. But he! He was asleep, for he knew not remorse. . . .

For it is by muteness that a dog becomes for one so utterly beyond value; with him one is at peace, where words play no torturing tricks. When he just sits, loving, and knows that he is being loved, those are the moments that I think are precious to a dog; when, with his adoring soul coming through his eyes, he feels that you are really thinking of him. But he is touchingly tolerant of one's other occupations. The subject of these memories always knew when one was too absorbed in work to be so close to him as he thought proper; yet he never tried to hinder or distract, or asked for attention. It dinged his mood, of course, so that the red under his eyes and the folds of his crumply cheeks – which seemed to speak of a touch of bloodhound introduced a long way back into his breeding – grew deeper and more manifest. If he could have spoken at such times, he would have said: 'I have been a long time alone, and I cannot always be asleep; but you know best, and I must not criticize.'

He did not at all mind one's being absorbed in other humans; he seemed to enjoy the sounds of conversation lifting round him, and to know when they were sensible. He could not, for instance, stand actors or actresses giving readings of their parts, perceiving at once that the same had no connection with the minds and real feelings of the speakers; and, having wandered a little to show his disapproval, he would go to the door and stare at it till it opened and let him out. Once or twice, it is true, when an actor of large voice was declaiming an emotional passage, he so far relented as to go up to him and pant in his face. Music, too, made him restless, inclined to sigh, and to ask questions. Sometimes, at its first sound, he would cross to the window and remain there looking for Her. At others, he would simply go and lie on the loud pedal, and we never could tell whether it was from sentiment, or because he thought that in this way he heard less. At one special Nocturne of Chopin's he always whimpered. He *was*, indeed, of rather Polish temperament – very gay when he was gay, dark and brooding when he was not.

On the whole, perhaps his life was uneventful for so far-travelling a dog, though it held its moments of eccentricity, as when he leaped through the window of a four-wheeler into Kensington, or sat on a Dartmoor adder. But that was fortunately of a Sunday afternoon – when adder and all were torpid, so nothing happened, till a friend, who was following, lifted him off the creature with his large boot.

If only one could have known more of his private life – more of his relations with his own kind! I fancy he was always rather a dark dog to them, having so many thoughts about us that he could not share with anyone, and being naturally fastidious, except with ladies, for whom he had a chivalrous and catholic taste, so that they often turned and snapped at him. He had, however, but one lasting love-affair, for a liver-coloured lass of our village, not quite of his own caste, but a wholesome if somewhat elderly girl, with loving and sphinx-like eyes. Their children, alas, were not for this world, and soon departed.

Nor was he a fighting dog; but once attacked, he lacked a sense of values, being unable to distinguish between dogs that he could beat and dogs with whom he had 'no earthly'. It was, in fact, as well to interfere at once, especially in the matter of retrievers, for he never forgot having in his youth been attacked by a retriever from behind. No, he never forgot, and never forgave, an enemy. Only a month before that day of which I cannot speak, being very old and ill, he engaged an Irish terrier on whose impudence he had long had his eye, and routed him. And how a battle cheered his spirit! He was certainly no Christian; but, allowing for essential dog, he was very much a gentleman. And I do think that most of us who live on this earth these days would rather leave it with that label on us than the other. For to be a Christian, as Tolstoy understood the word – and no one else in our time has had logic and love of truth enough to give it coherent meaning – is (to be quite sincere) not suited to men of Western blood. Whereas – to be a gentleman! It is a far cry, but perhaps it can be done. In him, at all events, there was no pettiness, no meanness, and no cruelty, and though he fell below his ideal at times, this never altered the true look of his eyes, nor the simple loyalty in his soul. . . .

Do they know, as we do, that their time must come? Yes, they know, at rare moments. No other way can I interpret those pauses of his latter life, when, propped on his forefeet, he would sit for long minutes quite motionless – his head dropped, utterly withdrawn; then turn those eyes of his and look at me. That look said more plainly than all words could: 'Yes, I know that I must go!' If *we* have spirits that persist – *they* have. If *we* know, after our departure, who we were – *they* do. No one, I think, who really longs for truth, can ever glibly say which it will be for dog and man – persistence or extinction of our consciousness. There is but one thing certain – the childishness of fretting over that eternal question. Whichever it be, it must be right, the only possible thing. He felt that too, I know; but then, like his master, he was what is called a pessimist.

My companion tells me that, since he left us, he has once come back. It was Old Year's Night, and she was sad, when he came to her in visible shape of his black body, passing round the dining-table from the window-end, to his proper place beneath the table, at her feet. She saw him quite clearly; she heard the padding tap-tap of his paws and very toe-nails; she felt his warmth brushing hard against the front of her skirt. She thought then that he would settle down upon her feet, but something disturbed him, and he stood pausing, pressed against her, then moved out towards where I generally sit, but was not sitting that night. She saw him stand there, as if considering; then at some sound or laugh, she became self-conscious, and slowly, very slowly, he was no longer there. Had he some message, some counsel to give, something he would say, that last night of the last year of all those he had watched over us? Will he come back again?

No stone stands over where he lies. It is on our hearts that his life is engraved.

From *Memories*

GEORGE BERNARD SHAW

Dog versus Motor

SIR, – MR PLUNKET GREENE'S letter is not one for which anyone who likes dogs and appreciates their friendship will blame him; yet I, who claim to be in that position myself, have acted precisely as those two gentleman, whom Mr Plunket Greene calls heartless cads, acted. I have more than once run over a dog and driven away as if nothing had happened, and on every such occasion there has been a lady in the car. Will Mr Greene tell us what he would do in the same circumstances? I take it that a good deal depends on the lady. If she is a heartless cad, no doubt the correct thing is to stop the car, so that she may enjoy the 'ghastly business of some minutes' duration,' and perhaps laugh at the distress of the dog's owners. But suppose she is a humane and sensitive person, very fond of dogs, and likely to suffer acute distress for some days after witnessing ghastly businesses – what then? Is it so clear, as Mr Plunket Greene thinks, that it is the duty of the driver, who can do no earthly good to the unfortunate animal, and whose apologies are much more likely to lead to a painful and undignified scene than to be of much comfort at such a moment, to stop and call the attention of his lady passenger to what has happened?

It is so far from being clear to me that I am quite sure that if Mr Plunket Greene is ever inconsiderate enough to act once as he suggests, he will not do it twice. When I have had nobody's feelings to consult but my own and those of my *chauffeur*, I have stopped, and the experience I have gathered in this way does not justify me in advising other people to follow my example. When you are unfortunate enough to kill a dog, and can neither restore the dead to life nor achieve an extraordinary display of tact in consoling people who, for the moment, loathe you, by far your best plan is to withdraw as rapidly as possible, especially if you are disposed to resent being treated as if you did it on purpose.

How unreasonable people can be when they are upset by the loss of a pet animal is shown by Mr Plunket Greene's complaint that the Andover motorists who killed his dog 'left to his children all that remained of it.' If they had carried it off, he would hardly have regarded that as an extenuating circumstance. If they had stopped, and Mr Plunket Greene had appeared on the scene, does it not seem at least possible that in his distress he might have said things to them – perhaps even done things to them – that would have convinced them that it is impossible to undo or mitigate a really painful accident by a few polite speeches, however sincere they may be?

Besides, what is the motorist to say? If he says it was not his fault, his exculpation irritates the owner by implicating the dog. And he can hardly be expected to say that it *was* his fault. No doubt he might simply say the right thing. But the man who can say the right thing at the right moment under agitating and probably provocative circumstances is a man in ten thousand. For the other nine thousand nine hundred and ninety-nine, the safest rule is, 'If you can do no good, hold your tongue and clear out.' If you stop to apologise you will presently find yourself stopping to argue: and that is not likely to improve matters. You begin by saying that you are extremely sorry. You end by pointing out that if people choose to allow their dogs to stray about the roads they must take the consequences; that you have already apologised, and that you have heard as much of the affair as you are disposed to stand. . . .

I hope I am not showing any want of sympathy with Mr Plunket Greene. If I had run over his dog, I should have felt miserable about it for a considerable time afterwards. Many motorists would feel the same. But our sympathy must not lead us into hypocrisy. The flat truth is that the slain dog for which a motorist stops is his first dog. No man stops for his tenth dog unless the circumstances are unusual, or he can do something more to the purpose than making sympathetic speeches, whilst politely but firmly refusing to admit that he is responsible, pecuniarily, legally, or morally, for the casualties which are inevitable as long as carriageways for fast traffic are used as fowl-runs, pastures, and playgrounds for pet animals, and even for infants. Every good-natured motorist will do what he can to avoid these casualties, for the sake of his own feelings as well as those of others; but he will kill a dog rather than a child, and a hen rather than a dog; and though to the end he will make more allowances for a puppy than for a dog, there will inevitably come a time (usually after about his twelfth act of involuntary slaughter) when he will think a little less of the need for motorists to train their drivers to avoid dogs, and a little more of the need for dog owners to train their dogs to avoid motors.

I may mention that when my driver, by a miracle of address, saved the life of a huge black collie in an Irish village last year, the inspector of police reproached him strenuously for losing an opportunity of extirpating a brute that flew at everything, and was a terror to the whole place. The public sympathy is not always with the dog. Mr Plunket Greene's dogs, however, were not savage black collies. One of them was an Aberdeen, the other a dachshund. Now if there is one dog that is less to be trusted to take care of itself in traffic than an Aberdeen, it is a dachshund. Both are slow, and almost invariably preoccupied. And the moral is that they had better be kept off our main roads. The motorist cannot always avoid them, and when he kills them it is useless to expect him to stop and apologise.

Although I am exceptionally squeamish about hurting animals, and for that reason cannot endure shooting, fishing, or hunting, I can recall at least thirteen cases in which cars in which I was seated (sometimes at the wheel) have gone over dogs. In one case I stopped and the owner of the dog, a little girl, went into violent hysterics when I spoke to her. I bought her a new dog. In another, when a poor man's sheep dog was the victim, I did not stop; but I sent a postal order from the next town to provide a substitute. In another, I managed to extricate an old retriever whimpering from beneath the car, and to pet him back into good humour, before restoring him with no bones broken to his proprietors, a couple of ladies, who scolded him energetically. In the remaining ten cases, I behaved like the 'heartless cads,' of whom Mr Plunket Greene complains; that is, I left the slain on the field, and fled on, either concealing the accident completely from my lady passengers (most men would do as much for their wives, I hope), or persuading them that nothing very dreadful had happened.

Letter to *The Car*, 22 February 1911

S IR – MAY I reply on the whole debate, which has now, I presume, exhausted itself?

First, let me deal with the writer of 'Automobile Notes' in the *Times*. His words carry weight and deserve it; and he has put it to me that if my argument justifies flight after running over and killing a dog, it equally justifies flight after running over and killing a child. Certainly it does, even *a fortiori*. . . .

Do I then advise the motorist to run away? Certainly not. There are limits to the self-sacrifice that can be demanded even from a motorist who has run over a child. As long as juries are thoughtless enough to regard flight on such occasions as evidence of callous ferocity, no motorist can be advised to attempt it under existing circumstances, because successful evasion is impossible. In the case of a dog it is easy enough; the distracted dog owner, and the bystanders, look at the dog instead of at the motorist's number; and the police will not trace a fugitive who has committed no crime, it not being their business to apprehend persons in order that they may be sued in the county court. But as the killing of a child involves an inquest, which may result in a verdict of manslaughter or even murder, the whole national machinery for the apprehension of criminals will be turned upon the motorist. His attempt to spare the feelings of the mother by flight will fail; he will be ignominiously dragged from his hiding place, and brought to trial; and the mother will be dragged to court to testify against him, and face his counsel, just as if he had surrendered at once. He will have accomplished nothing, except the loss of all hope of being considerately dealt with. His flight may have been well meant and chivalrous; but chivalry that does more harm than good is Quixotism, and I cannot recommend Quixotism as a rule of the road.

On the whole, when you kill a human being, stop. Do not apologise, nobody will trouble themselves about your gentility at such a moment, but give your name and address, and, heartless as it may seem, call attention to any facts that may tend to put the deceased in the wrong. I do not say that the rule has no exceptions. If I killed a tramp fifty miles from anywhere, and there was nobody about, I might perhaps bury him and say nothing for the sake of saving trouble; but even this, though natural, would be extremely imprudent.

As to the dog, the correspondence has left me not only unshaken in my opinion, but strongly confirmed in it. I repeat, if you can do no good – nay, if you can do no good that cannot be done equally well by the bystanders – do not stop. I have already given my reasons, and only two sections of your correspondents have taken any position that I did not deal with in my first communication. Let me deal with these two briefly now.

The first section claims that it is the duty of the motorist to put the moribund animal out of pain. I picture the motorist descending from his car, and returning on foot to his victim and his victim's owner, with his cap in one hand and a tyre lever in the other. Between each sentence of apology he delivers a smashing blow on the skull of the dying friend of man. And when he has battered its head to pieces he says, in his gentlest accent, 'I think I can assure you that your poor pet no longer suffers.' Now I do not deny that this course might save the dog some useless suffering. But I cannot pretend to think that it would make a good impression. People are not always reasonable about these things. I shall not try to dissuade any motorist from trying it if he likes; but I shall not try it myself. After all, the owner can always borrow a poker, and if he shrinks from using it, he is more likely to know the way to the nearest veterinary surgeon than the motorist. I should not leave a maimed and lonely dog to his fate in a desert, out of reach of assistance; but, as a matter of fact, lonely dogs do not occur in deserts, any more than babies do.

The second remonstrant section points out that the motorist who runs away loses an opportunity of demonstrating that he is a gentleman, and thereby defeats the main purpose for which, in the opinion of many respectable Englishmen, the universe was created. I confess I have no answer to this. I even recommend the deliberate pursuit and slaughter of dogs as an effective mean of providing occasions for these displays of *bon ton*. But let nobody suppose that the test of good breeding will be a light one. Gentlemen who rehearse imaginary comedies of exquisite good manners as they sit at home reading *The Car* may easily find, when their romance becomes reality, the owner of the dog, instead of listening in gentle distress to the hero of the piece until his or her tears give way to grateful and comforted smiles, taking a tone so unjust, so unappreciative, perhaps so grossly abusive, not impossibly even so violent, that the easy-chair dream of gentility may come untrue to the extent of anything from a deplorable altercation to several rounds of personal combat.

Letter to *The Car*, 15 March 1911

André Gide

Toby's Phobias

SINCE YESTERDAY WE have adopted a poor black poodle that was starving to death and prowling around our door for three days. His coat is all thick and matted from the plaster debris on which he has been sleeping in the house that is being built next door. At two a.m. Em. makes me go down to see if he isn't barking in the cellar, where we locked him up. I don't think he is intelligent, but he is affectionate.

I have bathed, I have soaped my poor dog in my tub. I hoped that cleanliness would give some lustre to his coat! But now he looks more than ever like a blind man's dog. And I who wanted a pedigreed dog, I've got what was coming to me! No matter; it is time to learn once more to prefer the events that choose me to those I should have chosen myself.

From his *Journal*, 27 April 1906

To AIR OUT the linen-room I leave two windows open, but with the shutters closed, and this darkens the room rather lugubriously. To divert my starling I risked taking him down onto the lawn at tea-time, when only the Moune, Miquette, and Toby were with us. The last-named was so excited that he trembled all over. Em. ran in fright to get the lead and tie him up. As for the Moune and Miquette, they are so obedient that I had no fear about them; the bird even approached and hopped around Miquette, who, probably finding her position humiliating, turned her head aside and pretended not to see him. I left the starling out about ten minutes; then I took him back into the linen-room, without holding him, freely perched on my finger.

ibid 23 June 1914

THIS MORNING I had to go and fetch Toby, who ran away yesterday to the Dumonts', attracted by their bitch. He allowed himself to be brought home without resisting; I didn't even have to attach his leash. Miquette went along with me, like a legitimate wife going to get her husband at a prostitute's. I should like to know whether or not bitches are capable of jealousy. I doubt it. I fancy that, even among birds, jealousy belongs only to the male.

ibid 21 July 1914

TOOK MIQUETTE BACK to Fellow; the bitch is just as willing as can be and even tries to help, but he insists on being out of line despite all I do to help him. Since, eventually, I left him to himself and he got nowhere, he came to get me, pulling and pushing me toward the bitch, again begging for my help.

I wish it were forbidden for anyone to make statements about sex who had not had experience in breeding and observing animals. Perhaps they would finally come to understand that many difficulties, deviations, and irregularities that they insist on calling abnormal and 'against nature' are no less *natural* than others.

ibid 5 October 1914

TOBY DIED LAST night. I reproach myself for not having noted from day to day the phases of his illness. I have just written to the Criquetot pork-butcher, who has assumed the veterinary's functions since the mobilization, to come with the necessary instruments to perform an autopsy. I have no idea of what he died . . .? Of a tumour, says Mathilde Roberty. Whatever the complaint was, it was strangely complicated by his nervous state. He was certainly the most neurasthenic dog one could possibly imagine. He had every possible phobia: hugged hedges and walls; always took the longest way around to come to a call; was seized with dizziness as he climbed the stairs; dared to eat only when no one was looking. He adored sugar; but if you offered him a piece, he would let it fall on the floor and go off into a corner to play the martyr. Whence it was impossible ever to reward him; untrainable, you could have got him only through hunger, and even then – I believe he never forgave me the spoonful of sugared coffee that I had made him take just after his arrival, when I did not yet know him and thought I could tame him. But the least approach to a blow put him in a snarling mood, or else he would run miles away as soon as I would raise my cane, or else he would squirt on the ground. It was just as impossible to help him; if you wanted to take a tick off of him, you had to put on gloves or else muzzle him; even then I had to give up more than once. And with his mania for rubbing up against old walls and bushes along the way, he swept up everything bad on his path; even to comb him required a thousand precautions and I had to give up combing his belly. How often he bit me like a mad dog!

With other dogs he tried to be dashing and would offer himself to their caresses. Although excited to the point of frenzy by the odour of our bitch on heat, he could never achieve anything with her, any more than with any other bitch whatever and any more, it goes without saying, than with our old cat, although she nevertheless excited him as much as a bitch and, on her side, would provoke and pursue him as much as if he had been a tomcat. You cannot imagine a more absurd and more dumbfounding game; Toby would wear himself out after her for hours and days on end.

He would spend most of the day seated, like a macaque, on his lumbar vertebrae with his legs and his whole hindquarters paradoxically brought forward between his front legs and sporting his cock like a rosette of the Légion d'Honneur on a lapel.

Porto-Riche had given him to me after having learned from Copeau, who frequented him, that we had a bitch of the same breed. Most certainly he wanted to get rid of him. Probably after having seen him at work, he had named him Joseph.

And for the last six weeks Toby had refused to eat. Em. kept him alive with pieces of sugar, which, I believe, stopped the diarrhoea that he had first had very seriously. We thought he was going to die of inanition, when suddenly – But I shall tell that after the autopsy has been made.

ibid, 19 January 1917

MIQUETTE'S DEATH. LONG blind, deaf, frightfully swollen, she seemed to remain attached to life only through fidelity to her mistress.

ibid 31 December 1920

RUDYARD KIPLING

The Power of the Dog

There is sorrow enough in the natural way
From men and women to fill our day;
But when we are certain of sorrow in store,
Why do we always arrange for more?
Brothers and sisters, I bid you beware
Of giving your heart to a dog to tear.

Buy a pup and your money will buy
Love unflinching that cannot lie –
Perfect passion and worship fed
By a kick in the ribs or a pat on the head.
Nevertheless it is hardly fair
To risk your heart for a dog to tear.

When the fourteen years which Nature permits
Are closing in asthma, or tumour, or fits,
And the Vet's unspoken prescription runs
To lethal chambers or loaded guns,
Then you will find – it's your own affair,
But . . . you've given your heart to a dog to tear.

When the body that lived at your single will,
With its whimper of welcome, is stilled (how still!),
When the spirit that answered your every mood
Is gone – wherever it goes – for good,
You will discover how much you care,
And will give your heart to a dog to tear!

We've sorrow enough in the natural way,
When it comes to burying Christian clay.
Our loves are not given, but only lent,
At compound interest of cent per cent.
Though it is not always the case, I believe,
That the longer we've kept 'em, the more do we grieve;
For, when debts are payable, right or wrong,
A short-time loan is as bad as a long –
So why in – Heaven (before we are there)
Should we give our hearts to a dog to tear?

The Dog Hervey

MY FRIEND ATTLEY, who would give away his own head if you told him you had lost yours, was giving away a six-months-old litter of Bettina's pups, and a half-a-dozen women were in raptures at the show on Mittleham lawn.

We picked by lot. Mrs Godfrey drew first choice; her married daughter, second. I was third, but waived my right because I was already owned by Malachi, Bettina's full brother, whom I had brought over in the car to visit his nephews and nieces, and he would have slain them all if I had taken home one. Milly, Mrs Godfrey's younger daughter, pounced on my rejection with squeals of delight, and Attley turned to a dark, sallow-skinned, slack-mouthed girl, who had come over for tennis, and invited her to pick. She put on a pair of pince-nez that made her look like a camel, knelt clumsily, for she was long from the hip to the knee, breathed hard, and considered the last couple.

'I think I'd like that sandy-pied one,' she said.

'Oh, not him, Miss Sichliffe!' Attley cried. 'He was overlaid or had sunstroke or something. They call him The Looney in the kennels. Besides, he squints.'

'I think that's rather fetching,' she answered. Neither Malachi nor I had ever seen a squinting dog before.

'That's chorea – St Vitus's dance,' Mrs Godfrey put in. 'He ought to have been drowned.'

'But I like his cast of countenance,' the girl persisted.

'He doesn't look a good life,' I said, 'but perhaps he can be patched up.' Miss Sichliffe turned crimson; I saw Mrs Godfrey exchange a glance with her married daughter, and knew I had said something which would have to be lived down.

'Yes,' Miss Sichliffe went on, her voice shaking, 'he isn't a good life, but perhaps I can – patch him up. Come here, sir.' The misshapen beast lurched toward her, squinting down his own nose till he fell over his own toes. Then, luckily, Bettina ran across the lawn and reminded Malachi of their puppyhood. All that family are as queer as Dick's hatband, and fight like man and wife. I had to separate them, and Mrs Godfrey helped me till they retired under the rhododendrons and had it out in silence.

'D'you know what that girl's father was?' Mrs Godfrey asked.

'No,' I replied. 'I loathe her for her own sake. She breathes through her mouth.'

'He was a retired doctor,' she explained. 'He used to pick up stormy young men in the repentant stage, take them home, and patch them up till they were sound enough to be insured. Then he insured them heavily, and let them out into the world again – with an appetite. Of course, no one knew him while he was alive, but he left pots of money to his daughter.'

'Strictly legitimate – highly respectable,' I said. 'But what a life for the daughter!'

'Mustn't it have been! *Now* d'you realise what you said just now?'

'Perfectly; and now you've made me quite happy, shall we go back to the house?'

When we reached it they were all inside, sitting on committee of names.

'What shall you call yours?' I heard Milly asked Miss Sichliffe.

'Harvey,' she replied – 'Harvey's Sauce, you know. He's going to be quite saucy when I've' – she saw Mrs Godfrey and me coming through the French window – 'when he's stronger.'

Attley, the well-meaning man, to make me feel at ease, asked what I thought of the name.

'Oh, splendid,' I said at random. 'H with an A, A with an R, R with a – '

'But that's Little Bingo,' some one said, and they all laughed.

Miss Sichliffe, her hands joined across her long knees, drawled, 'You ought always to verify your quotations.'

It was not a kindly thrust, but something in the word 'quotation' set the automatic side of my brain at work on some shadow of a word or phrase that kept itself out of memory's reach as a cat sits just beyond a dog's jump. When I was going home, Miss Sichliffe came up to me in the twilight, the pup on a leash, swinging her big shoes at the end of her tennis-racket.

'Sorry,' she said in her thick schoolboy-like voice. 'I'm sorry for what I said to you about verifying quotations. I didn't know you well enough and – anyhow, I oughtn't to have.'

'But you were quite right about Little Bingo,' I answered. 'The spelling ought to have reminded me.'

'Yes, of course. It's the spelling,' she said, and slouched off with the pup sliding after her. Once again my brain began to worry after something that would have meant something if it had been properly spelled. I confided my trouble to Malachi on the way home, but Bettina had bitten him in four places, and he was busy.

Weeks later, Attley came over to see me, and before his car stopped Malachi let me know that Bettina was sitting beside the chauffeur. He greeted her by the scruff of the neck as she hopped down; and I greeted Mrs Godfrey, Attley, and a big basket.

'You've got to help me,' said Attley tiredly. We took the basket into the garden, and there staggered out the angular shadow of a sandy-pied, broken-haired terrier, with one imbecile and one delirious ear, and two most hideous squints. Bettina and Malachi, already at grips on the lawn, saw him, let go, and fled in opposite directions.

'Why have you brought that fetid hound here?' I demanded.

'Harvey? For you to take care of,' said Attley. 'He's had distemper, but *I*'m going abroad.'

'Take him with you. I won't have him. He's mentally afflicted.'

'Look here,' Attley almost shouted, 'do I strike you as a fool?'

'Always,' said I.

'Well, then, if you say so, and Ella says so, that proves I ought to go abroad.'

'Will's wrong, quite wrong,' Mrs Godfrey interrupted; 'but you must take the pup.'

'My dear boy, my dear boy, don't you ever give anything to a woman,' Attley snorted.

Bit by bit I got the story out of them in the quiet garden (never a sign from Bettina and Malachi), while Harvey stared me out of countenance, first with one cuttlefish eye and then with the other.

It appeared that, a month after Miss Sichliffe took him, the dog Harvey developed distemper. Miss Sichliffe had nursed him herself for some time; then she carried him in her arms the two miles to Mittleham, and wept – actually wept – at Attley's feet, saying that Harvey was all she had or expected to have in this world, and Attley must cure him. Attley, being by wealth, position, and temperament guardian to all lame dogs, had put everything aside for this unsavoury job, and, he asserted, Miss Sichliffe had virtually lived with him ever since.

'She went home at night, of course,' he exploded, 'but the rest of the time she simply infested the premises. Goodness knows, I'm not particular, but it was a scandal. Even the servants! . . . Three and four times a day, and notes in between, to know how the beast was. Hang it all, don't laugh! And wanting to send me flowers and goldfish. Do I look as if I wanted goldfish? Can't you two stop for a minute?' (Mrs Godfrey and I were clinging to each other for support.) 'And it isn't as if I was – was so alluring a personality, is it?'

Attley commands more trust, goodwill, and affection than most men, for he is that rare angel, an absolutely unselfish bachelor, content to be run by contending syndicates of zealous friends. His situation seemed desperate, and I told him so.

'Instant flight is your only remedy,' was my verdict. 'I'll take care of both your cars while you're away, and you can send me over all the greenhouse fruit.'

'But why should I be chased out of my house by a she-dromedary?' he wailed.

'Oh, stop! Stop!' Mrs Godfrey sobbed. 'You're both wrong. I admit you're right, but I *know* you're wrong.'

'Three *and* four times a day,' said Attley, with an awful countenance. 'I'm not a vain man, but – look here, Ella, I'm not sensitive, I hope, but if you persist in making a joke of it – '

'Oh, be quiet!' she almost shrieked. 'D'you imagine for one instant that your friends would ever let Mittleham pass out of their hands? I quite agree it is unseemly for a grown girl to come to Mittleham at all hours of the day and night – '

'I told you she went home o' nights,' Attley growled.

'Specially if she goes home o' nights. Oh, but think of the life she must have led, Will!'

'I'm not interfering with it; only she must leave me alone.'

'She may want to patch you up and insure you,' I suggested.

'D'you know what *you* are?' Mrs Godfrey turned on me with the smile I have feared for the last quarter of a century. 'You're the nice, kind, wise, doggy friend. You don't know how wise and nice you are supposed to be. Will has sent Harvey to you to complete the poor angel's convalescence. You know all about dogs, or Will wouldn't have done it. He's written her that. You're too far off for her to make daily calls on you. P'r'aps she'll drop in two or three times a week, and write on other days. But it doesn't matter what she does, because you don't own Mittleham, don't you see?'

I told her I saw most clearly.

'Oh, you'll get over that in a few days,' Mrs Godfrey countered. 'You're the sporting, responsible, doggy friend who – '

'He used to look at me like that at first,' said Attley, with a visible shudder, 'but he gave it up after a bit. It's only because you're new to him.'

'But, confound you! he's a ghoul – ' I began.

'And when he gets quite well, you'll send him back to her direct with your love, and she'll give you some pretty four-tailed goldfish,' said Mrs Godfrey, rising. 'That's all settled. Car, please. We're going to Brighton to lunch together.'

They ran before I could get into my stride, so I told the dog Harvey what I thought of them and his mistress. He never shifted his position, but stared at me, an intense, lopsided stare, eye after eye. Malachi came along when he had seen his sister off, and from a distance counselled me to drown the brute and consort with gentlemen again. But the dog Harvey never even cocked his cockable ear.

And so it continued as long as he was with me. Where I sat, he sat and stared; where I walked, he walked beside, head stiffly slewed over one shoulder in single-barrelled contemplation of me. He never gave tongue, never closed in for a caress, seldom let me stir a step alone. And, to my amazement, Malachi, who suffered no stranger to live within our gates, saw this gaunt, growing, green-eyed devil wipe him out of my service and company without a whimper. Indeed, one would have said the situation interested him, for he would meet us returning from grim walks together and look alternately at Harvey and at me with the same quivering interest that he showed at the mouth of a rat-hole. Outside these inspections, Malachi withdrew himself as only a dog or a woman can.

Miss Sichliffe came over after a few days (luckily I was out) with some elaborate story of paying calls in the neighbourhood. She sent me a note of thanks next day. I was reading it when Harvey and Malachi entered and disposed themselves as usual, Harvey close up to stare at me, Malachi half under the sofa, watching us both. Out of curiosity I returned Harvey's stare, then pulled his lopsided head on to my knee, and took his eye for several minutes. Now, in Malachi's eye I can see at any hour all that there is of the normal decent dog, flecked here and there with that strained half-soul which man's love and association have added to his nature. But with Harvey the eye was perplexed, as a tortured man's. Only by looking far into its deeps could one make out the spirit of the proper animal, beclouded and cowering beneath some unfair burden.

Leggatt, my chauffeur, came in for orders.

'How d'you think Harvey's coming on?' I said, as I rubbed the brute's gulping neck. The vet had warned me of the possibilities of spinal trouble following distemper.

'He ain't *my* fancy,' was the reply. 'But *I* don't question his comings and goings so long as I 'aven't to sit alone in a room with him.'

'Why? He's as meek as Moses,' I said.

'He fair gives me the creeps. P'r'aps he'll go out in fits.'

But Harvey, as I wrote his mistress from time to time, throve, and when he grew better, would play by himself grisly games of spying, walking up, hailing, and chasing another dog. From these he would break off of a sudden and return to his normal stiff gait, with the air of one who had forgotten some matter of life and death, which could be reached only by staring at me. I left him one evening posturing with the unseen on the lawn, and went inside to finish some letters for the post. I must have been at work nearly an hour, for I was going to turn on the lights, when I felt there was somebody in the room whom, the short hairs at the back of my neck warned me, I was not in the least anxious to face. There was a mirror on the wall. As I lifted my eyes to it I saw the dog Harvey reflected near the shadow by the closed door. He had reared himself full-length on his hind legs, his head a little one side to clear a sofa between us, and he was looking at me. The face, with its knitted brows and drawn lips, was the face of a dog, but the look, for the fraction of time that I caught it, was human – wholly and horribly human. When the blood in my body went forward again he had dropped to the floor, and was merely studying me in his usual one-eyed fashion. Next day I returned him to Miss Sichliffe. I would not have kept him another day for the wealth of Asia, or even Ella Godfrey's approval.

Miss Sichliffe's house I discovered to be a mid-Victorian mansion of peculiar villainy even for its period, surrounded by gardens of conflicting colours, all dazzling with glass and fresh paint on ironwork. Striped blinds, for it was a blazing autumn morning, covered most of the windows, and a voice sang to the piano an almost forgotten song of Jean Ingelow's –

> Methought that the stars were blinking bright,
> And the old brig's sails unfurled –

Down came the loud pedal, and the unrestrained cry swelled out across a bed of tritomas consuming in their own fires –

> When I said I will sail to my love this night
> On the other side of the world.

I have no music, but the voice drew. I waited till the end:

> Oh, maid most dear, I am not here
> I have no place apart –
> No dwelling more on sea or shore,
> But only in thy heart.

It seemed to me a poor life that had no more than that to do at eleven o'clock of a Tuesday forenoon. Then Miss Sichliffe suddenly lumbered through a French window in clumsy haste, her brows contracted against the light.

'Well?' she said, delivering the word like a spear-thrust, with the full weight of a body behind it.

'I've brought Harvey back at last,' I replied. 'Here he is.'

But it was at me she looked, not at the dog who had cast himself at her feet – looked as though she would have fished my soul out of my breast on the instant.

'Wha – what did you think of him? What did *you* make of him?' she panted. I was too taken aback for the moment to reply. Her voice broke as she stooped to the dog at her knees. 'O Harvey, Harvey! You utterly worthless old devil!' she cried, and the dog cringed and abased himself in servility that one could scarcely bear to look upon. I made to go.

'Oh, but please, you mustn't!' She tugged at the car's side. 'Wouldn't you like some flowers or some orchids? We've really splendid orchids, and' – she clasped her hands – 'there are Japanese goldfish – real Japanese goldfish, with four tails. If you don't care for 'em, perhaps your friends or somebody – oh, please!'

Harvey had recovered himself, and I realised that this woman beyond the decencies was fawning on me as the dog had fawned on her.

'Certainly,' I said, ashamed to meet her eye. 'I'm lunching at Mittleham, but – '

'There's plenty of time,' she entreated. 'What do *you* think of Harvey?'

'He's a queer beast,' I said, getting out. 'He does nothing but stare at me.'

'Does he stare at you all the time he's with you?'

'Always. He's doing it now. Look!'

We had halted. Harvey had sat down, and was staring from one to the other with a weaving motion of the head.

'He'll do that all day,' I said. 'What is it, Harvey?'

'Yes, what *is* it, Harvey?' she echoed. The dog's throat twitched, his body stiffened and shook as though he were going to have a fit. Then he came back with a visible wrench to his unwinking watch.

'Always so?' she whispered.

'Always,' I replied, and told her something of his life with me. She nodded once or twice, and in the end led me into the house.

There were unaging pitch-pine doors of Gothic design in it; there were inlaid marble mantelpieces and cut-steel fenders; there were stupendous wall-papers, and octagonal, medallioned Wedgewood what-nots, and black-and-gilt Austrian images holding candelabra, with every other refinement that Art had achieved or wealth had bought between 1851 and 1878. And everything reeked of varnish.

'Now!' she opened a baize door, and pointed down a long corridor flanked with more Gothic doors. 'This was where we used to – to patch 'em up. You've heard of us. Mrs Godfrey told you in the garden the day I got Harvey given me. I' – she drew in her breath – 'I live here by myself, and I have a very large income. Come back, Harvey.'

He had tiptoed down the corridor, as rigid as ever, and was sitting outside one of the shut doors. 'Look here!' she said, and planted herself squarely in front of me. 'I tell you this because you – you've patched up Harvey, too. Now, I want you to remember that my name is Moira. Mother calls me Marjorie because it's more refined; but my real name is Moira, and I am in my thirty-fourth year.'

'Very good,' I said. 'I'll remember all that.'

'Thank you.' Then with a sudden swoop into the humility of an abashed boy – 'Sorry if I haven't said the proper things. You see – there's Harvey looking at us again. Oh, I want to say – if ever you want anything in the way or orchids or goldfish or – or anything else that would be useful to you, you've only to come to me for it. Under the will I'm perfectly independent, and we're a long-lived family, worse luck!' She looked at me, and her face worked like glass behind driven flame. 'I may reasonably expect to live another fifty years,' she said.

'Thank you, Miss Sichliffe,' I replied. 'If I want anything, you may be sure I'll come to you for it.' She nodded. 'Now I must get over to Mittleham,' I said.

'Mr Attley will ask you all about this.' For the first time she laughed aloud. 'I'm afraid I frightened him nearly out of the county. I didn't think, of course. But I dare say he knows by this time he was wrong. Say good-bye to Harvey.'

'Good-bye, old man,' I said. 'Give me a farewell stare, so we shall know each other when we meet again.'

The dog looked up, then moved slowly toward me, and stood, head bowed to the floor, shaking in every muscle as I patted him; and when I turned, I saw him crawl back to her feet.

That was not a good preparation for the rampant boy-and-girl-dominated lunch at Mittleham, which, as usual, I found in possession of everybody except the owner.

'But what did the dromedary say when you brought her beast back?' Attley demanded.

'The usual polite things,' I replied. 'I'm posing as the nice doggy friend nowadays.'

'I don't envy you. She's never darkened my doors, thank goodness, since I left Harvey at your place. I suppose she'll run about the county now swearing you cured him. That's a woman's idea of gratitude.' Attley seemed rather hurt, and Mrs Godfrey laughed.

'That proves you were right about Miss Sichliffe, Ella,' I said. 'She had no designs on anybody.'

'I'm always right in these matters. But didn't she even offer you a goldfish?'

'Not a thing,' said I. 'You know what an old maid's like where her precious dog's concerned.' And though I have tried vainly to lie to Ella Godfrey for many years, I believe that in this case I succeeded.

When I turned into our drive that evening, Leggatt observed half aloud:

'I'm glad Zvengali's back where he belongs. It's time our Mike had a look in.'

Sure enough, there was Malachi back again in spirit as well as flesh, but still with that odd air of expectation he had picked up from Harvey.

It was in January that Attley wrote me that Mrs Godfrey, wintering in Madeira with Milly, her unmarried daughter, had been attacked with something like enteric; that the hotel, anxious for its good name, had thrust them both out into a cottage annexe; that he was off with a nurse, and that I was not to leave England till I heard from him again. In a week he wired that Milly was down as well, and that I must bring out two more nurses, with suitable delicacies.

Within seventeen hours I had got them all aboard the Cape boat, and had seen the women safely collapsed into sea-sickness. The next few weeks were for me, as for the invalids, a low delirium, clouded with fantastic memories of Portuguese officials trying to tax calves'-foot jelly; voluble doctors insisting that true typhoid was unknown in the island; nurses who had to be exercised, taken out of themselves, and returned on the tick of change of guard; night slides down glassy, cobbled streets, smelling of sewage and flowers, between walls whose every stone and patch Attley and I knew; vigils in stucco verandahs, watching the curve and descent of great stars or drawing auguries from the break of dawn; insane interludes of gambling at the local Casino, where we won heaps of unconsoling silver; blasts of steamers arriving and departing in the roads; help offered by total strangers, grabbed at or thrust aside; the long nightmare crumbling back into sanity one forenoon under a vine-covered trellis, where Attley sat hugging a nurse, while the others danced a noiseless, neat-footed breakdown never learned at the Middlesex Hospital. At last, as the tension came out all over us in aches and tingles that we put down to the country wine, a vision of Mrs Godfrey, her grey hair turned to spun-glass, but her eyes triumphant over the shadow of retreating death beneath them, with Milly, enormously grown, and clutching life back to her young breast, both stretched out on cane chairs, clamouring for food.

In this ungirt hour there imported himself into our life a youngish-looking middle-aged man of the name of Shend, with a blurred face and deprecating eyes. He said he had gambled with me at the Casino, which was no recommendation, and I remember that he twice gave me a basket of champagne and liqueur brandy for the invalids, which a sailor in a red-tasselled cap carried up to the cottage for me at 3 A.M. He turned out to be the son of some merchant prince in the oil and colour line, and the owner of a four-hundred-ton steam yacht, into which, at his gentle insistence, we later shifted our camp, staff, and equipage, Milly weeping with delight to escape from the horrible cottage. There we lay off Funchal for weeks, while Shend did miracles of luxury and attendance through deputies, and never once asked how his guests were enjoying themselves. Indeed, for several days at a time we would see nothing of him. He was, he said, subject to malaria. Giving as they do with both hands, I knew that Attley and Mrs Godfrey could take nobly; but I never met a man who so nobly gave and so nobly received thanks as Shend did.

'Tell us why you have been so unbelievably kind to us gipsies,' Mrs Godfrey said to him one day on deck.

He looked up from a diagram of some Thames-mouth shoals which he was explaining to me, and answered with his gentle smile:

'I will. It's because it makes me happy – it makes me more than happy – to be with you. It makes me comfortable. You know how selfish men are? If a man feels comfortable all over with certain people, he'll bore them to death, just like a dog. You always make me feel as if pleasant things were going to happen to me.'

'Haven't any ever happened before?' Milly asked.

'This is the most pleasant thing that has happened to me in ever so many years,' he replied. 'I feel like the man in the Bible, "It's good for me to be here." Generally, I don't feel that it's good for me to be anywhere in particular.' Then, as one begging a favour. 'You'll let me come home with you – in the same boat, I mean? I'd take you back in this thing of mine, and that would save you packing your trunks, but she's too lively for spring work across the Bay.'

We booked our berths, and when the time came, he wafted us and ours aboard the Southampton mailboat with the pomp of plenipotentiaries and the precision of the Navy. Then he dismissed his yacht, and became an inconspicuous passenger in a cabin opposite to mine, on the port side.

We ran at once into early British spring weather, followed by sou'west gales. Mrs Godfrey, Milly, and the nurses disappeared. Attley stood it out, visibly yellowing, till the next meal, and followed suit, and Shend and I had the little table all to ourselves. I found him even more attractive when the women were away. The natural sweetness of the man, his voice, and bearing all fascinated me, and his knowledge of practical seamanship (he held an extra master's certificate) was a real joy. We sat long in the empty saloon and longer in the smoking-room, making dashes downstairs over slippery decks at the eleventh hour.

It was on Friday night, just as I was going to bed, that he came into my cabin, after cleaning his teeth, which he did half a dozen times a day.

'I say,' he began hurriedly, 'do you mind if I come in here for a little? I'm a bit edgy.' I must have shown surprise. 'I'm ever so much better about liquor than I used to be, but – it's the whisky in the suitcase that throws me. For God's sake, old man, don't go back on me to-night! Look at my hands!'

They were fairly jumping at the wrists. He sat down on a trunk that had slid out with the roll. We had reduced speed, and were surging in confused seas that pounded on the black port-glasses. The night promised to be a pleasant one!

'You understand, of course, don't you?' he chattered.

'Oh yes,' I said cheerily; 'but how about – '

'No, no; on no account the doctor. 'Tell a doctor, tell the whole ship. Besides, I've only got a touch of 'em. You'd never have guessed it, would you? The tooth-wash does the trick. I'll give you the prescription.'

'I'll send a note to the doctor for a prescription, shall I?' I suggested.

'Right! I put myself unreservedly in your hands. 'Fact is, I always did. I said to myself – 'sure I don't bore you? – the minute I saw you, I said, "Thou art the man."' He repeated the phrase as he picked at his knees. 'All the same, you can take it from me that the ewe-lamb business is a rotten bad one. I don't care how unfaithful the shepherd may be. Drunk or sober, 'tisn't cricket.'

A surge of the trunk threw him across the cabin as the steward answered my bell. I wrote my requisition to the doctor while Shend was struggling to his feet.

'What's wrong?' he began. 'Oh, I know. We're slowing for soundings off Ushant. It's about time, too. You'd better ship the dead-lights when you come back, Matchem. It'll save you waking us later. This sea's going to get up when the tide turns. That'll show you,' he said as the man left, 'that I am to be trusted. You – you'll stop me if I say anything I shouldn't, won't you?'

'Talk away,' I replied, 'if it makes you feel better.'

'That's it; you've hit it exactly. You always make me feel better. I can rely on you. It's awkward soundings but you'll see me through it. We'll defeat him yet. . . . I may be an utterly worthless devil, but I'm not a brawler. . . . I told him so at breakfast. I said, "Doctor, I detest brawling, but if ever you allow that girl to be insulted again as Clements insulted her, I will break your neck with my own hands." You think I was right?'

'Absolutely,' I agreed.

'Then we needn't discuss the matter any further. That man was a murderer in intention – outside the law, you understand, as it was then. They've changed it since – but he never deceived *me*. I told him so. I said to him at the time, "I don't know what price you're going to put on my head, but if ever you allow Clements to insult her again, you'll never live to claim it." '

'And what did he do?' I asked, to carry on the conversation, for Matchem entered with the bromide.

'Oh, crumpled up at once. 'Lead still going, Matchem?'

'I 'aven't 'eard,' said that faithful servant of the Union-Castle Company.

'Quite right. Never alarm the passengers. Ship the dead-light, will you?' Matchem shipped it, for we were rolling very heavily. There were tramplings and gull-like cries from on deck. Shend looked at me with a mariner's eye.

'That's nothing,' he said protectingly.

'Oh, it's all right for you,' I said, jumping at the idea. '*I* haven't an extra master's certificate. I'm only a passenger. I confess it funks me.'

Instantly his whole bearing changed to answer the appeal.

'My dear fellow, it's as simple as houses. We're hunting for sixty-five fathom water. Anything short of sixty, with a sou'west wind means – but

I'll get my Channel Pilot out of my cabin and give you the general idea. I'm only too grateful to do anything to put your mind at ease.'

And so, perhaps, for another hour – he declined the drink – Channel Pilot in hand, he navigated us round Ushant, and at my request up-channel to Southampton, light by light, with explanations and reminiscences. I professed myself soothed at last, and suggested bed.

'In a second,' said he. 'Now, you wouldn't think, would you' – he glanced off the book toward my wildly swaying dressing-gown on the door – 'that I've been seeing things for the last half-hour? 'Fact is, I'm just on the edge of 'em, skating on thin ice round the corner – nor'east as near as nothing – where that dog's looking at me.'

'What's the dog like? ' I asked.

'Ah, that *is* comforting of you! Most men walk through 'em to show me they aren't real. As if I didn't know! But *you*'re different. Anybody could see that with half an eye.' He stiffened and pointed. 'Damn it all! The dog sees it too with half an – Why, he knows you! Knows you perfectly. D'you know *him*?'

'How can I tell if he isn't real?' I insisted.

'But you can! *You*'re all right. I saw that from the first. Don't go back on me now or I shall go to pieces like the *Drummond Castle*. I beg your pardon, old man; but, you see, you *do* know the dog. I'll prove it. What's that dog doing? Come on! *You* know.' A tremor shook him, and he put his hand on my knee, and whispered with great meaning: 'I'll letter or halve it with you. There! You begin.'

'S,' said I to humour him, for a dog would most likely be standing or sitting, or may be scratching or sniffing or staring.

'Q,' he went on, and I could feel the heat of his shaking hand.

'U,' said I. There was no other letter possible; but I was shaking too.

'I.'

'N.'

'T-i-n-g,' he ran out. 'There! That proves it. I knew you knew him. You don't know what a relief that is. Between ourselves, old man, he – he's been turning up lately a – a damn sight more often than I cared for. And a squinting dog – a dog that squints! I mean that's a bit *too* much. Eh? What?' He gulped and half rose, and I thought that the full tide of delirium would be on him in another sentence.

'Not a bit of it,' I said as a last chance, with my hand over the bellpush. 'Why, you've just proved that I know him; so there are two of us in the game, anyhow.'

'By Jove! that *is* an idea! Of course there are. I knew you'd see me through. We'll defeat them yet. Hi, pup! ... He's gone. Absolutely disappeared!' He sighed with relief, and I caught the lucky moment.

'Good business! I expect he only came to have a look at me,' I said. 'Now, get this drink down and turn in to the lower bunk.'

He obeyed, protesting that he could not inconvenience me, and in the midst of apologies sank into a dead sleep. I expected a wakeful night, having a certain amount to think over; but no sooner had I scrambled into the top-bunk than sleep came on me like a wave from the other side of the world.

In the morning there were apologies, which we got over at breakfast before our party were about.

'I suppose – after this – well, I don't blame you. I'm rather a lonely chap, though.' His eyes lifted dog-like across the table.

'Shend,' I replied, 'I'm not running a Sunday school. You're coming home with me in my car as soon as we land.'

'That is kind of you – kinder than you think.'

'That's because you're a little jumpy still. Now, I don't want to mix up in your private affairs – '

'But I'd like you to,' he interrupted.

'Then, would you mind telling me the Christian name of a girl who was insulted by a man called Clements?'

'Moira,' he whispered; and just then Mrs Godfrey and Milly came to table with their shore-going hats on.

We did not tie up till noon, but the faithful Leggatt had intrigued his way down to the dock-edge, and beside him sat Malachi, wearing his collar of gold, or Leggatt makes it look so, as eloquent as Demosthenes. Shend flinched a little when he saw him. We packed Mrs Godfrey and Milly into Attley's car – they were going with him to Mittleham, of course – and drew clear across the railway lines to find England all lit and perfumed for spring. Shend sighed with happiness.

'D'you know,' he said, 'if – if you'd chucked me – I should have gone down to my cabin after breakfast and cut my throat. And now – it's like a dream – a good dream, you know.'

We lunched with the other three at Romsey. Then I sat in front for a little while to talk to my Malachi. When I looked back, Shend was solidly asleep, and stayed so for the next two hours, while Leggatt chased Attley's fat Daimler along the green-speckled hedges. He woke up when we said good-bye at Mittleham, with promises to meet again very soon.

'And I hope,' said Mrs Godfrey, 'that everything pleasant will happen to you.'

'Heaps and heaps – all at once,' cried long, weak Milly, waving her wet handkerchief.

'I've just got to look in at a house near here for a minute to inquire about a dog,' I said, 'and then we will go home.'

'I used to know this part of the world,' he replied, and said no more till Leggatt shot past the lodge at the Sichliffes's gate. Then I heard him gasp.

Miss Sichliffe, in a green waterproof, an orange jersey, and a pinkish leather hat, was working on a bulb-border. She straightened herself as the car stopped, and breathed hard. Shend got out and walked towards her. They shook hands, turned round together, and went into the house. Then the dog Harvey pranced out corkily from under the lee of a bench. Malachi, with one joyous swoop, fell on him as an enemy and an equal. Harvey, for his part, freed from all burden whatsoever except the obvious duty of a man-dog on his own ground, met Malachi without reserve or remorse, and with six months' additional growth to come and go on.

'Don't check 'em!' cried Leggatt, dancing round the flurry. 'They've both been saving up for each other all this time. It'll do 'em worlds of good.'

'Leggatt,' I said, 'will you take Mr Shend's bag and suitcase up to the house, and put them down just inside the door? Then we will go on.'

So I enjoyed the finish alone. It was a dead heat, and they licked each other's jaws in amity till Harvey, one imploring eye on me, leaped into the front seat, and Malachi backed his appeal. It was theft, but I took him, and we talked all the way home of r-rats and r-rabbits and bones and baths and the other basic facts of life. That evening after dinner they slept before the fire, with their warm chins across the hollows of my ankles – to each chin an ankle – till I kicked them upstairs to bed.

I was not at Mittleham when she came over to announce her engagement, but I heard of it when Mrs Godfrey and Attley came, forty miles an hour, over to me, and Mrs Godfrey called me names of the worst for suppression of information.

'As long as it wasn't me, I don't care,' said Attley.

'I believe you knew it all along,' Mrs Godfrey repeated. 'Else what made you drive that man literally into her arms?'

'To ask after the dog Harvey,' I replied.

'Then, what's the beast doing here?' Attley demanded, for Malachi and the dog Harvey were deep in council of the family with Bettina, who was being out-argued.

'Oh, Harvey seemed to think himself *de trop* where he was,' I said. 'And she hasn't sent after him. You'd better save Bettina before they kill her.'

'There's been enough lying about that dog,' said Mrs Godfrey to me. 'If he wasn't born in lies, he was baptized in 'em. D'you know why she called him Harvey? It only occurred to me in those dreadful days when I was ill, and one can't keep from thinking, and thinks everything. D'you know your Boswell? What did Johnson say about Hervey – with an e?'

'Oh, *that's* it, is it?' I cried incautiously. 'That was why I ought to have verified my quotations. The spelling defeated me. Wait a moment, and it will come back. Johnson said: "He was a vicious man,"' I began.

'"But very kind to me,"' Mrs Godfrey prompted. Then, both together, '"If you call a dog Hervey, I shall love him."'

'So you *were* mixed up in it. At any rate, you had your suspicions from the first? Tell me,' she said.

'Ella,' I said, 'I don't know anything rational or reasonable about any of it. It was all – all woman-work, and it scared me horribly.'

'Why?' she asked.

That was six years ago. I have written this tale to let her know – wherever she may be.

O. HENRY

Memoirs of a Yellow Dog

I DON'T SUPPOSE IT will knock any of you people off your perch to read a contribution from an animal. Mr Kipling and a good many others have demonstrated the fact that animals can express themselves in remunerative English, and no magazine goes to press nowadays without an animal story in it, except the old-style monthlies that are still running pictures of Bryan and the Mont Pelée horror.

But you needn't look for any stuck-up literature in my piece, such as

Bearoo, the bear, and Snakoo, the snake, and Tammanoo, the tiger, talk in the jungle books. A yellow dog that's spent most of his life in a cheap New York flat, sleeping in a corner on an old sateen underskirt (the one she spilled port wine on at the Lady 'Longshoremen's banquet), mustn't be expected to perform any tricks with the art of speech.

I was born a yellow pup; date, locality, pedigree, and weight unknown. The first thing I can recollect, an old woman had me in a basket at Broadway and Twenty-third trying to sell me to a fat lady. Old Mother Hubbard was boosting me to beat the band as a genuine Pomeranian-Hambletonian-Red-Irish-Cochin-China-Stoke-Pogis fox terrier. The fat lady chased a note round among the samples of gros grain flannelette in her shopping bag till she cornered it, and gave up. From that moment I was a pet – a mamma's own wootsey squidlums. Say, gentle reader, did you ever have a 100-pound woman breathing a flavour of Camembert cheese and Peau d'Espagne pick you up and wallop her nose all over you, remarking all the time in an Emma Eames tone of voice: 'Oh, oo's um oodlum, doodlum, woodlum, toodlum, bitsy-witsy skoodlums?'

From a pedigreed yellow pup I grew up to be an anonymous yellow cur looking like a cross between an Angora cat and a box of lemons. But my mistress never tumbled. She thought that the two primeval pups that Noah chased into the ark were but a collateral branch of my ancestors. It took two policemen to keep her from entering me at the Madison Square Garden for the Siberian bloodhound prize.

I'll tell you about that flat. The house was the ordinary thing in New York, paved with Parian marble in the entrance hall and cobblestones above the first floor. Our flat was three fl – well, not flights – climbs up. My mistress rented it unfurnished, and put in the regular things – 1903 antique upholstered parlour set, oil chromo of geishas in a Harlem tea house, rubber plant and husband.

By Sirius! there was a biped I felt sorry for. He was a little man with sandy hair and whiskers a good deal like mine. Henpecked? – well, toucans and flamingoes and pelicans all had their bills in him. He wiped the dishes and listened to my mistress tell about the cheap, ragged things the lady with the squirrel-skin coat on the second floor hung out on her line to dry. And every evening while she was getting supper she made him take me out on the end of a string for a walk.

If men knew how women pass the time when they are alone they'd never marry. Laura Jean Libbey, peanut brittle, a little almond cream on the neck muscles, dishes unwashed, half an hour's talk with the iceman, reading a package of old letters, a couple of pickles and two bottles of malt extract, one hour peeping through a hole in the window blind into the flat across the air-shaft – that's about all there is to it. Twenty minutes before time for him to come home from work she straightens up the house, fixes her rat so it won't show, and gets out a lot of sewing for a ten-minute bluff.

I led a dog's life in that flat. 'Most all day I lay there in my corner watching that fat woman kill time. I slept sometimes and had pipe dreams about being out chasing cats into basements and growling at old ladies with black mittens, as a dog was intended to do. Then she would pounce upon me with a lot of that drivelling poodle palaver and kiss me on the nose – but what could I do? A dog can't chew cloves.

I began to feel sorry for Hubby, dog my cats if I didn't. We looked so much alike that people noticed it when we went out; so we shook the streets that Morgan's cab drives down, and took to climbing the piles of last December's snow on the streets where cheap people live.

One evening when we were thus promenading, and I was trying to look like a prize St Bernard, and the old man was trying to look like he wouldn't have murdered the first organ-grinder he heard play Mendelssohn's wedding-march, I looked up at him and said, in my way:

'What are you looking so sour about, you oakum-trimmed lobster? She don't kiss you. You don't have to sit on her lap and listen to talk that would make the book of a musical comedy sound like the maxims of Epictetus. You ought to be thankful you're not a dog. Brace up, Benedick, and bid the blues begone.'

The matrimonial mishap looked down at me with almost canine intelligence in his face.

'Why, doggie,' says he, 'good doggie. You almost look like you could speak. What is it, doggie – Cats?'

Cats! Could speak!

But, of course, he couldn't understand. Humans were denied the speech of animals. The only common ground of communication upon which dogs and men can get together is in fiction.

In the flat across the hall from us lived a lady with a black-and-tan terrier. Her husband strung it and took it out every evening, but he always came home cheerful and whistling. One day I touched noses with the black-and-tan in the hall, and I struck him for an elucidation.

'See here, Wiggle-and-Skip,' I says, 'you know that it ain't the nature of a real man to play dry nurse to a dog in public. I never saw one leashed to a bow-wow yet that didn't look like he'd like to lick every other man that looked at him. But your boss comes in every day as perky and set up as an amateur prestidigitator doing the egg trick. How does he do it? Don't tell me he likes it.'

'Him!' says the black-and-tan. 'Why, he uses Nature's Own Remedy. He gets spifflicated. At first when we go out he's as shy as the man on the steamer who would rather play pedro when they make 'em all jackpots. By the time we've been in eight saloons he doesn't care whether the thing on the end of his line is a dog or a catfish. I've lost two inches of my tail trying to sidestep those swinging doors.

The pointer I got from that terrier – vaudeville please copy – set me to thinking.

One evening about 6 o'clock my mistress ordered him to get busy and do the ozone act for Lovey. I have concealed it until now, but that is what she called me. The black-and-tan was called 'Tweetness.' I consider that I have the bulge on him as far as you could chase a rabbit. Still 'Lovey' is something of a nomenclatural tin-can on the tail of one's self-respect.

At a quiet place on a safe street I tightened the line of my custodian in front of an attractive, refined saloon. I made a dead-ahead scramble for the doors, whining like a dog in the press dispatches that lets the family know that little Alice is bogged while gathering lilies in the brook.

'Why, darn my eyes,' says the old man, with a grin: 'darn my eyes if the saffron-coloured son of a seltzer lemonade ain't asking me in to take a drink. Lemme see – how long's it been since I saved shoe leather by keeping one foot on the foot-rest? I believe I'll – '

I knew I had him. Hot Scotches he took, sitting at a table. For an hour he kept the Campbells coming. I sat by his side rapping for the waiter with my tail, and eating free lunch such as mamma in her flat never equalled with her home-made truck bought at a delicatessen store eight minutes before papa comes home.

When the products of Scotland were all exhausted except the rye bread the old man unwound me from the table leg and played me outside like a fisherman plays a salmon. Out there he took off my collar and threw it into the street.

'Poor doggie,' says he; 'good doggie. She shan't kiss you any more. 'Sa darned shame. Good doggie, go away and get run over by a street car and be happy.'

I refused to leave. I leaped and frisked around the old man's legs happy a a pug on a rug.

'You old flea-headed woodchuck-chaser,' I said to him – 'you moon-baying, rabbit-pointing, egg-squealing old beagle, can't you see that I don't want to leave you? Can't you see that we're both Pups in the Wood and the missis is the cruel uncle after you with the dish towel and me with the flea liniment and a pink bow to tie on my tail. Why not cut that all out and be pards for ever more?'

Maybe you'll say he didn't understand – maybe he didn't. But he kind of got a grip on the Hot Scotches, and stood still for a minute, thinking.

'Doggie,' sayd he, finally, 'we don't live more than a dozen lives on this earth, and very few of us live to be more than 300. If I ever see that flat any more I'm a flat, and if you do you're flatter; and that's no flattery. I'm offering 60 to 1 that Westward Ho! wins out by the length of a dachshund.'

There was no string, but I frolicked along with my master to the Twenty-third Street ferry. And the cats on the route saw reason to give thanks that prehensile claws had been given them.

On the Jersey side my master said to a stranger who stood eating a currant bun:

'Me and my doggie, we are bound for the Rocky Mountains.'

But what pleased me most was when my old man pulled both of my ears until I howled, and said:

'You common, monkey-headed, rat-tailed, sulphur-coloured son of a door mat, do you know what I'm going to call you?'

I thought of 'Lovey', and I whined dolefully.

'I'm going to call you "Pete"', says my master; and if I'd had five tails I couldn't have done enough wagging to do justice to the occasion.

HENRY JAMES

A Tenant at Lamb House

THE SERVANTS WERE expected to look after Henry's pet dog, particularly during their master's absences. Tosca, who will be remembered at De Vere Mansions, died at Lamb House in 1899 and was buried in a corner of the garden – 'my domestic mortuary', he called it. She was followed by Tim and then by Peter, 'my admirable little Peter', ('He passed away ... at St Leonard's, fondly attended by the local "canine specialist" – after three days of dreadful "little dysentery".') And after that by Nick, a terrier, who died in 1902. Nick's place in his master's affections was taken by Max, a 'very beautiful and valuable little Dachshund pup of the "red" species, who has been promising to be the joy of my life up to a few hours since', so he wrote to his brother on May 24th, 1903, 'when he began to develop a mysterious and increasing tumification of one side of his face, about which I must immediately have advice. The things my dogs have, and the worries I have in consequence! I already see this one settled beneath monumental alabaster in the little cemetery in the angle of my garden, where he will make the fifth.' However, thanks to the attentions of the 'canine specialist' in St Leonards, Max survived, to become, as Henry told Mrs Boit and her sister 'the best and gentlest and most reasonable and well-mannered as well as most beautiful small animal of his kind to be easily come across – so that I think you will speedily find yourselves loving him for his own sweet sake.'

> The Servants, who are very fond of him and good to him, know what he 'has', and when he has it; and I shall take it kindly if he be not too often gratified with tid-bits between meals. Of course what he most intensively dreams of is being taken out on walks, and the more you are able so to indulge him the more he will adore you and the more all the latent beauty of his nature will come out. He is, I am happy to say, and has been from the first (he is about a year and half old) in very good, plain, straightforward health, and if he is not overfed and is sufficently exercised, and adequately brushed (his brush being always in one of the bowls on the hall-table – a convenient little currycomb) and Burgess is allowed occasionally to wash him, I have no doubt he will remain very fit. In the event, however, of his having anything at all troublesome the matter with him, kindly remember that there is an excellent 'Vet' a dozen miles away, who already knows him, and would come by to see him, for a moderate fee on any sign made. This person is 'Mr Percy Woodroffe Hill,' Canine Specialist, St Leonard's-on-Sea – a telegram would promptly reach him.

Indeed Henry felt the parting from Max as keenly as he did from the house itself. 'I left L. H. yesterday looking so dreadfully sorry to part with me', he wrote a week later, 'and so easy and pleasant to stay in withal, that I took refuge in burying my nose in Max's little gold-coloured back and wetting it (the back) with my tears'. Four months later, he was writing to Mrs Boit from his brother's home in Cambridge, Mass., and thanking his tenants for their kindness to the dog. 'Yes, I am homesick and I even yearn at times a little for curtsying Mrs P[addington] – no one curtseys to me here! But the heartbreak is nearest when I think of poor sweet-pawing little Max, for all of your patience with whom I effusively thank you. I hope he isn't too constant a burden.'

H. Montgomery Hyde, from *Henry James at Home*

IN 1891 ... [James] had a dachshund bitch with a beautiful countenance. He sat with the dachshund in his lap much of the time. We were speaking on the subject of sex in women and were comparing European women with American women in this regard. I had a notion that American women had less of this quality than European women, that in many American women it was negative, and in European women positive, and that many American girls looked like effeminate boys ... James said, stroking the head of the dachshund: 'She's got sex, if you like, and she's quite intelligent enough to be shocked by this conversation.'

E. S. Nadal, from 'Personal Recollections of Henry James'

E. F. BENSON

Another Tenant at Lamb House

WALT WHITMAN PROTESTS somewhere that for the future he intends to live entirely with animals (cows I think he says) because they do not make him sick with talking about their souls. No one has loved the human race more than he, but coming across that illuminating passage, I felt I knew exactly what he meant and warmed to it. I did not see my way to living with a cow, but the house – I do not know how it happened – had long been dogless, and the fire kindled. So when my cook on holiday in Wales asked if she might bring home a black collie puppy I hailed the suggestion. When I returned to London one summer from the pickling fountains of Droitwich (where I had been thinking too much not about my soul but my body) he was carried upstairs to be introduced, for he had not yet learned how to negotiate such puzzling contrivances as staircases. At once and automatically he was Taffy, globular in figure with a black coat of short and curly puppy hair, a white shirt front and white tips to his paws. He had gay, inquiring brown eyes, and he set himself diligently to study the domestic etiquette of genteel houses.

From the first it was clear that we had got hold of a very intelligent young gentleman, and he very soon mastered domestic etiquette. But he manifested also odd signs of knowing things which he had never studied, and which it is difficult to refer to instinct. His father and mother both came from generations of working dogs, but Taffy had been brought up to London as soon as he no longer needed his mamma to feed him, and had never been out with the shepherd. But a very queer thing happened. One of his new friends was playing with him and teaching him to retrieve a piece of rolled-up paper which he threw about the room. Taffy missed seeing where it was thrown, and his instructor with a downward movement of his hand pointed to where it lay on the floor. That is the gesture a shepherd makes when he wants his dog to efface himself and wait for further orders, and Taffy instantly lay down with his head flat on his paws. Again, he was taken for a walk in Hyde Park, and there, careering about, he sighted some sheep feeding near by. He stopped with a paw up, and then made a wide circuit round them exactly as a trained dog would do. This is rather mysterious: it looks as if, through the generations of his working ancestors, he had inherited knowledge which was not instinctive with them, but was the result of education.

My house soon passed into his guardianship, and he had a cordial welcome for all visitors, upstairs or downstairs, whom his people brought in. But he required that guarantee, for he could not allow unvouched-for folk to enter, and a tradesman, accustomed to let himself in and go to the kitchen with his goods was met with furious barking. Taffy shed his short puppy-coat, and put up a sweeping black plume on his tail and plumes at the back of his forepaws, and round his neck a silky Elizabethan ruff. He took but little interest in other dogs, with one exception, and consecrated himself to the service of his adopted people. A young dog's brain should be kept alert and active, especially if he comes of a stock that is accustomed to think. He enjoys having tasks set him on which he must exercise his wits. He went out for a short early walk, and then accompanied the bearer of my breakfast-tray up to my bedroom, carrying the kitchen-book which contained my cook's suggestions for the meals of the day. This was discipline, for the kitchen-book was a slim paper-covered volume which seemed specially designed to be firmly grasped in the paws and torn to shreds. Having resisted this temptation as he mounted three flights of stairs Taffy jumped on to my bed and gave me the book. He carried it down to the kitchen again, and went out for his morning's shopping. At the butcher's he was sometimes entrusted with his own dinner, pieces of raw liver wrapped up in thick paper, and he carried it home running at the mouth with the anticipation of what should then follow. Later in the morning he heard a step coming down from upstairs, and at that he bundled up the kitchen stairs and waited by the door into the hall, for that step certainly meant a run in the garden of the square. The key to the garden with a wooden tab attached to it was kept in the sitting-room by the front-door, and it was his duty to carry this to the garden gate. Very soon he made the correct connection between the key and the garden and fetched the key himself. Sometimes it had been put for educational purposes, in some unusual place, and then he searched for it. Often there were small dogs in the garden, Pekinese particularly, but he took no notice of their yappings, except when they fussed him by running about under him. Then he lifted a leg and, having performed the contemptuous office on any small Oriental who chanced to be there, he trotted away.

There was exercise in the park in the afternoon, a little slumber, and then work began again. Taffy went out with one of his friends to fetch the evening paper from the vendor in the Brompton Road and carry it home. After a week or two he grasped the hang of this expedition, and of his own accord he trotted on ahead to the vendor and waited, very much pleased with himself, for his paper to be given him. That became the custom (for the man knew that somebody would follow with the price of Taffy's purchase) and Taffy got impatient if he was not served immediately and was known to snatch a paper which had just been handed to somebody else. Occasionally this expedition started too soon; and the last edition had not yet come in, and then he was given an old poster folded up. Otherwise he stood there barking, and impeded traffic. One evening on his way home he met the only dog in whom he felt the slightest interest, a large Alsatian lady of strong sex appeal; he dropped his paper on the pavement to have a few words with her, and the lady stood on it. Taffy made his decision without delay, for, as

Queen Victoria wrote of John Brown 'his sense of duty ever went before every feeling of self.' He pushed her off it and trotted home with it.

He attended lunch and dinner, lying on the floor and forbidden, under pain of expulsion, to call attention to himself and nudge guests with his nose. But there was a chair set for him next me, and if he thought that something smelt unusually pleasant, he might jump on to his chair and speak to me. Speaking was not barking, which was not allowed, but making a low melodious singing noise. (Melba said that his voice-production was the best she had ever heard. She sang to us afterwards herself, and her voice-production was very good, too!) One night I had not noticed that he was sitting on his chair and had spoken. With the idea of putting his paw on my arm to remind me, he put it by mistake into a dish that was being handed me. Everybody laughed, and Taffy was quite aware that they were laughing at him. He jumped down from his chair, deeply offended.

A domestic problem that gave little anxiety at first was his relations with my young black cat. Peter had come to live in the London house while Taffy was with his family down at Rye, and he did not approve of the advent of a dog who, while he was daintily lapping his milk of a morning, swallowed the whole of it in a few comprehensive licks, and chased the saucer about the floor with his tongue to make sure he had secured the last drop. Peter leaped on to the dresser and regarded this rude black robber with malignant eyes. For a while he had his meals served there out of reach, but presently he developed a *schwärm*. When Taffy was asleep he crept near him, sat down and watched him, and then put out a sheathed paw and touched him gently on the nose. Taffy opened an eye, saw who it was, and went to sleep again. Presently he began to like Peter: he was seen, as if rather ashamed of such a weakness, surreptitiously to lick Peter's face, he let Peter play with his ball; and before long, Peter cuddled up close to him as he lay on the floor. They were both black as night, and silky haired: it was impossible to see where dog stopped and cat began.

As soon as Taffy saw his other home at Rye, he fell for it: from the first moment it enchanted him. But he did not enchant the large marmalade-coloured cat who lived there. Sandy spat and scolded, and never in the eight years they were there together did they become friendly. Again and again they were on the verge of a scrap, but they got to understand that they must put up with each other as best they could. The garden particularly took Taffy's fancy; he was quick to learn that the lawn and the path were his but not the flower-beds, and when he bit off a small bough from my miniature oak-tree he did it from the path. . . . His duties presented no fresh features, except that when he went shopping in the morning he carried a market basket, like the ladies of Rye: every evening he went to fetch the paper, which he brought to the garden-room. He understood that Sandy had a right to use the garden (and even sit in the flower-beds, since no one could prevent him) but other cats were not allowed. He galloped round in search of trespassers, and if he encountered Sandy he jumped over him. . . . The dogs of Rye liked him as little as he liked them: I think he gave himself airs as being a fashionable London dog on holiday. There was no fight, because he was not a fighter by nature and nobody felt inclined to be the aggressor against so large and powerful an adversary; but there were critical moments, when he and two or three others walked round in circles on tip-toe, very slowly and stiffly with various rituals for which I can offer no explanation. When dogs are behaving like that, any interference on the part of owners will almost certainly precipitate a row. Left to themselves they will probably solve the dangerous situation by these diplomatic exchanges and go on their ways without loss of prestige. . . .

There were expeditions to the sea. The sea proved not to be drinkable, but it was fringed with sand dunes among which on his first visit, he put up a rabbit. They were difficult country for hunting, for the steep slopes poured down avalanches of dry sand that smothered the feet, but the hope of some day finding another rabbit never left him. It was thirsty work under a summer sun, and so a bottle of proper water was carried by the expedition, and after Taffy had finished with the sand dunes, it was tilted into his mouth and he was very adroit in swallowing without spilling much. To get to the sea he had to travel by the steam-tram from Rye, which started on the far side of the River Rother, and if his afternoon walk lay in that direction, Taffy used to rush on ahead, get into a tram if there was one standing in the station, and wait for his friends. If they did not intend to go to the sea, it was disappointing after so pretty a piece of inductive reasoning to be hauled out. At tea-time the dining-room was reserved exclusively for Sandy, for that was his hour for drinking vast quantities of milk, and the presence of the blasted black dog filled him with such disgust that his appetite completely vanished. Punctually at ten every night, when drinks were brought out to the garden-room, Taffy made his last tour of the garden, barking loudly, so that any trespassing cat had plenty of time to get away, and with the sense of duty done, he retired to his rug in the pantry.

From *Final Edition*

W. H. DAVIES

D is for Dog

My dog went mad and bit my hand,
  I was bitten to the bone:
My wife went walking out with him,
  And then came back alone.

I smoked my pipe, I nursed my wound,
  I saw them both depart:
But when my wife came back alone,
  I was bitten to the heart.

A Poet and his Dog

Still do I claim no man can reach
  His highest soul's perfection,
Until his life, from day to day,
  Deserves a dog's affection.

We will now go back to the Mont Blanc, where Edward Garnett presided over the midday meal. Now, after that meal, Edward Thomas and myself would go along to the St George's Restaurant in St Martin's Lane, where there would be another gathering to tea, presided over by

Edward Thomas. The regular attendants were Edward Thomas, Ralph Hodgson, myself, and one or two others. Strange young writers came occasionally, being invited by Edward Thomas after he had reviewed their books in the various papers.

Hodgson was a man to my own mind, for we both preferred to talk of dogs and prizefighters instead of poets and poetry. He was very seldom seen without his dog, and the same words could be applied to him, with a little difference, as to the Mary of our childhood days, when we read –

> 'And everywhere that Mary went,
> The lamb was sure to go.'

The sight of Hodgson and his dog always reminded me of those words, altered to fit his particular case –

> 'And everywhere that Hodgson went,
> The dog was sure to go.'

*   *   *

At one time Hodgson used to come to my place to lunch once a week, bringing his bull-terrier along with him, for whom a special meal had been prepared. The dog knew this so well that he no sooner turned the corner of my street than it took all his master's strength to keep him in hand. And when they were in the house the dog used so much strength in entering the room that his master had to follow in the best shape he could command.

One day Hodgson was white with temper. It seems that a small black cat had chased the two of them up Charing Cross Road, and Hodgson had to run – not for his own life or his dog's – but for the cat's life. Hodgson knew that the cat was behind him, but the dog did not. So when he gave his dog more freedom to run, the dog took advantage and pulled harder and harder, until both master and dog were running for their lives. Seeing her enemies in full flight increased the cat's courage, of course, and she followed faster and faster, until she had chased them the whole length of Charing Cross Road. What made Hodgson so indignant was this – that Mooster, his big, strong bull-terrier, could have killed twenty cats in as many minutes, and yet he had to be made to run away from *one*, and a small one at that.

However, Hodgson soon got over this, and looking affectionately at his dog, said – 'Why doesn't Davies sell his books and buy a bull pup?'

This advice may sound amusing to others, expecially literary men, but to me it was quite a serious matter. For I would never think of keeping a dog or, for that matter, any other pet animal, unless I could give it close and proper attention; and it would only be as a married man that I would be able to do that. What has kept me from keeping pet animals has not been my indifference to them, but my great love of them. My life has been in danger on several occasions, but I have always counted my adventure with a certain strange dog as one of my most trying experiences. This was in the wilds of America, when I had to threaten a dog for over ten minutes, to prevent him from becoming more friendly and making me his master. Under the circumstances, I persuaded myself that I acted wisely for the both of us, in giving that poor creature a chance to find a more prosperous master.

*　　*　　*

Some time after this Hodgson and I went there again to dinner, again accompanied by a third friend – Mooster, his big, brown bull-terrier, who quickly won the admiration of the head waiter. For before either Hodgson or myself received one little morsel of food, that waiter had brought Mooster a large dish of bones, with the remark – 'This is yours, sir.' These bones the dog, with his strong, white dreadnoughts of teeth, crunched through with so much ease that we were all frightened at the sound. And it was no wonder that the gentleman who sat in the seat at the back of us was afraid to offer one word of complaint, when Mooster sat up and began to lick him all over his bald head. As the gentleman with the bald head did not appear to relish this as much as the dog, the latter had to be drawn back by force and quietly rebuked for his greed in wanting a second meal, when he had already had several pounds of meaty bones.

When we had finished dinner Hodgson asked me if I was in any hurry to get back home. On hearing that I was not, he proposed a walk, and off we went. But although I made every effort to start a conversation with Hodgson, and to sustain it, I failed every time. Sometimes, when I had asked him a question, and was expecting an answer, I saw, to my surprise, that Hodgson was five or six feet away from me, either in front or behind. At first I thought he must have had something serious on his mind and was unhappy. One moment we would be standing in the full light, and the next moment we would be standing in a dark doorway.

One moment we would be in the main street, and the next moment in a dark, narrow alley. But although I could not account for this, I was determined not to question Hodgson, but to wait and find out the meaning for myself. However, I now began to realize that the dog was not following his master, but that the master was following his dog. I began to wonder why I was there at all. For instance, the dog went where he liked and ignored the both of us; and his master could not give me the attention that was due to me as a friend and a companion, however much he would have liked to do so.

This strange behaviour of man and beast went on until we came to Carlton House Terrace, and it was now that I began to have some fear of the consequence. For it was soon obvious to me that we were trespassing on private property, and that Mooster was to blame for it. Not only that, but the houses, which had been in darkness until then, suddenly began to show lights in their porches and windows, and there were sounds of the opening and bolting of doors. Our presence had been discovered, that was certain; not because we made a great noise, but because the place had a churchyard quietness about it.

'Hodgson,' I said, 'we'll be arrested, for I believe we are trespassing.'

'It's all right now,' answered Hodgson in a happy voice, 'Mooster is very particular where he raises his leg, but it's all right now.'

It was now, for the first time, that I had the least idea of why we had undertaken that strange walk. 'Particular,' thought I, 'so I should think, seeing that we are in the neighbourhood of palaces and select clubs.'

The walk back home was much less exciting, for we all kept close together, Hodgson and I talking, and the dog listening to our conversation.

From *Later Days*

RALPH HODGSON

Dulcina, a Bull Terrier

Dulcina was, then suns rebelled
And trod th'eternal word;
To every ball its limits held,
The universe was stirred.

World embryons, in chaos rolled,
Knew system at her cry,
And hoary planets ages cold
Policed anew the sky.

Suns came and sun's star's satellites
To sing Dulcina's power,
And myriad moons left myriad nights
To keep a pagan hour.

In rebel red extravagance
The flaming legions came;
In her transplendent brilliance
They paled to candle flame,

And praised above all dams her dam,
And gave her sire reward,
And hailed me blest o'er all who am
Her bondman and her lord;

Who sees in her all things glassed fair
And Paradise would fly,
That wanting her were angel bare
And drear felicity.

JOHN WEST

The Dog Orchestra

THE 'DOG ORCHESTRA' is the property of Mr Louis Lavater and a very respectable property it is. Anyone with a head for figures can calculate the profits on the investment. Mr Lavater pays from eighteenpence to five shillings (never more) for a dog, and the orchestra brings him in £50 or £60 a week.

The orchestra consists of six dogs, gorgeously dressed, and provided with specially made instruments. They are not remarkable for pedigree, but they *are* remarkable for intelligence. Let us introduce these canine instrumentalists.

Jack is the trombone player. Next comes Tim, the bass; followed by Patsey, the first violin; Prince, the big drum; Peter, the cymbals; and Bob, the small drum. The bows, drumsticks, etc., are fixed to the dogs' paws by means of little bracelets.

Mr Lavater has been a public entertainer (and a lover of dogs) all his life. Many years ago, whilst performing with a circus at Copenhagen, he resolved to set about getting his dog orchestra together for it had long been his pet idea. He therefore went to the Dogs' Home in the Danish capital and paid five kroner for a nondescript cur. He took that cur home, fastened a stick on his paw, and persuaded him to beat a tea-tray. This same mongrel's musical education was in a fair way to be completed, when his master had to get rid of him on account of his pugnacious disposition.

Here is Jack, the trombone player. Now, it is a comparatively easy matter to get a dog to stand upon his hind legs, but give him a relatively heavy instrument to hold in his front paws the while, and see if he does not overbalance himself and relapse into his natural position. Jack had to be taught to stand on his hind legs for half an hour at a time; next, to balance himself, holding the trombone in position; then to work the instrument properly; and, finally, to act in conjunction with his colleagues. And this with six different dogs, having six different instruments, to say nothing of the 'funny' dog, who makes blunders purposely, and is betrayed by his neighbour, who leaves his instrument and 'informs' in his master's ear! The thing seems impossible, but was not so to Mr Lavater, to whose skill and patience and humour and fertility of imagination the dog orchestra is a living monument.

But look at Jack, the trombone player. Long association with that doleful instrument has made Jack a mournful dog. It took him three months to learn to keep his balance. Mr Lavater was almost in despair at the end of the first, and bought Jack a pair of cymbals, each weighing 8oz. 'This,' thought Jack, 'is *not* beyond me,' and he pounded away at the 'sounding brasses' with no regard for tune. This dog has had an adventurous career. He was once locked up in Basle for wandering at large without a muzzle. He swam across Niagara rapids, and has been 'held up' by robbers in America.

It is Mrs Lavater who makes the dresses for members of the orchestra. Tim, the bass viol player, wears an almost painfully sumptuous suit of bright green satin. He is a Maltese, is Tim, and this is probably why he wears at all times an air of dignified alertness, as who should say, 'I'm doing my very best, but don't trifle with me.' Tim's immediate predecessor had a rooted objection to all forms of work. He was as obstinate as he was lazy, and so he had to go.

Mr Lavater was years getting together his orchestra and rehearsing before he ventured to appear in public. The *debut* took place in a theatre near Amsterdam, and the trainer won't forget it this side of his grave. 'They came out reluctantly,' he said, 'dazed by the glare of the footlights. When they *were* out, they sat there looking helplessly at each other as if to say: "What on earth are we doing here?" Then they did wrong things at wrong moments. Prince fell over his big drum. The others got up and tore aimlessly about the stage, scared by the trailing of their instruments behind them; and to crown all Jack, the trombone "man," fell into the (human) orchestra. My Dutch audience were hysterical with merriment and even my wife, who stood in the wings, couldn't help laughing in spite of her vexation and dismay.'

The first violin is next represented – a quiet, sober dog, of evident culture and refinement. Not even the highly inappropriate clown cap, stuck rakishly one one side of his head, can detract from this animal's musicianly appearance. Patsey – a hideous name for a canine Sarasate – is clothed in a dress of green and mauve-striped silk. We fear his real character belies his appearance, however. He is always in trouble, being – like Esau – a mighty hunter, mainly of cats and people's pets generally.

Prince, who plays the big drum, has but one fault – he is too excitable, too strenuous. He is panting with excitement; his sharp little teeth are showing; he is pounding away for dear life. And yet he occupies the position of deputy-conductor under Mr Lavater himself! However, although Prince may lack the composure of a Mottl, a Richter, or a

Seidl, yet he makes up for it in feverish zeal. He is a Yorkshire, and affects a suit of pink and white satin.

'The first big drummer I had,' remarked Mr Lavater, 'I bought at Frankfort. He was a half-bred terrier. I took him away and tied him up, but he broke loose time after time and ran back to his master, who was a stableman. He was a queer dog. At rehearsals, and even on the stage during public performances, he would wait until I wasn't looking and then he'd give his nearest neighbour a sharp nip. For a long time I could never make out what caused those frightful yowls now and again, because, after biting his fellow, Prince would thump his drum anxiously, as though his soul was in his work and he wanted to get along with the show.'

This dog went mad on board a steamer going from Rotterdam to Antwerp. It was the funniest sight imaginable. The dog had the deck to himself in less than ten seconds. The captain wanted to have Prince thrown overboard, but Mr Lavater wouldn't hear of his property being disposed of in that way. The trainer threw some water over the dog, and that brought him round – for a time. Not long afterwards he went mad again, and finally ran himself to death in the streets of Antwerp. Another member of the orchestra was torn to pieces by pariah dogs in the streets of Constantinople. The present big drummer, Prince, was bought from a butcher in Hamburg, so they are a cosmopolitan lot, these performers.

It took one or two of the dogs some time to forget their former owners after passing into Mr Lavater's possession. Bob, the small drum, belonged to a widow who kept a perfumery shop, and for years that dog would run after ladies with black dresses.

Next comes Peter, the cymbal player. Many vicissitudes has Peter seen. Originally he belonged to a Paris *chiffonier*, or rag-picker. He used to go out o' nights with his master and mind the little cart, whilst unconsidered trifles were being gathered in. Peter is an Irish terrier, and he is a little sentimental. Peter seems to be crooning a simple love song, accompanying himself on the cymbals. This is the manner of the whole performance, as told by Mr Lavater:–

'The dogs follow me on to the stage and take their seats – the small drum first, then the big drum, the bass, the first violin, the cymbals, and last of all, the serious trombone. I stand up in the middle and commence by playing "The Girl I left Behind Me." A waltz comes next, and then the dogs follow with "The Last Rose of Summer" – played, I should explain, by means of bells on their paws, and not by their several instruments. It was an awful job to get them to play the bells properly. Either they would all play together or not at all. Later on in the performance, I call upon the dogs to sound a preliminary chord. They do so, and I say, "That is a false chord." Prince, the big drum, then hops up officiously and whispers something in my ear, whereupon I say, aloud, "Oh, is he, indeed? Tim, I hear it is you who are out of tune."'

Mr Lavater tells us that each dog knows his own dress, so that the moment it is held up he runs forward to push his little head into it. The dogs are fed well – their ordinary diet consisting of biscuit, soup, bread, rice, and occasionally boiled cabbage. Each acting member has an understudy, so as to avoid hitches when the unforeseen happens. A former 'big drum' came to a bad end on board an Atlantic liner by swallowing a lot of tow or jute, with which the engineers had been cleaning the machinery.

The last member of the orchestra to be introduced is Bob, the little drum. Bob is a water-spaniel, whose lines are cast in pleasant places. He is a painstaking dog, devoted to his profession. He is apt to thieve a little, but he is very lovable with it. 'He forgot himself one night,' remarked Mr Lavater, sternly, 'and made away with a pound of steak. I didn't beat him; I never do. I ignored him. He became penitent at once, and tried to attract my attention, but I would not look up from my paper. At last he was struck with an idea. He knew that whenever he did a smart thing he was applauded, so patting my knee eagerly with his paw to attract my attention for a moment, he began to parade across the hearth-rug, on his hind legs!'

Asked as to whether the dogs and their instruments were inter-changeable so to speak, Mr Lavater sadly replied that they were not. 'One night I tried it,' he said. 'I put the first violin on the big drum, and *vice-versa*. The result was comic in the extreme. The big drum began to bang his fiddle as though he would knock a hole through it, whilst the first violin seized his stick and began to draw it slowly across his drum.'

At the same time, the dogs have a keen sense of duty. Mr Lavater was one evening taking them in his brougham to the theatre, when suddenly a Volunteer band struck up outside. The effect was extraordinary. The dogs leaped up in their baskets. One commenced to saw the air, another to clap his paws together, and so on. They thought they had received their cue, and they hastened to respond according to their lights, notwithstanding the trying circumstances.

Strand Magazine, 1897

A. E. HOUSMAN
Curmudgeon

IT WAS A great comfort to me not to have you with me in Constantinople: it would have been 'poor doggie!' every step of the way, and
we should never have got a hundred yards from the hotel. They lie all
about the streets and the pavement, mostly asleep, and almost all have
got something the matter with them. They are extremely meek and
inoffensive: Turkey is a country where dogs and women are kept in
their proper place, and consequently are quite unlike the pampered and
obstreperous animals we know under those names in England. The
Turkish dog spends his life much like the English cat: he sleeps by day,
and at night he grows melodious. He does not bark over his quarrels so
much as English dogs do, and when he does bark it is sometimes rather
like the quacking of a soprano duck; but he wails: whether he is winning
or losing seems to make no difference, so dejected are his spirits. I soon
got used to the noise, however, and it did not spoil my sleep. The
people are very good in not treading on them, and so are the beasts of
burden; but wheeled vehicles, which have got much commoner of late
years, are less good to them, and the trams are not good to them at all.
One night in the dark I trod on a dog lying exactly in the middle of the
road: he squealed in a bitterly reproachful tone for a certain time; when
he had finished, the next dog barked in an expostulatory manner for the
same period, and then the incident was closed.

Letter to his stepmother, 1904

HENRY LAWSON
The Loaded Dog

DAVE REGAN, JIM BENTLY, and Andy Page were sinking a shaft
at Stony Creek in search of a rich gold quartz reef which was
supposed to exist in the vicinity. There is always a rich reef supposed to

exist in the vicinity; the only questions are whether it is ten feet or hundreds beneath the surface, and in which direction. They had struck some pretty solid rock, also water which kept them bailing. They used the old-fashioned blasting-powder and time-fuse. They'd make a sausage or cartridge of blasting-powder in a skin of strong calico or canvas, the mouth sewn and bound round the end of the fuse; they'd dip the cartridge in melted tallow to make it watertight, get the drill-hole as dry as possible, drop in the cartridge with some dry dust, and wad and ram with stiff clay and broken brick. Then they'd light the fuse and get out of the hole and wait. The result was usually an ugly pot-hole in the bottom of the shaft and half a barrow-load of broken rock.

There was plenty of fish in the creek, fresh-water bream, cod, cat-fish, and tailers. The party were fond of fish, and Andy and Dave of fishing. Andy would fish for three hours at a stretch if encouraged by a nibble or a bite now and then – say once in twenty minutes. The butcher was always willing to give meat in exchange for fish when they caught more than they could eat; but now it was winter, and these fish wouldn't bite. However, the creek was low, just a chain of muddy waterholes, from the hole with a few bucketfuls in it to the sizeable pool with an average depth of six or seven feet, and they could get fish by bailing out the smaller holes or muddying up the water in the larger ones till the fish rose to the surface. There was the cat-fish, with spikes growing out of the sides of its head, and if you got pricked you'd know it, as Dave said. Andy took off his boots, tucked up his trousers, and went into a hole one day to stir up the mud with his feet, and he knew it. Dave scooped one out with his hand and got pricked, and he knew it too; his arm swelled, and the pain throbbed up into his shoulder, and down into his stomach, too, he said, like a toothache he had once, and kept him awake for two nights – only the toothache pain had a 'burred edge', Dave said.

Dave got an idea.

'Why not blow the fish up in the big waterhole with a cartridge?' he said. 'I'll try it.'

He thought the thing out and Andy Page worked it out. Andy usually put Dave's theories into practice if they were practicable, or bore the blame for the failure and the chaffing of his mates if they weren't.

He made a cartridge about three times the size of those they used in the rock. Jim Bently said it was big enough to blow the bottom out of the river. The inner skin was of stout calico; Andy stuck the end of a six-foot piece of fuse well down in the powder and bound the mouth of the bag firmly to it with whipcord. The idea was to sink the cartridge in the water with the open end of the fuse attached to a float on the surface, ready for lighting. Andy dipped the cartridge in melted bees-wax to make it watertight. 'We'll have to leave it some time before we light it,' said Dave, 'to give the fish time to get over their scare when we put it in, and come nosing round again; so we'll want it well watertight.'

Round the cartridge Andy, at Dave's suggestion, bound a strip of sail canvas – that they used for making water-bags – to increase the force of the explosion, and round that he pasted layers of stiff brown paper – on the plan of the sort of fireworks we called 'gun-crackers'. He let the paper dry in the sun, then he sewed a covering of two thicknesses of canvas over it, and bound the thing from end to end with stout fishing-line. Dave's schemes were elaborate, and he often worked his inventions out to nothing. The cartridge was rigid and solid enough now – a formidable bomb; but Andy and Dave wanted to be sure. Andy sewed on another layer of canvas, dipped the cartridge in melted tallow, twisted a length of fencing-wire round it as an afterthought, dipped it in tallow again, and stood it carefully against a tent-peg, where he'd know where to find it, and wound the fuse loosely round it. Then he went to the camp-fire to try some potatoes which were boiling in their jackets in a billy, and to see about frying some chops for dinner. Dave and Jim were at work in the claim that morning.

They had a big black young retriever dog – or rather an overgrown pup, a big, foolish, four-footed mate, who was always slobbering round them and lashing their legs with his heavy tail that swung round like a stockwhip. Most of his head was usually a red, idiotic slobbering grin of appreciation of his own silliness. He seemed to take life, the world, his two-legged mates, and his own instinct as a huge joke. He'd retrieve anything; he carted back most of the camp rubbish that Andy threw away. They had a cat that died in hot weather, and Andy threw it a good distance away in the scrub; and early one morning the dog found the cat, after it had been dead a week or so, and carried it back to camp, and laid it just inside the tent-flaps, where it could best make its presence known when the mates should rise and begin to sniff suspiciously in the sickly smothering atmosphere of the summer sunrise. He used to retrieve them when they went in swimming; he'd jump in after them, and take their hands in his mouth, and try to swim out with them, and scratch their naked bodies with his paws. They loved him for his good-heartedness and his foolishness, but when they wished to enjoy a swim they had to tie him up in the camp.

He watched Andy with great interest all the morning making the cartridge, and hindered him considerably, trying to help; but about noon he went off to the claim to see how Dave and Jim were getting on, and to come home to dinner with them. Andy saw them coming, and put a panful of mutton-chops on the fire. Andy was cook today; Dave and Jim stood with their backs to the fire, as bushmen do in all weathers, waiting till dinner should be ready. The retriever went nosing after something he seemed to have missed.

Andy's brain still worked on the cartridge; his eye was caught by the glare of an empty kerosene-tin lying in the bushes, and it struck him that it wouldn't be a bad idea to sink the cartridge packed with clay, sand, or stones in the tin, to increase the force of the explosion. He may have been all out, from a scientific point of view, but the notion looked all right to him. Jim Bently, by the way, wasn't interested in their 'damned silliness'. Andy noticed an empty treacle-tin – the sort with the little tin neck or spout soldered on to the top for the convenience of pouring out the treacle – and it struck him that this would have made the best kind of cartridge-case: he would only have had to pour in the powder, stick the fuse in through the neck, and cork and seal it with bees-wax. He was turning to suggest this to Dave, when Dave glanced over his shoulder to see how the chops were doing – and bolted. He explained afterwards that he thought he heard the pan spluttering extra, and looked to see if the chops were burning. Jim Bently looked behind and bolted after Dave. Andy stood stock-still, staring after them.

'Run, Andy! Run!' they shouted back at him. 'Run! Look behind you, you fool!' Andy turned slowly and looked, and there, close behind him, was the retriever with the cartridge in his mouth – wedged into his broadest and silliest grin. And that wasn't all. The dog had come round the fire to Andy, and the loose end of the fuse had trailed and waggled over the burning sticks into the blaze; Andy had slit and nicked the firing end of the fuse well, and now it was hissing and spitting properly.

Andy's legs started with a jolt; his legs started before his brain did, and he made after Dave and Jim. And the dog followed Andy.

Dave and Jim were good runners – Jim the best – for a short distance; Andy was slow and heavy, but he had the strength and the wind and could last. The dog capered round him, delighted as a dog could be to find his mates, as he thought, on for a frolic. Dave and Jim kept shouting back, 'Don't foller us! Don't foller us, you coloured fool!' But Andy kept on, no matter how they dodged. They could never explain, any more than the dog, why they followed each other, but so they ran,

Dave keeping in Jim's track in all its turnings, Andy after Dave, and the dog circling round Andy – the live fuse swishing in all directions and hissing and spluttering and stinking. Jim yelling to Dave not to follow him, Dave shouting to Andy to go in another direction – to 'spread out', and Andy roaring at the dog to go home. Then Andy's brain began to work, stimulated by the crisis: he tried to get a running kick at the dog, but the dog dodged; he snatched up sticks and stones and threw them at the dog and ran on again. The retriever saw that he'd made a mistake about Andy, and left him and bounded after Dave. Dave, who had the presence of mind to think that the fuse's time wasn't up yet, made a dive and a grab for the dog, caught him by the tail, and as he swung round snatched the cartridge out of his mouth and flung it as far as he could; the dog immediately bounded after it and retrieved it. Dave roared and cursed at the dog, who, seeing that Dave was offended, left him and went after Jim, who was well ahead. Jim swung to a sapling and went up it like a native bear; it was a young sapling, and Jim couldn't safely get more than ten or twelve feet from the ground. The dog laid the cartridge, as carefully as if it were a kitten, at the foot of the sapling, and capered and leaped and whooped joyously round under Jim. The big pup reckoned that this was part of the lark – he was all right now – it was Jim who was out for a spree. The fuse sounded as if it were going a mile a minute. Jim tried to climb higher and the sapling bent and cracked. Jim fell on his feet and ran. The dog swooped on the cartridge and followed. It all took but a very few moments. Jim ran to a digger's hole, about ten feet deep, and dropped down into it – landing on soft mud – and was safe. The dog grinned sardonically down on him, over the edge, for a moment, as if he thought it would be a good lark to drop the cartridge down on Jim.

'Go away, Tommy,' said Jim feebly, 'go away.'

The dog bounded off after Dave, who was the only one in sight now; Andy had dropped behind a log, where he lay flat on his face, having suddenly remembered a picture of the Russo-Turkish war with a circle of Turks lying flat on their faces (as if they were ashamed) round a newly-arrived shell.

There was a small hotel or shanty on the creek, on the main road, not far from the claim. Dave was desperate, the time flew much faster in his stimulated imagination than it did in reality, so he made for the shanty. There were several casual bushmen on the veranda and in the bar; Dave rushed into the bar, banging the door to behind him. 'My dog!' he gasped, in reply to the astonished stare of the publican, 'the blanky retriever – he's got a live cartridge in his mouth – '

The retriever, finding the front door shut against him, had bounded round and in by the back way, and now stood smiling in the doorway leading from the passage, the cartridge still in his mouth and the fuse spluttering. They burst out of that bar; Tommy bounded first after one and then after another, for, being a young dog, he tried to make friends with everybody.

The bushmen ran round corners, and some shut themselves in the stable. There was a new weatherboard and corrugated-iron kitchen and wash-house on piles in the backyard, with some women washing clothes inside. Dave and the publican bundled in there and shut the door – the publican cursing Dave and calling him a crimson fool, in hurried tones, and wanting to know what the hell he came here for.

The retriever went in under the kitchen, amongst the piles, but, luckily for those inside, there was a vicious yellow mongrel cattle-dog sulking and nursing his nastiness under there – a sneaking, fighting, thieving canine, whom neighbours had tried for years to shoot or poison. Tommy saw his danger – he'd had experience from this dog – and started out and across the yard, still sticking to the cartridge. Half-way across the yard the yellow dog caught him and nipped him. Tommy dropped the cartridge, gave one terrified yell, and took to the bush. The yellow dog followed him to the fence and then ran back to see what he had dropped. Nearly a dozen other dogs came from round all the corners and under the buildings – spidery, thievish, cold-blooded kangaroo-dogs, mongrel sheep- and cattle-dogs, vicious black and yellow dogs – that slip after you in the dark, nip your heels, and vanish without explaining – and yapping, yelping small fry. They kept at a respectable distance round the nasty yellow dog, for it was dangerous to go near him when he thought he had found something which might be good for a dog or cat. He sniffed at the cartridge twice, and was just taking a third cautious sniff when –

It was very good blasting-powder – a new brand that Dave had recently got up from Sydney; and the cartridge had been excellently well made. Andy was very patient and painstaking in all he did, and nearly as handy as the average sailor with needles, twine, canvas and rope.

Bushmen say that that kitchen jumped off its piles and on again. When the smoke and dust cleared away, the remains of the nasty yellow dog were lying against the paling fence of the yard looking as if he had been kicked into a fire by a horse and afterwards rolled in the dust under a barrow, and finally thrown against the fence from a distance. Several saddle-horses, which had been 'hanging-up' round the veranda, were galloping wildly down the road in clouds of dust, with broken bridle-reins flying; and from a circle round the outskirts, from every point of the compass in the scrub, came the yelping of dogs. Two of them went home, to the place where they were born, thirty miles away, and reached it the same night and stayed there; it was not till towards evening that the rest came back cautiously to make inquiries. One was trying to walk on two legs, and most of 'em looked more or less singed; and a little, singed, stumpy-tailed dog, who had been in the habit of hopping the back half of him along on one leg, had reason to be glad that he'd saved up the other leg all those years, for he needed it now. There was one old one-eyed cattle-dog round that shanty for years afterwards, who couldn't stand the smell of a gun being cleaned. He it was who had taken an interest, only second to that of the yellow dog, in the cartridge. Bushmen said that it was amusing to slip up on his blind side and stick a dirty ramrod under his nose: he wouldn't wait to bring his solitary eye to bear – he'd take to the bush and stay out all night.

For half an hour or so after the explosion there were several bushmen round behind the stable who crouched, doubled up, against the wall, or rolled gently on the dust, trying to laugh without shrieking. There were two white women in hysterics at the house, and a half-caste rushing aimlessly round with a dipper of cold water. The publican was holding his wife tight and begging her between her squawks, to 'Hold up for my sake, Mary, or I'll lam the life out of ye!'

Dave decided to apologize later on, 'when things had settled a bit', and went back to camp. And the dog that had done it all, Tommy, the great, idiotic mongrel retriever, came slobbering round Dave and lashing his legs with his tail, and trotted home after him, smiling his broadest, longest, and reddest smile of amiability, and apparently satisfied for one afternoon with the fun he'd had.

Andy chained the dog up securely, and cooked some more chops, while Dave went to help Jim out of the hole.

And most of this is why, for years afterwards, lanky, easygoing bushmen, riding lazily past Dave's camp, would cry, in a lazy drawl and with just a hint of the nasal twang:

"Ello, Da-a-ve! How's the fishin' getting on, Da-a-ve?"

SIR PERCY FITZPATRICK

Encounters en route

ON TREK THERE were always new places to see, new roads to travel, and new things to examine, tackle or avoid. He learnt something fresh almost every day: he learnt, for instance, that, although it was shady and cool under the waggon, it was not good enough to lie in the wheel track, not even for the pleasure of feeling the cool iron tyre against your back or head as you slept; and he knew that, because one day he had done it and the wheel had gone over his foot; and it might just as easily have been his back or head. Fortunately the sand was soft and his foot was not crushed; but he was very lame for some days, and had to travel on the waggon.

He learned a good deal from Jess: among other things, that it was not necessary to poke his nose up against a snake in order to find out what it was. He knew that Jess would fight anything; and when one day he saw her back hair go up and watched her sheer off the footpath wide into the grass, he did the same; and then when we had shot the snake, both he and Jess came up very very cautiously and sniffed at it, with every hair on their bodies standing up.

He found out for himself that it was not a good idea to turn a scorpion over with his paw. The vicious little tail with a thorn in it whipped over the scorpion's back, and Jock had such a foot that he must have thought a scorpion worse than two waggons. He was a very sick dog for some days; but after that, whenever he saw a thing that he did not understand, he would watch it very carefully from a little way off and notice what it did and what it looked like, before trying experiments.

So, little by little, Jock got to understand plenty of things that no town dog would ever know, and he got to know – just as some people do – by what we call instinct, whether a thing was dangerous or safe, even though he had never seen anything like it before. That is how he knew that wolves or lions were about – and that they were dangerous – when he heard or scented them; although he had never seen, scented or heard one before to know what sort of animal it might be. You may well wonder how he could tell whether the scent or the cry belonged to a wolf which he must avoid, or to a buck which he might hunt, when he had never seen either a wolf or a buck at the time; but he did know;

and he also knew that no dog could safely go outside the ring of the camp fires when wolf or lion was about. I have known many town-bred dogs that could scent them just as well as Jess or Jock could, but having no instinct of danger they went out to see what it was, and of course they never came back.

* * *

A friend of my mine once told me a story about a dog of his and the trouble he had with fowls. Several of us had been discussing the characters of dogs, and the different emotions they feel and manage to express, and the kind of things they seem to think about. Every one knows that a dog can feel angry, frightened, pleased, and disappointed. Any one who knows dogs will tell you that they can also feel anxious, hopeful, nervous, inquisitive, surprised, ashamed, interested, sad, loving, jealous, and contended – just like human beings.

We had told many stories illustrating this, when my friend asked the question: 'Have dogs a sense of humour?' Now I know that Jock looked very foolish the day he fought the table-leg – and a silly old hen made him look just as foolish another day – but that is not quite what my friend meant. On both occasions Jock clearly felt that he had made himself look ridiculous; but he was very far from looking amused. The question was: Is a dog capable of sufficient thinking to appreciate a simple joke, and is it possible for a dog to feel amused. If Jess had seen Jock bursting to fight the table-leg would she have seen the joke? Well, I certainly did not think so; but he said he was quite certain some dogs have a sense of humour; and he had had proof of it.

He told the story very gravely, but I really do not even now know whether he – Well, here it is: He had once owned a savage old watch-dog, whose box stood in the back-yard where he was kept chained up all day; he used to be fed once a day – in the mornings – and the great plague of his life was the fowls. They ran loose in the yard and picked up food all day, besides getting a really good feed of grain morning and evening; possibly the knowledge of this made the old dog particularly angry when they would come round by ones or twos or dozens trying to steal part of his one meal. Anyhow, he hated them, and whenever he got a chance killed them. The old fowls learned to keep out of his way and never ventured within his reach unless they were quite sure that he was asleep or lying in his kennel where he could not see them; but there were always new fowls coming, or young ones growing up; and so the war went on.

One Sunday morning my friend was enjoying a smoke on his back stoep when feeding time came round. The cook took the old dog's food to him in a high three-legged pot, and my friend, seeing the fowls begin to gather round and wishing to let the old dog have his meal in peace, told the cook to give the fowls a good feed in another part of the yard to draw them off. So the old fellow polished off his food and licked the pot clean, leaving not a drop or a speck behind.

But fowls are very greedy; they were soon back again wandering about, with their active-looking eyes searching everything. The old dog, feeling pretty satisfied with life, picked out a sandy spot in the sunshine, threw himself down full stretch on his side, and promptly went to sleep – at peace with all the world. Immediately he did this, out stepped a long-legged athletic-looking young cockerel and began to advance against the enemy. As he got nearer he slowed down, and looked first with one eye and then with the other so as to make sure that all was safe, and several times he paused with one foot poised high before deciding to take the next step. My friend was greatly amused to see all the trouble that the fowl was taking to get up to the empty pot, and, for the fun of giving the conceited young cockerel a fright, threw a pebble at him. He was so nervous that when the pebble dropped near him, he gave one great bound and tore off flapping and screaming down the yard as if he thought the old dog was after him. The old fellow himself was startled out of his sleep, and raised his head to see what the row was about; but, as nothing more happened, he lay down again, and the cockerel, finding also that it was a false alarm, turned back not a bit ashamed for another try.

The cockerel had not seen the old dog lift his head; my friend had, and when he looked again he saw that, although the underneath eye – half buried in the sand – was shut, the top eye was open and was steadily watching the cockerel as he came nearer and nearer to the pot. My friend sat dead still, expecting a rush and another fluttering scramble. At last the cockerel took the final step, craned his neck to its utmost and peered down into the empty pot. The old dog gave two gentle pats with his tail in the sand, and closing his eye went to sleep again.

*   *   *

I took the rifle and went with the herd boy; Jim followed close behind, walking on his toes with the waltzy springy movement of an ostrich, eager to get ahead and repeatedly silenced and driven back by me in the few hundred yards' walk to the river.

A queer premonitory feeling came over me as I saw we were making straight for the bathing pool; but before reaching the bank the herd boy squatted down, indicating that somewhere in front and below us the enemy would be found. An easy crawl brought me to the river bank and, sure enough, on the very spot where I had stood to wash, only fifty yards from us, there was an enormous crocodile. He was lying along the sand-spit with his full length exposed to me. Such a shot would have been a moral certainty, but as I brought the rifle slowly up it may have glinted in the sun, or perhaps the crocodile had been watching us all the time, for with one easy turn and no splash at all he slid into the river and was gone.

It was very disgusting and I pitched into Jim and the other boys behind for having made a noise and shown themselves; but they were still squatting when I reached them and vowed they had neither moved nor spoken. We had already turned to go when there came a distant call from beyond the river. To me it was merely a kaffir's voice and a sound quite meaningless: but to the boys' trained ears it spoke clearly. Jim pressed me downwards and we all squatted again.

'He is coming out on another sandbank,' Jim explained.

Again I crawled to the bank and lay flat, with the rifle ready. There was another sand streak a hundred yards out in the stream with two out-croppings of black rock at the upper end of it – they were rock right enough, for I had examined them carefully when bathing. This was the only other sankbank in sight: it was higher than it appeared to be from a distance and the crocodile whilst hidden from us was visible to the natives on the opposite bank as it lay in the shallow water and emerged inch by inch to resume its morning sun bath. The crocodile was so slow in showing up that I quite thought it had been scared off again, and I turned to examine other objects and spots up and down the stream; but presently glancing back at the bank again I saw what appeared to be a third rock, no bigger than a loaf of bread. This object I watched until my eyes ached and swam; it was the only possible crocodile; yet it was so small, so motionless, so permanent looking, it seemed absurd to doubt that it really was a stone which had passed unnoticed before.

As I watched unblinkingly it seemed to grow bigger and again contract with regular swing, as if it swelled and shrank with breathing; and knowing that this must be merely an optical delusion caused by staring too long, I shut my eyes for a minute. The effect was excellent:

the rock was much bigger; and after that it was easy to lie still and wait for the cunning old reptile to show himself.

It took half an hour of this cautious manœuvring and edging on the part of the crocodile before he was comfortably settled on the sand with the sun warming all his back. In the meantime the waggon boys behind me had not stirred; on the opposite side of the river kaffirs from the neighbouring kraal had gathered to the number of thirty or forty, men, women and children, and they stood loosely grouped, instinctively still silent and watchful, like a little scattered herd of deer. All on both sides were watching me and waiting for the shot. It seemed useless to delay longer; the whole length of the body was showing, but it looked so wanting in thickness, so shallow in fact, that it was evident the crocodile was lying, not on the top, but on the other slope of the sand spit; and probably not more than six or eight inches – in depth – of body was visible.

It was little enough to aim at, and the bullet seemed to strike the top of the bank first, sending up a column of sand, and then, probably knocked all out of shape, ploughed into the body with a tremendous thump.

The crocodile threw a back somersault – that is, it seemed to rear up on its tail and spring backwards; the jaws divided into a huge fork as, for a second, it stood up on end; and it let out an enraged roar, seemingly aimed at the heavens. It was a very sudden and dramatic effect, following on the long silence.

Then the whole world seemed to burst into indescribable turmoil; shouts and yells burst out on all sides; the kaffirs rushed down to the banks – the men armed with sticks and assegais, and the women and children with nothing more formidable than their voices; the crocodile was alive – very much alive – and in the water; the waggon boys, headed by Jim, were all round me and all yelling out together what should or should not be done, and what would happen if we did or did not do it. It was Babel and Bedlam let loose.

With the first plunge the crocodile disappeared, but it came up again ten yards away thrashing the water into foam and going up stream like a paddle-boat gone roaring mad – if one can imagine such a thing! I had another shot at him the instant he reappeared, but one could neither see nor hear where it struck; and again and again I fired whenever he showed up for a second. He appeared to be shot through the lungs; at any rate the kaffirs on the other bank, who were then quite close enough to see, said that it was so. The waggon boys had run down the bank out on to the first sand spit and I followed them shouting to the kaffirs opposite to get out of the line of fire, as I could no longer shoot without risk of hitting them.

The crocodile after his first straight dash up stream had tacked about in all directions during the next few minutes, disappearing for short spells and plunging out again in unexpected places. One of these sudden reappearances brought him once more abreast, and quite near to us, and Jim with a fierce yell and with his assegai held high in his right hand dashed into the water, going through the shallows in wild leaps. I called to him to come back but against his yells and the excited shouts of the ever-increasing crowd my voice could not live; and Jim, mad with excitement, went on. Twenty yards out, where increasing depth steadied him, he turned for a moment and seeing himself alone in the water called to me with eager confidence, 'Come on, Baas.'

It had never occurred to me that any one would be such an idiot as to go into water after a wounded crocodile. There was no need to finish off this one, for it was bound to die, and no one wanted the meat or skin. Who, then, would be so mad as to think of such a thing? Five minutes earlier I would have answered very confidently for myself; but there are times when one cannot afford to be sensible. There was a world of unconscious irony in Jim's choice of words '*Come* on!' and '*Baas!*'

The boy giving the lead to his master was too much for me; and in I went!

I cannot say that there was much enjoyment in it for the first few moments – not until the excitement took hold and all else was forgotten. The first thing that struck me was that in the deep water my rifle was worth no more than a walking-stick, and not nearly as useful as an assegai; but what drove this and many other thoughts from my mind in a second was the appearance of Jock on the stage and his sudden jump into the leading place.

In the first confusion he had passed unnoticed, probably at my heels as usual, but the instant I answered Jim's challenge by jumping into the water he gave one whimpering yelp of excitement and plunged in too; and in a few seconds he had outdistanced us all and was leading straight for the crocodile. I shouted to him, of course in vain – he heard nothing; and Jim and I plunged and struggled along to head the dog off.

As the crocodile came up Jock went straight for him – his eyes gleaming, his shoulders up, his nose out, his neck stretched to the utmost in his eagerness – and he ploughed along straining every muscle to catch up. When the crocodile went under he slackened and looked anxiously about, but each fresh rise was greeted by the whimpering yelps of intense suppressed excitement as he fairly hoisted himself out of the water with the vigour of his swimming.

The water was now breast-high for us, and we were far out in the stream, beyond the sand spit where the crocodile had lain, when the kaffirs on the bank got their first chance and a flight of assegais went at the enemy as he rose. Several struck and two remained in him; he rose again a few yards from Jim, and that sportsman let fly one that struck well home. Jock who had been toiling close behind for some time and gaining slowly, was not five yards off then; the floundering and lashing of the crocodile were bewildering, but on he went as grimly and eagerly as ever. I fired again – not more than eight yards away – but the water was then up to my arms, and it was impossible to pick a vital part; the brain and neck were the only spots to finish him, but one could see nothing beyond a great upheaval of water and clouds of spray and blood-stained foam.

The crocodile turned from the shot and dived up stream, heading straight for Jock: the din of yelling voices stopped instantly as the huge open mouthed thing plunged towards the dog; and for one sick horrified moment I stood and watched – helpless.

Had the crocodile risen in front of Jock that would have been the end – one snap would have done it; but it passed clear underneath, and, coming up just beyond him, the great lashing tail sent the dog up with the column of water a couple of feet in the air. He did as he had done, when the koodoo bull tossed him: his head was round straining to get at the crocodile before he was able to turn his body in the water; and the silence was broken by a yell of wild delight and approval from the bank.

Before us the water was too deep and the stream too strong to stand in; Jim in his eagerness had gone in shoulder high, and my rifle when aimed only just cleared the water. The crocodile was the mark for more assegais from the bank as it charged up stream again, with Jock tailing behind, and it was then easy enough to follow its movements by the shafts that were never all submerged. The struggles became perceptibly weaker, and as it turned again to go with the stream every effort was concentrated on killing and landing it before it reached the rocks and rapids.

I moved back for higher ground and, finding that the bed shelved up rapidly down stream, made for a position where there would be enough elevation to put in a brain shot. The water was not more than waist high then, and as the crocodile came rolling and thrashing down I waited for his head to show up clearly. My right foot touched a sloping rock which rose almost to the surface of the water close above the rapids, and anxious to get the best possible position for a last shot, I took my stand there. The rock was the ordinary shelving bedrock, uptilted at an easy angle and cut off sheer on the exposed side, and the wave in the current would have shown this to any one not wholly occupied with other things; but I had eyes for nothing except the crocodile which was then less than a dozen yards off, and in my anxiety to secure a firm footing for the shot I moved the right foot again a few inches – over the edge of the rock. The result was as complete a spill as if one unthinkingly stepped backwards off a diving board: I disappeared in deep water, with the knowledge that the crocodile would join me there in a few seconds.

One never knows how these things are done or how long they take: I was back on the rock – without the rifle – and had the water out of my eyes in time to see the crocodile roll helplessly by, six feet away, with Jock behind making excited but ridiculously futile attempts to get hold of the tail; Jim – swimming, plunging and blowing like a maddened hippo – formed the tail of the procession, which was headed by my water-logged hat floating heavily a yard or so in front of the crocodile.

From *Jock of the Bushveld*

JOHN DAVIDSON

Two Dogs

Two dogs on Bournemouth beach: a mongrel, one,
With spaniel plainest on the palimpsest,
The blur of muddled stock; the other, bred,
With tapering muzzle, rising brow, strong jaw –
A terrier to the tail's expressive tip.
Magnetic, nimble, endlessly alert.

The mongrel, wet and shivering, at my feet
Deposited a wedge of half-inch board,
A foot in length and splintered at the butt;
Withdrew a yard and crouched in act to spring,
While to and fro between his wedge and me
The glancing shuttle of his eager look
A purpose wove. The terrier, ears a-cock,
And neck one curve of sheer intelligence,
Stood sentinel: no sound, no movement, save
The mongrel's telepathic eyes, bespoke
The object of the canine pantomime.

I stooped to grasp the wedge, knowing the game;
But like a thing uncoiled the mongrel snapped
It off, and promptly set it out again,
The terrier at his quarters, every nerve
Waltzing inside his lithe rigidity.

'More complex than I thought!' Again I made
To seize the wedge; again the mongrel won,
Whipped off the jack, relaid it, crouched and watched,
The terrier at attention all the time.
I won the third bout: ere the mongrel snapped
His toy, I stayed my hand; he halted, half
Across the neutral ground, and in his pause
Of doubt I seized the prize. A vanquished yelp
From both; and then intensest vigilance.

Together, when I tossed the wedge, they plunged
Before it reached the sea. The mongrel, out
Among the waves, and standing to them, meant
Heroic business; but the terrier dodged
Behind adroitly scouting in the surf,
And seized the wedge, rebutted by the tide,

In shallow water, while the mongrel searched
The English Channel on his hind-legs poised.
The terrier laid the trophy at my feet;
And neither dog protested when I took
The wedge: the overture of their marine
Diversion had been played out once for all.

A second match the reckless mongrel won,
Vanishing twice under the heavy surf,
Before he found and brought the prize to land.
Then for an hour the aquatic sport went on,
And still the mongrel took the heroic rôle,
The terrier hanging deftly in the rear.
Sometimes the terrier when the mongrel found
Betrayed a jealous scorn, as who should say,
'Your hero's always a vulgarian! Pah!'
But when the mongrel missed, after a fight
With such a sea of troubles, and saw the prize
Grabbed by the terrier in an inch of surf,
He seemed entirely satisfied, and watched
With more pathetic vigilance the cast
That followed.

                'Once a passion, mongrel, this
Retrieving of a stick,' I told the brute,
'Has now become a vice with you. Go home!
Wet to the marrow and palsied with the cold,
You won't give in; and, good or bad, you've earned
My admiration. Go home now and get warm,
And the best bone in the pantry.' As I talked
I stripped the water from his hybrid coat,
Laughed and made much of him – which mortified
The funking terrier.

'I'm despised, it seems!'
The terrier thought. 'My cleverness (my feet
Are barely wet!) beside the mongrel's zeal
Appears timidity. This biped's mad
To pet the stupid brute. Yap! Yah!' He seized
The wedge and went; and at his heels at once,
Without a thought of me, the mongrel trudged.

Along the beach, smokers of cigarettes,
All sixpenny-novel-readers to a man,
Attracted Master Terrier. Again the wedge,
Passed to the loyal mongrel, was teed with care;
Again the fateful overture began.
Upon the fourth attempt, and not before,
And by a feint at that, the challenged youth,
(Most equable, be sure, of all the group:
Allow the veriest dog to measure men!)
Secured the soaked and splintered scrap of deal.
Thereafter, as with me, the game progressed,
The breathless, shivering mongrel, rushing out
Into the heavy surf, there to be tossed
And tumbled like a floating bunch of kelp,
While gingerly the terrier picked his steps
Strategic in the rear, and snapped the prize
Oftener than his more adventurous, more
Romantic, more devoted rival did.

The uncomfortable moral glares at one!
And, further, in the mongrel's wistful mind
A primitive idea darkly wrought:
Having once lost the prize in the overture
With his bipedal rival, he felt himself
In honour and in conscience bound to plunge
For ever after it at the winner's will.

But the smart terrier was an Overdog,
And knew a trick worth two of that. He thought –
If canine cerebration works like ours,
And I interpret canine mind aright –
'Let men and mongrels worry and wet their coats!
I use my brains and choose the better part.
Quick-witted ease and self-approval lift
Me miles above this anxious cur, absorbed,
Body and soul, in playing a game I win
Without an effort. And yet the mongrel seems
The happier dog. How's that? Belike, the old
Compensatory principle again:
I have pre-eminence and conscious worth;
And he his power to fling himself away
For anything or nothing. Men and dogs,
What an unfathomable world it is!'

JACK LONDON

Bâtard

BÂTARD WAS A devil. This was recognized throughout the North-land. 'Hell's Spawn' he was called by many men, but his master, Black Leclère, chose for him the shameful name 'Bâtard'. Now Black Leclère was also a devil, and the twain were well matched. There is a saying that when two devils come together, hell is to pay. This is to be expected, and this certainly was to be expected when Bâtard and Black Leclère came together. The first time they met, Bâtard was a part-grown puppy, lean and hungry, with bitter eyes; and they met with a snap and snarl, and wicked looks, for Leclère's upper lip had a wolfish way of lifting and showing the white, cruel teeth. And it lifted then, and his eyes glinted viciously, as he reached for Bâtard and dragged him out from the squirming litter. It was certain that they divined each other, for on the instant Bâtard had buried his puppy fangs in Leclère's hand, and Leclère, thumb and finger, was coolly choking his young life out of him.

'Sacredam,' the Frenchman said softly, flirting the quick blood from his bitten hand and gazing down on the little puppy choking and gasping in the snow.

Leclère turned to John Hamlin, storekeeper of the Sixty Mile Post. 'Dat fo' w'at Ah lak heem. 'Ow moch, eh, you, *M'sieu*'? 'Ow moch? Ah buy heem, now; Ah buy heem queek.'

And because he hated him with an exceeding bitter hate, Leclère brought Bâtard and gave him his shameful name. And for five years the twain adventured across the Northland, from St Michael's and the Yukon delta to the head-reaches of the Pelly and even so far as the Peace River, Athabasca, and the Great Slave. And they acquired a reputation for uncompromising wickedness, the like of which never before attached itself to a man and dog.

Bâtard did not know his father – hence his name – but, as John Hamlin knew, his father was a great grey timber wolf. But the mother of Bâtard, as he dimly remembered her, was snarling, bickering, obscene, husky, full-fronted and heavy-chested, with a malign eye, a cat-like grip on life, and a genius for trickery and evil. There was neither faith nor trust in her. Her treachery alone could be relied upon, and her wild-wood amours attested her general depravity. Much of evil and much of strength were there in these, Bâtard's progenitors, and, bone and flesh of their bone and flesh, he had inherited it all. And then came Black Leclère, to lay his heavy hand on the bit of pulsating puppy life, to press and prod and mould till it became a big bristling beast, acute in knavery, overspilling with hate, sinister, malignant, diabolical. With a proper master Bâtard might have made an ordinary, fairly efficient sled-dog. He never got the chance: Leclère but confirmed him in his congenital iniquity.

The history of Bâtard and Leclère is a history of war – of five cruel, relentless years, of which their first meeting is fit summary. To begin with, it was Leclère's fault, for he hated with understanding and intelligence, while the long-legged, ungainly puppy hated only blindly, instinctively, without reason or method. At first there were no refinements of cruelty (these were to come later), but simple beatings and crude brutalities. In one of these Bâtard had an ear injured. He never regained control of the riven muscles, and ever after the ear drooped limply down to keep keen the memory of his tormentor. And he never forgot.

His puppyhood was a period of foolish rebellion. He was always worsted, but he fought back because it was his nature to fight back. And he was unconquerable. Yelping shrilly from the pain of lash and club, he none the less contrived always to throw in the defiant snarl, the bitter vindictive menace of his soul which fetched without fail more blows and beatings. But his was his mother's tenacious grip on life. Nothing could kill him. He flourished under misfortune, grew fat with famine, and out of his terrible struggle for life developed a preternatural intelligence. His were the stealth and cunning of the husky, his mother, and the fierceness and valour of the wolf, his father.

Possibly it was because of his father that he never wailed. His puppy yelps passed with his lanky legs, so that he became grim and taciturn, quick to strike, slow to warn. He answered curse with snarl, and blow with snap, grinning the while his implacable hatred; but never again, under the extremest agony, did Leclère bring from him the cry of fear nor of pain. This unconquerableness but fanned Leclère's wrath and stirred him to greater devilries.

Did Leclère give Bâtard half a fish and to his mates whole ones, Bâtard went forth to rob other dogs of their fish. Also he robbed caches and expressed himself in a thousand rogueries, till he became a terror to all dogs and masters of dogs. Did Leclère beat Bâtard and fondle Babette – Babette who was not half the worker he was – why Bâtard threw her down in the snow and broke her hind leg in his heavy jaws, so that Leclère was forced to shoot her. Likewise, in bloody battles, Bâtard mastered all his team-mates, set them the law of trail and forage, and made them live to the law he set.

In five years he heard but one kind of word, received but one soft stroke of a hand, and then he did not know what manner of things they were. He leaped like the untamed thing he was, and his jaws were together in a flash. It was the missionary at Sunrise, a newcomer in the country, who spoke the kind word and gave the soft stroke of the hand. And for six months after, he wrote no letters home to the States, and the surgeon at McQuestion travelled two hundred miles on the ice to save him from blood-poisoning.

Men and dogs looked askance at Bâtard when he drifted into their camps and posts. The men greeted him with feet threateningly lifted for the kick, the dogs with bristling manes and bared fangs. Once a man did kick Bâtard, and Bâtard, with quick wolf snap, closed his jaws like a steel trap on the man's calf and crunched down to the bone. Whereat the man was determined to have his life, only Black Leclère, with ominous eyes and naked hunting-knife, stepped in between. The killing of Bâtard – ah, *sacredam, that* was a pleasure Leclère reserved for himself. Some day it would happen, or else – bah! who was to know? Anyway, the problem would be solved.

For they had become problems to each other. The very breath each drew was a challenge and a menace to the other. Their hate bound them together as love could never bind. Leclère was bent on the coming of the day when Bâtard should wilt in spirit and cringe and whimper at his feet. And Bâtard – Leclère knew what was in Bâtard's mind, and more than once had read it in Bâtard's eyes. And so clearly had he read that, when Bâtard was at his back, he made it a point to glance often over his shoulder.

Men marvelled when Leclère refused large money for the dog. 'Some day you will kill him and be out his price,' said John Hamlin once, when Bâtard lay panting in the snow where Leclère had kicked him, and no one knew whether his ribs were broken, and no one dared look to see.

'Dat,' said Leclère, dryly, 'dat is my biz'ness, *M'sieu'*.'

And the men marvelled that Bâtard did not run away. They did not understand. But Leclère understood. He was a man who lived much in the open, beyond the sound of human tongue, and he had learned the voices of wind and storm, the sigh of night, the whisper of dawn, the clash of day. In a dim way he could hear the green things growing, the running of the sap, the bursting of the bud. And he knew the subtle speech of the things that moved, of the rabbit in the snare, the moody raven beating the air with hollow wing, the baldface shuffling under the moon, the wolf like a grey shadow gliding betwixt the twilight and the dark. And to him Bâtard spoke clear and direct. Full well he understood why Bâtard did not run away, and he looked more often over his shoulder.

When in anger, Bâtard was not nice to look upon, and more than once he had leapt for Leclère's throat, to be stretched quivering and senseless in the snow, by the butt of the ever ready dogwhip. And so Bâtard learned to bide his time. When he reached his full strength and prime of youth, he thought the time had come. He was broad-chested, powerfully muscled, of far more than ordinary size, and his neck from head to shoulders was a mass of bristling hair – to all appearances a full-blooded wolf. Leclère was lying asleep in his furs when Bâtard deemed the time to be ripe. He crept upon him stealthily, head low to earth and lone ear laid back, with a feline softness of tread. Bâtard breathed gently, very gently, and not till he was close at hand did he raise his head. He paused for a moment and looked at the bronzed full throat, naked and knotty, and swelling to a deep steady pulse. The slaver dripped down his fangs and slid off his tongue at the sight, and in that moment he remembered his drooping ear, his uncounted blows and prodigious wrongs, and without a sound sprang on the sleeping man.

Leclère awoke to the pang of the fangs in his throat, and, perfect animal that he was, he awoke clear-headed and with full comprehension. He closed on Bâtard's windpipe with both his hands, and rolled out of his furs to get his weight uppermost. But the thousands of Bâtard's ancestors had clung at the throats of unnumbered moose and caribou and dragged them down, and the wisdom of those ancestors was his. When Leclère's weight came on top of him, he drove his hind legs upwards and in, and clawed down chest and abdomen, ripping and tearing through skin and muscle. And when he felt the man's body wince above him and lift, he worried and shook at the man's throat. His team-mates closed around in a snarling circle, and Bâtard, with failing breath and fading sense, knew that their jaws were hungry for him. But that did not matter – it was the man, the man above him, and he ripped and clawed, and shook and worried, to the last ounce of his strength. But Leclère choked him with both his hands, till Bâtard's chest heaved and writhed for the air denied, and his eyes glazed and set, and his jaws slowly loosened, and his tongue protruded black and swollen.

'Eh? *Bon*, you devil!' Leclère gurgled mouth and throat clogged with his own blood, as he shoved the dizzy dog from him.

And then Leclère cursed the other dogs off as they fell upon Bâtard. They drew back into a wider circle, squatting alertly on their haunches and licking their chops, the hair on every neck bristling and erect.

Bâtard recovered quickly, and at the sound of Leclère's voice, tottered to his feet and swayed weakly back and forth.

'A-h-ah! You beeg devil!' Leclère spluttered, 'Ah fix you; Ah fix you plentee, by *Gar*!'

Bâtard, the air biting into his exhausted lungs like wine, flashed full into the man's face, his jaws missing and coming together with a metallic clip. They rolled over and over on the snow, Leclère striking madly with his fists. Then they separated, face to face, and circled back and forth before each other. Leclère could have drawn his knife. His rifle was at his feet. But the beast in him was up and raging. He would do the thing with his hands – and his teeth. Bâtard sprang in, but Leclère knocked him over with a blow of the fist, fell upon him, and buried his teeth to the bone in the dog's shoulder.

It was a primordial setting and a primordial scene, such as might have been in the savage youth of the world. An open space in a dark forest, a ring of grinning wolf-dogs, and in the centre two beasts, locked in combat, snapping and snarling raging madly about, panting, sobbing, cursing, straining, wild with passion, in a fury of murder, ripping and tearing and clawing in elemental brutishness.

But Leclère caught Bâtard behind the ear with a blow from his fist, knocking him over, and, for the instant, stunning him. Then Leclère leaped upon him with his feet, and sprang up and down, striving to grind him into the earth. Both Bâtard's hind legs were broken ere Leclère ceased that he might catch breath.

'A-a-ah! A-a-ah!' he screamed, incapable of speech, shaking his fist, through sheer impotence of throat and larynx.

But Bâtard was indomitable. He lay there in a helpless welter, his lip feebly lifting and writhing to the snarl he had not the strength to utter. Leclère kicked him, and the tired jaws closed on the ankle, but could not break the skin.

Then Leclère picked up the whip and proceeded almost to cut him to pieces, at each stroke of the lash crying: 'Dis taim Ah break you! Eh? By *Gar*! Ah break you!'

In the end, exhausted, fainting from loss of blood, he crumpled up and fell by his victim, and when the wolf-dogs closed in to take their vengeance, with his last consciousness dragged his body on top of Bâtard to shield him from their fangs.

This occurred not far from Sunrise, and the missionary, opening the door to Leclère a few hours later, was surprised to note the absence of Bâtard from the team. Nor did his surprise lessen when Leclère threw back the robes from the sled, gathered Bâtard into his arms and staggered across the threshold. It happened that the surgeon of McQuestion, who was something of a gadabout, was up on a gossip, and between them they proceeded to repair Leclère.

'*Merci, non*,' said he. 'Do you fix firs' de dog. To die? *Non*. Eet is not good. Becos' heem Ah mus' yet break. Dat fo' w'at he mus' not die.'

The surgeon called it a marvel, the missionary a miracle, that Leclère pulled through at all; and so weakened was he, that in the spring the fever got him, and he went on his back again. Bâtard had been in even worse plight, but his grip on life prevailed, and the bones of his hind legs knit, and his organs righted themselves, during the several weeks he lay strapped to the floor. And by the time Leclère, finally convalescent, sallow and shaky, took the sun by the cabin door, Bâtard had reasserted his supremacy among his kind, and brought not only his own team-mates but the missionary's dogs into subjection.

He moved never a muscle, nor twitched a hair, when, for the first time, Leclère tottered out on the missionary's arm, and sank down slowly and with infinite caution on the three-legged stool.

'*Bon!*' he said. 'Bon! De good sun!' And he stretched out his wasted hands and washed them in the warmth.

Then his gaze fell on the dog, and the old light blazed back in his eyes. He touched the missionary lightly on the arm. '*Mon père*, dat is one beeg devil, dat Bâtard. You will bring me one pistol, so, dat Ah drink de sun in peace.'

And thenceforth for many days he sat in the sun before the cabin door. He never dozed, and the pistol lay always across his knees. Bâtard had a way, the first thing each day, of looking for the weapon in its wonted place. At sight of it he would lift his lip faintly in token that he understood, and Leclère would lift his own lip in an answering grin. One day the missionary took note of the trick.

'Bless me!' he said. 'I really believe the brute comprehends.'

Leclère laughed softly. 'Look you, *mon père*. Dat w'at Ah now spik, to dat does he lissen.'

As if in confirmation, Bâtard just perceptibly wriggled his lone ear up to catch the sound.

'Ah say "keel".'

Bâtard growled deep down in his throat, the hair bristled along his neck, and every muscle went tense and expectant.

'Ah lift de gun, so, like dat.' And suiting action to word, he sighted the pistol at Bâtard.

Bâtard, with a single leap, sideways, landed around the corner of the cabin out of sight.

'Bless me!' the missionary repeated at intervals.

Lecère grinned proudly.

'But why does he not run away?'

The Frenchman's shoulders went up in the racial shrug that means all things from total ignorance to infinite understanding.

'Then why do you not kill him?'

Again the shoulders went up.

'*Mon père*,' he said after a pause, 'de taim is not yet. He is one beeg devil. Some taim Ah break heem, so an' so, all to leetle bits. Hey? some taim. *Bon*!'

A day came when Leclère gathered his dogs together and floated down in a bateau to Forty Mile, and so on to the Porcupine, where he took a commission from the P. C. Company, and went exploring for the better part of a year. After that he poled up the Koyokuk to deserted Arctic City, and later came drifting back, from camp to camp, along the Yukon. And during the long months Bâtard was well lessoned. He learned many tortures, and, notably, the torture of hunger, the torture of thirst, the torture of fire, and, worst of all, the torture of music.

Like the rest of his kind, he did not enjoy music. It gave him exquisite anguish, racking him nerve by nerve, and ripping apart every fibre of his being. It made him howl, long and wolf-like, as when the wolves bay the stars on frosty nights. He could not help howling. It was his one weakness in the contest with Leclère, and it was his shame. Leclère, on the other hand, passionately loved music – as passionately as he loved strong drink. And when his soul clamoured for expression, it usually uttered itself in one or the other of the two ways, and more usually in both ways. And when he had drunk, his brain a-tilt with unsung song and the devil in him aroused and rampant, his soul found its supreme utterance in torturing Bâtard.

'Now we will haf a leetle museek,' he would say. 'Eh? W'at you t'ink, Bâtard?'

It was only an old and battered harmonica, tenderly treasured and patiently repaired; but it was the best that money could buy, and out of its silver reeds he drew weird vagrant airs that men had never heard before. Then Bâtard, dumb of throat, with teeth tight clenched, would back way, inch by inch, to the farthest cabin corner. And Leclère, playing, playing, a stout club tucked under his arm, followed the animal up, inch by inch, step by step, till there was no further retreat.

At first Bâtard would crowd himself into the smallest possible space, grovelling close to the floor; but as the music came nearer and nearer, he was forced to uprear, his back jammed into the logs, his fore legs fanning the air as though to beat off the rippling waves of sound. He still kept his teeth together, but severe muscular contractions attacked his body, strange twitchings and jerkings, till he was all a-quiver and writhing in silent torment. As he lost control, his jaws spasmodically wrenched apart, and deep throaty vibrations issued forth, too low in the register of sound for human ear to catch. And then, nostrils distended, eyes dilated, hair bristling in helpless rage, arose the long wolf howl. It came with a slurring rush upwards, swelling in a great heart-breaking burst of sound, and dying away in sadly cadenced woe – then the next rush upward, octave upon octave; the bursting heart; and the infinite sorrow and misery, fainting, fading, falling, and dying slowly away.

It was fit for hell. And Leclère, with fiendish ken, seemed to divine each particular nerve and heartstring, and with long wails and tremblings and sobbing minors to make it yield up its last shred of grief. It was frightful, and for twenty-four hours after, Bâtard was nervous and unstrung, starting at common sounds, tripping over his own shadow, but, withal, vicious and masterful with his team-mates. Nor did he shows signs of a breaking spirit. Rather did he grow more grim and taciturn, biding his time with an inscrutable patience that began to puzzle and weigh upon Leclère. The dog would lie in the firelight, motionless, for hours, gazing straight before him at Leclère, and hating him with his bitter eyes.

Often the man felt that he had bucked against the very essence of life – the unconquerable essence that swept the hawk down out of the sky like a feathered thunderbolt, that drove the great grey goose across the zones, that hurled the spawning salmon through two thousand miles of boiling Yukon flood. At such times he felt impelled to express his own unconquerable essence; and with strong drink, wild music, and Bâtard, he indulged in vast orgies, wherein he pitted his puny strength in the face of things, and challenged all that was, and had been, and was yet to be.

'Dere is somet'ing dere,' he affirmed, when the rhymed vagaries of his mind touched the secret chords of Bâtard's being and brought forth the long lugubrious howl. 'Ah pool eet out wid bot' my han's, so, an' so. Ha! ha! Eet is fonee! Eet is ver' fonee! De priest chant, de womans pray, de mans swear, de leetle bird go *peep-peep*, Bâtard, heem go *yow-yow* – an' eet is all de ver' same t'ing. Ha! ha!'

Father Gautier, a worthy priest, once reproved him with instances of concrete perdition. He never reproved him again.

'Eet may be so, *mon père*,' he made answer. 'An' Ah t'ink ah go troo hell a-snappin', lak de hemlock troo de fire. Eh, *mon père*?'

But all bad things come to an end as well as good, and so with Black Leclère. On the summer low water, in a poling boat, he left McDougall for Sunrise. He left McDougall in company with Timothy Brown, and arrived at Sunrise by himself. Further, it was known that they had quarrelled just previous to pulling out; for the *Lizzie*, a wheezy ten-ton stern-wheeler, twenty-four hours behind, beat Leclère in by three days.

And when he did get in, it was with a clean-drilled bullet-hole through his shoulder muscle, and a tale of ambush and murder.

A strike had been made at Sunrise, and things had changed considerably. With the infusion of several hundred gold-seekers, a deal of whisky, and half-a-dozen equipped gamblers, the missionary had seen the page of his years of labour with the Indians wiped clean. When the squaws became preoccupied with cooking beans and keeping the fire going for the wifeless miners, and the bucks with swapping their warm furs for black bottles and broken time-pieces, he took to his bed, said 'Bless me' several times, and departed to his final accounting in a rough-hewn, oblong box. Whereupon the gamblers moved their roulette and faro tables into the mission house, and the click of chips and clink of glasses went up from dawn till dark and to dawn again.

Now Timothy Brown was well beloved among these adventurers of the North. The one thing against him was his quick temper and ready fist – a little thing, for which his kind heart and forgiving hand more than atoned. On the other hand, there was nothing to atone for Black Leclère. He was 'black', as more than one remembered deed bore witness, while he was as well hated as the other was beloved. So the men of Sunrise put an antiseptic dressing on his shoulder and hauled him before Judge Lynch.

It was a simple affair. He had quarrelled with Timothy Brown at McDougall. With Timothy Brown he had left McDougall. Without Timothy Brown he had arrived at Sunrise. Considered in the light of his evilness, the unanimous conclusion was that he had killed Timothy Brown. On the other hand, Leclère acknowledged their facts, but challenged their conclusion, and gave his own explanation. Twenty miles out of Sunrise he and Timothy Brown were poling the boat along the rocky shore. From that shore two rifle-shots rang out. Timothy Brown pitched out of the boat and went down bubbling red, and that was the last of Timothy Brown. He, Leclère, pitched into the bottom of the boat with a stinging shoulder. He lay very quiet, peeping at the shore. After a time two Indians stuck up their heads and came out to the water's edge, carrying between them a birch-bark canoe. As they launched it, Leclère let fly. He potted one, who went over the side after the manner of Timothy Brown. The other dropped into the bottom of the canoe, and then canoe and poling boat went down the stream in a drifting battle. After that they hung up on a split current, and the canoe passed on one side of an island, the poling boat on the other. That was the last of the canoe, and he came on into Sunrise. Yes, from the way the Indian in the canoe jumped, he was sure he had potted him. That was all.

This explanation was not deemed adequate. They gave him ten hours' grace while the *Lizzie* steamed down to investigate. Ten hours later she came wheezing back to Sunrise. There had been nothing to investigate. No evidence had been found to back up his statements. They told him to make his will, for he possessed a fifty-thousand dollar Sunrise claim, and they were a law-abiding as well as a law-giving breed.

Leclère shrugged his shoulders. 'Bot one t'ing,' he said; 'a leetle, w'at you call, favour – a leetle favour, dat is eet. I gif my feefty t'ousan' dollair to de church. I gif my husky dog, Bâtard, to de devil. De leetle favour? Firs' you hang heem, an' den you hang me. Eet is good, eh?'

Good it was, they agreed, that Hell's Spawn should break trail for his master across the last divide, and the court was adjourned down to the river bank, where a big spruce tree stood by itself. Slackwater Charley put a hangman's knot in the end of a hauling-line, and the noose was slipped over Leclère's head and pulled tight around his neck. His hands were tied behind his back, and he was assisted to the top of a cracker box. Then the running end of the line was passed over an overhanging branch, drawn taut, and made fast. To kick the box out from under would leave him dancing on the air.

'Now for the dog,' said Webster Shaw, sometime mining engineer. 'You'll have to rope him, Slackwater.'

Leclère grinned. Slackwater took a chew of tobacco, rove a running noose, and proceeded leisurely to coil a few turns in his hand. He paused once or twice to brush particularly offensive mosquitoes from off his face. Everybody was brushing mosquitoes, except Leclère, about whose head a small cloud was visible. Even Bâtard, lying full-stretch on the ground with his fore paws rubbed the pests away from eyes and mouth.

But while Slackwater waited for Bâtard to lift his head, a faint call came from the quiet air, and a man was seen running across the flat from Sunrise. It was the storekeeper.

'C-call 'er off, boys,' he panted, as he came in among them.

'Little Sandy and Bernadotte's jes' got in,' he explained with returning breath. 'Landed down below an' come up by the short cut. Got the Beaver with 'm. Picked 'm up in his canoe, stuck in a back channel, with a couple of bullet-holes in 'm. Other buck was Klok Kutz, the one that knocked spots out of his squaw and dusted.'

'Eh? W'at Ah say? Eh?' Leclère cried exultantly. 'Dat de one fo'sure! Ah know. Ah spik true.'

'The thing to do is to teach these damned Siwashes a little manners,' spoke Webster Shaw. 'They're getting fat and sassy, and we'll have to bring them down a peg. Round in all the bucks and string up the Beaver for an object lesson. That's the programme. Come on and let's see what he's got to say for himself.'

'Heh, *M'sieu*!' Leclère called, as the crowd began to melt away through the twilight in the direction of Sunrise. 'Ah lak ver' moch to see de fon.'

'Oh, we'll turn you loose when we come back,' Webster Shaw shouted over his shoulder. 'In the meantime meditate on your sins and the ways of Providence. It will do you good, so be grateful.'

As is the way with men who are accustomed to great hazards, whose nerves are healthy and trained in patience, so it was with Leclère who settled himself to the long wait – which is to say that he reconciled his mind to it. There was no settling of the body, for the taut rope forced him to stand rigidly erect. The least relaxation of the leg muscles pressed the rough-fibred noose into his neck, while the upright position caused him much pain in his wounded shoulder. He projected his under lip and expelled his breath upwards along his face to blow the mosquitoes away from his eyes. But the situation had its compensation. To be snatched from the maw of death was well worth a little bodily suffering, only it was unfortunate that he should miss the hanging of the Beaver.

And so he mused, till his eyes chanced to fall upon Bâtard, head between fore paws and stretched on the ground asleep. And then Leclère ceased to muse. He studied the animal closely, striving to sense if the sleep were real or feigned. Bâtard's sides were heaving regularly, but Leclère felt that the breath came and went a shade too quickly; also he felt that there was a vigilance or alertness to every hair that belied unshackling sleep. He would have given his Sunrise claim to be assured that the dog was not awake, and once, when one of his joints cracked, he looked quickly and guiltily at Bâtard to see if he roused. He did not rouse then but a few minutes later he got up slowly and lazily, stretched, and looked carefully about him.

'Sacredam,' said Leclère under his breath.

Assured that no one was in sight or hearing, Bâtard sat down, curled his upper lip almost into a smile, looked up at Leclère, and licked his chops.

'Ah, see my feenish,' the man said, and laughed sardonically aloud.

Bâtard came nearer, the useless ear wabbling, the good ear cocked forward with devilish comprehension. He thrust his head on one side quizzically, and advanced with mincing, playful steps. He rubbed his body gently against the box till it shook and shook again. Leclère teetered carefully to maintain his equilibrium.

'Bâtard,' he said calmly, 'look out. Ah keel you.'

Bâtard snarled at the word and shook the box with greater force. Then he upreared, and with his fore paws threw his weight against it higher up. Leclère kicked out with one foot, but the rope bit into his neck and checked so abruptly as nearly to overbalance him.

'Hi, ya! *Chook! Mush-on!*' he screamed.

Bâtard retreated, for twenty feet or so, with a fiendish levity in his bearing that Leclère could not mistake. He remembered the dog often breaking the scum of ice on the water hole by lifting up and throwing his weight upon it; and remembering, he understand what he now had in mind. Bâtard faced about and paused. He showed his white teeth in a grin, which Leclère answered; and then hurled his body through the air, in full charge, straight for the box.

Fifteen minutes later, Slackwater Charley and Webster Shaw returning, caught a glimpse of a ghostly pendulum swinging back and forth in the dim light. As they hurriedly drew in closer, they made out the man's inert body, and a live thing that clung to it, and shook and worried, and gave to it the swaying motion.

'Hi ya! Chook! you Spawn of Hell!' yelled Webster Shaw.

But Bâtard glared at him, and snarled threateningly, without loosing his jaws.

Slackwater Charley got out his revolver, but his hand was shaking, as with a chill, and he fumbled.

'Here you take it,' he said, passing the weapon over.

Webster Shaw laughed shortly, drew a sight between the gleaming eyes, and pressed the trigger. Bâtard's body twitched with the shock, threshed the ground spasmodically for a moment, and went suddenly limp. But his teeth still held fast locked.

VIRGINIA WOOLF

On a Faithful Friend

THERE IS SOME impertinence as well as some foolhardiness in the way in which we buy animals for so much gold and silver and call them ours. One cannot help wondering what the silent critic on the hearthrug thinks of our strange conventions – the mystic Persian, whose ancestors were worshipped as gods whilst we, their masters and mistresses, grovelled in caves and painted our bodies blue. She has a vast heritage of experience, which seems to brood in her eyes, too solemn and too subtle for expression; she smiles, I often think, at our late-born civilisation, and remembers the rise and fall of dynasties. There is something, too, profane in the familiarity, half contemptuous, with which we treat our animals. We deliberately transplant a little bit of simple wild life, and make it grow up beside ours, which is neither simple nor wild. You may often see in a dog's eyes a sudden look of the primitive animal, as though he were once more a wild dog hunting in the solitary places of his youth. How have we the impertinence to make these wild creatures forego their nature for ours, which at best they can but imitate? It is one of the refined sins of civilization, for we know not what wild spirit we are taking from its purer atmosphere, or who it is – Pan, or Nymph, or Dryad – that we have trained to beg for a lump of sugar at tea.

I do not think that in domesticating our lost friend Shag we were guilty of any such crime; he was essentially a sociable dog, who had his near counterpart in the human world. I can see him smoking a cigar at the bow window of his club, his legs extended comfortably, whilst he discusses the latest news on the Stock Exchange with a companion. His best friend could not claim for him any romantic or mysterious animal nature, but that made him all the better company for mere human beings. He came to us, however, with a pedigree that had all the elements of romance in it; he, when, in horror at his price, his would-be purchaser pointed to his collie head and collie body, but terribly Skye-terrier legs – he, we were assured, was no less a dog than the original Skye – a chieftain of the same importance as the O'Brien or the O'Connor Don in human aristocracy. The whole of the Skye-terrier tribe – who, that is, inherited the paternal characteristics – had somehow been swept from the earth; Shag, the sole scion of true Skye blood, remained in an obscure Norfolk village, the property of a low-born blacksmith, who, however, cherished the utmost loyalty for his person, and pressed the claims of his royal birth with such success that we had the honour of buying him for a very substantial sum. He was too great a gentleman to take part in the plebeian work of killing rats for which he was originally needed, but he certainly added, we felt, to the respectability of the family. He seldom went for a walk without punishing the impertinence of middle-class dogs who neglected the homage due to his rank, and we had to enclose the royal jaws in a muzzle long after that restriction was legally unnecessary. As he advanced in middle life he became certainly rather autocratic, not only with his own kind, but with us, his masters and mistresses; such a title though was absurd where Shag was concerned, so we called ourselves his uncles and aunts. The solitary occasion when he found it necessary to inflict marks of his displeasure on human flesh was once when a visitor rashly tried to treat him as an ordinary pet-dog and tempted him with sugar and called him 'out of his name' by the contemptible lap-dog title of 'Fido'. Then Shag, with characteristic independence, refused the sugar and took a satisfactory mouthful of calf instead. But when he felt that he was treated with due respect he was the most faithful of friends. He was not demonstrative; but failing eyesight did not blind him to his master's face, and in his deafness he could still hear his master's voice.

The evil spirit of Shag's life was introduced into the family in the person of an attractive young sheep-dog puppy – who, though of authentic blood, was unhappily without a tail – a fact which Shag could not help remarking with satisfaction. We deluded ourselves into the thought that the young dog might take the place of the son of Shag's old age, and for a time they lived happily together. But Shag had ever been contemptuous of social graces and had relied for his place in our hearts upon his sterling qualities of honesty and independence; the puppy, however, was a young gentleman of most engaging manners, and, though we tried to be fair, Shag could not help feeling that the young dog got most of our attention. I can see him now, as in a kind of blundering and shamefaced way he lifted one stiff old paw and gave it to me to shake, which was one of the young dog's most successful tricks. It almost brought the tears to my eyes. I could not help thinking, though I smiled, of old King Lear. But Shag was too old to acquire new graces; no second place should be his, and he determined that the matter should be decided by force. So after some weeks of growing tension the battle was fought; they went for each other with white teeth gleaming – Shag was the aggressor – and rolled round and round on the grass, locked in each other's grip. When at last we got them apart, blood was running, hair was flying, and both dogs bore scars. Peace after that was impossible; they had but to see each other to growl and stiffen; the question was – Who was the conqueror? Who was to stay and who to go? The decision we came to was base, unjust, and yet, perhaps, excusable. The old dog has had his day, we said, he must give place to the new generation. So old Shag was deposed, and sent to a kind of dignified dower-house at Parson's-green, and the young dog reigned in his stead. Year after year passed, and we never saw the old friend who had known us in the days of our youth; but in the summer holidays he revisited the house in our absence with the caretaker. And so time went on till this last year, which, though we did not know it, was to be the last year of his life. Then, one winter's night, at a time of great sickness and anxiety, a dog was heard barking repeatedly, with the bark of a dog who waits to be let in, outside our kitchen-door. It was many years since that bark had been heard, and only one person in the kitchen was able to recognise it now. She opened the door, and in walked Shag, now almost quite blind and stone deaf, as he had walked in many times before, and, looking neither to right nor left, went to his old corner by the fireside, where he curled up and fell asleep without a sound. If the usurper saw him he slunk guiltily away, for Shag was past fighting for his rights any more. We shall never know – it is one of the many things that we can never know – what strange wave of memory or sympathetic instinct it was that drew Shag from the house where he had lodged for years to seek again the familiar doorstep of his master's home. And it befell that Shag was the last of the family to live in the old house, for it was in crossing the road which leads to the gardens where he was taken for his first walks as a puppy, and bit all the other dogs and frightened all the babies in their perambulators, that he met his death. The blind, deaf dog neither saw nor heard a hansom; and the wheel went over him and ended instantly a life which could not have been happily prolonged. It was better for him to die thus out among the wheels and the horses than to end in a lethal-chamber or be poisoned in a stable-yard.

So we say farewell to a dear and faithful friend, whose virtues we remember – and dogs have few faults.

(1904)

Gipsy, the Mongrel

'SHE HAD SUCH a lovely smile,' said Mary Bridger, reflectively. They were talking, the Bridgers and the Bagots, late one night over the fire about old friends. This one, Helen Folliott, the girl with the lovely smile, had vanished. None of them knew what happened to her. She had come to grief somehow, they had heard, and, they agreed, each of them had always known that she would, and, what was odd, none of them had ever forgotten her.

'She had such a lovely smile,' Lucy Bagot repeated.

And so they began to discuss the oddities of human affairs – what a toss up it seems whether you sink or swim, why one remembers and forgets, what a difference trifles make, and how people, who used to meet every day, suddenly part and never see each other again.

Then they were silent. That was why they heard a whistle – was it a train or a siren? – a faint far whistle that sounded over the flat Suffolk fields and dwindled away. The sound must have suggested something, to the Bagots anyhow, for Lucy said, looking at her husband, '*She* had such a lovely smile.' He nodded. 'You couldn't drown a puppy who grinned in the face of death,' he said. It sounded like a quotation. The Bridgers looked puzzled. 'Our dog,' said Lucy. 'Tell us the story of your dog,' the Bridgers insisted. They both liked dogs.

Tom Bagot was shy at first, as people are who catch themselves feeling more than is reasonable. He protested too that it wasn't a story; it was a character study, and they would think him sentimental. But they urged him, and he began straight off – ' "You can't drown a puppy who grins in the face of death." Old Holland said that. He said it that snowy night when he held her over the water butt. He was a farmer, down in Wiltshire. He'd heard gipsies – that's to say a whistle. Out he went into the snow with a dog whip. They'd gone; only they'd left something behind them, a crumpled piece of paper it looked like in the hedge. But it was a basket, one of those rush baskets that women take to market, and in it, stitched up so that she couldn't follow, was a little scrap of a dog. They'd given her a hunk of bread and a twist of straw – '

'Which shows,' Lucy interrupted, 'that they hadn't the heart to kill her.'

'Nor had he,' Tom Bagot went on. 'He held her over the water and then – ' he raised his little grizzled moustache over his upper teeth, 'she grinned up at him like that, in the moonlight. So he spared her. She was a wretched little mongrel, a regular gipsies' dog, half fox terrier, half the lord knows what. She looked as if she'd never had a square meal in her life. Her coat was as rough as a door scraper. But she had – what d'you call it when you forgive a person a dozen times a day against your better judgment? Charm? Character? Whatever it was, she had that. Or why did he keep her? Answer me that. She made his life a burden to him. Put all the neighbours against him. Chased their hens. Worried the sheep. A dozen times he was on the point of killing her. Yet he couldn't bring himself to do it – not until she'd killed the cat, his wife's favourite. It was the wife who insisted. So once more he took her out into the yard, stood her against the wall, and was about to pull the trigger. And again – she grinned; grinned right into the face of death, and he hadn't the heart to do it. So they left it to the butcher; he must do what they couldn't. And then – chance again. It was a little miracle in its way – our letter coming that very morning. A pure fluke, look at it which ever way you will. We lived in London then – we'd a cook, an old Irish body, who swore she'd heard rats. Rats in the wainscot. Couldn't sleep another night in the place and so on. By chance again – we'd spent a summer there – I thought of Holland, wrote and asked him if he'd a dog to sell us, a terrier, to catch rats. The postman met the butcher; it was the butcher who delivered the letter. So by the skin of her teeth Gipsy was saved again. He was glad I can tell you, – old Holland. He popped her straight into the train with a letter. "Her looks are against her",' Bagot quoted again. '"But believe me, she's a dog of character – a dog of remarkable character." We stood her out on the kitchen table. A more miserable object you never saw. "Rats? Why they'd eat her," said old Biddy. But we heard no more of that tale.'

Here Tom Bagot paused. He had come it seemed to a part of his story that he found it difficult to tell. It is difficult for a man to say why he fell in love with a woman, but it is still more difficult to say why he fell in love with a mongrel terrier. Yet that was what had happened evidently – the little beast had exerted over him some indescribable charm. It was a love story he was telling. Mary Bridger was sure of that by something in his voice. A fantastic idea came to her that he had been in love with Helen Folliot, the girl with the lovely smile. He connected the two somehow. Aren't all stories connected? she asked herself, and thus dropped a sentence or two of what he was saying. The Bagots, when she listened, were remembering absurd little stories that they hardly liked to tell, and yet they meant so much.

'She did it all off her own bat,' Tom Bagot was saying. 'We never taught her a thing. Yet every day she'd have something new to show us. One little trick after another. She'd bring me letters in her mouth. Or, Lucy lighting a match, she'd put it out' – he brought his fist down upon a match – 'so. With her naked paw. Or she'd bark when the telephone rang. "Curse that bell" she'd say as plain as anything. And visitors – d'you remember how she'd size our friends up as if they were her own? "You may stay" – she'd jump and lick your hand; "No, we don't want you" and she'd rush to the door as if to show them the way out. And she'd never make a mistake. She was as good a judge of people as you are.'

'Yes,' Lucy confirmed him, 'she was a dog of character. And yet,' she added, 'lots of people didn't see it. Which was another reason for liking her. There was that man who gave us Hector.'

Bagot took up the story.

'Hopkins by name,' he said. 'By calling a stockbroker. Very proud of his little place in Surrey. You know the sort – all boots and gaiters, like the pictures in the sporting papers. It's my belief he didn't know one end of a horse from the other. But he "couldn't endure to see us with a wretched little mongrel like that".' Bagot was quoting again. The words had evidently had a sting in them. 'So he made so bold as to give us a present. A dog called Hector.'

'A red setter,' Lucy explained.

'With a tail like a ramrod,' Bagot continued, 'and a pedigree as long as your arm. She might have sulked – Gipsy. She might have taken it amiss. But she was a dog of sense. Nothing petty about her. Live and let live – it takes all sorts to make a world. That was her motto. You'd meet 'em in the High Street – arm in arm, I was going to say, trotting round together. She taught him a thing or two I'll be bound . . .'

'Give him his due, he was a perfect gentleman,' Lucy interrupted.

'A little lacking in the upper storey,' said Tom Bagot tapping his forehead.

'But with perfect manners,' Lucy argued.

There is nothing like a dog story for bringing out people's characters, Mary Bridger reflected. Of course, Lucy had been on the side of the gentleman; Tom on the side of the lady. But the lady's charms had vanquished even the Lucy Bagot who was inclined to be hard on her sex. So she must have had something in her.

'And then?' she prompted them.

'All went smoothly. We were a happy family,' Tom continued.

'Nothing to break the harmony until – ' here he hesitated. 'Come to think of it,' he blurted out, 'you can't blame nature. She was in the prime of life – two years old. What's that for a human being? Eighteen? Twenty? And full of life – full of fun – as a girl should be.' He stopped.

'You're thinking of the dinner party,' his wife helped him. 'The night the Harvey Sinnotts dined with us. The fourteenth of February – which,' she added with a queer little smile, 'is St Valentine's day.'

'Coupling day they call it in my part of the country,' Dick Bridger interposed.

'So it was,' Tom Bagot resumed. 'St Valentine's day – the God of love isn't he? Well, people of the name of Harvey Sinnott were dining with us. Never met 'em before. Connected with the firm,' (Tom Bagot was the London partner in the great Liverpool engineering firm of Harvey, Marsh and Coppard). 'It was a formal occasion. For simple people like ourselves a bit of an ordeal. We wished to show them hospitality. We did our best. *She*,' he indicated his wife, 'took no end of trouble, fussed about for days beforehand. Everything must be just so. You know Lucy . . .' He gave her a little pat on the knee. Mary Bridger knew Lucy. She could see the table spread; the silver shining, everything as Tom said 'just so' for the honoured guest.

'It was a slap up affair and no mistake about it,' Tom Bagot went on. 'A trifle on the formal side . . .'

'She was one of those women,' Lucy struck in, 'who seemed to be asking themselves "What's it cost? Is it real?" while they talk to you. And rather over dressed. She was saying – dinner half through – what a pleasure it was – they were staying as they always did at the Ritz, or at the Carlton – to have a quiet little meal. So simple, so homely. It was such a rest. . . .'

'No sooner were the words out of her mouth,' Bagot broke in, 'than there was an explosion . . . A sort of under table earthquake. A scuffle. A squeak. And she rose to her feet in all her . . .' he spread his arms wide to show the voluminous lady, 'panoply,' he hazarded, 'and screamed, "Something's biting me! Something's biting me!"' he squeaked in imitation. 'I ducked under the table.' (He looked under the flounce of a chair.) 'Oh that abandoned little creature! That imp of mischief! There on the floor at the good lady's feet . . . she'd given birth . . . she'd had a puppy!'

The memory was too much for him. He lay back in his chair shaking with laughter.

'So,' he continued, 'I wrapped a napkin round 'em. I carried 'em both out. (Mercifully the puppy was dead, stone dead.) I faced her with the fact. I held it under her nose. Out in the back yard. Out in the moonlight, under the pure gaze of the stars. I could have beaten her within an inch of her life. But how can you beat a dog that grins . . .'

'In the face of morality?' Dick Bridger suggested.

'If you like to put it that way,' Bagot smiled. 'But her spirit! By Jove! She scampered round the yard, the little hussy, chasing a cat . . . No, I hadn't the heart to do it.'

'And the Harvey Sinnotts were very nice about it,' Lucy added. 'It broke the ice. We were all good friends after that.'

'We forgave her,' Tom Bagot continued. 'We said it mustn't happen again. And it didn't. Never again. But other things did. Lots of things. I could tell you one story after another. But the truth is,' he shook his head, 'I don't believe in stories. A dog has a character just as we have, and it shows itself just as ours do, by what we say, by all sorts of little things.'

'You'd find yourself asking, when you came into a room – it sounds absurd but its's true,' Lucy added, 'now why did she do that? just as if she were a human being. And being a dog one had to guess. Sometimes one couldn't. The leg of mutton for instance. She took it off the dinner table, held it in her forepaws, laughing. By way of a joke? At joke at our expense? It seemed so. And one day we tried to play a trick on her. She had a passion for fruit – raw fruit, apples, plums. We gave her a plum with a stone in it. What'll she do with it? we asked. Rather than hurt our feelings, if you'll believe me, she held that plum in her mouth, and then, when she thought we weren't looking, dropped the stone in her bowl of water and came back wagging her tail. It was as if she'd said, "Had you there!"'

'Yes,' said Tom Bagot, 'she taught us a lesson. I've often wondered,' he went on, 'what she was thinking of us – down there among all the boots and old matches on the hearthrug? What was her world? Do dogs see what we see or is it something different?'

They too looked down at the boots and old matches, tried for a moment to lie nose on paws gazing into the red caverns and yellow flames with a dog's eyes. But they couldn't answer that question.

'You'd see them lying there,' Bagot continued, 'Gipsy on her side of the fire, Hector on his, as different as chalk from cheese. It was a matter of birth and breeding. He was an aristocrat. She a dog of the people. It was natural with her mother a poacher, her father the lord knows who, and her master a gipsy. You'd take them out together. Hector prim as a policeman, all on the side of law and order. Gipsy jumping the railings, scaring the royal ducks, but always on the side of the sea gulls. Vagabonds like herself. We'd take her along the river, where people feed the gulls. "Take your bit of fish," she'd say. "You've earned it." I've seen her, if you'll believe me, let one of them feed out of her mouth. But she had no patience with the pampered rich – the pug dogs, the lap dogs. You could fancy they argued the matter, down there on the hearthrug. And by Jove! she converted the old Tory. We ought to have known better. Yes, I've often blamed myself. But there it is – after a thing's over, it's easy to see how it could have been prevented.'

A shadow crossed his face, as if he remembered some little tragedy that, as he said, could have been prevented, and yet to the listener would mean nothing more than the fall of a leaf, or the death of a butterfly by drowning. The Bridgers set their faces to hear whatever it was. Perhaps a car had run over her, or perhaps she had been stolen.

'It was that old fool Hector,' Bagot continued. 'I never like handsome dogs,' he explained. 'There's no harm in them, but there's no character. He may have been jealous. He hadn't her sense of what's fitting. Just because she did a thing, he'd tried to go one better. To cut the matter short – one fine day he jumped over the garden wall, crashed through a neighbour's glass house, ran between an old chap's legs, collided with a car, never hurt himself but made a dint in the bonnet – that day's work cost us five pound ten and a visit to the police court. It was all her doing. Without her he'd have been as tame as an old sheep. Well, one of them had to go. Strictly speaking it should have been Gipsy. But look at it this way. Say you've two maids; you can't keep them both; one's sure of a place, but the other – she's not everybody's money, might find herself out of a job, in the soup. You wouldn't hesitate – you'd do as we did. We gave Hector to friends; we kept Gipsy. It was unjust perhaps. Anyhow, that was the beginning of the trouble.'

'Yes, things went wrong after that,' said Lucy Bagot. 'She felt she'd done a good dog out of a home. She showed it in all sorts of ways, those queer little ways that are all a dog has after all.' There was a pause. The tragedy whatever it was came closer, the absurd little tragedy which both these middle-aged people found it so hard to tell and so hard to forget.

'We never knew till then,' Bagot continued, 'how much feeling she had in her. With human beings, as Lucy says, they can speak. They can say "I'm sorry" and there's an end of it. But with a dog it's different. Dogs can't talk. But dogs,' he added, 'remember.'

'She remembered,' Lucy confirmed him. 'She showed it. One night for instance she brought an old rag doll into the drawing-room. I was sitting there alone. She took it and laid on the floor, as if it was a present – to make up for Hector.'

'Another time,' Bagot went on, 'she brought home a white cat. A wretched beast, covered with sores, hadn't even a tail. And he wouldn't leave us. We didn't want him. She didn't either. But it meant something. To make up for Hector? Her only way? Perhaps . . .'

'Or there may have been another reason,' Lucy went on. 'That's what I never could decide. Did she want to give us a hint? To prepare us? If only she could have spoken! Then we could have reasoned with her, tried to persuade her. As it was we knew vaguely all that winter that something was wrong. She'd fall asleep and start yelping, as if she were dreaming. Then she'd wake up, run round the room with her ears cocked as if she'd heard something. Often I'd go to the door and look out. But there wasn't anyone. Sometimes she'd begin trembling all over, half afraid, half eager. If she'd been a woman, you'd have said that some temptation was gradually overcoming her. There was something she tried to resist, but couldn't, something in her blood so to speak that was too strong for her. That was the feeling we had . . . And she wouldn't go out with us any longer. She would sit there on the hearthrug listening. But it's better to tell you the facts and let you judge for yourselves.'

Lucy stopped. But Tom nodded at her. 'You tell the end,' he said, for the plain reason that he couldn't trust himself, absurd though it seemed, to tell the end himself.

Lucy Bagot began; she spoke stiffly as if she were reading from a newspaper.

'It was a winter's evening, the sixteenth of December 1937. Augustus, the white cat, sat on one side of the fire, Gipsy on the other. Snow was falling. All the street sounds were dulled I suppose by the snow. And Tom said: "You could hear a pin drop. It's as quiet as the country." And that of course made us listen. A bus passed in a distant street. A door slammed. One could hear footsteps retreating. Everything seemed to be vanishing away, lost in the falling snow. And then – we only heard it because we were listening – a whistle sounded – a long low whistle – dwindling away. Gipsy heard it. She looked up. She trembled all over. Then she grinned . . .' She stopped. She controlled her voice and said, 'Next morning she was gone.'

There was dead silence. They had a sense of vast empty space round them, of friends vanishing for ever, summoned by some mysterious voice away into the snow.

'You never found her?' Mary Bridger asked at length.

Tom Bagot shook his head.

'We did what we could. Offered a reward. Consulted the police. There was a rumour – someone had seen gipsies passing.'

'What do you think she heard? What was she grinning at?' Lucy Bagot asked. 'Oh I still pray,' she exclaimed, 'that it wasn't the end!'

(1937)

J. M. BARRIE

Nana

MRS DARLING LOVED to have everything just so, and Mr Darling had a passion for being exactly like his neighbours; so, of course, they had a nurse. As they were poor, owing to the amount of milk the children drank, this nurse was a prim Newfoundland dog, called Nana, who had belonged to no one in particular until the Darlings engaged her. She had always thought children important, however, and the Darlings had become acquainted with her in Kensington Gardens, where she spent most of her spare time peeping into perambulators, and was much hated by careless nursemaids, whom she followed to their homes and complained of to their mistresses. She proved to be quite a treasure of a nurse. How thorough she was at bath-time; and up at any moment of the night if one of her charges made the slightest cry. Of course her kennel was in the nursery. She had a genius for knowing when a cough is a thing to have no patience with and when it needs stocking round your throat. She believed to her last day in old-fashioned remedies like rhubarb leaf, and made sounds of contempt over all this new-fangled talk about germs, and so on. It was a lesson in propriety to see her escorting the children to school, walking sedately by their side when they were well behaved, and butting them back into line if they strayed. On John's footer days she never once forgot his sweater, and she usually carried an umbrella in her mouth in case of rain. There is a room in the basement of Miss Fulsom's school where the nurses wait. They sat on forms, while Nana lay on the floor, but that was the only difference. They affected to ignore her as of an inferior social status to themselves, and she despised their light talk. She resented visits to the nursery from Mrs Darling's friends, but if they did come she first whipped off Michael's pinafore and put him into the one with blue braiding, and smoothed out Wendy and made a dash at John's hair.

No nursery could possibly have been conducted more correctly, and Mr Darling knew it, yet he sometimes wondered uneasily whether the neighbours talked.

He had his position in the City to consider.

From *Peter and Wendy*

Porthos

IT WAS IN Lucerne that the Barries saw that litter of St Bernard puppies, and it was Mrs Barrie, at first, who had simply got to have one. She loved animals, and they loved her, too. But it was Barrie who could put them under another of his own and special spells. So they made their choice, but as the puppy was still too young to leave its mother, it would have to follow them a little later by itself. Farewell to Lucerne, to Pontresina and the rest of their holiday tour . . . .

In the early autumn they paid a longish visit to the Winters at Medstead. The puppy had arrived now – about twice as large as when they had last seen him – and was still growing almost visibly every day. His name at first was Glen, and then it was Porthos or occasionally Glen Porthos, and finally Glen was dropped altogether. Just Porthos, which was also, you may remember, the name of Peter Ibbetson's St Bernard; but if it comes to that, when dogs are large and gloriously greedy, it's as apt a name as anyone could find. He was brown and white, with the saddest and noblest of expressions, and the red haws which the ignorant always take to be a symptom of sore eyes. But at present he seemed strong enough, barked boomingly, panted deafeningly, and when he stood on his hind legs was already nearly as tall as his master and mistress. The latter washed, brushed, and combed incessantly. The former immediately began introducing him to a number of ingenious games. He was a lucky dog, but he was also a dog of immense character. A literary dog, too, not only because he comes into *The Little White Bird* but because for years he was always sleeping or watching patiently while his master wrote . . . .

In the afternoons you may picture the two of them taking Porthos up to Kensington Gardens, through streets in which traffic, as we know it now, hardly existed, and in which a big dog could still saunter safely and at his ease. Barrie, in overcoat and bowler-hat, as worn by all, but with a scarf to protect his chest, and a thick stick more suited to a country walk. Mrs Barrie, dressed attractively and still looking remarkably young and pretty. Porthos – or Glen sometimes – vast, gentle, and apparently melancholy. But not really. For he isn't delicate yet, as he will become, alas, all too soon; he adores both his master and mistress, and this is one of the happiest times in the day. Watch him. He knows what's going to happen now. There's a toy-shop, and as he waits outside (he has stopped here, as he always does now, and stands waving his tail), one or other of his owners will go in and buy him a toy. He likes dolls even more than a ball to take up to the Gardens – 'What age is the child, madam?' such shopkeepers are apt to ask – and has a passion, though in this case he must wait till he gets home again, for anything that is wound up and runs about by itself. Not exactly mechanically-minded. There is something more maternal in his pleasure – though he has been known to show his love by swallowing or attempting to swallow a number of such gifts. The deep, booming bark shows that he has gratefully accepted another. The trio passes on, through Palace Gates, into the Broad Walk. . . .

They had taken [a house] near Grandtully, on the Tay. Barrie did some simple fishing in little burns, while Porthos watched him or, as a sport of his own, encouraged rabbits to run away from him by pushing them gently forward with his nose. But never caught them, and wouldn't have hurt them if he had. For Porthos was always the gentlest of gentlemen, though he had one habit that was perhaps less courteous than it seemed. He didn't much care for visitors, and had a notion that if he continued to shake hands with them they would go. They were flattered and delighted. 'Your dog seems to like me,' they would say, and Porthos lay down again, gazing at them mournfully and nobly from his tragic, reproachful eyes.

Luath

IN THE GARDEN between the house and the study at Leinster Corner there was a large, new kennel. Barrie passed it as he went to and fro, and it may even have occurred to him that it was amply large enough for human occupation, though he hadn't yet thought of a father called Mr Darling. But in any case there was no dog in it, for the new, black-and-white Newfoundland puppy – a Landseer, the breeder called it – had resolutely put its four feet down about sleeping out of doors. Had also raised its voice when an attempt had been made to enforce this arrangement, and had been let in again and hadn't gone back. So that presently the kennel, having served its secret purpose, disappeared from the scene.

It was Mrs Barrie who had first discovered, as dog-lovers do, that mourning for Porthos was no protection against the same risks and responsibilities again. A new dog there had got to be. She found it, bought it, and Barrie again provided it with a name. Luath. The ignorant found it a strange name indeed. The educated recalled *The Twa Dogs* of Robert Burns, in which Luath is the poor man's dog, and is supposed to represent the peasantry. The still more scholarly may have realised that Burns, in all probability, took the name from Ossian's *Fingal*. They may also have considered that the present Luath's master was anything but a poor man – though they didn't know, as can now be revealed, that his gross income this year would come to only just under sixteen thousand pounds. But then Burn's other dog, Caesar, isn't supposed to represent wealth so much as gentility, and anyhow Luath, with its suggestion of sonorous bark, was a fine name for a very fine animal indeed.

Never quite the same, for Barrie, as his beloved and almost human St Bernard. Never quite so good at those special and intimate games. But a dog of character as he, too, soon grew to an immense size. Famous in his own era for such a passion for motoring that he would force his way into strange vehicles when the occupants were trying to alight, and only his master or mistress could get him out again. It was Luath, too, who caught hedgehogs in the garden at Black Lake, and brought them carefully to Barrie and the little Davieses, to show, it would seem, that he also knew how to play at being wrecked on an island. It was Luath, as was said before, whose head and coat were copied for Nana in *Peter Pan*. He played a scene in it himself once,

having first studied his imitator's performance from a box. But always –
though again now he walked miles with Barrie in the country and in
Kensington Gardens – he was actually just a little more his mistress's
dog. Presently he would be hers entirely, and then his master would
never have a dog again. It seems impossible that Porthos could ever
have gone out of his life like that.

Denis Mackail from *The Story of J. M. B.*

'SAKI'

Louis

'IT WOULD BE JOLLY to spend Easter in Vienna this year,' said
Strudwarden, 'and look up some of my old friends there. It's about
the jolliest place I know of to be at for Easter – '

'I thought we had made up our minds to spend Easter at Brighton,'
interrupted Lena Strudwarden, with an air of aggrieved surprise.

'You mean that you had made up your mind that we should spend
Easter there,' said her husband; 'we spent last Easter there, and
Whitsuntide as well, and the year before that we were at Worthing, and
Brighton again before that. I think it would be just as well to have a real
change of scene while we are about it.'

'The journey to Vienna would be very expensive,' said Lena.

'You are not often concerned about economy,' said Strudwarden,
'and in any case the trip to Vienna won't cost a bit more than the rather
meaningless luncheon parties we usually give to quite meaningless
acquaintances at Brighton. To escape from all that set would be a
holiday in itself.'

Strudwarden spoken feelingly; Lena Strudwarden maintained an
equally feeling silence on that particular subject. The set that she
gathered round her at Brighton and other South Coast resorts was
composed of individuals who might be dull and meaningless in themselves, but who understood the art of flattering Mrs Strudwarden. She

had no intention of foregoing their society and their homage and flinging herself among unappreciative strangers in a foreign capital.

'You must go to Vienna alone if you are bent on going,' she said; 'I couldn't leave Louis behind, and a dog is always a fearful nuisance in a foreign hotel, besides all the fuss and separation of the quarantine restrictions when one comes back. Louis would die if he was parted from me for even a week. You don't know what that would mean to me.'

Lena stooped down and kissed the nose of the diminutive brown Pomeranian that lay, snug and irresponsive, beneath a shawl on her lap.

'Look here,' said Strudwarden, 'this eternal Louis business is getting to be a ridiculous nuisance. Nothing can be done, no plans can be made, without some veto connected with that animals's whims or convenience being imposed. If you were a priest in attendance on some African fetish you couldn't set up a more elaborate code of restrictions. I believe you'd ask the Government to put off a General Election if you thought it would interfere with Louis's comfort in any way.'

By way of answer to this tirade Mrs Strudwarden stooped down again and kissed the irresponsive brown nose. It was the action of a woman with a beautifully meek nature, who would, however, send the whole world to the stake sooner than yield an inch where she knew herself to be in the right.

'It isn't as if you were in the least bit fond of animals,' went on Strudwarden, with growing irritation; 'when we are down at Kerryfield you won't stir a step to take the house dogs out, even if they're dying for a run, and I don't think you've been in the stables twice in your life. You laugh at what you call the fuss that's being made over the extermination of plumage birds, and you are quite indignant with me if I interfere on behalf of an ill-treated, over-driven animal on the road. And yet you insist on every one's plans being made subservient to the convenience of that stupid little morsel of fur and selfishness.'

'You are prejudiced against my little Louis,' said Lena, with a world of tender regret in her voice.

'I've never had the chance of being anything else but prejudiced against him,' said Strudwarden; 'I know what a jolly responsive companion a doggie can be, but I've never been allowed to put a finger near Louis. You say he snaps at any one except you and your maid, and you snatched him away from Old Lady Peterby the other day, when she wanted to pet him, for fear he would bury his teeth in her. All that I ever see of him is the tip of his unhealthy-looking little nose, peeping out from his basket or from your muff, and I occasionally hear his wheezy little bark when you take him for a walk up and down the corridor. You can't expect one to get extravagantly fond of a dog of that sort. One might as well work up an affection for the cuckoo in a cuckoo-clock.'

'He loves me,' said Lena, rising from the table, and bearing the shawl-swathed Louis in her arms. 'He loves only me, and perhaps that is why I love him so much in return. I don't care what you say against him, I am not going to be separated from him. If you insist on going to Vienna you must go alone, as far as I am concerned. I think it would be much more sensible if you were to come to Brighton with Louis and me, but of course you must please yourself.'

'You must get rid of that dog,' said Strudwarden's sister when Lena had left the room; 'it must be helped to some sudden and merciful end. Lena is merely making use of it as an instrument for getting her own way on dozens of occasions when she would otherwise be obliged to yield gracefully to your wishes or to the general convenience. I am convinced that she doesn't care a brass button about the animal itself. When her friends are buzzing round her at Brighton or anywhere else and the dog would be in the way, it has to spend whole days alone with the maid, but if you want Lena to go with you anywhere where she doesn't want to go instantly she trots out the excuse that she couldn't be separated from her dog. Have you ever come into a room unobserved and heard Lena talking to her beloved pet? I never have. I believe she only fusses over it when there's some one present to notice her.'

'I don't mind admitting,' said Strudwarden, 'that I've dwelt more than once lately on the possibility of some fatal accident putting an end to Louis's existence. It's not very easy, though, to arrange a fatality for a creature that spends most of its time in a muff or asleep in a toy kennel. I don't think poison would be good; it's obviously horribly over-fed, for I've seen Lena offer it dainties at table sometimes, but it never seems to eat them.'

'Lena will be away at church on Wednesday morning,' said Elsie Strudwarden reflectively; 'she can't take Louis with her there, and she is going on to the Dellings for lunch. That will give you several hours in which to carry out your purpose. The maid will be flirting with the chauffeur most of the time, and, anyhow, I can manage to keep her out of the way on some pretext or other.'

'That leaves the field clear,' said Strudwarden, 'but unfortunately my brain is equally a blank as far as any lethal project is concerned. The little beast is so monstrously inactive; I can't pretend that it leapt into the bath and drowned itself, or that it took on the butcher's mastiff in unequal combat and got chewed up. In what possible guise could death come to a confirmed basket-dweller? It would be too suspicious if we invented a Suffragette raid and pretended that they invaded Lena's boudoir and threw a brick at him. We should have to do a lot of other damage as well, which would be rather a nuisance, and the servants would think it odd that they had seen nothing of the invaders.'

'I have an idea,' said Elsie, 'get a box with an air-tight lid, and bore a small hole in it, just big enough to let in an india-rubber tube. Pop Louis, kennel and all, into the box, shut it down, and put the other end of the tube over the gas-bracket. There you have a perfect lethal chamber. You can stand the kennel at the open window afterwards, to get rid of the smell of the gas, and all that Lena will find when she comes home late in the afternoon will be a placidly defunct Louis.'

'Novels have been written about women like you,' said Strudwarden; 'you have a perfectly criminal mind. Let's come and look for a box.'

Two mornings later the conspirators stood gazing guiltily at a stout square box, connected with the gas-bracket by a length of india-rubber tubing.

'Not a sound,' said Elsie; 'he never stirred; it must have been quite painless. All the same I feel rather horrid now it's done.'

'The ghastly part has to come,' said Strudwarden, turning off the gas. 'We'll lift the lid slowly, and let the gas out by degrees. Swing the door to and fro to send a draught through the room.'

Some minutes later, when the fumes had rushed off, he stooped down and lifted out the little kennel with its grim burden. Elsie gave an exclamation of terror. Louis sat at the door of his dwelling, head erect and ears pricked, as coldly and defiantly inert as when they had put him into his execution chamber. Strudwarden dropped the kennel with a jerk, and stared for a long moment at the miracle-dog; then he went into a peal of chattering laughter.

It was certainly a wonderful imitation of a truculent-looking toy Pomeranian, and the apparatus that gave forth a wheezy bark when you pressed it had materially helped the imposition that Lena, and Lena's maid, had foisted on the household. For a woman who disliked animals, but liked getting her own way under a halo of unselfishness, Mrs Strudwarden had managed rather well.

'Louis is dead,' was the curt information that greeted Lena on her return from her luncheon party.

'Louis *dead*!' she exclaimed.

'Yes, he flew at the butcher-boy and bit him, and he bit me too, when I tried to get him off, so I had to have him destroyed. You warned me that he snapped, but you didn't tell me that he was down-right dangerous. I shall have to pay the boy something heavy by way of compensation, so you will have to go without those buckles that you wanted to have for Easter; also I shall have to go to Vienna to consult Dr Schroeder, who is a specialist on dogbites, and you will have to come too. I have sent what remains of Louis to Rowland Ward to be stuffed; that will be my Easter gift to you instead of the buckles. For Heaven's sake, Lena, weep, if you really feel it so much; anything would be better than standing there staring as if you thought I had lost my reason.'

Lena Strudwarden did not weep, but her attempt at laughing was an unmistakable failure.

THOMAS THORNELY

Cat and Dog

(*A Difference of Temperament*)

O Slighted useless pains! What profit lies
In pouring praise on dull regardless ears?
I dubbed thee beautiful, acclaimed thee wise
And called the world to witness that thine eyes
Outshone in lustre all the starry spheres.
    That cold inscrutable heart I could not stir,
    Nor win so much as one approving purr!

Were but the half of what I squandered spent
In adulation on thine enemy,
It had upreared such mountains of content,

Unsealed such founts of slobbering sentiment,
As had turned love to flat idolatry.
   Thy finer taste counts such ebullience crude,
   And deems emotion but disquietude!

MARCEL PROUST

Puzzlement

EVERYONE WAS SO well known in Combray, animals as well as people, that if my aunt had happened to see a dog go by which she 'didn't know at all' she would think about it incessantly, devoting to the solution of the incomprehensible problem all her inductive talent and her leisure hours.

'That will be Mme Sazerat's dog,' Françoise would suggest, without any real conviction, but in the hope of peace, and so that my aunt should not 'split her head.'

'As if I didn't know Mme Sazerat's dog!' – for my aunt's critical mind would not so easily admit any fresh fact.

'Ah, but that will be the new dog M. Galopin has brought her from Lisieux.'

'Oh, if that's what it is!'

'It seems, it's a most engaging animal,' Françoise would go on, having got the story from Théodore, 'as clever as a Christian, always in a good temper, always friendly, always everything that's nice. It's not often you see an animal so well-behaved at that age.'

From *Du Côté de Chez Swann*
Trans. C. K. Scott Moncrieff

ST JOHN LUCAS
My Dog

The curate thinks you have no soul;
   I know that he has none. But you,
Dear friend! whose solemn self-control
   In our four-square, familiar pew

Was pattern to my youth – whose bark
   Called me in summer dawns to rove –
Have you gone down into the dark
   Where none is welcome, none may love?

I will not think those good brown eyes
   Have spent their light of truth so soon;
But in some canine Paradise
   Your wraith, I know, rebukes the moon,

And quarters every plain and hill,
   Seeking its master . . . As for me,
This prayer at least the gods fulfil:
   That when I pass the flood, and see

Old Charon by the Stygian coast
   Take toll of all the shades who land,
Your little, faithful, barking ghost
   May leap to lick my phantom hand.

RUPERT BROOKE

The Little Dog's Day

All in the town were still asleep,
When the sun came up with a shout and a leap.
In the lonely streets unseen by man,
A little dog danced. And the day began.

All his life he'd been good, as far as he could,
And the poor little beast had done all that he should.
But this morning he swore, by Odin and Thor
And the Canine Valhalla – he'd stand it no more!

So his prayer he got granted – to do just what he wanted,
Prevented by none, for the space of one day.
'*Jam incipiebo,*[1] *sedere facebo,*'[2]
In dog-Latin he quoth, '*Euge! sophos! hurray!*'

He fought with the he-dogs, and winked at the she-dogs,
A thing that had never been *heard* of before.
'For the stigma of gluttony, I care not a button!' he
Cried, and ate all he could swallow – and more.

He took sinewy lumps from the shins of old frumps,
And mangled the errand-boys – when he could get 'em.
He shammed furious *rabies,*[3] and bit all the babies,[3]
And followed the cats up the trees, and then ate 'em!

They thought 'twas the devil was holding a revel,
And sent for the parson to drive him away;

[1] Now we're off.
[2] *I'll* make them sit up.
[3] Pronounce either to suit rhyme.

For the town never knew such a hullabaloo
As that little dog raised – till the end of that day.

When the blood-red sun had gone burning down,
And the lights were lit in the little town,
Outside, in the gloom of the twilight grey,
The little dog died when he'd had his day.

FRANCES CORNFORD
A Child's Dream

I had a little dog, and my dog was very small;
He licked me in the face, and he answered to my call;
Of all the treasures that were mine, I loved him most of all.

His nose was fresh as morning dew and blacker than the night;
I thought that it could even snuff the shadows and the light;
And his tail he held bravely, like a banner in a fight.

His body covered thick with hair was very good to smell;
His little stomach underneath was pink as any shell;
And I loved him and honoured him, more than words can tell.

We ran out in the morning, both of us, to play,
Up and down across the fields for all the sunny day;
But he ran so swiftly – he ran right away.

I looked for him, I called for him, entreatingly. Alas,
The dandelions could not speak, though they had seen him pass.
And nowhere was his waving tail among the waving grass.

The sun sank low – I ran; I prayed: 'If God has not the power
To find him, let me die. I cannot bear another hour.'
When suddenly I came upon a great yellow flower.

And all among its petals, such was Heaven's grace,
In that golden hour, in that golden place,
All among its petals, was his hairy face.

CAPTAIN ROBERT SCOTT
Incidents on The Last Expedition

MEARES AND THE dogs were out early, and have been running to and fro most of the day with light loads. The great trouble with them has been due to the fatuous conduct of the penguins. Groups of these have been constantly leaping on to our floe. From the moment of landing on their feet their whole attitude expressed devouring curiosity and a pig-headed disregard for their own safety. They waddle forward, poking their heads to and fro in their usually absurd way, in spite of a string of howling dogs straining to get at them. 'Hulloa!' they seem to say, 'here's a game – what do all you ridiculous things want?' And they come a few steps nearer. The dogs make a rush as far as their leashes or harness allow. The penguins are not daunted in the least, but their ruffs go up and they squawk with semblance of anger, for all the world as though they were rebuking a rude stranger – their attitude might be imagined to convey 'Oh, that's the sort of animal you are; well, you've come to the wrong place – we aren't going to be bluffed and bounced by you,' and then the final fatal steps forward are taken and they come within reach. There is a spring, a squawk, a horrid red patch on the snow, and the incident is closed. Nothing can stop these silly birds. Members of our party rush to head them off, only to be met with evasions – the penguins squawk and duck as much as to say, 'What's it got to do with you, you silly ass? Let us alone.'

With the first spilling of blood the skua gulls assemble, and soon, for them at least, there is a gruesome satisfaction to be reaped. Oddly enough, they don't seem to excite the dogs; they simply alight within a few feet and wait for their turn in the drama, clamouring and quarrelling amongst themselves when the spoils accrue. Such incidents were happening constantly to-day, and seriously demoralising the dog teams. Meares was exasperated again and again.

January 1911

THE SURFACE CRUST which breaks with a snap and sinks with a snap, startling men and animals.

Custom robs it of dread but not of interest to the dogs, who come to imagine such sounds as the result of some strange freak of hidden creatures. They become all alert and spring from side to side, hoping to catch the creature. The hope clings in spite of continual disappointment.

A dog must be either eating, asleep, or *interested*. His eagerness to snatch at interest, to chain his attention to something, is almost pathetic. The monotony of marching kills him.

This is the fearfullest difficulty for the dog driver on a snow plain without leading marks or objects in sight. The dog is almost human in its demand for living interest, yet fatally less than human in its inability to foresee.

The dog lives for the day, the hour, even the moment. The human being can live and support discomfort for its future.

4 February

WE MADE A start as usual about 10 P.M. The light was good at first, but rapidly grew worse till we could see little of the surface. The dogs showed signs of wearying. About an hour and a half after starting we came on mistily outlined pressure ridges. We were running by the sledges. Suddenly Wilson shouted 'Hold on to the sledge,' and I saw him slip a leg into a crevasse. I jumped to the sledge, but saw nothing. Five minutes after, as the teams were trotting side by side, the middle dogs of our team disappeared. In a moment the whole team were sinking – two by two we lost sight of them, each pair struggling for a foothold. Osman the leader exerted all his great strength and kept a foothold – it was wonderful to see him. The sledge stopped and we drew it aside. The situation was clear in another moment. We had been actually travelling along the bridge of a crevasse, the sledge had stopped on it, whilst the dogs hung in their harness in the abyss, suspended between the sledge and the leading dog. Why the sledge and ourselves didn't follow the dogs we shall never know. I think a fraction of a pound of added weight must have taken us down. As soon as we grasped the position, we hauled the sledge clear of the bridge and anchored it. Then we peered into the depths of the crack. The dogs were howling dismally, suspended in all sorts of fantastic positions and evidently terribly frightened. Two had dropped out of their harness, and we could see them indistinctly on a snow bridge far below. The rope at either end of the chain had bitten deep into the snow at the side of the crevasse, and with the weight below, it was impossible to move it. By this time Wilson and Cherry-Garrard, who had seen the accident, had come to our assistance. At first things looked very bad for our poor team, and I saw little prospect of rescuing them. I had luckily inquired about the Alpine rope before starting the march, and now Cherry-Garrard hurriedly brought this most essential aid. It takes one a little time to make plans under such sudden circumstances, and for some minutes our efforts were rather futile. We could get not an inch on the main trace of the sledge or on the leading rope, which was binding Osman to the snow with a throttling pressure. Then thought became clearer. We unloaded our sledge, putting in safety our sleeping-bags with the tent and cooker. Choking sounds from Osman made it clear that the pressure on him must soon be relieved. I seized the lashing off Meares' sleeping-bag, passed the tent poles across the crevasse, and with Meares managed to get a few inches on the leading line; this freed Osman, whose harness was immediately cut.

Then securing the Alpine rope to the main trace we tried to haul up together. One dog came up and was unlashed, but by this time the rope had cut so far back at the edge that it was useless to attempt to get more of it. But we could now unbend the sledge and do that for which we should have aimed from the first, namely, run the sledge across the gap and work from it. We managed to do this, our fingers constantly numbed. Wilson held on to the anchored trace whilst the rest of us laboured at the leader end. The leading rope was very small and I was fearful of its breaking, so Meares was lowered down a foot or two to secure the Alpine rope to the leading end of the trace; this done, the work of rescue proceeded in better order. Two by two we hauled the animals up to the sledge and one by one cut them out of their harness.

Strangely the last dogs were the most difficult, as they were close under the lip of the gap, bound in by the snow-covered rope. Finally, with a gasp we got the last poor creature on to firm snow. We had recovered eleven of the thirteen.

Then I wondered if the last two could not be got, and we paid down the Alpine rope to see if it was long enough to reach the snow bridge on which they were trapped. The rope is 90 feet, and the amount remaining showed that the depth of the bridge was about 65 feet. I made a bowline and the others lowered me down. The bridge was firm and I got hold of both dogs, which were hauled up in turn to the surface. Then I heard dim shouts and howls above. Some of the rescued animals had wandered to the second sledge, and a big fight was in progress. All my rope-tenders had to leave to separate the combatants; but they soon returned, and with some effort I was hauled to the surface.

All is well that ends well, and certainly this was a most surprisingly happy ending to a very serious episode. We felt we must have refreshment, so camped and had a meal, congratulating ourselves on a really miraculous escape. If the sledge had gone down Meares and I *must* have been badly injured, if not killed outright. The dogs are wonderful, but have had a terrible shaking – three of them are passing blood and have more or less serious internal injuries. Many were held up by a thin thong round the stomach, writhing madly to get free. One dog better placed in its harness stretched its legs full before and behind and just managed to claw either side of the gap – it had continued attempts to climb throughout, giving vent to terrified howls. Two of the animals hanging together had been fighting at intervals when they swung into any position which allowed them to bite one another. The crevasse for the time being was an inferno, and the time must have been all too terribly long for the wretched creatures. It was twenty minutes past three when we had completed the rescue work, and the accident must have happened before one-thirty. Some of the animals must have been dangling for over an hour.

21 February

DURING OUR TRIP to the ice and sledge journey one of our dogs, Vaida, was especially distinguished for his savage temper and generally uncouth manners. He became a bad wreck with his poor coat at Hut Point, and in this condition I used to massage him; at first the operation was mistrusted and only continued to the accompaniment of much growling, but later he evidently grew to like the warming effect and sidled up to me whenever I came out of the hut, though still with some suspicion. On returning here he seemed to know me at once, and he comes and buries his head in my legs whenever I go out of doors; he allows me to rub him and push him about without the slightest protest and scampers about me as I walk abroad. He is a strange beast – I imagine so unused to kindness that it took him time to appreciate it.

May 15

O N ARRIVAL AT the hut they [Debenham and Gran] found poor little 'Mukáka' coiled up outside the door, looking pitifully thin and weak, but with enough energy to bark at them.

This dog was run over and dragged for a long way under the sledge runners whilst we were landing stores in January (the 7th). He has never been worth much since, but remained lively in spite of all the hardships of sledging work. At Hut Point he looked a miserable object, as the hair refused to grow on his hindquarters. It seemed as though he could scarcely continue in such a condition, and when the party came back to Cape Evans he was allowed to run free alongside the sledge.

On the arrival of the party I especially asked after the little animal and was told by Demetri that he had returned, but later it transpired that this was a mistake – that he had been missed on the journey and had not turned up again later as was supposed.

I learned this fact only a few days ago and had quite given up the hope of ever seeing the poor little beast again. It is extraordinary to realise that this poor, lame, half-clad animal has lived for a whole month by himself. He had blood on his mouth when found, implying the capture of a seal, but how he managed to kill it and then get through its skin is beyond comprehension. Hunger drives hard.

13 June

O NE OF OUR best sledge dogs, 'Julick,' has disappeared. I'm afraid he's been set on by the others at some distant spot and we shall see nothing more but his stiffened carcass when the light returns. Meares thinks the others would not have attacked him and imagines he has fallen into the water in some seal hole or crack. In either case I'm afraid we must be resigned to another loss. It's an awful nuisance.

29 July

THE FIRST ADDITION to our colony came last night, when 'Lassie' produced six or seven puppies – we are keeping the family very quiet and as warm as possible in the stable.

15 August

THE WRETCHED LASSIE has killed every one of her litter. She is mother for the first time, and possibly that accounts for it. When the poor little mites were alive she constantly left them, and when taken back she either trod on them or lay on them, till not one was left alive. It is extremely annoying.

17 August

PONTING AND GRAN went round the bergs late last night. On returning they saw a dog coming over the floe from the north. The animal rushed towards and leapt about them with every sign of intense joy. Then they realised that it was our long-lost Julick.

His mane was crusted with blood and he smelt strongly of seal blubber – his stomach was full, but the sharpness of backbone showed that this condition had only been temporary.

By daylight he looks very fit and strong, and he is evidently very pleased to be home again.

We are absolutely at a loss to account for his adventures. It is exactly a month since he was missed – what on earth can have happened to him all this time? One would give a great deal to hear his tale. Everything is against the theory that he was a wilful absentee – his previous habits and his joy at getting back. If he wished to get back, he cannot have been lost anywhere in the neighbourhood, for, as Meares says, the barking of the station dogs can be heard at least 7 or 8 miles away in calm weather, besides which there are tracks everywhere and unmistakeable landmarks to guide man or beast. I cannot but think the animal has been cut off, but this can only have happened by his being carried away on broken sea ice, and as far as we know the open water has never been nearer than 10 or 12 miles at the least. It is another enigma.

28 August

WALTER DE LA MARE

The Bandog

Has anybody seen my Mopser? –
  A comely dog is he,
With hair of the colour of a Charles the fifth,
  And teeth like ships at sea,
His tail it curls straight upwards,
  His ears stand two abreast,
And he answers to the simple name of Mopser,
  When civilly addressed.

From *Peacock Pie*

LYTTON STRACHEY

An Unhappy Visit to Scotland

THE ARRIVAL WAS worst of all. A DOG! – One of those dreadful vast ones, standing higher than a table – ugh – belonging to the young woman – imagine my anguish, cooped up in the pouring rain in the tiny sitting-room with four other persons, and IT coiled about my ankles – day after day – Splitting headaches, nerves racked, yellow eyes revolving wildly in despair – and then at night having to make my way through the mist to a dark wooden outhouse where a bed had been rigged up for me, and where my agonised soles were pierced with icy oilcloths.

Letter to Henry Lamb, 24 September 1913

JULIAN GRENFELL

To a Black Greyhound

Shining black in the shining light
  Inky black in the golden sun,
Graceful as the swallow's flight,
  Light as swallow, winged one,
Swift as driven hurricane –
  Double-sinewed stretch and spring,
Muffled thud of flying feet,
  See the black dog galloping,
    Hear his wild foot-beat.

See him lie when the day is dead,
  Black curves curled on the boarded floor.
Sleepy eyes, my sleepy-head –
  Eyes that were aflame before.
Gentle now, they burn no more,
  Gentle now and softly warm,
With the fire that made them bright
  Hidden – as when after storm
    Softly falls the night.

God of speed, who makes the fire –
  God of peace, who lulls the same –
God who gives the fierce desire,
  Lust for blood as fierce as flame –
God who stands in Pity's name –
  Many may ye be or less,
Ye who rule the earth and sun:
  Gods of strength and gentleness,
    Ye are ever one.

GRAHAM GREENE

Pug, Terrier and Boxer

THE FIRST THING I remember is sitting in a pram at the top of a
hill with a dead dog lying at my feet. It was close by the fields
which were later to become, thanks to the beneficence of my rich Uncle
Edward – known for mysterious reasons as Eppy – the playing-fields of
Berkhamsted School, for even the geography of the little town was
influenced by the two big families of Greenes (seventeen Greenes
resident in one small place would seem even today an unduly high
proportion of the population, and at holiday times the Greenes could
nearly reach a quarter of a century). The dog, as I know now, was a pug
owned by my elder sister. It had been run over – by a horse-carriage? –
and killed and the nurse thought it convenient to bring the cadaver
home this way. The memory may well be a true one, as my mother once
told me how surprised she had been months later by some reference
which I made to the 'poor dog'; they were almost the first words I had
spoken.

* * *

Once on my free day I walked over the hills to Chesterfield and found
a dentist. I described to him the symptoms, which I knew well, of an

abscess. He tapped a perfectly good tooth with his little mirror and I reacted in the correct way. 'Better have it out,' he advised.

'Yes,' I said, 'but with ether.'

A few minutes' unconsciousness was like a holiday from the world. I had lost a good tooth, but the boredom was for the time being dispersed.

The only other distraction lay in the old ladies – a gay crowd who insisted on playing paper games they didn't properly understand after dinner under the direction of an elderly gentleman: 'Famous general beginning with the letter B', the sort of thing to which family life had accustomed me. They were regarded with cynical impatience by the only other young people, a pale slang-ridden schoolboy and a girl with bobbed hair who wanted a hotel flirtation. She went with me to the pub where the landlord showed us into a private room, where we sat gingerly on the edge of a table and kissed dryly, then took refuge in a half of bitter and a gin and lime. She offered me a mongrel wire-haired terrier as a souvenir, which was to be sent by rail from Leicester to Berkhamsted and was to prove the bane of my life. Later the dog played an off-stage part in a play of mine, *The Potting Shed*, and Mr Kenneth Tynan, for reasons which remain mysterious to me, believed that he represented God.

*   *   *

After the first week in Nottingham I found cheap lodgings for myself and my dog Paddy in a grim grey row with a grim grey name, Ivy House, All Saints Terrace. My landlady was a thin complaining widow with a teenaged daughter, and, when my future wife, Vivien, visited me for a holiday weekend, the girl let down a cotton-reel from upstairs and banged it on my ground-floor window to disturb our loving quiet. My high tea before work consisted almost invariably of tinned salmon which I shared with Paddy, so that most days he was sick on the floor. On overcast mornings, before going on with my hopeless novel, I would take him for a walk in the nearby park where, when you touched the leaves, they left soot on the fingers. Once I took a lace worker to high tea, but she didn't sleep with me for all that. Oxford seemed more than six months away and London very far. I had fallen into a pocket out of life and out of time, but I was not unhappy.

*   *   *

I was happy on *The Times*, and I could have remained happy there for a lifetime, if I had not in the end succeeded in publishing a novel, but not the one I was about to finish when I left Nottingham . . . Paddy I could no longer retain. I left him at Berkhamsted without regret. Luckily he had wormed his way into my mother's affection. He was the first dog she had ever cared for – perhaps because like a difficult child he was both nervous and independent. He never quite recovered his mental equilibrium after a picture in the drawing-room fell down beside him, and in those days there was no psychoanalyst for dogs.

* * *

In 1945, when the second war was over, I began to plan a novel set in Nottingham, and I revisited the city on the excuse of refreshing my memory, though it wasn't a 'necessary' journey, the only kind which in those days we were expected to make. I found the essentials were still the same, though the 'boots' had disappeared from the Black Dog Inn. I wrote no more than the first chapter of the novel before I turned instead to *The Heart of the Matter*, but in 1957 I adapted the idea into an unsatisfactory play, *The Potting Shed*, in which I gave an off-stage part to my unsatisfactory dog. Our walks together along the River Trent and down to the goose-market forced their way into the play, and 'My landlady has a penchant for tinned salmon,' I remarked through a character's mouth. 'My dog likes it, but it often makes him sick. He's not a very good dog – parents unknown.' No, whatever Tynan might think, Paddy was never intended to be God. He was just himself.

From *A Sort of Life*

T HE TELEPHONE RANG from the table by the sofa. He lifted the receiver and said 'Hello,' but no one replied. 'Hello.' He silently counted four, then put the receiver down when he heard the connection break.

'Nobody?'

'I expect it was a wrong number.'

'It's happened three times this month. Always when you are late at the office. You don't think it could be a burglar checking up to see if we are at home?'

'There's nothing worth a burglary here.'

'One reads such horrible stories, darling – men with stockings over their faces. I hate the time after sunset before you come home.'

'That's why I bought you Buller. Where *is* Buller?'

'He's in the garden eating grass. Something has upset him. Anyway, you know what he's like with strangers. He fawns on them.'

'He might object to a stocking mask all the same.'

'He would think it was put on to please him. You remember at Christmas . . . with the paper hats . . .'

'I'd always thought before we got him that boxers were fierce dogs.'

'They are – with cats.'

The door creaked and Castle turned quickly: the square black muzzle of Buller pushed the door fully open, and then he launched his body like a sack of potatoes at Castle's flies. Castle fended him off. 'Down, Buller, down.' A long ribbon of spittle descended Castle's trouser leg. He said, 'If that's fawning, any burglar would run a mile.' Buller began to bark spasmodically and wriggle his haunches, like a dog with worms, moving backwards towards the door.

'Be quite, Buller.'

'He only wants a walk.'

'At this hour? I thought you said he was ill.'

'He seems to have eaten enough grass.'

'Be quiet, Buller, damn you. No walk.'

Buller slumped heavily down and dribbled onto the parquet to comfort himself.

'The meter man was scared of him this morning, but Buller only meant to be friendly.'

'But the meter man knows him.'

'This one was new.'

'New. Why?'

'Oh, our usual man has got the flu.'

'You asked to see his card?'

'Of course. Darling, are *you* getting scared of burglars now? Stop it, Buller. Stop.' Buller was licking his private parts with the gusto of an alderman drinking soup.

*   *   *

In the afternoon he took Sam and Buller for a walk across the Common, leaving Sarah to sleep. He would have liked to leave Buller behind, but his angry protest would have wakened Sarah, so he comforted himself with the thought that Buller was unlikely to find a cat astray on the Common. The fear was always there since one summer three years before, when providence played an ill trick by providing suddenly a picnic party among the beech woods who had brought with them an expensive cat with a blue collar round its neck on a scarlet silk leash. The cat – a Siamese – had not even time to give one cry of anger or pain before Buller snapped its back and tossed the corpse over his shoulder like a man loading a sack on to a lorry. Then he had trotted attentively away between the trees, turning his head this way and that – where there was one cat there ought surely to be another – and Castle was left to face alone the angry and grief-sticken picnickers.

In October however picnickers were unlikely. All the same Castle waited till the sun had nearly set and he kept Buller on his chain all the way down King's Road past the police station at the corner of the High Street. Once beyond the canal and the railway bridge and the new houses (they had been there for a quarter of a century, but anything which had not existed when he was a boy seemed new to Castle), he let Buller loose, and immediately, like a well-trained dog, Buller splayed out and dropped his *crotte* on the edge of the path, taking his time. The eyes stared ahead, inward-looking. Only on these sanitary occasions did Buller seem a dog of intelligence. Castle did not like Buller – he had bought him for a purpose, to reassure Sarah, but Buller had proved inadequate as a watchdog, so now he was only one responsibility more, though with canine lack of judgement he loved Castle more than any other human being.

* * *

Once a month on his day off Castle was in the habit of taking Sarah and Sam for an excursion into the sandy conifered countryside of East Sussex in order to see his mother. No one ever questioned the necessity of the visit, but Castle doubted whether even his mother enjoyed it, though he had to admit she did all she could to please them – according to her own idea of what their pleasures were. Invariably the same supply of vanilla ice-cream was waiting for Sam in the deep freeze – he preferred chocolate – and though she only lived half a mile from the station, she ordered a taxi to meet them. Castle, who had never wanted a car since he returned to England, had the impression that she regarded him as an unsuccessful and impecunious son, and Sarah once told him how *she* felt – like a black guest at an anti-apartheid garden party too fussed over to be at ease.

A further cause of nervous strain was Buller. Castle had given up arguing that they should leave Buller at home. Sarah was certain that without their protection he would be murdered by masked men, though Castle pointed out that he had been bought to defend them and not to be defended himself. In the long run it proved easier to give way, though his mother profoundly disliked dogs and had a Burmese cat which it was Buller's fixed ambition to destroy. Before they arrived the cat had to be locked in Mrs Castle's bedroom, and her sad fate, deprived of human company, would be hinted at from time to time by his mother during the course of the long day. On one occasion Buller was found spread-eagled outside the bedroom door waiting his chance, breathing heavily like a Shakespearian murderer. Afterwards Mrs Castle wrote a long letter of reproach to Sarah on the subject. Apparently the cat's nerves had suffered for more than a week. She had refused to eat her diet of Friskies and existed only on milk – a kind of hunger strike.

From *The Human Factor*

EDWARD THOMAS

Man and Dog

''Twill take some getting.' 'Sir, I think 'twill so.'
The old man stared up at the mistletoe
That hung too high in the poplar's crest for plunder
Of any climber, though not for kissing under:
Then he went on against the north-east wind –
Straight but lame, leaning on a staff new-skinned,
Carrying a brolly, flag-basket, and old coat, –
Towards Alton, ten miles off. And he had not
Done less from Chilgrove where he pulled up docks.
'Twere best, if he had had 'a money-box',
To have waited there till the sheep cleared a field
For what a half-week's flint-picking would yield.
His mind was running on the work he had done
Since he left Christchurch in the New Forest, one
Spring in the 'seventies, – navvying on dock and line

From Southampton to Newcastle-on-Tyne, –
In 'seventy-four a year of soldiering
With the Berkshires, – hoeing and harvesting
In half the shires where corn and couch will grow.
His sons, three sons, were fighting, but the hoe
And reap-hook he liked, or anything to do with trees.
He fell once from a poplar tall as these:
The Flying Man they called him in hospital.
'If I flew now, to another world I'd fall.'
He laughed and whistled to the small brown bitch
With spots of blue that hunted in the ditch.
Her foxy Welsh grandfather must have paired
Beneath him. He kept sheep in Wales and scared
Strangers, I will warrant, with his pearl eye
And trick of shrinking off as he were shy,
Then following close in silence for – for what?
'No rabbit, never fear, she ever got,
Yet always hunts. Today she nearly had one:
She would and she wouldn't. 'Twas like that. The bad one!
She's not much use, but still she's company,
Though I'm not. She goes everywhere with me.
So Alton I must reach tonight somehow:
I'll get no shakedown with that bedfellow
From farmers. Many a man sleeps worse tonight
Than I shall.' 'In the trenches.' 'Yes, that's right.
But they'll be out of that – I hope they be –
This weather, marching after the enemy.'
'And so I hope. Good luck.' And there I nodded
'Good-night. You keep straight on.' Stiffly he plodded;
And at his heels the crisp leaves scurried fast,
And the leaf-coloured robin watched. They passed,
The robin till next day, the man for good,
Together in the twilight of the wood.

ALEXANDER WOOLLCOTT

Verdun Belle

I FIRST HEARD THE saga of Verdun Belle's adventure as it was being told one June afternoon under a drowsy apple-tree in the troubled valley of the Marne.

The story began in a chill, grimy Lorraine village, where, in hovels and haymows, a disconsolate detachment of United States marines lay waiting the order to go up into that maze of trenches of which the crumbling traces still weave a haunted web around the citadel bearing the immortal name of Verdun.

Into this village at dusk one day in the early spring of 1918 there came out of space a shabby, lonesome dog – a squat setter of indiscreet, complex and unguessable ancestry.

One watching her as she trotted intently along the aromatic village street would have sworn that she had an important engagement with the mayor and was, regretfully, a little late.

At the end of the street she came to where a young buck private lounged glumly on a doorstep. Halting in her tracks, she sat down to contemplate him. Then, satisfied seemingly by what she sensed and saw, she came over and flopped down beside him in a most companionable manner, settling herself comfortably as if she had come at last to her long journey's end. His pleased hand reached over and played with one silken chocolate-coloured ear.

Somehow that gesture sealed a compact between those two. There was thereafter no doubt in either's mind that they belonged to each other for better or for worse, in sickness and in health, through weal and woe, world without end.

She ate when and what he ate. She slept beside him in the day, her muzzle resting on his leg so that he could not get up in the night and go forgetfully back to America without her noticing it.

To the uninitiated onlookers her enthusiasm may not have been immediately explicable. In the eyes of his top sergeant and his company clerk he may well have seemed an undistinguished warrior, freckle-faced and immensely indifferent to the business of making the world safe for democracy.

Verdun Belle thought him the most charming person in all the world. There was a loose popular notion that she had joined up with the company as mascot and belonged to them all. She affably let them think so, but she had her own ideas on the subject.

When they moved up into the line she went along and was so obviously trench-broken that they guessed she had already served a hitch with some French regiment in that once desperate region.

They even built up the not implausible theory that she had come to them lonely from the grave of some little soldier in faded horizon blue.

Certainly she knew trench ways, knew in the narrowest of passages how to keep out from underfoot and was so well aware of the dangers of the parapet that a plate of chicken bones up there would not have interested her. She even knew what gas was, and after a reminding whiff of it became more than reconciled to the regulation gas mask, which they patiently wrecked for all subsequent human use because an unimaginative War Department had not foreseen the peculiar anatomical specifications of Verdun Belle.

In May, when the outfit was engaged in the exhausting activities which the High Command was pleased to describe as 'resting', Belle thought it a convenient time to present an interested but amply forewarned regiment with seven wriggling casuals, some black and white and mottled as a mackerel sky, some splotched with the same brown as her own.

These newcomers complicated the domestic economy of the leathernecks' haymow, but they did not become an acute problem until that memorable night late in the month when breathless word bade these troops be up and away.

The Second Division of the AEF was always being thus picked up by the scruff of the neck and flung across France. This time the enemy had snapped up Soissons and Rheims and were pushing with dreadful ease and speed towards the remembering Marne.

Foch had called upon the Americans to help stem the tide. Ahead of the marines, as they scrambled across the monotonous plain of the Champagne, there lay amid the ripening wheat fields a mean and hilly patch of timber called Belleau Wood. Verdun Belle went along.

The leatherneck had solved the problem of the puppies by drowning four and placing the other three in a basket he had begged from a village woman.

His notion that he could carry the basket would have come as a shock to whatever functionary back in Washington designed the marine pack, which, with its neat assortment of food supplies, extra clothing, emergency restoratives, and gruesome implements for destruction, had been so painstakingly calculated to exhaust the capacity of the human back. But in his need the young marine somehow contrived to add an item not in the regulations – namely, one basket containing three unweaned and faintly resentful puppies.

By night and by day the troop movement was made, now in little wheezing trains, now in swarming lorries, now afoot.

Sometimes Belle's crony rode. Sometimes (under pressure of popular clamour against the room he was taking up) he would yield up his place to the basket and jog along with his hand on the tail-board, with Belle trotting behind him.

All the soldiers in Christendom seemed to be moving across France to some nameless crossroads over the hill. Obviously this was no mere shift from one quiet sector to another. They were going to war.

Everyone had assured the stubborn youngster that he would not be able to manage, and now misgivings settled on him like crows.

He guessed that Verdun Belle must be wondering too. He turned to assure her that everything would be all right. She was not there. Ahead of him, behind him, there was no sign of her. No one within call had seen her quit the line. He kept telling himself she would show up. But the day went and the night came without her.

He jettisoned the baskest and pouched the pups in his forest-green shirt in the manner of kangaroos. In the morning one of the three was dead. And the problem of transporting the other two was now tangled by the circumstance that he had to feed them.

An immensely interested old woman in the village where they halted at dawn, vastly amused by this spectacle of a soldier trying to carry two nursing puppies to war, volunteered some milk for the cup of his mess kit, and with much jeering advice from all sides, and, by dint of the eye-dropper from his pack, he tried sheepishly to be a mother to the two waifs. The attempt was not shiningly successful.

He itched to pitch them over the fence. But if Verdun Belle had not been run over by some thundering camion, if she lived she would find him, and then what would he say when her eyes asked what he had done with the pups?

So, as the order was shouted to fall in, he hitched his pack to his back and stuffed his charges back into his shirt.

Now, in the morning light, the highway was choked. Down from the lines in agonized, grotesque rout came the stream of French life from the threatened countryside, jumbled fragments of fleeing French regiments. But America was coming up the road.

It was a week in which the world held its breath.

The battle was close at hand now. Field hospitals, jostling in the river of traffic, sought space to pitch their tents. The top sergeant of one such outfit was riding on the driver's seat of an ambulance. Marines in endless number were moving up fast.

It was one of these who, in a moment's halt, fell out of line, leaped to the step of the blockaded ambulance, and looked eagerly into the medico top sergeant's eyes.

'Say, buddy,' whispered the youngster, 'take care of these for me. I lost their mother in the jam.'

The Top found his hands closing on two drowsy pups.

All that day the field-hospital personnel was harried by the task of providing nourishment for the two casuals who had been thus unexpectedly attached to them for rations. Once established in a farmhouse (from which they were promptly shelled out), the Top went over the possible provender and found that the pups were not yet equal to a diet of bread, corn syrup and corned willy. A stray cow, loosed from her moorings in the great flight, was browsing tentatively in the next field, and two orderlies who had carelessly reminisced of life on their farms back home were detailed to induce her co-operation.

But the bombardment had brought out a certain moody goatishness in this cow, and she would not let them come near her. After a hot and maddening chase that lasted two hours, the two milkmen reported a complete failure to their disgusted chief.

The problem was still unsolved at sundown, and the pups lay faint in their bed of absorbent cotton out in the garden, when, bringing up the rear of a detachment of marines that straggled past, there trotted a brown-and-white setter.

'It would be swell if she had milk in her,' the top sergeant said reflectively, wondering how he could salvage the mascot of an outfit on the march.

But his larcenous thoughts were waste. At the gate she halted dead in her tracks, flung her head high to sniff the air, wheeled sharp to the left and became just a streak of brown and white against the ground. The entire staff came out and formed a jostling circle to watch the family reunion.

After that it was tacitly assumed that these casuals belonged. When the hospital was ordered to shift farther back beyond the reach of the whining shells, Verdun Belle and the pups were entrusted to an ambulance driver and went along in style. They all moved – bag, baggage and livestock – into the deserted little Château of the Guardian Angel, of which the front windows were curtained against the eyes and dust of the road, but of which the rear windows looked out across drooping fruit trees upon a sleepy, murmurous, multi-coloured valley, fair as the Garden of the Lord.

The operating tables, with acetylene torches to light them, were set up in what had been a tool shed. Cots were strewn in the orchard alongside. Thereafter for a month there was never rest in that hospital.

The surgeons and orderlies took spells, snatching morsels of sleep and returning a few hours later to relieve the others. But Verdun Belle took no time off. Between cat naps in the corner, due attentions to her restive brood and an occasional snack for herself, she managed some-how to be on hand for every ambulance, cursorily examining each casualty as he was lifted to the ground.

Then, in the four o'clock dark of one morning, the orderly bending over a stretcher that had just been rested on the ground was hit by something that half-bowled him over.

The projectile was Verdun Belle. Every quivering inch of her proclaimed to all concerned that here was a case she was personally in charge of. From nose to tail tip she was taut with excitement, and a kind of eager whimpering bubbled up out of her as if she ached to sit back on her haunches and roar to the star-spangled sky but was really too busy at the moment to indulge herself in any release so satisfying to her soul. For here was this mess of a leatherneck of hers to be washed up first. So like him to get all dirty the moment her back was turned! The first thing he knew as he came to was the feel of a rough pink tongue cleaning his ears.

I saw them all next day. An ambling passer-by, I came upon two cots shoved together under an apple-tree. Belle and her ravenous pups occupied one of these. On the other the young marine – a gas case, I think, but maybe his stupor was shell-shock and perhaps he had merely had a crack on the head – was deep in a dreamless sleep. Before drifting off he had taken the comforting precaution to reach out one hand and close it tight on a silken ear.

Later that day he told me all about his dog. I doubt if I ever knew his name, but some quirk of memory makes me think his home was in West Philadelphia and that he had joined up with the marines when he came out of school.

I went my way before dark and never saw them again, nor ever heard tell what became of the boy and his dog. I never knew when, if ever, he was shipped back into the fight, nor where, if ever, those two met again. It is, you see, a story without an end, though there must be those here and there in this country who witnessed and could set down for us the chapter that has never been written.

I hope there was something prophetic in the closing paragraph of the anonymous account of Verdun Belle which appeared the next week in the AEF newspaper, *The Stars and Stripes*. That paragraph was a benison which ran in this wise:

Before long they would have to ship him on to the evacuation hospital, on from there to the base hospital, on and on and on. It was not very clear to anyone how another separation could be prevented. It was a perplexing question, but they knew in their hearts they could safely leave the answer to someone else. They could leave it to Verdun Belle.

J. C. SQUIRE

To a Bull-dog

(*W. H. S., Capt. [Acting Major] RFA; killed April 12, 1917*)

We shan't see Willy any more, Mamie,
    He won't be coming any more:
He came back once and again and again,
    But he won't get leave any more.

We looked from the window and there was his cab,
    And we ran downstairs like a streak,
And he said 'Hullo, you bad dog,' and you crouched to the floor,
    Paralysed to hear him speak.

And then let fly at his face and his chest
    Till I had to hold you down,

While he took off his cap and his gloves and his coat,
  And his bag and his thonged Sam Browne.

We went upstairs to the studio,
  The three of us, just as of old,
And you lay down and I sat and talked to him
  As round the room he strolled.

Here in the room where, years ago
  Before the old life stopped,
He worked all day with his slippers and his pipe,
  He would pick up the threads he'd dropped,

Fondling all the drawings he had left behind,
  Glad to find them all still the same,
And opening the cupboards to look at his belongings
  . . . Every time he came.

But now I know what a dog doesn't know,
  Though you'll thrust your head on my knee,
And try to draw me from the absent-mindedness
  That you find so dull in me.

And all your life you will never know
  What I wouldn't tell you even if I could,
That the last time we waved him away
  Willy went for good.

But sometimes as you lie on the hearthrug
  Sleeping in the warmth of the stove,
Even through your muddled old canine brain
  Shapes from the past may rove.

You'll scarcely remember, even in a dream,
   How we brought home a silly little pup,
With a big square head and little crooked legs
   That could scarcely bear him up,

But your tail will tap at the memory
   Of a man whose friend you were,
Who was always kind though he called you a naughty dog
   When he found you on his chair;

Who'd make you face a reproving finger
   And solemnly lecture you
Till your head hung downwards and you looked very sheepish!
   And you'll dream of your triumphs too.

Of summer evening chases in the garden
   When you dodged us all about with a bone:
We were three boys, and you were the cleverest,
   But now we're two alone.

When summer comes again,
   And the long sunsets fade,
We shall have to go on playing the feeble game for two
   That since the war we've played.

And though you run expectant as you always do
   To the uniforms we meet,
You'll never find Willy among all the soldiers
   In even the longest street,

Nor in any crowd; yet, strange and bitter thought,
   Even now were the old words said,
If I tried the old trick and said 'Where's Willy?'
   You would quiver and lift your head,

And your brown eyes would look to ask if I were serious,
  And wait for the word to spring.
Sleep undisturbed: I shan't say *that* again,
  You innocent old thing.

I must sit, not speaking, on the sofa,
  While you lie asleep on the floor;
For he's suffered a thing that dogs couldn't dream of,
  And he won't be coming here any more.

GEOFFREY DEARMER

The Turkish Trench Dog

Night held me as I crawled and scrambled near
The Turkish lines. Above, the mocking stars
Silvered the curving parapet, and clear
Cloud-latticed beams o'erflecked the land with bars;
I, crouching, lay between
Tense-listening armies peering through the night,
Twin giants bound by tentacles unseen.
Here in dim-shadowed light
I saw him, as a sudden movement turned
His eyes towards me, glowing eyes that burned
A moment ere his snuffling muzzle found
My trail; and then as serpents mesmerize
He chained me with these unrelenting eyes,
That muscle-sliding rhythm, knit and bound
In spare-limbed symmetry, those perfect jaws
And soft approaching pitter-patter paws.
Nearer and nearer like a wolf he crept –

That moment had my swift revolver leapt –
But terror seized me, terror born of shame
Brought flooding revelation. For he came
As one who offers comradeship deserved,
An open alley of the human race,
And sniffling at my prostrate form unnerved
He licked my face!

COLETTE

The Bitch

W HEN THE SERGEANT arrived in Paris on leave, he found his
mistress not at home. He was nevertheless greeted with tremulous
cries of surprise and joy, embraced and covered with wet kisses. His
bitch, Voracc, the sheep dog whom he had left with his young
sweetheart, enveloped him like a flame and licked him with a tongue
pale with emotion.

Meanwhile, the charwoman was making as much noise as the dog
and kept exclaiming: 'Of all the bad luck! Madame's just gone to
Marlotte for a couple of days to shut up her house there. Madame's
tenants have just left and she's going through the inventory of the
furniture. Fortunately, it isn't all that far away! Will Monsieur write out
a telegram for Madame? If it goes immediately, Madame will be here
tomorrow morning before lunch. Monsieur must sleep here. Shall I
turn on the water heater?'

'My good Lucie, I had a bath at home. Soldiers on leave are pretty
good at washing!'

He eyed his reflection in the glass; he was both bluish and ruddy,
like the granite rocks of Brittany. The Briard sheep dog, standing close
to him in a reverent silence, was trembling in every hair. He laughed
because she looked so like him, gray and blue and shaggy.

'Vorace!'

She raised her head and looked lovingly at her master, and the sergeant's heart turned over as he suddenly thought of his mistress, Jeannine, so young and so gay – a little too young and often too gay.

During dinner the dog faithfully observed all the ritual of their former life, catching the pieces of bread he tossed for her and barking at certain words. So ardent was the worship in which she was rooted that the moment of return abolished for her the months of absence.

'I've missed you a lot,' he told her in a low voice. 'Yes, you too!'

He was smoking now, half lying on the divan. Crouching like a greyhound on a tombstone, the dog was pretending to be asleep, her ears quite still. Only her eyebrows, twitching at the slightest noise, revealed that she was on the alert.

Worn out as he was, the silence gradually lulled the man, until his hand which held the cigarette slid down the cushion, scorching the silk. He roused himself, opened a book, fingered a few new knickknacks and a photograph, which he had not seen before, of Jeannine in a short skirt, with bare arms, in the country.

'An amateur snapshot . . . How charming she looks!'

On the back of the unmounted print he read: '*June 5, 1916.* Where was I on June the fifth? . . . Oh, I know, over in the direction of Arras. June the fifth. I don't know the writing.'

He sat down again and was overcome by a sleep which drove all thought away. Ten o'clock struck; he was still just sufficiently awake to smile at the rich and solemn sound of the little clock whose voice, Jeannine used to say, was bigger than its stomach. But as it struck ten the dog got up.

'Quiet!' said the sleepy sergeant. 'Lie down!'

But Vorace did not lie down. She snorted and stretched her paws, which, for a dog, is the same as putting on a hat to go out. She went up to her master and her yellow eyes asked plainly: 'Well?'

'Well,' he answered, 'what's the matter with you?'

Out of respect she dropped her ears while he was speaking, raising them again immediately.

'Oh, what a bore you are?' sighed the sergeant. 'You're thirsty! D'you want to go out?'

At the words 'go out,' Vorace grinned and began to pant gently, showing her beautiful teeth and the fleshy petal of her tongue.

'All right, then, we'll go out. But not for long, because I'm absolutely dropping with sleep.'

In the road Vorace was so excited that she barked like a wolf, jumped

right up to her master's neck, charged a cat, and spun around playing
'inner circle' with her tail. Her master scolded her tenderly and she did
all her tricks for him. Finally, she sobered down again and walked along
sedately. The sergeant suited his pace to hers, enjoying the warm night
and making a little song out of two or three idle thoughts.

'I'll see Jeannine tomorrow morning . . . I'm going to sleep in a comfy
bed . . . I've got seven more days to spend here . . .'

He became aware that his dog, which had trotted ahead, was waiting
for him under a gas lamp with the same look of impatience. Her eyes,
her wagging tail, and her whole body asked: 'Well? Are you coming?'

As soon as he caught up with her, she turned the corner at a
determined trot. It was then that he realized she was going somewhere.

'Perhaps,' he thought to himself, 'the charwoman usually . . . Or
Jeannine . . .'

He stood still for a moment, then went on again, following the dog,
without even noticing that he had, all at once, stopped feeling tired, and
sleepy, and happy. He quickened his pace and the delighted dog went
ahead, like a good guide.

'Go on, go on!' ordered the sergeant from time to time.

He looked at the name of a road, then went on again. They passed
gardens with lodges at the gates; the road was dimly lit and they met no
one. In her excitement, the dog pretended to bite the hand that hung at
his side, and he had to restrain a brutal impulse, which he could not
explain, in order not to beat her.

At last she stopped, as though saying: 'Well, here we are!' before an
old, broken-down railing, protecting the garden of a little low house
smothered in vines and bignonia, a timid, shrouded little house.

'Well, why don't you open it?' said the dog, which had taken up a
position before the wooden wicket gate.

The sergeant lifted his hand to the latch and let it fall again. He bent
down to the dog, pointed with his finger to a thread of light along the
closed shutters, and asked her in a low voice: 'Who's there? . . .
Jeannine?'

The dog gave a shrill 'Hi!' and barked.

'Shhh!' breathed the sergeant, clapping his hands over her cool, wet
mouth.

Once more he stretched out a hesitant arm toward the door and the
dog bounded forward. But he held her back by her collar and led her to
the opposite pavement, whence he gazed at the unknown house and the
thread of rosy light. He sat down on the pavement beside the dog. He

had not yet gathered together all those images and thoughts which spring up around a possible betrayal, but he felt singularly alone, and weak.

'Do you love me?' he murmured in the dog's ear.

She licked his cheek.

'Come on; let's go away.'

They set off, he in front this time. And when they were once more in the little sitting room, she saw that he was putting his linen and slippers in a sack that she knew well. Desperate but respectful, she followed all his movements, while tears, the color of gold, trembled in her yellow eyes. He laid his hand on her neck to reassure her.

'You're coming too. I'm not going to leave you anymore. Next time you won't be able to tell me what happened "after." Perhaps I'm mistaken. Perhaps I haven't understood you properly. But you mustn't stay here. Your soul wasn't meant to guard any secrets but mine.'

And while the dog shivered, still uncertain, he held her head in his hands, saying to her in a low voice: 'Your soul ... Your doggy soul ... Your beautiful soul ...'

Trans. *Enid McLeod*

CHARLIE CHAPLIN

Purps

EVERYTHING WAS READY for shooting to start on 15 January 1918. The first production was provisionally titled *I Should Worry*: only when it was completed did Chaplin decide on the title *A Dog's Life*. It remains one of his most perfect films. Louis Delluc called it 'the cinema's first total work of art'. It is as fast and prodigal of gags as a Karno sketch; its individual scenes cohere into a purposeful structure; at the same time it has a harder core of reality than any film that Chaplin had made before. It is about street life, low life, poverty and hunger, prostitution and exploitation. Without pretension and without sacrificing anything of its comic verve, Chaplin drives home the parallel between the existence of a stray dog, Scraps, and two human unfortunates – Charlie the Tramp and Edna, the bar singer. *A Dog's Life*, said *Photoplay* 'though only a grimy little backyard tableau, ranks with the year's few real achievements.' . . .

A Dog's Life has a strange and charming little coda. The last image of Charlie's escape from the crooks ends on an iris-out. This is followed by an iris-in on a vast ploughed field. Charlie, in a big straw hat, astride a ridge between the furrows, waddles along, dibbing holes with his forefinger and planting a seed in each. He looks up and waves happily towards the camera and to Edna, awaiting him in their idyllic little cottage, all cretonne and Home Sweet Home. A cradle stands beside the fire, and the couple gaze into it with pride. The audience is permitted to jump to the obvious conclusion before the interior of the cradle is revealed: within lies a proud Scraps amongst a litter of puppies. The pride is not unjustified – in earlier scenes Scraps' male sex has been more than evident.

Charlie had perceived the comic possibilities of dogs at least as early as *The Champion* – and Sydney had introduced canine comedy into Karno's *Flats* sketch years earlier. More than a year before he began *A Dog's Life*, in December 1916, the newspapers were carrying the headline 'Chaplin Wants A Dog with Lots of Comedy Sense'. Chaplin told the reporters:

> For a long time I've been considering the idea that a good comedy dog would be an asset in some of my plays, and of course the first that was offered me was a dachshund. The long snaky piece of hose got on my nerves. I bought him from a fat man named Ehrmentraut, and when Sausages went back to his master I made no kick.
>
> The second was a Pomeranian picked up by Miss Purviance, who had him clipped where he ought to have worn hair and left him with whiskers where he didn't need 'em. I got sick of having 'Fluffy Ruffles' round me so I traded the 'Pom' for Helene Rosson's poodle. That moon-eyed snuffling little beast lasted two days.

After this he was reported to have tried a Boston bull terrier, and in March 1917 he was said to have been seen in the company of a pedigree English bulldog called Bandy, whose grandmother, appropriately, was Brixton Bess.

'What I really want,' he said, 'is a mongrel dog. The funniest "purps" I ever set eyes on were mongrels. These studio beasts are too well kept. What I want is a dog that can appreciate a bone and is hungry enough to be funny for his feed. I'm watching all the alleys and some day I'll come home with a comedy dog that will fill the bill.' If the news reports are to be believed, after starting work on *A Dog's Life* Chaplin had taken into the studio twenty-one dogs from the Los Angeles pound. In response to complaints from the neighbours, however, the city authorities insisted that he reduce the number to twelve. The studio petty cash accounts show entries for dogs' meat starting from the second week of production and continuing until the end of shooting. The star of the film, a charming little mongrel called Mut (or Mutt), certainly became resident and remained on staff until his untimely death.

David Robinson, from *Chaplin: His Life and Art*

KATHERINE MANSFIELD

An Evening in Fulham

THE SKY IS PALE AND clear: the silly piano is overcome and reels out waltzes – old waltzes, spinning, drunk with sentiment – gorged with memory.

This is the hour when the poor underfed dog appears, at a run, nosing the dry gutter. He is so thin that his body is like a cage on four wooden pegs. His lean triangle of a head is down, his long straight tail is out, and up and down, up and down he goes, silent and fearfully eager. The street watches him from its creeper-covered balconies, from its open windows – but the fat lady on the ground floor who is no better than she should be comes out, down the steps to the gate, with a bone. His tail, as he waits for her to give it him, bangs against the gate post, like a broom-handle – and the streets says she's a fool to go feeding strange dogs. Now she'll never be rid of him.

(What I'd like to convey is that, at this hour, with this half light and the pianos and the open, empty sounding houses, he is the spirit of the

[Redcliffe] street – running up and down, poor dog, when he ought to have been done away with years ago.)

From *Journal*, July 1918

A Visitor in Menton

CONNIE [BEAUCHAMP] CAME yesterday to see me carrying a baby Pekinese. Have you ever seen a really *baby* one about the size of a fur glove – covered with pale gold down with paws like minute seal flappers – very large impudent eyes & ears like fried potatoes? Good God! What creatures they are. This one is a perfect complement to Wing. We *must* have one. They are not in the least pampered or fussy or spoilt. They are like fairy animals. This one sat on my lap, cleaned both my hands really very carefully, polished the nails then bit off carefully each finger & thumb & then exhausted and blown with 8 fingers & two thumbs inside him gave a great sigh & crossed his front paws & listened to the conversation. He lives on beef steaks and loaf sugar. His partner in life when he is at home is a pale blue satin bedroom slipper. Please let us have one at the Heron.

To John Middleton Murry, 23 January 1920

ADOLF HITLER

A Super Race

HOW MANY TIMES, at Fromelles, during the first World War, I've studied my dog Foxl. When he came back from a walk with the huge bitch who was his companion, we found him covered with bites. We'd no sooner bandaged him, and had ceased to bother about him, than he would shake off this unwanted load.

A fly began buzzing. Foxl was stretched out at my side, with his muzzle between his paws. The fly came close to him. He quivered, with his eyes as if hypnotised. His face wrinkled up and acquired an old man's expression. Suddenly he leapt forward, barked and became agitated. I used to watch him as if he'd been a man – the progressive stages of his anger, of the bile that took possession of him. He was a fine creature.

When I ate, he used to sit beside me and follow my gestures with his gaze. If by the fifth or sixth mouthful I hadn't given him anything, he used to sit up on his rump and look at me with an air of saying: 'And what about me, am I not here at all?' It was crazy how fond I was of the beast. Nobody could touch me without Foxl's instantly becoming furious. He would follow nobody but me. When gas-warfare started, I couldn't go on taking him into the front line. It was my comrades who fed him. When I returned after two days' absence, he would refuse to leave me again. Everybody in the trenches loved him. During marches he would run all round us, observing everything, not missing a detail. I used to share everything with him. In the evening he used to lie beside me.

To think that they stole him from me! I'd made a plan, if I got out of the war alive, to procure a female companion for him. I couldn't have parted from him. I've in my life never sold a dog. Foxl was a real circus dog. He knew all the tricks.

I remember, it was before we arrived at Colmar. The railway employee who coveted Foxl came again to our carriage and offered me two hundred marks. 'You could give me two hundred thousand, and you wouldn't get him!' When I left the train at Harpsheim, I suddenly noticed that the dog had disappeared. The column marched off, and it was impossible for me to stay behind! I was desperate. The swine who stole my dog doesn't realise what he did to me.

It was in January 1915 that I got hold of Foxl. He was engaged in pursuing a rat that had jumped into our trench. He fought against me, and tried to bite me, but I didn't let go. I led him back with me to the rear. He constantly tried to escape. With exemplary patience (he didn't understand a word of German), I gradually got him used to me. At first I gave him only biscuits and chocolate (he'd acquired his habits with the English, who were better fed than we were). Then I began to train him. He never went an inch from my side. At that time, my comrades had no use at all for him. Not only was I fond of the beast, but it interested me to study his reactions. I finally taught him everything:

how to jump over obstacles, how to climb up a ladder and down again. The essential thing is that a dog should always sleep beside its master. When I had to go up into the line, and there was a lot of shelling, I used to tie him up in the trench. My comrades told me that he took no interest in anyone during my absence. He would recognise me even from a distance. What an outburst of enthusiasm he would let loose in my honour! We called him Foxl. He went through all the Somme, the battle of Arras. He was not at all impressionable. When I was wounded, it was Karl Lanzhammer who took care of him. On my return, he hurled himself on me in frenzy.

When a dog looks in front of him in a vague fashion and with clouded eyes, one knows that images of the past are chasing each other through his memory.

* * *

I love animals, and especially dogs. But I'm not so very fond of boxers, for example. If I had to take a new dog, it could only be a sheepdog, preferably a bitch. I would feel like a traitor if I became attached to a dog of any other breed. What extraordinary animals they are – lively, loyal, bold, courageous and handsome!

The blind man's dog is one of the most touching things in existence. He's more attached to his master than to any other dog. If he allows a bitch to distract his attention for a moment, it's for hardly any time and he has a bad conscience. With bitches it's more difficult. When they're in heat, they can't be restrained.

During the winter of 1921–22, I was offered a sheep dog. He was so sad at the thought of his old master that he couldn't get accustomed to me. I therefore decided to part with him. His new master had gone a few steps, when he gave him the slip and took refuge with me, putting his paws on my shoulders. So I kept him.

When Graf made me a present of Muck, the process of getting accustomed was quicker. He came up the stairs rather hesitantly. When he saw Blondi, he rushed towards her, wagging his tail. Next day, it was indescribable. A dog gets used to a new master more quickly when there's already a dog in the house. It's enough even if he learns from the scent that his new master has recently had a dog; he feels himself trusted. The dog is the oldest of the domestic animals. He has been man's companion for more than thirty thousand years. But man, in his pride, is not capable of perceiving that even between dogs of the same breed there are extraordinary differences. There are stupid dogs and others who are so intelligent that it's agonising.

*　　*　　*

In many ways, my sheepdog Blondi is a vegetarian. There are lots of herbs which she eats with obvious pleasure, and it is interesting to see how she turns to them if her stomach is out of order. It is astonishing to see how wise animals are, and how well they know what is good for them.

I once watched how a cat went about eating a mouse. She did not gobble it at once, but first of all played with it, as if giving it the chance to escape. It was only when the mouse was bathed in sweat with all this running hither and thither that the cat gave it the *coup de grâce* and ate it. Obviously it is in this state that the mouse appears most succulent and savoury to the cat.

From *Table Talk*

GERTRUDE STEIN

Polybe

IT WAS DURING this stay at Palma de Mallorca that most of the plays afterwards published in *Geography and Plays* were written. She always says that a certain kind of landscape induces plays and the country around Terreno certainly did.

We had a dog, a mallorcan hound, the hounds slightly crazy, who dance in the moonlight, striped, not all one colour as the spanish hound of the continent. We called this dog Polybe because we were pleased with the articles in the Figaro signed Polybe. Polybe was, as Monsieur Marchand said, like an arab, *bon accueil à tout le monde et fidèle à personne.* He had an incurable passion for eating filth and nothing would stop him. We muzzled him to see if that would cure him, but this so outraged the russian servant of the english consul that we had to give it up. Then he took to annoying sheep. We even took to quarrelling with Cook about Polybe. Cook had a fox-terrier called Marie-Rose and we were convinced that Marie-Rose led Polybe into mischief and then virtuously withdrew and let him take the blame. Cook was convinced that we did not know how to bring up Polybe. Polybe had one nice trait. He would sit in a chair and gently smell large bunches of tube-roses with which I always filled a vase in the centre of the room on the floor. He never tried to eat them, he just gently smelled them. When we left we left Polybe behind us in the care of one of the guardians of the old fortress of Belvar. When we saw him a week after he did not know us or his name. Polybe comes into many of the plays Gertrude Stein wrote at that time.

From *The Autobiography of Alice B. Toklas*

THOMAS HARDY

Grave Concern

FORSTER'S ACQUAINTANCE with the Hardys, engineered by Sasson, had flourished, and this July [1922], as several times later, he went down on a visit to Max Gate. He wondered about his own motives, a little; for as a conversationalist he found Hardy very boring. Especially so about books. Forster determined, on this visit, to keep the talk away from books, and he did quite well, with topics like the discomfort of charabancs and whether 'chicken' was a singular or a plural. However, eventually Hardy sensed his drift and, Forster told Sasson, 'with commendable pique he insisted on revealing the secrets of his art'. Forster noticed how anxious Hardy was to make a good impression, no matter upon whom. While they were having tea, a reporter was announced, at which Hardy sprang up with alacrity, saying 'Reporters are very important people, you know.' Being very deaf, he had not heard the reporter's knock, but the dog 'Wessie', who had, had given a bark: Hardy, in a tone of significance, said '*They* know,' as if Wessie had displayed some preternatural faculty. Someone had said that Wessie looked like Robert Bridges, and Hardy, who was envious of Bridges, repeated this with relish. (Forster later remembered this with pleasure, when Bridges, who was envious of Hardy, said to him, when preparing an anthology of recent verse: 'I tried to find two poems by Hardy to include, but I couldn't, you know, I really couldn't.') Hardy showed Forster the graves of his pets, each with a headstone, now overgrown with ivy. They all seemed to have come to violent ends: 'This is Snowball – she was run over by a train. . . . This is Pella, the same thing happened to her. . . . This is Kitkin, she was cut clean in two . . .' Forster asked: 'How is it, Mr Hardy, that so many of your cats have been run over? Is the railway near?' 'Not at all near, not at all near. I don't know how it is. . . . But of course we have only buried those pets whose bodies were recovered. Many were never seen again.' Forster, reporting the scene to his mother (19 July 1922) said he could hardly keep grave, it was so like one of Hardy's novels or poems.

P. N. Furbank, from *E. M. Forster: A Life*

The Mongrel

In Havenpool Harbour the ebb was strong,
And a man with a dog drew near and hung,
And taxpaying day was coming along,
   So the mongrel had to be drowned.
The man threw a stick from the paved wharf-side
Into the midst of the ebbing tide,
And the dog jumped after with ardent pride
   To bring the stick aground.

But no: the steady suck of the flood
To seaward needed, to be withstood,
More than the strength of mongrelhood
   To fight its treacherous trend.
So, swimming for life with desperate will,
The struggler with all his natant skill
Kept buoyant in front of his master, still
   There standing to wait the end.

The loving eyes of the dog inclined
To the man he held as a god enshrined,
With no suspicion in his mind
   That this had all been meant.
Till the effort not to drift from shore
Of his little legs grew slower and slower,
And, the tide still outing with brookless power,
   Outward the dog, too, went.

Just ere his sinking what does one see
Break on the face of that devotee?
A wakening to the treachery
   He had loved with love so blind?
The faith that had shone in that mongrel's eyes
That his owner would save him by and by
Turned to much like a curse as he sank to die,
   And a loathing of mankind.

Why She Moved House

(*The Dog Muses*)

Why she moved house, without a word,
   I cannot understand;
She'd mirrors, flowers, she'd book and bird,
   And callers in a band.

And where she is she gets no sun,
   No flowers, no book, no glass;
Of callers I am the only one,
   And I but pause and pass.

A Popular Personage at Home

'I live here: "Wessex" is my name:
I am a dog known rather well:
I guard the house; but how that came
To be my whim I cannot tell.

'With a leap and a heart elate I go
At the end of an hour's expectancy
To take a walk of a mile or so
With the folk I let live here with me.

'Along the path, amid the grass
I sniff, and find out rarest smells
For rolling over as I pass
The open fields towards the dells.

'No doubt I shall always cross this sill,
And turn the corner, and stand steady,
Gazing back for my mistress till
She reaches where I have run already,

'And that this meadow with its brook,
And bulrush, even as it appears
As I plunge by with hasty look,
Will stay the same a thousand years.'

Thus 'Wessex'. But a dubious ray
At times informs his steadfast eye,
Just for a trice, as though to say,
'Yet, will this pass, and pass shall I?'

Dead 'Wessex' the Dog to the Household

Do you think of me at all,
  Wistful ones?
Do you think of me at all
  As if nigh?
Do you think of me at all
At the creep of evenfall,
Or when the sky-birds call
  As they fly?

Do you look for me at times,
  Wistful ones?
Do you look for me at times
  Strained and still?
Do you look for me at times,
When the hour for walking chimes,
On that grassy path that climbs
  Up the hill?

You may hear a jump or trot,
  Wistful ones,
You may hear a jump or trot –
  Mine, as 'twere –
You may hear a jump or trot
On the stair or path or plot;
But I shall cause it not,
  Be not there.

Should you call as when I knew you,
  Wistful ones,
Should you call as when I knew you,
  Shared your home;
Should you call as when I knew you,

I shall not turn to view you,
I shall not listen to you,
Shall not come.

SOMERVILLE & ROSS

Divagations

IN CONSIDERING THE relations between dogs and ourselves I feel
that it must be allowed that we have done them a wrong in inflicting
upon them a human conscience, a perfectly artificial Sensitiveness, that
condemns nearly all their natural tastes and wishes, even though – and
again I am reminded of human consciences – it sometimes fails to
interfere. For example, the creature that may be called the Natural
Dog, which – (if we are to believe what we are told) – has been evolved
from a wolf-cub is, by birth and heredity, accustomed to select the
warmest and softest resting-place within reach. Master's bed obviously
meets these requirements, and inherent good sense insists that so
fortunate an opportunity as an open door should be availed of. But here
the synthetic conscience comes into play, and Satisfaction in the resting-
place is shot through with anxiety. Master, approaching the bedroom
door, hears the guilty flop from bed to board, which is followed by
retreat beneath the couch whose feather-quilt had conduced so pleasantly to repose, and he knows that the knowledge of Good and Evil has
been imparted, and that the parallel case of Adam and Eve has been
repeated. I have even, on two separate occasions, witnessed the extreme
instance of restitution to a smaller companion of the bone wrested from
her by force of arms. On one of these, an awful voice from an upper
window (as from Heaven) uttered only the name of the offender. The
bone was immediately restored. In both cases conscience, combined
with awareness of Sin, was the compelling force.

*   *   *

Earlier in the course of these divagations I have spoken of the psychic
power of perception of which horses are possessed, and then, in

unaggressive brackets, I added 'and dogs.' I will now withdraw those timid brackets, and will declare my belief that Dogs possess an equal, if not even a higher share, with horses – and I am half-inclined to say with ourselves – of the same perceptiveness. Of this I have, more than once, been given proofs, and I believe that the following incident also confirms what I have claimed.

A few years ago, at a luncheon-party in London, I had the pleasure of meeting the late Mrs Thomas Hardy, the widow of the novelist. She and I were seated on either side of our host, a very distinguished dramatist, an old friend, whose wife was my cousin, and whose well-known initials are G. B. S.

At the farther end of the long table, at the moment of which I wish to speak, a great and celebrated surgeon, was engaged in argument with our host. The length of the table – it was a large party – separated the contestants, but their voices carried well. In fact, I felt as though a double barrage was roaring over my head. G. B. S., whose anti-vivisection views were consistently coupled with vegetarianism, put knife-edged arguments that would have cut deep into his carnivorous guests had they not compelled them to laughter. While the great surgeon, Sir Almroth Wright – (who has since gone on to a sphere in which it may be hoped these questions need not be discussed) – thundered back, hurling as it were shells, loaded with such terrible facts as, mercifully, are not often released in public. Conversation for those situated, as were Mrs Hardy and myself, in the storm-centre, was not possible, but – I speak for myself – I was well entertained. After all, to be seated in comfort, eating an admirable lunch, and listening to the super-heated cut-and-thrust of two of the cleverest men in London (who were not, I think, unaware of an attentive audience) may be considered a favourable position.

Mrs Hardy, no more than I, attempted to interpose a word into the barrage. I eyed her across the table, but met no responsive eye. I decided that she was one of those little ladies who look as if they have been small widows from the cradle to the grave. The argument roared on, but there came a regrettable interruption. A messenger came in and whispered to our host. He turned to me and said hurriedly.

'A man to see me – must go – talk to Mrs Hardy – ' He was gone.

Up to this moment I do not think Mrs Hardy had spoken a word. Her costume proclaimed her to be what St Paul has called 'a widow indeed,' but now, in the absence of a rather (perhaps) intimidating celebrity, she came forth from her crêpe-shrouded silence, and conversation became possible, and also, as I presently found, agreeable. Having, in the usual way, fenced with various subjects, we discovered one that we possessed in common, *Dogs*! It is one that may strike a warmly responsive chord, or may bore to desperation. An old cousin of mine was accustomed to say, autocratically, 'Children and Dogs destroy conversation!' (and I think that, on the whole, she was right). But Dogs undoubtedly made smooth the path of conversation for me, and, also, I venture to say, Mrs Hardy, and I can at least feel that my recital of the psychic endowments of two of my little dogs, provoked my companion guest to the following tale, which she told with obvious sincerity, and, I could see, with serious regard for truth.

She said that she and 'Mr Hardy' (thus she spoke of him) were accustomed to take their 'supper' in a sitting-room whose door opened 'out of doors,' and to this outside door, a special friend, a near neighbour, was in the habit of coming.

'Nearly every evening,' she said, 'after supper, when the day's work was over, he would announce himself with a peculiar knock, and then he would come in and would have a chat with Mr Hardy.'

She paused and looked apprehensively at the door, and glanced at the still empty chair of our host. I gave her an encouraging touch of the spur, and she took heart and went on with her story.

'We had a little white dog that we were very fond of, and she was devoted to our friend, and would always run to meet him when she heard his knock. And when he came in she would jump up and put her paws against him and be delighted to see him. Well, there came an evening, and after supper, we heard our neighbour's knock. I said 'come in', and he came in, and our little dog ran to welcome him, as she always did, wagging her little tail and putting up her paws against him – '

Mrs Hardy leaned against the table and looked across it, hard, at me.

'And then,' she went on, firmly, '*Immediately*, she dropped down and ran away and hid under the sofa! We called her, and so did our friend, but she wouldn't come out. We couldn't understand what had frightened her.'

She paused again, and her eyes held mine. Then, in a lowered voice, she said, 'Next morning, very early, our poor friend's son rushed into the house, and up to our room, and told us that his father had died in the night!'

*　　*　　*

Some years ago an opportunity came to me to visit a great, grave Dog Show. This took place in Bath, and it was, I am sure, a model of the best possible arrangements. I was a visitor to Bath and knew no one there. I wandered, solitary and friendless, through aisles and corridors, resounding with the protests of the exhibits. Their despairing chorus seemed to turn to hatred as I strayed by. I felt that they regarded me as a lone Irish wolf, and that if their restraining chains gave way, I should immediately be torn in pieces.

With this in mind I found myself in a palatial chamber, lined all round with Labradors, whose angry eyes were fixed on me. Keeping carefully in the centre of the gangway, I was aware of a long black arm outstretched as if to stop me. It belonged to a very large, shining, black bitch. I paused and spoke to her, from a cautious distance, but her yellow eyes implored me.

'Hold my hand!' they said, 'Be kind to me!'

Thus, in a South Carolina Slave-market, might some forlorn Aunt Chloe or Topsy have supplicated a passer-by. I took the great paw that she extended to me and held it, and comforted her as best I could. I hated having to let it go and leave her. But, (as I said to her) *'since there's no help, come, let us kiss and part.'*

As I passed on into the free sunlight that she could see but could not share, I heard a heart-broken cry. I hurried away.

From *Happy Days*

MARCIA DAVENPORT

Bach

EVER SINCE I can remember, a phrase or a melody or a characteristic ornamentation or resolution of Mozart's has struck something in me like a shiver of recognition. It may seem flippant to cite the following, but that is not my intention; I do it to show how physical such a thing might be. I once had a dog, the only time I have ever had a dog instead of my essential cat; and that dog, like any creature in my house, heard music around it all the time. What is music to a dog? But if I played a record of the Fifth Brandenburg Concerto, the dog would come running from wherever he was and plant himself in front of the gramo-phone. Incredible? A possibility that a flute and a cembalo in the key of D major made an agreeable vibration on the dog's ear-drums? There is lots of other music in the same key with similar scoring, and it was played all the time. Can a dog recognise a melody? I do not know. But my first reactions to any music of Mozart's were like those of that dog.

From *Too Strong for Fantasy*

HERBERT ASQUITH
The Hairy Dog

My dog's so funny I've not seen
His face for years and years:
His eyes are buried out of sight,
I only guess his ears.

When people ask me for his breed,
I do not know or care:
He has the beauty of them all
Hidden beneath his hair.

THOMAS MANN
Bashan

OUT YONDER, HOWEVER, in the woods or in the broad meadows alongside the brook, I often halt and watch when I catch him digging for a mouse, even though it should be late and I in danger of exceeding the time I have apportioned for my walk. The passionate devotion with which he goes to work is so fascinating to observe, his profound enthusiasm is so contagious, that I cannot but wish him success with all my heart, and naturally I also wish to be a witness of this success. The spot he is attacking may have made quite an innocent impression in its outward aspect – it is, let us say, some mossy little mound at the foot of a birch and possibly penetrated by its roots. But did not my Bashan hear the quarry, scent it, perhaps even see it as it switched away? He is absolutely certain that his bit of game is sitting there under the earth in some snug runlet or burrow; all that is necessary is to get at it, and so he goes digging away for all he is worth in absolute devotion to his task and oblivious to the world. He proceeds not ragingly, but with a certain fine deliberation, with the tempered passion of the real sportsman – it is wonderful to see. His small, tiger-striped body beneath the smooth coat of which the ribs align themselves and the muscles play, is hollowed, is concave in the middle; his hindquarters, with the stump of a tail vibrating to quick time, is erected vertically. His head is between his forepaws and thrust into the slant hole he has already dug. With averted face he continues with the rapid strokes of his iron claws to tear up the earth more and more – lumps of sod, pebbles, shreds of glass, and bits of roots fly all about me. Sometimes his snortings are heard in the silence of the fields – that is when he has succeeded in penetrating some little distance, and in wedging his snout into the entrance to the burrow in order, by means of his scent, to keep check upon the clever, still, and timid creature within there.

His breathing sounds muffled, he ejects his breath in a blast in order to be able to empty his lungs quickly – and to draw in the delicate, acrid, distant, and yet disguised odour of the mice. What emotions must surge through the breast of the little animal down there when it hears this hollow and muffled snorting? Well, that is its own affair, or perhaps God's affair, who has decreed that Bashan shall be the enemy and persecutor of these earth-mice. And then – is not fear only an intensified feeling for life? If no Bashan existed the little mouse would very likely be bored to death. And what use or purpose would then be served by its beady-eyed cleverness and its art of swift mining operations, factors that fairly well equalise the conditions of the battle, so that the success of the party upon the offensive always remains highly problematical, even improbable. Indeed I feel no compassion for the mouse; inwardly I take sides with Bashan, and sometimes I cannot remain content with the rôle of a mere spectator. I get my walking-stick into play whenever some firmly-bedded pebble, some tough cord of a root is in his way and help him to get rid of these obstacles. Then sometimes, in the midst of his hot and furious activity, he will throw up his head and bestow upon me a swift and fervent glance of gratitude and approval. With munching jaws and glinting teeth he goes working his way into the stubborn, fibrous ground, – tears away clods, throws them aside, sends his resonant snorts once more into the depths, and then, fired to renewed action by the provocative scent, sets his claws once more into furious action . . .

In the great majority of cases this is all love's labour lost. With the moist earth clinging to his nose and sprinkled about his shoulders, Bashan makes another quick and superficial survey of the territory and then gives it up and jogs indifferently on.

'There was nothing doing, Bashan,' I remark to him, when he chances to look at me. 'Nothing doing,' I repeat, shaking my head and raising my brows and my shoulders, so as to make the message plainer. But it is not at all necessary to comfort him; his failure does not depress him for a moment. To hunt is to hunt, the titbit of game is the least of all considerations. It was, take it all in all, a magnificent effort he thinks – in so far as he still happens to think of this violent business he has just been through. For now he is already on new adventure bent – adventures of which there is, indeed, no lack in the three zones of this domain.

Sometimes, however, he happens to catch the mouse. And then something occurs which never fails to strike me with horror – for Bashan devours his prey alive, with hide and hair. Perhaps the unfortunate creature had not been properly advised by its instincts of self-preservation and had chosen a spot for its burrow which was too soft, too unprotected and too easily excavated. Perhaps the little creature's tunnels had not been sunk deep enough, or it had been paralysed by fright and prevented from burrowing to deeper levels. Or it had perchance lost its head and, crouching a few inches under the surface with its little beady eyes popping out of their sockets with horror, listened to that terrible snorting coming nearer and nearer. No matter, the iron claws disinter it, uncover it, fling it into the air, into the pitiless glare of the day! Hapless little mouse! you had good cause to be frightened, and it is well that this immense and comprehensible fright has already reduced you to a kind of semi-unconsciousness. For now the tiny rodent is to be converted into pap and pulp.

Bashan has caught it by the tail; he tosses it upon the ground twice or thrice; a very faint squeak is heard, the last that is vouchsafed to the god-forsaken little mouse. And then Bashan snaps it up, and it disappears between his jaws and the white, gleaming teeth. He stands there with legs four square and forepaws braced. His neck is lowered and thrust forth as he chews – he catches at the titbit again and again and throws it into the proper position in his mouth. The tiny bones are heard to crack, a shred of fur hangs for a moment from the corner of his mouth; he draws it in and then all is over. Bashan then executes a kind of dance of joy and triumph, circling around me as I stand leaning on my cane with cold shudders rushing up and down my spine.

'You're a fine fellow!' I say to him in a kind of gruesome recognition of his victory. 'You scoundrel! you murderer! you cannibal!'

These words cause him to dance still more wildly, and, one might say, almost to laugh aloud. So I proceed on my way, somewhat chilled in the limbs owing to the tragedy I have just witnessed, and yet inwardly enlightened by the brutal humour of life. The thing, after all, is quite in order, in Nature's order. A mouselet which had been ill-advised by its faulty instincts has simply been converted into pap and pulp. Nevertheless I am inwardly gratified when in such instances as the foregoing, it did not become necessary for me to help along the natural order of things with my cane, but remained a simple and passive spectator.

Startling and even terrifying is it when some pheasant suddenly bursts from the thicket in which, sleeping or waking, it had hoped to remain undiscovered, some coign of concealment from which Bashan's delicate and unobtrusive nose had after a little searching managed to rouse it. Thumping and flapping, with frightened and indignant cries and cacklings, the large, rust-red and long-tailed bird lifts itself a-wing, and with all the silly heedlessness of a hen, goes scattering upon some tree from which it begins to scold, whilst Bashan, erect against the trunk, barks up at the fowl, stormily, savagely. The meaning behind this barking is clear. It says plainly enough: 'Get off! get off that perch! Tend to business. Fly off, so I can have my bit o' fun. Get off – I want to chase you!' The pheasant cannot, apparently, resist this powerful voice, and off it scuds, making its way with heavy flight through the branches, still cackling and complaining, whilst Bashan, full of manly silence, pursues it smartly along the level ground.

This is sufficient for Bashan's bliss; his wish and his will go no farther. What would have happened had he caught the bird? Nothing, I assure you, absolutely nothing. I once saw him with a bird between his claws. He had probably come upon it whilst it lay in deep sleep, so that the clumsy thing had had no time to lift itself from the ground. On that occasion Bashan had stood over the fowl, an utterly bewildered victor, and did not know what to do next. With one wing raked wide open and with its head drawn aside to the very limit of its neck, the pheasant lay in the grass and screamed, screamed without a single pause – a passer-by might have thought that some old woman was being murdered in the bushes. I hurried up, bent upon preventing something horrible. But I was soon convinced that there was nothing to fear. Bashan's all-too conspicuous confusion, the half-curious, half-disgusted mien with which, head aslant, he looked down upon his prisoner, assured me of that. This old wives' screeching and dinning in his ears, very likely got upon his nerves – the whole affair apparently caused him more embarrassment than triumph. Was it in victory or in shame that he pulled a couple of feathers out of his victim's dress, very, very cautiously with his mouth, refraining from all use of his teeth, and then threw them aside with an angry toss of his head?

He followed this tribute to his predatory instincts by taking his paw off his victim and letting it go free – not out of magnanimity, to be sure, but simply because the situation bored him, and because it really had nothing in common with the stir and gaiety of the chase. Never had I seen a more astonished bird! It had closed its account with life, and for a brief space it seemed that it no longer knew what use to make of life, for it lay in the grass as though dead. It then tottered along the ground for a bit, swung clumsily upon a tree, appeared about to fall from it, summoned its strength, and then with heavily-dragging feathery raiment went fluttering off into the distance. It no longer squawked, but kept its bill shut. Silently the bird flew across the park, the river, the forest beyond the river, away, away, as far as its short wings could carry it. It is certain that this particular pheasant never returned to this particular spot.

From *Bashan and I*

To Jack

[a dog who had 'written' to him]

ALAS MY GOOD Jack, poor Bashan, to whom you so cordially and nicely wrote, has long been dead – gone to the happy hunting grounds, to put it in consoling terms. A severe distemper, combined with pneumonia, carried him off very soon after I had told people about him; in other words, after he had come to life on another plane, so to speak, and sometimes I cannot repress the thought that there might be a connection and that perhaps what I did to the poor creature was not well done, but sinful. Who knows? In any case he had a very fine obituary in the newspaper here, entitled *Bashan* with a heavy cross after the name; so much he had, but it did him no good. There can be no doubt, given his temperament, that he would have been delighted by your letter. Thank you.

Munich, 10 May 1922

D. H. LAWRENCE

Perr-rr-rro!!

THE PARROTS WHISTLE exactly like Rosalino, only a little more so. And this little-more-so is extremely sardonically funny. With their sad old long-jowled faces and their flat disillusioned eyes, they reproduce Rosalino and a little-more-so without moving a muscle. And Rosalino, sweeping the *patio* with his twig broom, scraping and tittering leaves into little heaps, covers himself more and more with the cloud of his own obscurity. He doesn't rebel. He is powerless. Up goes the wild, sliding Indian whistle into the morning, very powerful, with an immense energy seeming to drive behind it. And always, always a little more than life-like.

Then they break off into a cackling chatter, and one knows they are shifting their clumsy legs, perhaps hanging on with their beaks and clutching with their cold, slow claws, to climb to a higher bough, like rather raggedy green buds climbing to the sun. And suddenly the penetrating, demonish mocking voices:

'Perro! Oh, Perro! Perr-rro! Oh, Perr-rro! Perro!'

They are imitating somebody calling the dog. *Perro* means dog. But that any creature should be able to pour such a suave, prussic-acid sarcasm over the voice of a human being calling a dog, is incredible. One's diaphragm chuckles involuntarily. And one thinks: *Is it possible?* Is is possible that we are so absolutely, so innocently, so *ab ovo* ridiculous?

And not only is it possible, it is patent. We cover our heads in confusion.

Now they are yapping like a dog: exactly like Corasmin. Corasmin is a little, fat, curly white dog who was lying in the sun a minute ago, and has now come into the verandah shade, walking with slow resignation, to lie against the wall near-by my chair. 'Yap-yap-yap! Wouf! Wouf! Yapyapyapyap!' go the parrots, exactly like Corasmin when some stranger comes into the *zaguán*, Corasmin and a little-more-so.

With a grin on my face I look down at Corasmin. And with a silent, abashed resignation in his yellow eyes, Corasmin looks up at me, with a touch of reproach. His little white nose is sharp, and under his eyes there are dark marks, as under the eyes of one who has known much trouble. All day he does nothing but walk resignedly out of the sun, when the sun gets too hot, and out of the shade, when the shade gets too cool. And bite ineffectually in the region of his fleas.

Poor old Corasmin: he is only about six, but resigned, unspeakably resigned. Only not humble. He does not kiss the rod. He rises in spirit above it, letting his body lie.

'Perro! Oh, Perr-rro! Perr-rro! Perr-rr-rro!!' shriek the parrots, with that strange penetrating, antediluvian malevolence that seems to make even the trees prick their ears. It is a sound that penetrates one straight at the diaphragm, belonging to the ages before brains were invented. And Corasmin pushes his sharp little nose into his bushy tail, closes his eyes because I am grinning, feigns to sleep and then, in an orgasm of self-consciousness, starts up to bite in the region of his fleas.

'Perr-rro! Perr-rro!' And then a restrained, withheld sort of yapping. The fiendish rolling of the Spanish 'r', malevolence rippling out of all the vanished spiteful aeons. And following it, the small, little-curly-dog sort of yapping. They can make their voices so devilishly small and futile, like a little curly dog. And follow it up with that ringing malevolence that swoops up the ladders of the sunbeams right to the stars, rolling the Spanish 'r'.

Corasmin slowly walks away from the verandah, his head drooped, and flings himself down in the sun. No! He gets up again, in an agony of self-control, and scratches the earth loose a little, to soften his lie. Then flings himself down again.

Invictus! The still-unconquered Corasmin! The sad little white curly pendulum oscillating ever slower between the shadow and the sun.

> In the fell clutch of circumstance
> I have not winced nor cried aloud,
> Under the bludgeonings of chance
> My head is bloody, but unbowed.

But that is human bombast, and a little too ridiculous even for Corasmin. Poor old Corasmin's clear yellow eyes! He is going to be master of his own soul, under all the vitriol those parrots pour over him. But he's not going to throw out his chest in a real lust of self-pity. That belongs to the next cycle of evolution.

From Mornings in Mexico

Rex

SINCE EVERY FAMILY has its black sheep, it almost follows that every man must have a sooty uncle. Lucky if he hasn't two. However, it is only with my mother's brother that we are concerned. She had loved him dearly when he was a little blond boy. When he grew up black, she was always vowing she would never speak to him again. Yet when he put in an appearance, after years of absence, she invariably received him in a festive mood, and was even flirty with him.

He rolled up one day in a dog-cart, when I was a small boy. He was large and bullet-headed and blustering, and this time, sporty. Sometimes he was rather literary, sometimes coloured with business. But this time he was in checks, and was sporty. We viewed him from a distance.

The upshot was, would we rear a pup for him. Now my mother detested animals about the house. She could not bear the mix-up of human with animal life. Yet she consented to bring up the pup.

My uncle had taken a large, vulgar public-house in a large and vulgar
town. It came to pass that I must fetch the pup. Strange for me, a
member of the Band of Hope, to enter the big, noisy, smelly plate-glass
and mahogany public-house. It was called The Good Omen. Strange
to have my uncle towering over me in the passage, shouting 'Hello
Johnny, what d'yer want?' He didn't know me. Strange to think he was
my mother's brother, and that he had his bouts when he read Browning
aloud with emotion and *éclat*.

I was given tea in a narrow, uncomfortable sort of living-room, half
kitchen. Curious that such a palatial pub should show such miserable
private accommodation, but so it was. There was I, unhappy, and glad
to escape with the soft fat pup. It was winter-time, and I wore a big-
flapped black overcoat, half cloak. Under the cloak-sleeves I hid the
puppy, who trembled. It was Saturday, and the train was crowded, and
he whimpered under my coat. I sat in mortal fear of being hauled out
for travelling without a dog-ticket. However, we arrived, and my
torments were for nothing.

The others were wildly excited over the puppy. He was small and fat
and white, with a brown-and-black head: a fox terrier. My father said
he had a lemon head – some such mysterious technical phraseology. It
wasn't lemon at all, but coloured like a field bee. And he had a black
spot at the root of his spine.

It was Saturday night – bath-night. He crawled on the hearth-rug
like a fat white tea-cup, and licked the bare toes that had just been
bathed.

'He ought to be called Spot,' said one. But that was too ordinary. It
was a great question, what to call him.

'Call him Rex – the King,' said my mother, looking down on the fat,
animated little tea-cup, who was chewing my sister's little toe and
making her squeal with joy and tickles. We took the name in all
seriousness.

'Rex – the King!' We thought it was just right. Not for years did I
realise that it was a sarcasm on my mother's part. She must have wasted
some twenty years or more of irony, on our incurable naïveté.

It wasn't a successful name, really. Because my father, and all the
people in the street failed completely to pronounce the monosyllable
Rex. They all said *Rax*. And it always distressed me. It always suggested
to me seaweed, and rack-and-ruin. Poor Rex!

We loved him dearly. The first night we woke to hear him weeping and whinneying in loneliness at the foot of the stairs. When it could be borne no more, I slipped down for him, and he slept under the sheets.

'I won't have that little beast in the beds. Beds are not for dogs,' declared my mother callously.

'He's as good as *we* are!' we cried, injured.

'Whether he is or not, he's not going in the beds.'

I think now, my mother scorned us for our lack of pride. We were a little *infra dig.*, we children.

The second night, however, Rex wept the same and in the same way was comforted. The third night we heard our father plod downstairs, heard several slaps administered to the yelping, dismayed puppy, and heard the amiable, but to us heartless voice saying 'Shut it then! Shut thy noise, 'st hear? Stop in thy basket, stop there!'

'It's a shame!' we shouted, in muffled rebellion, from the sheets.

'*I'll* give you shame, if you don't hold your noise and go to sleep,' called our mother from her room. Whereupon we shed angry tears and went to sleep. But there was a tension.

'Such a houseful of idiots would make me detest the little beast, even if he was better than he is,' said my mother.

But as a matter of fact, she did not detest Rexie at all. She only had to pretend to so do, to balance our adoration. And in truth, she did not care for close contact with animals. She was too fastidious. – My father, however, would take on a real dog's voice, talking to the puppy: a funny, high, sing-song falsetto which he seemed to produce at the top of his head. – ''s a pretty little dog! 's a pretty little doggy! – ay! – yes! – he is, yes! – Wag thy strunt, then! Wag thy strunt, Raxie! – Ha-ha! – Nay, tha munna – ' – This last as the puppy, wild with excitement at the strange falsetto voice, licked my father's nostrils and bit my father's nose with his sharp little teeth.

''E makes blood come,' said my father.

'Serves you right for being so silly with him,' said my mother.

It was odd to see her as she watched the man, my father, crouching and talking to the little dog and laughing strangely when the little creature bit his nose and toused his beard. What does a woman think of her husband at such a moment? –

My mother amused herself over the names we called him.

'He's an angel! – he's a little butterfly – Rexie, my sweet!'

'Sweet! A dirty little object!' interpolated my mother.

She and he had a feud from the first. Of course he chewed boots and worried our stockings and swallowed our garters. The moment we took off our stockings he would dart away with one, we after him. Then as he hung, growling vociferously, at one end of the stocking, we at the other, we would cry:

'Look at him mother! He'll make holes in it again.'

Whereupon my mother darted at him and spanked him sharply.

'Let go, Sir, you destructive little fiend.'

But he didn't let go. He began to growl with real rage, and hung on viciously. Mite as he was, he defied her with a manly fury. He did not hate her, nor she him. But they had one long battle with one another.

'I'll teach you, my Jockey! Do you think I'm going to spend my life darning after your destructive little teeth! I'll show you if I will.'

But Rexie only growled more viciously. They both became really angry, whilst we children expostulated earnestly with both. He would not let *her* take the stocking from him.

'You should tell him properly, mother. He won't be driven,' we said.

'I'll drive him further than he bargains for. I'll drive him out of *my* sight for ever, that I will,' declared my mother, truly angry. He would put her into a real temper, with his tiny, growling defiance.

'He's sweet! A Rexie, a little Rexie!'

'A filthy little nuisance! Don't think I'll put up with him.'

And to tell the truth, he *was* dirty at first. How could he be otherwise, so young? But my mother hated him for it. And perhaps this was the real start of their hostility. For he lived in the house with us. He would wrinkle his nose and show his tiny dagger-teeth in fury when he was thwarted, and his growls of real battle-rage against my mother rejoiced us as much as they angered her. But at last she caught him *in flagrante*. She pounced on him, rubbed his nose in the mess, and flung him out into the yard. He yelped with shame and disgust and indignation. I shall never forget the sight of him as he rolled over, then tried to turn his head away from the disgust of his own muzzle, shaking his little snout with a sort of horror, and trying to sneeze it off. My sister gave a yell of despair, and dashed out with a rag and a pan of water, weeping wildly. She sat in the middle of the yard with the befouled puppy, and shedding bitter tears she wiped him and washed him clean. Loudly she reproached my mother. 'Look how much bigger you are than he is. It's a shame, it's a shame!'

'You ridiculous little lunatic, you've undone all the good it would do him, with your soft ways. Why is my life made a curse with animals! Haven't I enough as it is – '

There was a subdued tension afterwards. Rex was a little white chasm between us and our parent.

He became clean. But then another tragedy loomed. He must be docked. His floating puppy-tail must be docked short. This time my father was the enemy. My mother agreed with us, that it was an unnecessary cruelty. But my father was adamant. 'The dog'll look a fool all his life if he's not docked.' And there was no getting away from it. To add to the horror, poor Rex's tail must be *bitten* off. Why bitten?, we asked aghast. We were assured that biting was the only way. A man would take the little tail and just nip it through with his teeth, at a certain joint. My father lifted his lips and bared his incisors, to suit the description. We shuddered. But we were in the hands of fate.

Rex was carried away, and a man called Rowbotham bit off the superfluity of his tail in the *Nags Head*, for a quart of best and bitter. We lamented our poor diminished puppy, but agreed to find him more manly and *comme il faut*. We should always have been ashamed of his little whip of a tail, if it had not been shortened. My father said it had made a man of him.

Perhaps it had. For now his true nature came out. And his true nature, like so much else, was dual. First he was a fierce, canine little beast, a beast of rapine and blood. He longed to hunt, savagely. He lusted to set his teeth in his prey. It was no joke with him. The old canine Adam stood first in him, the dog with fangs and glaring eyes. He flew at us when we annoyed him. He flew at all intruders, particularly the postman. He was *almost* a peril to the neighbourhood. But not quite. Because close second in his nature stood that fatal need to love, the *besoin d'aimer* which at last makes an end of liberty. He had a terrible, terrible necessity to love, and this trammelled the native, savage hunting beast which he was. He was torn between two great impulses: the native impulse to hunt and kill, and the strange, secondary, supervening impulse to love and obey. If he had been left to my father and mother, he would have run wild and got himself shot. As it was, he loved us children with a fierce, joyous love. And we loved him.

When we came home from school we would see him standing at the end of the entry, cocking his head wistfully at the open country in front of him, and meditating whether to be off or not: a white, inquiring little figure, with green savage freedom in front of him. A cry from a far distance from one of us, and like a bullet he hurled himself down the road, in a mad game. Seeing him coming, my sister invariably turned and fled, shrieking with delighted terror. And he would leap straight up her back, and bite her and tear her clothes. But it was only an ecstasy of savage love, and she knew it. She didn't care if he tore her pinafores. But my mother did.

My mother was maddened by him. He was a little demon. At the least provocation, he flew. You only had to sweep the floor, and he bristled and sprang at the broom. Nor would he leave go. With his scruff erect and his nostrils snorting rage, he would turn up the whites of his eyes at my mother, as she wrestled at the other end of the broom. 'Leave go, Sir, leave *go*!' She wrestled and stamped her foot, and he answered with horrid growls. In the end it was *she* who had to let go. Then *she* flew at him, and he flew at her. All the time we had him, he was within a hair's-breadth of savagely biting her. And she knew it. Yet he always kept sufficient self-control.

We children loved his temper. We would drag the bones from his mouth, and put him into such paroxysms of rage that he would twist his head right over and lay it on the ground upside-down, because he didn't know what to do with himself, the savage was so strong in him and he *must* fly at us. 'He'll fly at your throat one of these days,' said my father. Neither he nor my mother dared have touched Rex's bone. It was enough to see him bristle and roll the whites of his eyes when they came near. How near he must have been to driving his teeth right into *us*, cannot be told. He was a horrid sight snarling and crouching at us. But we only laughed and rebuked him. And he would whimper in the sheer torment of his need to attack us.

He never did hurt us. He never hurt anybody, though the neighbourhood was terrified of him. But he took to hunting. To my mother's disgust, he would bring large dead bleeding rats and lay them on the hearth-rug, and she had to take them up on a shovel. For he would not remove them. Occasionally he brought a mangled rabbit, and sometimes, alas, fragmentary poultry. We were in terror of prosecution. Once he came home bloody and feathery and rather sheepish-looking. We cleaned him and questioned him and abused him. Next day we heard of six dead ducks. Thank heaven no one had seen him.

But he was disobedient. If he saw a hen he was off, and calling would not bring him back. He was worst of all with my father, who would take him walks on Sunday morning. My mother would not walk a yard with him. Once, walking with my father, he rushed off at some sheep in a field. My father yelled in vain. The dog was at the sheep, and meant business. My father crawled through the hedge, and was upon him in time. And now the man was in a paroxysm of rage. He dragged the little beast into the road and thrashed him with a walking stick.

'Do you know you're thrashing that dog unmercifully?' said a passer-by.

'Ay, an' mean to,' shouted my father.

The curious thing was that Rex did *not* respect my father any the more, for the beatings he had from him. He took much more heed of us children, always.

But he let us down also. One fatal Saturday he disappeared. We hunted and called, but no Rex. We were bathed, and it was bed-time, but we would not go to bed. Instead we sat in a row in our night-dresses on the sofa, and wept without stopping. This drove our mother mad.

'*Am* I going to put up with it? *Am* I? And all for that hateful little beast of a dog! He shall go! If he's not gone now, he shall go.'

Our father came in late, looking rather queer, with his hat over his eye. But in his staccato tippled fashion he tried to be consoling.

'Never mind, my duckie, I s'll look for him in the morning.'

Sunday came – Oh, such a Sunday. We cried, and didn't eat. We scoured the land, and for the first time realised how empty and wide the earth is, when you're looking for something. My father walked for many miles – all in vain. Sunday dinner, with rhubarb pudding, I remember, and an atmosphere of abject misery that was unbearable.

'Never,' said my mother, 'never shall an animal set foot in this house again, while *I* live. I knew what it would be! I knew.'

The day wore on, and it was the black gloom of bed-time, when we heard a scratch and an impudent little whine at the door. In trotted Rex, mud-black, disreputable, and impudent. His air of off-hand 'How d'ye do!' was indescribable. He trotted round with *suffisance*, wagging his tail as if to say 'Yes, I've come back. But I didn't need to. I can carry on remarkably well by myself.' Then he walked to his water, and dranked noisily and ostentatiously. It was rather a slap in the eye for us.

He disappeared once or twice in this fashion. We never knew where he went. And we began to feel that his heart was not so golden as we had imagined it.

But one fatal day re-appeared my uncle and the dog-cart. He whistled to Rex, and Rex trotted up. But when he wanted to examine the lusty, sturdy dog, Rex became suddenly still, then sprang free. Quite jauntily he trotted round – but out of reach of my uncle. He leaped up, licking our faces, and trying to make us play.

'Why what ha' you done wi' the dog – You've made a fool of him.

He's softer than grease. You're ruined him. You've made a damned fool of him,' shouted my uncle.

Rex was captured and hauled off to the dog-cart and tied to the seat. He was in a frenzy. He yelped and shrieked and struggled, and was hit on the head, hard, with the butt-end of my uncle's whip, which only made him struggle more frantically. So we saw him driven away, our beloved Rex, frantically, madly fighting to get to us from the high dog-cart, and being knocked down, whilst we stood in the street in mute despair.

After which, black tears, and a little wound which is still alive in our hearts.

I only saw Rex once again, when I had to call just once at the *Good Omen*. He must have heard my voice, for he was upon me in the passage before I knew where I was. And in the instant I knew *how* he loved us. He really loved us. And in the same instant there was my uncle with a whip, beating and kicking him back, and Rex cowering, bristling, snarling.

My uncle swore many oaths, how we had ruined the dog for ever, made him vicious, spoiled him for showing purposes, and been altogether a pack of mard-soft fools not fit to be trusted with any dog but a gutter-mongrel.

Poor Rex! We heard his temper was incurably vicious, and he had to be shot.

And it was our fault. We had loved him too much, and he had loved us too much. We never had another pet.

It is a strange thing, love. Nothing but love has made the dog lose his wild freedom, to become the servant of man. And this very servility or completeness of love makes him a term of deepest contempt. – 'You dog!'

We should not have loved Rex so much, and he should not have loved us. There should have been a measure. We tended, all of us, to overstep the limits of our own natures. He should have stayed outside human limits, we should have stayed outside canine limits. Nothing is more fatal than the disaster of too much love. My uncle was right, we had ruined the dog.

My uncle was a fool, for all that.

Bibbles

Bibbles.
Little black dog in New Mexico,
Little black snub-nosed bitch with a shoved-out jaw
And a wrinkled reproachful look;

Little black female pup, sort of French bull, they say,
With bits of brindle coming through, like rust, to show you're not
    pure;
Not pure, Bibbles,
Bubsey, bat-eared dog;
Not black enough!

First live thing I've 'owned' since the lop-eared rabbits when I
    was a lad,
And those over-prolific white mice, and Adolph, and Rex whom I
    didn't own.
And even now, Bibbles, little Ma'am, it's you who appropriated
    me, not I you.
As Benjamin Franklin appropriated Providence to his purposes.

Oh Bibbles, black little bitch,
I'd have never let you appropriate me, had I known.
I never dreamed, till now, of the awful time the Lord must have,
    'owning' humanity,
Especially democratic live-by-love humanity.

Oh Bibbles, oh Pips, oh Pipsey,
You little black love-bird!
Don't you love *everybody*!
Just everybody.
You love 'em all.
Believe in the One Identity, don't you,

You little Walt-Whitmanesque bitch?
First time I lost you in Taos plaza,
And found you after endless chasing,
Came upon you prancing round the corner in exuberant, bibbling
    affection
After the black-green skirts of a yellow-green old Mexican woman
Who hated you, and kept looking round at you and cursing you in
    a mutter,
While you pranced and bounced with love of her, you
    indiscriminating animal,
All your wrinkled *miserere* Chinese black little face beaming
And your black little body bouncing and wriggling
With indiscriminate love, Bibbles;
I had a moment's pure detestation of you.

As I rushed like an idiot round the corner after you
Yelling: *Pips! Pips! Bibbles!*

I've had moments of hatred of you since,
Loving everybody!
'To you, whoever you are, with endless embrace!' –
That's you, Pipsey,
With your imbecile bit of a tail in a love-flutter.
You omnipip.

Not that you're merely a softy, oh dear me, no.
You know which side your bread is buttered.
You don't care a rap for anybody.
But you love lying warm between warm human thighs,
    indiscriminate,
And you love to make somebody love you, indiscriminate,
You love to lap up affection, to wallow in it,
And then turn tail to the next comer, for a new dollop.

And start prancing and licking and cuddling again, indiscriminate.

O yes, I know your little game.

Yet you're so nice,
So quick, like a little black dragon.
So fierce, when the coyotes howl, barking like a whole little lion,
    and rumbling,
And starting forward in the dusk, with your little black fur all
    bristling like plush
Against those coyotes, who would swallow you like an oyster.
And in the morning, when the bedroom door is opened,
Rushing in like a little black whirlwind, leaping straight as an
    arrow on the bed at the pillow
And turning the day suddenly into a black tornado of *joie de vivre*,
    Chinese dragon.

So funny
Lobbing wildly through deep snow like a rabbit,
Hurtling like a black ball through the snow,
Champing it, tossing a mouthful,
Little black spot in the landscape!

So absurd
Pelting behind on the dusty trail when the horse sets off home at a
    gallop:
Left in the dust behind like a dust-ball tearing along,
Coming up on fierce little legs, tearing fast to catch up, a real little
    dust-pig, ears almost blown away,
And black eyes bulging bright in a dust-mask
Chinese-dragon-wrinkled, with a pink mouth grinning, under jaw
    shoved out
And white teeth showing in your dragon-grin as you race, you
    split-face,
Like a trundling projectile swiftly whirling up,
Cocking your eyes at me as you come alongside, to see if I'm I on
    the horse,

And panting with that split grin,
All your game little body dust-smooth like a little pig,
　　　　　　　　　　　poor Pips.

Plenty of game old spirit in you, Bibbles.
Plenty of game old spunk, little bitch.

How you hate being brushed with the boot-brush, to brush all
　　　that dust out of your wrinkled face,
Don't you?
How you hate being made to look undignified, Ma'am:
How you hate being laughed at, Miss Superb!
Blackberry face!

Plenty of conceit in you.
Unblemished belief in your own perfection
And utter lovableness, you ugly-mug;
Chinese puzzle-face,
Wrinkled underhung physiog that looks as if it had done with
　　　everything,
Through with everything.

Instead of which you sit there and roll your head like a canary
And show a tiny bunch of white teeth in your underhung
　　　blackness,
Self-conscious little bitch,
Aiming again at being loved.

Let the merest scallywag come to the door, and you leap your very
　　　dearest love at him,
As if now, at last, here was the one you *finally* loved,
Finally loved;
And even the dirtiest scallywag is taken in,
Thinking: *This dog sure has taken a fancy to me.*

You miserable little bitch of love-tricks,
I know your game.

Me or the Mexican who comes to chop wood
All the same,
All humanity is jam to you.

Everybody so dear, and yourself so ultra-beloved
That you have to run out at last and eat filth,
Gobble up filth, you horror, swallow utter abomination and fresh-
  dropped dung.

You stinker.
You worse than a carrion-crow.
Reeking dung-mouth.
You love-bird.
Reject nothing, sings Walt Whitman.
So you, you go out at last and eat the unmentionable,
In your appetite for affection.

And then you run in to vomit it in my house!
I get my love back.
And I have to clean up after you, filth which even blind Nature
  rejects
From the pit of your stomach;
But you, you snout-face, you reject nothing, you merge so much
  in love
You must eat even that.

Then when I dust you a bit with a juniper twig
You run straight away to live with somebody else,
Fawn before them, and love them as if they were the ones you had
  really loved all along.
And they're taken in.

They feel quite tender over you, till you play the same trick on
   them, dirty bitch.

Fidelity! Loyalty! Attachment!
Oh, these are abstractions to your nasty little belly.
You must always be a-waggle with LOVE.
Such a waggle of love you can hardly distinguish one human from
   another.

You love one after another, on one condition, that each one loves
   you most.
Democratic little bull-bitch, dirt-eating little swine.

But now, my lass, you've got Nemesis on your track,
Now you've come sex-alive, and the great ranch-dogs are all after
   you.
They're after what they can get, and don't you turn tail!
You loved 'em all so much before, didn't you, loved 'em
   indiscriminate.
You don't love 'em now.
They want something of you, so you squawk and come pelting
   indoors.

Come pelting to me, now the other folk have found you out, and
   the dogs are after you.
Oh yes, you're found out. I heard them kick you out of the ranch
   house.
Get out, you little, soft fool!!

And didn't you turn your eyes up at me then?
And didn't you cringe on the floor like any inkspot!
And crawl away like a black snail!
And doesn't everybody loathe you then!
And aren't your feelings violated, you high-bred little love-bitch!

For you're sensitive,
In many ways very finely bred.
But bred in conceit that the world is all for love
Of you, my bitch: till you get so far you eat filth.
Fool, in spite of your pretty ways, and quaint, know-all, wrinkled
    old aunty's face.

So now, what with great Airedale dogs,
And a kick or two,
And a few vomiting bouts,
And a juniper switch,
You look at me for discrimination, don't you?
Look up at me with misgiving in your bulging eyes,
And fear in the smoky whites of your eyes, you nigger;
And you're puzzled,
You think you'd better mind your P's and Q's for a bit,
Your sensitive love-pride being all hurt.

All right, my little bitch.
You learn loyalty rather than loving,
And I'll protect you.

JAMES JOYCE

The Enemy Without

'WHAT DO YOU do?' Joyce inquired. I told him about Shakespeare and Company. The name, and mine, too, seemed to amuse him, and a charming smile came to his lips. Taking a small notebook out of his pocket and, as I noticed with sadness, holding it very close to his eyes, he wrote down the name and address. He said he would come to see me.

Suddenly a dog barked, and Joyce turned pale; he actually trembled. The bark came from across the road. I looked out of the window and saw a dog running after a ball. It had a loud bark but, as far as I could tell, no bite.

'Is it coming in? Is it fierce?' Joyce asked me, very uneasy. (He pronounced it 'feerrce'.) I assured him it wasn't coming in, and didn't look at all fierce, but he was still apprehensive and startled by every bark. He told me he had been afraid of dogs since the age of five, when one of 'the animals' had bitten him on the chin. Pointing to his goatee, he said that it was to hide the scar.

We talked on. Joyce's manner was so extremely simple that, overcome though I was in the presence of the greatest writer of my time, I somehow felt at ease with him. This first time, and afterwards, I was always conscious of his genius, yet I knew no one so easy to talk with.

Now the guests were leaving, and Adrienne was looking for me to say good-bye to the Spires. As I thanked Spire for his hospitality, he said he hoped I hadn't been bored. Bored? I had met James Joyce.

Sylvia Beach, from *Shakespeare and Company*

Tatters

A BLOATED CARCASS of a dog lay lolled on bladderwrack. Before him the gunwhale of a boat, sunk in sand. *Un coche ensablé*, Louis Veuillot called Gautier's prose. These heavy sands are language tide and wind have silted here. And there, the stoneheaps of dead builders, a warren of weasel rats. Hide gold there. Try it. You have some. Sands and stones. Heavy of the past. Sir Lout's toys. Mind you don't get one bang on the ear. I'm the bloody well gigant rolls all them bloody well boulders, bones for my steppingstones. Feefawfum. I zmellz de bloodz odz an Iridzman.

A point, live dog, grew into sight running across the sweep of sand. Lord, is he going to attack me? Respect his liberty. You will not be master of others or their slave. I have my stick. Sit tight. From farther away, walking shoreward across from the crested tide, figures, two. The two maries. They have tucked it safe among the bulrushes. Peekaboo. I see you. No, the dog. He is running back to them. Who?

Galleys of the Lochlanns ran here to beach, in quest of prey, their bloodbeaked prows riding low on a molten pewter surf. Danevikings, torcs of tomahawks aglitter on their breasts when Malachi wore the collar of gold. A school of turlehide whales stranded in hot noon, spouting, hobbling in the shallows. Then from the starving cagework city a horde of jerkined dwarfs, my people, with flayers' knives, running, scaling, hacking in green blubbery whalemeat. Famine, plague and slaughters. Their blood is in me, their lusts my waves. I moved among them on the frozen Liffey, that I, a changeling, among the spluttering resin fires. I spoke to no-one: none to me.

The dog's bark ran towards him, stopped, ran back. Dog of my enemy. I just simply stood pale, silent, bayed about. *Terribilia meditans.* A primrose doublet, fortune's knave, smiled on my fear. For that are you pining, the bark of their applause? Pretenders: live their lives. The Bruce's brother, Thomas Fitzgerald, silken knight, Perkin Warbeck, York's false scion, in breeches of silk of whiterose ivory, wonder of a day, and Lambert Simnel, with a tail of nans and sutlers, a scullion crowned. All kings' sons. Paradise of pretenders then and now. He saved men from drowning and you shake at a cur's yelping. But the courtiers who mocked Guido in Or san Michele were in their own house. House of . . . We don't want any of your medieval abstrusiosities. Would you do what he did? A boat would be near, a lifebuoy. *Natürlich*, put there for you. Would you or would you not? The man that was drowned nine days ago off Maiden's rock. They are waiting for him now. The truth, spit it out. I would want to. I would try. I am not a strong swimmer. Water cold soft. When I put my face into it in the basin at Clongowes. Can't see! Who's behind me? Out quickly, quickly! Do you see the tide flowing quickly in on all sides, sheeting the lows of sands quickly, shellcocoacoloured? If I had land under my feet. I want his life still to be his, mine to be mine. A drowning man. His human eyes scream to me out of horror of his death. I . . . With him together down . . . I could not save her. Waters: bitter death: lost.

A woman and a man. I see her skirties. Pinned up, I bet.

Their dog ambled about a bank of dwindling sand, trotting, sniffing on all sides. Looking for something lost in a past life. Suddenly he made off like a bounding hare, ears flung back, chasing the shadow of a lowskimming gull. The man's shrieked whistle struck his limp ears. He turned, bounded back, came nearer, trotted on twinkling shanks. On a field tenney a buck, trippant, proper, unattired. At the lacefringe of the tide he halted with stiff forehoofs, seawardpointed ears. His snout lifted barked at the wavenoise, herds of seamorse. They serpented towards his feet, curling, unfurling many crests, every ninth, breaking, plashing, from far, from farther out, waves and waves.

Cocklepickers. They waded a little way in the water and, stooping, soused their bags, and, lifting them again, waded out. The dog yelped running to them, reared up and pawed them, dropping on all fours, again reared up at them with mute bearish fawning. Unheeded he kept by them as they came towards the drier sand, a rag of wolf's tongue redpanting from his jaws. His speckled body ambled ahead of them and then loped off at a calf's gallop. The carcass lay on his path. He stopped, sniffed, stalked round it, brother, nosing closer, went round it, sniffing rapidly like a dog all over the dead dog's bedraggled fell. Dogskull, dogsniff, eyes on the ground, moves to one great goal. Ah, poor dogsbody. Here lies dogsbody's body.

– Tatters! Out of that, you mongrel.

The cry brought him skulking back to his master and a blunt bootless kick sent him unscathed across a spit of sand, crouched in flight. He slunk back in a curve. Doesn't see me. Along by the edge of the mole he lolloped, dawdled, smelt a rock and from under a cocked hindleg pissed against it. He trotted forward and, lifting his hindleg, pissed quick short at an unsmelt rock. The simple pleasures of the poor. His hindpaws then scattered sand: then his forepaws dabbled and delved. Something he buried there, his grandmother. He rooted in the sand, dabbling, delving and stopped to listen to the air, scraped up the sand again with a fury of his claws, soon ceasing, a pard, a panther, got in spousebreach, vulturing the dead.

From *Ulysses*

From the Carriage: an Echo of Argus

GASWORKS. WHOOPING COUGH they say it cures. Good job Milly never got it. Poor children! Doubles them up black and blue in convulsions. Shame really. Got off lightly with illness compared. Only measles. Flaxseed tea. Scarlatina, influenza epidemics. Canvassing for death. Don't miss this chance. Dogs' home over there. Poor old Athos!

Be good to Athos, Leopold, is my last wish. Thy will be done. We obey them in the grave. A dying scrawl. He took it to heart, pined away. Quiet brute. Old men's dogs usually are.

ibid

Garryowen

BLOOM: Fish and taters. N. g. Ah!

(He disappears into Olhousen's, the pork butcher's, under the downcoming rollshutter. A few moments later he emerges from under the shutter, puffing Poldy, blowing Bloohoom. In each hand he holds a parcel, one containing a lukewarm pig's crubeen, the other a cold sheep's trotter, sprinkled with wholepepper. He gasps, standing upright. Then bending to one side he presses a parcel against his rib and groans.) . . .

BLOOM: My spine's a bit limp. Go or turn? And this food? Eat it and get all pigsticky. Absurd I am. Waste of money. One and eightpence too much. *(The retriever drives a cold snivelling muzzle against his hand, wagging his tail)* Strange how they take to me. Even that brute today. Better speak to him first. Like women they like *rencontres*. Stinks like a polecat. *Chacun son gout.* He might be mad. Fido. Uncertain in his movements. Good fellow! Garryowen! *(The wolfdog sprawls on his back, wriggling obscenely with begging paws, his long black tongue lolling out)* Influence of his surroundings. Give and have done with it. Provided nobody. *(Calling encouraging words he shambles back with a furtive poacher's tread, dogged by the setter into a dark stalestunk corner. He unrolls one parcel and goes to dump the crubeen softly but holds back and feels the trotter)* Sizeable for threepence. But then I have it in my left hand. Calls for more effort. Why? Smaller from want of use. O, let it slide. Two and six.

(With regret he lets unrolled crubeen and trotter slide. The mastiff mauls the bundle clumsily and gluts himself with growling greed, crunching the bones. Two raincaped watch approach, silent, vigilant. They murmur together.)

THE WATCH: Bloom. Of Bloom. For Bloom. Bloom.

(Each lays a hand on Bloom's shoulder.)

FIRST WATCH: Caught in the act. Commit no nuisance.

BLOOM: *(Stammers)* I am doing good to others.

(A covey of gulls, storm petrels, rises hungrily from Liffey slime with Banbury cakes in their beaks.)

THE GULLS: Kaw kave kankury kake.

BLOOM: The friend of man. Trained by kindness.

(He points. Bob Doran, toppling from a high barstool, sways over the munching spaniel.)

BOB DORAN: Towser. Give us the paw. Give the paw.

(The bulldog growls, his scruff standing, a gobbet of pig's knuckle between his molars through which rabid scumspittle dribbles. Bob Doran falls silently into an area.)

SECOND WATCH: Prevention of cruelty to animals.

BLOOM: *(Enthusiastically)* A noble work! I scolded that tramdriver on Harold's cross bridge for illusing the poor horse with his harness scab. Bad French I got for my pains. Of course it was frosty and the last tram. All tales of circus life are highly demoralising.

ibid

RADCLYFFE HALL

Forthright Spirits

THE [LIBEL] CASE did not come up until the autumn. In the meantime, dogs were becoming a growing preoccupation. In February Olaf the Great Dane, still only a year old, had to be shot by the vet when it developed an epileptic condition. John [i.e. Radclyffe Hall] was heartbroken. 'I can suddenly remember John's face as we sat waiting for the sound of that shot,' Una wrote many years later. In April Una's dachshund Thora developed incurable follicular mange and had to be put down too. Both women wept miserably.

But owning dogs had its compensations too. Breeding and exhibiting was now an integral part of their life. They attended together all the main dog shows in and around London, kitting themselves out in fedoras, capes, boots and riding breeches. They specialized in Brabançonnes, or griffons as they are usually called, and they brought to their new-found hobby all the zeal and thoroughness which had characterized their psychical work. They quickly excelled, bringing home trophies from almost every contest they entered. Griffons are delicate, neurotic small dogs providing many difficulties for the breeder. When the drawing-room kennel at Chip Chase was full, the mess and the noise (not to speak of the stench) frequently got on their nerves – John's in particular – provoking further 'upheavals' between them. On one occasion Tinkie disgraced herself by having an attack of diarrhoea in Sir George Lewis's office.

John and Una presented a formidable, somewhat intimidating couple in the arcane world of professional exhibiting. They did not hesitate to criticize other dog owners whose standards of love and care fell short of their own. They were against anthropomorphism. 'One must bear in mind,' declared Una, 'that the dog has as good a right to be purely canine as the human being has to be purely human.' The central question was 'whether the dog has as good a cause for satisfaction in his owner as that owner has cause for gratification in ownership'. To John and Una, the owners were more often found wanting.

Michael Baker, from *Our Three Selves*

FRANZ KAFKA

A Philosopher Speculates

FOR IT MUST not be assumed that, for all my peculiarities, which lie open to the day, I am in the least exempt from the laws of my species. Indeed when I reflect on it – and I have time and disposition and capacity enough for that – I see that dogdom is in every way a marvellous institution. Apart from us dogs there are all sorts of creatures in the world, wretched, limited, dumb creatures who have no language but mechanical cries: many of us dogs study them, having given them names, try to help them, educate them, uplift them, and so on. For my part I am quite indifferent to them except when they try to disturb me,

I confuse them with one another, I ignore them. But one thing is too obvious to have escaped me; namely how little inclined they are, compared with us dogs, to stick together, how silently and unfamiliarly and with what a curious hostility they pass each other by, how mean are the interests that suffice to bind them together for a little in ostensible union, and how often these very interests give rise to hatred and conflict. Consider us dogs, on the other hand! One can safely say that we all live together in a literal heap, all of us, different as we are from one another on account of numberless and profound modifications which have arisen in the course of time. All in one heap! We are drawn to each other and nothing can prevent us from satisfying that communal impulse; all our laws and institutions, the few that I still know and the many that I have forgotten, go back to this longing for the greatest bliss we are capable of, the warm comfort of being together. But now consider the other side of the picture. No creatures to my knowledge live in such wide dispersion as we dogs, none have so many distinctions of class, of kind, of occupation, distinctions too numerous to review at a glance; we, whose one desire is to stick together – and again and again we succeed at transcendent moments in spite of everything – we above all others are compelled to live separated from one another by strange vocations that are often incomprehensible even to our canine neighbours, holding firmly to laws that are not those of the dog world, but are actually directed against it. How baffling these questions are, questions on which one would prefer not to touch – I understand that standpoint too, even better than my own – and yet questions to which I have completely capitulated. Why do I not do as the others: live in harmony with my people and accept in silence whatever disturbs the harmony, ignoring it as a small error in the great account, always keeping in mind the things that bind us happily together, not those that drive us again and again, although by sheer force, out of our social circle?

I can recall an incident in my youth; I was at the time in one of those inexplicable blissful states of exaltation which every one must have experienced as a child; I was still quite a puppy, everything pleased me, everything was my concern, I believed that great things were going on around me of which I was the leader and to which I must lend my voice, things which must be wretchedly thrown aside if I did not run for them and wag my tail for them – childish fantasies that fled with riper years. But at the time their power was very great, I was completely under their spell, and presently something actually did happen, something so extraordinary that it seemed to justify my wild expectations. In itself it was nothing very extraordinary, for I have seen many such things, and more remarkable things too, often enough since, but at the time it struck me with all the force of a first impression, one of those impressions which can never be erased and influence much of one's later conduct. I encountered, in short, a little company of dogs, or rather I did not encounter them, they appeared before me. Before that I had been running along in darkness for some time, filled with a premonition of great things – a premonition that may well have been delusive, that the world of dogs, as your researches make more and more evident, is pledged to silence and always will be? How long will you be able to endure it? That is the real great question of my life, before which all smaller ones sink into insignificance; it is put to myself alone and concerns no one else. Unfortunately I can answer it more easily than the smaller, specific questions: I shall probably hold out till my natural end; the calm of old age will put up a greater and greater resistance to all disturbing questions. I shall very likely die in silence and surrounded by silence, indeed almost peacefully, and I look forward to that with composure. An admirably strong heart, lungs that it is impossible to use up before their time, have been given to us dogs as if in malice; we survive all questions, even our own, bulwarks of silence that we are.

Recently I have taken more and more to examining my life, looking for the decisive, the fundamental, error that I must surely have made; and I cannot find it. And yet I must have made it, for if I had not made it and yet were unable by the diligent labour of a long life to achieve my desire, that would prove that my desire is impossible, and complete hopelessness must follow. Behold, then, the work of a lifetime. First of all my inquiries into the question: Whence does the earth procure the food it gives us? A young dog, at bottom naturally greedy for life, I renounced all enjoyments, apprehensively avoided all pleasures, buried my head between my front paws when I was confronted by temptation, and addressed myself to my task. I was no scholar, neither in the information I acquired, nor in method, nor in intention. That was probably a defect, but it could not have been a decisive one. I had had little schooling, for I left my mother's care at an early age, soon got used to independence, led a free life; and premature independence is inimical to systematic learning. But I have seen much, listened to much, spoken with dogs of all sorts and conditions, understood everything, I believe, fairly intelligently, and correlated my particular observations fairly intelligently: that has compensated somewhat for my lack of scholarship, not to mention that independence, if it is a disadvantage in learning things, is an actual advantage when one is making one's own inquiries. In my case it was all the more necessary as I was not able to employ the real method of science, to avail myself, that is, of the labours of my predecessors, and establish contact with contemporary investigators. I was entirely cast on my own resources, began at the very beginning, and with the consciousness, inspiriting to youth, but utterly crushing to age, that the fortuitous point to which I carried my labours must also be the final one. Was I really so alone in my inquiries, at the beginning and up to now? Yes and no. It is inconceivable that there must not always have been and that there are not today individual dogs in the same case as myself. I cannot be so accursed as that. I do not deviate from the dog nature by a hairbreadth. Every dog has like me the impulse to question, and I have like every dog the impulse not to answer. Every one has the impulse to question. How otherwise could my questions have affected my hearers in the slightest – and they were often affected, to my ecstatic delight, an exaggerated delight, I must confess – and how otherwise could I have been prevented from achieving much more than I have done? And that I have the compulsion to remain silent needs unfortunately no particular proof. I am at bottom, then, no different from any other dog; everybody, no matter how he may differ in opinion from me and reject my views, will gladly admit that, and I in turn will admit as much of any other dog. Only the mixture of the elements is different, a difference very important for the individual, significant for the race. And how can one credit that the composition of these available elements has never chanced through all the past and present to result in a mixture similar to mine, one, moreover, if mine be regarded as unfortunate, more unfortunate still? To think so would be contrary to all experience. We dogs are all engaged in the strangest occupations, occupations in which one would refuse to believe if one had not the most reliable information concerning them. The best example I can quote is that of the hovering dog. The first time I heard of one I laughed and simply refused to believe it. What? One was asked to believe that there was a very tiny species of dog, not much bigger than my head even when it was full grown, and this dog, who must of course be a feeble creature, an artificial, weedy, brushed and curled fop by all accounts, incapable of making an honest jump, this dog was supposed, according to people's stories, to remain for the most part high up in the air, apparently doing nothing at all but simply resting there? No, to try to make me swallow such things was exploiting the simplicity of a young dog too outrageously, I told myself. But shortly afterwards I heard from another source an account of another hovering dog. Could there be a conspiracy to fool me? But after that I saw the dog musicians with my own eyes, and from that day I considered everything possible, no prejudices fettered my powers of apprehension, I investigated the most senseless rumours, following them as far as they could take me, and the most senseless seemed to me in this senseless world more probable than the sensible, and moreover particularly fertile for investigation. So it was too with the hovering dogs. I discovered a great many things about them; true, I have succeeded to this day in seeing none of them, but of their existence I have been firmly convinced for a long time, and they occupy an important place in my picture of the world. As usual it is not, of course, their technique that chiefly gives me to think. It is wonderful – who can gainsay it? – that these dogs should be able to float in the air: in my amazed admiration for that I am at one with my fellow-dogs. But far more strange to my mind is the senselessness, the senselessness of these existences. They have no relation whatever to the general life of the community, they hover in the air, and that is all, and life goes on its usual way; someone now and then refers to art and artists, but there it ends. But why, my good dogs, why on earth do these dogs float in the air? What sense is there in their occupation? Why can one get no word of explanation regarding them? Why do they hover up there, letting their legs, the pride of dogs, fall into desuetude, preserving a detachment from the nourishing earth, reaping without having sowed? being particularly well provided for as I hear, and at the cost of the dog community too. I can flatter myself that my inquiries into these matters made some stir. People began to investigate after a fashion, to collect data; they made a beginning, at least, although they are never likely to go farther. But after all that is something. And though the truth will not be discovered by such means – never can that stage be reached – yet they throw light on some of the profounder ramifications of falsehood. For all the senseless phenomena of our existence, and the most senseless most of all, are susceptible of investigation. Not completely, of course – that is the diabolical jest – but sufficiently to spare one painful questions. Take the hovering dogs once more as an example; they are not haughty as one might imagine at first, but rather particularly dependent upon their fellow-dogs; if one tries to put oneself in their place one will see that. For they must do what they can to obtain pardon, and not openly – that would be a violation of the obligation to keep silence – they must do what they can to obtain pardon for their way of life, or else divert attention from it so that it may be forgotten – and they do this, I have been told, by means of an almost unendurable volubility. They are perpetually talking, partly of their philosophical reflections, with which, seeing that they have completely renounced bodily exertion, they can continuously occupy themselves, partly of the observations which they have made from their exalted stations; and although, as is very understandable considering their lazy existence, they are not much distinguished for intellectual power, and their philosophy is as worthless as their observations, and science can make hardly any use of their utterances, and besides is not reduced to draw assistance from such wretched sources, nevertheless if one asks what the hovering dogs are really doing one will invariably receive the reply that they contribute a great deal to knowledge. 'That is true,' remarks someone, 'but their contributions are worthless and wearisome.' The reply to that is a shrug, or a change of the subject, or annoyance, or laughter, and in a little while, when you ask again, you can learn once more that they contribute to knowledge, and finally when you are asked the question you yourself will reply – if you are not careful – to the same effect. And perhaps indeed it is well not to be too obstinate, but to yield to public sentiment, to accept the extant hovering dogs, and without recognizing their right to existence, which cannot be done, yet to tolerate them. But more than this must not be required; that would be going too far, and yet the demand is made. We are perpetually being asked to put up with new hovering dogs who are always appearing. One does not even know where they come from. Do these dogs multiply by propagation? Have they actually the strength for that? – for they are nothing much more than a beautiful coat of hair, and what is there in that to propagate? But even if that improbable contingency were possible, when could it take place? For they are invariably seen alone, self-complacently floating high up in the air, and if for once in a while they descend to take a run, it lasts only for a minute or two, a few mincing struts and once more they are back in strict solitude, absorbed in what is supposed to be profound thought, from which, even when they exert themselves to the utmost, they cannot tear themselves free, or at least so they say. But if they do not propagate their kind, is it credible that there can be dogs who voluntarily give up life on the solid ground, voluntarily become hovering dogs, and merely for the sake of the comfort and a certain technical accomplishment choose that empty life on cushions up there? It is unthinkable; neither propagation nor voluntary transition is thinkable. The facts, however, show that there are always new hovering dogs in evidence; from which one must conclude that, in spite of obstacles which appear insurmountable to our understanding, no dog species, however curious, ever dies out, once it exists, or, at least, not without a tough struggle, not without being capable of putting up a successful defence for a long time.

But if that is valid for such an out-of-the-way, externally odd, inefficient species as the hovering dog, must I not also accept it as valid for mine?

From *Investigations of a Dog*

DENIS MACKAIL

. . . and Bark Oneself

BY 1929, TOPSY HAD certainly invented her favourite game with me. It began very quietly, with a kind of thought-transference; for I would be sitting reading in a chair, when I suddenly felt that I must raise my eyes. There had been no sound, but I was quite right. Topsy was now lying on her back, on another arm-chair – no rules against this in the Mackail household, for they would have been quite useless with Pekes – gazing at me steadfastly from her benign brown eyes. I knew just what I was supposed to do then. I had to start growling – gently at first, but with a slight crescendo – and at the end of the growl I had to say 'Wuff!' At the first murmur a look of rapture would pass over Topsy's inverted features; and at the 'Wuff!' she would give a violent, convulsive movement – still on her back – which would sometimes throw her right across the chair. Or, as a slight variant, she would roll on to her feet, tuck her head into a corner, and – still managing to eye me – would butt in much the same manner as she had previously kicked.

This wasn't the end of the game, but it was the end of the variations. I continued to growl and say 'Wuff!', and Topsy continued to react in one way or the other; until quite suddenly there was a Wuff that produced no reaction at all. She was sitting up and looking at me with mild though still friendly surprise. 'Poor old fellow,' she seemed to be saying. 'A pity he's so childish in some ways.'

'Topsy!' I would say accusingly. 'You *know* you started it!'

She just blinked at me, though there was a slight flutter from the end of her tail.

'Oh, all right,' I said. 'I shan't play next time.'

But of course I always did. I had to, when that silent summons came. Besides, I was getting so remarkably good at growling.

From *Life with Topsy*

JOHN HAMPSON

A Bad Mascot

IVY, TOO, THOUGHT of her husband as a lover. He'd been such a nice chap when they courted, and mad about herself. Suddenly she burst out passionately, 'I wish I hated him, Tom; I wish I hated him, but I can't. If only he'd try. We'd do well in the summer. What with teas and that. Food's nearly all profit.' That story Tom had heard before, but summer would not find them at the Greyhound. God alone knew where they'd be then. He fumbled in his trouser pocket and found a scrap of crumpled paper which he handed across to Ivy.

'That's Grinds's receipt; he was pleased to get it, though he didn't say "thank you". I dare say he'll stop shouting the odds now.' Smoothing out the piece of paper, Ivy read: 'Dr. to Samuel Grinds, 30/9 for two prize hens and a turkey. Paid Saml. Grinds.' She questioned: 'Did he say anything about it?' The boy answered, ''Bout time, too. I'd a got somebody to knock that dog of his on the head if you'd not brought it soon.' Putting the receipt in her purse, Ivy commented shortly, 'Fred's a fool. It did us a bit of no good in the village, owing that poor old cripple thirty bob.' 'Of course it did,' agreed Tom angrily. 'But you couldn't make Fred see that. That damn dog of his. Two hens and a turkey in one night; it's never brought home a hare or a rabbit yet.' Going to the door Ivy called softly, 'Naxi, Naxi'. The dog came quickly, its proud head borne on too slender shoulders. It would never catch a rabbit, for she and Fred spoilt it, she knew that. Wrapt up in Pertinax, lay her fortune, Ivy felt. A chain of slight coincidences made her believe firmly in the dog's virtue as mascot to the inn. His very breed and her first sight of the animal made Ivy want him. Its owner, seeing her eagerness to possess the dog, rooked Freddy over the deal. She resented that on her husband; it was a bad omen. She failed to see that Fred had bought it to please her chiefly. Tom and she had known the greyhound was faulty, not worth half the sum Fred paid for him. From a breeder's point of view the animal should have been destroyed. That made Fred furious; the dog was a wonder. Instead of giving Ivy the dog he kept it for himself, extolling its many virtues and maintaining that he had bought it cheaply. In spite of this they were all fond of Naxi. The dog had beauty in their eyes, though on most showing points he was under-developed, and had the naughty vice of chicken-killing.

The Grovelace villagers watched, amused; they all knew Pertinax and his tricks. Every time a fowl met with accidental death, its owner would carry it bleeding up to the Greyhound, accusing Naxi and demanding compensation. Fred soon tired of that and kept the dog chained up. Then one night he got away; several people saw him hanging round Grinds's place. Next morning the old cobbler came up the hill in his wheeled chair, a bloody cargo of mangled flesh and feathers with him. The landlord denied liability, and the old man, already in a furious rage, threatened what would happen to Naxi. The villagers having enjoyed making Fred pay for the damage done by rats and other enemies of poultry, were incensed at his refusal to pay the cripple. This was a genuine case. Naxi was known to be a killer, and old Grinds had an extra hard time of things. Ivy and Tom took the cripple's side, too; it was only right and just that he should be paid. Fred remained obstinate; he had said he would not pay, and no one could make him. Ivy, because of her pity for the cripple, and her fear that some horrid vengeance might be Naxi's fate, took the money out of the till and gave it to Tom. The bill paid and Naxi, naughty dog, was safe, she felt.

Tom asked, 'Did he miss it?' In her dream, stroking the pet's silken coat, Ivy was startled. 'Miss what?' she said. 'The money you took out of the till to pay Grinds with?' Ivy shook her head. 'No. That proves what a fool he is. It would not be safe to leave him alone in the house for half a day,' her brother said. That was true enough; if Tom was out she had to stay in.

From Saturday Night at the Greyhound

EVELYN WAUGH

Cruttwell: the Loathed Tutor

CRUTTWELL'S APPEARANCE WAS not prepossessing. He was tall, almost loutish, with the face of a petulant baby. He smoked a pipe which was usually attached to his blubber-lips by a thread of slime. As he removed the stem, waving it to emphasise his indistinct speech, this glittering connection extended until finally it broke leaving a dribble on his chin. When he spoke to me I found myself so distracted by the speculation of how far this line could be attenuated that I was often inattentive to his words.

He was, I now recognise, a wreck of the war in which he had served gallantly. No doubt a modern doctor would have named, even if he could not cure, his various neuroses. It was as though he had never cleaned himself of the muck of the trenches. His conspectus of history was narrowed to the few miles of the Low Countries where he had fought, and the ultimate, unattainable frontier towards which he had gazed through his periscope over the barbed wire. He was obsessed by the Rhine and it was the first, sharp difference between us that I was ignorant of its course.

He had a kind of rough geniality which found expression in coarse soldiers' language and quickly gave place to a frustrated pugnacity. He had been a fellow of All Souls before 1914 and must then have been a young man of more polished manners, for he was of perfectly respectable origins; but all were blown and gassed away in two years' fighting. As Dean of the college he seemed often to fancy himself in command of a recalcitrant platoon. . . .

It was Terence [Greenidge] who first imaginatively imputed to Cruttwell sexual connection with dogs and purchased a stuffed one in a junk-shop in Walton Street, which we set in the quad as an allurement for him on his return from dining in All Souls. For the same reason we used rather often to bark under Cruttwell's windows at night.

From *A Little Learning*

On Guard

I

MILLICENT BLADE HAD a notable head of naturally fair hair; she had a docile and affectionate disposition, and an expression of face which changed with lightning rapidity from amiability to laughter and from laughter to respectful interest. But the feature which, more than any other, endeared her to sentimental Anglo-Saxon manhood was her nose.

It was not everybody's nose; many prefer one with greater body; it was not a nose to appeal to painters, for it was far too small and quite without shape, a mere dab of putty without apparent bone structure; a nose which made it impossible for its wearer to be haughty or imposing or astute. It would not have done for a governess or a 'cellist or even for a post office clerk, but it suited Miss Blade's book perfectly, for it was a nose that pierced the thin surface crest of the English heart to its warm and pulpy core; a nose to take the thoughts of English manhood back to its schooldays, to the doughy-faced urchins on whom it had squandered its first affection, to memories of changing room and chapel and battered straw boaters. Three Englishmen in five, it is true, grow snobbish about these things in later life and prefer a nose that makes more show in public – but two in five is an average with which any girl of modest fortune may be reasonably content.

Hector kissed her reverently on the tip of this nose. As he did so, his senses reeled and in momentary delirium he saw the fading light of the November afternoon, the raw mist spreading over the playing-fields; overheated youth in the scrum; frigid youth at the touchline, shuffling on the duck-boards, chafing their fingers and, when their mouths were emptied of biscuit crumbs, cheering their house team to further exertion.

'You will wait for me, won't you?' he said.

'Yes, darling.'

'And you will write?'

'Yes, darling,' she replied more doubtfully, 'sometimes ... at least I'll try. Writing is not my best thing, you know.'

'I shall think of you all the time Out There,' said Hector. 'It's going to be terrible – miles of impassable waggon track between me and the nearest white man, blinding sun, lions, mosquitoes, hostile natives, work from dawn until sunset single handed against the forces of nature, fever, cholera ... But soon I shall be able to send for you to join me.'

'Yes, darling.'

'It's bound to be a success. I've discussed it all with Beckthorpe – that's the chap who's selling me the farm. You see, the crop has failed every year so far – first coffee, then sisal, then tobacco, that's all you can grow there, and the year Beckthorpe grew sisal everyone else was making a packet in tobacco, but sisal was no good; then he grew tobacco, but by then it was coffee he ought to have grown, and so on. He stuck it nine years. Well if you work it out mathematically, Beckthorpe says, in three years one's bound to strike the right crop. I can't quite explain why, but it is like roulette and all that sort of thing, you see.'

'Yes, darling.'

Hector gazed at her little, shapeless, mobile button of a nose and was lost again ... 'Play up, play up,' and after the match the smell of crumpets being toasted over a gas-ring in his study ...

2

Later that evening he dined with Beckthorpe, and, as he dined, he grew more despondent.

'Tomorrow this time I shall be at sea,' he said, twiddling his empty port glass.

'Cheer up, old boy,' said Beckthorpe.

Hector filled his glass and gazed with growing distaste round the reeking dining-room of Beckthorpe's club. The last awful member had left the room and they were alone with the cold buffet.

'I say, you know, I've been trying to work it out. It *was* in three years you said the crop was bound to be right, wasn't it?'

'That's right, old boy.'

'Well, I've been through the sum and it seems to me that it might be eighty-one years before it comes right.'

'No, no, old boy, three or nine, or at the most twenty-seven.'

'Are you sure?'

'Quite.'

'Good ... you know it's awful leaving Milly behind. Suppose it *is* eighty-one years before the crop succeeds. It's the devil of a time to expect a girl to wait. Some other blighter might turn up, if you see what I mean.'

'In the Middle Ages they used to use girdles of chastity.'

'Yes, I know. I've been thinking of them. But they sound damned uncomfortable. I doubt if Milly would wear one even if I knew where to find it.'

'Tell you what, old boy. You ought to give her something.'

'Hell, I'm always giving her things. She either breaks them or loses them or forgets where she got them.'

'You must give her something she will always have by her, something that will last.'

'Eighty-one years?'

'Well, say twenty-seven. Something to remind her of you.'

'I could give her a photograph – but I might change a bit in twenty-seven years.'

'No, no, that would be most unsuitable. A photograph wouldn't do at all. I know what I'd give her. I'd give her a dog.'

'Dog?'

'A healthy puppy that was over distemper and looked like living a long time. She might even call it Hector.'

'Would that be a good thing, Beckthorpe?'

'Best possible, old boy.'

So next morning, before catching the boat train, Hector hurried to one of the mammoth stores of London and was shown the livestock department. 'I want a puppy.'

'Yes, sir. Any particular sort?'

'One that will live a long time. Eighty-one years, or twenty-seven at the least.'

The man looked doubtful. 'We have some fine healthy puppies, of course,' he admitted, 'but none of them carry a guarantee. Now if it was longevity you wanted, might I recommend a tortoise? They live to an extraordinary age and are very safe in traffic.'

'No, it must be a pup.'

'Or a parrot?'

'No, no, a pup. I would prefer one named Hector.'

They walked together past monkeys and kittens and cockatoos to the dog department, which, even at this early hour, had attracted a small congregation of rapt worshippers. There were puppies of all varieties in wire-fronted kennels, ears cocked, tails wagging, noisily soliciting attention. Rather wildly, Hector selected a poodle and, as the salesman disappeared to fetch him his change, he leant down for a moment's intense communion with the beast of his choice. He gazed deep into the sharp little face, avoided a sudden snap and said with profound solemnity:

'You are to look after Milly, Hector. See that she doesn't marry anyone until I get back.'

And the pup Hector waved his plume of tail.

3

Millicent came to see him off, but, negligently, went to the wrong station; it could not have mattered, however, for she was twenty minutes late. Hector and the poodle hung about the barrier looking for her, and not until the train was already moving did he bundle the animal into Beckthorpe's arms with instructions to deliver him at Millicent's address. Luggage labelled for Mombasa 'Wanted on the voyage' lay in the rack above him. He felt very much neglected.

That evening as the ship pitched and rolled past the Channel lighthouses, he received a radiogram: MISERABLE TO MISS YOU WENT PADDINGTON LIKE IDIOT, THANK YOU THANK YOU FOR SWEET DOG I LOVE HIM FATHER MINDS DREADFULLY LONGING TO HEAR ABOUT FARM DONT FALL FOR SHIP SIREN ALL LOVE MILLY.

In the Red Sea he received another: BEWARE SIRENS PUPPY BIT MAN CALLED MIKE.

After that Hector heard nothing of Millicent except for a Christmas card which arrived in the last days of February.

4

Generally speaking, Millicent's fancy for any particular young man was likely to last four months. It depended on how far he had got in that time whether the process of extinction was sudden or protracted. In the case of Hector, her affection had been due to diminish at about the time that she became engaged to him; it had been artificially prolonged during the succeeding three weeks, during which he made strenuous, infectiously earnest efforts to find employment in England; it came to an abrupt end with his departure for Kenya. Accordingly the duties of the puppy Hector began with his first days at home. He was young for the job and wholly inexperienced; it is impossible to blame him for his mistake in the matter of Mike Boswell.

This was a young man who had enjoyed a wholly unromantic friendship with Millicent since she first came out. He had seen her fair hair in all kinds of light, in and out of doors, crowned in hats in succeeding fashions, bound with ribbon, decorated with combs, jauntily stuck with flowers; he had seen her nose uplifted in all kinds of weather, had even, on occasions, playfully tweaked it with his finger and thumb, and had never for one moment felt remotely attracted by her.

But the puppy Hector could hardly be expected to know this. All he knew was that two days after receiving his commission, he observed a tall and personable man of marriageable age who treated his hostess with the sort of familiarity which, among the kennel maids with whom he had been brought up, meant only one thing.

The two young people were having tea together. Hector watched for some time from his place on the sofa, barely stifling his growls. A climax was reached when, in the course of some barely intelligible back-chat, Mike leant forward and patted Millicent on the knee.

It was not a serious bite, a mere snap, in fact; but Hector had small teeth as sharp as pins. It was the sudden, nervous speed with which Mick withdrew his hand which caused the damage; he swore, wrapped his hand in a handkerchief, and at Millicent's entreaty revealed three or four minute wounds. Millicent spoke harshly to Hector and tenderly to Mike, and hurried to her mother's medicine cupboard for a bottle of iodine.

Now no Englishman, however phlegmatic, can have his hand dabbed with iodine without, momentarily at any rate, falling in love.

Mike had seen the nose countless times before, but that afternoon, as it was bowed over his scratched thumb, and as Millicent said, 'Am I hurting terribly?', as it was raised towards him, and as Millicent said, 'There. Now it will be all right,' Mike suddenly saw it transfigured as its devotees saw it and from that moment, until long after the three months of attention which she accorded him, he was Millicent's besotted suitor.

The pup Hector saw all this and realized his mistake. Never again, he decided, would he give Millicent the excuse to run for the iodine bottle.

5

He had on the whole an easy task, for Millicent's naturally capricious nature could, as a rule, be relied upon, unaided, to drive her lovers into extremes of irritation. Moreover, she had come to love the dog. She received very regular letters from Hector, written weekly and arriving in batches of three or four according to the mails. She always opened them; often she read them to the end, but their contents made little impression upon her mind and gradually their writer drifted into oblivion so that when people said to her 'How is darling Hector?' it came naturally to her to reply, 'He doesn't like the hot weather much, I'm afraid, and his coat is in a very poor state. I'm thinking of having him plucked,' instead of, 'He had a go of malaria and there is black worm in his tobacco crop.'

Playing upon this affection which had grown up for him, Hector achieved a technique for dealing with Millicent's young men. He no longer growled at them or soiled their trousers; that merely resulted in his being turned from the room; instead, he found it increasingly easy to usurp the coversation.

Tea was the most dangerous time of day, for then Millicent was permitted to entertain friends in her sitting-room; accordingly, though he had a constitutional preference for pungent, meaty dishes, Hector heroically simulated a love of lump sugar. Having made this apparent, at whatever cost to his digestion, it was easy to lead Millicent on to an interest in tricks; he would beg and 'trust', lie down as though dead, stand in the corner and raise a fore paw to his ear.

'What does SUGAR spell?' Millicent would ask, and Hector would walk round the tea table to the sugar-bowl and lay his nose against it, gazing earnestly and clouding the silver with his moist breath.

'He understands everything,' Millicent would say in triumph.

When tricks failed Hector would demand to be let out of the door. The young man would be obliged to interrupt himself to open it. Once on the other side Hector would scratch and whine for re-admission.

In moments of extreme anxiety Hector would affect to be sick – no difficult feat after the unwelcome diet of lump sugar; he would stretch out his neck, retching noisily, till Millicent snatched him up and carried him to the hall, where the floor, paved in marble, was less vulnerable –

but by that time a tender atmosphere had been shattered and one wholly prejudicial to romance created to take its place.

This series of devices spaced out through the afternoon and tactfully obtruded whenever the guest showed signs of leading the conversation to a more intimate phase, distracted young man after young man and sent them finally away, baffled and despairing.

Every morning Hector lay on Millicent's bed while she took her breakfast and read the daily paper. This hour from ten to eleven was sacred to the telephone and it was then that the young men with whom she had danced overnight attempted to renew their friendship and make plans for the day. At first Hector sought, not unsuccessfully, to prevent these assignations by entangling himself in the wire, but soon a subtler and more insulting technique suggested itself. He pretended to tele-phone too. Thus, as soon as the bell rang, he would wag his tail and cock his head on one side in a way that he had learned was engaging. Millicent would begin her conversation and Hector would wriggle up under her arm and nuzzle against the receiver.

'Listen,' she would say, '*someone* wants to talk to you. Isn't he an angel?' Then she would hold the receiver down to him and the young man at the other end would be dazed by a shattering series of yelps. This accomplishment appealed so much to Millicent that often she would not even bother to find out the name of the caller but, instead, would take off the receiver and hold it directly to the black snout, so that some wretched young man half a mile away, feeling perhaps, none too well in the early morning, found himself barked to silence before he had spoken a word.

At other times young men badly taken with the nose would attempt to waylay Millicent in Hyde Park when she was taking Hector for exercise. Here, at first, Hector would get lost, fight other dogs and bite small children to keep himself constantly in her attention, but soon he adopted a gentler course. He insisted upon carrying Millicent's bag for her. He would trot in front of the couple and whenever he thought an interruption desirable he would drop the bag; the young man was obliged to pick it up and restore it first to Millicent and then, at her request, to the dog. Few young men were sufficiently servile to submit to more than one walk in these degrading conditions.

In this way two years passed. Letters arrived constantly from Kenya, full of devotion, full of minor disasters – blight in the sisal, locusts in the coffee, labour troubles, drought, flood, the local government, the world market. Occasionally Millicent read the letters aloud to the dog, usually she left them unread on her breakfast tray. She and Hector moved together through the leisurely routine of English social life. Wherever she carried her nose, two in five marriageable men fell temporarily in love; wherever Hector followed their ardour changed to irritation, shame and disgust. Mothers began to remark complacently that it was curious how that fascinating Blade girl never got married.

6

At last in the third year of this régime a new problem presented itself in the person of Major Sir Alexander Dreadnought, Bart, M.P., and Hector immediately realized that he was up against something altogether more formidable than he had hitherto tackled.

Sir Alexander was not a young man; he was forty-five and a widower. He was wealthy, popular and preternaturally patient; he was also mildly distinguished, being joint-master of a Midland pack of hounds and a junior Minister; he bore a war record of conspicuous gallantry. Millie's father and mother were delighted when they saw that her nose was having its effect on him. Hector took against him from the first, exerted every art which his two and a half years' practice had perfected, and achieved nothing. Devices that had driven a dozen young men to frenzies of chagrin seemed only to accentuate Sir Alexander's tender solicitude. When he came to the house to fetch Millicent for the evening he was found to have filled the pockets of his evening clothes with lump sugar for Hector; when Hector was sick Sir Alexander was there first, on his knees with a page of *The Times*; Hector resorted to his early, violent manner and bit him frequently and hard, but Sir Alexander merely remarked, 'I believe I am making the little fellow jealous. A delightful trait.'

For the truth was that Sir Alexander had been persecuted long and bitterly from his earliest days – his parents, his sisters, his schoolfellows, his company-sergeant and his colonel, his colleagues in politics, his wife, his joint-master, hunstman and hunt secretary, his election agent, his constituents and even his parliamentary private secretary had one and all pitched into Sir Alexander, and he accepted this treatment as a matter of course. For him it was the most natural thing in the world to have his ear-drums outraged by barks when he rang up the young woman of his affections; it was a high privilege to retrieve her handbag when Hector dropped it in the Park; the small wounds that Hector was able to inflict on his ankles and wrists were to him knightly scars. In his more ambitious moments he referred to Hector in Millicent's hearing as 'my little rival'. There could be no doubt whatever of his intentions, and when he asked Millicent and her mamma to visit him in the country, he added at the foot of the letter, 'Of course the invitation includes Hector.'

The Saturday to Monday visit to Sir Alexander was a nightmare to the poodle. He worked as he had never worked before; every artifice by which he could render his presence odious was attempted and attempted in vain. As far as his host was concerned, that is to say. The rest of the household responded well enough, and he received a vicious kick when, through his own bad management, he found himself alone with the second footman, whom he had succeeded in upsetting with a tray of cups at tea-time.

Conduct that had driven Millicent in shame from half the stately homes of England was meekly accepted here. There were other dogs in the house – elderly, sober, well-behaved animals at whom Hector flew; they turned their heads sadly away from his yaps of defiance, he snapped at their ears. They lolloped sombrely out of reach and Sir Alexander had them shut away for the rest of the visit.

There was an exciting Aubusson carpet in the dining-room to which Hector was able to do irreparable damage; Sir Alexander seemed not to notice.

Hector found a carrion in the park and conscientiously rolled in it – although such a thing was obnoxious to his nature – and, returning, fouled every chair in the drawing-room; Sir Alexander himself helped Millicent wash him and brought some bath salts from his own bathroom for the operation.

Hector howled all night; he hid and had half the household searching for him with lanterns; he killed some young pheasants and made a sporting attempt on a peacock. All to no purpose. He staved off an actual proposal, it is true – once in the Dutch garden, once on the way to the stables, and once while he was being bathed – but when Monday morning arrived and he heard Sir Alexander say, 'I hope Hector enjoyed his visit a little. I hope I shall see him here *very, very* often,' he knew that he was defeated.

It was now only a matter of waiting. The evenings in London were a time when it was impossible for him to keep Millicent under observation. One of these days he would wake up to hear Millicent telephoning to her girl friends, breaking the good news of her engagement.

Thus it was that after a long conflict of loyalties he came to a desperate resolve. He had grown fond of his young mistress; often and often when her face had been pressed down to his he had felt sympathy with that long line of young men whom it was his duty to persecute. But Hector was no kitchen-haunting mongrel. By the code of all well-born dogs it is money that counts. It is the purchaser, not the mere feeder and fondler, to whom ultimate loyalty is due. The hand which had once fumbled with the fivers in the livestock-department of the mammoth store, now tilled the unfertile soil of equatorial Africa, but the sacred words of commission still rang in Hector's memory. All through the Sunday night and the journey of Monday morning, Hector wrestled with his problem; then he came to the decision. *The nose must go.*

7

It was an easy business; one firm snap as she bent over his basket and the work was accomplished. She went to a plastic surgeon and emerged some weeks later without scar or stitch. But it was a different nose; the surgeon in his way was an artist and, as I have said above, Millicent's nose had no sculptural qualities. Now she has a fine aristocratic beak – worthy of the spinster she is about to become. Like all spinsters she watches eagerly for the foreign mails and keeps carefully under lock and key a casket full of depressing agricultural intelligence; like all spinsters she is accompanied everywhere by an ageing lap-dog.

From *Work Suspended, and Other Stories*

Hired Compassion

DENNIS BARLOW WENT to work after dinner. He drove towards Burbank, past luminous motels, past the golden gates and floodlit temples of Whispering Glades Memorial Park, almost to the extremity of the city, to his place of business. His colleague, Miss Myra Poski, was waiting for relief, hatted and freshly painted.

'I hope I'm not late.'

'You're sweet. I've a date at the Planetarium or I'd stay and fix you some coffee. There's been nothing to do all day except mail a few remembrance cards. Oh, and Mr Schultz says if anything comes in put it straight on the ice this hot weather. Good-bye;' and she was gone leaving Dennis in sole charge of the business.

The office was furnished in sombre good taste that was relieved by a pair of bronze puppies on the chimney-piece. A low trolley of steel and white enamel alone distinguished the place from a hundred thousand modern American reception-rooms; that and the clinical smell. A bowl of roses stood beside the telephone; their scent contended with the carbolic, but did not prevail.

Dennis sat in one of the armchairs, put his feet on the trolley and settled himself to read. Life in the Air Force had converted him from an amateur to a mere addict. There were certain trite passages of poetry which from a diverse multitude of associations never failed to yield the sensations he craved; he never experimented; these were the branded drug, the sure specific, big magic. He opened the anthology as a woman opens her familiar pack of cigarettes.

Outside the windows the cars swept past continuously, out of town, into town, lights ablaze, radios at full throttle.

'*I wither slowly in thine arms,*' he read. '*Here at the quiet limit of the world,*' and repeated to himself: 'Here at the quiet limit of the world. Here at the quiet limit of the world' . . . as a monk will repeat a single pregnant text, over and over again in prayer.

Presently the telephone rang.

'The Happier Hunting Ground,' he said.

A woman's voice came to him, hoarse, it seemed, with emotion; in other circumstances he might have thought her drunk. 'This is Theodora Heinkel, Mrs Walter Heinkel, of 207 Via Dolorosa, Bel Air. You must come at once. I can't tell you over the phone. My little Arthur – they've just brought him in. He went out first thing and never came back. I didn't worry because he's sometimes been away like that before. I said to Mr Heinkel, "But, Walter, I can't go out to dine when I don't know where Arthur is" and Mr Heinkel said, "What the heck? You can't walk out on Mrs Leicester Scrunch at the last minute," so I went and there I was at the table on Mr Leicester Scrunch's right hand when they brought me the news . . . Hullo, hullo, are you there?'

Dennis picked up the instrument which he had laid on the blotting-pad. 'I will come at once, Mrs Heinkel. 207 Via Dolorosa I think you said.'

'I said I was sitting at Mr Leicester Scrunch's right hand when they brought me the news. He and Mr Heinkel had to help me to the automobile.'

'I am coming at once.'

'I shall never forgive myself as long as I live. To think of his being brought home alone. The maid was out and the city wagon-driver had to telephone from the drug store . . . Hullo, hullo. Are you there? I said the city scavenger had to telephone from the drug store.'

'I am on my way, Mrs Heinkel.'

Dennis locked the office and backed the car from the garage; not his own, but the plain black van which was used for official business. Half an hour later he was at the house of mourning. A corpulent man came down the garden path to greet him. He was formally dressed for the evening in the high fashion of the place – Donegal tweeds, sandals, a grass-green silk shirt, open at the neck with an embroidered monogram covering half his torso. 'Am I pleased to see you!' he said.

'Mr W. H., all happiness,' said Dennis involuntarily.

'Pardon me?'

'I am the Happier Hunting Ground,' said Dennis.

'Yes, come along in.'

Dennis opened the back of the wagon and took out an aluminium container. 'Will this be large enough?'

'Plenty.'

They entered the house. A lady, also dressed for the evening in a long, low gown and a diamond tiara, sat in the hall with a glass in her hand.

'This has been a terrible experience for Mrs Heinkel.'

'I don't want to see him. I don't want to speak of it,' said the lady.

'The Happier Hunting Ground assumes all responsibility,' said Dennis.

'This way,' said Mr Heinkel. 'In the pantry.'

The Sealyham lay on the draining-board beside the sink. Dennis lifted it into the container.

'Perhaps you wouldn't mind taking a hand?'

Together he and Mr Heinkel carried their load to the wagon.

'Shall we discuss arrangements now, or would you prefer to call in the morning?'

'I'm a pretty busy man mornings,' said Mr Heinkel. 'Come into the study.'

There was a tray on the desk. They helped themselves to whisky.

'I have our brochure here setting out our service. Were you thinking of interment or incineration?'

'Pardon me?'

'Buried or burned?'

'Burned, I guess.'

'I have some photographs here of various styles of urn.'

'The best will be good enough.'

'Would you require a niche in our columbarium or do you prefer to keep the remains at home?'

'What you said first.'

'And the religious rites? We have a pastor who is always pleased to assist.'

'Well, Mr – ?'

'Barlow.'

'Mr Barlow, we're neither of us what you might call very church-going people, but I think on an occasion like this Mrs Heinkel would want all the comfort you can offer.'

'Our Grade A service includes several unique features. At the moment of committal, a white dove, symbolizing the deceased's soul, is liberated over the crematorium.'

'Yes,' said Mr Heinkel, 'I reckon Mrs Heinkel would appreciate the dove.'

'And every anniversary a card of remembrance is mailed without further charge. It reads: *Your little Arthur is thinking of you in heaven today and wagging his tail.*'

'That's a very beautiful thought, Mr Barlow.'

'Then if you will just sign the order . . .'

Mrs Heinkel bowed gravely to him as he passed through the hall. Mr Heinkel accompanied him to the door of his car. 'It has been a great pleasure to make your acquaintance, Mr Barlow. You have certainly relieved me of a great responsibility.'

'That is what the Happier Hunting Ground aims to do,' said Dennis, and drove away.

At the administrative building, he carried the dog to the refrigerator. It was a capacious chamber, already occupied by two or three other small cadavers. Next to a Siamese cat stood a tin of fruit juice and a plate of sandwiches. Dennis took this supper into the reception room and, as he ate it, resumed his interrupted reading.

From *The Loved One*

STEVIE SMITH

The Hound of Ulster

Little boy
Will you stop
And take a look
In the puppy shop –
Dogs blue and liver
Noses aquiver
Little dogs big dogs
Dogs for sport and pleasure
Fat dogs meagre dogs
Dogs for lap and leisure.
Do you see that wire-haired terrier?
Could anything be merrier?
Do you see that Labrador retriever?
His name is Belvoir.
   Thank you courteous stranger, said the child,
   By your words I am beguiled,
   But tell me I pray
   What lurks in the gray
   Cold shadows at the back of the shop?
Little boy do not stop
Come away
From the puppy shop.
For the Hound of Ulster lies tethered there
Cuchulain tethered by his golden hair
His eyes are closed and his lips are pale
Hurry little boy he is not for sale.

To the Dog Belvoir

Whom I saw in a Dream Push Baby N.
from under a Brewer's Dray and Die in His Place

The stricken Belvoir raised a paw and said:
I die a perfect gentle quadruped.

O Pug!

To the Brownes' pug dog, on my lap, in their car,
coming home from Norfolk.

O Pug, some people do not like you,
But I like you,
Some people say you do not breathe, you snore,
I don't mind.
One person says he is always conscious of your behind,
Is that your fault?

Your own people love you,
All the people in the family that owns you
Love you: Good pug, they cry, Happy pug,
Pug-come-for-a-walk.

You are an old dog now
And in all your life
You have never had cause for a moment's anxiety,
Yet,
In those great eyes of yours,
Those liquid and protuberant orbs,
Lies the shadow of immense insecurity. There
Panic walks.

Yes, yes, I know,
When your mistress is with you,
When your master
Takes you upon his lap,
Just then, for a moment,
Almost you are not frightened.

But at heart you are frightened, you always have been.

O Pug, obstinate old nervous breakdown,
In the midst of *so* much love,
And such comfort,
Still to feel unsafe and be afraid,

How one's heart goes out to you!

ELIZABETH VON ARNIM

In Dock

AUTUMN, THOUGH, DOESN'T last for ever; nor, as I found out later, does widowhood. Dogs, too, come and go; and before, so it seems, one can turn round, everything that has been has also gone. If it weren't for this, I don't know what we should do, there would be such an accumulation.

So, in due course, did our time in Devonshire end, and it ended, oddly enough, because of Prince. That dog, whom I had never liked and who never liked me, was the real cause of our release from enervation and listlessness to vigour, and renewed appreciation of the happy possibilities of life, though the poor thing paid for it with his own. He took to chasing sheep; and the ultimate effect was to send us rocketing up from the soft hollows of Devonshire, from the veils of mist with callers looming through them, to the hard and brilliant solitude of Swiss mountains.

As long as the sheep weren't there, naturally they couldn't be chased, but one day, after a year of decent black, and a further six months, so as to be well on the side of propriety, of greys and tentative, timid mauves, the seemly inertia in which I had been steeped began to lift, and looking out of my bedroom window at the fields, lush with buttercups but otherwise empty, it being May my sap rose.

'Why not,' I thought, burgeoning suddenly into enterprise, 'let all this to a farmer, and make a little money?'

I let; the farmer filled the fields with sheep; Prince chased them; and a painful period set in of indignation on one side and concern on the other, of threats and of apologies. But no apologies were of any use any more directly that devilish dog not only chased but killed, and I could see for myself that it was bound then to become a case for magistrates and penalties.

Now all persons who have spent much of their time in Germany, and certainly all born Germans, have a great fear of the law. Their one idea is not to attract its attention, to be inconspicuous, to crawl in time, as it were, under tables. Accordingly, when I saw myself within reach of its clutches, even though it was English law and presumably more mild, I began to tremble, while the children, being born Germans, trembled harder, and Elsa the maid, not only born German but of the class which can least easily defend itself, trembled hardest of anybody.

Here indeed was a pretty state of things for a widow, the sole protector of a set of orphans, to have got herself involved in, and all because of a dog she had never liked. From the start I cut a poor figure – anybody who trembles, does, – but I had witnessed the sheep being killed, and had no nerves left.

Hauled before a magistrate, the figure I cut continued poor, for, recognising him as one who several times had been to tea, I was inexperienced enough to regard this as a link, and, relieved and reassured, began, out of my turn, to talk.

Instantly I was silenced. I could hardly credit my ears. Incredible that a man who had several times been to tea should silence me; and I stood there outraged, all that was still left in me of *hochgeboren* up in arms, while I listened to him fining me. Why, only a week before, that very man was sitting in my drawing-room being plied with cake. Why, I indignantly remembered, he had actually had three lumps of sugar in every cup. Never again should he hear me offering him another slice of cake. Never again should sugar of mine be lavished on him. He had drunk the last of my cups of tea.

Poor indeed, though, did the figure I cut become when I was informed that Prince was to be handed over to the police to be shot, for on hearing this dreadful sentence, after one gasp of horror, I was sick. Then and there; before everybody; and in spite of the fact that I had never really liked him. But to have to go home, and in cold blood take a poor dog from his dinner, and let him be led away to die . . .

The magistrate, trying to pretend nothing was happening, trying to pretend the room wasn't being rent by unseemly sounds, fixed his eyes on a point well above my convulsed head, and said, 'Next case.'

From *All the Dogs of my Life*

Norman Douglas

Reality

WE KNOW THAT the Greeks were appreciative of the graces and virtues of canine nature – is not the Homeric Argus still the finest dog-type in literature? Yet to them the dog, even he of the tender Anthology, remained what he is: a tamed beast. The Greeks, sitting at dinner, resented the insolence of a creature that, watching every morsel as it disappeared into the mouth of its master, plainly discovered by its physiognomy the desire, the presumed right, to devour what he considered fit only for himself. Whence that profound word κυνῶπης – dog-eyed, shameless. In contrast to this sanity, observe what an Englishman can read into a dog's eye:

> That liquid, melancholy eye,
>   From whose pathetic, soul-fed springs
> Seemed surging the Virgilian cry –
>   The sense of tears in mortal things . . .

That is how Matthew Arnold interprets the feelings of Fido, watching his master at work upon a tender beefsteak . . .

From Old Calabria

RAY BOURBON

A Sad End

BOURBON WORKED steadily throughout the '40s, but by 1950 or so his act seemed so passé that jobs became scarce. He devised a ploy to get publicity. Wrote the *New York Journal-American* (May 28, 1956):

> Female impersonator Ray Bourbon, who wore dresses when he performed with Mae West on the Broadway stage, has undergone sex transformation surgery and today can wear dresses all the time.
>
> 'Yes, it's true,' said Ray – oops, it's been changed to Rae – 'I am now a woman.'
>
> According to Rae . . . the operation was performed last September by a Hungarian refugee doctor in Juarez, Mexico . . . The doctor also gave Rae a certificate that reads in part, 'Bourbon is now more woman than man.'
>
> 'And there's no doubt about it,' Rae asserted. 'My hair is thicker, my voice is higher, and my shape is like a woman's – a big woman's. I measure 44-36-40. That beats Mae West, doesn't it?'

It was all a hoax, of course, but it brought him little attention. Now sixty-four and penniless, Bourbon accepted any job, often driving hundreds of miles to small towns. He was humbler now and desperately lonely, but since most of his old friends no longer saw him he turned to his dogs for affection. He eventually acquired fifteen, which he loved so obsessively that he purchased a rickety trailer and took them with him around the country.

In 1965 he was driving through Texas on a 105-degree day. His old jalopy suddenly burst into flames, and the trailer caught fire. Luckily a nearby farmer came to his assistance and doused the vehicles with crop spray. Bourbon and his pets were unharmed, but the car and trailer were destroyed, along with most of his gowns. He was forced to leave the animals in the care of the owner of a local pet shop.

Over the next three years his fortunes went from bad to worse. Whenever possible, he sent money for the care of his 'kids', but by 1968 there was so little work that he couldn't spare a penny. The next time he called the store he learned that his dogs had been sold.

A few weeks later the pet-shop owner was found murdered. Bourbon, then appearing at the Jewel Box in Kansas City, was arrested and charged with masterminding the murder. He pleaded innocent, claiming that he would never have killed the one man who could help him reclaim his dogs, but the State of Texas gave him ninety-nine years. His lawyer filed for an appeal, but Bourbon's prison record made this hopeless. On June 3, 1970, *Variety* published the following letter:

Editor, *Variety*:
   This is the town where they pulled 'Midnight Cowboy' for being obscene. I am sure it must be obvious to you now what chance I had here for getting a fair trial.
   I'm hoping you will mention this as I seem to have been completely forgotten by everyone, especially ones I have done favors for.
   I'll be grateful for anything you can say to attract any kind of aid. I am now on an appeal. But I need help.
   The address of the jail where I'm in is 212 N. Broadway, Brownwood, Texas 76801.

Ray Bourbon

Nothing came of the appeal or of his plea for help. On Christmas Day, 1970, a friend called him in prison, where Bourbon had entered the final stages of a three-year bout with leukemia. 'All I want is to die on the outside,' he said. But a heart attack claimed him on July 19, 1971, and he died in the state hospital under confinement. Bourbon outlived by at least twenty years the shock value of his act, making it rather pathetic that so few noticed his genuinely sad demise.

James Gavin, from *Intimate Nights: The Golden Age of New York Cabaret*

LORD DUNSANY

Spiritual Guidance

THE DAY CAME and at the appointed hour, Dean Spanley arrived at my house. I had champagne for him and no Tokay, and noticed a wistful expression upon his face that increased all through dinner; until by the time that the sweet was served, and still there was no Tokay, his enquiring dissatisfied glances, though barely perceptible, reminded me, whenever I did perceive them, of those little whines that a dog will sometimes utter when gravely dissatisfied, perhaps because there is another dog in the room, or because for any other reason adequate notice is not being taken of himself. And yet I do not wish to convey that there was ever anything whatever about Dean Spanley that in the least suggested a dog; it was only in my own mind, preoccupied as it was with the tremendous discovery to the verge of which I had strayed, that I made the comparison. I did not offer Dean Spanley any Tokay during dinner, because I knew that it was totally impossible to break down the barrier between him and his strange memories even with Tokay, my own hope being to bring him not so far from that point by ordinary methods, I mean by port and champagne, and then to offer him the Tokay, and I naturally noted the exact amount required with the exactitude of a scientist; my whole investigations depended on that. And then the moment came when I could no longer persuade the Dean to take another drop of wine; of any ordinary wine, I mean; and I put the Tokay before him. A look of surprise came into his face, surprise that a man in possession of Tokay should let so much of the evening waste away before bringing it out. 'Really,' he said, 'I hardly want any more wine, but . . .'

'It's a better vintage than the other one,' I said, making a guess that turned out to be right.

And it certainly was a glorious wine. I took some myself, because with that great bundle of keys to the mysterious past, that the Maharajah's dozen bottles had given me, I felt I could afford this indulgence. A reminiscent look came over Dean Spanley's face, and deepened, until it seemed to be peering over the boundaries that shut in this life. I waited a while and then I said: 'I was wondering about rabbits.'

'Among the worst of Man's enemies,' said the Dean.

And I knew at once, from his vehemence, that his memory was back again on the other side of that veil that shuts off so much from the rest of us. 'They lurk in the woods and plot, and give Man no proper allegiance. They should be hunted whenever met.'

He said it with so much intensity that I felt sure the rabbits had often eluded him in that other life; and I saw that to take his side against them as much as possible would be the best way to keep his memory where it was, on the other side of the veil; so I abused rabbits. With evident agreement the Dean listened, until, to round off my attack on them, I added: 'And over-rated animals even to eat. There's no taste in them.'

'Oh, I wouldn't say that,' said the Dean. 'A good hot rabbit that has been run across a big field has certainly an, an element of . . .' And he did not complete his sentence; but there was a greedy look in his eyes.

I was very careful about refilling the Dean's glass; I gave him no more for some while. It seemed to me that the spiritual level from which he had this amazing view, back over the ages, was a very narrow one; like a ridge at the top of a steep, which gives barely a resting-place to the mountaineer. Too little Tokay and he would lapse back to orthodoxy; too much, and I feared he would roll just as swiftly down to the present day. It was the ridge from which I feared I had pushed him last time. This time I must watch the mood that Tokay had brought, and neither intensify it nor let it fade, for as long as I could hold it with exactly the right hospitality. He looked wistfully at the Tokay, but I gave him no more yet.

'Rabbits,' I said to remind him.

'Yes, their guts are very good,' he said. 'And their fur is very good for one. As for their bones, if they cause one any irritation, one can always bring them up. In fact, when in doubt always bring anything up: it's easily done. But there is one bit of advice I would give to you. Out-of-doors. It's always best out-of-doors. There are what it is not for us to call prejudices: let us rather say preferences. But while these preferences exist amongst those who hold them, it is much best out-of-doors. You will remember that?'

'Certainly,' I said. 'Certainly.'

And as I spoke I carefully watched his eyes, to see if he was still on that narrow ledge that I spoke of, that spiritual plane from which a man could gaze out on past ages. And he was. A hand strayed tentatively towards the Tokay, but I moved it out of his reach.

'Rats!' I said. And he stirred slightly, but did not seem greatly interested.

And then, without any further suggestion from me, he began to talk of the home-life of a dog, somewhere in England in the days long before motors.

'I used to see off all the carts that drove up to the back-door every day. Whenever I heard them coming I ran round; I was always there in time; and then I used to see them off. I saw them off as far as a tree that there was, a little way down the drive. Always about a hundred barks, and then I used to stop. Some were friends of mine, but I used to see them off the same as the rest. It showed them that the house was well guarded. People that didn't know me used to hit at me with a whip, until they found out that they were too slow to catch me. If one of them ever had hit me I should have seen him off the whole way down the drive. It was always pleasant to trot back to the house from one of these little trips. I have had criticism for this, angry words, that is to say; but I knew from the tone of the voices that they were proud of me. I think it best to see them off like that, because, because . . .'

I hastily said: 'Because otherwise they might think that the house wasn't properly guarded.'

And the answer satisfied him. But I filled the Dean's glass with Tokay as fast as I could. He drank it, and remained at that strange altitude from which he could see the past.

'Then sooner or later,' he continued, 'the moon comes over the hill. Of course you can take your own line about that. Personally, I never trusted it. It's the look of it I didn't like, and the sly way it moves. If anything comes by at night I like it to come on footsteps, and I like it to have a smell. Then you know where you are.'

'I quite agree,' I said, for the Dean had paused.

'You can hear footsteps,' he went on, 'and you can follow a smell, and you can tell the sort of person you have to deal with, by the kind of smell he has. But folk without any smell have no right to be going about among those that have. That's what I didn't like about the moon. And I didn't like the way it stared one in the face. And there was a look in his stare as though everything was odd and the house not properly guarded. The house was perfectly well guarded, and so I said at the time. But he wouldn't stop that queer look. Many's the time I've told him to go away and not to look at me in that odd manner; and he pretended not to hear me. But he knew all right, he knew he was odd and strange and in league with magic, and he knew what honest folks thought of him: I've told him many a time.'

'I should stand no nonsense from him,' I said.

'Entirely my view,' said the Dean.

There was a silence then such as you sometimes see among well-satisfied diners.

'I expect he was afraid of you,' I said; and only just in time, for the Dean came back as it were with a jerk to the subject.

'Ah, the moon,' he said. 'Yes, he never came any nearer. But there's no saying what he'd have done if I hadn't been there. There was a lot of strangeness about him, and if he'd come any nearer everything might have been strange. They had only me to look after them.

'Only me to look after them,' he added reflectively. 'You know, I've known them talk to a man that ought at least to be growled at; stand at the front door and talk to him. And for what was strange or magical they never had any sense; no foreboding I mean. Why, there were sounds and smells that would make my hair rise on my shoulders before I had thought of the matter, while they would not even stir. That was why they so much needed guarding. That of course was our *raison d'être*, if I may put it that way. The French often have a way of turning a phrase, that seems somehow more deft than anything that we islanders do. Not that our literature cannot hold its own.'

'Quite so,' I said to check this line of thought, for he was wandering far away from where I wanted him.

From *My Talks With Dean Spanley*

LADY OTTOLINE MORRELL

Misunderstanding

WHEN LADY OTTOLINE went out, she had attached to her, or to her shepherdess's crook, by ribbons, two or three pekinese dogs. She never ceased to be surprised that people stared at her in the street. Having heard of my socialist sympathies, she explained to me once that she had much sympathy for the workers – was prepared to love them – but there was this difficulty – they would stare so. For example, only two days previously, she had boarded a tram (Bloomsbury was a district where trams were indigenous) – she loved sailing through the streets in a tram – such a beautiful, billowing motion – on a London tram she felt like Queen Elizabeth floating down the Thames in the royal barge. But, of course, she had to be helped with her pekinese on to the top by the conductor, and then of course she liked the front (or was it the back?) seat ... and everyone had stared so ... and 'there was a man who I think must have been slightly under the weather who made a *rude* remark, and some rather silly children. ...' She was prepared to be *most friendly*, but she had met with *such concentrated hostility* that it was impossible not to be impressed by the fact that she was *not* welcome among them.

Stephen Spender, from *World Within World*

ERROL FLYNN

Honour Defended

M Y DOG ARNO, GIVEN to me by Robert Lord, a producer, became very famous about Hollywood. Everybody knew the dog. He went with me to the studio, on my yacht, even to night clubs once or twice.

Arno got lost at sea during one of my *Sirocco* trips. I felt pretty bad. I got a call from the Coast Guard saying Arno was identified by his collar. They asked me if I wanted to claim the dog's body. I said no, just send me the collar. I buried the collar in the animal cemetery I had in the rear of Mulholland House.

The movie columnist Jimmy Fidler printed an item saying in effect: *Errol Flynn, whose love for his dog Arno has been much heralded, didn't even bother to go get his body when it was washed up on shore. That's how much he cared for him.*

Just that, but it was enough. Each man mourns in his own way and no one can tell another's feelings.

A little later I went with Bruce Cabot to the Morambo. As we arrived, Cabot remarked, 'Hey, there's your pal Fidler.'

At that moment I mourned Arno afresh. I walked over to Fidler's table. He saw me coming through the dancers and got up with a smile, ready to extend his hand. I said, 'I won't dignify you with a closed fist but – ' and I gave him an open-handed wallop, hard. He went over the dance floor.

At that instant I felt a sharp pain in my ear. His wife had picked up the nearest fork and jabbed me with it.

Jimmy brought me into court on a charge of assault. I tried to lighten the proceedings with a crack, 'The lady obviously has good table manners. She used the right fork.'

Jack Warner was upset because it became a national scandal. You are not supposed to bop the press. Today Fidler and I are excellent friends.

From *My Wicked, Wicked Ways*

SIR HUGH WALPOLE

Mistaken Identity

STRAIGHT UP TO Brackenburn they drove, for a week of quiet before the Jubilee celebrations in London. Hugh's last dog Bingo had taken to killing chickens and had been disposed of. Now his friends and neighbours the Zanazzis presented him with the last of his long succession of pets. This was a black retriever called Ranter, a gentle, quiet, affectionate beast to which Hugh became very attached. One day, accompanied by Ranter, he set out for a walk, carrying a long shepherd's crook which he had brought home from Greece. Along the road he became entangled with a flock of sheep, and an irate motorist yelled out at him: 'Why the hell can't you keep your bloody sheep on the fell?' It was the only time he was ever taken for a native Cumbrian, and he used to tell this story locally with pride.

Rupert Hart-Davis, from *Hugh Walpole*

JAMES THURBER

Nomenclature

ABOUT FIFTEEN YEARS ago, when I was looking for a house to buy in Connecticut, I knocked on the front door of an attractive home whose owner, my real-estate agent had told me, wanted to sell it and go back to Iowa to live. The lady agent who escorted me around had informed me that the owner of this place was a man named Strong, but a few minutes after arriving at the house, I was having a drink in the living-room with Phil Stong, for it was he. We went out into the yard after a while and I saw Mr Stong's spaniel. I called to the dog and snapped my fingers, but he seemed curiously embarrassed, like his master. 'What's his name?' I asked the latter. He was cornered and there was no way out of it. 'Thurber,' he said, in a small frightened voice. Thurber and I shook hands, and he didn't seem to me any more depressed than any other spaniel I have met. He had, however, the expression of a bachelor on his way to a party he has tried in vain to get out of, and I think it must have been this cast of countenance that had reminded Mr Stong of the dog I draw. The dog I draw is, to be sure, much larger than a spaniel and not so shaggy, but I confess, though I am not a spaniel man, that there are certain basic resemblances between my dog and all other dogs with long ears and troubled eyes.

From: *The Beast in Me*

SIR NEVILE HENDERSON

High Station

HIP WAS THE Slovenian name given him at birth. In view of its obvious suitability I naturally did not alter it. He was one of seven or eight born in the kennels of a keeper's lodge in the hamlet of Lom, which lies in a fold of the hills forming part of the lovely Slovenian mountains, themselves an extension of the Julian Alps so famous for the luxuriance and variety of the flowers which cover their Alps or meadows in the spring. Lom itself lay just above Trzic, not far from Llublyana where two English brothers named Gassner owned a cotton factory. It was from one of them that I learned of Hippy's existence in September, 1930. It was just the kind of sporting dog that I wanted in a country like Yugoslavia, which is a sportsman's paradise, so I climbed up to Lom to have a look at him. He was of distinguished ancestry and both his parents had won prizes at Graz and elsewhere. He was then just over three months old and, knowing nothing about the good or bad points of the dachsbracke, I chose him from among his brothers and sisters solely because he seemed to me the liveliest and most enterprising of the litter. He cost me five hundred dinars, or about two English pounds, but, as I was shortly going on leave, I gave the keeper another hundred dinars to look after him for the next five months for me, and to teach him the rudiments of his profession and house manners. He cost me mints of money later as the result of his various escapades, but there never was such a bargain since Long Island was bought from the Indians for a handful of beads. A million pounds down in cash would literally not have bought him later; and there was far more to it than that. Sixty years of experience have taught me that Providence, at any rate in my case and throughout my life, tempers the wind to the shorn lamb. Hippy came into my existence just when I had lost my mother and my home, or in other words what I cared for most in the world; and more than anybody or anything else he, as my constant companion, helped to tide me over and to compensate me for those two great sorrows.

My mother had died in January, 1931, and when I returned to Belgrade after her death I had brought back with me to Yugoslavia a large and very powerful golden retriever called Rufus.

Throughout my diplomatic career I had always kept at my home in Sussex a sporting dog of sorts for use during the holidays and, when I realised that Sedgwick was shortly going to be sold, there was nothing else for me to do but to take Rufus away with me. He was about seven years old and was the first dog to occupy the Belgrade Legation, and as long as he lived he was the master there of all canine newcomers.

Once Rufus was installed, I lost no time in sending for Hippy. It was a long journey from Lom, involving a whole night in the train and, as Hippy reached Belgrade about seven o'clock in the morning, I sent my faithful Montenegrin servant, Louis, and my car to fetch him from the station. Louis was unused to dogs and having extracted Hippy from the crate in which he had been travelling for so many hours, he hustled him into the motor and straight up to my room where I was still in bed, without giving him the chance to relieve himself on the way. I can see the picture now. As soon as Louis took him off the lead, Hippy stood quite still on all his four feet in the middle of the room and let out a flood which I thought would never stop flowing. I can still see, too, the expression on his face as he looked at me, and no dog ever had a more expressive face. It said as clearly as if the words had been spoken, 'I know this is all wrong but I simply can't help myself, and you would do the same if you had been shut up in a crate for twelve hours.' Never once again did he offend in my house, though I fear that he was not always so particular in the houses of others where there happened to be dogs less refined in their manners than Hippy was. For he himself was scrupulously clean in that respect. When I used to go for the summer months to Bled and live in the hotel there, the dogs always slept in the sitting-room with the door to my bedroom and a window on to a balcony both open. The balcony had bars through which Hippy could just squeeze himself sideways while outside there ran a narrow ledge some eight inches wide. On one occasion Hippy was taken ill in the night. Even the balcony would not serve his cleanly purpose, so he got through the bars and turning his stern outwards dropped what he had to drop, not even on the ledge but on to the street some fifty or sixty feet below him. Certain traces were of course left on the ledge and it was by means of them that I reconstructed the scene the next morning. Such were his ideals about cleanliness in the home.

*   *   *

Whether he did or not put sport above his master mattered not at all, for if ever there was a one man's dog it was Hippy. He himself would have put it the other way round, namely that Nevile Henderson was a one dog's man.

To the whole of the rest of the world he was utterly and completely indifferent, though always perfectly courteous and polite to everybody, unless he thought they were hostile to me. If he thought that they were that, then he gave them unmistakable warning that he was there to defend me. Once in the summer of 1933 a very bumptious and offensive young Nazi tried to come up to speak to me when I was sitting in the park at Bled. It was a very hot day and my two dogs were lying concealed under the branches of the beech tree beside which I was sitting. I watched the man coming up with a smirk on his face with great distaste and my feelings must have been communicated by telepathy to Hippy, for just as he was about to say something to me out sprang Hippy, growling fiercely, followed by the other dog. The German fled for his life. On another occasion I was travelling by train down to Bosnia with Dimnik, the King's chief jäger. The conductor was not satisfied about the free railway pass which the Yugoslav Government had given me and began to argue about it in a whisper to Dimnik. Hippy was lying on the seat just opposite Dimnik and, realising that I was the subject of these suspicious whisperings, he slowly got up and very deliberately snapped his teeth with a terrifying click just an inch from the conductor's hand. The warning was so obvious and yet so scrupulously tactful that it was incredibly amusing, and the conductor troubled us no more. No, I was Hippy's property and he would suffer nobody else to interfere with or to worry me.

His natural dignity, which he preserved even under the most difficult circumstances, was another distinctive trait in his make-up. He was never ruffled or self-conscious. It was as if he had set his own value on himself and nobody could take a liberty with him without being made to realise it. Colonel Oxley came to stop with me once for about a month at the Legation, while his wife was away. One evening after dinner as we were going upstairs, with Hippy as usual leading the way, to the little sitting-room next to my bedroom in which I used to do most of my work at night, Oxo leaned forward and insolently smacked him across the buttocks with a copy of *The Times* which he had in his hand. Hippy stopped dead short and slowly turning his head round gave Oxo one look. The expression on Queen Victoria's face when she said 'We are not amused' must have been very like it. It was so shattering in its utter contempt, scorn and reproof that Oxley and I were left speechless with laughter. I can only remember one occasion in his life when that natural dignity that was his appeared even slightly shaken and that was when he returned to me one day in the Argentine from a hunt in which he had for the first time met with a skunk and had got the worst of the encounter. He was smelling to high heaven, and he realised it. For forty-eight hours while the smell lasted he continued to look ashamed of himself and he gave all skunks thereafter a very wide berth.

The curious part was that though Hippy treated the rest of the world with such complete and utter indifference, everyone who came into contact with him was devoted to him. It was his immense personality which made him so irresistible to all from the highest to the lowest. The late King Alexander of Yugoslavia had never in his life cared for dogs and there was not one in the Palace, but he, like all the others, fell a victim to Hippy's charm. Hippy had a standing invitation to the Palace, whether I went there for an audience or to dine, or for any other purpose, and if I failed to bring him with me, there was trouble. He was allowed to sit with impunity on any of the royal chairs or on the royal knees in the motor car. So much so that one day when the King himself rang me up on the telephone, as he sometimes used to do, to suggest I should go for a drive with him, I said I would with pleasure, though I fully realised that it was Hippy and not me that His Majesty wanted to accompany him. All foresters and jägers were, of course, enthusiastic about the dog and there was no trouble they would not take about him. Sometimes, when the woods were full of ticks, Hippy would come back with hundreds of them on him. However long and tiring the day may have been, the first thing the jägers would do, and would compete to do, was to go over him inch by inch and pick every one of these ticks off him. Hippy fell very seriously ill with pneumonia once when I was away on a holiday in England. My Serbian kitchenmaid and the Russian who did the odd jobs, Boris the boy, as he was called, sat up with him, literally night after night on end, changing his poultices and keeping him warm. When I got back to Belgrade the excellent vet there told me that Hippy would never have recovered but for their devotion. It was quite extraordinary how the strangest and most unlikely people, cat-lovers included, fell for his charm, even though they were often piqued by his utter indifference to their attentions.

* * *

Few dogs can have travelled as much as Hippy did in all forms of conveyances from aeroplanes and steamers and yachts to trains, motor cars and horse carriages. He never rode on a bicycle, but otherwise I can think of no form of locomotion which he did not take in his stride. He was sick the first time he went as a puppy after a heavy meal in a motor car but never again, not even in the air or on the sea, and he crossed the South Atlantic Ocean twice. King Alexander used to say that after himself there was no one who had travelled so much in Yugoslavia as the British Minister, and I never went anywhere without Hippy. As for other foreign countries, he hunted with me in Austria, Czechoslovakia and Hungary, the Argentine and Uruguay, Germany and at long last England. But in the course of his journeys he also visited Italy and Portugal, Brazil and Holland. A round dozen countries anyway, and more than falls to the lot of most human individuals in the course of their much longer lives.

Wherever he went everybody always fell for his charm and, with one exception, he treated everyone, human or animal, with the same charming, though completely indifferent courtesy and civility. He was not even a cat-hater at heart, though he loved to chase them and though he had helped Rufus to kill two or three in the Legation garden at Belgrade. I remember once staying at a keeper's cottage up in the mountains in Bosnia. There was a cat in the house and Hippy made its daily life a misery by chasing it all over the place till it found safety generally behind a large stack of wood. Early one morning I returned with Hippy from stalking roe or capercailzie. We came in very quietly and the cat, which was standing on the stairs with its back towards us, apparently did not hear us. All Hippy did was to go up to it and lick its behind. Whereupon the surprised cat let out a terrified screech and fled for its life, hotly pursued by Hippy yelling blue murder. But he really meant it no ill will; it was just something to chase.

The one exception referred to above were Chows. All his life Hippy hated a chow and would invariably attack one at sight. That lifelong hatred was the result of an incident which occurred when he was a puppy and consequently at an impressionable age. Princess Olga, the sister of the Duchess of Kent and the wife of Prince Paul of Yugoslavia, had a chow, whom she also used to take for walks in the park at Koshudniak. One day Hippy, Rufus and I in the course of our daily walk met Princess Olga and her two boys and the chow. While I was talking to Her Royal Highness, there was a bit of a fight between Rufus and the chow, undoubtedly started by the latter. I may be prejudiced, since for Hippy's sake I dislike chows as much as he did, but I do regard them, even though they are Chinese, as treacherous orientals, and though I did not actually see what happened I have no doubt that it was a Pearl Harbour affair and that the chow nipped Rufus when he wasn't looking. Only once, for no chow, however thick his coat, could have stood up to Rufus in fair fight. Anyway, as blood had been drawn, Princess Olga, who had her car with her, decided to move off elsewhere; the chow was shut up inside it while, as there was deep snow on the ground, her Royal Highness and one of the boys got on to a toboggan and were towed behind the car. Hippy of course ran after them, as he always pursued anything that seemed to be trying to escape from him. Unfortunately at the first turn in the road Princess Olga decided that that form of tobogganing was not much fun and stopped the car. As she opened the door to get into the car the chow jumped out and went straight for the unsuspecting Hippy who was then only a few yards behind. Princess Olga with the utmost courage ran to separate them and by the time I reached the scene she was, at the price of a severely bruised arm from a snap of her own chow, holding the latter up in the air by the scruff of the neck, while the youthful Hippy, only slightly injured, was leaping frantically in the air in an attempt to seize the chow's tail.

Never did Hippy forget that treacherous attack and in future if ever I saw a chow a mile off, I hurriedly put him on the lead. Nevertheless he did manage to have two more battles with them, one final one with Princess Olga's and one in Austria.

After this first incident, the Princess and I had agreed that, if we were likely to meet, we would muzzle our dogs beforehand. And so we did, but nevertheless it happened one day that we both went to a very unfrequented part of Koshudniak where we felt pretty certain not to meet each other. Even so I had luckily muzzled Rufus but not Hippy. Princess Olva was with Prince Paul, and I with Mrs Oxley, my Military Attaché's wife. My dogs were running ahead when suddenly out of the bushes appeared Princess Olga's chow. There was no question as to who started it, they were all mad keen for battle. Fortunately Rufus got in the first blow and rolled the chow over on his back, and held him there. The chow was innocuous since all he could bite was Rufus' wire muzzle, while Rufus, on the other side of it, could do no damage either to the chow. But Hippy could, and wisely at first he went for the chow's tail which he chewed to such good effect that it did not curl again for several days. As soon as I could reach the battlefield, I seized Hippy, thrust him into Mrs Oxley's arms for safe custody and then went back to separate the other two. Before I had even got there Hippy had wriggled out of his collar and Mrs Oxley's embrace and had returned to the fray. But this time foolishly he attacked in front, where all he succeeded in doing was to stick his head between Rufus' muzzle and the chow's jaws and to get a good slash on the cheek. Once more I got Hippy back to Mrs Oxley and by the time Prince Paul and Princess Olga arrived, I had managed to separate the other two, though not without being wounded myself by the chow in the leg. I must admit that after this Princess Olga sent the chow to a vet and got a dalmatian in its place, though she used to show me later a picture of the chow lying down with a cat sitting on its back to prove what a sweet-tempered animal it was!

The other chow battle was at Enzefeld, the lovely home in Austria of the Eugene Rothschilds where the Duke of Windsor lived for the first six months after his abdication. I was on my way from Germany down to Yugoslavia where I was going to shoot stags and was consequently obliged to take Hippy with me to Enzesfeld, in spite of the chow. However, we made arrangements in advance to the effect that at certain hours the chow would be kept shut up and at others Hippy. Even with the best of arrangements there is always a chance of a slip-up and one afternoon just as I was starting for the golf course with Kitty Rothschild, Hippy and the chow met at the front door, one going out just as the other was coming in. Honestly I believe that the chow would have avoided the conflict if it could have done, but Hippy gave it no chance. Up went his tail and his ears, without a moment's hesitation and quite silently he went straight into battle. It was all over in two seconds, in the course of the first of which Hippy got severely slashed on the ear and just over the eye but in the second of which he got a firm grip on the chow's throat where he hung on like a limpet. It was exactly like the end of the fight between the bulldog and White Fang in Jack London's great story. The wretched chow was utterly helpless and choking and it took three of us, another guest, Count Rex, a footman and myself to unclamp that tenacious hold on its neck. And we all three got bitten in the hands by Hippy in the process. That, luckily, was Hippy's last encounter with chows, for I was always afraid of them since they were three times his size and had such a thick coat on them that practically their only vulnerable spot was their throat. Apart from chows every other kind of dog, big or small, was, so far as Hippy was concerned, a friendly or at least a neutral animal.

From *Hippy, In Memoriam: The Story of a Dog*

GERALD DURRELL
Mother's Delight; Vicar's Shock

THE MAGENPIES LIKED the dogs, although they seized every opportunity to tease them. They were particularly fond of Roger, and he would frequently go and call on them, lying down close to the wire netting, ears pricked, while the Magenpies sat on the ground inside the cage, three inches away from his nose, and talked to him in soft, wheezy chucks, with an occasional raucous guffaw, as though they were telling him dirty jokes. They never teased Roger as much as they teased the other two, and they never attempted to lure him close to the wire with soft blandishment so that they could flap down and pull his tail, as they frequently did with both Widdle and Puke. On the whole the Magenpies approved of dogs, but they liked them to look *and* behave like dogs; so when Dodo made her appearance in our midst the Magenpies absolutely refused to believe that she was a dog, and treated her from the beginning with a sort of rowdy, jeering disdain.

Dodo was a breed known as a Dandy Dinmont. They look like long, fat, hair-covered balloons, with minute bow legs, enormous and protuberant eyes, and long flopping ears. Strangely enough it was due to Mother that this curious misshapen breed of dog made its appearance among us. A friend of ours had a pair of these beasts which had suddenly (after years of barrenness) produced a litter of six puppies. The poor man was at his wits' end trying to find good homes for all these offspring, and so Mother, good-naturedly and unthinkingly, said she would have one. She set off one afternoon to choose her puppy and, rather unwisely, selected a female. At the time it did not strike her as imprudent to introduce a bitch into a household exclusively populated by very masculine dogs. So, clasping the puppy (like a dimly conscious sausage) under one arm, Mother climbed into the car and drove home in triumph to show the new addition to the family. The puppy, determined to make the occasion a memorable one, was violently and persistently sick from the moment she got in the car to the moment she got out. The family, assembled on the veranda, viewed Mother's prize as it waddled up the path towards them, eyes bulging, minute legs working frantically to keep the long, drooping body in motion, ears flapping wildly, pausing now and then to vomit into a flower-bed.

'Oh, isn't he *sweet?*' cried Margo.

'Good God! It looks like a sea-slug,' said Leslie.

'Mother! Really!' said Larry, contemplating Dodo with loathing, 'where did you dig up that canine Frankenstein?'

'Oh, but he's *sweet,*' repeated Margo. 'What's wrong with him?'

'It's not a him, it's a her,' said Mother, regarding her acquisition proudly; 'she's called Dodo.'

'Well, that's two things wrong with it for a start,' said Larry. 'It's a ghastly name for an animal, and to introduce a bitch in the house with those other three lechers about is asking for trouble. Apart from that, just look at it! Look at the shape! How did it get like that? Did it have an accident, or was it born like that?'

'Don't be silly, dear; it's the breed. They're *meant* to be like that.'

'Nonsense, mother; it's a monster. Who would want to deliberately produce a thing that shape?'

I pointed out that dachshunds were much the same shape, and they had been bred specially to enable them to get down holes after badgers. Probably the Dandy Dinmont had been bred for a similar reason.

'She looks as though she was bred to go down holes after sewage,' said Larry.

'Don't be disgusting, dear. They're very nice little dogs, and very faithful, apparently.'

'I should imagine they have to be faithful to anyone who shows interest in them: they can't possibly have many admirers in the world.'

'I think you're being very nasty about her, and, anyway, you're in no position to talk about beauty; it's only skin deep after all, and before you go throwing stones you should look for the beam in *your* eye,' said Margo triumphantly.

Larry looked puzzled.

'Is that a proverb, or a quotation from the *Builders' Gazette*?' he inquired.

'I think she means that it's an ill-wind that gathers no moss,' said Leslie.

'You make me sick,' said Margo, with dignified scorn.

'Well, join little Dodo in the flower-bed.'

'Now, now,' said Mother, 'don't argue about it. It's my dog and I like her, so that's all that matters.'

So Dodo settled in, and almost immediately showed faults in her make-up which caused us more trouble than all the other dogs put together. To begin with she had a weak hind-leg, and at any time during the dog or night her hip joint was liable to come out of its socket, for no apparent reason. Dodo, who was no stoic, would greet this catastrophe with a series of piercing shrieks that worked up to a crescendo of such quivering intensity that it was unbearable. Strangely enough, her leg never seemed to worry her when she went out for walks, or gambolled with elephantine enthusiasm after a ball on the veranda. But invariably in the evening when the family were all sitting quietly, absorbed in writing or reading or knitting, Dodo's leg would suddenly leap out of its socket, she would roll on her back and utter a scream that would make everybody jump and lose control of whatever they were doing. By the time we had massaged her leg back into place Dodo would have screamed herself to exhaustion, and immediately fall into a deep and peaceful sleep, while we would be so unnerved that we would be unable to concentrate on anything for the rest of the evening.

We soon discovered that Dodo had an extremely limited intelligence. There was only room for one idea at a time in her skull, and once it was there Dodo would retain it grimly in spite of all opposition. She decided quite early in her career that Mother belonged to her, but she was not over-possessive at first until one afternoon Mother went off to town to do some shopping and left Dodo behind. Convinced that she would never see Mother again, Dodo went into mourning and waddled, howling sorrowfully, round the house, occasionally being so overcome with grief that her leg would come out of joint. She greeted Mother's return with incredulous joy, but made up her mind that from that moment she would not let Mother out of her sight, for fear she escaped again. So she attached herself to Mother with the tenacity of a limpet, never moving more than a couple of feet away at the most. If Mother sat down, Dodo would lie at her feet; if Mother had to get up and cross the room for a book or a cigarette, Dodo would accompany her, and then they would return together and sit down again, Dodo giving a deep sigh of satisfaction at the thought that once more she had foiled Mother's attempts at escape. She even insisted in being present when Mother had a bath, sitting dolefully by the tub and staring at Mother with embarrassing intensity. Any attempts to leave her outside the bathroom door resulted in Dodo howling madly and hurling herself at the door-panels, which almost invariably resulted in her hip slipping out of its socket. She seemed to be under the impression that it was not safe to let Mother go alone into the bathroom, even if she stood guard over the door. There was always the possibility, she seemed to think, that Mother might give her the slip by crawling down the plughole.

At first Dodo was regarded with tolerant scorn by Roger, Widdle, and Puke; they did not think much of her, for she was too fat and too low slung to walk far, and if they made any attempts to play with her it seemed to bring on an attack of persecution mania, and Dodo would gallop back to the house, howling for protection. Taken all round they were inclined to consider her a boring and useless addition to the household, until they discovered that she had one superlative and overwhelmingly delightful characteristic: she came into season with monotonous regularity. Dodo herself displayed an innocence about the facts of life that was rather touching. She seemed not only puzzled but positively scared at her sudden bursts of popularity, when her admirers arrived in such numbers that Mother had to go about armed with a massive stick. It was owing to this Victorian innocence that Dodo fell an easy victim to the lure of Puke's magnificent ginger eyebrows, and so met a fate worse than death when Mother inadvertently locked them in the drawing-room together while she supervised the making of tea. The sudden and unexpected arrival of the English padre and his wife, ushering them into the room in which the happy couple were disporting themselves, and the subsequent efforts to maintain a normal conversation, left Mother feeling limp, and with a raging headache.

To everyone's surprise (including Dodo's) a puppy was born of this union, a strange, mewling blob of a creature with its mother's figure and its father's unusual liver-and-white markings. To suddenly become a mother like that, Dodo found, was very demoralizing, and she almost had a nervous breakdown, for she was torn between the desire to stay in one spot with her puppy and the urge to keep as close to Mother as possible. We were, however, unaware of this psychological turmoil. Eventually Dodo decided to compromise, so she followed Mother around and carried the puppy in her mouth. She had spent a whole morning doing this before we discovered what she was up to; the unfortunate baby hung from her mouth by its head, its body swinging to and fro as Dodo waddled along at Mother's heels. Scolding and pleading having no effect, Mother was forced to confine herself to the bedroom with Dodo and her puppy, and we carried their meals up on a tray. Even this was not altogether successful, for if Mother moved out of the chair, Dodo, ever alert, would seize her puppy and sit there regarding Mother with starting eyes, ready to give chase if necessary.

'If this goes on much longer that puppy'll grow into a giraffe,' observed Leslie.

'I know, poor little thing,' said Mother; 'but what can I *do*? She picks it up if she sees me lighting a cigarette.'

'Simplest thing would be to drown it,' said Larry. 'It's going to grow into the most horrifying animal, anyway. Look at its parents.'

'No, indeed you won't drown it!' exclaimed Mother indignantly.

'Don't be *horrible*,' said Margo; 'the poor little thing.'

'Well, I think it's a perfectly ridiculous situation, allowing yourself to be chained to a chair by a dog.'

'It's my dog, and if I want to sit here I *shall*,' said Mother firmly.

'But for how long? This might go on for months.'

'I shall think of something,' said Mother with dignity.

The solution to the problem that Mother eventually thought of was simple. She hired the maid's youngest daughter to carry the puppy for Dodo. This arrangement seemed to satisfy Dodo very well, and once more Mother was able to move about the house. She pottered from room to room like some Eastern potentate, Dodo pattering at her heels, and young Sophia bringing up the end of the line, tongue protruding and eyes squinting with the effort, bearing in her arms a large cushion on which reposed Dodo's strange offspring. When Mother was going to be in one spot for any length of time Sophia would place the cushion reverently on the ground, and Dodo would surge on to it and sigh deeply. As soon as Mother was ready to go to another part of the house, Dodo would get off her cushion, shake herself, and take up her position in the cavalcade, while Sophia lifted the cushion aloft as though it carried a crown. Mother would peer over her spectacles to make sure the column was ready, giving a little nod, and they would wind their way off to the next job.

Every evening Mother would go for a walk with the dogs, and the family would derive much amusement from watching her progress down the hill. Roger, as senior dog, would lead the procession, followed by Widdle and Puke. Then came Mother, wearing an enormous straw hat, which made her look like an animated mushroom, clutching in one hand a large trowel with which to dig any interesting wild plants she found. Dodo would waddle behind, eyes protruding and tongue flapping, and Sophia would bring up the rear, pacing along solemnly, carrying the imperial puppy on its cushion. Mother's Circus, Larry called it, and would irritate her by bellowing out of the window:

'Oi! Lady, wot time does the big top go up, hay?'

He purchased a bottle of hair restorer for her so that, as he explained, she could conduct experiments on Sophia and try to turn her into a bearded lady.

'That's wot your show *needs*, lady,' he assured her in a hoarse voice – 'a bit of clarse, see? Nothing like a bearded lady for bringin' a bit o' clarse to a show.'

But in spite of all this Mother continued to lead her strange caravan off into the olive-groves at five o'clock every evening.

From *My Family and Other Animals*

ROBERT SERVICE

Abandoned Dog

They dumped it on the lonely road,
   Then like a streak they sped;
And as along the way I strode
   I thought that it was dead:
And then I saw that yelping pup
   Rise, race to catch them up.

You know how silly wee dogs are.
   It thought they were in fun.
Trying to overtake their car
   I saw it run and run:
But as they faster, faster went,
   It stumbled, sore and spent.

I found it prone upon the way;
   Of life was little token.
As limply in the dust it lay
   I thought its heart was broken:
Then one dim eye it opened and
   It sought to lick my hand.

Of course I took it gently up
   And brought it to my wife
Who loves all dogs, and now that pup
   Shares in our happy life:
Yet how I curse the bastards who
   Its good luck never knew!

PEGGY LEE

Nursing

O H, WHAT A LOVING dog Rex was. I named him Rex because even though he was a mixed breed, he was king to me. He was a silver-grey and his eyes were amber and full of adoration – adoration for me but not for the pack of hounds who were his mortal enemies. They got him one day and ripped him from one end to the other. He managed to drag himself home, and I cried so hard I could hardly see him.

I did manage to carry him upstairs and make a bed for him. Then I cleaned his wounds and tried to get him to drink some water. The poor dear couldn't even raise his head, but he feebly wagged his tail to let me know he appreciated my love.

He died that night and I sadly carried him down by the railroad bridge. The ground was frozen, so I covered him with an old khaki army blanket and put stones around him so the wind wouldn't whip the blanket away.

Many times during the winter I went to visit him there and in the spring I buried him.

From *Miss Peggy Lee*

GEORGE ORWELL

An Experiment

T HERE WERE AT least a few times in Spain when Orwell thought that he might never get back to his small cottage in Wallington, but in July he and Eileen returned to the village and resumed their quiet life. Aunt Nellie had not taken good care of the place while they were away. There were more mice than usual in the cottage, and the garden was in 'a ghastly mess', according to Orwell. No attempt was made to reopen the shop. Instead the couple began raising chickens, ducks and goats. There was a patch of common ground nearby where the goats were able to graze, and a shed in the back garden where they were stabled. Fanciful names were given to the animals. The cock, for example, was known as 'Henry Ford'. As Orwell explained to Jack Common, this name seemed to fit the bird 'because he had such a brisk, businesslike way of going about his job, in fact, he trod his first hen literally within 5 seconds of being put into the run'. They called their dog – a large, unclipped poodle – 'Marx', who presumably barked a great deal at 'Henry Ford'.

Orwell's voice was growing stronger, though he was still unable to speak loudly. He also discovered that he was unable to sing – 'But people tell me this doesn't matter.' He was feeling well enough to begin asking a few friends to come down for visits. A couple of men from his ILP contingent who had recently returned from Spain paid a visit to give him the latest news about the continuing campaign against the POUM. One former member of his unit, Douglas Moyle, remembered being invited down for a day and taking a long walk with Orwell and Marx. 'It was a nice dog, but of course I was amused by the name, and Eric told me he liked to see how people responded to it. Some guessed that the dog was named after Karl Marx, but others said Groucho Marx, or even Marks and Spencer.'

Michael Shelden, from *George Orwell*

National Folly

PERHAPS THE MOST horrible spectacles in England are the Dogs' Cemeteries in Kensington Gardens, at Stoke Poges (it actually adjoins the churchyard where Gray wrote his famous 'Elegy') and at various other places. But there were also the Animals' A.R.P. Centres, with miniature stretches for cats, and in the first year of the war there was the spectacle of Animal Day being celebrated with all its usual pomp in the middle of the Dunkirk evacuation. Although its worst follies are committed by the upper-class women, the animal cult runs right through the nation and is probably bound up with the decay of agriculture and the dwindled birthrate. Several years of stringent rationing have failed to reduce the dog and cat population, and even in poor quarters of big towns the bird-fanciers' shops display canary seed at prices ranging up to twenty-five shillings a pint.

From 'As I Please'

DOROTHY PARKER

Verse for a Certain Dog

Such glorious faith as fills your limpid eyes,
    Dear little friend of mine, I never knew.
All-innocent are you, and yet all-wise.
    (For Heaven's sake, stop worrying that shoe!)
You look about, and all you see is fair;
    This mighty globe was made for you alone.
Of all the thunderous ages, you're the heir.
    (Get off the pillow with that dirty bone!)

A skeptic world you face with steady gaze;
    High in young pride you hold your noble head,
Gayly you meet the rush of roaring days.
    (*Must* you eat puppy biscuit on the bed?)
Lancelike your courage, gleaming swift and strong,
    Yours the white rapture of a wingèd soul,
Yours is a spirit like a Mayday song.
    (God help you, if you break the goldfish bowl!)

'Whatever is, is good' – your gracious creed.
    You wear your joy of living like a crown.
Love lights your simplest act, your every deed.
    (Drop it. I tell you – put that kitten down!)
You are God's kindliest gift of all – a friend.

Your shining loyalty unflecked by doubt.
You ask but leave to follow to the end.
(Couldn't you wait until I took you out?)

Up Against It

WHEN DOROTHY RETURNED to Hollywood, her moment in the sun over, it was to the heat of a California summer at the Chateau Marmont. Weekends, she and Evans drove to Malibu or Arrowhead, but mostly their life settled into a routine: studio jobs, revisions on *The Coast of Illyria*, discussion of ideas for another play, a modern work this time because she didn't want to be typecast as writing exclusively about the Romantics. By now, there had been an addition to their household, a boxer named Flic, who was a few months old when they got him. Flic turned out to be an affectionate but timid animal who was terrified of just about everybody and everything. Dorothy, giving him the benefit of the doubt, decided that he must have been mistreated by his previous owners and began a program of assertiveness training. It didn't work. Norman Mailer urged her to bring Flic over to meet his dog, a large, black, ferocious German shepherd, apparently on the theory that if Flic could manage to make friends with Karl, he would be cured. Dorothy admired Mailer's best-selling *The Naked and the Dead*. When he sought her out upon his arrival in Los Angeles that summer, she had found the young war novelist and his pregnant wife, Beatrice, to be amusing company. Mailer, exhibitionist as only an insecure, twenty-six-year-old first novelist can be, seemed pathetically eager to be liked. Not so with Karl, whom Dorothy and Ross agreed had a shifty look. She doubted that a confrontation would be a good idea. Mailer said she overestimated the danger and assured her that Karl would behave himself.

When Dorothy and Ross drove up to Mailer's house, Flic must have caught a whiff of Karl because he seemed reluctant to leave the car. When they finally persuaded him to enter the living room, he immediately urinated on the carpet. Everyone could hear Karl breathing noisily in another part of the house. Dorothy, nervous, got ready to bolt, but Mailer swore he could control the situation.

At last Karl was led out on a leash. Advancing pleasantly, he first eyeballed Flic and sniffed his nose. Then he exploded like a bursting watermelon, his fleshy pink jaws spraying streams of spittle. As Mailer wrestled Karl back to a bedroom, Ross tried to quiet the petrified Flic and got his finger bitten.

As they were getting ready to drive off, Dorothy watched Mailer come scampering after them, shouting and waving his arms. Although outraged, she forced herself to speak. 'I said it wouldn't work,' she told him. Mailer said that he was sorry, but he did not look contrite. It would be nine years before she saw him again, and then she would remember only the harrowing encounter with his dog. In her eyes there was nothing he could do to redeem himself.

Marion Meade, from *Dorothy Parker: What Fresh Hell is This?*

WILLIAM PLOMER

In the Park

'MRS GAMBITT HAS been given a dog,' she said. 'Such a sweet little thing.'

This was not a good opening. Miss Haymer was not fond of dogs.

'How could a dog possibly be sweet?' she said.

'Oh, I thought you'd lost your old prejudice against them! I love them, as you know. I sometimes feel I ought to keep one myself.'

'What, in London! I must say I greatly prefer cats. They're so independent and mysterious, so elegant. Oh, these old women and their dogs! Connie, it's disgusting. I may be an old woman, but at least I don't have myself lugged about by a gross, overfed, flabby dog. . . . You know why the English are so fond of dogs, don't you? It's because they're so like themselves. Dogs are simply full of public-school spirit and cheerful stupidity and false pride – all the things the English admire so much in themselves. And then look, when one is abroad, and one sees two English people meeting for the first time in some outlandish spot. Watch them circling round and round each other with a growl and an angry but inquisitive stare, trying to find if they're of the same breed or rather class. Watch the careful top-and-bottom sniffing to see if the stranger is a friend or an enemy. What could be more doggy than all that? And then the War – an unthinking cheerfulness, a blind faithfulness, hard fighting, tail-wagging at the end, and then two minutes' silence, with the head on the paws. . . . And just because dogs are what they call "plucky" people will overlook all their filthy habits, and the same people love to tell you that dogs are "so clever", just because they can tell the difference between the smell of their owners and the smell of other people you would otherwise think were indistinguishable from them.'

'Fanny, what a tirade!' said Miss Brixworth. 'I think you're most unjust.'

'Oh, but I could say a lot more,' said Miss Haymer. 'They smell, they have fleas, they're greedy, they make sudden noises.'

'Well, so do human beings.'

'Not nice human beings.'

'Nor do nice dogs, Fanny. And they're often much more faithful and affectionate and better companions than human beings.'

'That's not saying much,' said Miss Haymer. 'And if it's true, it's no doubt because they're often more kindly treated than human beings. If you like them, I'll try and admit that dogs may be very nice, because I like you. I once knew a man in Morocco who said scorpions were the most faithful and affectionate little creatures, and I'm pretty sure he said they were intelligent, too. And he was a very nice man. . . . But I must say, what annoys me is that dogs always like me. It's most galling.'

'They're probably better judges of you,' said Miss Brixworth, 'than you are of them.'

Miss Haymer grunted, then she said:

'No, it's all very well, Connie; look at that woman over there fussing over that vile little mongrel. It's disgusting! She wants a man or a child. It's unhealthy, it's repulsive.'

Miss Brixworth put up her lorgnon and looked in the direction where Miss Haymer was pointing with her stick, its rubber end fastening on the landscape like a huge tentacle.

'She's actually kissing it,' said Miss Haymer.

'Why, it's Mrs Gambitt!' cried Miss Brixworth.

'My dear, what an awful-looking woman! What on earth does she dress like that for? Why doesn't she learn how to put her clothes on? And she's as thin as a scarecrow!'

From *The Case is Altered*

ALDOUS HUXLEY
Sunbathing in 1933

A FAINT RUSTLING caressed the half-conscious fringes of their torpor, swelled gradually, as though a shell were being brought closer and closer to the ear, and became at last a clattering roar that brutally insisted on attention. Anthony opened his eyes for just long enough to see that the aeroplane was almost immediately above them, then shut them again, dazzled by the intense blue of the sky.

'These damned machines!' he said. Then, with a little laugh, 'They'll have a nice God's-eye view of us here,' he added.

Helen did not answer; but behind her closed eyelids she smiled. Pop-eyed and with an obscene and gloating disapproval! The vision of that heavenly visitant was irresistibly comic.

'David and Bathsheba,' he went on. 'Unfortunately at a hundred miles an hour . . .'

A strange yelping sound punctuated the din of the machine. Anthony opened his eyes again, and was in time to see a dark shape rushing down towards him. He uttered a cry, made a quick and automatic movement to shield his face. With a violent but dull and muddy impact the thing struck the flat roof a yard or two from where they were lying. The drops of a sharply spurted liquid were warm for an instant on their skin, and then, as the breeze swelled up out of the west, startlingly cold. There was a long second of silence. 'Christ!' Anthony whispered at last. From head to foot both of them were splashed with blood. In a red pool at their feet the almost shapeless carcass of a fox-terrier. The roar of the receding aeroplane had diminished to a raucous hum, and suddenly the ear found itself conscious once again of the shrill rasping of the cicadas.

Anthony drew a deep breath; then, with an effort and still rather unsteadily, contrived to laugh. 'Yet another reason for disliking dogs,' he said, and, scrambling to his feet, looked down, his face puckered with disgust, at his blood-bedabbled body. 'What about a bath?' he asked, turning to Helen.

She was sitting quite still, staring with wide-open eyes at the horribly shattered carcass. Her face was very pale, and a glancing spurt of blood had left a long red streak that ran diagonally from the right side of the chin, across the mouth, to the corner of the left eye.

'You look like Lady Macbeth,' he said, with another effort at jocularity. '*Allons*.' He touched her shoulder. 'Out, vile spot. This beastly stuff's drying on me. Like seccotine.'

For all answer, Helen covered her face with her hands, and began to sob.

For a moment Anthony stood quite still, looking at her crouched there, in the hopeless abjection of her blood-stained nakedness, listening to the painful sound of her weeping. 'Like seccotine': his own words re-echoed disgracefully in his ears. Pity stirred within him, and then an almost violent movement of love for this hurt and suffering woman, this *person*, yes, this person whom he had ignored, deliberately, as though she had no existence except in the context of pleasure. Now, as she knelt there sobbing, all the tenderness he had ever felt for her body, all the affection implicit in their sensualities and never expressed, seemed suddenly to discharge themselves, in a kind of lightning flash of accumulated feelings, upon this person, this embodied spirit, weeping in solitude behind concealing hands.

From *Eyeless in Gaza*

LOUIS MACNEICE
With the Kennel Club

THE PLACE WHERE A dog show is held is called a venue. The Kennel Club's venue used to be the Crystal Palace where, when bored with the dogs, one could look at the goldfish. Their latest exhibition last week, their seventy-sixth, was held at Olympia. Both the dogs and their owners seemed to enjoy Olympia and there was comparatively little grumbling or migraine on the part of either. (If you want to see what difference a venue makes, go to the great winter dog show at the Bingley Hall, Birmingham.) As for the owners, I was sorry to notice better manners and less eccentricity. In the toy department I missed the customary six-foot Sapphos in breeches, while among the St Bernards and Great Danes I missed the tiny sentimental old ladies with game legs who feed their pets upon bull's-eyes.

The dogs themselves remain as odd as ever. I have little sympathy with the people who complain that breeding for show purposes produces an artificial type of dog. Dogs lead such artificial lives that they may as well look artificial into the bargain. But the fancies should keep their breeds differentiated and this is counteracted by excess of trimming – witness the flashier terriers. Kerry Blues do not look themselves at all when they are pruned like Airedales. And there are many developments which I would criticize on æsthetic rather than functional grounds. The Sealyam, say the older breeders, is becoming a sissy – no good for badger. But what does that matter to the countless Sealyam owners in NW8 or SW1? What does matter is that when Sealyams get too narrow in the head, they lose their expression of bonhomie.

On the whole I prefer big dogs to small and smooth-haired dogs to rough-haired. Among the bigger breeds I was sorry to notice that there was a very poor entry of mastiffs, the bitch certificate not being awarded, though the dog certificate went to a fine-looking fawn who is a son of that late prince among mastiffs, Champion Joseph of Hellingly. It was nice to see twenty-one Newfoundlands, walking about like sofas, but why so few Landseers? And I should have liked some more bull-mastiffs, for the bull-mastiff, in my opinion, has the greatest appeal of any dog on the bench, with his plodding feet, his thumpability, his piggy eyes, his casual ears and his fascinating manner of yawning. Great Danes, I think, have developed for the worse and are now too gawky. Bloodhounds had a very fair entry, several champions being defeated, and were slobbering less than usual. Being a Borzoi owner, I was disappointed that I could only look at the Borzois on the bench, for you cannot judge a Borzoi unless he is standing up. Most of them seemed to be lacking in coat and their owners were less made-up than usual. I noticed several dogs with the famous Mythe profile – one of the triumphs of breeding for a special feature. (The Mythe profile is more convex than that of the most decadent human aristocrat.)

Among the native breeds which are less often shown, it was pleasing to see bassets, beagles, smooth collies, Irish water spaniels and Stafford-shire bullterriers – the last-named a very *natural*-looking dog. Among the more exotic novelties I have no use at all for anything which comes out of Tibet except the pleasingly grumpy Tibetan mastiff. The other Tibetan breeds are what you would expect from a country where people are holy and never undress. The two specimens of Chihuahua, which got such a wonderful press, could beat the miniature black-and-tan terrier for any comic strip part as an insect. The Zoo lent a husky with a very falsetto voice. Shaggy Bernese mountain dogs and black-and-tan broad-headed Rottweilers both had appeal, but the prize for charm must go to the solitary specimen of a Chesapeake Bay retriever, a dog of a most unnatural fusty liver colour. And there were twenty-five Boston terriers, which are charming but not terriers.

Of toy breeds the best is the pug, inadequately represented at this show. I cannot understand why this classic little beast with its Quaker-like elegance and its marvellous dark popeyes full of *Sehnsucht*, should be so much less popular than the vulgarly pretentious Pekinese. Some pugs also are very good mousers. There was a good turn-out of Afghans and I revised my opinions that these are essentially ludicrous dogs – baboons dressed up in pyjamas. Some of these Afghans had the presence of sheiks. As for gundogs, I say nothing of them because they are useful. Their praises are printed in that eternity where stuffed trout swim in glass cases and it is always the Twelfth of August. Old English Sheepdogs might also be claimed to be useful but only by their breeders, for all dog-breeders have Faith. I should be sorry to be a sheep in the care of one of these boisterous hundred-pounders. Alsatians are to me an abomination and I was glad to see that they were just outnumbered by bull-terriers. Some regard the modern bull-terrier as a monstrosity, but except for someone I knew at Oxford I have never met anything to match their albino allure and their blend of indecency and pathos.

For the rest, dachshunds were many and well-polished, schnauzers were noisy, poodles wore coronation ribbons, Bedlingtons, those nasty little zanies, sat quivering in overcoats. Old ladies in all directions produced sandwiches from handbags, not to mention small but attractive bones. England is still herself, I thought, as I left this parade of dogs and drove away towards Knightsbridge.

(*Night and Day*, 14 October 1937)

Dogs in the Park

The precise yet furtive etiquette of dogs
Makes them ignore the whistle while they talk
In circles round each other, one-man bonds
Deferred in pauses of this man-made walk
To open vistas to a past of packs

That raven round the stuccoed terraces
And scavenge at the mouth of Stone Age caves;
What man proposes dog on his day disposes
In litter round both human and canine graves,
Then lifts his leg to wash the gravestones clean,

While simultaneously his eyes express
Apology and contempt; his master calls
And at last and sidelong he returns,
Part heretic, part hack, and jumps and crawls
And fumbles to communicate and fails.

And then they leave the park, the leads are snapped
On to the spiky collars, the tails wag
For no known reason and the ears are pricked
To search through legendary copse and crag
For legendary creatures doomed to die
Even as they, the dogs, were doomed to live.

SHIRLEY TEMPLE

Protection

A FEW DAYS PRIOR to Christmas, Selznick requested I come to his office at ten o'clock the next Sunday morning.

'I'm thinking of making *Little Women*,' he said, a comment delivered without humour.

I thought he referred to the Louisa May Alcott book, and indeed he did have a very rough script. Midway in my reading, however, he raised his hand to stop me and abruptly veered off into another subject.

'Rumors,' he said, sighing. 'Public love can turn to public hate overnight. Just spatter on your image, you'll see. A terrible backlash.'

He crumpled a scrap of paper and dropped it to the floor. 'It would be curtains,' he said, flicking the corners of his mouth dry with both fingertips.

Coming around to my side of the desk, he continued in a less accusatory tone. 'Of course you have to be smart about it.' He reached and took my hand in his. Glancing down, I saw the telltale stocking feet.

Pulling free, I turned for the door, but even more quickly he reached back over the edge of his desk and flicked a switch I had learned from Colby was a remote door-locking device. I was trapped.

Like the cartoon of wolf and piglet, once again we circled and reversed directions around his furniture. Blessed with the agility of a young dancer and confronted by an amorous but overweight producer, I had little difficulty avoiding his passionate clumsiness.

'It's just the grease that oils Hollywood's wheels,' he laughed, feinting ineffectively. 'Makes them run smoothly.'

'Not grease,' I answered, grasping for a metaphor. 'Acid.'

In contrast to my encounters with the Wizard and Jessel, banter was more effective with Selznick than a knee. In this case humor eventually cooled his hot pursuit.

Raising both hands in mock surrender, he told me to take the script home, return the next day and let him know what I thought of it.

Determined to avoid a more resolute confrontation with my boss, I arrived tugged by my three leashed dogs: Duke, a fawn-colored Great Dane; Chris, the barrel-chested boxer; and Lanny, a shifty-eyed collie. All muscles and eagerness, they plunged up toward Selznick's desk, gagging and snorting.

Knowing him to be partial only to toy poodles, I was not surprised to see him bug-eyed with dismay. 'Okay,' he laughed, moving behind his chair out of range, 'I'm not going to bother you.'

That trip was the first useful duty any of my dogs had performed. For all the food I had shoved down them, they preferred to nuzzle rather than bite. One night a tramp had sought temporary shelter in our garage, but rather than alert the household, vicious Chris had curled up beside the trespasser, just to keep him warm.

Realizing the dogs were a genuine concern to Selznick, however, I commanded, 'Down, down!' Chris sank to his haunches stiff-legged, but continued to stare belligerently at Selznick.

'Sit, sit,' I repeated, until the collie obediently curled up at my feet and tucked his pointed nose under his furry rear haunches. Duke remained standing, his long, hairless tail pounding a friendly tattoo on a nearby chair arm.

Overnight I had read the entire *Little Women* script and was enthusiastic about the part of Jo. Selznick said he intended to go ahead, and we agreed the role was mine. The conference concluded. I started to rise, but he patted the air, indicating I should remain seated.

As we had spoken the only other sound was from Duke, his lustrous, long form unmoving by my chair, pinkish tongue lolling out the side of his gaped jaws, whimpering in excitement.

Selznick had switched subjects. After this film, he said, forget America. What my career needed was Italy. 'They are on a naturalistic kick, the Anna Magnani thing. Be a femme fatale.' He shot me a sidelong glance. 'Some people think you are anyway.'

I was beginning to feel like travel-stained luggage that had never actually gone anywhere.

From a moviemaking perspective he may have had a point. Playing a film vamp, a sex symbol in an Italian vineyard, just might have commercial possibilities. What his suggestion really tested was the strength of my desire to, first, change my image, and, second, to commit to an endless career making movies. I remembered the Italian option for months, my artistic heart hankering after something my head knew could not be. In the end Selznick was the one who took his own advice.

From *Child Star*

SIGMUND FREUD

Theory

WE KNOW THAT IN the nursery things are different. The excreta arouse no disgust in children. They seem valuable to them as being a part of their own body which has come away from it. Here upbringing insists with special energy on hastening the course of development which lies ahead, and which should make the excreta worthless, disgusting, abhorrent and abominable. Such a reversal of values would scarcely be possible if the substances that are expelled from the body were not doomed by their strong smells to share the fate which overtook olfactory stimuli after man adopted the erect posture. Anal erotism, therefore, succumbs in the first instance to the 'organic repression' which paved the way to civilization. The existence of the social factor which is responsible for the further transformation of anal erotism is attested by the circumstance that, in spite of all man's developmental advances, he scarcely finds the smell of *his own* excreta repulsive, but only that of other people's. Thus a person who is not clean – who does not hide his excreta – is offending other people; he is showing no consideration for them. And this is confirmed by our strongest and commonest terms of abuse. It would be incomprehensible, too, that man should use the name of his most faithful friend in the animal world – the dog – as a term of abuse if that creature had not incurred his contempt through two characteristics: that it is an animal whose dominant sense is that of smell and one which has no horror of excrement, and that it is not ashamed of its sexual functions.

From *Civilisation and its Discontents*

Practice

FREUD LEFT FOR HIS summer vacation on 16 June [1928] when he had the company of his first chow, with which Dorothy Burlingham, who was becoming intimate with the family, presented him. Like most Jews of his generation Freud had had little contact with animals, but a couple of years before an Alsatian dog Wolf, had been procured to accompany his daughter Anna on her walks through the forests of the Semmering. Freud had taken a considerable interest in observing canine ways, and from now on he became more and more fond of one dog after another. This first chow, called Lun Yu, unfortunately survived only fifteen months. In August of the following year Eva Rosenfeld was escorting her from Berchtesgaden to Vienna when the dog broke loose in the station of Salzburg and after three days was found run over on the line. Freud remarked that the pain they all felt resembled in quality, though not in intensity, that experienced after the loss of a child. Before long, however, she was replaced by another, Jo-fi, who was a constant companion for seven years.

* * *

In January of 1937 Freud suffered a novel loss, that of the female dog to which he had been very attached for the past seven years. He used often to exchange confidences with Marie Bonaparte, who also loved animals. Only a month before, on 6 December, he had written:

> Your card from Athens and the manuscript of the Topsy book have just arrived. I love it; it is so movingly real and true. It is, of course, not an analytic work, but the analyst's search for truth and knowledge can be perceived behind this creation. It really gives the real reasons for the remarkable fact that one can love an animal like Topsy (or my Jo-fi) so deeply: affection without any ambivalence, the simplicity of life free from the conflicts of civilization that are so hard to endure, the beauty of an existence complete in itself. And in spite of the remoteness in the organic development there is nevertheless a feeling of close relationship, of undeniably belonging together. Often when I stroke Jo-fi I find myself humming a melody which, unmusical though I am, I can recognize as the (Octavio) aria from *Don Juan*:
> A bond of friendship binds us both, etc.
> When you at a youthful 54 cannot avoid often thinking of death, you cannot be astonished that at the age of 80½ I fret whether I shall reach the age of my father and brother or further still into my mother's age, tormented on the one hand by the conflict between the wish for rest and the dread of fresh suffering that further life brings and on the other anticipation of the pain of separation from which I am still attached.

Jo-fi, however, had to be operated on because of two large ovarian cysts. It seemed succesful, but two days later she suddenly died. Freud then, feeling he could not get on without a dog, took back from Dorothy Burlingham another chow called Lün which he had had to transfer to her four years before on account of Jo-fi's jealousy.

Ernest Jones, from his *Life of Freud*

JOHN CROWE RANSOM

Dog

Cock-a-doodle-doo the brass-lined rooster says,
Brekekekex intones the fat Greek frog –
These fantasies do not terrify me as
The bow-wow-wow of dog.

I had a little doggie who used to sit and beg,
A pretty little creature with tears in his eyes
And anomalous hand extended on his leg;
Housebroken was my Huendchen, and so wise.

Booms the voice of a big dog like a bell.
But Fido sits at dusk on Madam's lap
And, bored beyond his tongue's poor skill to tell,
Rehearses his pink paradigm, To yap.

However. Up the lane the tender bull
Proceeds unto his kine; he yearns for them,
Whose eyes adore him and are beautiful;
Love speeds him and no treason nor mayhem.

But, on arriving at the gap in the fence,
Behold! again the ubiquitous hairy dog,
Like a numerous army rattling the battlements
With shout, though it is but his monologue,
With a lion's courage and a bee's virulence
Though he is but one dog.

Shrill is the fury of the proud red bull,
His knees quiver, and the honeysuckle vine
Expires with anguish as his voice, terrible,
Cries, 'What do you want of my twenty lady kine?'

Now the air trembles to the sorrowing Moo
Of twenty blameless ladies of the mead
Fearing their lord's precarious set-to.
It is the sunset and the heavens bleed.

The hooves of the red bull slither the claybank
And cut the green tendrils of the vine; his horn
Slices the young birch unto splinter and shank
But lunging leaves the bitch's boy untorn.

Across the red sky comes master, Hodge by name,
Upright, biped, tall-browed, and self-assured,
In his hand a cudgel, in his cold eye a flame:
'Have I beat my dog so sore and he is not cured?'

His stick and stone and curse rain on the brute
That pipped his bull of gentle pedigree
Till the leonine smarts with pain and disrepute
And the bovine weeps in the bosom of his family.

Old Hodge stays not his hand, but whips to kennel
The renegade. God's peace betide the souls
Of the pure in heart. But in the box that fennel
Grows round are two red eyes that stare like coals.

P. G. WODEHOUSE
Cave Canem

I HATE THESE SURREPTITIOUS prowlings. Bertram Wooster is a man who likes to go through the world with his chin up and both feet on the ground, not to sneak about on tiptoe with his spine tying itself into reefer knots.

It was precisely because I had anticipated some such reactions that I had been so anxious that Jeeves should accompany me and lend moral support, and I found myself wishing that he would buck up and lend a bit more than he was doing. Willing service and selfless co-operation were what I had hoped for, and he was not giving me them. His manner from the very start betrayed an aloof disapproval. He seemed to be disassociating himself entirely from the proceedings, and I resented it.

Owing to this aloofness on his part and this resentment on mine, we made the journey in silence, and it was in silence that we entered the room and switched on the light.

The first impression I received on giving the apartment the once-over was that for a young shrimp of her shaky moral outlook Stiffy had been done pretty well in the matter of sleeping accommodation. Totleigh Towers was one of those country houses which had been built at a time when people planning a little nest had the idea that a bedroom was not a bedroom unless you could give an informal dance for about fifty couples in it, and this sanctum could have accommodated a dozen Stiffys. In the rays of the small electric light up in the ceiling, the bally thing seemed to stretch for miles in every direction, and the thought that if that detective had not called his shots correctly, Gussie's notebook might be concealed anywhere in these great spaces, was a chilling one.

I was standing there, hoping for the best, when my meditations were broken in upon by an odd, gargling sort of noise something like static and something like distant thunder, and to cut a long story short this proved to proceed from the larynx of the dog Bartholomew.

He was standing on the bed, stropping his front paws on the coverlet, and so easy was it to read the message in his eyes that we acted like two minds with but a single thought. At the exact moment when I soared like an eagle on to the chest of drawers, Jeeves was skimming like a swallow on to the top of the cupboard. The animal hopped from the bed and, advancing into the middle of the room, took a seat, breathing through the nose with a curious whistling sound, and looking at us from under his eyebrows like a Scottish elder rebuking sin from the pulpit.

And there for a while the matter rested.

Jeeves was the first to break a rather strained silence.

'The book does not appear to be here, sir.'

'Eh?'

'I have searched the top of the cupboard, sir, but I have not found the book.'

It may be that my reply erred a trifle on the side of acerbity. My narrow escape from those slavering jaws had left me a bit edgey.

'Blast the book, Jeeves! What about this dog?'

'Yes, sir.'

'What do you mean – Yes, sir?'

'I was endeavouring to convey that I appreciate the point which you have raised, sir. The animal's unexpected appearance unquestionably presents a problem. While he continues to maintain his existing attitude, it will not be easy for us to prosecute the search for Mr Fink-Nottle's notebook. Our freedom of action will necessarily be circumscribed.'

'Then what's to be done?'

'It is difficult to say, sir.'

'You have no ideas?'

'No, sir.'

I could have said something pretty bitter and stinging at this – I don't know what, but something – but I refrained. I realized that it was rather tough on the man, outstanding though his gifts were, to expect him to ring the bell every time, without fail. No doubt that brilliant inspiration of his which had led to my signal victory over the forces of darkness as represented by R. Spode had taken it out of him a good deal, rendering the brain for the nonce a bit flaccid. One could but wait and hope that the machinery would soon get going again, enabling him to seek new high levels of achievement.

And, I felt as I continued to turn the position of affairs over in my mind, the sooner, the better, for it was plain that nothing was going to budge this canine excrescence except an offensive on a major scale, dashingly conceived and skilfully carried out. I don't think I have ever seen a dog who conveyed more vividly the impression of being rooted to the spot and prepared to stay there till the cows – or, in this case, his proprietress – came home. And what I was going to say to Stiffy if she returned and found me roosting on her chest of drawers was something I had not yet thought out in any exactness of detail.

Watching the animal sitting there like a bump on a log, I soon found myself chafing a good deal. I remember Freddie Widgeon, who was once chased on to the top of a wardrobe by an Alsatian during a country house visit, telling me that what he had disliked most about the thing was the indignity of it all – the blow to the proud spirit, if you know what I mean – the feeling, in fine, that he, the Heir of the Ages, as you might say, was camping out on a wardrobe at the whim of a bally dog.

It was the same with me. One doesn't want to make a song and dance about one's ancient lineage, of course, but after all the Woosters did come over with the Conqueror and were extremely pally with him: and a fat lot of good it is coming over with Conquerors, if you're simply going to wind up by being given the elbow by Aberdeen terriers.

These reflections had the effect of making me rather peevish, and I looked down somewhat sourly at the animal.

'I call it monstrous, Jeeves,' I said, voicing my train of thought, 'that this dog should be lounging about in a bedroom. Most unhygienic.'

'Yes, sir.'

'Scotties are smelly, even the best of them. You will recall how my Aunt Agatha's McIntosh niffed to heaven while enjoying my hospitality. I frequently mentioned it to you.'

'Yes, sir.'

'And this one is even riper. He should obviously have been bedded out in the stables. Upon my Sam, what with Scotties in Stiffy's room, and newts in Gussie's, Totleigh Towers is not far short of being a lazar house.'

'No, sir.'

'And consider the matter from another angle,' I said, warming to my theme. 'I refer to the danger of keeping a dog of this nature and disposition in a bedroom, where it can spring out ravening on anyone who enters. You and I happen to be able to take care of ourselves in an emergency such as has arisen, but suppose we had been some highly-strung housemaid.'

'Yes, sir.'

'I can see her coming into the room to turn down the bed. I picture her as a rather fragile girl with big eyes and a timid expression. She crosses the threshold. She approaches the bed. And out leaps this man-eating dog. One does not like to dwell upon the sequel.'

'No, sir.'

I frowned.

'I wish,' I said, 'that instead of sitting there saying "Yes, sir" and "No, sir", Jeeves, you would do something.'

'But what can I do, sir?'

'You can get action, Jeeves. That is what is required here – sharp, decisive action. I wonder if you recall a visit we once paid to the residence of my Aunt Agatha at Woollam Chersey in the county of Herts. To refresh your memory, it was the occasion on which, in company with the Right Honourable A. B. Filmer, the Cabinet Minister,

I was chivvied on to the roof of a shack on the island in the lake by an angry swan.'

'I recall the incident vividly, sir.'

'So do I. And the picture most deeply imprinted on my mental retina – is that the correct expression? – '

'Yes, sir.'

' – is of you facing that swan in the most intrepid "You-can't-do-that-there-here" manner and bunging a raincoat over its head, thereby completely dishing its aims and plans and compelling it to revise its whole strategy from the bottom up. It was a beautiful bit of work. I don't know when I have seen a finer.'

'Thank you, sir. I am glad if I gave satisfaction.'

'You certainly did, Jeeves, in heaping measure. And what crossed my mind was that a similar operation would make this dog feel pretty silly.'

'No doubt, sir. But I have no raincoat.'

'Then I would advise seeing what you can do with a sheet. And in case you are wondering if a sheet would work as well, I may tell you that just before you came to my room I had had admirable results with one in the case of Mr Spode. He just couldn't seem to get out of the thing.'

'Indeed, sir?'

'I assure you, Jeeves. You could wish no better weapon than a sheet. There are some on the bed.'

'Yes, sir. On the bed.'

There was a pause. I was loth to wrong the man, but if this wasn't a *nolle prosequi*, I didn't know one when I saw one. The distant and unenthusiastic look on his face told me that I was right, and I endeavoured to sting his pride, rather as Gussie in our *pourparlers* in the matter of Spode had endeavoured to sting mine.

'Are you afraid of a tiny little dog, Jeeves?'

He corrected me respectfully, giving it as his opinion that the undersigned was not a tiny little dog, but well above the average in muscular development. In particular, he drew my attention to the animal's teeth.

I reassured him.

'I think you would find that if you were to make a sudden spring, his teeth would not enter into the matter. You could leap on to the bed, snatch up a sheet, roll him up in it before he knew what was happening, and there we would be.'

'Yes, sir.'

'Well, are you going to make a sudden spring?'

'No, sir.'

A rather stiff silence ensued, during which the dog Bartholomew continued to gaze at me unwinkingly, and once more I found myself noticing – and resenting – the superior, sanctimonious expression on his face. Nothing can ever render the experience of being treed on top of a chest of drawers by an Aberdeen terrier pleasant, but it seemed to me that the least you can expect on such an occasion is that the animal will meet you half-way and not drop salt into the wound by looking at you as if he were asking if you were saved.

It was in the hope of wiping this look off his face that I now made a gesture. There was a stump of candle standing in the parent candlestick beside me, and I threw this at the little blighter. He ate it with every appearance of relish, took time out briefly in order to be sick, and resumed his silent stare. And at this moment the door opened and in came Stiffy – hours before I had expected her.

The first thing that impressed itself upon one on seeing her was that she was not in her customary buoyant spirits. Stiffy, as a rule, is a girl who moves jauntily from spot to spot – youthful elasticity is, I believe, the expression – but she entered now with a slow and dragging step like a Volga boatman. She cast a dull eye at us, and after a brief 'Hullo, Bertie. Hullo, Jeeves,' seemed to dismiss us from her thoughts. She made for the dressing-table and, having removed her hat, sat looking at herself in the mirror with sombre eyes. It was plain that for some reason the soul had got a flat tyre, and seeing that unless I opened the conversation there was going to be one of those awkward pauses, I did so.

'What ho, Stiffy.'

'Hullo.'

'Nice evening. Your dog's just been sick on the carpet.'

From *The Code of the Woosters*

A Business Proposition

'GOOD AFTERNOON, SIR,' said Bowles. 'A gentleman is waiting to see you. I fancy I heard him calling me a moment ago.'

'Who is he?'

'A Mr Ukridge, sir. He – '

A vast voice boomed out from above.

'Bowles, old horse!'

Bowles, like all other proprietors of furnished apartments in the south-western district of London, was an ex-butler, and about him, as about all ex-butlers, there clung like a garment an aura of dignified superiority which had never failed to crush my spirit. He was a man of portly aspect, with a bald head and prominent eyes of a lightish green – eyes that seemed to weigh me dispassionately and find me wanting. 'H'm!' they seemed to say, 'Young – very young. And not at all what I have been accustomed to in the best places.' To hear this dignitary addressed – and in a shout at that – as 'old horse' affected me with much the same sense of imminent chaos as would afflict a devout young curate if he saw his bishop slapped on the back. The shock, therefore, when he responded not merely mildly but with what almost amounted to camaraderie was numbing.

'Sir?' cooed Bowles.

'Bring me six bones and a corkscrew.'

'Very good, sir.'

Bowles retired, and I bounded upstairs and flung open the door of my sitting room.

'Great Scott!' I said, blankly.

The place was a sea of Pekingese dogs. Later investigation reduced their numbers to six, but in that first moment there seemed to be hundreds. Goggling eyes met mine wherever I looked. The room was a forest of waving tails. With his back against the mantelpiece, smoking placidly, stood Ukridge.

'Hallo, laddie!' he said, with a genial wave of the hand, as if to make me free of the place. 'You're just in time. I've got to dash off and catch a train in a quarter of an hour. Stop it, you mutts!' he bellowed, and the six Pekingese, who had been barking steadily since my arrival, stopped in mid-yap, and were still. Ukridge's personality seemed to exercise a magnetism over the animal kingdom, from ex-butlers to Pekes, which bordered on the uncanny. 'I'm off to Sheep's Cray, in Kent. Taken a cottage there.'

'Are you going to live there?'

'Yes.'

'But what about your aunt?'

'Oh, I've left her. Life is stern and life is earnest, and if I mean to make a fortune I've got to bustle about and not stay cooped up in a place like Wimbledon.'

'Something in that.'

'Besides which, she told me the very sight of me made her sick and she never wanted to see me again.'

I might have guessed, directly I saw him, that some upheaval had taken place. The sumptuous raiment which had made him such a treat to the eye at our last meeting was gone, and he was back in his pre-Wimbledon costume, which was, as the advertisements say, distinctly individual. Over grey flannel trousers, a golf coat, and a brown sweater he wore like a royal robe a bright yellow mackintosh. His collar had broken free from its stud and showed a couple of inches of bare neck. His hair was disordered, and his masterful nose was topped by a pair of steel-rimmed pince-nez cunningly attached to his flapping ears with ginger-beer wire. His whole appearance spelled revolt.

Bowles manifested himself with a plateful of bones.

'That's right. Chuck 'em down on the floor.'

'Very good, sir.'

'I like that fellow,' said Ukridge, as the door closed. 'We had a dashed interesting talk before you came in. Did you know he had a cousin on the music halls?'

'He hasn't confided in me much.'

'He's promised me an introduction to him later on. May be useful to be in touch with a man who knows the ropes. You see, laddie, I've hit on the most amazing scheme.' He swept his arm round dramatically, overturning a plaster cast of the Infant Samuel at Prayer. 'All right, all right, you can mend it with glue or something, and anyway, you're probably better without it. Yessir, I've hit on a great scheme. The idea of a thousand years.'

'What's that?'

'I'm going to train dogs.'

'Train dogs?'

'For the music-hall stage. Dog acts, you know. Performing dogs. Pots of money in it. I start in a modest way with these six. When I've taught 'em a few tricks, I sell them to a fellow in the profession for a large sum and buy twelve more. I train those, sell 'em for a large sum, and with the money buy twenty-four more. I train those – '

'Here, wait a minute.' My head was beginning to swim. I had a vision of England paved with Pekingese dogs, all doing tricks. 'How do you know you'll be able to sell them?'

'Of course I shall. The demand's enormous. Supply can't cope with it. At a conservative estimate I should think I ought to scoop in four or five thousand pounds the first year. That, of course, is before the business really starts to expand.'

'I see.'

'When I get going properly, with a dozen assistants under me and an organized establishment, I shall begin to touch the big money. What I'm aiming at is a sort of Dogs' College out in the country somewhere. Big place with a lot of ground. Regular classes and a set curriculum. Large staff, each member of it with so many dogs under his care, me looking on and superintending. Why, once the thing starts moving it'll run itself, and all I shall have to do will be to sit back and endorse the cheques. It isn't as if I would have to confine my operations to England. The demand for performing dogs is universal throughout the civilized world. America wants performing dogs. Australia wants performing dogs. Africa could do with a few, I've no doubt. My aim, laddie, is gradually to get monopoly of the trade. I want everybody who needs a performing dog of any description to come automatically to me. And I'll tell you what, laddie. If you like to put up a bit of capital, I'll let you in on the ground floor.'

'No, thanks.'

'All right. Have it your own way. Only don't forget that there was a fellow who put nine hundred dollars into the Ford Car business when it was starting and he collected a cool forty million. I say, is that clock right? Great Scott! I'll be missing my train. Help me mobilize these dashed animals.'

From 'Ukridge's Dog College'

Global Dogs

To Denis Mackail

Domaine de la Fréyère
Auribeau
Alpes-Maritimes

According to present plans, Ethel and I dash over to London at the end of the month for a week or two. This, of course, involves leaving Miss Winks here, and I doubt if, when the time comes, we shall be capable of it. What a curse that quarantine law is. It seems so damned silly to extend it to Pekes, who couldn't possibly give rabies to anyone.

9 October 1932

To William Townend: Low Wood
                                                            Le Touquet
Ethel went over to England for a week the other day, and I was sitting in porch here waiting for her, and out of her cab wriggled a yellow object. Boo!! Snorky's Peke. It was a stroke of genius bringing her. She makes all the difference to Winky. They are the most tremendous friends. And here is a great fact of life which everybody should know – two Pekes are no more trouble than one. In fact, less, as you can leave two Pekes where it would break your heart to leave one alone.

2 August 1934

To William Townend:

Boo is quite a different dog now. Her bad temper has quite gone, and she is all affection. I think the trouble at Snorky's place was that the other dogs were not Pekes. Pekes really are a different race and class. They may try to be democratic, but they don't really accept other dogs as their social equals.

15 October 1934

To William Townend: 17 Norfolk Street
                                                         Park Lane
                                                         London W1
There's no getting away from it, female Pekes are human. You get to love them just as much as you would a child. I think it is partly because they are so absolutely dependent on you, and the way they combine bossiness with utter collapse when anything goes wrong. I shall never forget the time when I was going to air Boo and Winky at Norfolk Street and I started to pick Winky up and Boo flew at her, and I was so irritated that I gave a sideways kick and it caught Boo in the mouth. She dropped all her toughness in a second and lay down with her face between her paws and *screamed*. I've never felt such a hound and swine

in my life. Of course, two seconds after I started petting her she was alright again and just as bossy as ever.

10 December 1934

To William Townend: Low Wood

Le Touquet

That hound Boo as near as toucher got killed last night. We were walking on left side of road. Two girls on bikes came along on right side. Boo dashed across and gave chase, spilling one girl. I stopped to pick her up, and Boo legged it after the other one. I was twenty yards behind when I saw a car coming and at that moment Boo swerved to the left. I gave a yell and the car stopped with the wheel right over Boo. Another revolution would have killed her. She then trotted back to Ethel and lay on her back, which is her idea of passing off the most delicate situation.

1 July 1935

To William Townend:

Winks and Boo do nothing nowadays but fight. I think it is because they aren't getting enough exercise. Have you ever studied the psychology of the Dirty Look in Pekes. Winks and Boo will be sleeping quite happily at different ends of the room and then suddenly one of them will lift her head and stare. The other then stares. This goes on for about ten seconds, and then they rush at one another. My theory is that dogs say things which the human ear can't hear. By the way, we're taking both Pekes to St Moritz.

20 January 1936

To William Townend: 1315 Angelo Drive
                                                      Beverly Hills
                                                      California

PS The pup is simply marvellous. Winky loves her and they play together all the time. It has made Winky quite a young dog again, having the pup.

28 December 1936

To William Townend:

Winks is very well. Also the puppy, who now has two names – Wonder and Sixpence. My day starts when I hear the puppy bark in Ethel's room. I open the door, and she, the puppy, comes leaping out. Winky then pokes her head out of my bed, in which she has been sleeping, and I take them downstairs and let them out. I bring them in when I come down to breakfast, and they then have to be let out again in order to bark at the gardener, whose arrival is always a terrific surprise and shock to them, though he has turned up at the same time every morning for four months.

They stand with their feet up against the window.

Puppy: Do you see what I see? Is that a man in the garden?

Winks: Egad, it is, and a low sinister, Mexican-looking man. Should we tear him to pieces?

Puppy: Undoubtedly. We must keep the home safe.

Winks (to me): Hey! Open this door and let's get at him.

I open the door, and they fly out, yelling, to subside instantly as the gardener pets them. Next day, the same.

The puppy is now in an interesting condition. Imagine – at six months old! Nature seems to me an absolute ass. It appears to want dogs to start breeding before they are out of the cradle.

28 January 1937

To William Townend: Low Wood
                                                      Le Touquet

Winkie is dead. I can hardly bear to write about it, but I had to let you know. The usual thing – tick fever. Same as Boo.

28 November 1938

E. B. WHITE

A Boston Terrier

I WOULD LIKE TO hand down a dissenting opinion in the case of the Camel ad which shows a Boston terrier relaxing. I can string along with cigarette manufacturers to a certain degree, but when it comes to the temperament and habits of terriers, I shall stand my ground.

The ad says: 'A dog's nervous system resembles our own.' I don't think a dog's nervous system resembles my own in the least. A dog's nervous system is in a class by itself. If it resembles anything at all, it resembles the New York Edison Company's power plant. This is particularly true of Boston terriers, and if the Camel people don't know that, they have never been around dogs.

The ad says: 'But when a dog's nerves tire, he obeys his instincts – he relaxes.' This, I admit, is true. But I should like to call attention to the fact that it sometimes takes days, even weeks, before a dog's nerves tire. In the case of terriers it can run into months.

I knew a Boston terrier once (he is now dead and, so far as I know, relaxed) whose nerves stayed keyed up from the twenty-fifth of one June to the sixth of the following July, without one minute's peace for anybody in the family. He was an old dog and he was blind in one eye, but his infirmities caused no diminution in his nervous power. During the period of which I speak, the famous period of his greatest excitation, he not only raised a type of general hell which startled even his closest friends and observers, but he gave a mighty clever excuse. He said it was love.

'I'm in love,' he would scream. (He could scream just like a hurt child.) 'I'm in love and I'm going *crazy*.'

Day and night it was all the same. I tried everything to soothe him. I tried darkness, cold water dashed in the face, the lash, long quiet talks, warm milk administered internally, threats, promises, and close confinement in remote locations. At last, after about a week of it, I went down the road and had a chat with the lady who owned the object of our terrier's affection. It was she who finally cleared up the situation.

'Oh,' she said, wearily, 'if it's that bad, let him out.'

I hadn't thought of anything as simple as that myself, but I am a creature of infinite reserve. As a matter of record, it turned out to be not so simple – the terrier got run over by a motor car one night while returning from his amorous adventures, suffering a complete paralysis of the hip but no assuagement of the nervous system; and the little Scotty bitch returned to Washington, DC, and a Caesarian.

I am not through with the Camel people yet. Love is not the only thing that can keep a dog's nerves in a state of perpetual jangle. A dog, more than any other creature, it seems to me, gets interested in one subject, theme, or object, in life, and pursues it with a fixity of purpose which would be inspiring to Man if it weren't so troublesome. One dog gets absorbed in one thing, another dog in another. When I was a boy there was a smooth-haired fox terrier (in those days nobody ever heard of a fox terrier that *wasn't* smooth-haired) who became interested, rather late in life, in a certain stone. The stone was about the size of an egg. As far as I could see, it was like a million other stones – but to him it was the Stone Supreme.

He kept it with him day and night, slept with it, ate with it, played with it, analysed it, took it on little trips (you would often see him three blocks from home, trotting along on some shady errand, his stone safe in his jaws). He used to lie by the hour on the porch of his house, chewing the stone with an expression half tender, half petulant. When he slept he merely enjoyed a muscular suspension: his nerves were still up and around, adjusting the bed clothes, tossing and turning.

He permitted people to throw the stone for him and people would. But if the stone lodged somewhere he couldn't get to he raised such an uproar that it was absolutely necessary that the stone be returned, for the public peace. His absorption was so great it brought wrinkles to his face, and he grew old before his time. I think he used to worry that somebody was going to pitch the stone into a lake or a bog, where it would be irretrievable. He wore off every tooth in his jaw, wore them right down to the gums, and they became mere brown vestigial bumps. His breath was awful (he panted night and day) and his eyes were alight with an unearthly zeal. He died in a fight with another dog. I have always suspected it was because he tried to hold the stone in his mouth all through the battle. The Camel people will just have to take my word for it: that dog was a living denial of the whole theory of relaxation. He was a paragon of nervous tension, from the moment he first laid eyes on his slimy little stone till the hour of his death.

The advertisement speaks of the way humans 'prod' themselves to endeavour – so that they keep on and on working long after they should quit. The inference is that a dog never does that. But I have a dog right now that can prod himself harder and drive himself longer than any human I ever saw. This animal is a dachshund, and I shall spare you the long dull inanities of his innumerable obsessions. His particular study (or mania) at the moment is a black-and-white kitten that my wife gave me for Christmas, thinking that what my life needed was something else that could move quickly from one place in the room to another. The dachshund began his research on Chistmas Eve when the kitten arrived 'secretly' in the cellar, and now, five months later, is taking his Ph.D, still working late at night on it, every night. If he could write a book about that cat, it would make *Middletown* look like the work of a backward child.

I'll be glad to have the Camel people study this animal in one of his relaxed moods, but they will have to bring their own seismograph. Even curled up cozily in a chair, dreaming of his cat, he quivers like an aspen.

From *One Man's Meat*

T. S. ELIOT

Of the Awefull Battle of the Pekes and the Pollicles

*Together with some Account of the Participation
of the Pugs and the Poms, and the Intervention
of the Great Rumpuscat*

The Pekes and the Pollicles, everyone knows,
Are proud and implacable passionate foes;
It is always the same, wherever one goes.
And the Pugs and the Poms, although most people say
That they do not like fighting, yet once in a way,
Or now and again, they join in to the fray
And they
          Bark bark bark bark
          Bark bark BARK BARK
     Until you can hear them all over the Park.

Now on the occasion of which I shall speak
Almost nothing had happened for nearly a week
(And that's a long time for a Pol or a Peke).
The big Police Dog was away from his beat –
I don't know the reason, but most people think
He'd slipped into the Wellington Arms for a drink –
And no one at all was about on the street
When a Peke and a Pollicle happened to meet.
They did not advance, or exactly retreat,
But they glared at each other, and scraped their hind feet,
And started to

> Bark bark bark bark
> Bark bark BARK BARK
> Until you could hear them all over the Park.

Now the Peke, although people may say what they please,
Is no British Dog, but a Heathen Chinese.
And so all the Pekes, when they heard the uproar,
Some came to the window, some came to the door;
There were surely a dozen, more likely a score.
And together they started to grumble and wheeze
In their huffery-snuffery Heathen Chinese.
But a terrible din is what Pollicles like,
For your Pollicle Dog is a dour Yorkshire tyke,
And his braw Scottish cousins are snappers and biters,
And every dog-jack of them notable fighters;
And so they stepped out, with their pipers in order,
Playing *When the Blue Bonnets Came Over the Border.*
Then the Pugs and the Poms held no longer aloof,
But some from the balcony, some from the roof,
Joined in
To the din
With a

> Bark bark bark bark

Bark bark BARK BARK
Until you could hear them all over the Park.

Now when these bold heroes together assembled,
The traffic all stopped, and the Underground trembled,
And some of the neighbours were so much afraid
That they started to ring up the Fire Brigade.
When suddenly, up from a small basement flat,
Why who should stalk out but the GREAT RUMPUSCAT.
His eyes were like fireballs fearfully blazing,
He gave a great yawn, and his jaws were amazing;
And when he looked out through the bars of the area,
You never saw anything fiercer or hairier.
And what with the glare of his eyes and his yawning,
The Pekes with the Pollicles quickly took warning.
He looked at the sky and he gave a great leap –
And they every last one of them scattered like sheep.

And when the Police Dog returned to his beat,
There wasn't a single one left in the street.

From *Old Possum's Book of Practical Cats*

DODIE SMITH

Her Own Dogs

MY MOTHER'S NEW fiancé, 'Uncle Ru' to me, was already installed
as our paying guest; a small man, devoted to large dogs, he had
when he first came to us an outsize Great Dane, but it died just as I
was getting fond of it. As a consolation he gave me a Deerhound, which
I called Gelert, after the devoted hound in the well-known poem. My

uncles called it Rags, and not without reason as it was not merely a shaggy dog, it was a tangled shaggy dog. I doubt if it was quite a Deerhound, or any one kind of hound. Uncle Ru had 'Ten shillings reward to anyone returning this dog to Miss Dodie Smith at Kingston House' engraved on its massive collar and it was returned three times in a week. We believed that a gang of boys kept luring it out so that they could bring it back. A new home was found for ruinous Rags-Gelert, though I can't now see why he wasn't simply provided with a new collar. I think the truth was that none of us had got fond of him and he had shown no sign of getting fond of us. It seemed best to wish him better luck next time.

* * *

Towards the end of that week came my birthday. I was having breakfast in bed when Alec and Phyllis arrived with a large hatbox, saying they had bought me a joint present of a hat. I couldn't think of a more idiotic present but I soon did, for the hatbox, placed on my bed, began to lurch about and out of it came a big, clumsy Dalmatian puppy who made a dead set at my breakfast tray. How could they have done this to me?

It was true that I hankered for a Dalmatian and had said so to some journalist, on the publication of whose interview a Dalmatian breeder offered me one. I had arranged to choose it just as soon as the cottage was ready for it to live in. Idiotically, Alec had forgotten this. Anyway, here was a puppy I hadn't had the pleasure of selecting and he wasn't even the kind of puppy I fancied. He wasn't young enough or small enough; he was nearly half-grown. Naturally I didn't say any of this to Alec and Phyllis who had taken enormous trouble; they regaled me with all the fun *they'd* had in doing the choosing. I heard of all their secret meetings and how Alec had driven out very early that morning to fetch the animal.

I thanked them effusively, said the pup was gorgeous, awarded him the name I had ready: 'Pongo'; it seemed to me a good Victorian name for a coach dog. Then the breakfast tray, flooded by an overturned tea cup, was rescued from his enormous paws (he looked as if he might grow as big as a Great Dane, and he certainly did his best) and I went off to my bath.

How was I going to manage in the evenings, with a maid who didn't sleep in? Phyllis would be no help; she was playing in Gordon Daviot's *The Laughing Woman*. How was I going to manage this very day, when it was the maid's half-day off? Pongo would have to come to the

Haymarket Theatre. I would ask the stage-door keeper for some dressing room where he could be kept, with frequent visits from Alec.

All the stage-door keeper said was that dogs were absolutely forbidden at the Haymarket Theatre. Luckily, while we were arguing, Horace Watson came downstairs and said an exception could be made for my dog. Pongo instantly showed his appreciation by making a pool on the floor. Mr Watson said gently, 'Well, he doesn't know any better' and went back to his office for a towel.

What happened to Alec and Pongo during that morning I've no idea, but they were waiting inside the stage door when I came out for lunch. With me came Marie Ney who grabbed Pongo lovingly and instantly dropped him on the hard pavement. Pongo yelped; if I didn't exactly scream, I certainly made a dismayed noise. Basil, arriving, said, 'You're going to make a fool of yourself about that dog.' How right he was! (He later told me that he had thought 'Pongo' the worst name for a dog he had ever heard, but then he got to like it. And he became absolutely devoted to Pongo, frequently offering him a home. And Pongo, not a particularly affectionate dog, developed a passion for Basil and would insist on sitting on his knee – no mean burden – lovingly washing Basil's face, with never a cross word between them.)

That evening we discovered there was something wrong with one of Pongo's legs. Alec had suspected it that morning, after seeing him fall off a table at his breeder's, and being dropped out of Marie Ney's arms hadn't improved matters. Anyway, he was now definitely limping, we hated to make him walk, and his house-training was nil. So we decided Alec should take him back to the Surrey kennels and leave him there until the play had opened. I was sorry to let him go as I was already getting fond of him, but I was also relieved.

He was not merely lacking in house-training, he was dead against it. Most puppies don't discriminate between indoors and out; Pongo did, and he opted for indoors. You could lug him round Dorset Square for twenty minutes without results, then carry him up seventy-two stairs – he refused to walk them – and the minute you put him down in the hall he would gladly make use of it. I had a theory, which I still firmly hold, that after a puppy makes a mistake indoors he should promptly be put outdoors and will then, by degrees, get the right idea. But seventy-two stairs down and up again with a heavy puppy was more than I could face, or demand of my maid, a second Ellen. She was a farmer's daughter of hefty proportions who had impressed me by asking what were then considered high wages (thirty shillings a week!). She was the worst cook I had had, but she was good-tempered and willing to come up and down to the cottage. And she was fond of Pongo, which counted a lot. He was about to put her affection to test.

Some time earlier Phyllis had given me a simulated spaniel as a nightdress case (not one of her more inspired presents). This wasn't real dogskin, but Pongo seemed to know what it represented, and he fought it victoriously and ate a major part of its cotton-wool stuffing before we could get the remains away from him. That evening Ellen kindly carried him down the seventy-two stairs to the square; by now he had been known to use it, possibly accidentally. Suddenly I heard the most ghastly screaming. I dashed to a window.

Had Pongo been run over? But he was safely on the leash being dragged along by Ellen. Was she hurting his neck? Then I saw that the trouble was not at that end. He appeared to have acquired an extra tail. The lower one, which was trailing along the ground after him, was composed of the cotton-wool stuffing from the nightdress-case spaniel. He shook himself desperately but could not get free, and all the time his ear-piercing screams persisted. Front doors were flung open, windows shot up. Passers-by stopped. I heard shouts, 'Leave him alone, can't you?' 'She's pulling his head off.' Then, thank heaven, the white rope fell off and I saw Ellen urge him towards the front steps.

I met her in the hall. She was panting and scarlet in the face. She said it had been awful. 'They all thought I was ill-treating him. I didn't know where to look.' Rather too apt a remark, I felt. However, both she and Pongo swiftly recovered.

*   *   *

And at this juncture, Pongo got ill and there was no mystery about his illness; it was his kidney trouble again, far worse than ever before, and in an unbelievably short time he was in such a state of emaciation that it seemed cruel to keep him alive. However, according to our vet Proby Cautley, he wasn't suffering, and there was still hope. But day after day, when we visited Pongo, he had sunk lower and expert opinion called in from the Royal College of Veterinary Surgeons thought he should be put down. Proby, a great fighter, said no, not yet. We said he should decide.

He then said that as he could go no higher for advice in the veterinary world, he would rather like to discuss Pongo's case with an ordinary doctor. Would my own doctor care to consult with him? My dear Dr Chance was more than willing and offered to take a Harley Street specialist with him. Perhaps all this may have been done in an effort to satisfy me, as well as to help Pongo, for I was so unhappy about my poor dog that I was getting iller and iller. To Proby's delighted surprise, the specialist turned out to be Horace Evans, who was far more famous than I then realised. Opinions about kidney disease in canines and humans were pooled at the consultation, but nothing helpful could be suggested and Pongo, it seemed, just moved one day nearer to death. Kind Horace Evans would only accept a nominal fee.

Alec must have felt almost worse than I did, for Pongo had long ago showed that he was a one-man dog and that man was Alec. I never felt jealous and took particular pleasure in watching them together. I have a vivid memory of many returns after first nights to find Pongo asleep in Alec's flat, lit by the dim glow from the tropical tank. The reunion was a sight worth seeing. And it seemed that I should never see it again.

Phyllis, too, was devoted to Pongo and she now suggested that I should consult her Christian Science practitioner. Phyl was a more orthodox Scientist than I was, going to the church and even doing the daily 'Lesson', which consisted of reading five or six specified extracts from Mrs Eddy and then extracts from the Bible which were supposed to link. It took quite a long time every day and then on Sundays one didn't get a day of rest because one had to do the whole six days' work all over again. This simply wasn't me. And I did *not* want to go to her practitioner or any other practitioner. Still . . . as a last hope for Pongo.

I regret to say that I took agin that practitioner on sight. Phyllis herself didn't like him very much, but said she felt he was 'strong'. To me he seemed plain bossy and very sententious. Then I rebuked myself. I was merely being prejudiced, disliking the Christian Science jargon; he was obviously well-intentioned and as he was an orthodox Christian Scientist I had no right to blame him for talking like one. *I* was the one at fault, trying to make use of a religion while considering myself superior to its language. I told myself to be humble . . . for Pongo's sake. The practitioner said he would only accept the case if I would undertake to do that daily Lesson and read *all* Mrs Eddy's books. I agreed. (And kept my word. I had always found reading *Science and Health* a bit of a penance, but compared with Mrs Eddy's other books, it seemed a work of genius.) The practitioner said that it wasn't really necessary for him to see the dog but, to please me, he would. And now couldn't he give *me* some help? I hastily assured him I wasn't in need of any – and just managed to get out of his office before I had a sneezing fit.

Alec and I visited Pongo the next morning. As usual he managed a twitch of his tail for Alec, but there was no improvement. I warned Proby Cautley that a Christian Scientist practitioner would be calling.

Late in the afternoon Proby rang up to say that a little man in a bowler hat had visited Pongo or, rather, visited the room where Pongo was. Proby had offered to open Pongo's pen, but the man had said there was no need. 'He just stood in the doorway,' said Proby, 'as far away from all the dogs as he could. And I got the impression that he was terrified of them. Then he went away. And I now have to tell you that Pongo has at last taken a turn for the better.'

I didn't believe it. Proby must simply be trying to cheer me up. But he swore it was true. Pongo had taken some faint interest in food. 'And his eyes are different,' said Proby. 'He's at last on the mend.' I said we would come down and see him at once but was told we mustn't; in fact Proby wanted us to discontinue visits. 'You'll unsettle him. It'll be weeks before he's anything like himself again and I'd like you to leave him to me. I'll ring you again tomorrow.'

I had an appointment with Dr Chance next morning. He showed so little surprise about Pongo that I guessed he already knew. I should mention that he already knew about my interest in Christian Science and he had one said that he would willingly work with Christian Scientists if only they would work with him. Now he said, in effect, 'About your own health. It's my job as a doctor to go on trying to find out what's wrong with you. I shall end up getting your tonsils out and probably your teeth as well. And if that doesn't work I shall try something else. Why don't you go back to your Christian Science and see what happens? Take a holiday. Get right out of England for at least six weeks. If your vet doesn't want you to see your dog . . .'

I said I would talk it over with Alec; and I found he was fully in favour of it. We decided to tour on the Continent. We would hire a car with a courier-driver and invite Murray Macdonald to come with us. . . .

While at Dubrovnik we rang Phyllis. There were times when I wondered if Proby might be exaggerating the extent of Pongo's improvement. But Phyllis assured us there was no exaggeration, though she warned us we must prepared ourselves for a shock: 'He's got so terribly fat.' Fat? The skin-and-bone dog we had left behind us? 'He's so fat,' said Phyllis, 'he looks like Henry the Eighth.'

Then why couldn't we go back to him? But Proby was still adamant. And I had really promised Dr Chance to stay away for six weeks. So from Dubrovnik we drove on to Austria, where eventually we found ourselves in a snowy twilight up in the mountains at Heiligenblut and were advised by our foolish courier to press on over the Gross Glockner Pass (over 12,000 feet). The snow and ice increased and the little German car began to slide dangerously backwards. We feared we were stranded for the night, but we were finally hauled by chain to the top of the pass. Next day we were thankful to reach Innsbruck where we released our courier who must have been thankful to see the last of us.

Before leaving by train for England, we paid a visit to my *Autumn Crocus* inn at Medratz; it was the last time I ever saw it. Indeed, it was the last Continental holiday we ever took. It had cost a fortune and I had enjoyed scarcely a minute of it. But I was returning in perfect health to a fully recovered dog.

Back at the flat, Helga told us he was waiting for us in the sitting room. I opened the door and, for one wild moment, really did think the wrong dog had been delivered. Then he proved himself Pongo by leaping at Alec – and it was a miracle that such an obese dog should leap so high. He was indeed the Henry VIII of dogs and frankly, he looked pretty hideous. But we knew that imprisoned in that fat dog was not only a slim dog, but also the one dog in the world for us. And he soon regained his normal figure, sturdy but never stout. The only real change in him was that he no longer chased rabbits. (The Christian Science practitioner took credit for this.)

The one sad thing about the linked illnesses of my dog and myself was that I never again saw Dr Chance. Of course I rang him up but he made it clear that, though he was there if wanted, he thought I should do better to lay off doctors as much as I could. He thus did himself out of a fairly lucrative patient and I am quite sure this was not because he was bored with me; during the three years I had been to him we had formed a genuine friendship, and had gradually taken to discussing life in general more than my health. He got rid of me simply because he wished me well.

My special brand of hay fever returned some seven years later, but less virulently and eventually settled into being occasional attacks of normal hay fever at the normal time of year. It was over a quarter-of-a-century before I went to a doctor, by which time my dear Maxwell Chance was dead. The doctor I went to was equally distinguished and very kind but, as I might have expected, he had no idea what was the matter with me, and before he had made up his mind what it was, it had stopped being it. Such a nice man he was; I'd have liked to see him again. One of the drawbacks to being a Christian Scientist is that it does one out of knowing doctors.

If I *am* a Christian Scientist, that is. I never again went to a practitioner nor so much as entered a Christian Science church. And I only forced myself to do that plaguey 'Lesson' for as long as Pongo lived; he had five happy years ahead of him. But I have continued my daily penance of reading Mrs Eddy out of gratitude for something which, whether or not it is Christian Science, undoubtedly came my way through her.

I onced asked Proby Cautley point blank if he believed Pongo had been saved by Christian Science. He said he could only repeat that the dog had been at death's door in the morning and on the road to recovery by the afternoon, and that in between those times he had been visited by a little man in a bowler hat who was obviously terrified of dogs.

*   *   *

On my voyage to America in January 1939 I began a Journal in a beautiful coral, leather bound, gilt-edged book, large and inspiring. It had been a present from my manager, Alec Beesley, whom I was soon to marry after seven years of all but legal marriage, following five years of devoted friendship, begun at Heal's where he was Advertising Manager and I was a Buyer. He was with me on the S.S. Manhattan, as was our much loved Dalmatian, Pongo, and our ex-actress house-keeper, Eileen Potter, whom we very much liked. This was to be no brief trip to New York (as my three previous ones had been) to help cast one of my plays and to go to theatres. This time we intended to see far more of America, certainly drive to California and then, possibly, go round the world.

I planned to write in the Journal every day and so, for many weeks, I did. Eventually the entries became less frequent, but much longer. Reading through the early pages I find the journal writer a stranger to me, not only to myself as I am now, but also to my remembered self. Could she have been quite sincere? Did I really like the S.S. Manhattan quite so much and enjoy the crossing more than any of my six previous Atlantic crossings? I now suspect I was out to sell myself happiness.

Someone who did, surprisingly, enjoy the voyage was Pongo. He was given a large double kennel from which he could see other dogs and swiftly started a flirtation with a brown lady spaniel. Alec exercised him round the decks every morning and, though always pleased to see Alec, he was also pleased to go back to his bed where he had churned his blankets into a nest. I spent much time with him and was encouraged to scratch his stomach but never permitted to tidy his bed. Sitting in his pen I learned to know owners who visited their dogs by their feet and legs.

*   *   *

Sometime after we settled down I was tempted to go back to Hollywood to work on the film of *Rebecca*. Alfred Hitchcock, who was to direct, had asked for me. I had known Hitchcock in London and liked him; I liked him even better after we now had two long telephone talks. The job was simply to supply dialogue; he was already working on the story-line with someone else and I doubted if I could turn out good dialogue for a story and characters so very unlike my own work and there was absolutely no scope for humour. Also I had not particularly liked the novel. I put all this to Hitchcock and asked him to think it over. He rang me next day to say I had given him a sleepless night but he still wanted me. He eventually persuaded me to agree but I regretted it afterwards, feeling sure I should let him down. I need not have worried. The terms of the contract were quite impossible. I should have had to remain for just as long as the studio wanted me. I bowed out with relief but regretted, and still regret, that I wasn't able to work with Hitchcock.

We settled down into our peaceful routine and I got on better with my play; I neared the end of the first act. Then disaster struck. Pongo bit a five-year-old child.

It happened by the swimming pool when Alec and Pongo were alone there. I was writing in my room. Pongo was safely tethered to a tree with his dinner dish beside him, in which he had left a few biscuits. Alec dived, swam under water, and came up to find Pongo barking and a child screaming. Alec had barely picked the child up before the bathing-pool attendant, who liked Pongo, rushed out of the hotel to say that he had seen the incident through a window and the child had both pulled Pongo's tail and attempted to steal Pongo's dinner. (Simultaneously?) The proprietors of the hotel then came out and were solidly on Pongo's side. The child was not a guest, but the son of people who lived nearby and who had been warned again and again not to let him come to the pool on his own. But he was both screaming and bleeding and a doctor had to be sent for, all the more so as the child's parents had now arrived and were most belligerent.

The doctor said it was a very small bite and Pongo, now at his affectionate best, was obviously a healthy dog, but as in America there was always a fear of rabies, the health authorities would have to be notified. We drove into Carmel and got Pongo an attorney.

The attorney couldn't have been kinder, nor could the health authorities who came next day to inspect Pongo and the child. We got the impression that they liked Pongo best. All that was asked of us was that we would stay in the locality for three weeks. Then another inspection took place, Pongo and the child were pronounced in perfect health. We gave the child a handsome present and Pongo's attorney refused to be paid for holding a watching brief. All was well – except that for me the peace of Robles had been shattered and my work on the play had dried up. So, too, had the Californian hills and though their uniform gold was almost more beautiful than their uniform green had been, for me they were now arid.

*　　*　　*

I don't remember any wintry weather but during the late autumn there was often a thick sea mist; once Pongo, out with us before going to bed, dashed off into the woods and came back smelling horrible after an encounter with a skunk. We rubbed him with some of the scented maquis-like herbs that grew all around hoping they might lessen the smell. They removed it entirely and the skunk discharge must have acted as a fixative for the herb scents, for Pongo smelt heavenly for days.

*　　*　　*

I had never felt such grief since my mother died when I was eighteen. The only thing which helped me at all was writing in my Journal, page after page about Pongo's life and death. At last I seemed to have written my worst grief out of my system, only to find it replaced by a frightening neurosis. I feared I had been responsible for Pongo's death.

One of the reasons we did not return to England was that we could not let him face the six month's quarantine. Had I, therefore, subconsciously wished him dead? If so, might I not now subconsciously wish Alec dead – because it was his attitude to war that was causing me to remain in America? To my conscious mind, he mattered more than anything in the world to me, but how did I know what my subconscious mind was up to? I had adored Pongo.

My subconscious mind must be firmly put in place. I would get another dog. I would get *two* dogs; that would be a double barrier against death wishes.

Of course I didn't let Alec know about my neurosis. I knew he was longing for another dog and we believed we should never get over Pongo's loss until we had one. I pointed out that *two* dogs might prevent our becoming so obsessed as we had been over Pongo. We must be sensible about these dogs.

There were no good Dalmatian puppies to be had anywhere near Carmel, but there were several well-known Dalmatian breeders near Beverly Hills. And the Rolls needed servicing. This would put it out of action for several days, but John van Druten at once offered us the use of his new car and chauffeur for the great Dalmatian hunt. So back to Beverly Hills.

We particularly wanted one of the puppies to be liver-spotted, not easy to find but we got one, a male aged two months, from a little-known kennels. And from Leo Meeker's famous 'Four-in-Hand' Kennels we were able to get a beautiful six months old black-and-white bitch. We eventually registered her as 'Four-in-Hand' Folly, and as the liver-spotted pup had no kennel name we registered him as 'Freckles of Finchingfield', hoping he would one day see our English village (which he did). He never learned to answer to 'Freckles' or any other name until we tried saying 'Buzz' very loudly. He took to that.

We boarded the pups with the Hollywood vet, who had once been Pongo's, until the Rolls was ready to take us back to Carmel. That return journey began disastrously; Folly was terribly car-sick. Fortunately, the car seats were protected by tough loose covers, but still we had to turn back; Alec had a theory that she might travel better by night. This proved to be the case. From darkness to dawn she was troubled by nothing but hunger; she had to be fed almost continuously. It took her six months to grow out of car sickness if she travelled by day. Hunger she never did grow out of. For her fourteen years of life she was the hungriest dog I ever knew.

So we came back at first light to the little house overlooking Seal Rock and at last the aching sense of loss for Pongo was assuaged. There is an old superstition that a good dog cannot enter heaven until his master has a new dog to guard him. I hoped that Pongo, now free even of his love for us, would find a shore as beautiful as Carmel's to gallop on and all his old desire to gallop.

*   *   *

Soon after Jack went back to New York, our vet examined Folly and said we might expect five or six puppies and, though they were not due for ten days or so, we had better settle her somewhere quiet. So back she went into the garden guest room, a large bedroom with a very small bathroom. She seemed quite happy there, but the next morning we found she had destroyed the upholstery of an armchair, ripped a mattress, damaged a rug beyond repair and had retired to the small, dark bathroom to which she returned every time we took her out. So we made up her bed there and tried to keep our minds off what the damage she had done was going to cost us.

A couple of days later, after having some friends to dinner, we went down to say goodnight to her and were astonished to find that three puppies had already been born and another was now arriving. Folly washed it, we dried it and then put it with the other puppies. She was showing no sign of distress and at this rate, if she was only going to have five or six, the whole litter would soon have arrived. But she didn't stop at six and it was when the seventh was being born that we noticed something frightening: the pups were being born *green*. We knew, of course, that Dalmatians have no spots when born, but surely the puppies ought to be white? Then a hideous suspicion struck us. As advised by a text book we had made the basis of Folly's bed a piece of carpet and that carpet was green. Was the dye coming off on the pups?

It was long after midnight but I dashed indoors and telephoned our vet. He said no, it was not the carpet, the pups had every right to be green – something to do with the afterbirth. He was very patient, poor man, but he drew the line at coming to help us. If we and Folly had achieved seven puppies, we were doing very nicely and there probably wouldn't be any more. He was going back to sleep.

I made sure that poor, deserted Buzz was sleeping peacefully in my bedroom, got some warm milk for Folly and returned to find the eighth puppy had arrived. Soon came the ninth. By now Folly was moaning a little and looking pretty exhausted – as well she might, poor girl, seeing this was her first litter. We told her and ourselves that this would be the last pup, but we were wrong. As the night wore on there was a tenth, then an eleventh, then a twelfth. Then the thirteenth pup was born seemingly dead.

We had read in a Dalmatian text book that patched puppies should instantly be put down (patches, unlike spots, show at birth) but we had already treated our one patched pup with the utmost care. Now, however, I felt that in view of this huge litter, I could well be resigned to the death of this last weak and particularly small puppy. Not so Alec. He massaged it and rubbed it with a towel. And then a seeming miracle happened. One moment it was limply motionless – its nose and the skin showing through its hair were a sickly yellow. And then gradually its whole body was suffused with pink, its mouth opened, its little legs wriggled. It was alive! Alec said he felt like God. (Its birth was to be described by me in a book written over twelve years later and eventually recreated in Walt Disney's wonderful cartoon film, *101 Dalmatians*.) The sun was up before Folly delivered her final puppy, making fifteen in all – a staggeringly high number for a first litter. Only then did I get out of my new and expensive, black lace dinner dress.

* * *

Alec spent much of the weekend with Folly, rotating the pups so that fifteen could share accommodation for eight. Obviously she couldn't go on feeding them all and on Monday, after much telephoning, Alec located a dog-pound where they had a stray with some milk to give. He drove off to get her, also bringing back a doll's feeding bottle and an old fashioned fountain pen filler. Astonishingly, the stray was a Dalmatian, too. We installed her in Alec's bathroom and gave her a enormous meal of meat and milk. Though pitifully thin, she had milk to give but would need a lot of feeding up. I stayed with her until she settled down to sleep on the bed we had made up for her; she was timid but very friendly. We now had eighteen Dalmatians in the house.

Alec spent the afternoon with Folly, doing duty as a foster mother; we felt the stray must have a long rest before we tried her on the job. The doll's feeding bottle worked well but took a very long time. The fountain pen filler was quicker, but it was difficult to regulate the flow. Still, Alec did extremely well, though in great discomfort. We had been advised to draw the bathroom curtains and make it resemble a dark cupboard, so Alec, sharing the cramped floor space, was continually bumping his head into the bath, the lavatory basin or the lavatory seat – and he was extremely hot in the California heat. By the time he came out he was tottering – and covered in milk.

The next day we introduced one of the puppies to the foster-mother. There was one frightening moment and then she took to it, fed it and washed it. We brought her two more – thanking heaven Folly couldn't count. All went well. We felt that was enough for one day and Alec again spent the afternoon feeding Folly's puppies. I tried my hand but was no good whatever; the puppies would not keep still. And anyway I had to cope with the house and visits from Charlie. By the Wednesday I felt I must have some help so Alec drove to the Employment Bureau for a cleaner.

* * *

Of the fourteen places mentioned in my Journal only one evokes a vivid memory. On the thirteenth day, at Blythe, California, I was on my way to get an early evening meal (Alec and I usually went separately, so that our dogs need not be left alone in the car) when I saw an old English sheepdog puppy, obviously lost. It was dashing in and out of the traffic; twice I saw it narrowly avoid being run over. I managed to catch it and found it was still small enough for me to carry, so I took it to a nearby petrol station and got it some water (unwillingly given) and was told it had been about all day. All I got for my suggestion that the police should be notified was a surly headshake.

So I carried it to a restaurant intending to buy it some food. There was a pleasant young police officer eating at the counter who told the cashier to telephone the police station. Before I had even got as far as ordering the pup's meal, I heard the strident sound of a police siren and along came a police car, bristling with policemen. They sprang out with guns drawn and hurled themselves into the restaurant, obviously expecting at least to quell a riot – they had only been told they were urgently needed. On being faced with one puppy, now being fed sweet biscuits, they exploded with laughter and set about soothing an obviously eccentric English woman. Sure, they would take the dog to the police station. Yes, indeed, they'd give it a good meal. No, of course, they wouldn't just turn it over to the dog pound; if they couldn't find its owner they would probably adopt it. One elderly Irish cop said he'd personally give it a home – anyone would be glad to have a cute pup like that. It was finally borne away, with the lights of the police car flashing, the siren blaring. I hoped the noise didn't frighten it as much as it always frightened me.

From *Look Back with Love*;
Look Back with Mixed Feelings;
Look Back with Astonishment;
Look Back with Gratitude

BOBBY SHORT

The Treachery of the Cat

A COUPLE OF OLD chickens, who laid an egg now and then, had the run of the yard. We had a grey cat named Bunny, because she'd been born on Easter Sunday, and a dog named Pal that my brother Reg had brought home as a pup. Pal, a mongrel with a dominant strain of German shepherd going for him, immediately attached himself to my mother, right to the source of all good things. He used to wait on the corner of Robinson and English for her to come home from work, watching fixedly all the way up past Lincoln Park to Logan Avenue until he saw that tiny, distant speck six or eight blocks away. Then he'd race headlong to meet her. He never chased cars like other dogs. Pal's personal quirk was uniquely his own – he chased shadows on the wall. We also had a goldfish, who'd be frozen in his bowl on those winter nights when we were without coal for the furnace. But in the morning, as soon as a fire got started in the kitchen range, the fish would thaw out, good as new, and pick up his leisurely route back and forth through his pink castle gate.

* * *

The Schanettes also told wonderful stories – Louisiana stories about the animals, the tar baby, and the devil baby who was a trickster, always handing out smart advice and scheming to get everyone else in trouble. And there was a story that explained why dogs and cats are enemies. The tale is an ancient one, solemnly recorded nowadays in one form or another by anthropologists and sociologists rummaging through the West African coastal countries. Well, *I* heard it from Daise Schanette in Chicago. And she told it charmingly.

Once upon a time, it seems, the dog and the cat were married.

One fine day, the cat said to the dog, 'Husband, I have good news. I'm going to have a baby.'

Yes, that certainly was good news, said the dog. And he had good news too. He had found a large pot of lard and hidden it down in the cellar. When winter came, they would have plenty of food in the house. So, the days went by, and one evening the dog was rocking on his front porch, playing his banjo and singing some little Creole song.

And he turned to his wife, the cat, and said, 'Well, wife, have you decided on a name for the child?' And the cat just couldn't think, so she licked her lips and she said, 'Yes, I've decided to call the child Top Off.'

What a strange name for a child, thought the dog, but he kept on rocking and singing.

A few weeks later he again said to his wife, 'Have you thought of a better name for the child?'

The cat couldn't think, so she licked her lips and said, 'Yes, Half Gone.' A few weeks later, the cat said 'All Gone' was the name of the child.

Then the dog went down cellar to find that the pot of lard was empty. 'Now I know where you got those names – Top Off, Half Gone, All Gone!' So he chased the cat out of the house. And ever since that day, dogs and cats have been mortal enemies.

From *Black and White Baby*

LUDWIG BEMELMANS

Dog Story

FOR MANY YEARS our summer vacations were spent in an old peasant house, and everybody who came to see us was breathless, partly on account of the beauty of the scenery, but chiefly because the house stood atop a steep hill, overlooking a village on the shore of a remote Austrian lake.

The landscape was as simple as bread and water. A ring of dark, green mountains which anyone could climb reflected themselves in the silent lake. At one side of this lake, a string of gay rowboats shifted back and forth in the currents of the green water. Each boat had the name of a girl painted on its side, and from the end of the pier to which they were tied I went swimming while Wally, my dachshund (she was so small that I carried her home in my coat pocket whenever we had walked too far), slept in one of the boats, in the shade of the bench that spans the center. Wally disliked both sun and water.

From the pier one walked into the garden of the White Horse

Tavern, a cool space, filled with yellow tables and chairs, shaded by an arbor of wild grapevines.

Here usually sat a man of good appetite; he was a butcher and Wally's best friend, a plain fat man with a round shaven head, a large mustache, the caricature of a German, and certainly a butcher. He owned the house to the left of ours, on the hill.

After he had finished eating and laid knife and fork aside, he would take a piece of bread, break it into two pieces, call for Wally, and, mopping up the rest of the sauce on his plate, carefully feed it to the dog.

He paid his bill, said good-morning, blew his nose into a large blue handkerchief, finished his beer, and took his cane from a hook, put on an alpine hat, and in a wide circle walked around the baroque, salmon colored church.

Next to the church was a fountain, with a statue of St Florian, the patron saint of firemen, standing on a tall column above it. As the butcher passed this fountain, the lower half of him was always hidden by the wide basin and only his hat, coat, and arms – rowing in the air – seemed to walk up the street. In a while we followed him up the hill.

The sounds of this remote place were as comfortable as its panorama. In the morning twilight, Wally was at the garden gate, barking at the cattle that were driven up to the high meadows. From their necks hung bronze bells, suspended from heavy, quill-embroidered leather straps. The bells clanged away into the distance, and their place was taken by the church bells below calling to early mass at about seven.

The little motor boat that zigzagged back and forth over the lake had another bell, which announced its first departure half an hour later. The bell on the schoolhouse rang at eight.

As the sun rose over the high wall of mountains it changed all the colors in the valley and lit up the underside of the clouds that hung in the thin clear air above. Children sang in the schoolhouse, the birds in the trees, carpets were beaten in gardens, and the cobbler started hammering.

At half-past ten followed the screech of the small wheels of the daily train from Salzburg as it slowed down to negotiate the sharp curve which carried it into the village. At this sound Wally sent up a long, high flute-like cry. She took that up again for another sound that came from the same direction as the train, the tearing howl of the whistle which announced that it was noon in the sawmill at the far end of the lake.

The worst sound, one that made the little dog's hair stand on end and sent her for protection under a couch, was the music that started at one, Mozart, Bach, Haydn, Schubert, and Beethoven. It came from the house on our right. In its living-room, little girls, in one-hour shifts, glared at études, cramped their small fingers into claws, and performed awful concertos on two old Bechstein grand pianos.

This went on until four. When the last of the little blond girls had left, Frau Dorothea von Moll, the music teacher, came out of the house, held her temples for a moment, and then walked slowly up and down in her kitchen garden. She wandered between even rows of spinach, kohlrabi, beets, celery, peas, and carrots and the large leaves of rhubarb.

She wore a severe black costume, on cold days a mantle trimmed with worn Persian lamb, an old grey bonnet, and a watch on a long thin golden chain. She looked like someone deliberately and carefully made up to play the role of a distinguished old lady in reduced circumstances.

She went out little; a few gentle, little old ladies formed a group that met in her garden house on Thursdays. She entertained them with coffee and Gugelhupf, a native cake, and with anecdotes of musicians and the great people she had known when her husband, the famous pianist Arnulf von Moll, was still alive.

As soon as the pianos were stilled, Wally ran down the steep stairs that led to Frau Dorothea's garden as if to thank her because the terrible concert was over. Wally see-sawed down the incline – front legs first, back legs after. Then she squeezed through an opening in the fence and attended the Thursday teas, eating cake and drinking milk. On other days she just walked up and down between the rows of vegetables, behind Frau Dorothea.

Wally's initial cost was very small, notwithstanding the fact that her father was the Bavarian champion Hasso von der Eulenburg, and that she personally was entered on her distinguished pedigree as Waltraut von der Eulenburg. However, she became expensive almost immediately.

One Sunday morning she pulled the cloth off the breakfast table and with it every cherished cup and saucer of a Sèvres tea set. The hot water from a falling pot scalded her, and Wally walked about for a week wrapped in bandages. As soon as this was forgotten she ate a box of matches, and when she had recovered from that experience and come back from the veterinary, she worked a whole night to rip the satin cover off a Biedermeier love seat, took all the horsehair carefully out of it, carrying small tufts of it all over the house, down to Frau Dorothea's, and over to the butcher's garden.

There were many more nice things in this old house of which we were very fond, and it seemed best to send Wally away to be trained. One day a forest ranger, who had trained many dogs, took her away in his knapsack. To this experience I owe the knowledge that dogs can recognize a picture, a fact often disputed.

The forest rangers are government employees; they wear green mountain uniforms and faded felt hats with plumes. Most of them have Santa Claus beards, and usually they smoke long pipes that hang down the middle of the beard and end over heavy silver watch chains that are weighted down with old thalers. They carry knapsacks and over their shoulders hang double-barreled shotguns.

This forester found Wally more stubborn than any dachshund he had ever trained. He was very strict with her, rubbed her nose on the floor whenever she had done indignities to his clean house, gave her a few slaps on the backside, and threw her out into the forest.

Wally came home to us a few weeks later a completely changed dog. A model dog. Soon after her return a new tobacco was put on the market. It was called 'Forester's Cut' and was wonderfully and widely advertised. Large posters were pasted up everywhere; on them appeared a package of 'Forester's Cut,' and the picture of a forester smoking it with delight. He wore the rakish hat with the plume, the grass-green uniform, the white beard, the shotgun, and was just such a one as Wally had been living with.

Wherever Wally saw this picture, she went for it. She strained on her leash, the little hair chest became a bellows and started to work in and out, the lips were pulled up from over her teeth, and long rolls of thunder came from her throat. She shook with anger and looked like an old woodcut of the devil in a peasant Bible. She did nothing about the picture when it was shown to her in magazines, where it appeared in full colors but was reduced to half a page, nor did she recognize it when she saw a poster that was life-sized but printed in black and white.

At the end of that summer's vacation, we took Wally to America with us. It was not a happy idea and we should have followed the advice of Frau Dorothea, who wanted to keep Wally for us until our return. Wally hated the big liner. She was in a good kennel and had the company of two theatrical black poodles, good-natured animals, used to travel, and able to ride a bicycle and to count up to ten. The food was excellent, the sailor who took care of her a friendly fellow. But Wally remained curled up in a corner of her compartment, an unhappy, defiant coil of dachshund. She looked with mistrust at the ocean, with despair at the masts, the funnels, and the ventilators of the ship. She never played with the other dogs and stopped trembling only when she was wrapped up and resting on my lap in a deck chair.

Wally did not like New York any better than the ship. Her memories were a nightmare of fire-engine sirens, revolving doors, backfiring automobiles, the absence of grass and bushes, the rarity of trees. We decided the next summer to leave her with Frau Dorothea, who took care of our house while we were away.

This also was a sad arrangement. Frau Dorothea wrote that Wally came home only for meals, that she ate little, became thinner and thinner, sat in front of the closed door of our house, and that even her friend the butcher, leaning over the fence from his side of the garden and holding up choice pieces of meat, could not console her. Once she almost bit him when he came up to the house to speak to her.

We asked a dog specialist for advice and he suggested that we send her some piece of personal wearing apparel. A pair of old slippers, an old skiing mitten to which I had lost the mate, and a sweater with a few holes were dispatched with the next mail.

This helped a good deal. We read in happier letters that Wally now had a basket on the porch of our house and busied herself packing and unpacking it. She carried the slippers or the glove proudly through the garden, slept inside, under, and on top of the sweater. She still sat on the porch waiting for us until dark, but she ate now, slept at night in Frau Dorothea's house, and the butcher was allowed to come into the garden, was welcome, with a bone, or even just as he was.

We did not open the house the next summer; it was the year of the Anschluss. From letters we gathered that the village was not noticeably disturbed; a new strategic highway was being built along the lake, new songs were being sung, some people had become very quiet and others too loud, and a few places had been renamed; but to a dog, Hermann Göring Strasse and Adolf Hitler Platz are as good as Heinrich Heine Strasse and Dollfuss Platz.

Early the next year, Frau Dorothea had a visitor at whom Wally barked. He was a portly, serious business man from Salzburg and he offered to buy her house. The man's name was Hermann Brettschneider.

Frau Dorothea said that she loved her home, had no reason to sell it, and would certainly never sell it at the price he offered her. She told him that our house was for sale. He did not want our house. He left.

A few weeks later he came back again, this time in the parade uniform of a captain of Storm Troopers, the medal of the Order of the

Blood, highest Nazi decoration, on his chest. He sat a long while in her garden house and talked, and he left finally, red in the face. Frau Dorothea still did not want to sell.

Soon after he was gone, the piano lessons stopped, the little blond girls were forbidden to come. The old ladies also sent their regrets and stayed away on Thursdays. One night windows were broken, and then the butcher was arrested because he had come out of his garden to beat up a young man in uniform. The young man in uniform had been busy with a pail of red paint and a brush; he had lettered on the wall of Frau Dorothea's house, 'Get out of town, Sarah – make haste, go back to Jerusalem.'

On the first of the next month the house was newly painted, the windows repaired; the balcony broke out in Nazi bunting, and Herr Hauptmann Brettschneider gave a garden party bright with uniforms.

Frau Dorothea moved out of the village, to a house near the sawmill, and during the daytime she stayed indoors or in her little garden.

Wally, of course, was Aryan. She could run around and she made the long run to our house twice a day. She climbed to the terrace, unpacked the dirty slippers, and carried the skiing glove about. The butcher was in a concentration camp, but the Brettschneider housekeeper gave Wally occasional pieces of ham, ends of sausages, cuts of pork. Storm Troopers keep good kitchens.

When it was time for her to come home, late at night, Frau Dorothea usually walked to meet her in the dark. It was a rather dangerous place to walk. It was a freightyard of a place; its contours were an uncertain smudge, much like a charcoal drawing. There was a lamp about sixty feet from the spot where the railroad tracks crossed the new cement highway. It was here that the wheels of the train screeched at half-past ten in the morning. The highway entered the village in a blind, sudden turn, something the engineers would have liked to avoid, but the alternative would have been to drill a tunnel through two mountains. At the side of the highway, on its outer curve, the ground was soft and the terrain dropped down to the rocky bed of a river, the outflow of the lake. About where the lamp was, the water thundered down over a dam. It was an ideal setting for accidents, this place.

The accident happened on the night of March 7, 1939. A battery of tanks was being rushed to the Eastern Front – Front is the right word, for Germany was in a state of war – and came to the sawmill somewhat ahead of a schedule, at the moment that Wally was about to cross the highway.

The beams of the strong headlights, the hellish clatter and tumult of the machinery, and the apparition of terror that a tank is, must have frozen the little dog to the middle of the road.

The driver of tank Number 1 tried to avoid her. He suddenly put on the brakes, that is, he retarded the left tractor belt and advanced the right. Four of the tanks behind him piled into one another, and his had turned too far, left the highway, and rolled over three times as it went down the river bed.

It went into the shallow water (the sawmill closes the locks at night, to have more water for the turbine the next morning) right side up, and the two men in it, in overalls, loosened their belts and climbed out of the machine. Tanks Number 2, 3, 4, and 5 were somewhat damaged.

From the tower of tank Number 6 jumped a baby of a lieutenant with his first mustache. The men had climbed out of the other tanks and stood in a ring about Wally. The lieutenant picked her up, patted her head, spoke soft words to her, and held her to his cheek.

When Frau Dorothea came forward he clicked his heels, saluted, and smiled. 'Dear lady, so sorry,' he said, and gave the dog to her. While the mechanics set to work repairing the damaged tanks, the young lieutenant lingered a moment or two, asking the dog's name and talking to Frau Dorothea about her. Then he went over to the edge of the highway.

At his direction, pulleys and spades appeared. Chains and cables were carried down the embankment. As two bugs might pull another, a dead one, under a leaf somewhere to eat him, two of the tanks above, without effort or strain, dragged the tank up out of the river bed and set it on the road. The lieutenant waved at Frau Dorothea and Wally as he got into the top of his machine. Tank Number 6 started forward, then the other tanks fell into line, one by one, and the procession continued on its way to the Czechoslovakian frontier.

From *Small Beer*

GUY GIBSON

Victim

NEXT DAY I BECAME the second war casualty. I had just been down to move my kit from C Charlie after the night before. When I entered the Mess I noticed a large black Labrador sitting in the hall. Being fond of dogs I went up to him and gave him a friendly pat to show that he was welcome to the Mess, but the dog did not agree. In a flash his great jaws had clamped down on my hand and then I was running into the washroom, hand streaming with blood and with half the seat of my pants missing. They were new ones, too. As the monster chased me, jaws dripping for another bite, Pitcairn happened to come out of the bar with his flying-boots on. A hefty man was Pit, and one kick lifted the brute into the air and it ran away howling. Then I was free, but the damage was already done. I could practically see daylight through the great holes in my hand, and even if I say it myself, it was extremely painful. The boys and I wanted the dog court-martialled on the spot, but it happened to belong to the Group-Captain, so he was given a free pardon and told not to do it again. The Group-Captain came to see me while I was having the fifth stitch put in. He was breathing heavily because he had just had his lunch. 'I hear you had some trouble with Zimba,' he said. 'Pity. You want to watch him.' Watch him! I nearly blew up on the spot. Of all the things to say. But then I wasn't feeling too good at the time. Poor old Zimba had to pay later for his crimes though. After running up the unenviable score of 2 certs, 4 probables and many damaged, he was finally posted elsewhere. Maybe his score is even greater today.

Wing-Commander Jordan, who had taken the squadron over, gave me thirty-six hours' sick leave for this incident. Jordan was a fine type, and in the few days he was in the squadron everyone got to know and like him well. He spent most of his time shouting. I remember one day I went into his office and he had two telephones, one on either ear. To the Group-Commander he was explaining that he only had nineteen aeroplanes and the nineteenth would not be serviceable for some days. On the other phone he was speaking to the Mess about the bad condition of the roast potatoes he had had for lunch. After a while I think he got mixed up between the two phones and the Adjutant had to close the door before he burst his sides. He was never afraid of taking decisions, and the thirty-six hours' leave he gave me was entirely off his own bat, as at that time there was definitely no leave for anybody in the Services.

My brother was getting married on the 5th and I was to be his best man, so the thirty-six hours came in handy. The journey to Rugby was most eventful in a browning-off sort of way. It was still boiling hot and the blood from my hand had begun to soak through the bandage and on to the sling. As I stood waiting for my train at Nottingham station an old woman came up. 'Bad luck, you poor young boy,' she said. 'Kiel, I suppose?'

Then a young man – 'My brother was on your do. Simpson's his name. He wasn't wounded too, was he?'

At the wedding an old man put the cap on it. He sidled up with the air of a man about to give away a great secret. 'I was in the last lot, my boy,' he whispered. 'I admire you for that.'

I nearly shot a cat. Can't a chap walk around with a bloody arm in a sling (and I mean bloody) without everyone pre-supposing he had had it shot off or something? Dogs bite sometimes. One bit me. But it was no good, and I reached for the bottle.

From *Enemy Coast Ahead*

GEORGE ABBOTT

Duty Calls

WE HAD SOME trouble with the costumes for *Look, Ma, I'm Dancin'!*, but Mary and The Mannequin came to our assistance nobly. It was almost a great show – but not quite. I don't think I can remember a funnier entrance than Nancy Walker coming down the New York Central platform with a gigantic wolfhound as tall as she was. My combination gardener and chauffeur, Lawrence Larry, had a chance to go on the stage as a redcap, and he was put in charge of the dog. One night, out of kindness, one of the stagehands brought the wolfhound a bone. When the time came for his entrance, the wolfhound didn't want to leave his bone; he became ferocious, and for a time it looked as though the dog would lose his entrance and the redcap would lose an arm. But Larry had a great way with animals, and he was able to drag the beast onstage just at the last minute, though the audience may have wondered why the dog was looking so longingly off-stage right. . . .

At this time Mary invited a couple of visitors from the West to come and live with us. One was a fierce collie named Val, known to all my friends as Fangs. He was a remarkable beast and a great individualist. He arrived in Sands Point groggy after five or six days in a baggage car. The family next door had two aggressive and disagreeable Doberman pinschers and a boxer. These dogs intruded upon our property frequently, snarling at us and making themselves generally unpleasant. Now, sensing that there was a newcomer on the premises, they came over to investigate. They found Val in the garage recuperating from his ride, but when they threatened him he rose on groggy feet and offered to give battle. We came to his rescue. The next day, however, we had to leave Val, for we were going on a trip for ten days. We gave the servants instructions to protect him as best they could and took off for the Adirondacks.

As our car came up the drive on return, a wild beast charged out snapping and barking as though he were going to tear the machine to pieces. Val had recovered. He became a cringing, affectionate, wonderful warm dog the minute he recognized Mary, but though he accepted me he would have nothing to do with me. From the servants we learned that Val had grown strong enough a day or two after our departure to take on the neighboring dogs singly and collectively until he had become master of the field.

One day we were all out on the terrace, and the dog was being patted as he went from one guest to another; as he passed by me I too gave him an affectionate tap, whereupon he turned and bit me in the face. Mary telephoned her mother in California to find if the dog had had rabies shots; there seemed to be a great deal of uncertainty, so to be safe Abbott had to have shots for a couple of weeks. But Val was contrite about his attack on me and became docile and friendly. When winter came we couldn't take him to the city and had to put him in a kennel. We went out to visit him a couple of times, but he always put on such a scene that it was more than we could bear. He was a rugged individual; he never gave in; he barked all winter long and never accepted the prison to which we had sentenced him. By spring, he had almost lost his voice, and he had certainly lost his health. I grew to like him better than any dog I ever knew, and when he died that summer I felt that I had brought this about by an unjust sentence. He was a terror to everybody but his friends, but he was loyal to them. The next year we got another collie, but he was a poor substitute. He was too aristocratic; he seemed a tepid dog after fierce old Val. He was very handsome, however, and somebody stole him.

From *Mister Abbot*

F. SCOTT FITZGERALD

Berating the Landlady

1403 North Laurel Avenue
Hollywood, California
July 29, 1940

Dear Mrs Neuville:

I thought the other day that a large rat had managed to insert itself into the plaster above my bedroom and workroom. I was, however, surprised that it apparently slept at night and worked in the day, causing its greatest din around high noon.

However, yesterday, much to my surprise, I deduced from the sounds it emitted that it was a dog, or rather several dogs, and evidently training for a race, for they ran round and round the tin roof. Now I don't know how these greyhounds climbed up the wall but I know dog-racing is against the law of California – so I thought you'd like to know. Beneath the arena where these races occur an old and harassed literary man is gradually going mad.

August 12, 1940

The woman across the hall takes her dog on that bare and resounding roof every morning. It is impossible to work or sleep while the riot is in progress. Today we had some words about it and she informed me of her intention to continue – though if I took to rapping on her roof she would doubtless consider it an outrage.

I believe that the roof was locked when I took this apartment and I request that it be locked again. As a respecter of the rights of others I know she has no legal or moral right to perpetuate this nuisance.

[F. Scott Fitzgerald died on 20 December]

EUGENE O'NEILL

From the Grave

SHORTLY AFTER THE couple had moved into the château they bought a fox terrier, an excitable creature that enjoyed swimming with O'Neill, but he faded into the background when they acquired Silverdene Emblem from England, an uncommonly bright Dalmatian who won the wholehearted love of both his masters. Indeed, Carlotta's feeling for her daughter and O'Neill's for his three children seem to have been markedly less than what they felt for their 'Blemie.' Until his death twelve years later, he was, in O'Neill's words, 'a comfort to [us] in time of sorrow, and a reason for added joy in [our] happiness,' while Carlotta said, 'He's the only one of our children who never disappointed us.' His collar, leash, overcoat and raincoat were made to order at Hermès of Paris, and he slept on quality linens in a miniature four-poster with a canopy. 'When Gene and I read by the fireplace,' Carlotta recalled, 'Blemie would lie first by one of us, then go over and lie by the other, so as not to show any partiality. He didn't want to hurt anyone's feelings. A diplomatic little gentleman, our Blemie.'

Lillian Gish, concurring that the Dalmatian was exceptionally winning, says that he was 'a person, a full-fledged member of the family, a regular host at the château. When breakfast was brought to you, he'd trot along with an air that suggested he wanted to make sure everything was all right. Carlotta wrote me that after I left, Blemie threw himself on the ground, stretched, and gave a deep sigh, as though to say, "Thank heaven, that's over." He was now free of responsibility.'

*   *   *

The latter months of 1940 found the O'Neills increasingly worried about Blemie; already half blind and deaf, he went lame from falling downstairs and had to be carried around like a baby. 'Gene and I spoil him no end,' Carlotta told Dorothy Commins, 'but always say he is the only one of our children who has not disillusioned us – & always seemed conscious (& grateful) of our efforts to do all we could for his welfare & happiness!'

Blemie died on December 17, after a long spell of dry weather, and as he was being buried in a grove not far from the house, the rattling of the leaves sounded to Carlotta like 'sad castanets.' Scarcely had the O'Neills returned indoors when a thunderstorm broke, the first rain in months, giving them the feeling that nature was mourning with them. To relieve his feelings that day, Eugene wrote 'The Last Will and Testament of Silverdene Emblem O'Neill,' a charming piece that contains echoes of Whitman's 'Song of Myself' (O'Neill had been rereading the poet earlier this year).

In the 'Will' O'Neill wrote under Blemie's name: 'I have little in the way of material things to leave. Dogs are wiser than men. They do not set great store upon things. They do not waste their days hoarding property. They do not ruin their sleep worrying about how to keep the objects they have, and to obtain the objects they have not. There is nothing of value I have to bequeath except my love and my faith . . . if I should list all those who have loved me it would force my Master to write a book. Perhaps it is vain of me to boast when I am so near death, which returns all beasts and vanities to dust, but I have always been an extremely lovable dog.

'I ask my Master and Mistress to remember me always, but not to grieve for me too long . . . It is painful for me to think that even in death I should cause them pain. Let them remember that while no dog has ever had a happier life (and this I owe to their love and care for me) now that I have grown blind and deaf and lame . . . my pride has sunk to a sick, bewildered humiliation. I feel life is taunting me with having over-lingered my welcome. It is time I said goodbye, before I become too sick a burden on myself and on those who love me. It will be sorrow to leave them, but not sorrow to die. Dogs do not fear death as men do. We accept it as part of life, not as something alien and terrible which destroys life. What may come after death, who knows? I would like to believe with those of my fellow Dalmatians who are devout Mohammedans, that there is a Paradise where one is always young and full-bladdered; where all the day one dillies and dallies with an amorous multitude of houris . . . .

'I am afraid this is too much for even such a good dog as I am to expect. But peace, at least, is certain. Peace and long rest for weary old heart and head and limbs, an eternal sleep in the earth I have loved so well. Perhaps, after all, this is best.'

After O'Neill gave Carlotta the 'Will,' he did not mention Blemie for months, but often, as they sat before the fireplace, she caught him glancing first at her feet, then at his own, where the Dalmatian used to divide his time. Often, too, Eugene walked up to the grave, which had a marble headstone inscribed, 'Sleep in Peace, Faithful Friend,' and would stand there a long time.

Louis Sheaffer, from *O'Neill: Son and Artist*

MICHAEL CURTIZ

A Spurned Extra in Casablanca

ONE MORE BRIEF delay was caused by Curtiz's mangled English. On the day he arrived to shoot the first Black Market scene, he informed the properties man, who already had assembled an impressive group of animals for the shot, that he needed a 'poodle, a black poodle.' The request seemed unusual, but the prop man was not about to argue with the temperamental director, so he set about finding the dog while everyone waited.

As luck would have it, there was just such an animal available, and the man got it to the set within half an hour. 'It's very nice,' said Curtiz, 'but I want a poodle.' When the poor technician tried to explain that

that's what the dog was, Curtiz exploded: 'I wanted a poodle in the street! A poodle of water! Not a goddamn dog!'

Frank Miller, from Casablanca

BEATRIX POTTER

A Fortnight Before Death

A T PRESENT I AM in bed recovering from a cold; *not* flue [sic] or any temperature, just a creaking & thumping. As my heart has never been normal since I had rheumatic fever as a girl – I don't think much about it, and I was often worse in London. But if an old person of 77 continues to play these games – well it can be done once too often. I have plenty to do indoors and the little dogs are great company – most efficient foot warmers.

To Stephanie Duke, 10 December 1943

FRANKLIN ROOSEVELT

Democratic Dog

H E RETURNED TO his quarters for lunch with members of his party and took a leisurely nap afterward. In the evening, in spite of orders for a darkened ship, he sat on the quarter deck with officers and some of the 1,600 sailors and Marines to watch a movie. It wasn't until the third day that he began to notice the absence of Fala from his side. [An earlier dog, Major, had bitten Ramsay Macdonald.] The dog disappeared below decks with monotonous regularity. In the evening the President thought he had discovered the reason.

Fala appeared to be shedding or shorn. There was little black hair left on his back. Mr Roosevelt ordered an aide to investigate. Within an hour he understood what had happened. Some of the sailors had coaxed Fala to the crew mess to feed him tidbits. The dog had been a conscious party to the wrongdoing. One sailor said he had a kid brother back home who would appreciate a lock of the hair of the President's dog. This led to a snip here and there a snip. Many sailors seemed to recollect the affection of loved ones for Fala. Mr Roosevelt issued an order, through Captain Walter L. Calhoun, that the dog was not to be fed, and not to be clipped.

*   *   *

On the evening of September 23 the President emerged in his wheelchair from draperies behind the big dais in the Presidential Room of the New Statler Hotel. Screened by Secret Service men, he was lifted up to his seat near the center of the dais and, as the friendly crowd of Teamsters and their friends roared approval, Mr Roosevelt beamed his great smile and held both hands aloft in greeting. To his left was Daniel Tobin, Teamster president; to the right was AFL president William Green. In front of his dinner plate stood an assortment of silvery microphones. He looked old but trim in his black tie and dinner jacket. While others ate, the President barely touched dinner, working instead on the final draft of his speech with a pen. . . .

As he marshaled his arguments and rolled his eyes ceilingward in disbelief, the President was working his way toward the 'crusher.' The paragraph, which would in time be one of the best remembered of all the Roosevelt speeches, was his own. At Quebec FDR had penned it and asked Grace Tully to mail it to Rosenman for inclusion in the speech:

'These Republican leaders have not been content with attacks on me, or my wife, or on my sons,' he said sorrowfully. 'No, not content with that, they now include my little dog Fala.' The audience began to roar. 'Well, of course, I don't resent attacks, and my family doesn't resent attacks, but Fala does resent them.' Then, archly, with both brows high on his forehead. 'You know, Fala is Scotch, and being a Scottie, as soon as he learned that the Republican fiction writers in Congress and out had concocted a story that I had left him behind on the Aleutian Islands and had sent a destroyer back to find him – at a cost to the taxpayers of two or three, or eight or twenty million dollars – his Scotch soul was furious. He has not been the same dog since.' The surf of laughter hit a high-water mark. The President had to wait to continue. 'I am accustomed to hearing malicious falsehoods about myself, such as that old worm-eaten chestnut that I have represented myself as indispensable. But I think I have a right to resent, to object to libelous statements about my dog.'

The success of the speech was assured. Millions of Americans at home, listening to radios, were laughing.

Jim Bishop, from *F. D. R.'s Last Year*

WYNDHAM LEWIS

Exile

WE ARE ON the grim side just now. The death of our hirsute gremlin has left an ugly gap. You will understand that people never forgive you for possessing more of anything than themselves – more reputation is a sore offence: and if you put yourself in their power they can make you tolerably uncomfortable. By coming to Canada – in the middle of a world-war – I did that. And my wife has had to pay as well as myself. So this small creature, which stood for all that was benevolent in the universe, sweetened the bitter medicine for her. Like the spirit of a simpler and saner time, this fragment of primitive life confided his destiny to her, and went through all the black days beside us. She feels she has been wanting in some care – for why should this growth in his side, almost as big as his head, have gone undetected? – Such are the reflections that beset her. Whereas I am just another human being – by no means a well of primitive joie-de-vivre: so not much comfort!

To Felix Giovanelli, 28 January 1944

HUMPHREY BOGART

Remedy

PROBABLY ONE OF the things that contributed most to the decline of Hollywood is the lack of replacements for people like the late Humphrey Bogart. I used to go to his house occasionally. I would invariably encounter the biggest hazard there (outside Bogie himself), which consisted of two very large boxer dogs. They would sleep all evening in the middle of the living room. Naturally, this heightened the decibel level of the conversation. It also resulted in everyone lighting kitchen matches all night long in the hope that somehow the sulphur smell would dispel the smell of the damn dogs.

Oscar Levant, from *The Unimportance of Being Oscar*

ERIC KNIGHT

For To Kill the Beasties

'ANDREW.'
     'Aye?'
  'Ye knaw, I were just thinking. It's curious that wi' us, a dog should be oor greatest helper and also oor greatest enemy.'
  'That's it, Jock. It's because they're so clever to help us, they become so clever to hurt us when they turn bad. And any of 'em can turn bad, too, Jock. Don't forget that. Even your ain beastie that ye treasure so much. Once they taste sheepblood, they become killers.'
  'Not ma Donnie!'
  'Nay, nor I think ma Vic, either. But it's true. Once ony of 'em kill, they're started, and they go on killing not for food, but for the joy o' bloody slaughtering.'
  'Ma Donnie wadn't!'
  'Ye can never tell, Jock. There's some dogs, now, that'll be pairfect and upricht wi' their ain flock. Then, comes nicht, they'll travel far awa'

– sometimes meeting like by appointment wi' ithers o' their kind. Then like a pack o' wolves they'll descend ravening on the flock, and they'll tear through 'em, killing and slaughtering, and they'll be awa' again afore help comes. Then they'll separate, and each steal back hame. And come the next day, they'll guard their ain flock as if butter wadn't melt i' their mouths.'

'Ah, but not ma Donnie. If I thocht he did . . .'

They were silent a while. Then Jock spoke again.

'It seems sad that us wha have the greatest fondness for dogs must destroy 'em.'

'Aye – but little destroying we'll do if we keep chattering all nicht. They'd never come.'

The silence settled again, and the patch of moonlight moved across the floor of the rude croft. And then, at last, the older man spoke again, this time his voice trembling with emotion.

'Here they come!'

The other jumped to position, leaning his rifle on the ledge. They both stared, breath-held, at the landscape far to their left.

'Aye, there!'

Jock sighted along his rifle. There was a movement by the stone wall. Then, beyond the lined sights of the gun he saw a dog. There was no air of stealth to it. It came over the wall and trotted plainly into view.

It was Lassie. It was a week since she had left her den, but she still travelled with a limp. She came over the field in the clear moonlight, going straight and steady as if following a compass route.

In the stone hut the older man released his pent breath.

'Let him have it, Jock,' he cried, in a hoarse whisper.

The younger man cuddled his rifle, but did not fire.

'Where's the others?'

'What's the odds? Let him have it.'

'It's a collie – d'ye ken wha's it is?'

'Nay. It's a stray – one o' them wild ones, forebye. Let it have it, lad. Don't miss, now.'

Jock turned his head.

'I handled one o' these things in the war, Andrew. I dinna miss – not when I pay for ma own ammuneetion.'

'Then let fly, Jock!'

The younger man cuddled the stock of his rifle again. He held his breath. Slowly he brought the sights in line – now he saw over the vee of the hindsight the steady, unwavering tip of the foresight. Above it was the tiny figure of a trotting collie. The collie moved, but it always stayed in the tip of the foresight as the gun followed it along.

Jock took up the slack on the trigger. He felt the 'second pull' beginning to take up.

'Hurry, Jock, now!'

Jock lifted his head and laid the rifle down.

'I canna do it, Andrew.'

'Shoot it, man, shoot it!'

'Na, na, Andrew. It doesna look like one o' they devils. Look, it pays no heed to aught. Let's see if it gangs near the sheep. For it seems to be paying no heed to them at all. Look.'

'It's a stray. We have a richt to shoot it!'

'Let's see if it gangs near the sheep. If it does . . .'

'Och, ye gormless! Shoot it!'

The older man's voice rose in urgent tones. The cry floated over the night to where Lassie trotted. She paused in her tracks and turned her head. Then it all struck her together – the sound of men, the scent of them, the movement in the window of the stone hut. It was man – man that would chain her, man that she must avoid.

She wheeled and sprang away in a sudden lope.

'There! It's seen us! Let him have it!'

The sudden dash of Lassie half convinced the younger man that he had misjudged the dog below. For Lassie's actions were like those of a guilty dog.

He lifted the rifle quickly, cuddled the stock, and fired.

At the crack that shattered the night, Lassie leaped away. The ugly whine of a bullet passing by her left shoulder made her veer quickly to the right. She raced across the field. There was another shot, and she felt a burning shock in her flank.

'Nay, I hit it.'

'Ye didna. Look at it go!'

Inside the small shelter the voices of the men mixed with those of the dogs, who now cried pandemonium.

'Let 'em out!'

The old man raced to the door and opened it. The dogs, then the men, tumbled out, and raced away after Lassie's tracks.

'Go get it! Sic 'em!' yelled Andrew.

The dogs raced along, baying at the chase. They went down the slope, bellies flat, and their bodies almost doubling in two with the urgency of their speed. Behind them came the men, but they were soon left behind. The dogs suddenly swerved, and bayed louder – for they had picked up the trail – the warm scent of new blood.

Ahead of them Lassie galloped. Twice she halted suddenly and snapped at the flank where the bullet had creased her leg muscles. She could hear the pursuing dogs behind, but she did not increase her pace. She had no fear of dogs. It was man she wished to leave behind, and her senses told her they were not near. But now she feared him more than ever. Not only could his hands chain and pen one up, but he could make the terrifying thunder noises that hurt the ears and that somehow reached out like a long, invisible whip and brought pain such as that which now tore at her.

Truly man was an evil menace.

Steadily she loped along, feeling that perhaps she would soon leave them all behind.

But the other dogs were fresh. They had not travelled, half-starved, for hundreds of weary miles. And they were soon within sight of her. They bayed a higher note, and despite the best speed that Lassie could attain, they were soon behind her. Then one charged at her flank, tearing it with his teeth and buffeting her with his shoulder to bring her down.

But one thing Lassie still had. She might be weary and starved. But she had no cowardice. She whirled like lightning and stood, fearless. Her mane stood erect, and her lips were drawn back from her fangs.

Her attitude halted the other dogs in their tracks, for though of a much rougher breed, they were of collie blood, too. And they understood the warning.

Here was no cur to be chivied and chased like rabbit.

As if she had driven away a petty worry, Lassie turned in obedience to the great driving force inside her. She must go on her way – south and ever south.

But the others took it for a signal of fear, and together they charged. They tore past her, as collies will, slashing as they went. For collies do not rush and hold. Their way of fighting is not like that of the bulldog; nor like that of the terrier which dodges and worries and shakes. They rather desire to run past an enemy, giving the long, slashing wounds that wear a foe down.

It was Lassie's own way of fighting, and instinctively she knew how to meet it. However, as she whirled to meet one adversary, the other would race in and slash from the other direction. But Lassie pivoted, waiting to meet the nearest foe. She stood, her head erect, watchful in the moonlight. The one behind her charged. She dodged it and started on her way again. But the other was racing in. She turned again – a second too late. The charge buffeted her and she half fell. The other raced in before she could regain her feet. The three became a snarling, composite pile. Lassie fought herself free. And then it began all over again – one dog charging, the other racing in as she turned to meet the first.

The battle was long, and it was still going on as the men arrived, panting from their long run. They stood and watched.

'Dinna ye shoot the noo, Jock,' Andrew puffed. 'Ye micht hit ma Vickie.'

Jock nodded, and cradled the gun on his arm. His head was thrust forward. He watched closely the battle that the one, tired, travel-weary dog put up against the two sturdy ones, rough and heavy and hard from their years of work. And often he thought that the two must win.

But Lassie had something that the others had not. She had blood. She was a pure-bred dog, and behind her were long generations of the proudest and best of her kind.

This theory of blood lines in animals is not an empty one, as any animal lover knows. Where the cold-blood horse will quit and give no more, the thoroughbred will answer and give another burst of speed gallantly, even if he is spending the last ounce of life strength: where the mongrel dog will whine and slink away, the pure-bred will still stand with uncomplaining fearlessness.

And it was this blood that won for Lassie. As one dog charged, she met him. Unmindful of the other coming at her flank, she drove him down. He lay in a moment of surrender.

Then Lassie did a curious thing. Instead of taking an easy victory and driving at his throat, she merely placed a forepaw stiffly over his body as if holding him there as a wrestler would. As long as he remained motionless, he would not suffer.

Then, as he lay still and unprotesting, Lassie faced the other dog. She lifted her head where the fangs gleamed white, and from her chest came the slow, low rumble of challenge.

The other dog looked at her, and then he, too, lay down and began licking a wound on his paw. It was armistice.

So the dogs stood for a moment – the one prone under Lassie's stiff paw, the other cleaning himself with an air that seemed to say:

'I didn't have anything to do with this whole affair at all!'

It was only for a moment that picture remained, and then the madness of the fight left Lassie. The growl died in her throat, and she remembered what she had to do. She turned calmly and trotted away.

Only then did one of the men behind dance and lift his voice.

'Now – now Jock! Shoot it!'

But the younger man did not move. For, in his mind, he was not seeing dogs, but men. He was remembering a certain day. And as he stood the tired collie passed out of sight.

'Losh, Jock, and why did ye not shoot?'

'I could 'na, Andrew.'

'And why not?'

'I were thinking o' March – March i' 1918, Andrew, when they come over us – and the regiment stood. It were like that, Andrew, yon collie. She fought the same way the Black Watch did, Andrew. I' March, back i' 1918 . . .'

'Are ye daft?'

'Nay, Andrew.'

The younger man wrinkled his brow.

'March, 1918,' the older man scoffed.

'Weel, it were a brave dog, anyhow, Andrew. And – and it were going somewheer – and – and – besides. I couldn'a shoot, for I forgot to load up again.'

'Och, now that's something. Forgot to load. I should think a sojer would never forget to load up again after he's fircd.'

'Weel – we ha' so mony things to remember, Andrew,' the younger man said.

Then, as they turned away, he clicked open the breech gently, took out the cartridge from the chamber of his rifle, and slipped it in his pocket silently. With the dogs following them the men went back to the rude shelter on the moonlit slope.

From *Lassie Come Home*

PETER LAWFORD

'LASSIE WAS A vicious bastard!' Peter said years after he made his next picture, *Son of Lassie*, a wartime saga set in England with the canine superstar. 'You want to know how we did those scenes [of affection between man and dog]? I had raw meat stuck under my arms and under my shirt and rubbed on my face and stuck up my clyde, and that animal was eating me alive! What you saw on the screen, what you thought was the true love of a dog for his master, wasn't that at all ... no, it was sheer animal hunger!'

When Peter first found out that MGM had assigned him to the picture, however, he was thrilled. The studio was giving him an extraordinary opportunity: for the first time, he would be the topbilled star of a motion picture, the actor on whose shoulders the film rested. It was a prospect that both excited and frightened him; he began to suffer from back pain, a problem he would frequently have in the future when under stress.

The box-office appeal of *Son of Lassie* was virtually guaranteed. Producer Sam Marx had scored a huge hit in 1943 with *Lassie Come Home*, the heartwarming story of the beautiful collie's struggle to be reunited with her owner, the young Roddy McDowall. Eleven-year-old Elizabeth Taylor, in her second movie, played a moppet who sets the animal free.

For the sequel, Peter's first Technicolor production, he and June Lockhart were cast to play the adult versions of Roddy and Elizabeth. Pal, a male dog who was called 'the only star who could play a bitch better than Bette Davis,' played the dual roles of Lassie and her pup, Laddie.

Peter played Joe Carraclough, a strapping young man strongly attached to Laddie, an adorable if none-too-bright animal. When Joe leaves home for RAF training, his girlfriend (Lockhart) promises to take care of Laddie, but the dog runs forty miles to follow Joe. After battles with Nazi soldiers and raging rapids, man and dog are reunited, Joe returns to his girl, Laddie rejoins his mother, and everyone lives happily ever after.

Location filming took place at Patricia Bay, near Vancouver, British Columbia in August and September 1944. Peter did his own swimming in the treacherous, thirty-two-degree waters of the Columbia River, a task made more difficult by his limited use of his right arm. He pointedly did not ask for a double to swim for him, however, because he never wanted his bosses to feel he wouldn't be up to the physical demands of whatever role they wanted him to play. He knew that such an attitude could severely limit his career.

Peter found himself amused during filming by the star treatment accorded his canine costar. While he went without a dressing room, he said, 'Lassie was checked into a two-bedroom suite, accompanied by a whole retinue – sort of like a small Frank Sinatra unit.'

The amusement turned to anger, however, when he realized that the studio provided Lassie with safety measures not accorded him. Shooting the scenes in the rapids, Peter noticed that Pal had been securely tethered to shore with rope to make sure he didn't drown, while Peter was left to his own devices. Neither was Peter pleased to learn that Pal had been insured for a million dollars. 'I had the suspicion that if I was insured at all, it was for a substantially smaller amount.'

There was no love lost between actor and dog; Peter nicknamed the film 'Son of a Bitch.' Even while doing publicity for the picture, he expressed reservations about working with an animal: 'As an actor you haven't a dog's chance when you act with a dog. You can be acting for all you're worth, sure you have audience attention. Then the dog wags its tail, or tosses a soulful glance, and the spectators whoop and coo. The human actor might as well not be there.'

James Spada, from *Peter Lawford*

ROBINSON JEFFERS

The House Dog's Grave

(*Haig, an English bulldog*)

I've changed my ways a little; I cannot now
Run with you in the evenings along the shore,
Except in a kind of dream; and you, if you dream a moment
You see me there.

So leave awhile the paw-marks on the front door
Where I used to scratch to go out or in,
And you'd soon open; leave on the kitchen floor
The marks of my drinking-pan.

I cannot lie by your fire as I used to do
On the warm stone,
Nor at the foot of your bed; no, all the nights through
I lie alone.

But your kind thought has laid me less than six feet
Outside your window where firelight so often plays,
And where you sit to read – and I fear often grieving for me –
Every night your lamplight lies on my place.

You, man and woman, live so long, it is hard
To think of you ever dying.
A little dog would get tired, living so long.
I hope that when you are lying

Under the ground like me your lives will appear
As good and joyful as mine.
No, dears, that's too much hope: you are not so well cared for
As I have been.

And never have known the passionate undivided
Fidelities that I knew.
Your minds are perhaps too active, too many-sided.
But to me you were true.

You were never masters, but friends. I was your friend.
I loved you well, and was loved. Deep love endures
To the end and far past the end. If this is my end,
I am not lonely. I am not afraid. I am still yours.

T. H. WHITE

Miraculous Recovery

H E KNEW THAT Brownie was jealous of the hawks and felt her
nose put out of joint. He had tended her when she got a thorn in
her foot, and after that she made several attempts to regain his attention
by limping and holding up a sound paw. When she went off her food
he commented, 'Brownie is on hunger strike as a protest against the
hawk.' In fact, she was developing distemper, which is usually a mortal
affair with a grown dog.

Six years later, in the *Biography of Brownie* written for his godson,
William Potts, he wrote:

> She had decided to die.
>
> She had had it for a day before I noticed, but when I did notice, the
> miracle happened all at once in my heart. Something in her dying look at
> last penetrated my thick skull. I wrapped her up in the best eiderdown; I
> bought bottles of brandy and port and stuff to make junket. I had a
> veterinary surgeon every day and even a human doctor twice, and I sat up
> beside her, day and night, with hot water bottles, for a week. She got rennet
> every two hours with a teaspoon of brandy, and I told her over and over
> again that if she would not die I would not keep hawks any more, or go to
> cinemas or to dances or to any place where she could not go as well.
>
> But I couldn't stop her. She got weaker and weaker, and it was awful to
> hear her breathe, and the doctor and the vet were useless, and you could
> hardly feel her heart. At last came a minute when I said:
>
> 'In a quarter of an hour she will be dead.'
>
> Then I said: 'Well, there is nobody left in it but me and Death! We will
> fight it out. I can't possibly make her any worse, so I will at least do
> something to see if I can make her better.'

He looked up Distemper in the *Encyclopaedia Britannica*, and found a
rather half-hearted recommendation of quinine.

> I gave her half a human dose, which burned her weak throat but she was
> too feeble to cough it up. When the quarter of an hour was up, she stood
> up on her shaky legs and was sick. The next time the whey came round she
> actually drank it, instead of having to have it poured down her throat.
>
> That night she suddenly ran out into the darkness, or rather tottered out,
> and vanished. It was pitch dark. I stayed for hours calling her and walking

about the wood with candles, but I could not find her and she did not come back. At last I knew she had died in a ditch, so I went back to the house and cried myself to sleep, but I got up again at dawn, and went to look for her body. I was calling and looking when she staggered out of the wood, not quite sure who she was or who I was, and I carried her home in floods of tears, but they were quite needless. She was cured.

They were both cured. The trick of withholding his heart, which shows so odiously in the courtship of the barmaid, was gone, abolished by the shock of finding himself essential to a living creature. 'I have always wanted to be somebody's best friend, but never succeeded' – so he once wrote to Potts. 'I have no friends, only acquaintances. You have no idea how curious it is to live one's whole life like a cat.' He remained unsecured, sharp-clawed and suspicious: these were in his lot, like the caution which his lot enforced on him. 'His own amorous feelings were, I think, all for boys, and he was very very very careful about them.' But his loving feelings were less strictly guarded, and at the realization that he might lose Brownie's love before he had allowed himself to love her 'the miracle happened all at once'. He dared to risk his heart on something that might be dead in another twenty-four hours. Whether or not this made much difference in his cat's life, it made a great difference to his next book.

Brownie was so sure of their new relationship that he was not even held to his promise. He went on keeping Cully and two sparrowhawks and presently added an owl, whom he called Archimedes.

Grief

BEFORE HE SETTLED to a duration of work he had to send *The Elephant and The Kangaroo* to America. This entailed going to Dublin. That evening, Mr McDonagh met him at the bus-stop. He said, 'Mr White, I'm afraid I have bad news for you.' His voice was solemn, and White with jesting gravity replied, 'I hope I haven't been arrested as a spy?'

'Brownie is dead.'

White's entry in the folio notebook was probably written in the early morning of November 26th. (The date refers to the day of her death.)

Brownie is dead. 25.xi.xliv.

She had a happy life, probably happier than most setters, except that the happier you are the more you want to be happy, so it evens out. Her major troubles were only being allowed to sit in my lap for 6 hours a day, and things like that.

She lived fairly long for a working setter. I can't be sure if she was 12 or 14, but could make a good guess if I had a copy of England Have My Bones.

She could have lived longer, but for the filthy piece of work that I was on one of my bi-annual trips (for 9 hours) to Dublin at the time she had one of her annual attacks. I could have saved her, perhaps. The people here didn't understand her. But it was impossible not to go to Dublin sometimes, since I had our living to earn. This trip was about getting The Elephant and the Kangaroo to America. I had to leave her for a few hours every year, or we shouldn't have earned a living at all.

All the same, I let her down in the end: she had trusted her whole life to me always, and I was not there to save it.

I had saved it at least twice before, which is something.

The dead body by my side is not Brownie. But what is? She was a sprite who danced before me through 12 perfect years of love. But she is not that now. It is gone. And the poor dead face is not it either. I have an actual physical feeling in my heart – muscular, not emotional – as if it were going to burst.

It means that I died last night. All that me is dead, because it was half her.

It is useless and ignoble to repine about one's lot. Is it any use repining about hers? Whose? The dead body's? The sprite's?

Might-have-beens are too agonizing, and not practical.

She was the central fact of my life.

It is only me who has lost anything. Brownie has lost nothing. For when the self itself is lost, that self cannot lose anything.

The handwriting is perfectly steady till the last paragraph where it slightly wavers. On the next page, written in a large stumbling, childish hand, as though by someone illiterate or almost blind, comes:

> Brownie, I am free of you,
> Who ruled my heart for 14 years!
> O Freedom, all begun anew,
> O iceblock heart, O tears!
>
> My gentleness, my trustfulness,
> My looker-up, my life,

My coward who leaned on my care
In vain, my child and wife,

My mother with the golden pelt,
Myself with melting eye,
My Brownie, rooted in the core,
My hoping lover-lie.

Then the steady handwriting resumes:

I must make myself realize that she is now entirely a thing of the past. It
is rather an effort not to follow her into it myself, as I have always followed
her everywhere else. But I must not, and I must face this, a little at a time.

He sat up with her corpse for two nights and buried her in the grounds
of Doolistown House. A lock of copper-red hair, tied very neatly with a
strand of blue silk, is fastened in the large diary, on a page where he
had stuck some photographs of her taken at Belmullet. It is still glowing,
silken and pliable, as though cut from a living head. With her death, he
lost the only being he dared to love, the only being who found security
in his insecurity. The trust she fixed on the handsome, rather showy,
not very attentive young man with a beautiful top hat, who accepted her
dependence as an embellishment – like a rich tassel – had become the
thing he depended on.

For three consecutive days after Brownie's death he wrote to Garnett.
The language of total bereavement can be heard as heartless, because
it is so practical. There is not much else it can be. Bereavement impales
one on practical considerations. They are all that is left to think about.

Please do not write to me at all about her for a very long time, but tell me
if I ought to buy another bitch or not, as I do not know what to think about
anything. I *might* live another 30 years, which would be two dog's lifetimes
at this, but of course they hamper one very much when one loves them so
desperately.

Her body was beside him as he wrote that. Then, after her burial:

Now I am to begin a new life and it is important to begin it right, but I
find it difficult to think straight. It is about whether I am to get another dog
or not. I am good to dogs, so from their point of view I suppose I ought.
But I might not survive another bereavement like this in 12 years' time, and

dread to put myself in the way of it. Or I could get two dogs and breed up
vast families of puppies, but what would be the good of that? It would only
be an occupation. Brownie was my life and I am lonely for just such
another reservoir for my love – not for an occupation. But if I did get such
a reservoir it would die in about 12 years and at present I feel I couldn't
face that. Do people get used to being bereaved? This is my first time.

Garnett replied:

You ask should you buy another bitch. One can only speak for oneself,
but I think the best antidote to the numbing obsession of grief is having
responsibility to a living creature. So I would say Yes: you should. But not
just any bitch. A gun-dog preferably as all the job of training will be good
for you. Often it will hurt you – but you will realize you cannot dodge the
responsibility.

It was the thought that by going to Dublin he had dodged his
responsibility to Brownie – the only responsibility he had – which
caused White his sharpest torment. He was to blame. And at the same
time his complicated conscience told him that he was more likely to be
blamed for having fixed his heart on a mere dog. Suddenly, in the third
letter, he regained himself.

The whole and single unnaturalness of the position is that dogs and men
have incompatible longevities. Everything else is perfectly natural and I
would not have it altered in any respect. I regret nothing about Brownie,
except the bitter difference of age.

Towards the end of December he wrote again:

I stayed with the grave for a week, so that I could go out twice a day and
say, 'Good girl: sleepy girl: go to sleep, Brownie.' It was a saying she
understood. I said it steadily. I suppose the chance of consciousness
persisting for a week is several million to one, but that was the kind of
chance I had to provide for. Then I went to Dublin, against my will, and
kept myself as drunk as possible for nine days, and came back feeling more
alive than dead.
I have done what you said I was to do, or at any rate I have bought a
puppy bitch. Brownie had taught me so much about setters that it seemed
silly to waste the education, so I stuck to them. No setter could never
remind me of her any more than one woman would remind you of another,
except in general terms.

The new arrangement looks like the foetus of a rat, but she has a pedigree rather longer than the Emperor of Japan's. She nibbles for fleas in my whiskers.

The new arrangement was named Killie. Presently there was another puppy; Garnett wanted a gun-dog – by 1945 a rational desire – and asked White to find and train a pointer for him.

Sylvia Townsend Warner, from her Life of T. H. White

H. L. MENCKEN

Dispute with a Neighbour

June 28, 1942.

Dear Charlie:

May I bother you to make some effort to abate the frequent and ear-splitting barking of your dog? The other morning he got me up at 7.15 A.M., and twice this afternoon he carried on in a deafening manner when I was trying to get a little rest, following illness. He barks very often at meal times, to my great embarrassment when I have guests. His barking in the house is as disturbing as his barking in the yard.

I suspect that he is too large and boisterous an animal for confinement in a city yard and house. I hope that you will find it possible to relieve your neighbours of this disturbance.

October 22, 1945.

Dear Charlie:

Your dog barked yesterday from about 5.30 P.M. to 7 or thereabout. I called up your house but got no answer; apparently there was no one home. As a result of this uproar I had to abandon some important work on which I was engaged. Such interruptions to my work cost me money, and disturbances of my rest, at my age, are dangerous to my health. I have been aroused from sleep as early as 6.45 A.M. and as late as 12.30 midnight.

I must ask you once more to stop this nuisance. So long as your sister was living I remembered her plea that she felt insecure in the house without the dog. But that reason is now gone. I am therefore trusting you either to teach your dog to stop disturbing the neighbourhood or to get a dog less noisy.

February 1, 1946.

Dear Charley:

On November 25 last you gave a solemn undertaking to Captain Harris, Mr Asner, my brother and me to abate the intolerable nuisance of your barking dog. This promise has been kept so far as the backyard is concerned, but the animal still barks furiously in the house, apparently while you are out. Today it made an ear-splitting din from 12.30 to nearly one o'clock, all through my lunch time. And it has barked loudly almost every day for weeks past.

This is my last notice to you that this nuisance must be ended as you agreed. If it is not stopped completely and permanently within five days I shall seek legal redress for the damage to my peace and comfort and the interference with my work.

[The whole country heard the barking of Fortenbaugh's dog. Mencken's move to file suit hit the wire services and even the radio networks. Exasperated beyond endurance he had engaged a legal friend, Richard Cleveland, to represent him. Confronted with the courts, Mencken's neighbour caved in. He exiled the dog to the precincts of the Baltimore Humane Society, many miles from 1524 Hollins Street; and the court enjoined him from ever bringing the animal back.]

From *The New Mencken Letters*, ed. Carl Bode

BILLIE HOLIDAY

Walk, Don't Walk

MOM WAS UNHAPPY about me living all alone in a little apartment on 104th Street. It was near her place on 99th Street, but she thought I should stay with her like I always had. I had no husband. Now we had something else in common – both of us were grass widows. She didn't know I had Joe Guy on the string then and I didn't tell her. Finally we compromised and I used to spend three evenings a week with her and the rest with Guy. But that wasn't enough. She was lonely without me and beginning to be real worried about me.

I tried to tell Mama she had the dog, Rajah Ravoy, to take care of her. Rajah was a skinny run-down mutt when Dr Carrington, a West Indian doctor friend of mine, had brought him to me to take care of. He was a sad dog then, and I didn't have time to take care of him so I took him to Mom.

Sometimes when I was working at Café Society I used to take him to work with me. He was so low, I figured he needed the grandest name in the world. So I borrowed the fancy name from a magician who was working a joint in the village at that time – Rajah Ravoy.

This dog was amazing, he was so smart. In the morning Mom would leave the Bronx and take the bus to 99th Street and Columbus to open her restaurant. Rajah would stand by until she got on the bus, then he'd take off. When she got to the restaurant, there he was, waiting at the door to be fed.

Sometimes he would bark and raise hell and try to keep Mom from going to work in the morning. She knew he was trying to tell her she shouldn't open up that day. And that dog knew what he was doing. She'd stay home and, sure enough, the Board of Health or somebody would be around to make trouble and there was nobody there.

Rajah would go off by himself without any damn leash and go in Central Park to take a bath. The cops and the SPCA people would try to catch him, but he could outwit them any time and come highballing to the apartment, up the stairs. He could do everything, almost ring the bell.

He could even make it all the way from the Bronx to my place on 104th Street. We could have thrown away our telephones, Mom and me. With Rajah we didn't need them.

Mom loved that dog. And the day he died Mom said he was all she had to live for and she wouldn't last long after. And she was so right.

From *Lady Sings the Blues*

INGRID BERGMAN

Up on the Roof

ROBERTO [ROSSELLINI] GAVE me a dog, a little black bulldog. That was all I needed! I put him down on the black lava sand, and he disappeared; he matched the sand so closely you couldn't see him. Dear little Stromboli – what else could we call him? [name of film] – stayed with me for years afterwards and barked at all the photographers . . . .

I had not left the apartment for five weeks because I saw that a car of photographers was waiting all day in the street. I took Stromboli to the terrace on the roof, we had nice walks there and I could sit and read and take sunbaths. I didn't need to go out. We used to look down into the street and see those cameras and we spit, just a little, down upon them. That is, I spit, Stromboli was not able to but I know he wanted to.

From *My Story*

ELVIS PRESLEY

Where All the Good Dogs Go

AFTER ELVIS GOT his famous first guitar for his tenth birthday and he learned to play it well enough to accompany himself singing 'Old Shep', he sang 'Old Shep' at every place and at every opportunity permitted so that it became a joke among his schoolmates – 'Oh no! Not another round of "Old Shep" today.' . . .

At the beginning of that school term, during morning devotions, Mrs Grimes asked her pupils if any of them could say a prayer.

Elvis got up and said one and then went straight into his rendition of 'Old Shep'.

Mrs Grimes was highly impressed. 'He sang it so sweetly,' she says, 'it liked to make me cry.' And it gave her an idea.

She took him along to the school principal, Mr Cole, and again Elvis sang 'Old Shep'. Mr Cole was similarly impressed. It was a few weeks before the Mississippi–Alabama Fair, held annually at Tupelo's fairground, which included among its many attractions a children's talent contest. Each school in the area selected its contestants. Elvis was promptly entered. . . .

On Wednesday afternoon, the second day of the 1945 Fair, when he was ten years old, Elvis, wearing overalls and accompanying himself on his guitar, stood on a chair to reach the microphone on the stage of the grandstand and sang 'Old Shep' in the children's singing contest. He won second prize – \$5 and free admission to all the amusement rides.

He had sung 'Old Shep' of course, many many times before. But as this can be considered his professional debut – he got money for it – it is worth noting that it took place not in a little theatre, or an actors' studio, or an obscure nightclub, but at a country fair, in front of a live audience of his own people – and in a grandstand that seated two thousand.

As the prizes were gauged by audience applause, Elvis' reaction to his success must certainly have been a magnification of Glady's [his mother's] reaction to *her* success dancing to Jimmie Rodgers. But if Gladys had tasted pleasure, Elvis – it might be said – had tasted blood. For, however many people were actually seated in the grandstand to watch a children's talent contest, his child's eye would have it filled to capacity.

*   *   *

One wonders what thoughts went fleetingly through the minds of those fellow students who knew him as an insignificant, not-much-liked, oddball senior, as Elvis came slouching out on stage, eyes on the ground, only his glistening hair and red shirt vibrating off the stage lights as he propped a foot on a chair and suddenly slid his guitar round to his front prior to raising the roof. How much initial resistance did he have to overcome? How many Elvis-baiters would be sitting there hoping he'd make a fool of himself. How long did it take for scoffing to switch to surrender; for thought to be conquered by feeling? Perhaps midway into his first number, 'Cold, Cold, Icy Fingers'. Perhaps earlier than that this born performer had again established the dominance of his eery twinship, his magical mutuality with a large audience.

And since many in the crowd were seen crying during his performance, we can be sure he had not forgotten to rely on dependable 'Old Shep'. According to Martha Wallace, a classmate of hers in eighth grade actually fainted during the song.

*   *   *

It was a very different Elvis from the one on the Steve Allen [television] show three months before in the harness of white tie and tails and the humiliation of having Steve Allen smirkingly present him with a roll that looks exactly like a large roll of toilet paper with, said Allen, the 'signatures of eight thousand fans'. With the audience on his side Elvis simply looked at Steve as if to say, 'It's all right, I've been made a worse fool of in my life', and after he patted the dog he was about to sing ['Hound Dog'] to, he wiped his hands on his trousers as if to wipe away Steve Allen, the dog and the whole show.

Elaine Dundy, from *Elvis and Gladys*

PATRICK WHITE

Passion

WHAT MATTERED MORE than anything in their lives were the dogs. P. V. M. White and E. G. Lascaris reintroduced the schnauzer to Australia. Soon after they arrived at Castle Hill they registered the name Grauvolk Kennels, and from 1949 the *Breeders' Directory* carried advertisements for their Grauvolk schnauzers. Other kennels were soon established, but the Grauvolk dogs dominated Sydney shows for five years from 1949 when Solomon and Maggy each won a 'challenge' at the Royal Easter Show. White boasted to Mollie McKie after that first triumph that the English judge had insulted a great many of the exhibitors through a loudspeaker, 'However, he announced that Maggy had the makings of a great Schnauzer bitch, also through the loudspeaker.'

Schnauzers are Austrian cattle dogs, hairy grey beasts with black snouts and a menacing growl. Those who love the breed say schnauzers are demanding, intelligent and so loyal that they haunt their owners' footsteps like pepper-and-salt ghosts. In the Australian world of dog intrigue, it mattered that Franz had come to Lascaris in Palestine without a pedigree. The problem was solved when local dog authorities were persuaded to declare Franz of pure blood. White gave the dog the pedigree name Ironsides of Erewhon and he became – and remains – a heroic animal in the memory of Australian schnauzer circles: smuggled out of central Europe by a Jewish refugee, saved from death by E. G. Lascaris to become the mascot of the Greek Sacred Regiment.

In Grauvolk's early days when litters were hard to sell White invited *Woman* magazine to visit the farm. 'An Author and his Dogs' records Dogwoods in spring, an old apple tree shimmering with blossom, the 'workmanlike' figure of Patrick White declaring he had written his last word, and a litter of schnauzer pups 'with satiny silk hair and the most appealing, bewhiskered faces'. When Lottie and Solomon were let out to be photographed they escaped across the paddock 'as if jet propelled. Patrick tried desperately to bring them to heel. Obedient? "Oh, yes, usually very obedient," said their master, with a suddenly sweet smile, "but behaving like fiends today!"' Male pups, reported *Woman*, sold for £20 and bitches for £15.

At its height Grauvolk had ten permanent dogs and four litters each year. The dog calendar built to a climax after a series of local shows on the fringes of Sydney, at which the schnauzers qualified for the big event of the Royal Easter Show in late summer. 'We took seven dogs to Sydney for the Dalwood Show,' White reported to Molly McKie in late 1949. 'It caused quite a sensation, a team of seven Schnauzers but it was a great strain to me, especially when two young dogs slipped their collars in the traffic outside the Cricket Ground. We won masses of prizes of course, but all wrongly awarded.' Each Easter, as if by fixed routine, White had an attack of asthma/influenza/bronchitis and reached the Sydney ring in an exhausted trance. 'One stands for days beside the dogs' benches, looking out through the bars, sees human beings pushing, sweating, goggling and joking, and worse still, one has to answer the questions that they ask.' Despite successes year after year,

Grauvolk's great object was never achieved, to produce a schnauzer that was 'Best in Show (All Breeds)' in Sydney and Melbourne.

Grauvolk lost money hand over fist. When the pups developed scour from cows' milk, White bought Saanen goats and began to breed them as his uncle Clem had done out on Barwon Vale. He loved goats but they were expensive, litters sold unprofitably, and show victories earned them no more than five shilling and ribbons. 'We spent all our money on the dogs. Manoly spent all his savings.' Lascaris earned no wages on the farm, and after the kennel catastrophes he was as poor as he had ever been in his life. The long road which began with Turkish expropriations in Anatolia, ended for this Lascaris at Grauvolk Kennels. He wanted to get a job but White insisted he stay with him on the farm.

*   *   *

There was a rambling place in North Sydney that seemed perfect, but a deal could not be struck with a couple of ancient sisters, 'hard as nails underneath all their vagueness'. Then Arrighi found a terrace in Queen Street, Woollahra, but there was no yard for the dogs and their needs were crucial.

Dogs were the two men's passion, and on them they lavished their love and care. There runs through all the letters he wrote in these years – even letters to London agents and New York publishers – a stream of pure domestic comedy: the story of Lucy and Fanny. Lucy was a miniature pinscher who arrived as the last of the schnauzers was, in Miss Docker's words, gathered to God. 'She is very elegant,' White reported to Ronald Waters when the pup arrived. 'Wears rhinestones in the evening, green jade for afternoon receptions, and red leather *pour le sport.*' Fanny came a few months later. She was a pug. 'You should have a pug before you die,' White advised his old friend. 'They are so like so many of one's friends.' He found them game and athletic.

When the decision was taken to do the right thing by Fanny, White arranged an assignation in Strathfield with a dog of the noble name Teng Wah Lo-Sze. Of the difficulties that followed, Dutton received a full account: 'Unfortunately Fanny has so far been terrified and Lo-Sze not all that interested. I wish you could see the house in which all this takes place. It is a real Home Beautiful in the right kind of brick, with pixies, storks, and toadstools on the lawn, dog ornaments inside – literally hundreds of them, from small china ones to enormous cloth Dismal Desmonds, the size of a man, standing in corners. Quite eerie. The matings take place in what the pug-lady refers to as the "dogs' TV lounge". Certainly there is a TV working madly all the time, which is perhaps what puts the dogs off. On the last occasion there was some dreadful musical, with a number, the chorus of which went: "Sit down! Sit down! Sit down!" Teng Wah Lo-Sze obediently did, and that was the end of the mating for that evening. We are also learning "terms", such as "showing colour" for bloody discharge, "tied", and "a slip mating" – all too Dekyvere.'

News of the litter born just before Christmas was widely broadcast. What gripped White at any moment went into his letters: 'Fanny gave birth to a litter of seven three days ago, refused to do anything for them and we live now by the alarm clock, feeding, and wiping the bottoms of pups. A pug is something to get ready-made.' Four pups survived. Two were sold, one was given to Doris Fitton, and the last remained at Dogwoods. She grew into the Divine Ethel. White wrote to Charles Osborne at the *London Magazine*, 'Pugs are probably going to be the vice of my old age.'

David Marr, from his *Life of Patrick White*

JEAN DUTOURD

A Child is Born

WHEN SHE WAS told, as tactfully as could be, that she had just given birth to a child with a dog's head, Mme Du Chaillu fainted. After twenty years of sterility, it was a severe blow. M. Du Chaillu was, if possible, even more distraught. For fifteen minutes he seriously felt like killing his spouse, but one glance at her innocent face made him blush for his hideous suspicions. He contented himself with sighing: 'My poor Henriette! We might have been spared this.'

Mme Du Chaillu burst out sobbing.

'It's ghastly! How could it have happened? I don't ever want to see it. Do you feel as miserable as I do, Léon?'

M. Du Chaillu pressed Mme Du Chaillu's hand, whereat she

redoubled her tears. Blushing, he enquired in a choking voice: 'Did you think of a dog while you were pregnant?'

'Never!' cried Mme Du Chaillu. 'Not once!'

'And . . . before?' murmured M. Du Chaillu, in a still more broken voice.

'Before?' asked Mme Du Chaillu in surprise.

The child snuffled in its cradle. The head of a puppy, frail and endearing, surmounted the swaddled body of this newborn human being. Its pink muzzle, its unopened eyes and its soft fur wrung from M. Du Chaillu his first tears.

'What will people say?' wondered Mme Du Chaillu.

'Quite likely it'll die,' said the midwife.

'We'll have no such luck,' said M. Du Chailu sadly.

'Anyway, we can't call him Pierre,' said Mme Du Chaillu.

They called him Edmond. Mme Du Chaillu could not bring herself to give him her breast, nor would the curé administer baptism.

'Let us wait till he talks,' said the curé. 'Suppose he has a dog's soul and barks? Ah, it is a great trial that the Lord has sent you, my friends. Prayer will help you to bear it.'

Edmond's tongue was examined: it was flat. A real dog's tongue. He would bark, there was no doubt. The unhappy parents became desperate. Contrary to the curé's assurances, prayer brought them no solace; one would rather have said that it bored them. Then, at the age of six months, Edmond distinctly pronounced the word 'papa', which gave ground for much rejoicing. He had the soul of a man!

In two years Edmond's head reached its definitive shape: it was a spaniel's, with long, flapping ears, wide, gaping jaws, and long hairs, masses of yellow and white hairs. For the rest, he was built like an ordinary human being. He was quite a charming child who talked, walked, filled his father's pipe and played with his mother's slippers. His parents could not help having some affection for him. One day, on his own initiative, he went to fetch the paper from the newsvendor and carried it home in his mouth.

'Little wretch!' cried M. Du Chaillu. 'Aren't you ashamed of yourself?'

Edmond received a whipping which made him cry a great deal.

'Never try to repeat that joke,' said M. Du Chaillu.

The first six years of Edmond's life slipped by much as the first six years of any small boy. Sometimes his mother cast him a look full of pity and sorrow, but he paid it no attention. His father did not like to see him in the proximity of dogs and was always chasing them away. Edmond would hear him say to his friends: 'That child had a canine predestination.'

Edmond understood that these words referred to him. Full of pride, he ran to the kitchen and confided to the cook: 'Madeleine, I have a canine predestination. Papa said so.'

'Run away to bed,' replied the cook. 'Don't bother me. I've my washing to do. Really! Your bite is worse than your bark!'

Edmond roared with laughter. He loved the girl's joviality.

The second whipping he was to remember was administered to him by his father one day when the latter caught him stroking a young poodle in the street. M. Du Chaillu, the chastiser, seemed to suffer more than Edmond, the chastised.

'Ah, Edmond,' he said, panting, 'what a difficult child you are! Hardly is my back turned before you're up to some dirty trick. Let me catch you at it again, and you'll see! My own son! Me, Léon Du Chaillu! In the middle of the street!'

Edmond could not comprehend his father's indignation. What could be reprehensible in stroking the nose of a playful poodle? But parental wiggings have a strange power. The more Edmond was whacked on the behind, the more he felt covered with shame. He had indeed stroked a dog, and in the street, too. There must definitely be something very wrong with him to have felt neither embarrassment at the time nor any sense of guilt later.

'I confess I cannot understand you,' declared M. Du Chaillu. 'You are quite beyond me. What are children coming to nowadays? When I was a boy . . . Edmond, listen to me: I'm not an unkind man. I'm your father. I'm prepared to forgive anything, but not that. If I ever find you again with a dog, I'll send you straight to a reformatory.'

Edmond went without dinner and was sent to think things over in his room. He spent an hour regretting that such an amusing occupation as stroking a dog in the street should make his father so unhappy and earn him a beating. After which, he fell asleep and dreamed of savage dogs, which disturbed his slumbers.

M. Du Chaillu, for his part, said to his wife: 'That child distresses me. He is unquestionably attracted by dogs, and we must avoid that at all costs. What can we do, Henriette? What can we do?'

Mme Du Chaillu was no less worried. 'Do you really think it's bad for him to be with dogs?' she queried.

'Bad? No! Catastrophic! Besides, there's the question of morality.

Understand me, Henriette. That boy has a canine predestination. We must do everything in our power to fight it. As far as I'm concerned, I shall be inflexible on that point.'

It was decided not to speak of dogs before Edmond. When that couldn't be avoided, they would shower abuse on these animals. They would depict them as terrible, cruel, treacherous brutes, etc. Might it not even be a good thing to have Edmond bitten by some mangy cur so as to imprint their hatred in his flesh? This last suggestion, however, upset Mme Du Chaillu and was provisionally abandoned. Two china King Charles' spaniels which adorned the mantelpiece were locked away in a cupboard, and a picture in the drawing-room representing a St Bernard rescuing a stray mountaineer was taken down – a rather second-rate painting, anyway. In three months dogs lost all their fascination for Edmond; he began to hate and fear them. They filled him with extraordinary repugnance. In order to frighten him, it was enough to say: 'I'm going to fetch the dog ...' and he would flee, shrieking. Nevertheless, his parents had not enough courage to carry their scheme through to its logical conclusion and inspire in Edmond a horror of himself as well. On the contrary, they did all they could to make him forget his spaniel's head. 'I don't want my son to develop any complexes,' declared M. Du Chaillu, who had heard talk of Freud. But in the long run it is rather difficult not to 'develop complexes' when one has a dog's head. The friends of the family had all been cautioned. They behaved just as if Edmond had an ordinary child's face. They spoke to him of his chubby cheeks, they referred to his fur as hair, to his fangs as milk-teeth, and so on. An old aunt said to him one day, without meaning any harm: 'Wipe your snout, it's covered with chocolate.' The word 'snout' made M. Du Chaillu jump several feet. He ordered the old lady to clear out and never come back.

From *A Dog's Head*

ROBERT CHALLONER

Arms and the Dog

We bivouacked in an April wood,
   Brewed up, and rolled our blankets out
To lie in silent company
Drinking the sweet enchanted tea
   Old soldiers dream about.

When, caught against the sunken fire,
   His ember-kindled eyes aglow,
Came that sad sycophantic hound
Who's immemorially bound
   To go where soldiers go.

I know him well. His myriad breed
   Are old and tried campaigning friends
Who've shared a hundred camps with me
From leaguers deep in Germany
   To Terrier week-ends.

And as he fussed with flattened ears
   Then crawled across to lick my hand
I took the dues his tribe have paid
In homage to the soldier's trade
   Since first they knew command.

He comes of that same lineage
   Which shared the shadowed blanket-arc
With men-at-arms and musketeers
Condottieri, cuirassiers,
   In his ancestral dark.

And this he knew; for, honours done
And ceremonials complete,
He sighed like one who'd travelled far
Down endless centuries of war
And slept across my feet.

From *Punch* 7 May 1952

RAYMOND CHANDLER

Maestro

A FAMILY ON THE street behind us has a black French poodle, small, toy size, I guess. The animal is taking piano lessons, $35 a month. As of now he can play Peter, Peter Pumpkin Eater, not technically very exacting, but one has to begin, *n'est-ce pas?* Little steps for little feet. Later one hopes he will make his debut in Carnegie Hall. The people can afford it and that's all it takes. One looks forward, perhaps a little hesitantly, to his scintillating performance of Chopin's Barcarolle, a difficult piece seldom played and never played really well since de Pachmann. Rubinstein is supposed to be a Chopin virtuoso, but to me he is very in and out. The poodle has a pretty clear field there. It's nice to have ambitious neighbours, and to live in a milieu where money is spent on Art, not just on Cadillacs, Jaguars, and colored butlers. This is true. $35 a month for lessons. Black toy French poodle.

To Hardwick Moseley, 23 March 1954

RICHARD NIXON

Checkers

ONE OTHER THING I probably should tell you, because if I don't they'll probably be saying this about me too. We did get something, a gift, after the election. A man down in Texas heard Pat on the radio mention the fact that our two youngsters would like to have a dog. And, believe it or not, the day before we left on this campaign trip we got a message from Union Station in Baltimore saying they had a package for us. We went down to get it. You know what it was? It was a little cocker spaniel dog in a crate that he sent all the way from Texas. Black and white spotted. And our little girl Tricia, the six-year old, named it Checkers. And you know, the kids love the dog, and I just want to say this right now, that regardless of what they say about it, we're gonna keep it.

YVOR WINTERS

Elegy on a Young Airedale Bitch Lost Some Years since in the Salt Marsh

> Low to the water's edge
> You plunged; the tangled herb
> Locked feet and mouth, a curb
> Tough with the salty sedge.
>
> Half dog and half a child,
> Sprung from that roaming bitch,
> You flung through dike and ditch,
> Betrayed by what is wild.

The old dogs now are dead,
Tired with the hunt and cold,
Sunk in the earth and old.
But your bewildered head,

Led by what heron cry,
Lies by what tidal stream? –
Drenched with ancestral dream,
And cast ashore to dry.

SHEILA BURNFORD

Allies

IN THE COLD hour before dawn, the bull terrier woke, then laboriously and painfully staggered to his feet. He was trembling with cold and was extremely hungry and thirsty. He walked slowly and stiffly in the direction of the pool nearby, passing on his way the cat who was crouched over something held between his paws. He heard a crunching sound as a cat's jaws moved, and wagging his tail in interest moved over to investigate. The cat regarded him coolly and distantly, then stalked away, leaving the carcass; but it was a disappointing mess of feathers only. He drank long and deeply at the pool and on his return tried the feathers again, for he was ravenous, but they stuck in his gullet and he retched them out. He nibbled at some stalks of grass, then delicately, his lips rolled back over his teeth, picked a few over-ripe raspberries from a low bush. He had always liked to eat domestic raspberries this way, and although the taste was reassuringly familiar, it did nothing to appease his hunger. He was pleased to see the young dog appear presently; he wagged his tail and licked the other's face and then followed resignedly when a move was made towards the direction of the road. They were followed a few moments later by the cat who was still licking his lips after his feathery breakfast.

In the grey light of dawn the trio continued down the side of the road until they reached a point where it took a right angled turn. Here they hesitated before an overgrown rutted trail that led from the side of the road, its entrance almost concealed by overhanging branches. It appeared to lead over the hills to the westward, and was an old disused tote road from some worked out timber operation deep in the bush. The leader lifted his head and appeared almost as though he were scenting for something, some reassurance, and apparently found it satisfactory for he led his companions up the trail between the overhanging trees. The going here was softer, for the middle was overgrown with grass and the ruts on either side were full of dead leaves. The close growing trees which almost met overhead would afford more shade when the sun rose higher. These were all consider-ations that the old dog needed, for he was tired today before he started and his pace was considerably slower.

Both dogs were very hungry and watched with mouth watering envy when the cat caught and killed a chipmunk while they were resting by a stream in the middle of the day. But when the old dog advanced with a hopeful wag of his tail the cat growlingly retreated into the bushes with his prey. Puzzled and disappointed, the terrier sat listening to the crunching sounds inside the bushes, saliva running from his mouth.

A few minutes later the cat emerged and sat down, daintily cleaning his whiskers. The old dog licked the black Siamese face with his panting tongue and was affectionately patted on the nose in return. Unlike human beings, there was no jealousy, and there were no recriminations or soul searchings as to who should eat and why. The cat was lucky to have something when he was hungry and so the cat ate it, and this was understood by the old dog who would certainly have done the same thing had he had the opportunity. But he was very hungry indeed; he nibbled a few more raspberries and gazed hopefully around with his short-sighted peering gaze, as though expecting the heavens to open and his own familiar brown dish marked 'Dog' to drop down filled with tasty dog manna.

The young dog too was hungry, but would have to be on the verge of starvation before the barriers of deep-rooted Labrador heredity would be broken down. For generations his ancestors had been bred to retrieve without harming and there was nothing of the hunter in his makeup, and as yet, any killing was abhorrent to him. He drank deeply at the stream and urged his companions on.

The trail ran high over the crest of this hilly wooded country and the surrounding countryside below was filled with an overwhelming beauty of colour; the reds and vermilions of the occasional maples; pale birch, and here and there the scarlet clusters of mountain ash berries against a rich dark green background of spruce and pine and fir, tamarack and cedar.

Several times they passed log ramps built into the side of the hill over which the logs would have been rolled down into the waiting timber toboggans years ago; and sometimes they passed derelict buildings in rank overgrown clearings, old stables for the bush horses and living quarters for the men who had worked there a generation ago. The windows were broken and sagging and weeds were growing up between the floorboards, and even one old rusted cooking stove had fireweed springing from the firebox. The animals, strangely enough, did not like this evidence of human occupation and would skirt them as far as possible, the hair raised along their backs.

Late in the afternoon the old dog's pace had slowed down to a stumbling walk and it seemed as though only sheer determination kept him on his feet at all. He was dizzy and swaying and his heart was pounding. The cat must have sensed this general failing for he now walked steadily beside the dogs, very close to his tottering, failing old friend, and uttering plaintive worried bleats. Finally, the old dog came to a standstill by a deep rut, half filled with muddy water. He stood there as though he did not even have the strength to step around it, his head sagging and his whole body trembling. Then, as he tried to lap the water, his legs seemed to crumble under him and he collapsed half in and half out the rut, lying quite still, eyes closed, and only the long shallow shuddering breaths to indicate he was still alive. The young dog became frantic now, barking and scratching with his paws at the edge of the rut, pushing at the still body with his nose, whining and barking again and doing everything in his power to rouse the limp white body. Again and again he barked and the cat growled softly and continuously, walking back and forth and rubbing his whole length against the dirty muddied head. There was no response to their attentions and the old dog lay unconscious and unheeding.

The other two animals grew silent, and sat by his side, disturbed and uneasy, until at last they turned and left him, neither looking back, the Labrador disappearing into the bushes where the crack of broken branches marked his progress further and further away; and the cat to stalk a partridge which had appeared at the side of the trail some hundred yards away, and was sitting contentedly in the evening sun, filling its crop with gravel preparatory to roosting in a tree. The partridge flew across the trail with a sudden whirr into the trees, while the cat was still some distance away. Undaunted, and licking his lips in anticipation, the cat continued around a bend in the trail in search of another, and was lost to sight.

The shadows lengthened across the track, deserted now save for the still white form in the middle. A curious squirrel peered in bright-eyed wonder from a nearby tree, clucking softly to himself. A shrew ran halfway across, paused and ran back; and there was a soft sound of wings as a whiskey jack landed and swayed to and fro on a birch branch, tilting his head to one side as he looked down and called to his mate to come and join him. A sudden hush descended over everything, and it seemed for a moment as though the whole scene was suspended in eternity.

Suddenly, there was a sound of a heavy body pushing through the undergrowth, accompanied by a sharp crackling of branches, and the spell was broken. Chattering shrilly in alarm and excitement, the squirrel ran up the trunk of the tree and the whiskey jacks flew off. And on to the trail on all fours scampered a young half grown bear cub, round furry ears pricked and small deepset eyes alight with curiosity in the sharp little face as he beheld the unconscious old dog. There was a grunting snuffling sound in the bush behind the cub: the mother was investigating a rotten tree stump. The cub stood for a moment and then hesitantly advanced towards the dog. He sniffed around, wrinkling his facile nose at the unfamiliar smell, then reached out a long curved black paw and tapped the white head. For a moment, the mists of unconsciousness cleared in the old dog's head, and he opened his eyes, aware of danger. The cub sprang back in alarm and watched from a safe distance. Seeing that there was no further movement, he loped back and cuffed again with his paw, this time harder, and watched for a response. Only enough strength was left in the old dog for a valiant baring of his teeth. He snarled faintly with pain and hatred when his shoulder was raked by the wicked claws of the excited cub, and made a pathetically gallant attempt to struggle to his feet. The smell of the drawn blood excited the cub further and he straddled the dog's body and started to play with the long white tail, nibbling at the end like a child with a new toy. His efforts had been too much for the old dog – even as he bared his teeth again with the faintest whisper of a snarl, merciful unconsciousness claimed him.

Around the bend in the trail, dragging a large dead partridge by the wing, came the cat. The wing sprung back softly from his mouth as he gazed transfixed at the scene before him. In one split second a terrible transformation took place; the blue eyes glittered hugely and evilly in the black masked face and every hair on the wheat-coloured body stood upright so that he appeared twice the size; even the chocolate-coloured tail puffed up as it switched angrily from side to side. He crouched low to the ground, tensed and ready, and uttered a high earsplitting scream, and as the startled cub turned, the cat sprang! He landed on the back of the dark furred neck, clinging with his monkey-like hind legs while he raked his long claws across the cub's eyes. Again and again he raked with his terrible talons, hissing and spitting in murderous devilry until the cub was screaming in pain and fear and blinded with blood, making ineffectual brushing movements with his paws to dislodge the unseen horror on his back. His screams were answered by a thunderous roar, and a huge brown she bear crashed through the bushes and rushed to the cub. She swiped at the clinging cat with a tremendous paw; but the cat was too quick for her and with a hiss of fury leaped to the ground and disappeared behind a tree. The unfortunate cub's head received the full force of the blow and it was sent spinning across the track into the bushes. In a blind, frustrated rage, maddened by the cries of her cub, the mother turned for something on which to vent her fury, and saw the still figure of the old dog. Even as she lumbered snarling towards him with vengeance in her heart, the cat distracted her attention, appearing suddenly, hissing and spitting at the side of the track. The bear halted, red eyes glinting savagely, before the attack, standing on her hind legs, neck up stretched and her head weaving from side to side in a menacing snake-like way. The cat uttered another banshee-like scream and took a step forward, fixing his squinting terrible eyes on his enormous adversary. Something like fear or indecision crept into the bear's eyes and it shuffled back a step and lowered its head: the cat took another slow deliberate step forward; the bear retreated again, bewildered by the tactics of this terrible small animal, and distraught by the cub's whimpering. The cat took more steps forward, crouching low and lashing his tail from side to side; the bear shifted its weight uneasily, longing to retreat and still retain some dignity, but afraid to turn its back. The rapidly approaching crackling of undergrowth, heralding the approach of possibly a mate to this vicious unknown animal turned the great animal into a statue, rigid with apprehension, and when a great golden dog sprang out of the bush and stood beside the cat, teeth bared and snarling, every hair on his back erect and a great golden ruff standing out, the bear threw the last presence of dignity to the winds: she dropped to all fours and with a swift lumbering run and a last growl of desperate bravado, fled into the bush to join her cub. The sounds of their flight receded in the distance, until finally all was quiet again and the curious squirrel climbed down from his ringside seat and slid further down the trunk of the tree.

The cat shrank back to his normal size, and his eyes regained their usual cool detached look. He shook each paw distastefully in turn, as though wishful to shake off all contact with the bear, and glanced briefly at the limp muddied bundle that lay unconscious and unheeding by his feet, blood oozing from four deep parallel gashes on the shoulder, then turned and sauntered slowly down the track towards his partridge.

The young dog nosed his friend all over, whining and trying to arouse him and attempting to staunch the blood with his rough tongue. But there was no response and he finally gave up and lay down panting on the grass. His eyes were uneasy and watchful and the hairs still stood upright in a ridge on his back, and from time to time he whined in perplexity. He watched as the cat dragged a large grey bird almost up to the nose of the unconscious dog then slowly and deliberately began to tear at the bird's flesh. He growled softly, but the cat ignored him and continued his tearing and eating. Presently, the enticing smell of raw warm meat filtered through into the old dog's unconsciousness and brought with it a well remembered memory. From that memory grew the desire to live – to live and eat again. He opened one eye and gave an appreciate sniff. The effect was galvanizing: his dirty muddied half-chewed tail stirred and he raised his shoulders, then his forelegs with a convulsive effort, like an old workhorse getting up after a fall.

He was a pitiful sight – the half of his body which had lain in the rut was black and soaking – the other side was streaked and stained with blood. He looked like some grotesque harlequin. He trembled violently and uncontrollably, but in the sunken depths of the little black currant slit eyes there was a faint gleam of interest returning, and it increased as he pushed his nose into the still warm bundle of soft grey feathers. This time there was no warning growl from the cat, or retreating with the prey, but instead a disdainful stepping back and a studiedly indifferent washing of the black stockinged paws, almost as though he disclaimed any part of the bird and the whole episode was incidental and trivial.

The old dog ate, crunching the bones ravenously with his blunt teeth. Even as his companions watched him, a miraculous strength slowly seeped back into his body. Muddied, bloodied, exhausted and half dead, the old bull terrier loved life and had no intention of letting an encounter with a mere bear wrest it from him. By nightfall he was able to walk over to the soft grass at the side of the track, where he lay down and blinked happily at his companions, wagging his pitiful tail. The Labrador lay down beside him and licked the wounded shoulder.

Two or three hours later the purring cat joined them, dropping as though by accident, another succulent morsel by his old friend's nose. This was a little deer mouse, a curious little creature with big eyes and long hind legs like a miniature kangaroo. This was swallowed in one satisfying gulp and soon the old dog slept.

But the cat, purring against his chest, and the young dog curled at his back were wakeful and alert most of the remaining night. The encounter with the bear had sharpened every sense and set every warning nerve in their bodies tingling. Death had walked too closely with them that day, and as yet they were not free of the shadow.

Who is to tell what thoughts pass through an animal's mind, or indeed if they are even capable of contemplation? It may have been that the young dog at least felt more reassured that night, for the 'frivolous feather-headed cat' of yesterday had today shown the ferocity and cunning of a tiger; and, too, had shown himself a capable provider. Perhaps he was aware of the gallantry and tenacity which had been displayed today by their elderly companion and sensed that some of the burden of leadership was being shared, and that the elements of a solid working partnership were being fused among the three.

*　　*　　*

It was lonely, uninhabited country, the nearest road lying many miles away to the south, so that there were no bridges, and the river if anything became wider as they trotted along the banks. After three or four miles the young dog could endure the frustration no longer; he plunged into the water and swam rapidly and strongly across to the far side, his tail streaming out behind like an otter's. He loved the water, and was as much at home in it as the other two hated and feared it. He stood on the far bank, barking encouragingly, but the old dog whined in such distress, the cat yowling in chorus, that he swam across again, paddling around in the shallows near the bank. The old dog walked gingerly into the shallow water, shivering and miserable, turning his head away. Once more the Labrador swam the river, climbed out on the far side, shook himself, and barked. There was no mistaking the command in his bark. The old dog took another reluctant step forward, whining piteously, his expressive tail curled well under. The barking continued; again he advanced; again the Labrador swam across to encourage him. Three times he swam across, and the third time the old dog waded in up to his chest and started swimming reluctantly. He was not a very good swimmer; he swam in jerky rapid movements, his head held high out of the water, his little black eyes rolling fearfully, but he was a bull terrier, a white cavalier, and he kept on, following the wake of the other, until at last he climbed out on the far side. His transports of joy on reaching dry land were like those of a shipwrecked mariner after six weeks at sea on a raft: he rushed in circles, he rolled on his back, he ran along with alternate shoulders low in the long grass to dry himself, until finally he joined the Labrador on the bank to bark encouragingly at the cat.

The poor cat showed the first signs of terror since leaving on his incredible journey; he was alone, and the only way to rejoin his friends lay in swimming across the terrible stretch of water. He ran up and down the bank, all the time keeping up his unearthly Siamese wailing. The young dog went through the same tiring performance that he had used before, swimming to and fro, trying to entice him into the water, but the cat was beside himself with terror and it was a long long time before he finally made up his mind; when he did it was with a sudden blind desperate rush at the water, completely un-cat-like. His expression of horror and distaste was almost comical as he started swimming towards the young dog who waited for him a few yards out. He proved to be a surprisingly good swimmer, and was making steady progress across, the dog swimming alongside, when tragedy struck, mocking the courage of the little vulnerable animal and turning triumph into disaster.

Many years ago a colony of beavers had dammed a small stream which had tumbled into the river about two miles upstream. Since the beavers had left, the dam had been crumbling and loosening gradually, and for a long time it had just been a question of time when it would give way altogether, releasing the eager little stream again to join the river. Fate loosened the dam this very day, this very hour, this very minute! Almost as the two animals reached midstream it broke altogether. The pent up force of the stream leaped through the gap in an ever widening torrent, carrying everything before it and surging into the river, where it became a swift mountainous wave carrying small trees, torn away branches, pieces of river bank and beaver dam before it on the crest. The young dog saw the onrushing terrifying wave several moments before it reached them, and frantically tried to swim into a position upstream of the cat, instinctively trying to protect it but he was too late, and the great curling, crested wave surged over, submerging them in a whirling chaos of debris. The end of a log struck the cat full on the head; he was swept under and over and over until his body was finally caught on a half submerged piece of the old dam, and was carried along on the impetus of the wave, as it tore down the river bed.

The old dog, barking wildly, and frantic with anxiety, for he had sensed the disaster although he could not see it, waded chest deep into the churning water, but the force knocked him back again, breathless and choking; and he was forced to retreat.

The other dog, strong swimmer though he was, made his way to the bank only with the greatest difficulty. Even then he was carried almost half a mile downstream before his feet were on firm ground. Immediately he set off down the river side following the swift flood.

Several times he saw the little figure of the cat, half under water, rushing madly ahead of him on the crest of the water, but he was never near enough, except at one point where the partially submerged piece of beaver dam caught on an overhanging branch. He plunged in immediately; but just as he was nearly within reach it tore free and once more went whirling and turning down the river until it was lost to sight. Although the dog pursued at full speed, he gradually fell further and further behind.

At last he was brought to a complete halt when the river entered a rocky gorge with no foothold on either side. He was forced to climb inland, and by the time he rejoined the river on the far side of the gorge there was no sign of the cat.

It was nearly dark when he returned to find the terrier, who was walking wearily along the river bank towards him; he was exhausted, limping badly from a cut paw, and utterly spent and miserable; so much so that he barely returned the greeting of the bewildered and lonely old dog but dropped to the ground, his flanks heaving, to lie there.

They spent that night where they were, by the banks of the river, peaceful again after the violence of the afternoon. They lay curled closely together for comfort and warmth, and when a thin, cold rain fell they moved under the spreading branches of an old spruce for shelter.

In the middle of the night the old dog sat up, trembling all over with cold. He threw his head back, howling his grief and loneliness to the heavy weeping sky, for he had dearly loved his friend the cat.

From *The Incredible Journey*

SAMUEL BECKETT

Trouble Saved

UNABLE TO REMEMBER the name of my town I resolved to stop by the kerb, to wait for a passer-by with a friendly and intelligent air and then to whip off my hat and say, with my smile, I beg your pardon Sir, excuse me Sir, what is the name of this town, if you please? For the word once let fall I would know if it was the right word the one I was seeking, in my memory, or another, and so where I stood. This resolution, actually formed as I rode along, was never to be carried out, an absurd mishap prevented it. Yes, my resolutions were remarkable in this, that they were no sooner formed than something always happened to prevent their execution. That must be why I am even less resolute now than then, just as then I was even less so than I once had been. But to tell the truth (to tell the truth!) I have never been particularly resolute, I mean given to resolutions, but rather inclined to plunge headlong into the shit, without knowing who was shitting against whom or on which side I had the better chance of skulking with success. But from this leaning too I derived scant satisfaction and if I have never quite got rid of it it is not for want of trying. The fact is, it seems, that the most you can hope is to be a little less, in the end, the creature you were in the beginning, and the middle. For I had hardly perfected my plan, in my head, when my bicycle ran over a dog, as subsequently appeared, and fell to the ground, an ineptness all the more unpardonable as the dog, duly leashed, was not out on the road, but in on the pavement, docile at its mistress's heels. Precautions are like resolutions, to be taken with precaution. The lady must have thought she lad left nothing to chance, so far as the safety of her dog was concerned, whereas in reality she was setting the whole system of nature at naught, no less surely than I myself with my insane demands for more light. But instead of grovelling in my turn, invoking my great age and infirmities, I made things worse by trying to run away. I was soon overtaken, by a bloodthirsty mob of both sexes and all ages, for I caught a glimpse of white beards and little almost angelfaces, and they were preparing to tear me to pieces when the lady intervened. She said in effect, she told me so later on and I believed her, Leave this poor old man alone. He has killed Teddy, I grant you that, Teddy whom I loved like my own child, but it is not so serious as it seems, for as it happens I was taking him to the veterinary surgeon, to have him put out of his misery. For Teddy was old, blind, deaf, crippled with rheumatism and perpetually incontinent, night and day, indoors and out of doors. Thanks then to this poor old man I have been spared a painful task, not to mention the expense which I am ill able to afford, having no other means of support than the pension of my dear departed, fallen in defence of a country that called itself his and from which in his lifetime he never derived the smallest benefit, but only insults and vexations. The crowd was begining to disperse, the danger was past, but the lady in her stride. You may say, she said, that he did wrong to run away, that he should have explained, asked to be forgiven. Granted. But it is clear he has not all his wits about him, that he is beside himself, for reasons of which we know nothing and which might put us all to shame, if we did know them. I even wonder if he knows what he has done. There emanated such tedium from this droning voice that I was making ready to move on when the unavoidable police constable rose up before me. He brought down heavily on my handlebars his big red hairy paw, I noticed it myself, and had it appears with the lady the following conversation. Is this the man who ran over your dog, Madam? He is, sergeant, and what of it? No, I can't record this fatuous colloquy. So I will merely observe that finally in his turn the constable too dispersed, the word is not too strong, grumbling and growling, followed by the last idlers who had given up all hope of my coming to a bad end. But he turned back and said, Remove that dog.

From *Molloy*

MARILYN MONROE

Miscreants

PETER [LAWFORD] WAS initially attracted to Marilyn because at that time in her life she did have a wholesome, down-to-earth side. She loved the beach, worked out with weights to firm up her figure, and had an abundance of girlish high spirits. But the more he got to know and like her, the less interested he was in her sexually. Many aspects of the private Norma Jeane appealed to him: he loved her subtle, skewed sense of humour, her vulnerability, her tentative intelligence. But he was put off by the Marilyn Monroe persona she adopted publicly, the brassy blonde in skin-tight dresses and plunging décolletage. It was precisely this dynamic between innocence and wantonness that made Marilyn so fascinating to the public, but the wanton side left Peter cold.

He was put off, too, by what he saw as Marilyn's lack of hygiene. Joe Naar recalled picking Marilyn up along with Peter and Joe's date, the actress Barbara Darrow. 'Peter went into her apartment and her dog had done something on the carpet and she didn't seem to care. He was so disgusted he said to me, "*You* take her out." So we switched dates. He knew Barbara because I'd dated her before, so he took Barbara home and I took Marilyn home.'

Peter later said that he had stepped in the dog's mess, and Marilyn poked her head out of the bathroom door and chirped, 'Oh dear, he's done it again!' The dog, Peter added, 'turned out to be the smallest chihuahua I've ever seen. Heaven knows how it had produced such a pile!'

James Spada, from Peter Lawford

PHILIP LARKIN

Take One Home for the Kiddies

On shallow straw, in shadeless glass,
Huddled by empty bowls, they sleep:
No dark, no dam, no earth, no grass –
Mam, get us one of them to keep.

Living toys are something novel,
But it soon wears off somehow.
Fetch the shoebox, fetch the shovel –
Mam, we're playing funerals now.

JOHN OSBORNE
Esmé Percy

M<small>Y ABIDING MEMORY</small> of the week is of dining with Peggy
Ashcroft and Esmé Percy at an Indian restaurant by the Martyrs'
Memorial. They talked entertainingly and Esme's beloved dog farted
incessantly under the table. Peggy grew impatient. 'Don't you think he
needs a bit of a clean-out?' 'Oh, but I only shampooed him this
morning.' 'I mean clean *within*, not without.'

Heroic Snoopy

W<small>HEN SHE</small> [M<small>ARY</small> U<small>RE</small>] came to in the late afternoon, she clearly
had almost no remembrance of her first-footing capers the night
before. It was soon obvious that we were both stricken with not only
hangovers but severe flu. I took our temperatures, which confirmed the
diagnosis . . .

I dosed us with hot whisky and a couple of sleeping-pills. It seemed
the only practical way of facing the first onslaught of the New Year. We
were both asleep long before midnight.

A few hours later I was woken by the sound of barking. Snoopy, our
lively but neurotic dachshund, was thumping his paws on my chest. The
bedroom was thick with smoke. The well of the staircase was consumed
with flames taller than a man. I grabbed Mary, who was still asleep,
thrust a pillow into her hands and dragged her to the study, opened the
window and perched her on the sloping roof. She clung there dazed
but fairly calm while I picked up the telephone, which was miraculously
still working.

Within minutes we could hear the bells of the fire-engines entering
the street. Then there was a delay and a great deal of shouting below.
A fleet of Hooray sports cars blocked the approach. Snoopy's barking
had stopped and flames were visible beneath the door. Suddenly a
figure appeared through the smoke, flipped Mary over his shoulder and
covered her in a blanket. I clutched the window-frame, burning from
the heat behind and wondering if I should resign myself to jumping and
the certainty of a broken limb or two. A helmeted figure scampered up

a ladder at astonishing speed, held out a strong arm and guided me down.

I was bundled into a waiting police-car where Mary was crouched unhurt, crying for Snoopy. It seemed unlikely he could have survived, but he was found later curled up beneath her dressing-table and returned to us at the Goring Hotel, where we were efficiently installed. It was almost light when we sat down in our Edwardian suite, congratulating the dog and drinking coffee laced with whisky.

From *Almost a Gentleman*

JOHN STEINBECK

Indigestion

IN THE MIDDLE of April [1936] he reported, 'I'm working rapidly now on *Of Mice and Men*. Pages are flying,' but at the end of the following month, he had what he called a 'minor tragedy.' After their return from Mexico, John had acquired a setter puppy, one in a long line of dogs called Toby. He recounted to Elizabeth Otis that his pup, 'left alone one night, made confetti of about half my manuscript book. Two months work to do over again. It sets me back. There was no other draft. I was pretty mad but the poor little fellow may have been acting critically' [27 May]. He didn't want to punish Toby severely, since what was the use of ruining 'a good dog for a manuscript I'm not sure is good at all.'

Jackson Benson, from *The True Adventures of John Steinbeck, Writer*

On the Road

NOW, CHARLEY is a mind-reading dog. There have been many trips in his lifetime, and often he has to be left at home. He knows we are going long before the suitcases come out, and he paces and worries and whines and goes into a state of mild hysteria, old as he is. During the weeks of preparation he was underfoot the whole time and made a damned nuisance of himself. He took to hiding in the truck, creeping in and trying to make himself look small.

* * *

Charley is a tall dog. As he sat in the seat beside me, his head was almost as high as mine. He put his nose close to my ear and said, 'Ftt.' He is the only dog I ever knew who could pronounce the consonant *F*. This is because his front teeth are crooked, a tragedy which keeps him out of dog shows; because his upper front teeth slightly engage his lower lip Charley can pronounce *F*. The word 'Ftt' usually means he would like to salute a bush or a tree. I opened the cab door and let him out, and he went about his ceremony. He doesn't have to think about it to do it well. It is my experience that in some areas Charley is more intelligent that I am, but in others he is abysmally ignorant. He can't read, can't drive a car, and has no grasp of mathematics. But in his own field of endeavour, which he was now practicing, the slow, imperial smelling over and anointing of an area, he has no peer. Of course his horizons are limited, but how wide are mine?

* * *

Charley likes to get up early, and he likes me to get up early too. And why shouldn't he? Right after his breakfast he goes back to sleep. Over the years he has developed a number of innocent-appearing ways to get me up. He can shake himself and his collar loud enough to wake the dead. If that doesn't work he gets a sneezing fit. But perhaps his most irritating method is to sit quietly beside the bed and stare into my face with a sweet and forgiving look on his face; I come out of deep sleep with the feeling of being looked at. But I have learned to keep my eyes tight shut. If I even blink he sneezes and stretches, and that night's sleep is over for me. Often the war of wills goes on for quite a time, I squinching my eyes shut and he forgiving me, but he nearly always wins. He liked travelling so much he wanted to get started early, and early for Charley is the first tempering of darkness with the dawn.

* * *

As I sat there fingering the first volume of *The Spectator* and considering how the mind usually does two things at once that it knows about and probably several it doesn't, a luxurious car drove in and a rather stout and bedizened woman released a rather stout and bedizened Pomeranian of the female persuasion. I would not have known this latter fact, but Charley knew. Emerging from behind the garbage can, he found her beautiful, his French blood flared up, and he proceeded to gallantries unmistakable even to the slack eyes of mademoiselle's mistress. This creature let out a shriek like a wounded rabbit, emerged from the car with an explosive ooze, and would have snatched her darling to her bosom if she could have bent down that far. The best she could do was to fetch a slap at tall Charley's head. He quite naturally and casually took a nip at her hand before proceeding toward romance. Until that moment I never quite knew the meaning of the phrase 'to make the welkin ring.' In the first place I didn't know what a welkin was. I looked it up later. And that bull bitch of a woman sure as hell made it ring. I grabbed her hand and saw that the skin wasn't even broken, so I grabbed her dog, which promptly bit me good and drew blood before I could get the little monster by the throat and gently throttle it.

Charley regarded the whole scene as nonsense. He wet on the garbage can for the twentieth time and called it a day.

It took time to calm the lady. I brought out the bottle of brandy, which might have killed her, and she took a slug that should have killed her.

After all I've done for him you'd think Charley would have come to my aid, but he dislikes neurotics and he detests drunks. He climbed in Rocinante, crawled under the table, and went to sleep. Sic semper cum Frogs.

At last milady flailed away with her hand brake on, and the kind of a day I had built lay in ruins. Addison had crashed in flames, the trout no longer ringed the pool, and a cloud covered the sun and put a chill in the air. I found myself driving faster than I wanted to and it began to rain, a cold steel rain. I didn't give the lovely villages the attention they deserved, and before long I had crossed into Maine and continued eastward.

*   *   *

Charley had no answer to my premise. Also, he was a mess. I had promised myself to keep him combed and clipped and beautiful, and I hadn't done it. His fur was balled and dirty. Poodles do not shed any more than sheep do. At night, when I had planned this virtuous grooming, I was always too busy with something else. Also I discovered a dangerous allergy I didn't know he had. One night I had pulled up at a trucker's park where huge cattle trucks put up and cleaned their beds; around the park there was a mountain of manure and a fog of flies. Although Rocinante was screened the flies got in in their millions and hid in corners and would not be dislodged. For the first time I got out the bug bomb and sprayed heavily, and Charley broke into a sneezing attack so violent and prolonged that I had finally to carry him out in my arms. In the morning the cab was full of sleepy flies and I sprayed it and Charley had another attack. After that, whenever flying visitors invaded I had to close Charley out and air out the house or cab after the pests were dead. I never saw such a severe allergy.

*   *   *

I must confess to a laxness in the matter of National Parks. I haven't visited many of them. Perhaps this is because they enclose the unique, the spectacular, the astounding – the greatest waterfall, the deepest canyon, the highest cliff, the most stupendous works of man or nature. And I would rather see a good Brady photograph than Mount Rushmore. For it is my opinion that we enclose and celebrate the freaks of our nation and of our civilization. Yellowstone National Park is no more representative of America than is Disneyland.

This being my natural attitude, I don't know what made me turn sharply south and cross a state line to take a look at Yellowstone. Perhaps it was a fear of my neighbours. I could hear them say, 'You mean you were that near to Yellowstone and didn't go? You must be crazy.' Again it might have been the American tendency in travel. One goes, not so much to see but to tell afterward. Whatever my purpose in going to Yellowstone, I'm glad I went because I discovered something about Charley I might never have known.

A pleasant-looking National Park man checked me in and then he said, 'How about that dog? They aren't permitted in except on leash.'

'Why?' I asked.

'Because of the bears.'

'Sir,' I said, 'this is an unique dog. He does not live by tooth or fang. He respects the right of cats to be cats although he doesn't admire them. He turns his steps rather than disturb an earnest caterpillar. His greatest fear is that someone will point out a rabbit and suggest that he chase it. This is a dog of peace and tranquility. I suggest that the greatest danger to your bears will be pique at being ignored by Charley.'

The young man laughed. 'I wasn't so much worried about the bears,' he said. 'But our bears have developed an intolerance for dogs. One of them might demonstrate his prejudice with a clip on the chin and then – no dog.'

'I'll lock him in the back, sir. I promise you Charley will cause no ripple in the bear world, and as an old bear-looker, neither will I.'

'I just have to warn you,' he said. 'I have no doubt your dog has the best of intentions. On the other hand, our bears have the worst. Don't leave food about. Not only do they steal but they are critical of anyone who tries to reform them. In a word, don't believe their sweet faces or you might get clobbered. And don't let the dog wander. Bears don't argue.'

We went on our way into the wonderland of nature gone nuts, and you will have to believe what happened. The only way I can prove it would be to get a bear.

Less than a mile from the entrance I saw a bear beside the road, and it ambled out as though to flag me down. Instantly a change came over Charley. He shrieked with rage. His lips flared, showing wicked teeth that have some trouble with a dog biscuit. He screeched insults at the bear, which hearing, the bear reared up and seemed to me to overtop Rocinante. Frantically I rolled the windows shut and, swinging quickly to the left, grazed the animal, then scuttled on while Charley raved and ranted beside me, describing in detail what he would do to that bear if he could get at him. I was never so astonished in my life. To the best of my knowledge Charley had never seen a bear, and in his whole history had showed great tolerance for every living thing. Besides all this, Charley is a coward, so deep-seated a coward that he has developed a technique for concealing it. And yet he showed every evidence of wanting to get out and murder a bear that outweighed him a thousand to one. I don't understand it.

A little farther along two bears showed up, and the effect was doubled. Charley became a maniac. He leaped all over me, he cursed and growled, snarled and screamed. I didn't know he had the ability to snarl. Where did he learn it? Bears were in good supply, and the road became a nightmare. For the first time in his life Charley resisted reason, even resisted a cuff on the ear. He became a primitive killer lusting for the blood of his enemy, and up to this moment he had had no enemies. In a bearless stretch, I opened the cab, took Charley by the collar, and locked him in the house. But that did no good. When we passed other bears he leaped on the table and scratched at the windows trying to get out at them. I could hear canned goods crashing as he struggled in his mania. Bears simply brought out the Hyde in my Jekyll-headed dog. What could have caused it? Was it a pre-breed memory of a time when the wolf was in him? I know him well. Once in a while he tries a bluff, but it is a palpable lie. I swear that this was no lie. I am certain that if he were released he would have charged every bear we passed and found victory or death.

It was too nerve-wracking, a shocking spectacle, like seeing an old, calm friend go insane. No amount of natural wonders, of rigid cliffs and belching waters, of smoking springs could even engage my attention while that pandemonium went on. After about the fifth encounter I gave up, turned Rocinante about, and retraced my way. If I had stopped the night and bears had gathered to my cooking, I dare not think what would have happened.

At the gate the park guard checked me out. 'You didn't stay long. Where's the dog?'

'Locked up back there. And I owe you an apology. That dog has the heart and soul of a bear-killer and I didn't know it. Heretofore he has been a little tender-hearted toward an underdone steak.'

'Yeah!' he said. 'That happens sometimes. That's why I warned you. A bear dog would know his chances, but I've seen a Pomeranian go up like a puff of smoke. You know, a well-favored bear can bat a dog like a tennis ball.'

I moved fast, back the way I had come, and I was reluctant to camp for fear there might be some unofficial non-government bears about. That night I spent in a pretty auto court near Livingston. I had my dinner in a restaurant, and when I had settled in with a drink and a comfortable chair and my bathed bare feet on a carpet with red roses, I inspected Charley. He was dazed. His eyes held a faraway look and he was totally exhausted, emotionally no doubt. Mostly he reminded me of a man coming out of a long, hard drunk – worn out, depleted, collapsed. He couldn't eat his dinner, he refused the evening walk, and once we were in he collapsed on the floor and went to sleep. In the night I heard him whining and yapping, and when I turned on the light his feet were making running gestures and his body jerked and his eyes were wide open, but it was only a night bear. I awakened him and gave him some water. This time he went to sleep and didn't stir all night. In the morning he was still tired. I wonder why we think the thoughts and emotions of animals are simple.

*   *   *

In the middle of the night Charley awakened me with a soft apologetic whining, and since he is not a whining dog I got up immediately. He was in trouble, his abdomen distended and his nose and ears hot. I took him out and stayed with him, but he could not relieve the pressure.

I wish I knew something of veterinary medicine. There's a feeling of helplessness with a sick animal. It can't explain how it feels, though on the other hand it can't lie, build up its symptoms, or indulge in the pleasures of hypochondria. I don't mean they are incapable of faking. Even Charley, who is as honest as they come, is prone to limp when his feelings are hurt. I wish someone would write a good, comprehensive book of home dog medicine. I would do it myself if I were qualified.

Charley was a really sick dog, and due to get sicker unless I could find some way to relieve the growing pressure. A catheter would do it, but who has one in the mountains in the middle of the night? I had a plastic tube for siphoning gasoline, but the diameter was too great. Then I remembered something about pressure causing muscular tension which increases the pressure, etc., so that the first step is to relax the muscles. My medicine chest was not designed for general practice, but I did have a bottle of sleeping pills – seconal, one and a half grains. But how about dosage? That is where the home medicine book would be helpful. I took a capsule apart and unloaded half of it and fitted it together again. I slipped the capsule back beyond the bow in Charley's tongue where he could not push it out, then held up his head and massaged it down his throat. Then I lifted him on the bed and covered him. At the end of the hour there was no change in him, so I opened a second capsule and gave him another half. I think that, for his weight, one and a half grains is a pretty heavy dose, but Charley must have a high tolerance. He resisted it for three quarters of an hour before his breathing slowed and he went to sleep. I must have dozed off, too. The next thing I knew, he hit the floor. In his drugged condition his legs buckled under him. He got up, stumbled, and got up again. I opened the door and let him out. Well, the method worked all right, but I don't see how one medium-sized dog's body could have held that much fluid. Finally he staggered in and collapsed on a piece of carpet and was asleep immediately. He was so completely out that I worried over the dosage. But his temperature had dropped and his breathing was normal and his heart beat was strong and steady. My sleep was restless, and when dawn came I saw that Charley had not moved. I awakened him and he was quite agreeable when I got his attention. He smiled, yawned, and went back to sleep.

I lifted him into the cab and drove hell for leather for Spokane. I don't remember a thing about the country on the way. On the outskirts I looked up a veterinary in the phone book, asked directions, and rushed Charley into the examination room as an emergency. I shall not mention the doctor's name, but he is one more reason for a good home book on dog medicine. The doctor was, if not elderly, pushing his luck, but who am I to say he had a hangover? He raised Charley's lip with a shaking hand, then turned up an eyelid and let it fall back.

'What's the matter with him?' he asked, with no interest whatever.

'That's why I'm here – to find out.'

'Kind of dopey. Old dog. Maybe he had a stroke.'

'He had a distended bladder. If he's dopey, it's because I gave him one and a half grains of seconal.'

'What for?'

'To relax him.'

'Well, he's relaxed.'

'Was the dosage too big?'

'I don't know.'

'Well, how much would you give?'

'I wouldn't give it at all.'

'Let's start fresh – what's wrong with him?'

'Probably a cold.'

'Would that cause bladder symptoms?'

'If the cold was there – yes, sir.'

'Well, look – I'm on the move. I'd like a little closer diagnosis.'

He snorted. 'Look here. He's an old dog. Old dogs get aches and pains. That's just the way it is.'

I must have been snappish from the night. 'So do old men,' I said. 'That doesn't keep them from doing something about it.' And I think for the first time I got through to him.

'Give you something to flush out his kidneys,' he said. 'Just a cold.'

I took the little pills and paid my bill and got out of there. It wasn't that this veterinary didn't like animals. I think he didn't like himself, and when that is so the subject usually must find an area for dislike outside himself. Else he would have to admit his self-contempt.

On the other hand, I yield to no one in my distaste for the self-styled dog-lover, the kind who heaps up his frustrations and makes a dog carry them around. Such a dog-lover talks baby talk to mature and thoughtful animals, and attributes his own sloppy characteristics to them until the dog becomes in his mind an alter ego. Such people, it seems to me, in what they imagine to be kindness, are capable of inflicting long and lasting tortures on an animal, denying it any of its natural desires and fulfillments until a dog of weak character breaks down and becomes the fat, asthmatic, befurred bundle of neuroses. When a stranger addresses Charley in baby talk, Charley avoids him. For Charley is not a human; he's a dog, and he likes it that way. He feels that he is a first-rate dog and has no wish to be a second-rate human. When the alcoholic vet touched him with his unsteady, inept hand, I saw the look of veiled contempt in Charley's eyes. He knew about the man, I thought, and perhaps the doctor knew he knew. And maybe that was the man's trouble. It would be very painful to know that your patients had no faith in you.

From *Travels with Charley*

Last Days

CHARLEY IS WELL but he is getting old. The hip he had broken as a pup gives him considerable trouble now, particularly when the weather changes. But in the morning he still thinks of himself as Youth.

To Otto Lindhardt, September 1962
From *A Life in Letters*

LAST WEEK WAS one of sadness. Charley dog died full of years but leaving a jagged hole nevertheless. He died of what would probably be called cirrhosis in a human. This degeneration is usually ascribed to indulgence in alcohol. But Charley did not drink, or if he did he was very secret about it.

To D.E.S. Montgomery, April 1963, *ibid*

JACQUELINE SUSANN

Josephine's Shyness

I WOULD LIKE TO be able to say it was just an accident – or fate. Like I was taking a walk and a stray poodle just happened to follow me home. But to begin with, stray poodles do not roam up and down Central Park South. And if a stray poodle did follow me home, it would immediately be followed by a hysterical owner and the police. So remember, whenever you see a poodle dragging some captive around on a leash, it's the captive who put his own head in the noose. Because a poodle never goes in search of its victim. The victim goes in search of a poodle.

To any smug individual who as yet does not share his worldly goods with a poodle – who *knows* it will never happen to him – I offer just two words of advice.

WATCH OUT!

It sneaks up on you. The most innocent little incident can trigger it off, and wham! suddenly you get the 'call.' The insatiable urge to give up all worldly pleasures and donate your life to the care and raising of a French Poodle.

It happened to me on a day that was like any other day. I had been lunching with my good friend Dorothy Strelsin. Late in the afternoon we went back to her apartment. She wanted me to see some new pictures she had acquired. The moment she opened the door, a small furry object rushed to greet her, prancing on its hind legs in sheer ecstasy.

'This is Tinker,' Dorothy said in a tender voice. Then she picked up three pounds of squirming, elated dog, which immediately started to saturate her with adoring kisses. I stood by silently while Dorothy received five minutes of this rapturous affection. Then she placed him on the floor, and we entered the living room with Tinker capering at her heels, squealing with joy at her mere presence. Her husband, Alfred, looked up from his paper and said, 'Hello, dear. Hello, Jackie.' Then he went back to his paper. (A very normal and husbandly thing to do.)

I know that when I come home late, and Irving is watching the news on television, he won't even fade me with a 'Hello, dear.' In fact he doesn't even acknowledge my presence until Chet has said good night to David, and David says, 'Good night, Chet.' Then he gives me a casual smile and a 'Hello, dear.'

Now I'm not knocking 'Hello dears.' They're very nice to hear. And a husband is a glorious thing to have around the house. But after seeing Dorothy and Tinker together, I wanted a little fanfare of my own. I wanted someone to bounce to the door to meet me, to cover my face with adoring kisses, to follow me around the apartment. And as much as Irving loves me, he just is not the prancing following type.

I began thinking. Thinking about poodles. It got so I stopped and stared every time I saw a poodle. And the more I stared, the more my convictions grew. EVERY poodle stared at its master with a look of complete idolatry. You've seen that look. The way a young painter looks at a Rembrandt or Titian. The way Liz Taylor looks at Richard Burton. The way Zsa Zsa looks at mink. That's how a poodle looks at its master.

I started staring in pet shot windows – but no longer as a spectator. Now I was a potential buyer. Let's face it! I was 'hooked.'

*　　*　　*

Of course, she didn't know what a 'walk' was. She had never heard the word before, but she knew something was up. She put down the satin throw pillow she was eating and gave me her undivided attention.

I showed her the leash. (Sure, I had bought a leash. No one had suggested a wheelchair. Who figured I was going to wind up with the Elizabeth Barrett of poodles?) Josie stared at the leash. Something definitely was up. She had never seen that before. She sniffed at it but didn't get the message. However, this dog would do anything for me, so she obligingly tried to eat it. I slipped it around her neck.

She suddenly turned into a whirling dervish. She rolled, leaped, and used all four feet in an effort to free this noose from her neck. It was obvious that, for the first time in our relationship, Josephine and I were having a 'difference of opinion.'

I picked her up, leash and all, and carried her to the park. I knew she'd get the idea when she saw other dogs sporting similar neckwear. She got the idea after almost choking to death three times. But as soon as she realized that the leash and I were merely an extension of her personality, she relaxed and got into the swing of things.

She smelled the benches, the grass, and even sniffed at the trunks of trees. Then I sat her down and told her the secrets of the grass and trees. They were not merely ornamental. I had plunked down two dollars for her license. That made her a taxpayer. She owned this park.

Therefore, the grass and trees were were for her convenience. To be used any time she saw fit. In place of *The New York Times*.

But she didn't seem to get the idea. However, I knew all she needed was a good illustration. I rushed her over to a boxer who was getting set to perform against a litter basket. This was a big mistake. I had expected a performance – not a tidal wave! We both ran for the hills!

Next, I let her view a Scotty as he gently lifted his leg against a tree. She wasn't frightened – just thought it was a disgusting display of bad taste. She watched a wire-haired perform the same ritual, followed by two cocker spaniels and a Maltese terrier. She yawned. After the boxer, all this was chicken feed!

I kept her out for twenty minutes. She enjoyed herself. But that's all she did. Enjoy herself. The moment she reached the privacy of our apartment, she made a dive for the kitchen and *The New York Times*.

However, I wasn't the least disheartened. Josie was very bright. I was positive that after one more outing the *Times* and *Tribune* would lose her patronage. She would have gotten the hang of the park first time out, if only that stupid boxer hadn't come on so strong!

*　　*　　*

The next day I tried Park Avenue. After all, I wanted to live, too. And I had read that both Cary Grant and Tony Curtis were in town. Well, Irving hadn't exaggerated. Josie sure was a smash. Like he said, we were stopped by every beautiful model. They all wanted to cuddle Josie. Since this wasn't exactly what I had in mind, I decided to try another avenue. I figured Madison Avenue might be different. It was. I spent ten minutes having a thrilling tête-à-tête with Arthur Murray. And on the next block I ran into Charles Coburn. You can see how my luck was running.

Thereafter I confined our walks to Central Park. At least there we'd meet dogs, and Josie might learn about the trees. But Josephine seemed to have a closed mind on this subject. I pointed out all the other dogs who dutifully lifted well-trained legs against the waiting trees. Josephine stared obediently, and sometimes even displayed a small amount of interest, but she never regarded it as anything but a spectator sport.

I coaxed. I pleaded. I finally resorted to physical instruction. I lifted her leg against a tree and held it there for ten minutes. I had no results other than to attract a curious group of onlookers. However, I stuck to it relentlessly. My motto: 'Let them stop and stare, it won't bother me.'

It got so I became a familiar sight in the park, holding Josie's leg against a tree. After a few days, I rarely attracted more than a passing stare.

One day, while I was in the midst of this new hobby, a fat woman with two pregnant Airedales passed. She paused to stare at me with interest.

After about ten minutes, she said, 'What is she supposed to be doing?' (Oh, you meet all kinds! What did she think Josephine was supposed to be doing? Ballet exercises?) But I couldn't be rude to a fat lady with two pregnant dogs, so I gave her a brief explanation.

The fat lady said, 'But she's a girl.'

I agreed and returned my attention to Josie and the tree. Josie, who has the disposition of an angel, obediently held her leg up, but of course, nothing happened. (I tell you, that dog would do anything for me, except give up *The New York Times.*)

The fat lady stood there and studied the situation with great interest. Finally she said, 'Girls don't lift their legs against trees.'

I put down Josie's leg. What did girl dogs do?

She said, 'They squat.'

Then, as if on command, her fat Airedales squatted and showed me how it was done. Even Josephine watched with interest, although she seemed slightly embarrassed at their lack of restraint. Then the fat lady and her Airdales waddled off with the air of personal satisfaction of a job well done.

The moment they were out of sight, I tried to push Josie into a squatting position. She went rigid and stared at me like I had suddenly lost my senses. The more I tried, and the more rigid she became.

That night I told Irving about my conversation with the fat lady. He said it made sense and agreed to give it a whirl. The following morning we took her to the park together. After three or four unsuccessful attempts on my part, Irving snatched her from me. What was I trying to do to this poor dog? First I had almost gotten her leg out of joint. Now she was a cinch for curvature of the spine.

He decided to take over.

From *Every Night, Josephine!*

JOHN LENNON

Good Dog Nigel

Arf, Arf, he goes, a merry sight,
Our little hairy friend,
Arf, Arf, upon the lampost bright
Arfing round the bend.
Nice dog! Goo boy,
Waggie tail and beg,
Clever Nigel, jump for joy

Because we're putting you to sleep at three of the clock, Nigel.

LYNDON JOHNSON

Aural Sense

PRESIDENT JOHNSON HAS made his first serious political error in weeks. He picked up his beagles by the ears yesterday to make them yelp, and the wrath of humane societies has fallen upon him today. 'It is good for them', the President blandly assured a surprised delegation of bankers as he yanked the beagles, Him and Her, up by the ears. 'It does them good to let them bark.'

The humane societies could not disagree more. One of them said today: 'A dog has a front end and a back end and appreciates support at both ends. The question is not how painful it is to beagles, but how painful it is to any living creature to be lifted by the ears. In our experience this is the wrong way to do it.'

Reuter, 28 April 1964

(It is sometimes said that this incident cost Johnson dearly; in fact, he was re-elected with an overwhelming majority the following November.)

JOHN CHEEVER

Sexual Confusion

M Y FATHER LOVED dogs. Cassiopeia, the black Labrador puppy he bought from a litter out of Phil Boyer's bitch Sable of Teatown in 1962, became his muse, his companion, his faithful and discreet confidante. Cassie was not really a dog at all but a dowager countess with all the airs of a stingy aristocrat, my father would explain to anyone who cared to listen. She and our next dog, Flora Macdonald (named for the woman who helped Bonnie Prince Charlie escape from Scotland), were actually 'formerly dorgs' – a term he had invented to explain the fact that they were really people temporarily trapped in hairy, rotund bodies. He had a special relationship with many medium-sized or large dogs (small dogs were too much like cats). He loved Arthur Spear's Minerva (Flora's daughter), and the Maxwells' Daisy, and the Swopes' Mowena, and Gene and Clare Thaw's Kelly, and my two golden retrievers Maisie and Bathsheba (everyone else called Bathsheba 'Sheba', but my father felt that she liked to be called by her full name), and the Boyers' Ezekiel, whom we had as a puppy because he was the son of our Labrador Cassiopeia.

'Dear Zeke,' my father wrote to him at the Boyers', in what he imagined was Cassie's inimitable tone.

> it was very good to hear from you, you will nevr know how much yr letters mean to me now that I am nearing the end of my journey. oh I know you will say mother dere, no, no, no, but the truth is that yr mother has got so

weak in these last months that she can no longer raise herself up to the lid
of an average-sized garbage pail. . . . daisy maxwell [the Maxwells' yellow
Labrador] came to visit. she is yellow all over and committed several
discourtesies that I do not choose to describe. The old fool got smeared
and invited his publisher [Cass Canfield] to dinner. This publisher is a rich
old man named Cassie and so naturally there were a lot of mix ups such as
when the old fool would shout cassie get your face out of the cracker dish
or cassie shut up. mrs. swope was there and she giggled. they had pasta to
eat with some kind of sauce that did not agree with me. pffffrt, pffffrt all
night long. I simply didn't shut my eyes once.

 please try to enjoy yourself and try not to let the thought of your lonely
impoverished and enfeebled old mother come between yourself and your
happiness. look away from the body into truth and light.

yr loving Mother

He also described his own affection for Cassie in his journal.

The old dog, my love. The difficulties with upholstered furniture. How she
began in her middle age to dislike long walks. Starting up the beach she
seemed to enjoy herself but if you took an eye off her she would swing
around and gallop back to the house. . . . That she always got to her feet
when I entered the room. That she enjoyed men very much and was
conspicuously indifferent to women. That her dislikes were marked and she
definitely preferred people from traditional and if possible wealthy origins.
That she had begun to resemble those imperious and somehow mannish
women who devilled my youth; the dancing teacher, the banker's wife, the
headmistress of the progressive school I attended. How when I was alone
and heard her wandering through the house my feelings for her were of
love and gratitude; that her heavy step put me to sleep. That she barked
when I talked loudly to myself.

Cassie was put down by the vet in 1968, because she had become too
crippled to walk, but when Flora died at home in my mother's arms,
almost ten years later, there was a problem. My father wrapped her in
burlap and put her on the porch bench, where the other dogs sniffed
her apprehensively. The next day, my mother insisted that my father
dig a grave for her. He had to drive to Vermont that evening to read at
Bennington, and he explained that he didn't have the energy to do both.
In the end, the man who came to mow the lawn dug the grave. Flora
rests at the end of the rose garden, next to a chrysanthemum planted in
her memory.

 My father's last dog was a scruffy golden retriever of indeterminate age. For a long time I thought this dog would be the exception to my father's passion for the canine species, but I underestimated his perversity and the dog's well-masked charm. She was a boisterous, leggy, badly bred dog with a square head and a habit of dropping wet rocks on your feet. My parents inherited her when my brother Ben didn't want her anymore. She was named Tara, after Scarlett O'Hara's ancestral home in *Gone With the Wind*. My father decided that Tara was an unsuitable name for a dog, and he rechristened her 'Edgar.' Although this resulted in some sexual confusion, he usually referred to her as 'him', altering the pronoun to go with her new name. The change seemed to give her oblivious stubbornness an endearing quality, and slowly Edgar became my father's dog just as Cassie and Flora had been before her. My father fed her and she slept at the foot of his bed. Edgar was photographed with my father for *Time* and *People* (her frequently successful efforts to knock over photographers notwithstanding); she appeared on book-jacket covers and in the newspapers.

'We are very close,' my father wrote me about Edgar when I was living in France in 1978.

He seems to feel it is his destiny to walk with me in these twilight years. When he wakes me, late at night, rooting noisily amongst his dingle-berries, we exchange the most profound and tender smiles before we both return to sleep. . . . In the evenings we watch the baseball games on TV and we both cry at triples. What has come between us is Tennis Balls.

Edgar led me to believe that he enjoys Tennis Balls. We have a new neighbour named Townsend who will give me a can of tennis balls if I will lunch with him. Townsend likes to talk about how undeserved is his failure as a novelist. I get three balls. I give these to Edgar, one by one, and he hides them all over the place and brings for me to throw for him sharp rocks, black walnuts and an occasional tomato. When I lecture him on the fact that I have ruined my day for a tin of tennis balls he brings me more rocks and walnuts. I sometimes raise my voice and the neighbours and their friends all come out to listen. . . . I don't know where this will end.

Edgar was a sort of noble savage, I suppose, a canine version of the dumb innocent who is wiser than all the scholars and professors and learned doctors. In the end, her prescience was spooky. When my father came back from his first visit to Memorial Hospital in 1981, just after his disease had been diagnosed as cancer, Edgar abandoned her place at her foot of his bed and went to sleep in the living room. My father was terribly upset by this defection. Although none of us said it, it was as if Edgar knew that my father was going to die. It took us a few days to lure her back, but about a month after that Edgar started to cough. She wouldn't eat. One afternoon she got caught in the snow under my father's car, and although he could hardly walk, he crawled underneath to free her. Later my mother took her to the vet. The next day they did a series of X-rays, and the vet called to explain that Edgar had lung cancer. It was too late to do anything about it. She died in March of 1982.

Susan Cheever, from *Home Before Dark*

CHARLES PANATI

In the money

I T WILL PERHAPS come as no surprise that the largest group of will makers who leave unusual bequests are pet lovers. Dogs and cats are the most frequent legatees, but estates have been left to guppies, cockatoos, marmosets, ferrets, and pythons. Research has turned up nothing of a lion's share.

The largest canine bequest on record was that of Eleanor Ritchey, heiress to the Quaker State Refining Corporation. She died in Fort Lauderdale, Florida, in 1968, will her entire fortune of $4.5 million to her 150 beloved dogs. The family contested. A court battle raged for 5 years, the dogs represented by a prestigious Southern law firm. By the time an agreement was reached in September 1973, Eleanor Ritchey's escrow estate had mushroomed to $14 million and 77 of the dogs had died (natural deaths). This meant the surviving dogs were even richer. As were their lawyers.

In the final settlement, the dogs were awarded $9 million, each receiving $123,287.67, to go for food, grooming, and housing. Two million dollars was divided among Eleanor Ritchey's brothers and sisters. The rest of the estate went as fees to the dogs' lawyers. But this was not the end of the issue. The Florida court, under Circuit Judge Leroy Moe, posed a thorny issue: What if two of the dogs mated and sired a pup? Upon the parents' deaths, was the pup entitled to the balance of their canine estate?

The legal answer: yes. To avoid dog trials in perpetuity, it was decided that the animals be tattooed to prove indelibly their identity as inheritors, then segregated by sex to prevent parenting. From their inheritances, the dogs 'contributed' seventeen thousand dollars each year for their food and housing, and another twelve thousand dollars annually for weekly grooming and periodic medical checkups. Upon a dog's death, its estate passed on to Auburn University in Alabama for research into canine diseases.

From *Panati's Extraordinary Endings of Practically Everything and Everybody*

BRIAN WILSON

Inspiration

T HEN, AS ALWAYS, I pulled myself out of bed, went to the piano to save myself, and resumed work with Tony [Asher]. It was mid-February. I played him the song I'd written titled 'Good, Good, Good Vibrations.' I had the chorus but no lyrics for the verses. He loved the song but was a little weirded out when I explained why I'd written the song and what I wanted it to convey.

'My mom told me dogs discriminate between people,' I said. 'They like some because the people give off good vibrations. They bite others because they give off bad vibrations. I have a feeling this is a very spiritual song, and I want it to give off good vibrations.'

*   *   *

It wasn't enough. I needed more. I had to get farther out.

That's when the carpenters arrived and began constructing a giant boxlike frame around the piano. It was gorgeous, two and a half feet high. A couple of days later, several dump trucks rumbled up the driveway and workmen emptied two tons of sand into the newly built box. Marilyn, who disapproved, reluctantly gave in to my search for inspiration.

'Who am I to argue with the creator?' she said, exasperated. . . . Clearly, these assemblages weren't an attempt to stimulate creativity as much as they were camouflaged, cleverly rationalized and crazy efforts to escape the pressure and the people in my life. I was looking for places to hide from the escalating demands made on me. I wanted to be by myself and not have to worry about delivering a new album or competing with Lennon and McCartney or Spector. I was getting tired and needed a place to rest. . . . Van Dyke [Parks] was less appreciative of the sandbox. He took one look at me sitting at this grand piano set in the middle of a giant sandbox and immediately let me know that he found the sight disgusting. Juvenile, irresponsible, and sickening. Then he discovered that the dogs had taken to the sandbox more than even I had.

'What's that?' he asked, pointing in front of the piano.

I looked around the instrument. My dog Banana had relieved himself in the sand.

'It's dog shit,' I answered.

Van Dyke smiled apprehensively. Then he pulled up a chair, refusing to walk in the sand. It wasn't the easiest of times between Van Dyke and me.

From *Wouldn't It Be Nice*

SIR NOËL COWARD

On the Brighton Front

TARQUIN OLIVIER: 'What are those two dogs doing?'

COWARD: 'Well, the one in front is blind, and the other one is kindly pushing her to St Dunstan's Home for the Blind.'

TENNESSEE WILLIAMS

Bitten

FROM ROCHESTER, THEY moved to a two-week engagement in Detroit. Revisions [to *The Night of the Iguana*, 1961] descended from Williams's hotel room daily – brought to director and cast by Frank Merlo, who usually reported that the playwright had been awake most of the night and so was sleeping until afternoon. It was in Detroit that an unfortunate accident severed any hope of a reconciliation with Merlo.

'As if it weren't bad enough that the cast was hardly on speaking terms,' Frank Corsaro recalled, 'we were told that Williams's dog had bit him on the ankle, and that an infection had set in. He had to be hospitalized.' He also had to be calmed with increased sedation, for he was not only in acute pain from the wound but he was virtually irrational with rage and fear. The dog, given to him by Anna Magnani (and aptly named Satan), had been set on him by Merlo, he raved: Frank wanted him dead, all Frank wanted was his money, the dog always loved Frank more – it was a first major explosion of unreason. Only Merlo knew what was responsible, and he was powerless now to prevent Williams's pattern of self-destruction.

But somehow, with his remarkable recuperative and resilient powers, Williams returned to work on the production, bandaged ankles and unstable nerves notwithstanding. For the five-week run in Chicago he lived quite soberly and sensibly – but without Merlo, who took the dreaded dog and returned to Key West. Merlo was himself strangely weak and livid from a constant hacking cough; and neither he nor Williams had the emotional or physical energy for dialogue. This was the major moment of rupture in the declining relationship.

Donald Spoto, from *The Kindness of Strangers*

I'M SPENDING A FEW restful days in New Orleans with Victor and our new English bull-dog, Madam [Sophia], before returning to casting in New York. Madam looks just like a much-magnified Froggy and is delightful except that she is not house-broken and is cutting her teeth on the furniture.

Tennessee Williams to Maria St Just, April 1975

WHILE I AM IN Malibu, poor Madam is staying in San Francisco with Andrew Lyndon. I called last night to check on things. Andrew, drunker than usual – if possible – tried to get Madam to speak to me on the phone but she refused . . .

Could not bring her here because of the cats which are very ill-natured. Is there no possible way to get her to England without quarantine?! Liz Taylor kept her dog in yacht on Thames.

ibid, 24 July 1976

THE MATTER OF THE dog's English visit did not go any further, for, on leaving San Franciso, Williams had been assured that the hold of the aircraft in which Madam Sophia was to travel back to New York was air-conditioned, but it was not, and upon arrival the dog was found dead of suffocation.

THOM GUNN

Yoko

All today I lie in the bottom of the wardrobe
feeling low but sometimes getting up
to moodily lumber across rooms
and lap from the toilet bowl, it is so sultry
and then I hear the noise of firecrackers again
all New York is jaggedy with firecrackers today
and I go back to the wardrobe gloomy
trying to void my mind of them.
I am confused, I feel loose and unfitted.

At last deep in the stairwell I hear a tread,
it is him, my leader, my love.

I run to the door and listen to his approach.
Now I can smell him, what a good man he is,
I love it when he has the sweat of work on him,
as he enters I yodel with happiness,
I throw my body up against his, I try to lick his lips,
I care about him more than anything.

After we eat we go for a walk to the piers.
I leap into the standing warmth, I plunge into
the combination of old and new smells.
Here on a garbage can at the bottom, so interesting,
what sister or brother I wonder left this message I sniff.
I too piss there, and go on.
Here a hydrant there a pole
here's a smell I left yesterday, well that's disappointing
but I piss there anyway, and go on.
I investigate so much that in the end
it is for form's sake only, only a drop comes out.

I investigate tar and rotten sandwiches, everything, and go on.

And here a dried old turd, so interesting
so old, so dry, yet so subtle and mellow.
I can place it finely, I really appreciate it,
a gold distant smell like packed autumn leaves in winter
reminding me how what is rich and fierce when excreted
becomes weathered and mild
                    but always interesting
and reminding me of what I have to do.

My leader looks on and expresses his approval.

I sniff it well and later I sniff the air well
a wind is meeting us after the close July day
rain is getting near too but first the wind.

Joy, joy,
being outside with you, active, investigating it all,
with bowels emptied, feeling your approval
and then running on, the big fleet Yoko,
my body in its excellent black coat never lets me down,
returning to you (as I always will, you know that)
and now
 filling myself out with myself, no longer confused,
my panting pushing apart my black lips, but unmoving,
I stand with you braced against the wind.

J. R. ACKERLEY

Petulance

I HAVE BEEN READING Joe's account of himself and his father [*My Father and Myself*]. What odd books he wrote, but he was an odd man. After years of friendship he quarrelled with me because, on one of his visits to Lewes, sitting in the garden having tea, we heard a snarling behind us and his dog Queenie and my dog Nigg were having the sort of yapping, snapping, snarling hysterical dust-up which shows the difference between a bitch fight and a dog fight. I took it calmly and in fact separated them without difficulty. Joe did not say anything to me, but he told Trekkie that I had behaved monstrously – my horrible dog had attacked his beloved Queenie and I had paid no attention to this and had not even said that I was sorry. Joe never came near me again.

Leonard Woolf, in a letter to William Plomer

E. M. FORSTER

An Apology

ANOTHER VISIT I paid him, again when he was out of sorts, to his Chiswick flat, has stayed in my memory and is relevant. It was some fifteen years ago. I had an Alsatian bitch at that time and, when he invited me over, asked if I might bring her. Starting early, I could walk much of the way from Putney and thus combine my visit with her exercise. Morgan did not like dogs (a bad mark!), he was, if anything in the animal line, a cat man, but he agreed and we reached him by noon. He was in bed and I sat beside him on the edge of it. There was something particular he wanted to tell me, naturally I forget what, and while he was speaking my dog barked. She had heard a latch-key turn in the flat's front door. It was Morgan's char arriving. I hushed her, but it was difficult to silence her in such matters in which she thought she knew best – and it was of course correct behaviour for her to bark. Morgan resumed his interrupted story, she barked again, for the char could now be heard moving about in the kitchen alongside us. With a gesture of fatigue and despair Morgan stopped once more, then resumed when I pulled the animal between my legs and tried to deprive her of further speech by gripping her jaws together with my hands. But she freed herself from this uncomfortable clamp and barked again. 'Bloody dog!' exclaimed Morgan. Much embarrassed I said 'I'm so sorry' and cuffed the good creature who was only trying to warn us that there was a stranger in the place, and the stranger that he or she had been detected. Then I glanced at Morgan who had become silent. Tears were trickling down his face. He said 'Joe, forgive me. It was so *rude*'. To some people this may not look a very saintly story, to me it seemed divinely beautiful that anyone should cry for such a reason. It may be added that later on, when I had published a book about this dog, he said 'Thank you, you have opened my eyes', and then chose it for one of the Sunday papers as the best book of the year.

J. R. Ackerley, from *E. M. Forster: A Portrait*

PHIL SPECTOR

A Wife's Adversaries

EXCEPT FOR MY drives, about the only other time I left the house was when I'd take a little walk around the grounds. And after Phil turned the yard over to his dogs, I couldn't even to that anymore.

Phil's dog phase stared out when he got Grishka, this big Russian wolfhound – you know those dogs with the big, long noses? This was a gigantic thing, and I was scared to death of it. But Phil loved that dog so much he even made poor George Johnson cook dinner for it every night. And this dog didn't eat Alpo – Grishka ate steak.

Of course, whenever Phil liked one of something, it was just a matter of time before he got more of them. And so, a few months after he got Grishka, he brought home these two giant borzois. Then he got a couple of German shepherds, too. Pretty soon our yard looked like a kennel, with five dogs barking and running around at all hours of the day and night.

The only reason Phil even kept these crazy dogs at all was to build up his image. He wanted everyone to see him as this eccentric genius, so whenever a reporter came to interview him at the mansion, he made sure Grishka and the two giant borzois were sitting on the living room sofa. The reporter would take a look at these three skinny dogs and think Phil was a little nuts, and he'd put that in his article. And Phil loved it. He figured everyone already thought he was nuts, so he was damn well going to act the part. The problem was that he got caught up in his own craziness, and after a while even Phil couldn't tell where the act ended and real life began.

*   *   *

My mouth felt like a big brown sponge, and I drank it all in one long gulp. It wasn't until I set the glass down that I heard the shouting outside the window. It sounded like Phil. 'Sit down!' he was yelling. 'Sit down!'

'What's going on out there?' I asked.

'Oh,' Mom said, walking over to the window. 'Phil's out there trying to train one of his dogs. Been at it all morning. I don't know why he don't just give up.'

She pulled the curtain open just wide enough so I could see. Phil was standing by the pool, dressed in these terrible little red shorts that he'd been wearing since high school. He was waving a stick in the air like a circus lion tamer, but this poor German shepherd just lay there shaking at his feet. And Phil kept staring this poor animal down the whole time.

I'll never forget the look in his eyes. Phil stared at that dog with a cold, killer gaze that said, 'I *will* control you.' I couldn't believe the man I loved was capable of such a cruel stare. Then, suddenly it dawned on me that I was seeing Phil in a true light for the first time in years. The sad part is, I should've recognized it sooner. He'd stared at me that exact same way at least a hundred times before. I stood at the window watching Phil for the longest time. When I'd finished, I turned calmly to my mother and said, 'I hate him.'

Up to then I'd felt disappointment toward Phil. And fear, and anger – but never hate. It was an odd feeling. The only thing that had kept me going for all these years of slow torture was the fact that I loved Phil without question. And now, suddenly, I didn't even have that anymore.

'You look like you seen a ghost,' my mother said.

I wish I had. It wouldn't have been as scary. 'Mom,' I confessed, 'I don't know how much longer I can stay here like this.'

'I know what you mean, Ronnie,' she said. 'Married life ain't never easy.'

Ronnie Spector, from *Be My Baby*

TURNING TO THE Ramones, pulling the Phil trips and control games on a ripened and off-the-wall band set in its own ways, his manic presence at once divided the group and obscured the rock-and-roll bond they shared. At an early idea meeting Phil insulted drummer Marky Ramone's girlfriend. As they drove to Phil's house for the first time, they thought they were entering a compound. 'You drive in there,' Joey said, 'and you see all the signs about dogs and electrified fences ... the barbed wire, the mine fields. I'm sure a good portion of it's a put-on, part of the persona, the psychosis, but it can be intimidating. It's like when you went there, you were there; you can't get out until he's ready to let you out, and he's never ready, 'cause I guess he didn't have company too often and I guess he likes to keep you around. You'd say, "Well, Phil, it's time for us to go now," and he'd disappear. Then he'd come back and he'd want to show you his terrarium or some of the hideous-looking things he had in there. The night had to belong to Phil, just like the studio does. . . . It was just too weird. One time I opened a closet door in his kitchen and this St. Bernard dog jumped out of the dark. It was locked in, just hangin' out in there.'

Mark Ribowsky, from He's A Rebel

JOHN SPARROW

S CENE: THE CORNMARKET. An RSPCA collector is shaking a collecting-tin.

JOHN SPARROW (puts hand in pocket as if to take out coins): Madam, does the RSPCA use its funds to help dogs?
COLLECTOR (eagerly): Oh yes, sir, we do a great deal indeed for dogs.
JOHN SPARROW: Then I'm afraid that I cannot give you any money.

*   *   *

scene: A country house. A dog comes in, and sits by John Sparrow, who pats it.
JOHN SPARROW: What a nice dog – almost as nice as not having a dog at all.

(Oxford tradition)

Unmanned Dogs

S IR, FOUR OR five years ago you printed a letter in which I endorsed the appeal that had then recently been launched for help to save Venice from damage by pollution. Much has since been done in that field by several bodies, not least by the English 'Save Venice' Committee, headed by Lord Norwich and, in Venice itself, by Sir Ashley Clarke: a visitor to the city today will see splendid evidence of their achievement. There is, however, one threat to the amenities of Venice that has grown more serious during the past few years, and has evoked no counter-measures: the threat constituted by that indefatigable and unsavoury engine of pollution, the dog.

Ten years ago there was hardly a dog to be seen in the city: a few rich people owned a few small dogs – that was all. Five years ago, as I pointed out in my previous letter, the canine threat was beginning to make itself felt, in more unpleasant ways than one. Today ownership of a dog has become, it seems, a 'status-symbol' with the Venetian populace, and the dog is ubiquitous – Alsatians, bull-terriers, Labradors, poodles, mongrels of every shape and size throng the *calli* and the *campi* – muzzled, indeed, as the law very properly requires, but still – alas! – at one end only.

It is all too easy to imagine what these animals must suffer, kept in a city of canals and stone streets, with hardly a square yard of earth or grass where they can run free; the consequences for human beings, unfortunately, do not have to be imagined: as they pick their way along the Venetian pavements, pedestrians find their footsteps horribly, and almost literally, dogged.

Only a fortnight ago the municipal authorities of Pisa enacted a by-law excluding dogs – '*con motivi*', says *La Stampa*. '*Di carratere igienico-sanitarii e di decoro*' – from the centre of their city. Lovers of dogs and lovers of Venice alike must hope that the Venetian authorities will follow without delay this excellent example.

The Times, 30 September 1975

W. H. AUDEN

Talking to Dogs

(In memoriam Rolfi Strobl, run over, June 9th, 1970)

From us, of course, you want gristly bones
and to be led through exciting odorscapes
   – their colors don't matter – with the chance
of a rabbit to chase or of meeting
   a fellow arse-hole to snuzzle at,
but your deepest fury is to be accepted
   as junior members of a Salon
suaver in taste and manners than a pack,
   to be scratched on the belly and talked to.
Probably, you only hear vowels and then only if
   uttered with lyrical emphasis,
so we cannot tell you a story, even
   when it is true, nor drily dissect
in the third person neighbors who are not there
   or things which can't blush. And what do we,
those of us who are householders, not shepherds
   or killers or polar explorers,
ask from you? The admiration of creatures
   to whom mirrors mean nothing, who never
false your expression and so remind us
   that we as well are still social retards
who have never learned to command our feelings
   and don't want to, really. Some great men,
Goethe and Lear, for instance, have disliked you,
   which seems eccentric, but good people,
if they keep one, have good dogs. (The reverse
   is not so, for some very bad hats
handle you very well.) It's those who crave
   a querulous permanent baby,

or a little detachable penis,
   who can, and often do, debase you.
Humor and joy to your thinking are one,
   so that you laugh with your whole body,
and nothing dismays you more than the noise
   of our local superior titters.
(But then our young males are dismayed by yours
   To whom, except when a bitch is air-borne,
chastity seems to present no problem.)
   Being quicker to sense unhappiness
without having to be told the dreary
   details or who is to blame, in dark hours
your silence may be of more help than many
   two-legged comforters. In citizens
obedience is not always a virtue,
   but yours need not make us uneasy
because, though child-like, you are complete, no New
   Generation whom it's our duty
to disappoint since, until they notice
   our failings, they will never bother
to make their own mistakes. Let difference
   remain our bond, yes, and the one trait
both have in common, a sense of theatre.

JEREMY THORPE

Why was Rinka Shot?

WEST SOMERSET IS buzzing with rumours of a most unsavoury description following reports in the *West Somerset Free Press* about an incident which occurred recently on Exmoor. Mr Norman Scott, a thirty-five-year-old writer, of Combe Martin, North Devon, who claims to have been a great friend of Jeremy Thorpe, the Liberal statesman, was found by an AA patrolman weeping beside the body of Rinka, his Great Dane bitch, which had been shot in the head.

Information about this puzzling incident has since been restricted, on Home Office orders, but a man arrested at London Airport on a firearms charge will be appearing before Minehead magistrates on 19 December, when we may learn more.

My only hope is that sorrow over his friend's dog will not cause Mr Thorpe's premature retirement from public life.

Auberon Waugh in 'Diary', *Private Eye*, 12 December 1975

A N EARLY MORNING summons to attend on Lord Gnome in person. I rush off to brush my teeth and shout at the dear Wife for not having cleaned my shoes properly. Trembling, I compose my face into the most *enthused* expression I can summon as I approach the Presence.

His Lordship receives me, as always, on the lavatory. He shows me a copy of the morning newspaper.

It says that Mr Thorpe has been adopted as Liberal candidate in North Devon and that the Lord Chief Justice has delayed his trial until a time more convenient to the exalted statesman. What is this to me?

Lord Gnome tells me that he has always been particularly fond of dogs. One day, he hopes to be able to own a dog for himself. Do I have any dogs? Yes, I babble, several. That is good, says Lord Gnome. Otherwise he would have to buy me some. He dismisses me with a nod.

What can this mean? Have I done something wrong?

ibid, 4 April 1979

T ODAY'S NEWSPAPERS EXPLAIN everything. Under huge photographs of myself, my dear Wife and my Dogs I learn that I am to stand as Dog Lovers' candidate in North Devon. As the election approaches, Lord Gnome has decided that the Liberal candidate for North Devon may not have quite the necessary qualities to appeal to the nation's dog lovers. So I am to be a Member of Parliament in his place.

Who would have thought if they had seen me during my schooldays in Lancashire – a regular scamp I was, I can tell you – that one day I would be mingling with the mightiest in the land and rubbing shoulders with television personalities like Dennis Howell and Cyril Smith in the Palace of Westminster?

Lord Gnome is paying all my expenses and any bribes which may be necessary, but I desperately need an agent in the constituency.

ibid, 5 April 1979

NOW I AM OFF to Rome until April 18. Gifts of money, flowers, Pedigree Chum etc. may be sent to Combe Florey, but genuine offers of help – as agent, sponsors, canvassers, envelope addressers, stewards at public meetings etc. – should be sent to the Campaign Manager at Gnome House. After I am elected, a Grand Ball and Dog Show will be held in the Town Hall, Barnstaple, to which all helpers will be invited. That is my first and only election promise.

ibid, 10 April 1979

WHILE THE ISSUE of Mr Thorpe's trial was undecided, I refrained from comment. This was partly out of deference to the legal process, partly because, as someone who proposes to follow the trial in person, I had a personal interest. My plans were to be in London on 30 April and stay throughout, thereby providing myself with a further reason for not being able to vote in the general election. Under the circumstances comment seemed inappropriate.

However, when it became known that the Lord Chief Justice of England had agreed to a deferment of the trial to suit Mr Thorpe's convenience – in defiance of all legal precedent and in face of objections from two of Mr Thorpe's co-defendants – it seemed that something more than comment was called for. That decision by the Lord Chief Justice, who is the embodiment of the Law, itself the only guarantee of Order and social tranquility, set me on the Road to Barnstaple.

One has no reason to doubt that it would have been most inconvenient for Mr Thorpe to have stood trial on 30 April, but one must also point out that the crimes of which he is accused are extremely serious ones, such as should bring him into the cordial dislike of all right-minded people, if he is guilty. If he should prove not guilty, of course, the non-deferment of his trial would have added to his misfortunes, already of such a magnitude that one can think only of the consolations of religion as a possible balm. But the risk of being wrongfully accused of a serious crime is one of the prices we must all accept for living in an ordered society, and it seems to me a gross miscarriage of justice, itself a crime against Order, that Mr Thorpe should be treated differently from any other alleged felon.

*   *   *

The choice of Dog Lovers' Party may seem opportunistic. Another objection to my candidature has been that it is hitting a man when he is down, although my chief reason for standing is that Mr Thorpe is not down: if he were, I would not stand. By the same logic, he should be unopposed at this election. If it is argued that the other candidates are standing on serious political issues like the national economy, I reply that no issue is more serious that the one on which I am standing, which concerns the moral climate of the country.

There is much to be said in favour of doggies. I have observed a hatred of doggies growing up in this country, especially among town-dwellers, which has unmistakable echoes of Weimar. *Of course* doggies will shit on the pavement if local government does not provide them with doggie toilets. So would anybody who had nowhere else. Doggies are being used as a scapegoat for the collapse of our society brought about by the loss of Empire. During the Weimar Republic and after, many university professors remained silent. Well, I am standing up to be counted.

From the *Spectator*, 14 April 1979

E VEN WHEN I HAVE disposed of the three main parties I still have to convince voters that the Dog Lovers are preferable to other parties on what the *Daily Telegraph* impolitely calls the 'cranky fringe'. The signs are that the election in North Devon will be one of the dirtiest in living memory. Already it is being said that I am conducting the campaign from my property in southern France. This is not true. Although I may not yet have found time to visit the constituency, I am well situated in West Somerset, scarcely thirty miles away. For my own part, I disdain such whispering methods, and will deal with my other opponents briefly. The Wessex Regionalist Candidate is Miss Henrietta Rous. Although she is unmarried, I suspect that she is not a virgin. The English National Party candidate, Dr Hansford-Miller, is said to wear a smock. Ecology is a disgusting word which should be spelled oecology, its use confined to scientists who know what it means. Commander Boaks seems quite a reasonable person, but I am not sure whether he is sound on dogs. There are very few black people in Barnstaple, so the National Front candidate is wasting his time. When a drowned monkey was washed ashore at Bideford during the Napoleonic War, the locals patriotically hanged it, after deciding it was a Frenchman.

* * *

Here is my Adoption Meeting Address, composed and delivered in a bathroom at Combe Florey on 23 April 1979:

CITIZENS OF BARNSTAPLE AND
VOTERS OF NORTH DEVON

Unaccustomed as I am to public Speaking, I offer myself as your Member of Parliament in the General Election on behalf of the nation's dog lovers to protest about the behaviour of the Liberal Party generally, and the North Devon Constituency Liberal Association in particular. Their candidate is a man about whose attitude to dogs – not to mention his fellow human beings – little can be said with any certainty at the present time.

But it is one thing to observe the polite convention that a man is innocent until proven guilty. It is quite another thing to take a man who has been publicly accused of crimes which would bring him into the cordial dislike of-all-right-minded citizens and dog-lovers, and treat him as a hero.

Before Mr Thorpe has had time to establish his innocence of these extremely serious charges, he has been greeted with claps, cheers and yells of acclamation by his admirers in the Liberal Party, both at the national conference in Southport and here in the constituency. I am sorry, but I find this disgusting.

I invite all the electors of North Devon, but especially the more thoughtful Liberals and dog-lovers, to register their disquiet by voting for me on 3 May, and I sincerely hope that at least 50 voters in this city will take the opportunity to do so.

Genesis XVIII 26: And the LORD said If I find in Sodom fifty righteous within the city, then I will spare all the place for their sakes.

1 Samuel XXIV 14: After whom dost thou pursue? after a dead dog, after a flea.

Rinka is *NOT* forgotten. Rinka lives. Woof woof. Vote Waugh to give *all* dogs the right to life, liberty and the pursuit of happiness.

From the *Spectator*, 28 April 1979

V ARIOUS COPIES WERE sent out to local and national newspapers, but only the *Guardian* printed it. One of the local North Devon newspapers thoughtfully gave its copy to the Liberal agent in North Devon, Mrs Lilian Prowse, who showed it to Mr Thorpe, with results which soon became apparent . . . .

No sooner had the *Guardian* article appeared than I received a telephone call from a journalist in London. He congratulated me on a great battle I had just won before the Lord Chief Justice and two other judges in the Queen's Bench Divisional Court. I replied that I knew nothing about it. It seemed that Mr Jeremy Thorpe through his counsel, Mr George Carman QC, had sought an injunction to ban my election address and commit me to prison for contempt of court on the grounds that it might prejudice a jury at Thorpe's subsequent trial. The Lord Chief Justice, in his wisdom, had refused to do anything of the sort. Knowing nothing of this move, I could only conjecture that Thorpe's motive might have been more concerned with the voters of North Devon than with jurors at the Old Bailey. Asked for a comment, I said that the Divisional Court's decision restored my faith in British justice, and suggested that things would have come to a pretty pass if alleged criminals could not only stand for Parliament, but send any opponents to prison who mentioned this circumstance.

I was celebrating this great victory quietly when the telephone rang again, about an hour later. Mr Thorpe had taken the Divisional Court's decision to appeal and been awarded his injunction by Lord Denning, sitting with two appeal judges. Next day Lord Denning listened to arguments hastily put together by counsel on my behalf and dismissed them with contumely, saying he had been reading my column in *Private Eye* and had no doubt that my motives in standing for Parliament were improper. Mr George Carman QC, enlarging on his client's case, said that two points at issue were who shot the dog Rinka and whether or not there had been a homosexual relationship with Norman Scott, both of which were hotly disputed, and both prejudiced by the election address. In point of fact, there was never any doubt about who had shot the dog – Andrew Newton – and when it came to trial Mr Carman conceded that his client was a man of homosexual tendencies at the relevant time, even though he continued to deny that Thorpe had ever exercised these tendencies on Norman Scott, who was not mentioned in the address. Nor did anyone at the trial deny for a moment that the dog was shot – with or without Mr Thorpe's connivance – in order to assist the Liberal cause and Liberal candidate in North Devon. But it is an unattractive and otiose occupation to moan about judicial decisions which have gone against one. Lord Denning, one of the greatest and best judges we ever had, plainly thought the Dog Lovers' candidature in bad taste, when he said it was as 'plain as plain can be' that the election address might prejudice Thorpe's trial, and was not prepared to consider the view that the Liberal's candidature was in even worse taste. The most interesting aspect of this episode, from my own point of view, was not so much that as a parliamentary candidate I now faced the electorate without an election address or any explanation of why I was standing – under the circumstances, it was a great tribute to North Devon Dog Lovers that seventy-nine of them were prepared to abdicate their democratic right of choosing a government by voting for me – but that Thorpe had overcome his handicaps. One began to take the measure of the enormous sympathy for this ex-barrister, ex-Oxford man, among his own kind.

But he did not do so at the election. At half past three in the morning of 4 May 1979 he learned that the seat he had won from the Conservatives in 1959 – the only Conservative loss in that election – was lost on a huge swing away from him. In February 1974, Thorpe received 34,052 votes to give him a majority of 11,072 over his Conservative opponent. By the General Election of October that year, his vote had sunk to 28,209 and his majority to 6,721. In May 1979, he received only 23,338 votes, and his Conservative opponent was elected to Parliament on a majority of 8,463 with 31,811 votes. The rag, tag and bobtail of 'fringe' party candidates – Labour, Ecology, National Front, English National, Dog Lovers, Wessex Regionalist and Democratic Monarchist Public Safety White Regionalist, in that order, made no noticeable difference to the result, all of them losing their deposits of £150.

To many, the most remarkable factor in this election result was that 23,338 voters were prepared to cast their votes for a man living under the cloud of a serious criminal charge. One will never know what proportion of that number was demonstrating its belief in his innocence and what proportion was demonstrating its continued support for him whether he was guilty or not. In the first instance the voters would appear to cast doubt on general beliefs about the effect of bad publicity; in the second, one can only draw one's own conclusions about the moral climate in North Devon, and possibly in the country at large.

The most interesting aspect may be that he lost only 5,000 votes as a result of the intense publicity given the committal proceedings in Minehead. There can be no doubt that he had a large personal following in North Devon, but the important point is that it was not quite large enough. His gamble had not paid off.

Auberon Waugh, from The Last Word

SEVENTY-NINE PEOPLE had the courage to vote for Dog Lovers despite everything. Lady Fartwell wept with emotion when she heard. At a huge £340 luncheon party in the Epicure restaurant, Romilly Street, given by my friends in the Socialist Workers Party, I point out that Dog Lovers secured more votes in Devon than Socialist Workers in the whole country.

Tony Cliff replies between mouthfuls of lobster thermidor that if legal expenses are taken into account with deposit and printing bills, each vote cost Lord Gnome about £40. Does this qualify for the Guinness Book of Records?

From 'Diary', Private Eye, 4 May 1979

IT IS HARD TO see how this trial can end happily for everyone. Sometimes I dream, in the long sleepy afternoons, that the Defence calls a surprise last minute witness, and Rinka bounds into the courtroom, panting eagerly and wagging her tail. But even this development, happy as it would be from nearly every point of view, would leave the Director of Public Prosecutions, Sir Thomas 'Tony' Hetherington, looking like the biggest fool in England.

ibid, 1 June 1979

THE JURY WAS out all the day. At nightfall, they were taken to a secret hotel, unable to talk to anyone except a court official to say whether or not they had reached a unanimous verdict. The four defendants were taken to Brixton Prison for the night. Three of them were shut up in circumstances of considerable privation in a cell with two other prisoners, one of them apparently an aggressive Negro who had been convicted of manslaughter. Thorpe, however, found himself afflicted by an upset stomach, and was taken to the prison hospital, where conditions were less austere. The prison authorities were reluctant to reveal whether it was normal to take people to hospital suffering from a stomach upset.

From *The Last Word*

THE VERDICT. THORPE declared not guilty, as we all knew he would be. How could it have occurred to any of us for a moment that he was anything but innocent?

Speaking for myself, I think it may have been something to do with the double-breasted waistcoats he wears. At my school, prefects were allowed to wear these absurd garments as a badge of office. So many of them were hypocrites, sodomites, and criminal psychopaths that I understandably jumped to the conclusion that Jeremy Thorpe might just possibly be one, too.

Now we know otherwise, perhaps he will consider wearing more conventional clothes in the future.

From Diary, *Private Eye*, 21 June 1979

EDWARD HOAGLAND

Dogs and the Tug of Life

IT USED TO be that you could tell just about how poor a family was by how many dogs they had. If they had one, they were probably doing all right. It was only American to keep a dog to represent the family's interests in the intrigues of the back alley; not to have a dog at all would be like not acknowledging one's poor relations. Two dogs meant that the couple were dog lovers, with growing children, but still might be members of the middle class. But if a citizen kept three, you could begin to suspect he didn't own much else. Four or five irrefutably marked the household as poor folk, whose yard was also full of broken cars cannibalized for parts. The father worked not much, fancied himself a hunter; the mother's teeth were black. And an old bachelor living in a shack might possibly have even more, but you knew that if one of them, chasing a moth, didn't upset his oil lamp some night and burn him up, he'd fetch up in the poorhouse soon, with the dogs shot. Nobody got poor feeding a bunch of dogs, needless to say, because the more dogs a man had, the less he fed them. Foraging as a pack, they led an existence of their own, but served as evidence that life was awfully lonesome for him and getting out of hand. If a dog really becomes a man's best friend his situation is desperate.

That dogs, low-comedy confederates of small children and ragged bachelors, should have turned into an emblem of having made it to the middle class – like the hibachi, like golf clubs and a second car – seems at the very least incongruous. Puppies which in the country you would have to carry in a box to the church fair to give away are bringing seventy-five dollars apiece in some of the pet stores, although in fact dogs are in such oversupply that one hundred and fifty thousand are running wild in New York City alone.

There is another line of tradition about dogs, however. Show dogs, toy dogs, foxhounds for formal hunts, Doberman guard dogs, bulldogs as ugly as a queen's dwarf. An aristocratic Spanish lady once informed me that when she visits her Andalusian estate each fall the mastiffs rush out and fawn about her but would tear to pieces any of the servants who have accompanied her from Madrid. In Mississippi it was illegal for a slave owner to permit his slaves to have a dog, just as it was to teach them how to read. A 'Negro dog' was a hound trained by a bounty hunter to ignore the possums, raccoons, hogs, and deer in the woods that other dogs were supposed to chase, and trail and tree a runaway. The planters themselves, for whom hunting was a principal recreation, whooped it up when a man unexpectedly became their quarry. They caught each other's slaves and would often sit back and let the dogs do the punishing. Bennet H. Barrow of West Feliciana Parish in Louisiana, a rather moderate and representative plantation owner, recounted in his diary of the 1840s, among several similar incidents, this for November 11, 1845: 'In 5 minutes had him up & a going, And never in my life did I ever see as excited beings as R & myself, ran ½ miles & caught him dogs soon tore him naked, took him Home

Before the other negro[es] at dark & made the dogs give him another over hauling.' Only recently in Louisiana I heard what happened to two Negroes who happened to be fishing in a bayou off the Blind River, where four white men with a shotgun felt like fishing alone. One was forced to pretend to be a scampering coon and shinny up a telephone pole and hang there till he fell, while the other impersonated a baying bounding hound.

Such memories are not easy to shed, particularly since childhood, the time when people can best acquire a comradeship with animals, is also when they are likely to pick up their parents' fears. A friend of mine hunts quail by jeep in Texas with a millionaire who brings along forty bird dogs, which he deploys in eight platoons that spell each other off. Another friend, though, will grow apprehensive at a dinner party if the host lets a dog loose in the room. The toothy, mysterious creature lies dreaming on the carpet, its paws pulsing, its eyelids open, the nictitating membranes twitching; how can he be certain it won't suddenly jump up and attack his legs under the table? Among Eastern European Jews, possession of a dog was associated with the hard-drinking *goyishe* peasantry, traditional antagonists, or else with the gentry, and many carried this dislike to the New World. An immigrant fleeing a potato famine or the hunger of Calabria might be no more equipped with the familiar British-German partiality to dogs – a failing which a few rugged decades in a great city's slums would not necessarily mend. The city had urbanized plenty of native farmers' sons as well, and so it came about that what to rural America had been the humblest, most natural amenity – friendship with a dog – has been transmogrified into a piece of the jigsaw of moving to the suburbs: there to cook outdoors, another bit of absurdity to the old countryman, whose toilet was outdoors but who was pleased to be able to cook and eat his meals inside the house.

There are an estimated forty million dogs in the United States (nearly two for every cat). Thirty-seven thousand of them are being destroyed in humane institutions every day, a figure which indicates that many more are in trouble. Dogs are hierarchal beasts, with several million years of submission to the structure of a wolf pack in their breeding. This explains why the Spanish lady's mastiffs can distinguish immediately between the mistress and her retainers, and why it is about as likely that one of the other guests at the dinner party will attack my friend's legs under the table as that the host's dog will, once it has accepted his presence in the room as proper. Dogs need leadership, however; they seek it, and when it's not forthcoming quickly fall into difficulties in a world where they can no longer provide their own.

From *Heart's Desire*

JOHN CLEESE/CONNIE BOOTH
Heart's Desire

(*The hotel bar; evening. Sybil is at the bar, Manuel is serving guests. The Major is sitting at a table with Mrs Chase, who is fondling a little lap dog.*)

MRS CHASE: And he loves pecans and walnuts and he simply adores those little cheese footballs . . . don't you, my darling . . . isn't he beautiful?

THE MAJOR: (*who is not that interested*) Very attractive little feller . . . what is it?

MRS CHASE: He's a little Chitzu.

THE MAJOR: Is he really? . . . Oh dear, dear, dear. What breed is it?

MRS CHASE: Well, they're lap dogs, aren't they.

THE MAJOR: A Lapp dog? Oh, hard to imagine him stalking a reindeer, what?

BASIL: (*coming up to the table*) Ah, Major, can I get you another one?

THE MAJOR: Ah . . . (*looks at watch*) Why not, why not?

BASIL: For you, Mrs Chase?

MRS CHASE: Oh, nothing for me, thank you, but Prince would like a little saucer of warm milk as it's nearly our bed-time . . .

BASIL: Yes . . . Manuel! (*to Mrs Chase*) Manuel will attend to its heart's desires. I'm afraid I'm lumbered with the people tonight . . . (*he moves off; Manuel hurries up*) Manuel – *por favor, el perro microscópico* . . .

*   *   *

(The dining room. Manuel approaches Mrs Chase's table with bowl and cushion. He puts the bowl on the floor.)

MRS CHASE: On the table . . . on the table. (*Manuel puts the cushion on the table*) No! *That!* (*Manuel puts the bowl on the table uncertainly; Mrs Chase picks up the dog*) Now put that under him. (*Manuel puts the bowl on the chair*) The cushion! The cushion!

Manuel puts the cushion under the dog, but the dog snaps at him, scoring a hit.

MANUEL: He bite me!

MRS CHASE: You frightened him.

MANUEL: *Qué?*

MRS CHASE: You make sudden movements like that, of course he's going to bite. Don't you have dogs in Calcutta?

POLLY: (*coming up*) Excuse me, but I have an order for eggs and sausage for this table.

MRS CHASE: Oh, yes. The sausages are for him. (*Polly puts the food down*)

MANUEL: Ooh!

POLLY: What's the matter, Manuel?

MANUEL: He bite me.

MRS CHASE: Cut them up. Cut them up into little pieces. (*Polly starts cutting up her eggs*) No, not my eggs, not my eggs. The sausages!

POLLY: Oh, sorry. (*she goes to cut them up but the dog takes a bite at her, too*)

MANUEL: He bite Polly, too. You see?

MRS CHASE: If dogs are allowed in the dining room at least the staff should know how to handle them.

POLLY: (*charmingly*) I'll cut them up in the kitchen, Mrs Chase.

MRS CHASE: *Little* pieces.

The kitchen. Terry is finishing the kippers.

TERRY: Kippers ready!

Polly and Manuel enter. She puts the plate down, hard.

MANUEL: He hurt you, Polly?

Basil is peering at the kippers.

SYBIL: Basil, what are you doing?

BASIL: . . . Do you know when the sixth *was*, Sybil?

SYBIL: Will you just take it upstairs.

TERRY: They're all right, Mr Fawlty.

BASIL: Are they supposed to be that colour?

SYBIL: Basil, will you just take it up. What's the matter, Manuel?

POLLY: That hairy mosquito just bit us both.

SYBIL: What?

MANUEL: Is not right in dining room like that.

SYBIL: Well, she pays extra for the dog, Manuel, you see . . . Basil, it's *after* eight.

BASIL: (*still peering at the kippers*) Poisoning is still an offence in this country, you know, Sybil.

SYBIL: Oh *do* get a move on, we've got a busy day, I've got the laundrymen coming . . .

BASIL: The laundrymen! My God! A woman's work is never delegated, is it. (*he exits*)

SYBIL: What are you doing, Polly?

POLLY: Just preparing some sausages. (*she adds some tabasco sauce to them*) Bangers à la Bang.

From *Fawlty Towers*: 'The Kipper and the Corpse'

LADY DIANA COOPER

Subterfuge

HER DOG WAS almost as great a solace to her as any friend. Writhing, twitching neurotically, as much an insect as an animal, 'Doggie' – and later Doggie II and Doggie III – was a chihuahua, charmless to most of those who knew it but to Diana possessed of supernatural loveliness. Lurking in her sleeve, wrapped loosely in a shawl, it went everywhere with her; to Covent Garden, to Buckingham Palace, the more inaccessible the venue the more determined Diana was that it should not be left behind. Usually it behaved, when it did not Diana quickly repaired the damage. In a smart Soho restaurant

Doggie escaped and defecated lavishly at the feet of a prosperous business man. Ugly scenes threatened but Diana rose to the occasion and within a few moments the bemused but enchanted business man was agreeing that really what was needed in the restaurant was a few more dogs; it was ridiculous of the head waiter to try to keep them out. In the innermost fastness of her bedroom, Doggie and the television helped to keep loneliness at bay, providing a soothing background of rustles, yaps and conversation, a convincing simulacrum of company when company was absent.

Philip Ziegler, from *Diana Cooper*

QUEEN ELIZABETH II
Corgi and Bess: Rabies Strikes

PONTIUS SAW HIS mistress hardly at all over the next fortnight; he wasn't singled out from the others for a solo walk again, and so saw only her legs with any regularity, from the dogs' privileged position under the dining-table. When she next properly took notice of him, it was in the great dim hall, where he was irritably cuffing at his sore nose and shuffling backwards and forwards on the floor. In the uncertain light the Queen had the sudden horrifying impression that Punchie was paying an absurd homage, retreating backwards before her and making one formal bow after another. This mirage struck her as horrifying because of the special position the pet dogs occupied in her life. With her family of course Her Majesty had an abundantly loving relationship, but that was in part a solidarity natural to people who were making the best of the same bad job.

(In previous, less regimented reigns, monarchs had engaged in family quarrels just like ordinary people, but for the Windsors a generation gap was a luxury they simply could not afford.)

Her feeling for her dogs was different. She loved them, purely and without limit, for their ignorance of her status; the eyes which gazed up at her as she mashed processed fodder with hallmarked fork could never be clouded by the thought that she wasn't theirs alone. That she had to be shared with so many million others.

However many Sundays the dogs see their mistress preparing for church, they will never come to guess that the diminutive woman, hardly even a flyweight, so tensely inspecting her appearance in the mirror, is uniquely and By the Grace of God Defender of the Faith.

Who is there to tell them that the hostess who somehow musters obliging interest in the technicalities of shooting, is Colonel-in-Chief of the Malawi Rifles?

And how can they know that the homebody who curls up at her ease on a sofa and sings breathily along with 'People Will Say We're in Love,' her very favourite tune, has degrees in music from the universities of London and Wales?

Freedom of the Drapers' Company hasn't spoiled her, nor has her incomparable wardrobe made her vain and luxury-loving; but her dogs see nothing of that. They see only her tweeds as rough as emery-boards, the preferred dowdiness of her private life.

All her honours and titles, from the Supreme Governorship of the Church of England to the Elephant of Denmark, are as nothing to her pets; and she relishes their unforced bad nature with unfailing eagerness and pleasure.

Santa Claus conspires yearly with her, to fill the corgis' individual stockings with chocolate drops, and rubber bones.

Enormously relieved that the dog hadn't after all guessed her secret identity (which couldn't be hidden as easily as Clark Kent's), Elizabeth Windsor padded in stockinged feet aross the thin carpeting to her pet. She picked him up and made much of him, pressing him to her without particularly noticing the way he wriggled, in his discomfort.

'Punchieluvvamummaduzzie?' she inquired dreamily. 'Punchieluvva-mummie?' In a gallant and uncharacteristic effort to give pleasure Punchie unrolled a red carpet of distended tongue, and drew it painfully once or twice across his mistress's smiling muzzle.

Adam Mars-Jones, 'Hoosh-Mi': from *Lantern Lecture*

A. L. ROWSE

Apollo, Glorious Labrador

for Harold and Joan Hartley

Apollo, glorious labrador,
Of golden coat and amber eyes,
Of your regal looks and gentle ways
We have so many memories.

What a kingdom you had here:
Trevissick Turn to Hallane Mill,
Trenarren village and Ropehawn,
Along the headland to flagstaff hill.

All the beaches here were yours,
Porthtowam, Gwendra, Silvermine,
When you were young and frolicsome,
In summer days, of sheen or shine.

Following your master into the sea,
Close on his track, treading the waves,
Bounding across seaweed and rocks,
Under the Vans, exploring the caves.

You toss your treasure trove in the air,
Flotsam and jetsam, wrack of the sea,
Pieces of spar, a cellophane square
To protect from the birds his cherry tree.

What days you had of bliss and joy
Splashing in the valley stream;
Back to the shelter of Rose Cottage
All the night, perchance to dream

How once you chased my favourite cat;
Peter, the white Persian, spat
Fury from the safety of a tree
At such a breach of his dignity:
Nor was I wholly pleased thereat –

But forgave you for your charming way
Of welcoming me, a visitor,
With a present of your bone or toy,
A shoe or slipper at your door.

You became with advancing age
A wise old dog, a sober sage,
Couchant before the friendly fire
Of the ever hospitable squire

Who made Rose Cottage what it is –
A haven of all felicities.
How much we miss you: there's not much fun
At your home now you are gone.
Yet, on reflection, I am glad
To think what a golden life you had.

DORIS DAY

Heart to Heart

ANYONE WHO KNOWS anything about me knows how involved I am
with dogs. Dogs are as important to me as people. The dogs I live
with are just as much my family as are my mother and son. During the
bleak, difficult years since Marty's death, my canine family has been a
source of joy and strength to me. I have found that when you are deeply

troubled, there are things you get from silent, devoted companionship of a dog that you get from no other source.

In a way I never got over what happened to Tiny, the little black and tan, who, when I was on crutches, was hit by a car and died in my arms. It was totally my fault for walking him without a leash, and I've had a lingering sense of guilt about his death all my life. How important Tiny was to me during that lonely, interminable strength when I was waiting for my leg to mend, and how tragic a death he suffered! I learned my lesson – no dog should ever be allowed to run free; to this day, if I see a dog in the street, I will hop out of my car, stop traffic, and try to lure the poor little thing into my car so that I can take him home (if he has a collar with identification) or turn him over to the volunteer group I'm associated with, Actors and Others for Animals, which will try to locate his owner or, failing that, find a home for him.

My passion for and understanding of dogs are really directly attributable to two remarkable books which I read as a girl – *Letters to Strongheart* and *Kinship with All Life*, both written by a man named J. Allen Boone. I'm sure they are still to be found in most public libraries. The books are primarily about a German shepherd named Strongheart, who was a big movie star long before Rin-Tin-Tin came on the scene. Boone lived alone with Strongheart for a long period of time, during which Boone, intrigued with the unusual and uncanny powers of the dog, began to experiment with ways and means of communicating with him, but not using the ordinary master-dog method of communication.

In *Kinship with All Life*, Boone taught me the difference between training a dog and educating one. Trained dogs, Boone points out, are relatively easy to turn out. All that's needed is a certain amount of bluff and bluster, and things that can be used for threatening and rewarding purposes. Educating a dog, though, demands keen intelligence, integrity, imagination, and a gentle touch – mentally, vocally, and physically.

Conventional training is mostly concerned with the physical. The trainer assumes that he is dealing with a dumb animal who has to be dominated so that he will be completely subservient to him, obeying his every command and focusing idolatrous attention on his master at all times. But *educating* a dog requires just the reverse of all that. Full emphasis is placed on the mental rather than on the physical. The dog owner must treat the dog as an intelligent fellow being whose capacity for development and expression he does not limit in any direction. He tries to help the dog make use of his thinking facilities.

Boone found ways to communicate with Strongheart during the long silences they shared, and it was those revelations that had such a profound effect on me. Boone relates how he freed himself of prejudices and purified his thinking to the point at which Strongheart was truly able to share precious dog wisdom with Boone, 'wonderful secrets having to do with the great dog art of living abundantly and happily in the present tense regardless of circumstances.' Boone found that after establishing a strong rapport with Strongheart, he was able to establish a mental two-way bridge between them, over which it was possible for Boone's thoughts freely to cross into Strongheart's thinking areas and for the dog's thoughts just as freely to cross over into his.

I realize that, summarized like this, Boone's account seems rather irrational, but I can assure you that with the details and documentation in the book it is all very rational indeed. In fact, it is this attitude towards communicating that I brought to my relations with my own dogs, with extraordinary results. I do indeed communicate with my dogs but not in the usual dog owner's manner of talking down to them in a way that smacks of baby talk.

What I have learned is that dogs are here on earth to teach us. They have taught me how to be serenely patient, and they have taught me about love – fundamental love, such as Jesus taught. No matter how abusive or inconsiderate its owner has been, a dog will turn his other cheek and continue to love him. And loyalty – I have never found in a human being loyalty that is comparable to a dog's loyalty. And yet people buy a dog as they buy a plant, and they treat him like a plant after they get him. They buy him from pet shops and backyard breeders without checking on the dog's condition. They breed the dog because they think it would be cute to have puppies. They haven't the slightest interest in or concept of the spiritual qualities of the dogs they buy.

My dogs were all strays, rejects, most of whom would have been put to sleep if I had not rescued them. My oldest dog, Myra Muffin, is a brown poodle, mostly, who was found wandering alone without identification by a roadside in Las Vegas. She had three sons, Red, Bo-Bo, and Charlie – but this was ten or eleven years ago, before I had learned the facts about the dog population. Bambi is the malamute-shepherd mix I mentioned whom I found running in the rain as I left CBS Studio City one day. She was in a run-down condition and had terrible mange which I treated for a long time. She is now absolutely gorgeous.

I found Ruby, a dachshund, limping along in the Valley. One of his eyes was badly infected. I went from house to house all up and down the street but the dachsi didn't belong to anyone, so I took him home and treated his foot and his eye. I gave him a good German name, Rudy. Schatzie is another dachshund, a refugee from the house Terry had in the mountains. El Tigre de Sassafrass is a little grey poodle who was brought to me by my set decorator. Tigre had been badly neglected by his owner, was completely neurotic, and spent most of his time under the bed. He is super cool now and spends most of his time *in* the bed.

Bubbles is a black schnoodle (mix of schnauzer and poodle) who was left at the poodle parlour by someone who never called for her. The owner of the parlour begged me to take her to avert having her put to sleep. Daisy June, a collie who is den mother of the group, came from the Holiday Humane shelter.[1] Bucky, a spaniel mix, was found roaming around Studio City. Big Tiger, or just plain Biggest, is a poodle mix who was brought to me by a former housekeeper who found him in a vacated house.

Obviously, I could not continue befriending every stray orphan who came my way. So I have turned my compassion and energy towards the Actors and Others for Animals organization. But personnel and finances limit the scope of what we can do. We raised substantial amounts at our annual bazaar and other fund-raising events, but all of it goes out as fast as it comes in, for emergencies, spaying and neutering, and housing strays and unwanted animals. Scarcely a day passes that someone does not call about or come by with some poor little creature who needs care and attention and a place to live. They break my heart. They really do. So beautiful, and vulnerable, and alone. Totally dependent upon a human being, who, if he takes the orphan to his heart, will become just as dependent on the dog for those unique qualities that only a dog can bring into your life.

I have previously mentioned the magnificient sycamore tree in my backyard. It soared ninety feet into the air and its limbs were the size of ordinary tree trunks. It towered over the roof of my house and was as wide as the house itself. It was truly a tree of majesty and splendour. One of my great pleasures, after coming home from a hectic day at the television studio, was to have a swim and then lie under that sycamore tree with my dogs all beside me – love above and all around.

I took very good care of the tree, having it regularly pruned and inspected by the tree men, and its huge branches wired to lessen strain.

---

[1] Holiday Humane is a simply marvellous place in North Hollywood with which Actors and Others is now affiliated. It's an orphanage with a clinic on the premises, and every dog is spayed or neutered on admission. It is a prototype of the kind of shelter, like Bide-A-Wee in New York, that we'd like to see established in cities all over the country.

It was a tree, I felt, that was destined to be the rock of ages. But then, one afternoon about two years ago, as I lay under the trees watching the clouds through the leaves, I became aware that a few pieces of bark were falling from the trunk. I called the tree men, who came to inspect it but assured me that the tree was sound and that the pieces of falling bark were meaningless.

That night around three in the morning, the dogs who were sleeping in my bedroom became restless and woke me. It was a very hot, humid night. I got out of bed and went to the screen door that gives onto the patio. The sycamore tree was located just outside that door, its main branches extending over the roof of my bedroom and the entire house. I opened the door to let the dogs out, intending to take a walk around the pool with them. But curiously, they did not leave the bedroom but stood at the door looking up at me. They were utterly quiet, and I remember thinking, as I stood there, how silent the night was. Just then, however, the silence was slightly broken by a little cracking sound, and then, after a moment, by another. Then I heard a small piece of bark fall from the trunk of the tree. The dogs didn't budge. Invariably, when I opened that door they would go bounding into the yard, especially if I was going to walk with them. But they just stood there, mute, looking up at me.

Something about the night, the eerie silence, the strange behaviour of the dogs, and the little squeaks of the sycamore's wood, made me step back into the room and close the screen door. Just as I did, at the precise moment that the screen door slid shut, there was a great, thunderous screeching sound and the huge tree fell with a roar of wrenching cascading wood – but miraculously it fell away from the house, towards the open area of the yard, the deadly branches completely avoiding the roof above my bedroom. If the tree had fallen the other way, there is no doubt it would have crashed through the roof and killed all of us. And if the dogs and I had stepped out of the door that night – I shudder to think.

The fallen tree completely filled the yard. It took a week to have it cut up and carted away. The tree men marvelled at the miraculous way the tree had fallen.

I sorely miss the tree, and grieve for it as I grieve for friends who have died. I often think about that night. I think about that moment when those dogs of mine stood there at the screen door and communicated something to me that kept me from leaving that room. Overall, I'm convinced, it was an act of God, and I think that God had chosen to speak to me through my dogs, who are looked after by Him as well as I am.

From *Doris Day: Her Story*

JOHN UPDIKE

Another Dog's Death

For days the good old bitch had been dying, her back
pinched down to the spine and arched to ease the pain,
   her kidneys dry, her muzzle gray. At last
I took a shovel into the woods and dug her grave

in preparation for the certain. She came along,
which I had not expected. Still, the children gone,
   such expeditions were rare, and the dog,
spayed early, knew no nonhuman word for love.

So she made her stiff legs trot and let her bent tail wag.
We found a spot we liked, where the pines met the field.
   The sun warmed her fur as she dozed and I dug;
I carved her a safe place while she guarded me.

I measured her length with the shovel's handle;
she perked in amusement, and sniffed the heaped earth.
   Back down at the house, she seemed friskier,
but gagged, eating. We called the vet a few days later.

They were old friends. She held up a paw, and he
injected a violet fluid. She swooned on the lawn,
   and we watched her breathing slowly ebb to naught.
In the wheelbarrow up to the hole, her fur took the sun.

DAVID STEEL AND CEAUSESCU

Remember Rinka

EVER SINCE READING about the overthrow and execution of the tyrant Ceausescu in Romania, I have worried about the fate of the black Labrador puppy which was presented to this cruel and evil man by David Steel, at a time when we must suppose the former Liberal leader thought he could do business with him.

A recent biography brings us up to date. Ceausescu rechristened the unfortunate dog Corbu, made him an honorary colonel in the Romanian Army, gave him his own car and chauffeur and fed him better than any Romanian citizen.

On one occasion, when visiting a hospital in Bucharest, Corbu was attacked by the hospital cat. Ceausescu had the hospital demolished. When Ceausescu was overthrown and shot, Corbu was also killed, riddled with bullets by an anonymous Romanian Andrew Newton.

A correspondent asks what is the attitude of the official Dog Lovers Party of Great Britain (of which I am President for Life) to these developments. This is the second time that a dog with Liberal Party connections has come to a sticky end.

My answer is that like the Communist Party of Great Britain, the Dog Lovers Party has recently changed its name. We are now the All Pets Welcome Classless Fun and Laughter Democratic Jesus Movement. The sad fate of Corbu is on the agenda for discussion at our next Glee Session, to be debated after the vexed question of animal ordinations.

Auberon Waugh in the *Daily Telegraph*, 1991

BOB DYLAN

Dogs Bob Dylan Seems To Have Abandoned

1 Hamlet: the pedigree shepherd-dog that turned out not to be; acquired by Dylan (a sibling went to Albert Grossman) in the Woodstock era. Dogs were a fashion then – see also items 2 and 3 on this list. Hamlet was given away to Band member Rick Danko when the unfortunate animal's pretensions to good breeding were exposed as phoney.

2 The Collie that Dylan owned, again in Woodstock, in 1968. It is pictured in the middle of the 1986 Australian Tour Programme.

3 The St Bernard ditto; pictured in *The Telegraph* (issue 15).

4 Sasha: the dog A.J. Weberman found evidence of in Dylan's garbage on MacDougal Street, Greenwich Village, in 1970. A.J.'s unique research established that the Dylans gave this wretched creature Gainsburgers and Ken-L Ration (she was well fed . . .), and that they had to call a vet in to treat her for an upset stomach.

5 Rover: the dog that was part of the family in 1972, and which was taken across the borderline down to Durango, Mexico, and installed as part of the Dylan entourage in his trailer on the set of *Pat Garrett and Billy The Kid.*

6 Peggy: the Beagle puppy mentioned in the *Rolling Thunder Logbook* by Sam Shepard as being less than fully house-trained, and which can be seen in *Renaldo & Clara* trying to insinuate herself between Shepard and Sara Dylan on the sofa in *that* trailer. Or caravan, as we say in Britain.

7 The black Labrador which Dylan had with him in his station-wagon (or estate-car, as we . . .) when he revisited his childhood home in Hibbing, Minnesota in April 1984.

N.B. Dylan's current dogs are two Great Danes called Brutus and Baby. How much longer?

Michael Gray, from *All Across the Telegraph*

(One of these dogs, or yet another, is to be heard barking its appreciation in the background on an early version of 'Every Grain of Sand'. The movie version of *Hard Rain* is dedicated to Rover, #5 above.)

MILAN KUNDERA

Two Rolls and a Bee

K ARENIN WAS NOT overjoyed by the move to Switzerland. Karenin hated change. Dog time cannot be plotted along a straight line; it does not move on and on, from one thing to the next. It moves in a circle like hands of a clock, which – they, too, unwilling to dash madly ahead – turn round and round the face, day in and day out following the same path. In Prague, when Tomas and Tereza bought a new chair or moved a flower pot, Karenin would look on in displeasure. It disturbed his sense of time. It was as though they were trying to dupe the hands of the clock by changing the numbers on its face.

Nonetheless, he soon managed to reestablish the old order and old rituals in the Zurich flat. As in Prague, he would jump up on their bed and welcome them to the day, accompany Tereza on her morning shopping jaunt, and make certain he got the other walks coming to him as well.

He was the timepiece of their lives. In periods of despair, she would remind herself she had to hold on because of him, because he was weaker than she, weaker perhaps even than Dubcek and their abandoned homeland.

* * *

The collective farm chairman became a truly close friend. He had a wife, four children, and a pig he raised like a dog. The pig's name was Mefisto, and he was the pride and main attraction of the village. He would answer his master's call and was always clean and pink; he paraded about on his hoofs like a heavy-thighed woman in high heels.

When Karenin first saw Mefisto, he was very upset and circled him, sniffing, for a long time. But he soon made friends with him, even to the point of preferring him to the village dogs. Indeed, he had nothing but scorn for the dogs, because they were all chained to their doghouses and never stopped their silly, unmotivated barking. Karenin correctly assessed the value of being one of a kind, and I can state without compunction that he greatly appreciated his friendship with the pig.

The chairman was glad to be able to help his former surgeon, though at the same time sad that he could do nothing more. Tomas became the driver of the pickup truck that took the farm workers out to the fields and hauled equipment.

The collective farm had four large cow sheds as well as a small stable of forty heifers. Tereza was charged with looking after them and taking them out to pasture twice a day. Because the closer, easily accessible meadows would eventually be mowed, she had to take her herd into the surrounding hills for grazing, gradually moving farther and farther out and, in the course of the year, covering all the pastureland round about. As in her small-town youth, she was never without a book, and the minute she reached the day's pasture she would open it and read.

Karenin always kept her company. He learned to bark at the young cows when they got too frisky and tried to go off on their own; he did so with obvious zest. He was definitely the happiest of the three. Never before had his position as keeper of the clock been so respected. The country was no place for improvisation; the time in which Tereza and Tomas lived was growing closer to the regularity of his time.

One day, after lunch (a time when they both had an hour to themselves), they took a walk with Karenin up the slope behind their cottage.

'I don't like the way he's running,' said Tereza.

Karenin was limping on a hind leg. Tomas bent down and carefully felt all along it. Near the hock he found a small bump.

The next day he sat him in the front seat of the pickup and drove, during his rounds, to the neighbouring village, where the local veterinarian lived. A week later, he paid him another visit. He came home with the news that Karenin had cancer.

Within three days, Tomas himself, with the vet in attendance, had operated on him. When Tomas brought him home, Karenin had not quite come out of the anesthesia. He lay on the rug next to their bed with his eyes open, whimpering, his thigh shaved bare and the incision and six stitches painfully visible.

At last he tried to stand up. He failed.

Tereza was terrified that he would never walk again.

'Don't worry,' said Tomas. 'He's still under the anesthetic.'

She tried to pick him up, but he snapped at her. It was the first time he'd ever tried to bite Tereza!

'He doesn't know who you are,' said Tomas. 'He doesn't recognize you.'

They lifted him onto their bed, where he quickly fell asleep, as did they.

At three o'clock that morning, he suddenly woke them up, wagging his tail and climbing all over them, cuddling up to them, unable to have his fill.

It was the first time he'd ever got them up, too! He had always waited until one of them woke up before he dared jump on them.

But when he suddenly came to in the middle of the night, he could not control himself. Who can tell what distances he covered on his way back? Who knows what phantoms he battled? And now that he was at home with his dear ones, he felt compelled to share his overwhelming joy, a joy of return and rebirth.

* * *

While the heifers grazed, Tereza sat on a stump with Karenin at her side, his head resting in her lap. She recalled reading a two-line filler in the papers ten or so years ago about how all the dogs in a certain Russian city had been summarily shot. It was that inconspicuous and seemingly insignificant little article that had brought home to her for the first time the sheer horror of her country's oversized neighbour.

That little article was a premonition of things to come. The first years following the Russian invasion could not yet be characterized as a reign of terror. Because practically no one in the entire nation agreed with the occupation regime, the Russians had to ferret out the few exceptions and push them into power. But where could they look? All faith in Communism and love for Russia was dead. So they sought people who wished to get back at life for something, people with revenge on the brain. Then they had to focus, cultivate, and maintain those people's aggressiveness, give them a temporary substitute to pratice on. The substitute they lit upon was animals.

All at once the papers stared coming out with cycles of features and organized letters-to-the-editor campaigns demanding, for example, the extermination of all pigeons within city limits. And the pigeons would be exterminated. But the major drive was directed against dogs. People were still disconsolate over the catastrophe of the occupation, but radio, television, and the press went on and on about dogs: how they soil our streets and parks, endanger our children's health, fulfill no useful function, yet must be fed. They whipped up such a psychotic fever that Tereza had been afraid that the crazed mob would do harm to Karenin. Only after a year did the accumulated malice (which until then had been vented, for the sake of training, on animals) find its true goal: people. People started being removed from their jobs, arrested, put on trial. At last the animals could breathe freely.

Tereza kept stroking Karenin's head, which was quietly resting in her lap, while something like the following ran through her mind: There's no particular merit in being nice to one's fellow man. She had to treat the other villagers decently, because otherwise she couldn't live there. Even with Tomas, she was *obliged* to behave lovingly because she needed him. We can never establish with certainty what part of our relations with others is the result of our emotions – love, antipathy, charity, or malice – and what part is predetermined by the constant power play among individuals.

True human goodness, in all its purity and freedom, can come to the fore only when its recipient had no power. Mankind's true moral test, its fundamental test (which lies deeply buried from view), consists of its attitude towards those who are at its mercy: animals. And in this respect mankind has suffered a fundamental debacle, a debacle so fundamental that all others stem from it.

* * *

Karenin gave birth to two rolls and a bee. He stared, amazed, at his own progeny. The rolls were utterly serene, but the bee staggered about as if drugged, then flew up and away.

Or so it happened in Tereza's dream. She told it to Tomas the minute he woke up, and they both found a certain consolation in it. It transformed Karenin's illness into a pregnancy and the drama of giving birth into something both laughable and touching: two rolls and a bee.

She again fell prey to illogical hopes. She got out of bed and put on her clothes. Here, too, her day began with a trip to the shop for milk, bread, rolls. But when she called Karenin for his walk that morning, he barely raised his head. It was the first time that he had refused to take part in the ritual he himself had forced upon them.

She went off without him. 'Where's Karenin?' asked the woman behind the counter, who had Karenin's roll ready as usual. Tereza carried it home herself in her bag. She pulled it out and showed it to him while still in the doorway. She wanted him to come and fetch it. But he just lay there motionless.

Tomas saw how unhappy Tereza was. He put the roll in his mouth and dropped down on all fours opposite Karenin. Then he slowly crawled up to him.

Karenin followed him with his eyes, which seemed to show a glimmer of interest, but he did not pick himself up. Tomas brought his face right up to his muzzle. Without moving his body, the dog took the end of the roll sticking out of Tomas's mouth into his own. Then Tomas let go of his end so that Karenin could eat it all.

Still on fours, Tomas retreated a little, arched his back, and stared yelping, making believe he wanted to fight over the roll. After a short while, the dog responded with some yelps of his own. At last! What they were hoping for! Karenin feels like playing! Karenin hasn't lost the will to live!

Those yelps were Karenin's smile, and they wanted it to last as long as possible. So Tomas crawled back to him and tore off the end of the roll sticking out of Karenin's mouth. Their faces were so close that Tomas could smell the dog's breath, feel the long hairs on Karenin's muzzle tickling him. The dog gave out another yelp and his mouth twitched; now they each had half a roll between their teeth. Then Karenin made an old tactical error: he dropped his half in the hope of seizing the half in his master's mouth, forgetting, as always, that Tomas was not a dog and had hands. Without letting his half of the roll out of his mouth, Tomas picked up the other half from the floor.

'Tomas!' Tereza cried. 'You're not going to take his roll away from him, are you?'

Tomas laid both halves on the floor in front of Karenin, who quickly gulped down the first and held the second in his mouth for an ostentatiously long time, flaunting his victory over the two of them.

Standing there watching him, they thought once more that he was smiling and that as long as he kept smiling he had a motive to keep living despite his death sentence.

The next day his condition actually appeared to have improved. They had lunch. It was the time of day when they normally took him out for a walk. His habit was to start running back and forth between them restlessly. On that day, however, Tereza picked up the leash and collar only to be stared at dully. They tried to look cheerful (for and about him) and pep him up a bit, and after a long wait he took pity on them, tottered over on his three legs, and let her put on the collar.

'I know you hate the camera, Tereza,' said Tomas, 'but take it along today, will you.'

Tereza went and opened the cupboard to rummage for the long-abandoned, long-forgotten camera. 'One day we'll be glad to have the pictures,' Tomas went on. 'Karenin has been an important part of our life.'

'What do you mean, "has been"?' said Tereza as if she had been bitten by a snake. The camera lay directly in front of her on the cupboard floor, but she would not bend to pick it up. 'I won't take it along. I refuse to think about losing Karenin. And you refer to him in the past tense!'

'I'm sorry,' said Tomas.

'That's all right,' said Tereza mildly. 'I catch myself thinking about him in the past tense all the time. I keep having to push it out of my mind. That's why I won't take the camera.'

They walked along in silence. Silence was the only way of not thinking about Karenin in the past tense. They did not let him out of their sight; they were with him constantly, waiting for him to smile. But he did not smile; he merely walked with them, limping along on his three legs.

'He's just doing it for us,' said Tereza. 'He didn't want to go for a walk. He's just doing it to make us happy.'

It was sad, what she said, yet without realizing it they were happy. They were happy not in spite of their sadness but thanks to it. They were holding hands and both had the same image in their eyes: a limping dog who represented ten years of their lives.

They walked a bit farther. Then, to their great disappointment, Karenin stopped and turned. They had to go back.

*　　*　　*

An old thought came back to her: Her home was Karenin, not Tomas. Who would wind the clock of their days when he was gone?

Transported mentally into the future, a future without Karenin, Tereza felt abandoned.

Karenin was lying in a corner whimpering. Tereza went out into the garden. She looked down at a patch of grass between two apple trees and imagined burying Karenin there. She dug her heel into the earth and traced a rectangle in the grass. That was where his grave would be.

'What are you doing?' Tomas asked, surprising her just as she had surprised him reading the letter a few hours earlier.

She gave no answer. He noticed her, hands trembling for the first time in many months. He grabbed hold of them. She pulled away from him.

'Is that a grave for Karenin?'

She did not answer.

Her silence grated on him. He exploded. 'First you blame me for thinking of him in the past tense, and then what do you do? You go and make the funeral arrangements!'

She turned her back on him.

Tomas retreated into his room, slamming the door behind him.

Tereza went in and opened it. 'Instead of thinking about yourself all the time, you might at least have some consideration for him,' she said. 'He was asleep until you woke him. Now he'll start whimpering again.'

She knew she was being unfair (the dog was not asleep); she knew she was acting like the most vulgar of women, the kind that is out to cause pain and knows how.

Tomas tiptoed into the room where Karenin was lying, but she would not leave him alone with the dog. They both leaned over him, each from his own side. Not that there was a hint of reconciliation in the move. Quite the contrary. Each of them was alone. Tereza with her dog, Tomas with his.

It is thus divided, each alone, that, sad to say, they remained with him until his last hour.

*   *   *

Why is it that a dog's menstruation made her lighthearted and gay, while her own menstruation made her squeamish? The answer seems simple to me: dogs were never expelled from Paradise. Karenin knew nothing about the duality of body and soul and had no concept of disgust. That is why Tereza felt so free and easy with him. (And that is why it is so dangerous to turn an animal into a *machina animata*, a cow into an automaton for the production of milk. By so doing, man cuts the thread binding him to Paradise and has nothing left to hold or comfort him on his flight through the emptiness of time.)

From this jumble of ideas came a sacrilegious thought that Tereza could not shake off: the love that tied her to Karenin was better than the love between her and Tomas. Better, not bigger. Tereza did not wish to fault either Tomas or herself; she did not wish to claim that they could love each other *more*. Her feeling was rather that, given the nature of the human couple, the love of man and woman is a priori inferior to that which can exist (at least in the best instances) in the love between man and dog, that oddity of human history probably unplanned by the Creator.

It is a completely selfless love: Tereza did not want anything of Karenin; she did not ever ask him to love her back. Nor had she ever asked herself the questions that plague human couples: Does he love me? Does he love anyone more than me? Does he love me more than I love him? Perhaps all the questions we ask of love, to measure, test, probe, and save it, have the additional effect of cutting it short. Perhaps the reason we are unable to love is that we yearn to be loved, that is, we demand something (love) from our partner instead of delivering ourselves up to him demand-free and asking for nothing but his company.

And something else: Tereza accepted Karenin for what he was; she did not try to make him over in her image; she agreed from the outset with his dog's life, did not wish to deprive him of it, did not envy him his secret intrigues. The reason she trained him was not to transform him (as a husband tries to reform his wife and a wife her husband), but to provide him with the elementary language that enabled them to communicate and live together.

Then too: No one forced her to love Karenin; love for dogs is voluntary. (Tereza was again reminded of her mother, and regretted everything that had happened between them. If her mother had been one of the anonymous women in the village, she might well have found her easygoing coarseness agreeable. Oh, if only her mother had been a stranger! From childhood on, Tereza had been ashamed of the way her mother occupied the features of her face and confiscated her 'I'. What made it even worse was that the age-old imperative 'Love your father and mother!' forced her to agree with that occupation, to call the aggression love! It was not her mother's fault that Tereza broke with her. Tereza broke with her not because she was the mother she was but because she was a mother.)

But most of all: No one can give anyone else the gift of the idyll; only an animal can do so, because only animals were not expelled from Paradise. The love between dog and man is idyllic. It know no conflicts, no hair-raising scenes; it knows no development. Karenin surrounded Tereza and Tomas with a life based on repetition, and he expected the same from them.

If Karenin had been a person instead of a dog, he would surely have long since said to Tereza, 'Look, I'm sick and tired of carrying that roll in my mouth every day. Can't you come up with something different?' And therein lies the whole of man's plight. Human time does not turn in a circle; it runs ahead in a straight line. That is why man cannot be happy: happiness is the longing for repetition.

Yes, happiness is the longing for repetition, Tereza said to herself.

When the chairman of the collective farm took his Mefisto out for a walk after work and met Tereza, he never failed to say, 'Why did he come into my life so late, Tereza? We could have gone skirt chasing, he and I! What woman could resist these two little pigs?' at which point the pig was trained to grunt and snort. Tereza laughed each time, even though she knew beforehand exactly what he would say. The joke did not lose its charm through repetition. On the contrary. In an idyllic setting, even humour is subject to the sweet law of repetition.

*   *   *

Dogs do not have many advantages over people, but one of them is extremely important: euthanasia is not forbidden by law in their case; animals have the right to a merciful death. Karenin walked on three legs and spent more and more of his time lying in a corner. And whimpering. Both husband and wife agreed that they had no business letting him suffer needlessly. But agree as they might in principle, they still had to face the anguish of determining the time when his suffering was in fact needless, the point at which life was no longer worth living.

If only Tomas hadn't been a doctor! Then they would have been able to hide behind a third party. They would have been able to go back to vet and ask him to put the dog to sleep with an injection.

Assuming the role of Death is a terrifying thing. Tomas insisted that he would not give the injection himself; he would have the vet come and do it. But then he realized that he could grant Karenin a privilege forbidden to humans: Death would come for him in a guise of his loved ones.

Karenin had whimpered all night. After feeling his leg in the morning, Tomas said to Tereza, 'There's no point in waiting.'

In a few minutes they would both have to go to work. Tereza went in to see Karenin. Until then, he had lain in his corner completely apathetic (not even acknowledging Tomas when he felt his leg), but when he heard the door open and saw Tereza come in, he raised his head and looked at her.

She could not stand his stare; it almost frightened her. He did not look that way at Tomas, only at her. But never with such intensity. It was not a desperate look, or even sad. No, it was a look of awful, unbearable trust. The look was an eager question. All his life Karenin had waited for answers from Tereza, and he was letting her know (with more urgency than usual, however) that he was still ready to learn the truth from her. (Everything that came from Tereza was the truth. Even when she gave commands like 'Sit!' or 'Lie down!' he took them as truths to identify with, to give his life meaning.)

His look of awful trust did not last long; he soon laid his head back down on his paws. Tereza knew that no one ever again would look at her like that.

They had never fed him sweets, but recently she had bought him a few chocolate bars. She took them out of the foil, broke them into pieces, and made a circle of them around him. Then she brought over a bowl of water to make sure that he had everything he needed for the several hours he would spend at home alone. The look he had given her just then seemed to have tired him out. Even surrounded by chocolate, he did not raise his head.

She lay down on the floor next to him and hugged him. With a slow and laboured turn of the head, he sniffed her and gave her a lick or two. She closed her eyes while the licking went on, as if she wanted to remember it forever. She held out the other cheek to be licked.

Then she had to go and take care of her heifers. She did not return until just before lunch. Tomas had not come home yet. Karenin was still lying on the floor surrounded by the chocolate, and did not even lift his head when he heard her come in. His bad leg was swollen now, and the tumor had burst in another place. She noticed some light red (not blood-like) drops forming beneath his fur.

Again she lay down next to him on the floor. She stretched one arm across his body and closed her eys. Then she heard someone banging on the door. 'Doctor! Doctor! The pig is here! The pig and his master!' She lacked the strength to talk to anyone, and did not move, did not open her eyes. 'Doctor! Doctor! The pigs have come!' Then silence.

Tomas did not get back for another half hour. He went straight to the kitchen and prepared the injection without a word. When he entered the room, Tereza was on her feet and Karenin was picking himself up. As soon as he saw Tomas, he gave him a weak wag of the tail.

'Look,' said Tereza, 'he's still smiling.'

She said it beseechingly, trying to win a short reprieve, but did not push for it.

Slowly she spread a sheet out over the couch. It was a white sheet with a pattern of tiny violets. She had everything carefully laid out and thought out, having imagined Karenin's death many days in advance. (Oh, how horrible that we actually dream ahead to the death of those we love!)

He no longer had the strength to jump up on the couch. They picked him up in their arms together. Tereza laid him on his side, and Tomas examined one of his good legs. He was looking for a more or less prominent vein. Then he cut away the fur with a pair of scissors.

Tereza knelt by the couch and held Karenin's head close to her own.

Tomas asked her to squeeze the leg because he was having trouble sticking the needle in. She did as she was told, but did not move her face from his head. She kept talking gently to Karenin, and he thought only of her. He was not afraid. He licked her face two more times. And Tereza kept whispering, 'Don't be scared, don't be scared, you won't feel any pain there, you'll dream of squirrels and rabbits, you'll have cows there, and Mefisto will be there, don't be scared . . .'

Tomas jabbed the needle into the vein and pushed the plunger. Karenin's leg jerked; his breath quickened for a few seconds, then stopped. Tereza remained on the floor by the couch and buried her face in his head.

Then they both had to go back to work and leave the dog laid out on the couch, on the white sheet with tiny violets.

They came back towards evening. Tomas went into the garden. He found the lines of the rectangle that Tereza had drawn with her heel between the two apples trees. Then he started digging. He kept precisely to her specifications. He wanted everything to be just as Tereza wished.

She stayed in the house with Karenin. She was afraid of burying him alive. She put her ear to his mouth and thought she heard a weak breathing sound. She stepped back and seemed to see his breast moving slightly.

(No, the breath she heard was her own, and because it set her own body ever so slightly in motion, she had the impression the dog was moving.)

She found a mirror in her bag and held it to his mouth. The mirror was so smudged she thought she saw drops on it, drops caused by his breath.

'Tomas! He's alive!' she cried, when Tomas came in from the garden in his muddy boots.

Tomas bent over him and shook his head.

They each took an end of the sheet he was lying on, Tereza the lower end, Tomas the upper. Then they lifted him up and carried him out to the garden.

The sheet felt wet to Tereza's hands. He puddled his way into our lives and now he's puddling his way out, she thought, and she was glad to feel the moisture on her hands, his final greeting.

They carried him to the apple trees and set him down. She leaned over the pit and arranged the sheet so that it covered him entirely. It was unbearable to think of the earth they would soon be throwing over him, raining down on his *naked* body.

Then she went into the house and came back with his collar, his leash, and a handful of chocolate that had lain untouched on the floor since morning. She threw it all in after him.

Next to the pit was a pile of freshly dug earth. Tomas picked up the shovel.

Just then Tereza recalled her dream: Karenin giving birth to two rolls and a bee. Suddenly the words sounded like an epitaph. She pictured a monument standing there, between the apple trees, with the inscription *Here lies Karenin. He gave birth to two rolls and a bee.*

It was twilight in the garden, the time between day and evening. There was a pale moon in the sky, a forgotten lamp in the room of the dead.

Their boots were caked with dirt by the time they took the shovel and spade back to the recess where their tools stood all in a row: rakes, watering cans, hoes.

From *The Unbearable Lightness of Being*

ANDY WARHOL

Double Whammy

AFTER GETTING BITTEN some more I decided that Archie must have fleas, so I checked and he did. Some years are good for fleas and this is one of them . . . .

I just stepped in dog shit. In my hall. And I'm usually wearing slippers but this time I wasn't. And usually you can smell it a mile away, but it just didn't smell, so I just finished cleaning it up. And I'm all fleabitten. When you know there's fleas, you keep feeling them all the time whether they're there or not. So I just took a shower to get the shit off my foot and now I'm thinking what disease I can pick up from this whole episode.

Diary, 28/29 August 1983

ALAN ROSS

The Walk to Work

A PAINTING BY Malcolm Green shows a worried-looking Dalmatian scrutinizing itself in a mirror; the object of concern is a large black spot on its muzzle. With just such apprehension do adolescents probe for blemishes or blackheads, and with similar anxiety did our bearded collie, Bella, peer though her fringe on first encountering daylight each morning – for bad weather could postpone departure or, alternatively, conflict with preconceived ideas of destination.

Although only three-quarters of a mile, or about 15 minutes' walk, from my house to my office, there are a dozen possible routes, all in the right general direction. Together Bella and I must have taken them more than 3,500 times and, on every occasion, it was Bella herself who decided which permutation of square, crescent, garden, terrace, and street should be followed. There seemed no rhyme or reason for her choice, other than whim, but whatever it was brooked no alternative. She set off as if no other way was thinkable, and on the rare occasions that I had specific cause to deny her she gave in with bad grace. Instead of head thrust forward and eagerly straining against the collar, she would lag behind, swerving every few yards, intent on distractions. It would take several minutes for her to recover her habitual good humour, the change signalled by an upward tilting of the head, a show of teeth, and a quickening of pace.

For more than ten years we did this daily journey to and fro. It might seem a boring business going over such familiar ground five or six times a week but, because of the uncertainties and different attractions *en route*, it never was.

For example, the marginally longest way, though the one involving fewest changes of direction, would take us across the death trap of the Fulham Road into Drayton Gardens. On one side there was the old Forum cinema, the South Kensington Squash Club and the Society of Authors. Sometimes a detour would have to be made over the cobbles of Cresswell Place, a leafy, villagey mews once inhabited by Agatha Christie. Cresswell Place exerted a strong pull over Bella, but if this could be deflected and we stuck to the right-hand side of the street, then we would pass Thomas Pink, purveyors of striped shirts and boxer shorts to the gentry, a garage specialising in Lancias, and the Paris

Pullman, now, alas, no longer an art-film house but a smart block of flats.

Once on the Old Brompton Road it would be a straight run past the library and the Chanterelle restaurant (originally owned by the novelist Walter Baxter), past Clareville Grove, the home of Rosamond Lehmann until her recent death, past the Onslow Hotel – almost everything round here bears the name Onslow, which is rather traumatic for me since the most nerve-racking hours of my life were spent in the Arctic in a destroyer called *Onslow* – with Reece Mews, where the artist Francis Bacon lives and works, on one side, and a branch of Christie's on the other.

In the best weather Bella preferred the mews and garden route – on one corner Laurie Lee, then the studio and house of R. B. Kitaj, and then the flat of Anita Brookner, and finally up Elm Park Gardens and into Cranley Gardens.

A marginal embellishment would take us into Old Church Street, past the Chelsea Arts Club, and behind the Marsden hospital. Here there used to be an old burial ground, almost adjacent to the tiny Jewish cemetery hidden behind a pair of antique shops. Cemeteries held a permanent fascination for Bella, corpses perhaps yielding rich subterranean odours, but there was no easy way into this one.

By limiting our time on the two main thoroughfares of Fulham Road and Old Brompton Road, the greater part of our journey would be along the sides of one of the many Onslow Gardens, and Onslow Square. There would always be cars, vans, lorries or people lost here, because the numbering of the houses is eccentric to the point of perversity, and there are, in any case, three quite separate Onslow Gardens. This area is the prettiest bit, all trees, lawns and churches, with well-dressed old gentlemen of military bearing exercising themselves and their animals.

Since there are numerous parallel streets leading out of the gardens, such as Sumner and Cranley Places, further variety can be introduced. There is the Michelin Building route, which involves passing one of Cecil Beaton's old houses in Pelham Place, and another up in Sydney Place.

The office as a focus for dog walking serves a purpose, but it has hazards. One day during lunch some years ago Bella managed to be allowed out through three lots of doors by helpful messengers and postmen. Finding her scavenging in Thurloe Square, a kindly lady took her in and eventually deposited her in Battersea Dogs' Home. On another occasion she was idling along when the guns were fired for the Queen's birthday salute. She took off like a bat out of hell to be retrieved very woebegone two days later from the police pound in Hyde Park.

No car was safe from her. Drivers who had briefly left their vehicles with a window half open would be astonished on their return to find Bella ensconced behind the wheel and reluctant to move over. She was indifferent to the company, the journey was what mattered.

Although bred for rough work in the country, she became a London office dog and took her duties very seriously. As we adapt to dogs so do they to us, with grace and goodwill.

I have barely scratched the surface of our various excursions which turned walking to work into a mystery tour. But, sadly, Bella is no more, there is no anxious face checking on the weather and meditating on our course. Left to myself I tend these days, unimaginatively, always to go the same way.

JILL BENNETT

Will

NOTEBOOK, 27 MAY 1991: Adolf [Jill Bennett] has left half a million to Battersea Dogs' Home. She never bought a bar of soap in all the time she lived with me. Always she cried poverty . . . It is the most perfect act of misanthropy, judged with the tawdry, kindless theatricality she strove to achieve in life. She had no love in her heart for people and only a little more for dogs.

John Osborne, from *Almost a Gentleman*

A. N. WILSON

E VERYONE PREFERS dogs to politicians.

From the *Evening Standard*, 29 January 1993

LARS GUSTAFSSON

Elegy for a Dead Labrador

Here there may be, in the midst of summer,
a few days when suddenly it's fall.
Thrushes sing on a sharper note.
The rocks stand determined out in the water.
They know something. They've always known it.
We know it, too, and we don't like it.
On the way home, in the boat, on just such evenings,
you would stand stock-still in the bow, collected,
scouting the scents coming across the water.
You read the evening, the faint streak of smoke
from a garden, a pancake frying
half a mile away, a badger
standing somewhere in the same twilight
sniffing the same way. Our friendship
was of course a compromise; we lived
together in two different worlds; mine,
mostly letters, a text passing through life;
yours, mostly smells. You had knowledge
I would have given much to have possessed:
the ability to let a feeling – eagerness, hate, or love –
run like a wave through your body
from nose to tip of tail, the inability

ever to accept the moon as fact.
At the full moon you always complained loudly against it.
You were a better Gnostic than I am. And consequently
you lived continually in paradise.
You had a habit of catching butterflies on the leap
and munching them, which some people though disgusting.
I always liked it. Why
couldn't I learn from you? And doors.
In front of closed doors you lay down and slept,
sure that sooner or later the one would come
who'd open up the door. You were right.
I was wrong. I ask myself, now this
long mute friendship is forever finished,
if possibly there was anything I could do
which impressed you. Your firm conviction
that I called up the thunderstorms
doesn't count. That was a mistake. I think
my certain faith that the ball existed,
even when hidden behind the couch,
somehow gave you an inkling of my world.
In my world most things were hidden
behind something else. I called you 'dog.'
I really wonder whether you conceived of me
as a larger, noisier 'dog,'
or as something else, forever unknown,
something that is what it is, existing in that attribute
it exists in, a whistle
in the nocturnal park one has got used to
returning to without actually knowing
what it is one is returning to. About you,
and who you were, I knew no more.
One might say, from this more objective
standpoint, we were two organisms. Two
of those places where the universe makes a knot

in itself, short-lived, complex structures
of proteins that have to complicate themselves
more and more in order to survive, until everything
breaks and turns simple once again, the knot
dissolved, the riddle gone. You were a question
asked of another question, nothing more,
and neither had the answer to the other.

(*Translated, from the Swedish, by Yvone L. Sandstroem.*)

DAVID HOCKNEY

Soulmates

DESPITE THE RAKISH homosexuality of his early work, he has always needed an extended family, composed of the lovers, helpers and hangers-on who beleaguer him in Jack Hazan's film *A Bigger Splash*. Now, however, he is a family man in earnest: the single parent of two dachshunds, careful to ration the food and the affection he doles out to them. 'You've to be very careful you pet them equally. They watch each other, and keep notes. They live for love. Oh, and for food I suppose; that's the only material interest they have. I got Stanley first, then his brother, who was run over when I was away in England – I rushed straight back. I replaced him with Boodgie. The name doesn't mean anything, it was just baby talk when I first had him. I suppose you could say that the two of them are an item now.' Hockney replaced Stanley on the floor and watched contentedly as Boodgie, now awake since there was no more opera to sleep through, set about medicinally licking his soulmate's eye. 'Stanley's a bit bunged up, and Boodgie is putting him right. They're great healers, dogs. Remember the ones in the Bible that licked Lazarus's sores for him?'

Like the objects of Hockney's affection, from his mother and on through a succession of lissom lads, the dogs have had their devotion repaid with immortality. In one painting, Stanley's tapering snout has been smashed into cubistic facets; redesigned as a harlequin, he romps through the 'home-made prints' Hockney has created on a photocopying machine. A terracotta dachshund guards the grate in his sitting room, and above it a trompe-l'oeil fireplace painted on to the wall is decorated with pretended snapshots of the same small tubular companion. 'They're not LA dogs,' Hockney insisted. 'They haven't had nose jobs, or done commercials.' Hockney's dogs have supplied him, perhaps for the first time, with a love which is unconditional and disinterested, not dependent on his celebrity; they are also a stabilising influence. 'I used to think I couldn't have dogs because I travelled so much. Now I have them, I don't feel the need to travel. As a matter of fact, I never go away for longer than three weeks now.'

Hockney proved his selfless fondness when, while he was dandling them, I noticed a dollop of what President Bush calls doo-doo on his natty, expensive trouser leg. He swabbed it off without fuss or revulsion. These are the proudly worn badges of parenthood, like the nursing mother's epaulette of sick. . . . The fax, a medium of communication, suits his irrepressible gregariousness. Likewise, he used a still video camera, one of only a few hundred manufactured, to photograph an assortment of picture dealers, plumbers, opera impresarios and delivery boys who just happened to turn up at his house. He wanted to see what the images looked like when printed. The results dangle from a high wall of his studio: an LA beach bum exudes attitude from every pumped-up muscle; Stanley Donen, the director of *Singin' in the Rain*, leans with his ankles crossed at an effortlessly debonair angle, and Dennis Hopper clasps a newborn baby and glowers satanically. 'I took the dogs with me once when I visited Dennis. Stanley went in and peed straight away in the middle of the carpet. You could see from the look on Dennis's face why he didn't make his career in musical comedy.'

The factory works at all hours: Hockney has a ravenous eagerness to learn, and an equal compulsion to teach. The most trivial observation can wind him up. The dozy indifference of his dogs to the television monitor prompted a dissertation on technology and perception: 'I've learned a lot from Stanley and Boodgie. They can't read the television picture. It's an abstract to them – which is exactly what it is to us, except that we've forgotten that. We assume it's reality, whereas it's as artificial as a painting.'

Peter Conrad in the *Observer*, 1992

COPYRIGHT ACKNOWLEDGEMENTS

It was with heartening enthusiasm that the following gave permission to use their material in this collection:

The Estate of Herbert Asquith, for 'The Hairy Dog' from *Pillicock Hill*; Michael Baker, for an extract from *Our Three Selves: A Life of Radclyffe Hall* (GMP publishers); William Heinemann, for an extract from *The True Adventures of John Steinbeck, Writer* by Jackson Benson; Bloomsbury publishers, for an extract from Peggy Lee's *Miss Peggy Lee*; Shirley Temple Black, for an extract from *Child Star*; Peter Conrad, for an extract from an interview with David Hockney in the *Observer*; Geoffrey Dearmer, for 'The Turkish Trench Dog', from *A Pilgrim's Song* (John Murray); P. N. Furbank, for an extract from *E. M. Forster: A Life, Volume 2*; Michael Gray and John Bauldie, for a list from *All Across the Telegraph: A Bob Dylan Handbook*; Sir Rupert Hart-Davis, for an extract from his *Hugh Walpole* and from *The Case is Altered* by William Plomer; Edward Hoagland, for an extract from 'Dogs and the Tug of Life' in *Heart's Desire*; Michael Holroyd, for an extract from *The Smith of Smiths* by Hesketh Pearson, and for a letter by Lytton Strachey as printed in his *Lytton Strachey*; Roger Hubank, for an extract from *Saturday Night at the Greyhound* by John Hampson; Michael Kennedy, for an extract from his *Portrait of Elgar*; Adam Mars-Jones, for an extract from *Lantern Lecture*; Hugh Montgomery-Massingberd, for an interview with James Lees-Milne, first published in the *Daily Telegraph*; Mary Oliphant for extracts from *Life With Topsy* and *The Story of J.M.B.* by Denis Mackail; Yoko Ono, for 'Good Dog, Nigel' from *In His Own Write* by John Lennon; the Estate of the late Sonia Brownwell Orwell, Martin Secker and Warburg Ltd, and Harcourt Brace Jovanovich for an extract from 'As I Please' in *The Collected Essays, Journalism and Letters* by George Orwell; the Estate of James Osborn for an extract from his edition of the *Anecdotes* of Joseph Spence (Oxford University Press); John Osborne, for extracts from *Almost a Gentleman*; Oxford University Press and the Sir Edward Elgar Will Trust, for an extract from a letter by Sir Edward Elgar, printed in *Letters of a Lifetime* ed. Jerrold Northrop

Moore; Charles Panati, for an extract from *Panati's Extraordinary Endings of Practically Everything and Everybody*; Mrs Trekkie Parsons, for a letter by Leonard Woolf, as printed in his *Letters* (ed. Frederic Spotts); Mrs Eva Reichmann for an extract from *Zuleika Dobson* by Max Beerbohm; David Robinson, for an extract from his *Chaplin: Life and Art*; Alan Ross, for an essay first published in the *Independent*; A. L. Rowse, for 'Apollo, Glorious Labrador' from *A Life: Collected Poems*; Professor Michael Shelden, for an extract from *George Orwell*; Bobby Short, for extracts from *Black and White Baby*; Sir Stephen Spender, for an extract from *World Within World*; Gore Vidal, for an extract from *Two Sisters*; Frederick Warne for an extract from *Letters* by Beatrix Potter (ed. Judy Taylor); Auberon Waugh, for various writings in *Private Eye*, the *Spectator*, *The Last Word* and the *Daily Telegraph*; Weidenfeld Publishing Group for La Fontaine's *Fables*, translated by Edward Marsh in Everyman's Library; A. N. Wilson, for an aphorism from the *Evening Standard*; Philip Ziegler, for an extract from *Diana Cooper*; David Marr and the Estate of Patrick White for extracts from *Patrick White: A Life*.

Permission has also been granted by the Peters Fraser and Dunlop Group Ltd for *Flaubert's Parrot* by Julian Barnes; David Higham Associates for *E. M. Forster: a Portrait* by J. R. Acklerley, for *Travels With My Aunt* © 1969 Verdant SA, *A Sort of Life* © 1971 Verdant SA and *The Human Factor* © 1978 Verdant SA by Graham Greene, and for 'With the Kennel Club' by Louis MacNeice, first published in *Night and Day* in 1937 (also available in *Night and Day* ed. Christopher Hawtree, Chatto and Windus, 1985); 'A Boston Terrier' from *One Man's Meat* by E. B. White, copyright 1939 by E. B. White. Reprinted by permission of HarperCollins Publishers Inc; Alfred A. Knopf and Hamish Hamilton Ltd. for 'Another Dog's Death' from *Facing Nature: Poems* by John Updike © John Updike 1976 (also available in *Collected Poems*, 1993); The Literary Trustees of Walter de la Mare and the Society of Authors as their representative for 'The Bandog' from *Peacock Pie* and *The Complete Poems*; Mrs Valerie Eliot, Faber and Faber Ltd and Harcourt Brace Jovanovich for 'The Pekes and the Pollicles' from *Old Possum's Book of Practical Cats* by T. S. Eliot; Faber and Faber Ltd and Farrar, Straus and Giroux for 'Yoko' by Thom Gunn from *Selected Poems 1950–79* © 1976, 1979 by Thom Gunn; Faber and Faber Ltd and HarperCollins Publishers Inc for *The Unbearable Lightness of Being* by Milan Kundera; Faber and Faber Ltd and Randon House Inc for 'Talking to Dogs' from *Collected Poems* by W. H. Auden (ed. Ed Mendelson); Faber and Faber Ltd for 'Dogs in the Park' from

Gertrude Stein; Methuen Ltd for an extract from *Letters* by Wyndham Lewis (ed. W. K. Rose); to Viking for extracts from *Journals 1889–1949* by André Gide (translated Justin O'Brien); to Curtis Brown Ltd for extracts from *My Family and Other Animals* by Gerald Durrell and from *My Talks with Dean Spanley* by Lord Dunsany; Hamish Hamilton for an extract from *The Beast in Me* by James Thurber; William Heinemann Ltd for an extract from *What Fresh Hell is This?* by Marion Meade; Laurence Pollinger Ltd for extracts from *The Letters of F. Scott Fitzgerald* (ed Andrew Turnbull); W. W. Norton for 'The House Dog's Grave' by Robinson Jeffers; the Enoch Pratt Free Library for extracts from *The New Mencken Letters* (ed Carl Bode); the Estate of Raymond Chandler for an extract from *Selected Letters* (ed Frank MacShane); the Estate of Andy Warhol for an extract from *Diaries* (ed Pat Hackett); the Estate of Tennessee Williams and Lady St Just for extracts from *Five O'Clock Angel*; William Heinemann Ltd for an extract from *My Wicked, Wicked Ways* by Errol Flynn; Weidenfeld and Nicolson Ltd for an extract from *Home Before Dark* by Susan Cheever; the Estate of Jacqueline Susann for extracts from Every *Night, Josephine!*; HarperCollins Publishers Inc for an extract from *Wouldn't It Be Nice* by Brian Wilson; Bodley Head Ltd for an extract from *The Kindness of Strangers: the Life of Tennessee Williams* by Donald Spoto; the Estate of Billie Holliday for an extract from *Lady Sings the Blues*; Methuen Ltd for an extract from *The Complete Fawlty Towers* by John Cleese and Connie Booth; Weidenfeld and Nicolson for extracts from *Elvis and Gladys* by Elaine Dundy; Random House Inc for an extract from *Mister Abbott* by George Abbott.

Every effort has been made to trace copyright holders but some have gone to earth and others are slow to surface. Any omissions can be rectified in future editions.

INDEX OF AUTHORS

GENERAL INDEX

The names of dogs have been distinguished from humans' by quotation marks